ACKNOWLEDGEMENT

THE ALMANAC OF THE UNELECTED would like to acknowledge its appreciation to a large number of individuals who contributed many long hours to this first edition. We are indebted to a long list of contributing researchers and writers many of whom are listed on page 749.

However, we would like to extend a special note of thanks to Meg Mullery for her editorial management, and to Kirsten Fedewa, Regina Mellon, Connie Lambert, Christopher Smith, Bob Witeck, Joe Tarver, Tom Needles and Diana Aldridge for their substantial editorial contributions and technical assistance.

Photography credits: Walter Nicholls, photography editor, and Sarah Helmstadter, chief photographer.

CONTENTS

FOREWORD

"Legislation is an aggregate, not a simple production. It is impossible to tell how many persons, opinions and influences have entered into its composition."

Woodrow Wilson

The staff of the United States Congress today play a vital role in helping the Members produce legislation and set national policies. These "unelected" public servants often serve with little recognition but they bring essential expertise and dedication to the Congress.

Choosing some 600 of these key Congressional staff to be recognized and profiled by virtue of their involvement in the legislative process was something of an art, something of an organizational science, and in many ways an impossibility.

After all, an estimated 14,000 individuals work for the leadership, for the committees or on the personal staffs of Representatives and Senators. Among their ranks are men and women, spread across hundreds of subcommittees and committees whose expertise and legislative know-how is crucial to the drafting and passage of legislation.

How to choose? Who can know them all?

Nearly all of the staff toil in anonymity, unknown to all but a few Washington insiders. They rightly defer the limelight to the Members of Congress themselves. Information on the staff up to now has been informal, compartmentalized and verbally transmitted—like a near-forgotten family history. Ask a veteran oil and gas attorney in Washington for the background on a particular longtime staffer on the Senate Energy Committee. Go to the Pentagon and ask their Congressional liaison specialists about a staff expert on the Armed Services Subcommittee on Military Installations and Facilities. In short, even those people in the nation's capital who are familiar with the Congressional staff, usually only know something about the staffers involved in their own specific fields.

The mission of *The Almanac of the Unelected* is to provide a comprehensive, reliable overview of these unelected public servants. The Almanac profiles some 600 of the key staffers, organized by committee, but not necessarily limited to committee staff. The Members' personal staff play too important a role not to be included. The Almanac attempts to give readers a subjective sense of the staffer's approach to the issues—his or her legislative expertise and professional background. In no way can the Almanac be definitive. What it does provide is that "sixth sense" of a person through the art of profile and personal interview which most staffers were gracious in granting.

At least one staffer is included for most standing, select or special committees. Several dozen staffers are profiled for some of the committees with the broadest jurisdictions. The selection process was based on a combination of factors. First, we focused on the obvious, including committee staff directors and chief counsels. After this, selections were discussed among committee insiders themselves. Lists of staffers were reviewed with veteran lobbyists, public interest group leaders, reporters and staffers.

In the end, selecting the key staffers to be profiled was subjective, sometimes bordering on searching for water with a "divining rod". It had to be. Surely we left out some staffers influential in the consideration and determination of legislation. We invite and welcome our readers'—staffers and Congress watchers alike—comments and suggestions. In subsequent volumes we will expand and update our coverage.

Likewise, there are certain to be staffers who will newly emerge as major contributors in the 2nd session of the 100th Congress. Future editions of the Almanac will include these individuals. There will be turnover among the staffers profiled. Some will leave Washington. Others will join the private sector. Some will join the new administration taking office in 1989. Still others will leave the Hill and eventually seek elective office, like one-time staffers Lyndon Johnson, Robert Kennedy, George Mitchell and Tony Coelho. Change is an integral part of the Congress, and we are committed to keeping our readers as up to date as possible.

Finally, we hope to provide a sense of the Congress itself through this "snapshot" of some 600 vivid characters, uniquely interesting individuals. Each in his or her own field is dedicated to an extraordinary degree to excellence in public service. We believe learning about these individuals in the Almanac is insightful. We hope, in some measure, it is reassuring, maybe even a little inspiring.

One of our writers put it best in a note to the Editor:

"I want to tell you what a delightful experience this has been and how impressed I am with all the men and women I interviewed. Their enthusiasm and commitment to the work they are doing is amazing and very genuine. To me, they are the true civil servants. It was fascinating to walk around Dirksen, looking for a quiet place to talk, and see heads popping out of doors, each one asking, "Have your heard?". The status of the legislation on which they were personally working was the issue. I saw very little of the arrogance or self-importance which is often thought to permeate Hill staffers. Instead, I saw incredibly hard-working and dedicated people who truly believe in what they are doing. I had the distinct impression that most them would live in their offices if it were permitted."

This, then, is the Staff of the U.S. Congress, 1988.

      Charles C. Francis
      Jeffrey B. Trammell

A HISTORY OF THE UNELECTED

by
Floyd M. Riddick
Parliamentarian Emeritus,
United States Senate

When I became an employee on Capitol Hill in 1947, the staffs were small, and very few staffers could be considered "professionals". When the two legislative bodies were in session, the Chambers were never overcrowded with professional staffs. Except for the Representatives and Senators themselves, only when a major proposed piece of legislation was under consideration would professional staff members be present. Even then, only very few staff members of the committee reporting the measure would be stationed near or close by the Chairman of the committee managing the bill. That was it.

The rules and practices of the two Chambers were very restrictive, and any staff members on the Floor not on duty with the bill at that time would be invited to leave the Chamber. As a matter of fact, at that time female secretaries and legislative aides did not have Senate Floor privileges when the Senate was in session.

At the beginning of our government in 1789, except for a few officials of the two houses—such as the Clerk of the House of Representatives, the Secretary of the Senate, and the Sergeant at Arms of the House—there were no legislative staffs. At that stage of our history, there was no need for such.

As a matter of fact, the "unelected staffs" are a modern development. Not until 1946, with the enactment of the "Legislative Reorganization Act of 1946," did the Congress begin generally to establish professional staffs for standing and special committees and other specialized services for the two Houses, as well as professional staffs for Members of the two Houses.

To illustrate the changes and the need therefore through the years, let's take a note of a few statistics on the number of employees and the amount of funds for the Congress and the Administration, as follows.

During the years of the George Washington administration, you could almost count the number of employees of each House on your fingers, and few of them could be considered as professional employees. The highest number of federal employees in the Administration during any year that George Washington was President totaled approximately 1,000.

In 1825, the Congress had fewer than 20 employees, and the President and his administration had approximately 6,500 employees. The federal budget for that year totaled $15,857,000.

In 1850, the Congress had fewer than 40 employees. The employees of the executive branch totaled 25,000.

In 1900, the congressional employees had increased to fewer than 300, and the number of employees of the Administration had increased to approximately 180,000.

The Joint Committee on Internal Revenue was created in 1926 by the Revenue Act of that year, fortified by a professional staff in the field of taxation, and that Committee is still a major adjunct to the Congress in writing tax legislation.

Each House of Congress has a Legislative Counsel to assist its committees, individual Members or their designees, and any groups of Members, in the drafting of proposed legislation or even in the interpretation of existing law. The Office of the Legislative Counsel for each House was created in the Revenue Act of 1919. These two staffs of the House and Senate have become indispensable aides of their respective Houses.

Except for the years the United States was engaged in war, the number of employees of the Administration was comparatively small until the Depression. During the Franklin D. Roosevelt administration the number of federal civilian employees increased-to 485,489 in 1930 and 766,828 in 1940.

The congressional personnel remained comparatively small until 1946. Until that date the budget for the legislative branch was smaller than that for the Bureau of Indian Affairs. In 1986, the staffs of the House of Representatives and the Senate had increased to a grand total of 19,430; the officers and employees of the Executive Branch had increased to 1,954,348, not including military.

The annual budget for each of the years mentioned above for each of the Congresses and Administrations follows:

	Congress	Administration
1850	NA	$ 39.54 million
1900	$ 4.4 million	520.86 million
1930/1940	20.1/23.0 million	3.32/9.6 billion
1946	54.1 million	61.7 billion
1986	1.7 billion	989.7 billion

To combat the Administration and to keep the Members of Congress informed to do their job, pressure had been building up from the days of the Depression in 1929 until it crystalized in 1946 with the enactment of the Legislative Reorganization Act.

The need for legislative professional staffs has grown greatly since the beginning of the twentieth century. Since 1900 there has been a rapid growth both in the number of laws and in the expansion of subject matter embodied in the laws. This expansion has created a legal maze reaching deeply into the daily lives of all our people. So great is this development that large professional staffs in both legislative branch and the administrative have been deemed necessary.

The industrial world has become so complicated in recent years that some system of regulation by the government has been considered necessary to prevent serious social conflicts. The government has concluded that in order to meet these needs laws must be enacted involving all phases of economic life, each phase covering such intricate details that the services of professional staffs became essential.

The congressional staffs are now basically responsible for taking the approved policies of the Members of the House and Senate committees and translating them into the reports of the committees to their respective Houses and preparing the proposed legislative language to be embodied in the statutory law.

Many members of the unelected professional staffs do not stay until their retirement. After some years of experience, some turn to more lucrative roles in both the private and public sectors. Some have moved to high roles in the United Nations; some to Deputy or Under Secretary of various Cabinet posts; some have joined the President's staff at the White House and a few have become members of the president's Cabinet, including one as Secretary of State. One who had been in the House employment became a Representative, then a Senator, then Vice President, and finally, President of the United States (Lyndon B. Johnson). A number of congressional staffers have moved up to being a Representative or a Senator; and many have become directors or members of commissions of the great number of independent agencies of the government, such as the Federal Trade Commission, the Federal Communications Commission, the Farm Credit Administration, FDIC, National Labor Relations Board, General Services Administration, NASA, SEC, TVA and Small Business Administration.

In the private sector, many former staff members have left their services with the Congress to represent industry, with the idea of seeing that laws enacted will not destroy or unduly hurt the interests of the private sector which they now represent.

Hence, this gives a brief picture of the development of the unelected professional staffs.

Floyd M. Riddick
Parliamentarian Emeritus

Washington, D.C.
1988
Most of historical data provided by Senate Historian, Richard Baker.

HOUSE OF REPRESENTATIVES

HOUSE OF REPRESENTATIVES
LEADERSHIP

Werner W. Brandt
Assistant to the Majority Leader
H-114 Capitol Bldg.
225-5604

Personal: born 8/29/38 in New York, New York. B.A. history, Hamilton Coll., 1960. Univ. of Pennsylvania, 1960-1961. 1961, U.S. Army Reserve. 1962-1972, Foreign Service Officer, Dept. of State. 1972-1981, Legislative Assistant, Rep. Thomas Foley, (D-WA). 1981-present, Assistant to the Majority Leader.

Expertise: Legislative process, political advisor & liaison to interest groups, political organizations & labor community

As one of Congressman Tom Foley's chief aides, Brandt is an affable, gracious man whose role is to act as the eyes and ears of the Majority Leader. He is Foley's principal liaison to major interest groups, trade associations, organized labor, the business community, state and local governments, and other groups who press their cases on Capitol Hill. Brandt has worked on all of Foley's political campaigns as media advisor, political strategist, and contact with voter and interest groups.

Brandt views himself as a "facilitator" for Foley, bringing diverse groups with often conflicting interests before the House leadership for a fair hearing of the issues: "My job is to ensure that the views of major political and policymaking actors are given a hearing by the House leadership." While Foley's office often concentrates on maintaining a well-oiled legislative machine, Brandt has been actively involved in legislation in a variety of areas. Since his stint as Chairman of the House Agriculture Committee, Foley has maintained his interest and involvement in the development of American farm policy. His long history of legislative accomplishments includes reforms of Congressional procedure during the 1970's, the development of U.S. nutrition and food stamp programs, chairing the 1987 Executive/Congressional budget summit, authoring major homeless legislation, serving on the House Iran/Contra Committee, and coordinating several major foreign policy initiatives. Brandt played a role in all of these.

While Brandt's position includes a wide range of responsibilities, his personal interests lie in the areas of foreign policy and national security, especially Soviet, Japanese, and European relations. He has travelled widely throughout these regions and is Foley's principal staffer on these issues.

Though Foley maintains a relatively small legislative staff in his capacity as Majority Leader, his staffers have earned a reputation for being well-prepared and well-connected. With George Kundanis, Foley's chief floor assistant handling much of the legislative load, Brandt is not as well known among fellow staffers. "Brandt is seen as the guy who interacts with the players around town, who stays in touch, who keeps those on the outside informed of the workings of the Leadership's inner circle," observes one long-time Hill staffer.

The father of two, Brandt divides his time between family and work. In his off-hours, he spends much of his time reading, travelling, touring museums and taking long walks with his family.

Steve Champlin
Executive Floor Assistant
Office of the Majority Whip
H-148 Capitol Bldg.
225-3130

Personal: born 6/6/51 in Providence, Rhode Island. B.A. Wesleyan Univ., 1974. M.A. Wesleyan Univ., 1976. Master in Divinity, Yale Divinity School, 1980. 1978-1980, lobbyist, director of Washington office, Vietnam Veterans of America. 1981-87, Legislative Director and Administrative Assistant for Deputy Whip Bonior. 1987-present, Executive Floor Assistant for Majority Whip Coelho. Married to Deborah Woitte Champlin. Publication: Vietnam Veteran: History of Neglect, (1984).

Expertise: Majority Whip operation

If you have ever looked behind the scenes when a major bill comes up for a vote on the floor of the House of Representatives, you may have seen the highly organized, intensive network of the Democratic Whip operation—and you may also have seen Steve Champlin.

As Executive Floor Assistant to Majority Whip Tony Coelho (D-CA), Champlin is a key figure in managing the Whip operation. His duties include developing floor strategy, tracking how Democratic Members are likely to vote based on counts provided by the Zone Whips (those Members designated in each geographic zone to keep tabs on his or her colleagues for the leadership) and reaching out to the various factions found among the House Democrats.

Champlin began his professional career in 1978 working with the Vietnam Veterans of America (VVA)—first as a lobbyist and later as the Director of the VVA's Washington office. While with the VVA, Champlin met Rep. David Bonior of Michigan and became involved with the early Vietnam Veterans legislation in the House. Bonior organized the Vietnam Veterans caucus in 1978, and Champlin helped draft the original Vietnam Veterans Act, which was introduced by Bonior in 1978 and enacted into law in the early 1980s. In January, 1981, Champlin joined Bonior's staff as Legislative Director, and then became his Administrative Assistant. Together with Bonior, Champlin wrote *Vietnam Veteran: A History of Neglect* in 1984. After Bonior became Chairman of the Leadership task force on Nicaragua, Champlin, during 1985 and 1986, became one of the principal Democratic staffers organizing the opposition to Contra aid.

In 1987, after moving over to the Majority Whip's office, Champlin was instrumental in assisting and managing Coelho's expansion of the Whip system. Coelho has been attempting to create a more effective Democratic Whip operation, reaching out and seeking to forge unity among the disparate groups comprising the House Democratic membership. Champlin is quite pleased with the success he believes his boss has already achieved in his first term as Majority Whip.

Issues such as the Contra resistance in Nicaragua and the nuclear arms race concern Champlin greatly. There are days, however, when he puts the worries of the world out of his mind, and instead goes searching through antique shops. A self-admitted "antique-freak," Champlin's favorite items are American period country furniture, and Chinese embroideries and porcelains.

Michael E. Grisso
Legislative Assistant
to the Speaker of the House
House Democratic Steering and
    Policy Committee
H-324 Capitol Bldg.
225-8550

Personal: Born 6/17/57, Cleburne, Texas A.A., Tarrant County Junior College, 1979. Univ. of Texas at Arlington. 1976-1977, Treasury Department, IRS, audit division. 1977-80, Investigative Agent. 1980-1982, Section Chief of IRS investigative groups working in West Texas. 1982-86, Legislative Assistant, Rep. Jim Wright (D-Tex).

Expertise: Taxes, banking, energy, health care, agriculture

When Rep. Jim Wright was elected Speaker of the House at the beginning of the 100th Congress, he had definite plans as to how to "get the House in order." Wright began assembling staff to assist him with his assertive style of leadership.

Mike Grisso, a legislative assistant to Wright since 1982 and a known worker, was an obvious choice to be on the new Speaker's team.

Grisso is a young man who, by his own admission, can't wait to get to the office each morning. Since joining the Steering and Policy Committee, the leadership panel which among other responsiblities makes committee assignments, Grisso says the opportunities to learn and meet new challenges have arisen daily.

He credits his achievements to the fact he knows "the language of legislation" and is not shy about asking questions when he does not know the fine points of particular issues.

In the first session of the 100th Congress, Grisso was the chief liaison with the financial institutions industry, including Texas savings and loans hit hard by the oil crisis. The troubles of Texas savings and loans had a substantial impact on H.R. 27 (P.L. 100-86), which President Reagan signed into law in the summer of 1987. This law allows the Federal Savings and Loan Insurance Corporation (FSLIC) to issue $10.8 billion in bonds to replenish its depleted capital.

Another major piece of legislation into which Grisso has put much work is the catastrophic health care legislation. The measure is aimed at protecting the elderly and disabled against catastrophic medical costs.

In 1983, while on the staff of Wright's Congressional office, Grisso worked on the Social Security reform bill, from conception to it's signature into law. This bill was designed to insure the short-term and long-term solvency of the system.

Free time is at a premium for Grisso, but when he does manage to break away from his office in the Capitol, he enjoys a variety of activities including sailing, golf and art. Antiquing is a special interest and he is often found exploring small antique shops in rural Virginia and Maryland.

Frederick W. Hatfield
Chief of Staff
Rep. Tony Coelho (D-CA)
H-148 Capitol
225-3130

Personal: born 3/15/55, Artesia, Ca. B.A. California State Univ. at Fresno, 1977; secondary teaching credential in American government, 1978. 1978, Instructor of American government to secondary education students. 1979-1980, Worked with a Fresno, California public relations firm. 1980-1984, field representative; 1984-1987, administrative assistant, Rep. Tony Coelho. 1987 to present, Chief of Staff, Rep. Tony Coelho.

Expertise: Agriculture, San Joaquin Valley politics

Fred Hatfield plays a dual role on Rep. Tony Coelho's staff. He not only oversees the day-to-day political operations of Coelho's congressional office, he is also Coelho's right-hand man in the Member's role as House Majority Whip.

Hatfield joined Coelho's staff in 1980 as a field representative in the Congressman's home district (CA-15). He served in this role until 1984 when Coelho asked him to join his Washington staff as Administrative Assistant. His outstanding leadership in this role prompted Coelho, when elected to the office of the Majority Whip in January, 1987, to name Hatfield Chief of Staff.

Hatfield describes his unique dual role as a vital link between the two staffs. It is Hatfield who makes certain Coelho sees the "right" people and briefs him on all sides of a concern. It is also Hatfield who takes on Coelho's overflow when time is tight.

Because his leadership responsibilities are so time-consuming, Hatfield claims he does not have the right to label himself an "expert" on any specific legislation other than San Joaquin Valley agriculture. "I spend a lot of time making sure both of Coelho's offices run smoothly and, while I make it a point to know both sides of an issue, I, unfortunately, am not always able to know all the intricacies of the issue."

But, when it comes to knowing the Congressman's district, Hatfield is a star. Hill observers describe Hatfield as "the epitome of what a good AA should be." One said, "Fred is as efficient as a supercomputer and as friendly as a basset hound. His personality and style are an unbeatable combination."

Hatfield knows the district, knows the issues and, most importantly, he reads Coelho well.

Hatfield's interests when off Capitol Hill include playing tennis and reading biographies.

Leadership

Mike Johnson
Chief of Staff
Minority Leader Robert H. Michel
 (R-IL)
H-229, The Capitol
225-0600

Expertise: Republican leadership

In late 1976, when the results of the November election caused a mass exodus from the White House, Ford staffer Mike Johnson thought his government duty was over, and he was headed back to Illinois. But an old friend, the same one who encouraged Johnson to come to Washington a year earlier, offered him a press position on then Minority Whip Bob Michel's staff. The move obviously paid off as Johnson is now the Chief of Staff for the Republican Leader of the House.

Since Michel has general authority over more than fifty staffers, Johnson has to cover a lot of territory. After you meet him, you can understand why the Minority Leader entrusts Johnson with such a commanding responsibility. A very personable individual with a good sense of humor, Johnson conducts the activities of many very distinct staffs in Washington and Illinois. Every Friday morning, Johnson brings them together to discuss events of the past week and to plan the week ahead for the Minority Leader.

In his capacity as Chief of Staff, Johnson is called upon to meet with lobbyists and constituents who wish to express their views to Michel. Johnson continues to deal with the press. He also stands as the point of connection between Michel and the various Republican organizations including the Republican National Committee, serving as an important link to the Minority Leader.

Johnson keeps a careful eye out for issues important to Michel and the GOP. He cites the Minority Leader's foremost responsibilities, "in no specific order," as the leadership of House Republicans, representation of the 18th District in Illinois, service to his country. . . . and reelection. Johnson makes those responsibilities his priorities.

Personal: born 12/6/46 in Danville, Illinois, reared in Sioux Falls, S.D. Northern State College, Aberdeen, SD, 1965-1967. 1968-1975, staff, Register-Mail, Galesburg, IL. Hired as reporter, promoted to Assistant Managing Editor, Managing Editor, Editor-in-Chief. 1976, Associate Director, Office of Presidential Messages, Ford Administration. 1977-1985, Press Secretary, Rep. Bob Michel (R-IL), 1985-present, Chief of Staff, Rep. Bob Michel.

Regarding the role of the minority in the House, Johnson is quick to say the GOP is indeed influential, dismissing any suggestion to the contrary. He believes "there has to be a minority constantly struggling to become the majority if our system is to work." One of the Hill's top generalists, Johnson helps make it work for Republicans.

Although golfing reigns supreme as Johnson's leisure time activity, he also enjoys playing the guitar, the piano, the clarinet, "anything musical."

George Kundanis
Executive Floor Assistant
House Majority Leader Tom Foley
  (D-WA)
H-114 Capitol Bldg.
225-5604

Personal: born 2/13/50, Chicago, IL. B.A. Northwestern Univ., 1971. M.A. 1972, Ph.D. 1982 Univ. of Wisconsin. 1976-77, American Political Science Association Fellow. 1977, Legislative Assistant to Rep. Thomas Foley. 1977-80, Assistant to Chairman of House Democratic Caucus. 1981-86, Floor Assistant to House Majority Whip; 1987-present, Executive Floor Assistant, Office of House Majority Leader.

Expertise: House leadership policy, strategy

George Kundanis had just completed his freshman year at Northwestern University when the Democratic Party chose to hold its national convention in his hometown. That was the summer of 1968. The events of that year proved important in American political history and from his ringside seat Kundanis was convinced that his pursuit of a career in politics was right. He majored in American Government and chose to focus on Congress, primarily because he felt it was the branch of government upon which the electorate could have the greatest impact. After meeting his B.A. requirements, Kundanis continued graduate studies at the University of Wisconsin and midway through his Ph.D. program, the American political Science Association offered him a fellowship to come to Washington for some hands-on experience with the U.S. political system.

"It couldn't have been a better opportunity because the Association covered our living expenses. Since the congressional offices get a full-time staff person at no charge and there were just six of us, we could choose among them. I particularly wanted experience on the House side because the political process tends to be more open and accessible. Kundanis chose the office of Representative Foley (D-WA) who had just been elected to chair the House Democratic Caucus. At the end of the year-long fellowship, Representative Foley offered him a permanent staff position.

In his capacity as floor assistant Kundanis's principal focus is coordinating floor schedules, seeing that the wants and needs of 258 Democratic representatives are met, figuring out which bills come up and when. Keeping the process running smoothly when 258 individuals, each with their own concerns, must share limited time and attention is not a trivial accomplishment. Colleagues agree his unique abilities to assess the positions of the House membership on party issues is a great asset and his low-keyed approach to working out inevitable conflicts among members is usually successful in bringing about consensus.

After nearly ten years working on the Hill, Kundanis still finds his greatest personal satisfaction comes from a favorable vote on an issue that he feels strongly about. Peace and arms control first attracted him to politics and they remain foremost as concerns. He's fascinated by the political process and particularly enjoys the ongoing challenges of individual actors and the dynamics of their interaction.

Leadership

Marshall L. Lynam
Administrative Assistant and Chief
 of Staff
House Speaker Jim Wright (D-TX)
H-209, Capitol Bldg.
225-8040

*Personal: born 11/27/24 in Bishop,
Texas. Attended Texas Arts and
Industries Coll. 1943-1945, gunner on
a B-17 with 97th Bomb Group in
Europe. 1946-1947, reporter,* Valley
Morning Star *and* Vernon Daily
Record. *1948, reporter; and 1949,
manag. editor,* Tyler Morning
Telegraph. *1950-1958, special
assignment reporter, Scripps Howard
Fort Worth Press. 1959, manag. editor,*
Longview *News and Journal. 1960-
1961, aviation and space editor, Fort
Worth Star Telegram. 1962-present,
administrative assistant and chief of
staff, Rep. Jim Wright (D-TX).*

Expertise: Administration, press relations

On the wall of Marshall Lynam's office in the Capitol hangs a sign bearing this message from his boss, House Speaker Jim Wright:

"Don't tell me why it can't be done. Show me how it can."

This sign suggests that the strong-willed, can-do Speaker from Texas expects from his administrative assistant and chief of staff at least three qualities—hard work, dedication, and lots of resourcefulness.

In Lynam, a tall, balding ex-newspaperman, Wright seems to have found all three. The two have worked together since 1962, when Wright brought Lynam aboard as a press aide.

Within a couple of years, Lynam advanced to the administrative assistant's job and today, as Wright's chief of staff, he directs and coordinates the efforts of the 44 legislative and administrative specialists who see that the Speaker's various offices are kept ticking.

Riding herd on all his varied responsibilities stretch Lynam pretty thin. "Someday," he laughs, "I'd like to be able to spend more than five minutes on one subject."

His primary job is to see that the whole operation runs smoothly. He huddles with the Speaker several times a day, and when Lynam makes a telephone call, knowledgeable people in Washington know that the message is from the Speaker.

Lynam says he is proud of Wright's staff. "Every member clearly understands that he or she is expected to treat every citizen with the same courtesy and respect that the Speaker does. After all, we don't own this place—the people do."

Colleagues both on and off Capitol Hill attest to Lynam's qualifications and philosophy where it concerns the Hill. As one Washington representative says, Lynam is "an ideal staffer. He is not out for self-aggrandizement, rather he puts his boss in the deserved forefront while he works through the mire of detail."

Besides his five grandchildren, Lynam's principal outside interest is boating, and enjoys spending time on his 28-foot cabin cruiser. Yet he laughs as he tells of the embroidered plaque that his wife has: "I love my husband, but damn that boat!"

John Mack
Executive Director
Democratic Steering and Policy
  Committee
H-209 Capitol Bldg.
225-2204

Personal: born 3/15/54 in Hutchinson, Kansas. George Mason Univ., 1972-1973. 1975-1979, Clerk and staff assistant, Rep. Jim Wright (D-TX). 1979-1986, Executive Assistant to House Majority Leader. 1987-present, Executive Director, Democratic Steering and Policy Committee.

Expertise: Legislative strategy, House floor procedure

John Mack is a humble man with an important position. As Executive Director of the Democratic Steering and Policy Committee, he is responsible for overseeing Speaker Jim Wright's legislative operations on behalf of all 258 Democrat members of the House of Representatives.

Mack is not one to talk about his role as the Speaker's chief strategist and general "right hand," and when asked to describe his duties, he says he "does a lot of things," but "I always do . . . whatever Jim Wright wants."

Mack's loyalty to Wright has been unswerving. Since he joined Wright's staff in 1975 as a file clerk, Mack moved up to a staff assistant position, which he held from 1975 to 1979, and served as the Executive Assistant to Majority Leader Wright from 1979 to 1986.

Upon Tip O'Neill's retirement and Jim Wright's election as Speaker, Mack was named Executive Director of the Democratic Steering and Policy Committee, a position held by Ari Weiss when O'Neill was Speaker. Weiss similarly was O'Neill chief legislative strategist. But where O'Neill had other well known and respected aides such as Gary Hymel and Kirk O'Donnell to whom he delegated considerable responsibility, Wright's style is different.

Mack's job is to see that it all works smoothly for the Democratic leadership and that the Speaker's interests are protected. He describes the legislative schedule of the House as, "What the Speaker is responsible for, what the Majority Leaders does and what the Majority Whip puts his name on."

Rep. Tony Coelho, House Majority Whip, describes Mack as, "not only a professional, but also a good friend. And, I think I express the views of many of my colleagues."

Tom Nides, special assistant to the Majority Whip, says "John Mack is duly respected by both Members and staffers—a difficult line to toe. John walks this thin line superbly."

When not working long and hard hours, Mack can be found on the golf course or waterskiing.

Leadership

Hyde H. Murray
505 Cannon House Office Bldg.
225-8888

Expertise: Parliamentary procedure, agriculture

Notwithstanding his use of quotes from the likes of Shakespeare to Plato, Hamilton to Aristotle, Hyde H. Murray is truly a legacy all in himself. Murray has continuously been elected to the position of Minority Counsel by the House Republican Membership and the full House since 1979. He also wears a multiplicity of hats, serving as Counsel to House Republican Leader Robert Michel (IL); as Minority Clerk of the House; as Minority Floor Assistant; and as a Staff Assistant to the Republican Committee on Committees. Some call him the "Prince of Ethiopia," a friendly reference to holding many titles without supporting armies.

Murray has also served as an agricultural and natural resource specialist with the platform committees of the Republican National Conventions in 1964, 1968, 1972, and 1984, and as Assistant Parliamentarian for the 1976 and 1980 Conventions. He is a co-author of the *Manual on Legislative Procedure in the U.S. House of Representatives*, has been an instructor of parliamentary procedure at Harvard University, and currently is an instructor on the legislative process at George Washington University.

Personal: born 8/2/30 in Iola, Wisconsin. B.A. Univ. of Wisconsin, 1952. J.D. Georgetown Univ., 1957. Member of the Wisconsin and D.C. Bar. 1952-1954, lieutenant, U.S. Army Corps of Engineers. 1957-1958, Office of the General Counsel, U.S. Department of Agriculture. 1958-1978, Counsel and Minority Staff Director, House Agriculture Committee. 1979-present, Minority Counsel, House of Representatives, and Counsel, House Republican Leadership .

It is Murray's "affection for the process" that continues to lure him back to the House year after year. Murray calls himself a hill "junkie" who has witnessed many changes within the system since his career started in 1958.

On a positive note, Murray sees the number of women in law school and in key staff positions greater than ever before. "It is no longer an oddity in the House for women to be in top legislative positions."

Murray stands strongly behind the Constitutional treatment of power. "Our system is based on Separation of Power—our ultimate insurance of freedom. The Minority has a duty to defeat legislation which it perceives to be counter to the best interests of the people. Often, success lies in events that do not happen, or events that people never hear about."

Active and vivacious, Murray submerges himself into numerous activities. He was the 1987 President of the Congressional Staff Club, Capitol Hill's oldest and largest bi-partisan and bi-cameral staff organization. He is a member of the Capitol Hill Toastmasters Club, the Federal Bar Association, the U.S. Capitol Historical Society, and the General Administration Board of the USDA Graduate School and the Board of the Capitol Hill Civil War Roundtable. He also has an ongoing agricultural experiment in his back yard called "suburban farming," and enjoys long distance running, art and sculpture.

Thomas R. Nides
Special Assistant
House Majority Whip Tony Coelho
   (D-CA)
H-148 Capitol Bldg.
225-3130

Expertise: Strategy, field organizing

Tom Nides entered politics at a relatively early age when he organized a statewide campaign in Minnesota to get Vice President Mondale to speak to his Duluth high school graduating class. For nearly a year, prominent Minnesotans barraged the White House with letters while Nides circulated petitions and collected signatures from northern Minnesota. The massive campaign paid off in the spring of 1979 when Vice President Mondale's legal counsel, Mike Berman, confirmed the engagement.

Not one to let talent go unnoticed, Vice President Mondale offered Nides a summer internship and years later Nides reciprocated by working on the Mondale for President campaign, first as political director for Minnesota, then one of the delegate coordinators for the Democratic National Convention, and finally Midwest field director for the general election. As the fates would have it, work for Mondale failed to secure him a position on the White House staff, so Nides went to work for the Democratic Congressional Campaign Committee for a year.

When Tony Coelho became House Majority Whip, he asked Nides to join his staff. "I really think he just thought it would be a good idea to have someone around who could make him laugh a lot," says Nides

Nides describes himself as an intermediary between his boss and constituent groups. "This job is so varied. One day you're counting votes on some big issue that's on the floor; the next day you're meeting with 50 representatives of an environmental group who want to establish a national park."

Personal: born 2/25/61, Duluth, Minnesota. B.A. Univ. of Minnesota 1983. 1984-85, PAC Director for the Democratic Congressional Campaign Committee. 1986-present, Special Assistant, House Majority Whip Tony Coelho.

For Nides, working in the House can have its frustrations. "Sometimes there's too much going on today to sit and plan about tomorrow. It's almost a forest and trees situation. Right now we're trying to develop long range legislative response to the deepening AIDS crisis. This is a tremendously complex problem that desperately requires level-headed approaches based on in-depth education. But every day brings the possibility of long-range efforts being blown off the tracks by some legislative bombshell or another. And there you are without a national policy based on a humane, well-considered response."

Nides loves his work in Washington. "This place is a magnet that draws the most knowledgeable people to it, and it gives those of us on the Hill an incredible opportunity to learn from them."

Leadership

William R. Pitts
Floor Assistant
Republican Leader Bob Michel (R-
   IL)
H-228 Capitol Bldg.
225-0600

Expertise: Floor procedure

A man who cherishes his anonymity, Bill Pitts seems to have very little left, at least among the close-knit circles of Members of Congress and their staff. Sometimes known as "Professor Pitts", he is well schooled in House rules and procedures. Pitts' father worked for the House Republican leadership for decades until retirement as aide to the Republican Whip in 1972.

Steeped in GOP politics and policies, Pitts began his career in the House at age 16 as a Congressional page and was mentored by such important insider figures as his father and Ralph Vinovich, former Administrative Assistant to Rep. Bob Michel (R-IL).

Pitts, 40, is Michel's key strategist, the point man for and the staff brains behind the Republican floor operation in the House. Pitts has played an important role in the Republican battles in the Reagan years, ranging from the 1981-1982 Reagan budget cuts to the continuing skirmishes over aid to the Contras.

In a recent profile, *The Washington Post* described Pitts' special role: "While many aides exert their influence by pushing a particular political ideology, Pitts' influence comes through sheer knowledge of the institution, its rules and the players on both sides of the aisle. . .Pitts is known for dredging up arcane rules or little-used maneuvers to help the GOP even the score."

In college he worked with the Capitol grounds crew, taking a temporary job in the Republican cloakroom after graduation. During Michel's tenure as House Minority Whip, Pitts was made floor assistant, the position he has held for 10 years.

On the occasion that the Republicans score a procedural legislative victory, word spreads on the Hill that Pitts actually thought of the maneuver or found the loophole. Adjectives often used by staff and Members to describe him include loyal, well-rounded, brilliant and complicated.

In 1986 Pitts was profiled in *Washingtonian* in the "People to Watch" column. The piece reported "During the summer recess he piles his cocker spaniel Oblio into his rebuilt Hudson and heads for Ocean City, where Pitts has built a Victorian porch on his old Cape Cod cottage."

Known for an unconventional sense of humor, Pitts is remembered by staffers as having arrived at a Halloween party dressed as a clothesline. When a delegation representing the Congress went to New York's Federal Hall to celebrate the bicentennial of the U.S. Constitution, the stocky Pitts was there to welcome them, dressed as an 18th century town crier, ringing a bell and crying "Hear ye, hear ye, hear ye, the Democrats want to raise your taxes!"

In 1986, Pitts was married in Bob Michel's office by the House chaplain.

Leadership

Peter D. Robinson
Deputy Staff Director
H-324, Capitol Bldg.
225-8550

Expertise: House procedure, legislative strategy

Although Peter Robinson entered law school with the hope of eventually pursuing a career in criminal law, a part-time position with a bail agency prompted him to alter those objectives.

One of Robinson's law professors, recognizing his talents, suggested contacting Lewis Deschler, then-Parliamentarian of the House of Representatives. At the time, Deschler was in the process of a major rewrite of the House Precedents, the ultimate authority on House floor procedures. Robinson, who found the work fascinating, was hired by Deschler and subsequently assisted in writing and editing various portions of the Precedents. Thus began a l2-year tenure as Assistant Parliamentarian.

Following that experience, Robinson secured a position with the House leadership. Currently, as deputy staff director of the House Democratic Steering and Policy Committee, Robinson helps develop and execute the party's legislative program.

Personal: born 4/29/47 in New London, Connecticut. B.A. Dartmouth Coll., 1969. J.D. Georgetown Univ., 1972. 1974-1986, Assistant Parliamentarian, U.S. House of Representatives. 1987-present, Deputy Staff Director, House Democratic Steering and Policy Committee.

Robinson serves the House leadership in a number of ways, including advising members on House procedure, helping devise and implementing legislative strategy, submitting recommendations for committee and subcommittee chairmanships, and lending advisory assistance to colleagues and members alike on the House's institutional prerogatives. In this last regard, Robinson assists House Democrats in the delineation of House responsibilities *vis a vis* the Senate and the executive branch.

Robinson finds especially challenging the need to balance the interests of all House members. A vital component for maintaining that balance is relying on orderly, reliable and time-tested procedures.

Perhaps Robinson's description of his job as "traffic cop" is most appropriate, since he must help coordinate House procedure with the legislative agenda advanced by the House leadership. This also includes assisting with the authorization and appropriation processes so that those processes are coordinated through the committee in a timely fashion.

Another facet of Robinson's job involves assisting individual House members with their own legislative initiatives, as well as special requests from the executive branch."Our responsibility as staff is to act for the members," says Robinson. "They tell us what they need and we fill in the details and help make it happen."

HOUSE OF REPRESENTATIVES
COMMITTEE ON AGRICULTURE

Agriculture

Mario A. Castillo
Chief of Staff
1301 Longworth House Office
    Bldg.
225-0420

Expertise: Agriculture, exports, trade policy

As chief of staff for the House Agriculture Committee, Castillo takes his responsibilities in food production and exports personally. In fact, he takes them all the way to his own kitchen on Capitol Hill, where several times a year, he hosts (and cooks for) a gathering of foreign agricultural counselors and ambassadors, and key Americans involved in agriculture, including his boss, Committee Chairman Kika de la Garza (D-TX). It is that personal commitment to his area of expertise that makes Castillo one of the most energetic and colorful committee chiefs of staff.

In that role, Castillo's responsibilities cover the universe of agricultural activities, from daily administration of over seventy staffers to helping draft language for specific farm bills. His special area of interest is the international promotion of agricultural products: "The international community is our customer. We may have our differences with the EEC and Japan, but they are customers for our products."

Castillo is instrumental in helping to organize the April 1988 agricultural summit with the European Economic Community, and he meets regularly with the agricultural liaisons of various foreign countries. At the request of the Soviet Ambassador, he recently put together a syllabus on agricultural issues for use by the Soviet Minister of Agriculture, Victor Nikinov. Also at the request of the Soviet Ambassador, he arranged a comprehensive field visit of key farm sites throughout the United States, headed by Nikinov and a high-ranking delegation of Soviet agricultural/politburo officials. For the spring of 1988, he has arranged a major promotion of U.S. wines in Italy, including some from the wine-growing regions of Texas, where his grandparents originally settled.

Personal: born September 16, 1947, San Angelo, Texas. B.A. Angelo State University, 1970. 1970, teacher, San Antonio. 1971, teacher and director of Bilingual Project, Colorado City, TX. 1973, Ford Foundation Fellowship in Education, special assistant to EEOC. 1974, permanent special assistant to Commissioner Telles, EEOC. 1976, special assistant to Director, Community Services Organization. 1977, campaign coordinator for W. Texas, Nelson Wolfe campaign for 21st District. 1978, staff assistant, Rep. Marvin Leath (D-TX). 1978-1979, staff assistant to Rep. Kika de la Garza. 1979-1980, Staff Director, Agriculture Subcommittee on Department Operations, Research and Foreign Agriculture. 1980-1981, Deputy Staff Director; 1981-present, Chief of Staff, House Committee on Agriculture.

Recent legislation Castillo helped to pass includes the Farm Bill of 1985, which set support prices and agricultural prices for the next four years, and the Farm Credit Act.

In 1980, Mayor Marion Barry appointed Castillo as a member of the D.C. Commission on Arts and Humanities. Through the commission, he developed the Larry Neal/Pen Faulkner writers conference for the eastern seaboard, a landmark effort to bring together writers of all races in a working environment. In 1985, the Congressional Hispanic Caucus selected Castillo as one of the top twenty Hispanic leaders in the United States.

Castillo's special concern is American agriculture beyond the year 2000. "We don't have the divine right to dominate the market," he says. "At best, we have the divine right to hustle."

Fred J. Clark
Staff Assistant
1301 Longworth House Office
  Bldg.
225-2171

Expertise: Credit & finance, commodity programs, conservation, rural development

Upon being elected to Congress in 1982, Rep. Richard Lehman (D-CA) brought Clark, then on his staff in the California State Assembly, to Washington. As legislative assistant for Lehman, Clark was primarily responsible for the congressman's work on the Committee on Banking, Finance, and Urban Affairs. Clark also worked with the House Agriculture Committee, where he was later hired as staff assistant, receiving his baptism-by-fire through his involvement with the 1985 farm bill.

More recently, Clark represented the full Agriculture Committee in its work on legislation in 1987 to bail out the Federal Farm Credit System (FCS) and assist borrowers of the Farmers Home Administration. Clark's previous work with the House Banking Committee paid dividends as the two committees worked together to write language creating "Farmer Mac"—the Federal Agricultural Mortgage Corporation. This new program will allow commercial banks and other farm lenders to make real estate loans to farmers and then to sell the loans into a secondary market, thereby allowing increased capital for farm real estate lending to flow from investors on Wall Street to farmer-borrowers in rural areas.

Clark's responsibilities also include work with other financial issues, such as commodity and stock index futures. This issue has drawn particular attention since last October's stock market crash, as well as the increasing interplay between he futures market and New York's equity markets.

Personal: born 3/19/57 in San Jose, California. B.S. California Polytechnic State Univ., 1983, magna cum laude. J.D. Georgetown Univ., 1988. 1981-1983, legislative aide, California State Assemblyman Richard Lehman (D). 1983-1985, legislative assistant, Rep. Richard Lehman (D-CA). 1985-present, staff assistant, House Committee on Agriculture

One of the things Clark quickly learned as a staff member of the committee was that oversight of agriculture programs is an ongoing necessity. Oftentimes, a program needs to be fine-tuned as a result of harsh weather conditions or the flux in agricultural prices. The committee has continued to have success in shepherding legislation to address the FCS's problems through the legislative process in three consecutive years—1985, 1986, and 1987. Clark will also be involved in the committee's oversight of the four billion dollars FCS bailout in the months ahead.

The 1985 farm bill had several conservation programs, all of which Clark monitors on a continuing basis. Included in the bill was an array of programs designed to encourage farmers to utilize sound conservation practices and standards. The committee, with Clark's assistance, has been overseeing this area and will no doubt have a good sense of how effective the programs are by the time the committee begins drafting the 1990 farm bill.

Rural development is another area in which Clark has been steadily developing an expertise. Legislation in this area may include cost-sharing for infrastructure development (e.g., bridges, roads, dams, etc.); the retraining of farmers who suffer or are forced out of business; and the promotion of expanded business development in rural areas.

In addition to assisting other committee staffers with drafting "committee reports and bill language, Clark is also responsible for the committee's work on the cotton and rice programs. Because of the interrelationship between all of the agricultural commodities, Clark must also be something of a generalist. Thus, his work also extends to wheat, corn and various other farm commodities. And although the committee addresses commodity programs every four to five years in the omnibus farm bill, the current budget climate has forced the committee and Clark to alter many of the programs each year in the budget reconciliation process.

Clark is recognized as a diligent student of American agricultural policy and congressional politics.

Howard (Chip) H. Conley III
Staff Economist
1301 Longworth House Office
  Bldg.
225-2171

Expertise: Budget and program cost analysis

When the Agriculture Committee began work on the landmark farm bill early in 1985, they sought an agricultural economist who could provide the Committee with sound judgment and economic analysis of the various federal farm programs. Perhaps, they thought, this person could inject some fresh ideas into the way the programs have been traditionally conceptualized and administered. It was going to be a long and difficult fight, and help would be needed in "shoe-horning" the bill into an already tight budget situation. As a result the Committee recruited Chip Conley, an agriculture specialist who has spent more than 17 years learning and working in the field.

Colleagues say Conley's background and expertise in agriculture economics give the House committee a real "leg up" in both soundness and credibility in its assessment of the issues. Conley's career has taken him from improving farming efficiency in rural India to program analysis at the USDA and the Congressional Budget office.

During consideration of the 1985 Farm Bill, Conley's job was to identify and analyze the core problems of the rapidly deteriorating farming sector, and to determine a variety of options that would maximize the cost-effectiveness of government programs.

Personal: born 11/27/47 in Norfolk, Virginia. B.A. Wesleyan Univ., 1970. M.S. Agricultural Economics, Univ. of Tennessee, 1976. 1970-72, Peace Corps Volunteer, Dairy Extension Program, India. 1973-76, Peace Corps Agricultural Representative. 1976-78, Agricultural Economist, U.S. Department of Agriculture. 1978-85, Principal Budget Analyst, Congressional Budget Office. 1985-present, Staff Economist, Committee on Agriculture.

Conley believes that the most important single effect of the 1985 bill has been the stabilization of land values in the farming industry, making it easier for debt-burdened farmers to make intelligent choices about their futures. Conley believes the major problem facing the industry is not a labor surplus, as many farm program critics argue, but a debt surplus caused by late-1970s inflation and overvalued land prices. Congress has already taken the next step, with the enactment of H.R. 3030, the Agricultural Credit Act of 1987, to address the debt problem, by requiring the restructuring of problem loans as an alternative to potential mass foreclosures.

Generally, Conley sees himself as an economist recommending "numbers alternatives" to the Committee members. He believes in leaving policy calls to elected officials.

Conley appreciates the bipartisan nature of the Committee, which observers have called the "key working ingredient of the Committee." During the consideration of the 1985 Farm Bill, Conley spent equal amounts of time consulting with members of the minority and the majority. He is reluctant to label himself ideologically, but says that as an economist, he is naturally somewhat conservative, and personally favors policy options that are more responsive to the market.

Timothy P. DeCoster
Staff Director
Subcommittee on Forests, Family
    Farms, and Energy
1301 Longworth House Office
    Bldg.
225-1867

*Personal: born 10/3/56 in Quincy,
Illinois. B.A. Grinnell Coll., 1978
(Grinnell Honors Scholarship). J.D.
Univ. of Missouri-Columbia 1981.
1981-1984, Legislative Assistant, Rep.
Harold Volkmer (D-MO). 1984-1987,
Legislative Director, Rep. Harold
Volkmer. 1987-present, Staff Director,
Subcommittee on Forests, Family
Farms, and Energy.*

Expertise: Forestry and Agriculture

When Tim DeCoster was growing up in Missouri, political
discussion was the centerpiece of the evening meal. His father
served in the Missouri State legislature near twenty years and the
young DeCoster naturally assumed a bent toward politics. After
graduating from law school, "Washington just seemed like a good
place to start." He contacted Congressman Harold Volkmer's (D-
MO) office to begin an internship. Shortly thereafter he was
promoted to Legislative Aide, and soon after Legislative Director.
In 1987, DeCoster moved over to become the Staff Director of the
Subcommittee on Forests, Family Farms, and Energy chaired by
Congressman Volkmer.

With the bulk of Subcommittee work taken up by forest-related
issues, DeCoster found that most of his time was dedicated to that
work. He soon learned that forest management embraces many
aspects: management of wildlife, timber, recreational activities,
water quality, road construction, research and others.

In 1982, as Legislative Assistant for Congressman Volkmer,
DeCoster entered a particularly tough battle involving two
wilderness bills. The issue had been debated for years and was
not finally resolved until 1984. The bills designated relatively small
parcels of land in Missouri as wilderness areas: Paddy Creek,
consisting of a little less than 17,000 acres, and the Irish
Wilderness of roughly 17,000 acres. The experience turned out to
be a baptism by fire; DeCoster learned a lot about forestry issues
very quickly. The opposition, well-funded and well-organized,
enjoyed support from the administration as well as from other
members of the Missouri delegation. The Paddy Creek bill was
approved in 1982, and the Irish in 1984. After the bills were
passed, an environmental lobbyist commented that it was, "acre
for acre, the toughest wilderness battle" they had ever fought.

DeCoster particularly enjoys his work now that he's on the
committee staff because it allows him to focus on a narrower
range of issues: "Working more closely with issues sometimes
allows you to see tangible results."

Philip L. Fraas
Chief Counsel
1301 Longworth House Office
  Bldg.
225-1663

Personal: born 1943. B.A. Rockhurst Coll., Kansas City, Mo., 1965. J.D. Univ. of Missouri, 1969. 1962-1968, U.S. Army Reserve. 1967-1968, insurance claims adjustor. 1969, estate and gift tax attorney. 1970-1973, prosecuting attorney, criminal justice grants manager, U.S. Department of Justice. 1975 Special Counsel; 1970-1980, Counsel, both with Senate Agriculture Committee. 1981-1984, Deputy Chief Counsel and Minority Staff Director, Senate Agriculture Committee. 1985 to present, Chief Counsel, House Agriculture Committee.

Expertise: U.S. agricultural policy, commodity futures trading

In his thirteen years on the Hill, Phil Fraas has seen a lot of battles fought over agriculture legislation. What's more, he has Witnessed them from both the Senate and the House. Fraas was a key player in the development of the 1977, 1981 and 1985 farm bills.

As Chief Counsel for the Committee, Fraas helps coordinate the Committee's agenda with those of the Foreign Affairs, Ways and Means, Energy and Commerce, and Banking Committees on issues such as trade, securities and farm credit policy.

Fraas also oversees the Committee's three-member legal staff. Since the subcommittees are without their in-house legal counsel, the full Committee's legal staff serve as counsel to the subcommittee chairmen as well.

"Phil Fraas is a trusted advisor to the chairman (Kika de la Garza of Texas)," says a lobbyist who works on agriculture issues. "He's a straight stick who listens well, and he's sharp." The committee recently saw the enactment of the Agriculture Credit Act of 1987, which is designed to revitalize the farm credit system. The Committee is now assessing current regulatory procedures and mechanisms in light of recent stock market volatility. Fraas says the Committee is examining in particular the use of program trading in the financial futures markets. "We're looking at legislative proposals to change the regulatory responsibilities of the Commodities Futures Trading Commission and its relationship to the Securities and Exchange Commission," he says.

The agriculture title of the Omnibus Trade Bill is another priority, he notes. "I'm very optimistic about getting some kind of legislation this year," he says. In addition, the Committee is looking at rewriting the Federal Insecticide, Fungicide and Rodentcide Act (FIFRA), which the House passed in the 99th Congress but which the Senate failed to act on. "Prospects for passage are good in the 100th Congress, he adds. One of the issues in FIFRA is an examination of the "re-registration" process of agricultural pesticides being conducted by the Environmental Protection Agency. The process involves the chemical analysis and registration of all pesticides used in the United States. Fraas says the Committee would like to accelerate EPA's review process by streamlining the procedures and providing more money and resources for the Agency to complete its work.

"EPA promised in 1972 that it would examine each pesticide under the newly established environmental regulations and complete the process in a few years," he notes. "Here we are in 1988 and the process is not finished."

Agriculture

Gregory Frazier
Staff Director
Subcommittee on Wheat,
 Soybeans, and Feed Grains
1301-A Longworth House Office
 Bldg.
225-1494

Personal: born 9/17/53 in Abilene, Kansas. B.S. in history and political science, Kansas State Univ., 1975. M.A. Univ. of Connecticut, 1976. 1977-1983, Staff Assistant, Representative Dan Glickman (D-KS), Wichita, KS. 1983-1985, Legislative Assistant, Representative Dan Glickman, Washington, D.C. 1985-1986, Legislative Director, Representative Dan Glickman. 1987-present, Staff Director, Subcommittee on Wheat, Soybeans, and Feed Grains, House Committee on Agriculture.

Expertise: Domestic farm commodities programs, trade issues affecti▮ wheat, soybeans, and feed grains

In a profession where staff turnover and fresh faces are common, Greg Frazier has become an uncommonly experienced and knowledgeable constant on Capitol Hill. As Staff Director for the House Subcommittee on Wheat, and Feed Grains, Frazier provides Subcommittee Chairman Dan Glickman (D-KS) with an 11-year background in farm-related legislation.

"Capitol Hill's not the easiest place in the world to work," Frazier bluntly states. "Unfortunately, Capitol Hill just grinds people up– that's the nature of the work here, and you either adapt to it or you don't."

Frazier has made it through the grind and, amazingly enough, has managed to do it without sacrificing the sense of loyalty which seems almost ingrained in his Midwestern roots. "I don't think that I could ever work for another Member besides Dan," says Frazier. "At some point I'm going to try something different–I don't know what that is. But it's very difficult to be thinking about that when you enjoy it."

As Staff Director for the Agriculture Committee's largest and most active subcommittee, Frazier usually has little time to think about anything other than his work. If you want to get to the heart of most major farm commodities legislation, you can't pass "GO" without first going through Frazier's subcommittee. In 1987, most of Frazier's activities centered around the budget process. "Both in reconciliation and in the Budget Summit, at least 75% of the farm program's savings will come out of our subcommittee," says Frazier.

As much as Frazier and the many hard-hit members of the Agriculture Committee would like to help American agriculture, the task this time has been to figure out how to reduce spending. As Frazier puts it, "If you're going to do something about the deficit, and if you're going to do something about agriculture, it means making some changes."

It is apparent that cutting back on farm expenditures has not been the easiest or most desired options–especially from the subcommittee point of view, but Frazier still sees some hope for America's farmers. "A lot of people say that the worst that we've had is over, that things are beginning to improve a bit," says Frazier. "There is some evidence for that."

"But for every example of a farmer doing better," Frazier is quick to add, "it's easy to come up with someone who's not."

Lynn Gallagher
Staff Consultant
1301 Longworth House Office
  Bldg.
225-2342

Expertise: Nutrition, public assistance, food stamps

"Socially conscious" is probably the best adjective a person could use to describe the professional life of Lynn Gallagher.

Since her days as an undergraduate at Merimack College in Andover, Mass. and the University of California in Long Beach, Gallagher has been concerned with the social welfare and public assistance issues which have become part of the nation's public policy over the last two decades. Today, with twenty years of experience under her belt, Gallagher serves as the minority staff consultant for the Domestic Marketing, Consumer Relations and Nutrition Subcommittee of the House Committee on Agriculture.

"It was a brand new experience for me in 1981 when I started on the Hill," says Gallagher. "I feel like an old hand at this kind of thing now."

Although the 1985 Farm Bill was the last major piece of legislation to deal at much length with the food stamp issue, Gallagher has been working on issues related to the simplification and coordination of major public assistance programs. Gallagher was an active participant in the formulation of public assistance and food stamp-related policy in the 1987 Stewart B. McKinney Homeless Assistance Act, as well as the Family Welfare Reform Act. Although Gallagher's background is public welfare programs, she also has contributed to related agricultural programs such as the marketing orders, surplus distribution and nutrition education dairy programs.

Personal: born 6/22/45 in Boston, Massachusetts. B.A. California State Univ., Long Beach, 1967. 1967, Social worker, working with aged and disabled persons, Los Angeles County. Chief of the Bureau of Public Assistance for the Virginia Department of Social Services.

Being on minority staff, Gallagher hasn't been able to play as prominent a role in the legislative process as some might like, but that doesn't seem to bother this polite, well-travelled daughter of a Naval officer. "For the time being," says Gallagher, "I'm pleased to be right here." When she's not working, Gallagher spends time with her family. Her father retired in the Washington, D.C, area after serving in the Navy, and Gallagher's four brothers and one sister have also managed to stay close-by.

Agriculture

Timothy J. Galvin
Professional Staff Member
1301 Longworth House Office
  Bldg.
225-2171

Expertise: Price support programs

Tim Galvin first discovered his interest in agriculture in high school when he worked part-time as a herdsman for a family-owned cow-calf operation near his home in Sioux City, Iowa. His interest in politics budded shortly thereafter when, during the summer between high school and college, he interned in Rep. Berkley Bedell's (D-IA) district office. It seemed logical, then, that Galvin's career would somehow fuse the two. He packed his bags for Washington, and he's been working on agricultural issues in Congress ever since.

Now, after more than ten years on Capitol Hill, Galvin has advanced to a top policy-making position on the Agriculture Committee. He has distinguished himself as a leading expert on the federal government's price support programs for wheat, feed grains, soybeans, sugar, and dairy; and on the volatile issue of pesticide safety reform. Colleagues say the depth of Galvin's knowledge and understanding of these issues has made him an asset to the Committee staff.

As Bedell's chief legislative aide, Galvin engineered his boss's push for stronger and more effective price supports for feed grains. Galvin contributed significantly to the senior Agriculture Committee member's initiative for a mandatory price support program and farmers referendum. This idea was ultimately unsuccessful but was widely hailed by the farming community as an important step toward re-thinking the country's farm support program.

Personal: born 11/22 in Sioux City, Iowa. B.A. George Washington Univ., 1979. M.S. Georgetown Univ., 1985. 1979-81, Legislative Assistant to Rep. Berkley Bedell (D-IA). 1981-85, Legislative Director to Rep. Bedell. 1983-1984, Member, Agricultural Working Group, Mondale for President. 1985-87, Staff Director, Subcommittee on Department Operations, Research and Foreign Agriculture, Committee on Agriculture. 1987 to present, Professional Staff Member, Committee on Agriculture.

Galvin serves as the Agriculture Committee's expert on the Federal Insecticide, Fungicide and Rodenticide Act (FIFRA), the country's pesticide control law. Under his direction as a staff director, the Subcommittee on Department Operations, Research and Foreign Agriculture reported legislation that passed the House three times in 1986 to significantly accelerate the EPA's review of pesticides for compliance with modern safety standards.

Galvin, was an agriculture advisor to the 1984 Mondale For President campaign, and has volunteered with the Dukakis presidential campaign to do likewise.

James R. Lyons
Staff Assistant
1301-A Longworth House Office
  Bldg.
225-2171

Expertise: Natural resources and environment, livestock and poultry, food safety and inspection, rural development and commodity programs.

Three years as a program analyst for the U.S. Fish and Wildlife service sparked Jim Lyons' interest in policy and the legislative process. In 1982, believing that experience is the best teacher, he turned down an opportunity to return to Yale to work toward a Ph.D and instead took a job representing the Society of American Foresters.

Having experience as a lobbyist, Lyons brings a different perspective to his position as a professional staff member with the House Agriculture Committee. The advantage, he believes, is that he has worked with many of the individuals and organizations seeking assistance from the Committee.

In his first two years with the Committee, Lyons has been involved in a wide range of issues such as legislation establishing the Columbia River Gorge National Scenic Area; a measure expanding the scope of current research on the effects of air pollution on forests; a bill to initiate a federal groundwater program; reauthorization of natural resource extension activities and the Endangered Species Act; and increasing assistance to family farmers and those who have been forced to leave farming due to financial stress. Lyons is a strong advocate of congressional oversight and believes that legislation and regulation are not the cure-all for every issue. In this regard, he has been instrumental in Committee efforts to review national forest management and planning activities and to seek greater balance in USDA's natural resources management programs.

Lyon believes that USDA programs and policies should have a solid scientific basis and that both the short- and the long-term ramifications of decisions need to be understood. He is an advocate of compromise and strives to ensure that Members "hear both sides" before deciding how to deal with an issue.

Personal: born 5/17/55 in Englewood, New Jersey. B.S. Cook Coll., Rutgers Univ., 1977. Master of Forestry, Yale Univ., 1979. 1979-82, Program Analyst, U.S. Fish & Wildlife Service. 1982-86, Director of Resource Policy, Society of American Foresters. 1986-87, Staff Director, Subcommittee on Forests, Family Farms, and Energy, House Committee on Agriculture. 1987-present, Staff Assistant, Committee on Agriculture.

Parks Shackelford
Consultant
Subcommittee on Cotton, Rice and
  Sugar
1336 Longworth House Office
  Bldg.
225-1867

As staff consultant for the Subcommittee on Cotton, Rice, and
Sugar, Parks Shackelford is involved in researching and promoting
these crops and the federal programs which affect them.

Shackelford first worked for Subcommittee Chairman Jerry
Huckaby (D-LA) as an intern during high school. Agricultural policy
was not a new thing to him even in high school. It was what he
knew best, having grown up on a farm in the small town of Jones,
LA, where his family cultivated, and still cultivates, rice and cotton,
two of the main cash crops of Huckaby 's Louisiana district

As an undergraduate Shackelford became interested in Latin
American studies and international relations. This took him to
Costa Rica for 10 months, after he received his B.A. in Latin
American studies,

He came to Washington, seeking a job in international relations in
which he could apply both his fluency in Spanish and first-hand
knowledge of Central America. He found jobs in this area scarce,
and decided instead to take a job tracking farm legislation for the
Subcommittee on Cotton, Rice, and Sugar.

*Personal: born 4/14/61 in Jones,
Louisiana. B.A. in Latin American
Studies Tulane Univ. New Orleans, LA,
1983. 1985, assistant to staff
consultant, House Subcommittee on
Cotton, Rice, and Sugar. 1986,
Legislative Assistant, National
Commission on Agricultural Trade and
Export Policy. Legislative Assistant,
Rep. Richard Durbin (D-IL). 1987-
present, Staff Consultant,
Subcommittee on Cotton, Rice and
Sugar.*

While it may have seemed like his second choice , the job involved
him once again in the field of agriculture. When he left the
subcommittee in 1986, it was to remain in the field of agriculture,
working on a legislative project for the National Commission on
Agriculture Trade and Export Policy. His work on the project
finished, and the position of staff consultant for the Subcommittee
on Cotton, Rice, and Sugar available, Shackelford naturally
returned to the subcommittee, where he remains.

When not working on the Hill, Shackelford prefers to be hunting
and fishing.

Daniel Waggoner
Staff Director
Subcommittee on Livestock, Dairy, and Poultry
1430 Longworth House Office Bldg.
225-1496

Expertise: Livestock, dairy & poultry

At the age of 26, Daniel Waggoner became the youngest staff director on Capitol Hill, and a key staff player on agricultural issues vital to much of rural America.

Waggoner got his start when he came to the attention of Rep. Charles Stenholm (D-TX), chairman of the Subcommittee. During a football reception at Texas State, where he had recently graduated with a masters in agribusiness and animal science, Waggoner met Stenholm and his wife. A few months later he was working in Washington.

Waggoner's responsibilities center on issues such as cattle disease, dairy price supports and regulation of the poultry industry. He notes the agricultural sectors covered by the Subcommittee represent "probably the largest industry in the country in terms of total sales and volume" and adds "we can no longer discuss policy on the basis of what we do and don't do within our borders. . .we are now in an international ag-market, and policies of yesterday will no longer meet the policies and demands of tomorrow."

The Texan, who grew up on a horse and cattle ranch, still enjoys riding horses and is adept at both English and Western riding styles. He works with youth in the 4-H organization and, when he's not playing tennis, the former member of the national Horse and Cattle Judge Team judges livestock at county fairs.

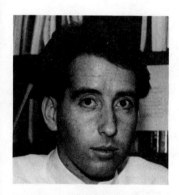

Personal: born 5/20/60 in Athens, Texas. B.A. Texas State Univ., 1983. M.A. Texas State Univ., 1984. 1985-86, Staff Aide, Rep. Charles Stenholm (D-TX). 1987-present, Staff Director, Subcommittee on Livestock, Dairy, and Poultry, House Committee on Agriculture.

HOUSE OF REPRESENTATIVES
COMMITTEE ON APPROPRIATIONS

Appropriations

John Berry
Associate Appropriations Staff
Representative Steny Hoyer (D-
  MD)
1513 Longworth House Office
  Bldg.
225-4131

Personal: born 2/10/59 in Rockville, Maryland. B.A. Univ. of Maryland, 1980 (summa cum laude). M.P.A. Maxwell School of Public Affairs, Syracuse Univ., 1981. 1982, Chief Administrative Office and Cable Television Office, Montgomery County government. 1983-84, Senate Finance Committee Staffer, Maryland General Assembly. 1985-present, Associate Appropriations Staff, U.S. Representative Steny Hoyer.

Expertise: Treasury, Postal Service and general government

Hoyer has a reputation for selecting sharp, articulate staffers and pushing them hard to perform to the maximum of their abilities. John Berry has been with Hoyer since 1985. He is young and bright, and is already considered to be a "rising star" among the many associate staffers of the Appropriations Committee. Many people his age might easily develop an inflated sense of importance about themselves when saddled with such a label— but not Berry. He is quick to point out that he works for a Member who has distinguished himself for his effectiveness.

Like his predecessor, John Moag, who is now a partner with the prestigious law firm of Patton, Boggs, and Blow, John Berry is delegated with considerable responsibility by Hoyer. With the exception of Hoyer's Labor and HHS Subcommittee assignment, (which Greg Gill handles), Berry is responsible for all the Congressman's appropriations work, including his Treasury, Postal Service and General Government Subcommittee assignment.

While the issues in the Treasury, Postal Service and General Government Subcommittee do not often attract national attention, they are bread-and-butter issues in Hoyer's district of Prince Georges County, Maryland. With 63,000 constituents who are federal employees, Hoyer gives priority, as those who have observed John Berry are aware, to negotiating solutions to problems affecting the federal workforce.

Consequently, Berry spends much of his time on civil service pay and benefits issues and staffing Hoyer's rear-guard actions against Administration efforts to nibble away at these programs. He works hard to maintain a dialogue with the Office of Management and Budget (OMB), which sometimes includes using what he refers to as a "carrot and stick" approach. Hoyer led the fight in the House against the Administration's plan to implement a mandatory drug testing program for federal employees. When Hoyer realized there were not enough votes on the Hill for a ban, he got an amendment added that enumerated stringent procedures, spelling out the exact process under which federal employees could be tested. Berry coordinated this successful effort by working with federal employee labor unions, the Administration and staffers in other Congressional offices to identify areas where consensus was possible.

Another issue Berry handled for Hoyer was resolving how money collected from federal employees through the Combined Federal Campaign was to be distributed to charitable organizations. While not a "hot" evening news item, it was nevertheless important to Hoyer and his constituents. As on the drug testing issue, Berry conducted long and arduous negotiations with groups such as the Office of Personnel Management, the United Way Campaign, the National Service Agencies, and International Service Agencies in an effort to develop a consensus position.

Berry also spends his time on a number of Treasury, Internal Revenue Service, and U.S. Customs issues. He worked with another branch of the Treasury Department, the Secret Service, on resolving problems related to extending protection to the Pope on his 1987 visit to the United States.

Like many Maryland natives, Berry enjoys eating seafood, particularly crabs, and water-skiing when he has the opportunity.

Delacroix Davis III
Staff Assistant
Subcommittee on Defense
H-144 Capitol Bldg.

Expertise: Procurement/Air Force aircraft & Army, Navy,& AF missiles

By some defense experts' reckoning, Del Davis is "still in the process of getting his feet wet" at the defense subcommittee.

It's no reflection on Davis, whom they say is very capable and thoroughly knowledgeable about his areas—procurement of Air Force aircraft and all missiles. Rather, it's more a function of his relatively short term as a staff assistant there, the long-time defense hands being a tough bunch to impress.

"Even though they may have real expertise in something," a former committee staffer explains, "the defense staff is moved around from Air Force aircraft to Army trucks until they have a broad-based feel of what the bill is about. And after a while, they find their niche."

The Subcommittee's professional track often includes working first for the full committee, or "the front office" as it's called. There, they learn the nuts and bolts of the appropriations process as well as what one calls "the guts" of the bill.

Davis has done both. He started out on the full committee in the mid-70s and moved to the Defense Subcommittee a couple of years ago to handle the operations and maintenance accounts. In 1987, he received his present responsibilities.

Davis's strong suit is the technical area, according to a Senate counterpart. "He is a consistent performer and straight-forward on his agenda. A very principled fellow. When he believes in something he is like a mad dog on your pant leg.

"He can be very accommodating, but he has the attitude of 'let's get the job done that we are supposed to do.' He can be very assertive in those things he feels strongly about."

A minority committee staffer has a similar impression of Davis. "He is very professional in how he goes about his job, but he can be brutally truthful when you ask his opinion. He has a dry wit."

His duties also include running hearings and conferences with the Senate. He may also be detailed to work on special projects that come up when they don't fit into other staffers' areas.

Davis also draws the admiration of his colleagues for his prowess in handling the ball on another type of "floor." Says one: "He's a helluva basketball player."

Jimmy R. Fairchild
Staff Assistant
1016 Longworth House Office
  Bldg.
225-0772

Expertise: Appropriations

Jim Fairchild takes a low-profile approach to his job. But he's really not out of place, because Republican staffers on the House Appropriations Committee as a rule are neither seen nor heard as often as their Democratic counterparts.

Fairchild, a Kansas native, has spent ten years on the Committee, all as a staff consultant.

Fairchild and his Republican staff colleagues operate at somewhat of a numerical disadvantage. "One of the drawbacks to the Committee is a limited number of slots that the Democrats are willing to provide for Republican staff members," says an official with the House Minority Whip's office.

As a result, all Republican staffers actually work for the full Committee and are assigned to follow from one to three subcommittees, depending on the area. Fairchild, for example, looks after three: Commerce, Justice, State and Judiciary; Foreign Operations; and Legislative.

Because the staff is stretched so thin, "Fairchild and the other Republican staff on the Committee don't have much time to breathe, let alone anything else," the Whip staffer adds.

But even with the time demands and the limited roles that Republican staff play on the committee, Fairchild prefers to stay out of the limelight.

Personal: born 11/8/40 in McPherson, Kansas. B.A. Kansas State Univ., 1963. Georgetown Univ., 1963-1964. 1963-1965, clerk, Rep. Garner Shriver, (R-KS). 1965-1966, research assistant, Rep. Archie Nelson, (R-MN). 1966-1976, appropriations associate staff, Rep. Garner Shriver. 1977-present, Staff Assistant, Committee on Appropriations.

Robert B. Foster
Staff Assistant
Subcommittee on Agriculture,
  Rural Development, Agriculture,
  and Related Agencies
2362 Rayburn House Office Bldg.
225-2368

Expertise: Agriculture and rural development

"In the pecking order around the Department of Agriculture, if your boss is on one telephone line, and Bob Foster is on the other, you ask your boss if he's willing to hold," says Mike Hoback, an assistant secretary of Agriculture. "A call from Bob Foster is a call from Chairman Whitten. He carries with him the clout of the chairman. You jump out of respect and because he's been very fair in his dealings with us."

No where does the Appropriations Committee Chairman's hand seem heavier or more evident than in the agriculture subcommittee he also heads. As the chief clerk, an important part of Foster's job is seeing that his chairman, who has been dubbed "The Permanent Secretary of Agriculture," gets to bring the "bacon" home to Mississippi.

"He's got the Chairman's confidence and his eyes and ears," explains one lobbyist. "He know when to go with it. He knows how to fill in the blanks, when Whitten hands him the appropriations bill he's handwritten on a yellow pad. He fits in cotton, rice, soybeans, fish and catfish for Mississippi. Republicans are out of the loop there.

"Whitten scares everybody—he does! You must swear not to tell anybody I said this—or we'll not be getting anything for a long time. Whitten is that powerful. He's the law."

The lobbyist adds, "Everyone thinks the world of Bob Foster."

So does Chairman Whitten. Asked about Foster's qualifications and why he was chosen for the top subcommittee staff slot, Whitten issued this statement: "Bob Foster has worked with me in defense for years, now with rural development. He is tops in his field. Does the fact that I've kept him speak loudly enough?"

Foster, himself from rural Ohio and a graduate of Ohio State, worked three years with Aerojet General and six years with the Small Business Administration before coming to the committee over 18 years ago.

He is given the highest marks from Democrats and Republicans for everything from his knowledge about agriculture to his soft-spoken, courteous manner.

Department of Agriculture budget director Steve Dewhurst calls him the consummate professional.

"Since 1978, I've been dealing with him on an everyday basis," he says. "He knows his subject matter, is cool in a crisis, and does his homework. He is just a class guy. He is very circumspect, not a wheeler-dealer. He protects the (Committee's) decisions and can negotiate better than most staff in Congress."

Mario Castillo, chief of staff of the House Agriculture Committee, returned a call for his comments on Foster within the hour—from Tokyo. "He understands the political and the functions of the department. He's not just a simple number cruncher.

"He's not one of the show horses. He's the type that gets things done behind the scenes and wields a great deal of power. I'd take his word to the bank."

When Castillo needs to talk with Foster about program specifics or to get his reaction, he doesn't call. He goes to visit Foster.

"If there is a situation where Mr. Whitten differs from the Agriculture Committee, Foster will lay it out for you. He's very honest. He'll listen to anything you have to say and discuss the basis on which he thinks your argument is erroneous."

John Victor, the budget director of the Agriculture Research Service, adds, "If he calls you for information, he knows exactly what he wants. He reviews it in painstaking detail and gets to the guts of the issue.

"He doesn't go into a lot of editorializing or gossip. He guards very carefully the individual personality and political thoughts of the members."

Says the lobbyist: "Bob Foster is one of those people you can trust. You know you are not going to get stabbed in the back. What you tell him stays in confidence."

A resident of Annapolis, Foster sails and plays golf. He has also researched his family's genealogy.

Terence Freese
Legislative Assistant
Rep. Norman Dicks (D-WA)
2301 Rayburn House Office Bldg.
225-5916

Expertise: Defense, military construction

When Rep. Norman Dicks was elected to the House in 1976, he brought to Washington one of his most valuable campaigners. Though he had just turned twenty-three, Terry Freese was already a campaign veteran with six years' experience behind him. At sixteen, Freese worked on a Washington state initiative to get the vote for 19-year-olds. In 1972, he campaigned throughout several states for presidential candidate George McGovern, and then applied his experience to various state and local campaigns. By the time Norman Dicks decided to run for the 6th District House seat, Freese was just coming off a city council campaign and took up the challenge of his first congressional campaign. He coordinated the door-to-door effort and "went through lots of shoe leather" himself.

Freese doesn't like political classifications, but often finds himself on the liberal side of many issues. He takes pride in his role in limiting the MX Missile project.

Personal: born 4/16/53 in Spokane, WA. B.A. (magna cum laude), Gonzaga Univ. 1975. 1977-1978, Legislative Assistant, Rep. Norman Dicks. 1979 to present, HAC.

Freese's concern about arms control issues is also reflected in his work to keep the U.S. within Salt II limits. Last year in the Appropriations Committee, he helped Dicks successfully delete four projects which would have created problems within the restrictive interpretation of the treaty. The programs were put back into the Defense Appropriation on the floor, however. More recently, the Reagan Administration's Strategic Defense Initiative program has raised similar questions, and Freese has helped Dicks in his efforts to ensure there would be no specific violations of the ABM treaty language.

Freese describes himself as "a political addict" and says that, although it took him awhile to get used to Washington D.C., he loves being directly involved in major issues. "My boss seems to have a hundred new ideas each day and we have our hands full just keeping up with him. Sometimes the hardest job is determining the possible."

Freese relaxes by playing limited-contact ice hockey. He and his wife enjoy following road races in the area. They met when she joined the Congressman's staff as Legislative Assistant, assigned primarily to Interior issues.

Aubrey A. "Tex" Gunnels
Staff Assistant
H-218 Capitol Bldg.
225-5834

Personal: born 4/20/18 in San Augustine County, Texas. Draughon's Business Coll., Lubbock, TX. A.A. American Univ., Dunham-Devor fellowship, 1950. CSC Sr. Admin. Intern Program (11th) 1950, Wash. 1942-1946, U.S.M.C. 1931-1938, Commercial teacher and accountant, Lubbock and Plainview, TX. 1938-1955, staff assignments in the field of military budget and requirements, Dept. of Defense, Wash. 1955-1956, Chief, Major Material Team, USRO, Paris, France. 1958-present, Staff Assistant to House Committee on Appropriations.

Expertise: Treasury, Postal Service, general government

In 1958, Aubrey A. "Tex" Gunnels was preparing to travel to New York and then on to Paris to join the U.S. delegation to NATO. Then a call came from the chairman of the House Appropriations Committee, Representative Clarence Cannon (D-MO). Cannon was looking for a capable individual to join his committee staff and had his eye on Gunnels. "I am prepared to offer you a permanent appointment on Appropriations," Cannon said, and Gunnels responded simply, "Yes, sir." He cancelled all plans for travelling to Paris.

As Staff director of the Treasury, Postal Service, and General Government Subcommittee on Appropriations, Gunnels handles appropriations for 65 government agencies. Politics, he says, plays no role in his recommendations, and because of that he has earned the trust of many Members. "I try to give the best advice possible to the entire committee," he says. "The staff is non-political here; we are professional, and this helps us to work together rather than constantly clashing over . . . partisan projects."

Gunnels has good reason to enjoy his job. He can see the results of his efforts. "When I was at DOD," he says, "I would write a letter and by the time it got signed I wouldn't recognize it. Here, I see language in law which we wrote years ago which is still being used and repeated each year. There is a certain satisfaction in knowing that these are examples of jobs well done, that they have withstood the test of time."

Since its establishment, Gunnels has fought hard for funds for the Federal Law Enforcement Training Center at Glynco, GA. In July, 1987, he attended the ground-breaking ceremonies for a new dormitory at Glynco, unaware that it would later be named the "Aubrey A. 'Tex' Gunnels Dormitory Complex." It is scheduled to be completed in January 1989.

Gunnels has never regretted the choice he made in 1958. During Lyndon Johnson's administration, he was offered the position of Commissioner of Customs. "I was sorely tempted but knew my efforts would get lost in the system," he says, "that I would not be able to influence certain outcomes for this country as much as I'd like. I'm happy where I am."

Gunnels has three children and is active in Masonic Order.

Lucy McLelland Hand
Appropriations Assistant
Rep. William Lehman (D-FL)
2347 Rayburn House Office Bldg.
225-4211

Personal: born 6/11/48 in Washington, D.C. A.B. Smith College, 1970. 1971, Muskie Presidential campaign. 1973-present, Rep. William Lehman: 1973-74, Receptionist; 1975, Office Manager; 1975-77, Legislative Assistant; 1977-79, Majority Associate staff for Lehman, House Budget Committee; 1980-Present, Associate Staff for Lehman, House Appropriations Committee.

Expertise: Transportation

Lucy McLelland Hand had been active in politics for several years before she began working on the Hill. At Smith College she was a volunteer for the presidential campaign of Senator Eugene McCarthy (D-MN) and later, after graduating, worked full-time on an unsuccessful 1970 congressional primary campaign for a liberal Democrat in Maryland, and, in 1971, on the ill-fated presidential campaign of Senator Edmund Muskie (D-ME).

Her transition from campaigner to Hill staffer was not automatic or easy, however. After a period of searching, while working in a department store, Hand finally got her opportunity to work on the Hill in late 1973 as receptionist for Florida Congressman Bill Lehman. Although it was not exactly a high-level policy position, Hand felt that being a receptionist was a way to gain "Hill experience." It gave her the chance to prove her value to Lehman, and she wasted no time in doing just that. Today, after holding almost every position in his office, Hand is Lehman's senior staffer and is responsible for managing his powerful Appropriations Committee assignment. She knows the importance of every position in a congressional office and the role each one plays in enhancing the reputation of its Congressman. Over the years, she has been at Lehman's side as he has developed a reputation for quiet effectiveness, particularly on transportation issues.

Initially, it might not appear that a southern Democratic office would be a natural place for a person with a history of working on liberal Democratic campaigns. Lehman's district, though, is not typical of the South. His Dade County (Miami and northern suburbs) constituency includes a large number of retirees from the Northeast and a significant black urban population. This is the only congressional district in Florida won by the Mondale-Ferraro ticket in 1984. Not surprisingly, Bill Lehman's voting habits are more like those of a northern Democrat.

First elected to Appropriations in 1979, Lehman went on the Subcommittee on Transportation in 1979 to serve as an advocate for Dade County's mass transit needs. Many of his constituents were used to having mass transit systems at their disposal in the Northeast and wanted the same type of service in Dade County, especially since many of them were retired. Hand has worked closely with staffers on the Committee to ensure that Lehman's promise to his constituents to develop Miami's bus and rail systems has been fulfilled.

Although Hand's first duty is to ensure that Lehman's Florida interests are promoted, she plays a much wider role among staffers on the Appropriations Committee. When Lehman assumed the Transportation Subcommittee chairmanship in 1982, she became an important conduit through which staffers of other

Members would make their transportation needs known to him. Over the years, she has developed a reputation for being unusually accessible and refreshingly frank in discussing these matters.

Because of Lehman's desire to help other Members on transportation matters, Hand has become a key player in the annual battle over federal funding levels for mass transit systems throughout the country. She has helped to coordinate Lehman's efforts to assist sunbelt cities such as Atlanta, Houston and Los Angeles that are moving toward comprehensive mass transit systems and to thwart the Administration's plan to slash funding for Washington's Metropolitan Area Transit Authority, which receives its funding through a separate budget account in the transportation bill. In addition to mass transit issues, Hand closely monitors air safety issues for Lehman. She has worked on the successful efforts to force the Administration to increase the budget for hiring and training additional air traffic controllers and to require altitude encoding transponders in aircraft to help avert mid-air collisions.

Hand works with Tom Kingfield, the Subcommittee's Staff Director, in seeing that Lehman's policies are implemented. While there is some overlap in their duties, the relationship between the two of them is characterized by mutual respect and friendly cooperation.

Less glamorous, perhaps, is Lehman's long-standing interest in injury prevention. Hand is coordinating his participation in the new five-year Children's Hospital/Johnson & Johnson/National Safety Council Safe Kids campaign, which will involve both issues of interest to the Select Committee on Children, Youth and Families' Task Force on Prevention Strategies, which Lehman also chairs, and the traffic safety issues of the Transportation Subcommittee.

In her spare time, Hand enjoys travel, photography, singing (currently with the Junior League's Washingtones) and gardening.

Francis M. Hugo
Minority Staff Director
1016 Longworth House Office
  Bldg.
225-3481

*Personal: born in Watertown, New
York. B.A. Cornell Univ., 1962 (Pi
Sigma Alpha). Graduate study,
American Univ., 1962-1968. 1956-
1959, U.S. Marine Corps. 1962,
Research Assistant, Legislative
Reference Service. 1963, Legislative
Assistant, Sen. James B. Pearson (R-
KS). 1964, Research Associate,
Republican Natl. Comm. 1964-1969,
Public Finance Analyst, American
Enterprise Institute. 1968, Presidential
Transition Task Force on the Federal
Budget. 1969-1972, Computer
Systems Analyst, and 1972-1973,
Asst. to the Asst. Director for Policy
Analysis, Congressional Research
Service. 1973-present, Minority Staff
Director, House Committee on
Appropriations.*

Expertise: Appropriations

Mike Hugo, Minority Staff Director of the House Appropriations Committee for the last fifteen years, says above all else a person in his position must understand the appropriations and budget processes.

What Hugo actually does—and what he knows—are far more extensive. He works on one of the most important committees in Congress, directing a staff of seven professionals.

"My role is more a counsel, or an adviser, than a director," he says. Hugo emphasizes the importance of procedural knowledge above all else. "You need to understand how the budget and legislative process works," he says. "And about the executive budget process and Gramm-Rudman. There are bodies of procedural knowledge that a staff director has to know to keep things moving." Hugo must also keep an eye on the endless stream of substantive appropriations issues on which House Republicans will be formulating positions.

Serving in the minority has been the challenge of House Republican staffers since Congressman Joe Martin (R-MA) served as the last Republican Speaker back in the 1950s. But fifteen years on the staff of the minority has not discouraged Hugo. His efforts over the years have won praise from a number of quarters, among them two former minority leaders, John Rhodes and Gerald Ford, whose photos and notes of appreciation hang on one of his office walls.

His proudest moment came in 1981, when the House and the Senate approved a resolution (H.J. Res. 370) aimed at curbing spending. "It's one of the few times in my 15 years that we went head-to-head with the Democrats, presented a Republican alternative and won."

Hugo's work also earned him plaudits from another well-known Republican. "Your efforts as minority clerk for the House Appropriations Committee are essential to our effort to reduce federal spending," President Reagan wrote in a 1982 letter. "It is reassuring to know that our Republican members of the Appropriations Committee have your support and counsel."

Hugo enjoys bicycling. He also is an avid computer programmer. At the American Enterprise Institute, where he worked from 1964-69, Hugo designed the computer systems to support the federal budget analyses he wrote. He later spent three years as a systems analyst at the Congressional Research Service and, in his current job, designed some of the systems that support the text-processing functions of his staff.

Dennis M. Kedzior
Staff Assistant
H218 Capitol Bldg.
225-2771

Expertise: Budget and appropriations process

When the House leadership wants to know what is going to happen on appropriations bills, Dennis Kedzior is the staffer the Appropriations Committee sends. And, along with Fred Mohrman and Ed Powers, he is part of the "front office triad" that keeps Chairman Whitten "really informed on where things stand and the committee proceeding on its chaotic schedule," says a former colleague.

As the number two staffer on the full committee, Kedzior assembles omnibus bills and the Concurrent Resolutions (CR) into which the thirteen appropriations bills have been rolled in recent years. He assists staff director Fred Mohrman in staff selection and supervision and is frequently the Committee's representative in coordinating bills crossing many committees' jurisdictions, such as the omnibus drug program of l985, from House consideration to conference.

He worked as a budget analyst for the State of Wisconsin prior to joining the full committee in a more junior slot. He was promoted to his current position two years ago.

A veteran observer of Appropriations comments, "He's (Kedzior) very expert at the whole budget and appropriations process from a process standpoint—the formatting of appropriations bills and the CR—and thinking them through procedurally. He always seems to know what's going on in all thirteen of the subcommittees."

A senior colleague says, "Dennis does an excellent job because he is very sensitive to things. That's why he is one of the few that is well liked and well respected.

"He has what I'd describe as a 'quasi-pastoral approach.' He listens to you. I think that's the key to his success. He listens to you and he translates what he hears very well. He is able to read between the lines, but is somewhat uncomfortable asking your thoughts beforehand."

Another former colleague adds, "They won't know if they've made a good or bad impression on him. He's very impartial. But he conveys what is told him to the subcommittee and full committee chairmen, accurately and without prejudice.

"He will analyze what's said in a professional pro and con manner and then present his analysis. He's not a policymaker. Staff that try to (make policy) don't last long there."

An avid sailor, Kedzior lives in Annapolis with his wife and commutes in a four-wheel drive vehicle.

Appropriations

Thomas J. Kingfield
Subcommittee on Transportation
2358 Rayburn House Office Bldg.
225-2141

Expertise: Transportation/FAA and Coast Guard

"No one in the federal government has more experience with the transportation budget and has heard more of the stories than Tom Kingfield," declares a former deputy budget director of the Department of Transportation. "Yet he manages to take a fresh look at the appropriations bill each year."

The expertise of the chief staffer of the Subcommittee on Transportation is well recognized. He's one of those staffers who is reverently referred to as a "survivor," having outlasted 10 Department of Transportation heads and four subcommittee chairmen.

"Surviving that long—and doing so in a way that maintains good relationships—is an accomplishment," one of the country's best known big city transportation executives notes. "He's always kept the subcommittee chairman's ability to control the subcommittee—to make sure each gets what he needs, from the chairman to the members." Jack Schenendorf, chief minority counsel for the House Public Works and Transportation Committee, says, "He's the consummate professional in all of his dealings. We have our policy differences but he is a straight shooter. His political assessment of pluses and minuses of the controversies is very good."

A former colleague notes: "He's quiet and stern which conceals, somewhat, a bright intellect. He's low-key, not flashy, a very hard person to read physically and verbally. It's clear in his mind that Members make the decisions. Anyone trying to lobby him should realize that."

Larry Barnett of the Air Transport Association considers Kingfield very accessible and a good source of information about the details of DOT program needs and the appropriations process. "He can give you all the numbers on these things," the government relations director says.

"Everything on the subcommittee is done by consensus. He doesn't deal directly with Mr. Whitten because he's been there so long. He's not automatically favorably disposed to industry."

While the FAA and Coast Guard are Kingfield's two primary areas of responsibility, some observers feel he is less supportive of the latter and point to its major spending cuts in recent years. Others say he only reflects the institutional prejudices of his bosses, whose wishes he carries out faithfully.

Kingfield resides in Bethesda with his wife and children. He's known to be a good tennis player.

Edward E. Lombard
Staff Assistant
Subcommittee on Legislative Branch
H-218 Capitol Bldg.
225-5338

Personal: born 1/26/34 in Youngstown, Ohio. John Carroll Univ., 1952-1954. B.A. Youngstown Univ., 1959. M.I.A. Yale Univ., 1961 (Yale Fellowship). M.S. Stanford Univ., 1968. 1968, National Institute of Public Affairs Fellowship. 1964-1974, partner, Lland Associates. 1961-1964, planning analyst, Brunswick Corp. 1964-1966, staff, Office of Postmaster General. 1966-1971, Data Management Director, Small Business Administration. 1971-1973, Assistant Director for Administration, Dept. of Commerce. 1973-present, Staff Assistant, Subcommittee on Legislative, House Committee on Appropriations.

Expertise: Legislative appropriations, economic analysis, business planning, and automatic data processing

In the early 1970's, the Committee on Appropriations, then under the chairmanship of George Mahon (D-TX), found that it needed a staffer who had both technical capabilities in the area of computers and data processing and strong management abilities. Ed Lombard was then working at the Economic Development Administration in the Department of Commerce. As the Director of Program Analysis and Chief of Information Systems, Lombard's responsibilities included evaluating government programs and supervising large-scale data processing systems' development and operations. When Chairman Mahon heard of Lombard's qualifications, he tapped him for the committee job.

It wasn't long before Chairman Mahon had the opportunity to assess if he had chosen the right individual. Lombard was given responsibility for organizing the Committee's scorekeeping procedures for dealing with the Congressional Budget and Impoundment Control Act of 1974, which in turn led to the installation of a budget database and information retrieval system for Congress and for linking the Congressional and OMB databases. Subsequently, he supervised a small staff of Committee computer and technical experts who operated several on-line appropriation scorekeeping systems.

His current assignment is as committee clerk on the legislative branch appropriations subcommittee, where he and his colleagues put together the appropriations bill which includes funds for salaries and office and committee allowances in the Congress. (Chairman Vic Fazio's willingness to fight for pay raises, despite their unpopularity with the public, has endeared him to most Members and staff.) In the past, Lombard has also acted in an advisory capacity in regard to procurement of automated data processing for the federal government, as well as operations and funding matters.

But there is more to Ed Lombard than being an appropriations staffer. Off the Hill, he has been active as a coach of Babe Ruth baseball and youth basketball, and is an avid golfer. He has also taught business statistics at the University of Baltimore and has served as Commissioner of the Fairfax County (Virginia) Economic Development Authority.

Kevin Lynch
Legislative Assistant
Representative Les AuCoin (D-OR)
2159 Rayburn House Office Bldg.
225-0855

*Personal: born 9/5/59 in New York,
N.Y. B.A. Dartmouth Coll., 1981.
L'Universite Laval, Quebec, 1979.
London School of Economics, 1980.
1983-1988, associate staff, Committee
on Appropriations.*

Expertise: Interior, public land management, energy

Kevin Lynch left Dartmouth with a B.A. degree and four years experience as a writer, editor and publisher of his college newspaper. Congressman William Ratchford (D-CT) hired him as a Legislative Assistant, promoted him to Press Secretary, then moved him over to a staff position on the House Appropriations Committee, Interior and Transportation Subcommittee. Congressman Les AuCoin of Oregon hired Lynch for that position in 1985 and told Lynch that a top priority would be to pull together The Columbia River Gorge National Scenic Area Act. Efforts to develop a coordinated land management process had been in the works for several years and pressure from both developers and conservationist was mounting to move toward a resolution.

In 1986 Congress passed the act, which turned out to be remarkably innovative land management package. In retrospect, Lynch credits its success to the active participation of potentially conflicting interests. Although industrial development of the area was not permitted in the legislation, residential projects were given the go ahead; real estate developers and home builders came away feeling reasonably happy. Some observers who initially expressed skepticism about the law's chances for resolution find themselves almost mystified at the smoothness with which it seems to be working.

Lynch seems to thrive on devising compromises between conflicting interests and AuCoin puts his talent to good use. The lumber industry dominates Oregon's economy, but dozens of other businesses related to fishing, recreation and tourism depend on careful management of the forest lands. Objectives are not always compatible but for Lynch, therein lies the challenge . . . and the fun.

Lynch has also spent considerable time on the issue of nuclear waste production. Many of AuCoin's constituents live downstream or near the Hanford site and feel their security threatened by forty-three years' accumulation of nuclear waste materials. Lynch feels that the Energy Department must be required by Congress to put safety and the protection of public health and well-being on an equal footing with the development of new defense systems that generate ever more waste for which there is as yet no adequate means of disposal. Lynch, whose youthful appearance belies his responsibilities, enjoys reading, classical music, and cooking.

Paul J. Magliocchetti
Staff Assistant
Subcommittee on Defense
H-144 Capitol Bldg.
225-2847

Expertise: Procurement/Navy Ships and Aircraft

Coming from the General Accounting Office to the Appropriations Committee a decade ago, Magliocchetti brought with him a keen sense of cost and efficiency. In the six-odd years he has been working with the Subcommittee on Defense, his knowledge of Navy shipbuilding and his innovative cost-saving economies have saved the federal government billions of dollars, according to defense experts.

"He is first rate," claims a Pentagon official. "He knows more about what it costs to build a Navy ship than the Navy. He fully understands it. He knows how to build a ship to make it do what it's supposed to do. He knows whether it's a good deal or not. "He has been the shepherd of the Navy's plan to raise to a 600-ship Navy. He's been looking at every ship and has saved the country billions of dollars."

"He's very hard on the Navy. They have to prove to him what they're telling him. And he's always right," one Pentagon official explains. "He'll scoop the savings up and apply them to another ship. The Navy was able to build six new ships without having to labor through the appropriations procedure because of Magliocchetti and his frugalness. Magliocchetti himself often refers to what he calls the Navy's "learning curve" — the first ship costs more dollars than subsequent ones. He makes a point of making sure the Navy learns its lessons early and well, so as to save money and time, producing more efficiently in the long run.

A minority committee colleague impressed by Magliocchetti's performance, notes, "He has a high level of trust from the members because he has such a track record—near close to perfect," the staffer explains. "Every year he comes up with some new idea for cutting costs. He spends a lot of energy on it and doesn't beat the same old bush. He then goes out to industry or the Pentagon to see if his idea works and to make sure it has a firm foundation in the real world. He's not a hipshooter when it comes to crunch time—he makes sure he has the facts."

He adds, "Paul is smart, aggressive and not shy in pursuing his ideas or in presenting his opinions. He'll kill you with his honesty. He's not afraid to burst anyone's bubble, including the Secretary of the Navy." Magliocchetti's expertise and political skills are readily acknowledged by his Senate counterparts. "He is a tough taskmaster and a very artful negotiator," says one staffer. "He never gets himself in a situation he's going to lose. He always has his bases covered."

Richard N. Malow
Staff Assistant
Subcommittee on HUD-
   Independent Agencies
H-143 Capitol Bldg.
225-3241

Expertise: HUD-Independent Agencies

Some of those who regularly deal with the chief subcommittee clerk refer to Richard Malow as "Congressman Malow" and claim he is one of the House's most aggressive staffers at wielding power on his turf and on his terms.

But even these sometime critics share the assessment of Pete Perkins, minority staff counsel for the Senate Commerce, Science, and Technology Committee: "Dick Malow is very talented and competent. He has intuitive, analytical abilities and a very broad-based understanding of the programs in his responsibilities. He's quite effective."

Adds a senior House staffer, "He's a politically in-tune guy and knows what his chairman [Ed Boland] needs and the power bases in the House. He keeps the HUD public housing programs funded when the Administration is trying to zero them out."

Perhaps a telling commentary on Malow's clout is that even his boosters are generally reluctant to offer comments, except with a promise of anonymity.

A HUD official offers this explanation: "Chairman Boland trusts him and uses his advice a lot. He gives him a lot of free rein in the administrative expense areas of a department's or agency's budget. He has a lot of discretionary power, and he uses it. If he wants to increase or decrease these areas, he can usually do it."

Department representatives recall all too painfully the penalty they paid for sending what Malow considered an overwhelming number of lobbyists to the Subcommittee's mark-up in a tiny room in the Capitol. Their legislative affairs budget for the next year was cut. "It ticked him off," says one. "You could call it punishment or getting the attention of the department. Whatever it is, it works."

The Subcommittee also determines the amount of spending for 16 agencies, including EPA, the VA, and NASA. With knowledge from experience, the advocates of these agencies tend to deal with Malow *very carefully*. "He scares the hell out of a lot of people within the NASA community," confides an industry lobbyist. "He has more to do with how much money it gets than anyone else. He really knows NASA inside and out—he's THE expert.

"But he's the kind who plays his cards close to the vest. He'll listen, but he won't tell you what he's up to. If he wants information, he calls you, but it's more difficult to get through to him."

Others agree. "If you supply him with inaccurate information, he'll blow your head off" says one budget officer. "He barks and growls and can be very rough. It takes a while to get used to him. He's good, but tough as nails.

"He sees his job as getting all sides of the story. His primary motivation is to serve the chairman and the committee and to ensure the legislative intent of a department or agency is carried out.

An Administration lobbyist considers Malow very partisan and suggests one makes sure the Subcommittee retains some leverage through the spending bill to involve itself in policy-making decisions of the department or agency.

"I don't think that Boland knows his methods," he charges. "But if you were to call him on it, I'd imagine nine times out of ten Boland would stick up for him."

Malow became the chief clerk of the subcommittee in 1977 after about half a dozen years as an assistant. He previously had worked at the Department of Agriculture.

He is married and likes to go fishing on the Chesapeake Bay.

William F. Marinelli
Staff Assistant
Subcommittee on Military
    Construction
B300 Rayburn House Office Bldg.
225-3047

Expertise: Military construction

Solid analytical skills and straight-shooting have earned Bill Marinelli wide respect as he oversees the staff of the subcommittee that parcels out $10 billion a year for military construction projects.

"Bill evaluates these policies judiciously on an even-handed basis. He has an ability to distinguish between a Pentagon requirement and *is very nonpartisan,* says a former colleague. "He was always candid on how he felt about certain policy projects. We don't measure a project in isolation but against the whole policy adopted by the Administration and earlier Congresses."

The former staffer adds, "He was very amenable to having an open discussion when our positions differed. He believes in compromising—to get along, you have to go along."

A minority committee staffer comments, "He's a straight-shooter and understands he works for the members. He's very thorough and capable."

Another colleague explains, "If Bill doesn't agree with you, he'll tell you right away. But, he is very non-partisan. He has a difficult job. Some might view the projects as pork, and, in a sense, it is. Jobs go to the local carpenters, construction crews. It boils down to bricks and mortar. He has to satisfy a lot of parochial interests as well as defense interests. Even members who vote against every thing in the defense bill want to work their district projects in. He does superb work." Subcommittee Chairman Bill Hefner concurs.

"Bill's background in the Corps of Engineers (15 years in the field and in Washington) gives him special skills to handle his present job as staff director," states Hefner. "His 10 years of experience with the budget process on the full committee staff make him especially qualified to serve as a bipartisan advisor to the subcommittee and its members.

Marinelli holds a B.S. degree in civil engineering from Villanova and a masters from Stanford. He has been the head of the subcommittee staff since 1984.

He is considered to have a good professional rapport with Hefner and to be influential in his decisions. Full Committee Chairman Jamie Whitten has traditionally let the subcommittee chairman have the final say on project funding. Marinelli is a sailor and a golfer who wins tournaments.

Patrick O. McGarey
Legislative Director/Counsel
Representative Daniel Akaka (D-HI)
2301 Rayburn House Office Bldg.
225-4906

Expertise: Agriculture

After knocking on Hill office doors for two weeks in January 1979, Patrick McGarey found and accepted a legislative staff position with Congressman Dan Akaka's office. He found himself exactly where he wanted to be. The year before, as a senior in college, he had landed a position as Legislative Intern in Senator Lowell Weicker's office. That experience and three more months as an H.H.S. paralegal convinced McGarey that he wanted to make Washington his home.

Because of the uniqueness of Hawaii as the state most recently admitted to the Union and its geographic isolation, a good deal of McGarey's attention is focused on constituent concerns, particularly in agriculture. Hawaii produces one fifth of the total U.S. sugar output and McGarey works to keep the domestic sugar industry strong and competitive in the marketplace. And when Hawaii's new multi-billion dollar interstate highway system became tangled in a legal logjam, McGarey's efforts led to a legislative solution to the problem which permitted road construction to continue.

McGarey takes a personal interest in energy issues and is particularly proud of his efforts with the House Appropriations Committee to require that the federal government purchase electricity from local utilities, thereby keeping down costs to residential customers. He also believes that development of renewable energy resources is critical to the national interest, and has worked against the budget cuts that inevitably threaten energy R&D programs.

McGarey has a strong sense of responsibility to his community: he serves as Planning Commissioner for Rockville, Maryland and also sits on the Board of Directors of the House of Representatives Child Care Center . He swims daily for exercise and enjoys the mountains with his family in the summer for water sports and in winter for downhill or cross-country skiing.

Personal: born 5/16/56 in New York, New York. B.A. Colgate Univ. 1978. J.D. George Washington Univ. Law School, 1985. 1979-1981, Legislative Assistant; 1985-present, Legislative Director and Counsel to Rep. Daniel Akaka and 1981-present, Associate Staff Member for Committee on Appropriations.

Appropriations

Americo S. Miconi
Staff Assistant
Subcommittee on the District of
   Columbia
H-302 Capitol Bldg.
225-5338

Expertise: District of Columbia

When Americo Miconi's daughter got married in late 1987, not only did the District Government's congressional lobbyist, its legislative director, and their two assistants attend, so did Mayor Marion Barry. This stands as testimonial to the clout of the clerk of the subcommittee holding the purse strings for the city's federal appropriation. Of course, those who deal regularly with "Mico," profess he's "just a wonderful guy," perhaps blurring somewhat the distinction between his influence and his personal popularity.

Moving from assistant clerk to the panel's top (and only) professional staff slot he's held for the past decade, Miconi is used to being courted by representatives of the city government or business community for this program or that project. He's equally familiar with being the dumping ground for complaints from private residents to Members of Congress on their pet concerns—budget-related or not.

A graduate of Fairmont State College, Miconi worked in budget and accounting positions at the Treasury Department prior to joining the Appropriations Committee in 1970. He considers himself "a budget man."

His sharp political skills combined with solid expertise in D.C. government budget matters have earned him the respect of colleagues and subcommittee members. Miconi enjoys a close relationship and communicates freely with Subcommittee Chairman Julian Dixon (D-CA), as well as key D.C. officials.

"He keeps in touch and calls us frequently," says Julius Hobson, assistant director for congressional and federal relations for the D.C. government. "He's very responsive to us. He's not difficult to reach day or night at the office or home, and he returns calls immediately.

Hobson says, "Miconi has a very strong budget background and manages to facilitate the budget process very well year after year."

Ed Sylvester, staff director of the House Committee on the District of Columbia, states: "He's a very well respected staff person . . . highly competent. He knows his business. There are nominal changes in the D.C. budget over the years."

"Not only does he have the technical expertise, he also knows how to get things done. He is able to do good work where there are many divergent pieces in the process—the Mayor, the Council, the Congress, and OMB. In most instances, he comes through and without too much public hoopla."

Frederick G. Mohrman
Staff Director
Full Committee
H218 Capitol
225-2771

Expertise: Appropriations, administration

Fred Mohrman heads what many consider the most tight-lipped, most powerful, and most professional committee staff in the House. With a passion for anonymity, their allegiance belongs to Chairman Jamie Whitten (D-MS) and the twelve other subcommittee chairmen, referred to as the "college of cardinals." Collectively representing nearly everything there is to know about the federal government, these committee elders determine where nearly half of the federal budget dollar is spent.

Providing continuity as panel chairmen come and go, some of the senior staff members have, themselves, become institutions. Members, congressional staffers, and lobbyists alike regularly tap their vast storehouses of information.

"They combine the breadth of knowledge and the depth of detail," says a long-time committee observer. "They work long hours to have it."

Staff members are generally recruited on loan on a trial basis from budget offices of the agencies to help out with a specific appropriations bill. Those who impress the committee are invited back when there is a suitable opening. They are not asked about their party affiliation.

Chairman Whitten elaborates: "Our staff is professional. If we have a vacancy, I ask the members to recommend someone to me who has worked for the committee on (agency) leave. Without exception, I have followed their recommendations. Each must have been trained and experienced in budgeting."

The staffers pride themselves on their ability to do anything. In the thick of the budget and appropriations process, they work for days without going home. When the President delivers the annual budget to Congress on a Saturday morning, the Committee staff presents a full briefing to Whitten by the next evening.

"It's the best budget briefing in Washington," says a former colleague, "It's at least as good as the President gets, including all the political pressures and considerations."

But despite their pivotal roles, the staff never forgets they are clerks there to serve the chairman and his members. "They never speak for themselves," adds the associate. "If they speak, they speak for the Chairman. They never express a view they are not authorized to express. That's part of their professionalism."

Mohrman is responsible for supervising the staff and handling all the administrative aspects of the committee. But he also wears the hat of legal counsel, head counter, reader of bills, and, some say, "shepherd."

Appropriations

Whitten tersely comments, "Fred Mohrman was chosen to head the staff after years of service. He is excellent."

A graduate of Kansas State College, Mohrman served as a budget analyst and then deputy budget officer at the Commerce Department. He also worked at the Office of Management and Budget. Joining the committee staff in 1975, he was the staff director for the Subcommittee on the Interior, chaired by Congressman Sid Yates, until being promoted to his current position.

Mohrman is considered one of the most powerful staff members on the Hill because of his critical role in the appropriations process. Some minority staffers have been known to chafe at his handling of their Members' concerns. Nonetheless, there is little question that on the Appropriations Committee Staff, Mohrman is "numero uno."

A veteran observer of the Appropriations Committee says,"He is an extremely capable and effective staff person. He's tough, but has to be—to represent the people he works for."

A senior staff member on the Budget Committee comments, "He's politically sensitive and relates well to the Members. He understands the constraints of the process. He's somewhat low-key in demeanor, but he carries a big pencil in the appropriations process. He's been very responsive to me."

Says a colleague, "Fred is peerless in the budget process. He's got it in his eyes, his ears, his toes. He has a photographic mind and an encylopedic knowledge." One of Mohrman's colleagues remembers him citing an obscure 1963 law during a Committee discussion over the intent of a program. If he doesn't know the answer, he knows exactly where to put his hands on it.

There is another side to Mohrman. According to a colleague: "He's fun and a good conversationalist with a great sense of humor. He's big-hearted, soft, as far as his kids. And he's a good bridge player."

Henry A. Neil, Jr.
Staff Assistant
Subcommittee on Labor-HHS-
    Education
2358 Rayburn House Office Bldg.
225-3508

Expertise: Labor, health, human services, education

Henry Neil is one of those model professional staff members about whom associates can't say enough good things. Nearly two decades of tenure have solidified his reputation as an expert who stands ready to assist congressional and department staffers and loyally serves his chairman and subcommittee.

He is universally described as "very low key" and those who have worked with him offer a variety of reasons for his effectiveness as the subcommittee's chief clerk. "He's extremely valuable because he knows his programs, his laws, their histories, and his chairman," explains Don Baker, a counsel to the Education and Labor Committee.

He has a great sense of what the chairman will or will not do. "He is a most sympathetic and thoughtful guy who has helped me a lot."

Jack Jennings also a counsel to Education and Labor Committee, says, "He's intelligent, knowledgeable, unflappable, cooperative, reliable, and goes about his job with a lot of competence."

Dennis Williams, deputy assistant secretary for budget at HHS, simply states, "He is clearly one of the most knowledgeable persons on HHS."

HHS budget officer James Becraft notes Neil "is a top-notch and first-rate budget man. He's very friendly, but firm. He's not the type of person who creates a furor, being mild-mannered, ethical, straight and above board. He's the kind of person who observes the rules."

Neil is especially held in high regard at the National Institutes on Health because of his advocacy for its programs.

Norm Mansfield, NIH's chief financial officer, comments, "He is a true professional in every sense of the word. He has an institutional memory, no ax to grind, and views himself as carrying out the will of the chairman and its subcommittee members.

Chairman William Natcher perhaps sums it up best. "Henry Neil is a dedicated, loyal staff assistant and one of the outstanding staff officials of the Committee," he states.

"He is not only well qualified from the standpoint of education and training, but he possesses all of the attributes that make him an excellent 'unelected official'."

Though a stroke kept Neil out for most of 1987, he was back on the job in January, 1988. Prior to coming to the committee in 1969, he had worked in budgeting areas at the old Health, Education, and Welfare Department. He has a degree from Princeton University and has done post-graduate work at Harvard and the Universities of Heidelberg and Hamburg in Germany.

Observers point out that Neil has established "quality relationships" with members of the Subcommittee and a "close friendship" with Natcher.

"He probably is at the level of confidante with Natcher," says Becraft. "He pretty much knows in advance what Natcher wants and can speak for him a lot of times. Although he's open, he can play his cards close to the vest."

"Chairman Natcher doesn't like anyone to know what is the subcommittee's bill until it's reported out," explains Jennings. "He puts an embargo on until it's at full committee. Henry won't tell people what's in it simply because Natcher doesn't want him to."

A department lobbyist notes that Natcher is a "hands-on chairman. He handles everything—nothing gets done without his approval." That arrangement seems to suit Neil just fine, who is more the behind-the-scenes-type of staff director.

"He's organized his office very well, " Becraft says. "He delegates a lot of responsibility to other people. It's indicative of his style. He doesn't need to be the star on all occasions. He lets the staff carry their own loads, yet it's clear the staff guy running the show is Henry.

"He's very fair and reasonable when it comes to getting information from the department. Nonetheless, he wants the stuff when he wants it."

Edd C. Nolan
Legislative Assistant
Representative Tom Bevill (D-AL)
2302 Rayburn House Office Bldg.
225-4876

Expertise: Energy and water appropriations

A soft-spoken man with an introspective nature, Edd Nolan has compiled more than twenty years of service to Alabama congressmen. Since 1976, he has served under Representative Tom Bevill (D-AL), the powerful Chairman of the House Appropriations Subcommittee on Energy and Water.

Home to Nolan and the powerful congressman he serves is north Alabama, a region that has benefited from an infusion of federal dollars through programs like the Tennessee Valley Authority (TVA) and the Appalachia Regional Commission. Populism is still strong among the people of north Alabama and Chairman Bevill personifies that tradition. Bevill views the public works programs funded through the Energy and Water Subcommittee as tools to building better lives for the less fortunate.

Since 1977, Bevill has presided over the appropriation of funds for TVA, the Appalachia Regional Commission, the Army Corps of Engineers and assorted water projects. Nolan joined Bevill's staff in 1976, the same year that Bevill got a seat on the Subcommittee. Even then, Nolan was no novice to public works projects. His former employer, Representative Robert Jones (D-AL), was a member of the Public Works Committee. Nolan handled Jones's authorization of TVA and was involved in the successful effort to create the Appalachia Regional Commission, one of President Kennedy's economic development initiatives.

Personal: born 3/22/40 in Alexander City, Alabama. American Univ., 1964-1966. B.A. George Mason Univ., 1974. 1958-1962, U.S. Navy, Machinist Mate Second Class. 1964, staffer in House of Representatives Post Office. 1965-1976, Legislative Assistant, Rep. Robert Jones (D-AL). 1976-present, Legislative Assistant and Associate Appropriations Staffer, Rep. Tom Bevill (D- AL).

Nolan now works for Bevill to appropriate what Jones once authorized. Knowing Bevill's sensitivity to charges that his bill is loaded with "pork," one of Nolan's tasks is to ensure that every potential project undergo a cost-benefit analysis before any funds are committed. He works closely with Hunter Spillan, the Subcommittee staff director, to ensure that the energy and water bill reflects Bevill's parochial and national interests. He also consults with Proctor Jones, the Senate Energy and Water staff director, when the need arises.

Nolan considers one of his major accomplishments under Bevill to be the appropriating of funds to complete the Tennessee-Tombigbee navigation channel. Opposed by the railroads and environmental groups, Tennessee-Tombigbee was authorized by Congress in 1945. Construction of the channel began in 1971. When faced with floor amendments in 1980 and 1981 proposing to cut off funds for the project, Nolan and Spillan staffed Bevill's campaign to keep Tennessee-Tombigbee alive. Bevill eventually prevailed, but only after three votes took place. The first amendment lost by 45 votes, the second by 20 votes, and the third in 1981 by 10 votes.

Appropriations

John Osthaus
Staff Director
Subcommittee on Commerce,
Justice, State, the Judiciary and
Related Agencies
H-309 Capitol Bldg.
225-3351

Expertise: Commerce, Justice and State

Like many of the professional Appropriations staffers, John Osthaus worked in the executive branch budget offices before coming to the Committee. For him, the advantages of working on the Capitol Hill end of Pennsylvania Avenue are clear: there is less bureaucracy and more contact with the people who make the policy decisions.

Ostahus's primary responsibility is managing the annual Commerce/Justice/State appropriations bill for Congressman Neal Smith (D-IA), the subcommittee chairman. From a technical point of view, Osthaus' job is to understand how spending patterns for programs affect future outlays. He must know which programs can have their funding "stretched out" in the event that spending authority in future years is less than anticipated. And he must know how much obligational authority for new programs can be committed without exceeding current or future budget figures.

Osthaus works with the Budget Committee and many of the authorizing committees to help him determine the bill's parameters. George Schafer, his colleague, helps lighten the load by concentrating on Department of Justice and Judiciary portions of the bill. Osthaus's coordination with the Budget Committee has increased over the past few years, especially in the wake of the Gramm-Rudman-Hollings bill and its restrictions on outlays. Assembling the Commerce/Justice/ State bill involves programs that are authorized in the Committees on Energy and Commerce, Merchant Marine and Fisheries, Foreign Affairs, Small Business, Judiciary, Science and Technology, Education and Labor and Ways and Means. Osthaus maintains an active dialogue with staffers on these committees.

Personal: born 9/5/41 in Toledo, Ohio. B.A. Kalamazoo Coll., 1963 (cum laude). LL.B. Univ. of Michigan, 1966. 1966-1969, Lieutenant Junior Grade, U.S. Navy. 1969-1972, budget examiner, Office of Management and Budget. 1972-1973, budget analyst, General Services Administration. 1972-present, Captain, U.S. Naval Reserve. 1973-1974, Staff Assistant, House Appropriations Subcommittee on Treasury. 1974-1979, Staff Assistant, House Appropriations Subcommittee on Commerce, Justice, State, the Judiciary and Related Agencies. 1980-present, Staff Director, House Appropriations Subcommittee on Commerce, Justice, State, the Judiciary and Related Agencies.

In recent years, the Subcommittee for which Osthaus works has been very busy beating back attempts by the Reagan Administration to dismantle a number of federal programs traditionally supported by the Democrats. These include the Legal Services Corporation, the Office of Juvenile Justice and the Small Business Administration. Commerce Department programs like Sea Grant, Coastal Zone Management, and the Economic Development Administration have also been on the Administration's hit list. Although much of the battle to protect these programs has taken place in the authorizing committees, Osthaus has carried out Smith's mandate to protect them on the appropriations end. Osthaus notes that Smith has been particularly supportive of the Legal Services Corporation and the Small Business Administration as well as the Economic Development Administration.

In addition to these duties, Osthaus works with Members, their staffers, and other groups on concerns of their districts or other special matters. Smith has a reputation for trying to accommodate Members as best he can, both on and off the Appropriations Committee and both Democrats and Republicans, when putting together his subcommittee's bill. Both Osthaus and Darold Dandy, who is one of Smith's associate staffers, serve as conduits to Smith on these matters. Those who have met with Osthaus on specific matters comment that he always gives a fair hearing and relates their views back to Smith.

Off the Hill, Osthaus spends time with his family and devotes two weeks a year and a weekend every month to the Naval Reserve.

Appropriations

Terry R. Peel
Staff Assistant
Subcommittee on Foreign
  Operations
H-308 Capitol Bldg.
225-2041

Expertise: Foreign operations

Terry Peel's low-key and open style complement the strong and active chairmanship of Rep. Dave Obey (D-WI), who is frequently butting heads with the Administration over foreign aid programs, especially on its requests to fund the Nicaraguan contras.

"Terry's personality lends itself to keeping the place on an even keel, even on controversial subject matters," says a subcommittee observer. "He's outgoing, pleasant, with real good interpersonal skills.

"He's smart and does his homework. He functions well as a consensus builder, working with members and their staffs to filter out competing demands. He's a results-oriented person who likes intractable issues where there appears to be no solution. He puts together coalitions and ideas that work."

A representative of the Agency for International Development comments, "He does not allow himself to get charged up. He's a capable, quiet, non-threatening guy, and as such lets down his defenses and gets down to business."

Those who deal with Peel also consider his ability to keep an open mind as part of his effectiveness. "He's very deliberative, doesn't come to quick judgments, and has a willingness to see all sides of an issue," says another Administration advocate. "He doesn't get locked into an issue and is willing to change his mind.

"Obey is a very strong and political person. He and the State Department are often at odds on certain issues. That makes Terry's job very difficult." All you can hope for is to get a fair hearing of your side in Congress and you get that from him. Obey will set certain limits for spending, and Terry will present the options to his boss."

State Department experts accord him good marks for his general knowledge of foreign assistance programs and international organizations under the Subcommittee. "He has picked up the specifics real well and is not afraid to admit what he doesn't know," points out one officer. "If he doesn't know, he asks the questions. He goes out and gets the answers.

He may not be in a position to tell us what the chairman is thinking, but he's honest about it. And he doesn't try to blow smoke to cover information he can't get. It's refreshing."

According to many observers, Obey dominates the subcommittee. He establishes the spending mark for a program. It's up to other members to challenge the level because there is no natural constituency from the public, and they are not overly inclined to wrestle with their chairman.

Obey calls Peel "an integral member of his team," one that he says encompasses two other staff assistants on the Subcommittee and an associate staff member in his personal office.
Administration lobbyists see Peel as the initial point person on the subcommittee with whom they touch base first. He serves as the clearinghouse where some issues are resolved, but others must be taken up at a higher level. Obey, they say, sets the policy, relying on Peel for facts and ideas to consider and for carrying out his bidding. Though skilled as an arbiter, Peel secures Obey's approval before suggesting any major compromise, the Administration representatives note. They credit him with having quietly resolved thousands of lesser issues through compromises worked out in conference with his Senate counterparts, leaving the House and Senate conferees to hammer out the several dozen larger differences between their bills.

He is viewed as a good manager of the Subcommittee staff and responsible for the panel's orderly and well-organized hearings and mark-ups.

Appropriations

Donald Richbourg
Staff Assistant
Subcommittee on Defense
H-144 Capitol Bldg.
225-2847

Expertise: Defense appropriations

Don Richbourg has been aptly described as "the glue that holds together" the Subcommittee that determined over $279 billion in defense outlays in 1988. In addition to supervising a dozen staff assistants, he also stood at the helm when then-Chairman Joe Addabbo fell ill, and guided his successor, Bill Chappell, in his new leadership responsibilities.

The chief subcommittee clerk is widely respected in all corners of the defense community. States a Pentagon official, "he is totally nonpartisan—he is as concerned about the Members of Congress he serves as he is about the Defense Department."

"He has the clout to get what he wants from DOD, but not in Congress as a whole, since defense spending is not a particularly popular subject."

"He presents the facts to the Subcommittee and reconciles the budget and the outlays like a watchful, panting dog," the official says. "He shapes a lot of the nuts and the bolts of the defense bill and makes the Defense Department stick within its outlays."

"His political instincts are without peer. He works in the art of the possible. Though the Subcommittee operates in a nonpartisan manner, he has to make sure the bill doesn't go to the floor and get rolled by others. He understands what the traffic will bear there. He holds back little nuggets from the House bill to get what he wants from the Senate in conference. He always comes back with more than the House bill had, but he doesn't get greedy."

No one understands the defense appropriations process, knows its laws, or writes a bill better than Richbourg, claims a minority committee staffer. "He's a whiz at juggling the numbers," the staffer says. "He's fair and has no ax to grind. The staff on both sides is all for one and one for all. He works for all the members. Of course, everyone wants Bill Chappell to come first as the chairman, but Richbourg plays no favorites among the other members.

"He's good at reading the (political) tea leaves in advance and knows where the minefields are in the House. He has to produce a product that the entire House will support, and he's very good at that. He is very sensitive to the up and down side of their decisions. An honest broker in the best sense of the word."

Richbourg became the head of the subcommittee staff four years ago. He previously served as the chief clerk of the foreign operations subcommittee and as a staff assistant on the full committee staff.

Pat Bogenberger, a defense budget analyst for the Budget Committee, says Richbourg "is very straight-forward and not one to beat around the bush. He doesn't string you along with what his influence can do. He has a good sense of what staff limits are."

A former associate says Richbourg is "a real gentleman and eminently fair" in all his dealings. "He never directly offers his views, but if a member asks him to develop a position, they get it. You never know whether he agrees with it or not."

A Senate colleague also gives Richbourg a high rating of approval.

"He knows the Subcommittee personalities and its traditions better than anyone else," the staffer explains. "He never missed a beat in the transition from Addabbo to Chappell.

Addabbo was still trying to exert himself with his mark for the bill from his hospital bed when Chappell was acting chairman. Richbourg showed a lot of professional acumen in what was an awkward situation. He never got caught in the middle of it.

"He doesn't stand on a lot of ceremony. He does what he has to do with everyone's confidence. He represents all sides fairly, with no loose ends. That he can work successfully for a liberal Northeast Democrat and then a conservative Southern Democrat speaks well of his professionalism.

"Richbourg," he adds, "is one of the easiest people to work with. He is very accommodating and never gets personal. He is strong on the technical side and not too mercurial or cute on the political end of the job. His attitude at conference is: 'Don't promise more than you can deliver.'"

Jan Schoonmaker
Chief Legislative Assistant
Representative Lindy Boggs (D-LA)
2353 Rayburn House Office Bldg.
225-6636

Personal: born 4/22/46 in New Orleans, Louisiana. B.A., Transylvania Univ. in political science, 1968. J.D. Tulane Univ. Law School, 1974. 1969-70, U.S. Army. 1974-present, Legislative Assistant, Rep. Lindy Boggs.

Expertise: Energy and water

Jan Schoonmaker is many things to Lindy Boggs–top political aide, savvy legislative assistant and longtime family friend.

His association with her began even before she represented Louisiana's Second District. In high school, under the sponsorship of Boggs's husband, the late Congressman Hale Boggs, Schoonmaker was a page in the House of Representatives. It was only after finishing law school and serving in Vietnam that Schoonmaker began to work for Boggs, who had just been elected to fill her husband's seat following the disappearance of his airplane in Alaska, while campaigning with his colleague Rep. Nick Begich.

During his years of service to Hale and Lindy Boggs, Schoonmaker has acquired first-hand knowledge about the House of Representatives as an institution. Having been a page and now an associate appropriations staffer, he knows where the real power resides in the House and how it exercises its might in subtle and sometimes not so subtle ways. Fiercely partisan and yet pragmatic, Schoonmaker's political disposition meshes well with prevailing sentiments on the Appropriations Committee.

Boggs's twenty-seven years as a politically active Congressional wife and fifteen years as a Member of Congress have made her one of the House's most respected and beloved Members. Schoonmaker's nuts-and-bolts understanding of the legislative process, has helped make her one of its most influential and effective Members.

Schoonmaker is responsible for Boggs' general committee work, her Energy and Water Subcommittee assignment, and most projects relating to the District and the state of Louisiana. He is a native of the district he serves, which is surprisingly unique among associate appropriations staffers in the House. His personal familiarity with New Orleans is a great asset to Boggs in her efforts to stay in touch with community and business leaders and to promote the region in Congress.

Schoonmaker coordinated her successful efforts to have funds appropriated in the 98th and the 100th Congresses for the deepening of the Mississippi River ship channel, which directly benefited the port of New Orleans. When Louisiana's energy sector began to boom in the 1970's, he managed her increasingly active role in the Committee on energy issues. South Louisiana is the center of the nation's offshore drilling industry and was hit hard by the Committee's moratoria on drilling activities in selected areas of the Outer Continental Shelf. Schoonmaker has been a key staffer behind the annual effort to abolish the moratoria. In recent years, he has also handled Boggs' successful efforts to obtain funds through various Appropriations Subcommittees for construction of research facilities at Tulane and Louisiana State University.

Not all of Schoonmaker's work for Boggs on the Appropriations Subcommittee is parochial. About half of the funds appropriated through the Energy and Water Bill are defense-related and have little impact on New Orleans. Boggs takes these duties seriously and Schoonmaker makes it his job to understand even the minute details of the nuclear weapons programs under the jurisdiction of the Department of Energy. He has enjoyed this aspect of his job so much that it has now turned into an interest that he pursues outside of the office.

With fourteen years service in Congress, it seems clear that Schoonmaker will be with Lindy Boggs as long as she decides to remain in Congress.

Appropriations

Timothy J. Shea
Staff Assistant
1016 Longworth House Office
   Bldg.
225-6626

Expertise: Appropriations

For Timothy J. Shea, there's nothing like a battle on the floor to get the blood going.

Shea, minority staff assistant on the House Appropriations Committee, isn't talking about a brawl in some dimly lit bar. He's referring to the give-and-take that often occurs on the House floor.

Shea has worked on the Committee for three years after spending two on the personal staff of Rep. Silvio Conte of Massachusetts, the ranking Republican on the Committee.

Like the other GOP staffers, Shea is assigned to several subcommittees, which is necessary because Republicans receive a limited number of staff slots on the Committee. His subcommittees include Interior and Related Agencies; Treasury Postal Service and General Government; and the District of Columbia.

He also spends a good deal of time on environmental concerns which come before the Committee.

"Environmental issues are interesting and they are very important to Mr. Conte," he says. "He has considerable influence in that area, so I have the opportunity to really make a dent in policy."

Conte, who has been ranking member since 1979, commands a great deal of respect on the Committee and in the House; Shea points out, "which makes it easier for our staff. We have access to meetings and markup sessions, more so than some of the junior Democratic staffers."

Also, Republican staffers work well with their Democratic counterparts on the Committee, which Shea says is largely non-partisan.

Personal: born 4/10/60 in Fall River, Massachusetts. A.B. Boston Coll., 1982. 1981-1982, Legislative Assistant to Lieutenant Governor of Massachusetts. 1982-1985, Legislative Assistant to Rep. Silvio Conte (R-MA). 1985-present, Staff Assistant, House Committee on Appropriations.

In addition to the subcommittees on which Shea works, he also tracks other committee issues of concern to Conte. The two are in constant communication, often for several hours a day.

"I wanted to work in Congress and wrote to several people," he says. Conte—"I had heard of him but wasn't that familiar with him"—answered his letter and offered him a job. After working on foreign affairs and other issues for Conte, he went to the Committee in 1985.

Shea has just begun law school at Georgetown University. With classes at night and his job during the day, "I manage to keep on my toes," he says.

Neal Sigmon
Staff Director
Subcommittee on the Interior
B-308 Rayburn House Office Bldg.
225-3081

Personal: born 7/14/43 in Charlotte, N.C. B.A. Duke Univ., 1965. M.P.A., George Washington Univ., 1973. 1968-72, staff sergeant, U.S. Air Force. 1974-76, Federal Power Commission. 1976-77, Federal Energy Administration. 1977-79, Dept. of Energy. 1980, Staff Asst., House Appropriations Subcommittee on the Interior. 1985-present, staff director, House Appropriations Subcommittee on the Interior.

Expertise: Interior

When Fred Mohrman left the Interior Subcommittee staff in 1985 to become the staff director of the Full Appropriations Committee, Neal Sigmon moved up to fill his spot on the Subcommittee.

Sigmon's background as a budget analyst in a variety of federal energy and power agencies was good preparation for this assignment. Like most of the Appropriations subcommittees, the jurisdiction of the Interior Subcommittee is wide-ranging. Bob Kripowicz, Sigmon's staff assistant, helps Sigmon cover the programs under the jurisdiction of the Subcommittee by concentrating on energy issues; Kathy Johnson covers Forest Service and Indian issues and Jocelyn Hunn staffs minerals related programs.

As staff director, Sigmon is known as low-key but effective. Working under Rep. Sidney Yates (D-IL), his style of managing the Subcommittee staff is a good complement to Yates' aggressive leadership.

Like all Appropriations subcommittees, the majority and minority work together on most issues in a fairly bipartisan fashion. Staffers for minority members on the Subcommittee have a close working relationship with Sigmon and have no qualms about relying upon him to accommodate their Member's interests.

The Subcommittee is a battleground each year between environmentalists and groups desiring to develop the nation's natural resources. Some of the more divisive issues Sigmon is involved in each year are the Outer Continental Shelf (OCS) moratoria on oil and gas exploration and determining funding levels for forest road construction.

The Senate Interior Appropriations Subcommittee has generally tilted in the pro-development direction during the Reagan years. Sigmon is known to be an effective voice for the more pro-environmental House Subcommittee positions during the staff-to-staff negotiations leading up to the House-Senate conference on the Interior bill.

Sigmon has always been particularly important to Chairman Yates in determining the amount of funds that are needed to care for the nation's extensive wildlife refuges, national parks and forest systems. Since it is impossible for Yates to spend the amount of time that is required to visit some of these far-flung installations, Sigmon does much of the legwork, reporting back to Yates on their needs and problems.

Hunter L. Spillan
Staff Assistant
Subcommittee on Energy And
    Water Development
2362 Rayburn House Office Bldg.
225-3421

Expertise: Energy and water development

In a body where some legislators can't remember the names of their own staff assistants, most everyone knows who Hunter Spillan is. He is the chief of staff for the subcommittee that makes the highly politicized decisions on funding for energy and water development projects, perhaps the last bastion of "pork barrel" politics in which a member can still directly influence the process.

When members want to put in a word or check the status of a particular pet project, they often talk directly to Spillan. House Interior Committee Chairman Mo Udall is one of them. "They probably don't want to bother (Subcommittee Chairman Tom) Bevill," Udall explains. "Hunter knows what Bevill thinks. He's a brilliant guy and knows what's in the bill off the top of his head. He's quiet, diligent, and tells it to you straight."

A veteran staff colleague adds: "He knows where the power is, and he has his hands on it. The Members of Congress know that, and they come to him."

Spillan has had a lot of practice. He has served nearly two decades on the Appropriations Committee. He has logged an equal amount of time among positions with the Civil Service Commission, the General Services Administration and the Small Business Administration. He was planning to retire in 1979 when Rep. Jamie Whitten (D-MS) became Committee Chairman and asked him to stay.

Described as "a Southern gentleman," Spillan enjoys wide respect among members and fellow staffers.

Chairman Bevill says, "Nobody can put together a bill like Hunter Spillan."

Dan Beard, staff director of the Interior Subcommittee on Water and Power Resources, agrees.

"He has a great deal of influence with the chairman, who has the ultimate say. But his views are highly respected and they can be crucial as he shares them with the Members."

David McCarthy, aide to ranking subcommittee member John Myers, says "The energy and water development bill was always the first or second appropriations bill enacted until it was consumed by the Continuing Resolution (CR). You got to give a lot of that credit to Hunter. His parliamentary floor maneuvering has been historically masterful."

Sandra K. Stuart
Chief of Staff
Rep. Vic Fazio (D-CA)
2433 Rayburn House Office Bldg.
225-5716

Personal: born 2/27/44 in Greensboro, N.C. B.A. Univ. of North Carolina in Greensboro, 1967. 1974-1976, Monterey Law School. 1978, legislative correspondent, Rep. John Moss (D-CA). 1979-1981, chief legislative assistant, Rep. Robert Matsui (D-CA). 1982-present, Rep. Vic Fazio.

Expertise: Appropriations, budget

When Sandra Stuart became an associate appropriations staffer for Rep. Vic Fazio (D-CA), one of her first priorities was to build strong relationships with the professional staffers on the Appropriations Committee.

Observing that associate staffers are parochial and that they can be a barrier between the Member and a committee staffer, Stuart has spent six years learning how to use her position to promote rather than hinder Fazio's ability to work directly with the Appropriations Committee. Evidently, her efforts have paid off. Today, she is singled out by committee staff as being one of the most effective voices for a Member on the Appropriations Committee.

Stuart worked for two other California representatives before coming to Fazio. Her ties to the state reach back to the mid-1970s, when her husband was transferred there by the Navy. In California, Stuart got involved in Democratic politics and, when time permitted, took in a little scuba-diving. When the Navy transferred her husband to Washington, D.C., Stuart's political experience helped her land a job as a legislative correspondent with Rep. John Moss (D-CA), the powerful chairman of an Energy and Commerce subcommittee. When Moss retired and was replaced in his Sacramento district by Bob Matsui, Stuart was asked to work for the new congressman.

Stuart is now chief-of-staff for Vic Fazio. At one time, she was responsible for his legislative and military construction subcommittee assignments in addition to transportation, defense, and foreign operations issues. With the 1987 departure of Pat Fulton, who ran Fazio's Energy and Water Subcommittee assignment, she assumed overall responsibility for Fazio's work on the Appropriations Committee.

In 1983, she worked on Fazio's successful drive to get funding for the restoration of the West Front of the U.S. Capitol.

Stuart's success in establishing a good rapport with Committee staff, combined with Fazio's good reputation on the Committee, has eased her job of coordinating his committee assignment. Insiders on Appropriations point out that once one has the trust of the Committee staff and understands the Members' priorities, one can achieve objectives in an appropriations bill that might otherwise not have been possible.

As an example, Stuart points to Fazio's advocacy of renewable fuels programs. With no strong constituency in the early 1980s, renewable fuels research was not a priority in the Energy and

Water bill. There were no Members or staffers on the Committee who were strongly supportive of solar and wind energy programs. Today, however, these programs enjoy a good deal of support among Committee members. Stuart indicates this change occurred because Fazio and his staff worked closely with Committee staffers to develop awareness of the potential benefits of renewable fuels to the nation.

Today, Stuart is less involved with the details of Fazio's Subcommittee work and more concerned with the broader policy questions relating to his Appropriations and Budget Committee assignments. Fazio is one of five Members serving on both the Appropriations and Budget Committees. Being an influential force in the Democratic Party Leadership, he is an important "policy bridge" between the two committees. Stuart serves in a similar fashion between the staffers of the two committees. She is often called upon by Appropriations full committee staff to elaborate on discussions that took place in the Budget Committee.

Her work in both committees has given her an understanding of how budget authority breaks down into spending patterns, outlays and finally line-items in appropriations bills. Stuart explains that her work is all about "learning what makes Johnny run". Obviously, her expertise is part of what makes "Fazio run" as well.

Barbara W. Wainman
Associate Staff & Press Secretary
Representative Ralph Regula (R-OH)
2209 Rayburn House Office Bldg.
225-3876

Personal: born 5/16/56 in Washington, D.C. B.A. Smith Coll., (dean's list), 1978. 1979-1981, analyst for House Republican Conference, Legislative Digest. 1981-present, Associate Staff & Press Secretary to Representative Ralph Regula (R-OH).

Expertise: Interior appropriations

Rep. Ralph Regula (R-OH), the Ranking Minority Member of the Appropriations Interior Subcommittee, is an influential force for the Republicans on the Committee. Barbara Wainman is his right hand and Associate Staff for the Appropriations Committee. She staffs his Subcommittee on the Interior assignment and is helpful in his efforts to influence the final version of the annual Interior bill and most other appropriations measures.

Regula does not always follow the traditional Republican line, but then neither do many of the Republicans on the Appropriations Committee. He represents a declining industrial district and is more protectionist in his views than most Republicans. He sometimes sides with environmentalists, but usually not on those issues that affect the economic livelihood of his district.

Her responsibilities for the Subcommittee require that she work closely with Neal Sigmon, the staff director of the Interior Subcommittee, and that she participate in all Interior Conferences between the House and the Senate. With much of the work of the Subcommittee enjoying bipartisan support, Wainman has an excellent relationship with Sigmon.

Wainman has recently spent much of her time monitoring U.S. Forest Service programs. Regula generally supports a higher Forest Service budget, but opposes programs in the budget that lack accountability and are not cost-efficient. The Tongass Timber Supply Fund in Alaska is a recent target. Wainman has been working hard to reform the program, which currently gets a permanent appropriation under the Alaska Land Act and benefits only a few logging companies.

Regula's Interior assignment also requires Wainman to have a good working knowledge of energy issues—an area she admits she knew nothing about when first starting to work in his office. Since 1981, though, Wainman has turned herself into an energy expert and has been effective in monitoring Regula's energy interests.

She helped coordinate his "clean coal" compromise in 1985 that eventually provided $400 million for research over a period of three years. Industry in Regula's district uses coal, much of which is mined in adjacent Ohio congressional districts. During her service to Regula, he became more active in the Outer Continental Shelf leasing issue and took a lead role in opposing imposition of moratoria on drilling, which had routinely been contained in the Interior appropriations bill. Wainman was likely an impetus to Regula's decision to become more involved in the OCS issue.

HOUSE OF REPRESENTATIVES
COMMITTEE ON ARMED SERVICES

Carl Thomas Bayer
Professional Staff Member
2117 Rayburn House Office Bldg.
225-6527

Personal: born 5/30/41 in St. Louis, Missouri. B.A. Westminster Coll. (Missouri), 1968. M.S. University of Rochester, 1973. Advanced studies in aerospace engineering, University of Alabama. 1963-1967, U.S. Navy, special assignment to National Aeronautics and Space Administration at Marshall Space Flight Center, Huntsville, AL. 1967-1983, Analyst for the U.S. Army Ballistic Missile Defense Organization, Huntsville, AL. 1983-present, Professional Staff Member, House Armed Services Committee.

Expertise: Defense, research, development

With the departure this year of influential, long-time Professional Staff Member Tony Battista from the House Committee on Armed Services, many with an interest in military research and development will turn their attention toward his teammate in the support of the Subcommittee on Research and Development. They will discover Carl Bayer, a modest workhorse who for five years has been advising the subcommittee on the authorization and oversight of Department of Defense research, development, testing, and evaluation. Bayer is a highly qualified expert with twenty-five years of experience in defense and aerospace research.

Carl Bayer tends to divert the focus of attention away from himself, his activities, and his individual role on the Committee. He insists that his hiring in January, 1983 came about quietly and without political implication. Bayer had served one prior stint with the Committee Staff on a fellowship in 1980. He will not attempt to distinguish his contributions from the aggregate output of the staff and emphasizes his team work with them and especially with Tony Battista.

After commissioning him in 1963, the Navy assigned Bayer to NASA at Marshall Space Flight Center in Huntsville where he researched projects in space exploration. Leaving the Navy four years later, Bayer was employed as a civilian by the U.S. Army Ballistic Missile Defense Organization in Huntsville. He spent the next sixteen years there until he came to Washington, except for a year's fellowship at the University of Rochester to study defense systems analysis. With the Army, Bayer became Chief of the Systems Definition Division. His office analyzed and developed many of the defense concepts and experiments that are now an integral part of the Strategic Defense Initiative (SDI) Program. This particular expertise of his will become critical within the Armed Services Committee as the current issue of the Strategic Defense System development is undertaken.

His arrival on the Armed Services Committee took place a timely two months before SDI was announced as a national initiative in March of 1983. SDI has been one of the greatest issues confronting the Committee during Bayer's tenure there.

Included among issues of concern to him besides SDI, Carl Bayer mentions the conventional force buildup, strategic force modernization, technology base programs, and the budgetary level of his subcommittee's oversight which has almost doubled in these five years.

Lawrence H. Cavaiola
Professional Staff Member
2343 Rayburn House Office Bldg.
225-4004

Expertise: Naval issues

After ten years with the navy, Lawrence Cavaiola has had the good fortune of finding positions which are well-suited to his broad expertise in naval operations and lifelong love affair with the sea. After stints with the Secretary of Defense's office and Congressional Budget Office, he has secured a spot with the House Armed Services Committee. Armed with a Ph.D. in Operations Research, Cavaiola's knowledge of naval weapons procurement and shipbuilding design is viewed as invaluable by fellow staff and House members alike.

Recognized as a team player who shuns the spotlight in favor of bipartisan consensus, he describes his views as "moderately independent," to the point of being apolitical. Says Cavaiola, "My job has nothing to do with partisanship, and everything to do with giving House members the information necessary to ensuring that the U.S. Navy is the best it can possibly be."

As a professional staff member with Armed Services since 1984, he has worked extensively on the annual Department of Defense authorization bills as well as issues relating to naval weapons systems and procurement. As the U.S. Navy builds toward its projected goal of a 600-ship fleet, a longstanding priority of the Reagan White House and strongly supported by Cavaiola, he has played a significant supporting role in the development of policy relating to shipbuilding design and overhaul.

Most recently, he helped author the legislation which established the Commission on Merchant Marine and Defense, a body which has just released a study concerning how best to provide the sealift that would be needed in time of war.

Personal: born 8/04/47 in Red Bank, New Jersey. B.S. U.S. Naval Academy, 1969. Ph.D. Johns Hopkins Univ., 1976. 1969-1980, Active Duty U.S. Navy. 1980-1982, Operations Research Analyst with the Office of the Secretary of Defense. 1982-1984, Principal Analyst with Congressional Budget Office. 1984-present, Professional Staff Member, House Armed Services Committee.

Long hours during busy legislative sessions make spare time "a luxury" for Cavaiola. His home in Severna Park, Maryland (near Annapolis) serves as a welcome retreat from the halls of Capitol Hill. Describing himself as a "sailor for life," his home's proximity to the ocean keeps him close to the water and his Naval Reserve duties.

Armed Services

Joseph Cirincione
Professional Staff Member
1606 Longworth House Office
  Bldg.
225-5971

Expertise: National security issues

Upon arriving on Capitol Hill in 1985, national security expert Joseph Cirincione hoped to find a House Democratic Member who shared his generally conservative defense views and keen interest in military reform. Recognizing Cirincione's impressive professional and educational credentials, including top graduation honors from Georgetown's graduate Foreign Service program and stints with the USIA and Center for Strategic and International Studies, Rep. Charles Bennett (D-FL) moved quickly to offer him a position as a professional staff member with the House Armed Services Committee. The choice, it would appear, was a wise one.

His primary areas of work include the Strategic Defense Initiative, NATO conventional defense, procurement policy reform, and strategic and tactical doctrine. Cirincione would like to see a refocusing of U.S. defense policy away from nuclear doctrine toward greater reliance on conventional defensive forces. He remains a bit skeptical of SDI, opting instead for additional arms pacts with Moscow and the hope of a renewed detente between the superpowers.

Another area of defense policy which holds great interest for Cirincione is procurement. A firm believer that the procurement process must be restructured to encourage increased efficiency and lower cost, he has worked to maximize the return of each defense dollar through his assistance in the crafting of new procurement legislation. Though strictly partisan when it comes to the voting booth, he is regarded as a sure and steady professional by his fellow staffers; one who values bipartisanship on military matters in support of a strong American military.

Personal: born 11/13/ in New York, New York. B.A. Boston Coll., 1971. M.Sc. Georgetown Univ., 1983. 1982, Research Analyst, Center for Strategic and International Studies in Washington, D.C. 1983, Special Assistant to the Associate Director for Programs at the United States Information Agency. 1983-1984, Associate Director of the Central America Project at the Carnegie Endowment for International Peace in Washington, D.C. 1985 to present, Professional Staff Member, House Armed Services Committee.

Cirincione's career on the Hill, though brief, includes a number of important legislative contributions. His work to require the Department of Defense to do live fire testing of new weapons under battlefield conditions has helped bring about a policy shift by the Pentagon institutionalizing such procedure. He has also worked extensively on a bill prohibiting defense contractors from hiring DOD employees who have worked on contracts involving the prospective employer for full two years after leaving DOD. The bill was adopted in 1986 and passed again in 1987. In a rebuke to SDI, he worked on what is called the Conventional Defense Initiative or CDI. This 1986 bill shifted funds from the Strategic Defense Initiative to the budgets of promising conventional weapons systems.

Cirincione enjoys running and swimming and prefers to spend weekends with his family.

Williston Bernard Cofer, Jr.
Professional Staff Member
2339 Rayburn House Office Bldg.
225-4151

Expertise: management technology

The wide range of activities for which the House Committee on Armed Services is responsible requires extensive coordination of resources. Not only does the committee have jurisdiction over defense activities, but also must ensure the well-being and morale of the men and women who serve in the armed forces is maintained. Williston Cofer, Jr., a professional staff member on the committee, plays an important role in coordinating these resources.

Cofer brings to the committee a wide range of work experience. He has worked as a cost analyst for Capitol Airlines and served for two years in the U.S. Army. His managerial skills were already apparent at this early stage of his career as he was rewarded the Army's certificate of Management Achievement Award.

Upon finishing his B.A., Cofer went to work for the General Accounting Office (GAO). At GAO, where he rose to the immediate staff of the comptroller general, he was involved in formulating policies for determining the direction of the agency. While at GAO, he worked on and gained a graduate degree in automatic data processing systems and a Master of Science in management technology. These studies assisted Cofer in helping to design a management information system for the agency.

Personal: born 6/22/36 in Washington, D.C. George Washington Univ., 1955-1956. B.A. Western new Mexico Univ., 1965. Graduate certificate American Univ., 1970. M.S. American Univ, 1972. 1956-1960, cost analyst, Capitol Airlines. 1960-1962, U.S. Army. 1965-1974, auditor, General Accounting Office. 1974-1977, team leader, House Committee on Appropriations. 1977-present, professional staff member, Committee on Armed Services.

Cofer's staff coordinator role on the Armed Services Committee involves many facets of the committee's work in relaying information to and from the subcommittees and panels. Cofer has found his work with the Morale, Welfare, and Recreation panel to be particularly interesting. Cofer's responsibilities have recently been increased to include involvement in authorizations for operations and maintenance.

Cofer is an individual who seems well-tuned to look after the morale and recreation of the military.

Steven K. Conver
Professional Staff Member
2340 Rayburn House Office Bldg.
225-9647

Expertise: Defense, operations research

When a professional staff position on the House Armed Services Committee became available in 1985, Steve Conver asked Rep. Bill Dickinson (R-AL), the committee's ranking Republican, to consider him for the job. Few applicants could have been more qualified. Conver, a former Air Force captain and a graduate of the U.S. Air Force Academy, had spent years studying defense operations and management while working at the Pentagon.

Although the Armed Services Committee staff is officially bipartisan, Conver, along with one other professional staff member, works primarily for the committee's Republican minority. He reports directly to Dickinson, one of the strongest defense advocates in Congress, who became the ranking Armed Services Republican in 1981. Conver views his role now as "trying to protect the defense budget" each year against attacks from the liberal members of Congress. Conver's major task is helping draft the minority's position on the annual Department of Defense authorization bill.

Personal: born 12/11/44 in Memphis, Tennessee. B.S. U.S. Air Force Academy, 1966. M.S. Ohio State Univ., 1970. 1966-1975, Commissioned Officer, U.S. Air Force. 1967-1970, USAF Foreign Technology Division Analyst. 1970-1973, USAF Systems Command Analyst. 1974-1975, USAF Studies and Analysis Operations Research Analyst. 1975-1978, U.S. Nuclear Regulatory Commission Operations Analyst. 1978-1981, Chief of Analysis and Planning, U.S. Nuclear Regulatory Commission. 1981-1985, Deputy Assistant Secretary of the Air Force for Programs and Budget/ Financial Management. 1985-present, Professional Staff Member, House Armed Services Committee.

A stout defender of "a strong national defense", he is also an advocate of improving the defense acquisition process. Reflecting the independent view his boss has sometimes taken on Defense Department spending requests, Conver says the Pentagon needs to "be more candid, forthright, and less bureaucratic" to improve efficiency and public trust as well as to fend off attacks from Defense Department critics in Congress. Conver cites Dickinson's efforts to persuade President Reagan to establish the 1985 Packard Commission on defense procurement reforms as evidence that congressional hawks are just as determined to increase Pentagon efficiency as are defense critics.

At the same time, Conver steadfastly defends the need for recently proposed weapons systems, such as the MX missile and chemical weapons, to maintain America's defense posture. He is more often an ally of the military than a critic of it.

For example, the former Air Force financial manager sees recent cuts in defense spending as being excessive. He says roughly half the automatic spending cuts under the Gramm-Rudman-Hollings deficit reduction law would come in defense programs, although defense accounts for only 29% of the federal budget.

Conver says a major concern of his is the tendency in recent years for lawmakers to attach amendments to the defense authorization bill which restricts the President's options in arms control and foreign policy matters. He describes those moves as "meddlesome" and decries Congress trying to "force its will" in areas he believes the President should have responsibility.

Robert J. Eastman
Professional Staff Member
2340 Rayburn House Office Bldg.
225-7991

Personal: born 2/18/42 in St. Augustine, Florida. B.A. Florida State Univ., 1964. 1965-1985, officer: department head; flag secretary; executive officer; commanding officer; and congressional liaison officer, U.S. Navy. 1985-present, Professional Staff Member, House Armed Services Committee.

Expertise: Military logistics, defense spending

As a career naval officer, Bob Eastman had 20 years of practical experience, including three years as a congressional liaison officer. This latter experience gave Eastman a first-hand understanding of the day-to-day working relationship between the Pentagon and Capitol Hill.

Since coming on to the House Armed Services, Eastman has been responsible for oversight of the Navy and Marine Corps' operation and maintenance account in the Defense Department's budget. That account, which was over $80 billion last year, involves everything from gas and oil for ships and aircraft to bacon and beans for sailors and marines.

Eastman is also involved with the ship maintenance and repair provisions of the yearly defense authorization bill. That responsibility involves monitoring Navy policy on ship repair and overhauls, which includes overseeing competition between the public and private sector as well as the scheduling of when and where ship repair work is performed.

As a result of past problems of U.S. military capabilities (e.g., the aborted 1980 Iran rescue mission), the Defense Department has established the Office of the Assistant Secretary of Defense for Special Operations and Low Intensity Conflicts. This office, with a budget of about $2.6 billion, coordinates the DOD's activities under new policy and strategy guidelines and serves as the focal point for issues concerning Special Operations Force (SOF). Eastman, who is the sole committee staffer responsible for overseeing SOF, was a pivotal player in providing staff support for the DOD Special Operations Reorganization legislation.

SOF's objective is to upgrade the U.S. conventional forces posture and to secure sufficient support and sustainability for these forces. Eastman is responsible for monitoring the organization and funding levels for the various forces.

Although Eastman has travelled throughout the world while in the Navy, he genuinely enjoys the Washington metropolitan area. In fact, the prospect of remaining in Washington and working on Capitol Hill was a strong factor in his decision to retire from the Navy. While off the Hill, Eastman enjoys following the Redskins and attending the theater.

Marilyn Elrod
Professional Staff Member
Subcommittee on Military
  Installations and Facilities
2119 Rayburn House Office Bldg.
225-7120

*Personal: born 2/26 in Indianapolis,
Indiana. B.A., Purdue Univ., 1967.
American Univ., 1967-68. 1969-71,
Administrative Assistant to Rep. Allard
K. Lowenstein. 1971-83, Legislative
Assistant and Military Caseworker for
Rep. Ron Dellums (D-CA). 1983-
Present, House Committee on Armed
Services, Subcommittee on Military
Installations and Facilities.*

Expertise: Military construction, homeporting

Although Marilyn Elrod has worked on Capitol Hill since completing her education in 1969, it is obvious she has maintained the sense of purpose of a newcomer.

Described by some as "a right arm" to the Chairman of the Subcommittee on Military Installations and Facilities, Ron Dellums (D-CA), Elrod graduated from her position as a military caseworker on his personal staff and has earned a reputation as a pleasant but "hardline" and non-compromising advocate for Dellums's views and programs. These include a trial program that requires five percent of all defense contracts be given to minorities.

How does she approach this task? "I go in with the facts, and know the people who support the issue." Elrod concedes she is not one who likes confrontation for confrontation's sake. She is most proud of her efforts on homeporting, and is considered the most knowledgeable staff member on this issue, although she says it is her "greatest headache."

Elrod has travelled to military facilities worldwide and encourages the local military personnel to be flexible in their search for solutions to construction needs. "Bricks and mortar" are not the cheapest means to solve a problem, she says with budget constraints in mind.

In the future, Elrod hopes to bring a different perspective to military construction issues so that members will think more about the overall policies of the country in deciding what and where to build—moving them from the traditional approach to construction summed up by the question, "what new facility will go in my district?" Between sessions of Congress, Elrod travels but says she has very little personal time because trips are most often scheduled to accommodate other military and congressional staff. She likes her work and considers herself a "lifer" on the Hill.

Karen S. Heath
Professional Staff Member
2343 Rayburn House Office Bldg.
225-7560

Expertise: Military personnel, manpower and health care

Karen Heath says that she became an "instant expert" in defense, military health care and manpower issues while working as a legislative assistant to a senior member of the House, Congressman Charles Wilson of California.

A former military spouse, Heath says she is sensitive to specific concerns of those receiving medical services during peacetime (younger members of the military and their families and retired personnel) but realizes the ultimate purpose of military medical capabilities is being ready during wartime. Therefore, she has focused much attention on the reserve component of medical services and is pushing for the military to find reserve personnel with the proper medical skills and training to increase wartime readiness.

Although reticent about discussing her accomplishments, Heath will admit she played a role in helping bring the matter of "danger pay" to military personnel stationed in the Persian Gulf to the attention of Congress and to the public and is happy that, after a series of hearings, a stubborn Pentagon finally agreed to change its policy and issue the pay. She also was quite active in the Montgomery GI bill.

Personal: born in Washington, D.C. Westhampton Coll. B.A. George Washington Univ. M.A. John Hopkins Univ. (Phi Beta Kappa). Baltimore County teacher. Legislative assistant and administrative assistant to Rep. Charles Wilson (D-CA). Professional staff member, Committee on Armed Services.

Today Heath works closely with Rep. Beverly Byron (D-MD), the chairman of the manpower and personnel subcommittee and an advocate of a strong national defense. Byron is the daughter of one of President Dwight Eisenhower's top naval advisors. With CHAMPUS and other major issues under the jurisdiction of this subcommittee unresolved, Byron is likely to be a busy chairman—with Heath at her side.

Others have recognized Heath's contribution to the military. The Fleet Reserve Association honored her with an award, a bell which sits unobtrusively on her credenza, for her work on survivor benefits in the ninety-sixth session of Congress.

When she does get away from the committee, Heath likes to spend time in her garden.

William H. Hogan, Jr.
General Counsel
2120 Rayburn House Office Bldg.
225-1181

*Personal: born 8/27/17 in Lynn,
Massachusetts. A.B. in economics,
Brown Univ. J.D. Boston Coll. Law
School. 1940-1968, U.S. Navy.
Captain, Judge Advocate General
Corps. Married to former Vivian Olson,
3 boys. 1968, Assistant, ranking
minority member, House Committee
on Armed Services. 1969, Assistant
Counsel, Investigations
Subcommittee. 1970, Assistant,
Personnel & Intelligence
Subcommittees. 1976-present,
General Counsel, House Armed
Services Committee.*

Expertise: Legal & procedural matters

Bill Hogan has seen a lot of change. In 1969, in his early days with the House Armed Services Committee as a professional staff member, there were only 8-10 individuals on the professional staff. The budget for Armed Services programs was discussed in terms of millions. Today, there are upward of fifty on staff and the budget is discussed in billions of dollars. Hogan has served as General Counsel since 1976, and just as the Committee's responsibilities have become increasingly complex, so has his role evolved over the years.

In the beginning of his term as General Counsel, Hogan was more active in the overall operations at the professional staff level; today his work largely pertains to advising Members and staff on the legislative process. This is his area of expertise. He is described by a colleague as "the institutional memory" of the Committee.

Hogan cites the annual, multi-billion dollar authorization bill as perhaps the most significant task of the Armed Services Committee. Also, within the annual budget process is the continuing priority of pay and benefits for military personnel, something about which Hogan feels very strongly.

He sees his most important challenge as that of trying to get the best national security and defense possible for the taxpayers' dollars. Most satisfying, he claims, is "the opportunity of providing for a successful deterrent to aggression while enhancing the lot of military personnel and their families."

"Middle of the road" is how Hogan describes his political philosophy. He votes for whoever he thinks will do the best job, regardless of party affiliation. Having seen military duty in three wars, he believes a strong national defense is absolutely essential to U.S. foreign policy.

A lover of sports and travel, Hogan, who is now seventy, has plans to retire in the near future–but no plans to stop working. He wants to keep contributing, but gives no specifics. He just says he's keeping his options open.

Edward J. Holton
Professional Staff Member
2340 Rayburn House Office Bldg.
225-1462

Personal: born 11/13/42 in Chicago, Illinois. B.S. Univ. of Maryland, 1970. M.B.A. Univ. of Maryland, 1973. 1962-66, United States Marine Corps. 1966-67, Central Intelligence Agency. 1974-82, Program Evaluator, General Accounting Office. 1982-present, Professional Staff Member, House Armed Services Committee.

Expertise: Air Force, Army, Navy and Marine Corps operations and maintenance accounts

"Everything from fuel to toilet paper, plus civilian personnel" is how Ed Holton describes the range of the $80 billion accounts which he is responsible for overseeing. As a staff member serving the Armed Services Investigations Subcommittee and the Readiness Subcommittee, he pays a lot of attention to the nuts and bolts of military "O & M" — Operation and Maintenance.

Holton has used his early experiences with the Marine Corps and the C.I.A. to advantage since joining the Armed Services Committee staff in 1982. There he has helped guide committee oversight of morale, welfare, and recreation issues, and authored legislation on budget, construction, and auditing issues. Holton also handles the issue of humanitarian aid to Afghanistan and Central America for the committee .

In addition to having practical "inside" knowledge of the armed forces, Holton has taken the time to make himself a skilled logistician. He received high honors as an undergraduate in business administration. His M.B.A. curriculum included a specialty in transportation, logistics and physical distribution.

Holton has managed a private tax accounting firm, and worked seven years as a Program Evaluator with the General Accounting Office in Washington, Panama, and Denver. Besides Defense programs, his special issues at G.A.O. included Amtrak, the Panama Canal Treaty, and numerous Indian aid programs.

A robust sportsman, Holton looks forward to fulfilling someday a dream of beachfront living, raising Irish wolfhounds and devoting Saturday afternoons in the fall to Notre Dame football.

Deborah Roche Lee
Professional Staff Member
2343 Rayburn House Office Bldg.
225-0759

Expertise: Military personnel, alliance defense

Deborah Lee is living proof that the world of defense policy is not controlled solely by male bureaucrats. Indeed, as she begins her fifth year on the House Armed Services Committee, she is recognized by both staff colleagues and Members as a leading expert in the areas of military personnel and alliance defense.

The youngest professional staff member on the committee, Lee shares with another staffer the panoply of issues addressed by the Subcommittee on Military Personnel and Compensation. Those issues range from the health care of service personnel to the role of women in the military to U.S. conventional force levels in Europe.

In addressing the military health care field, Lee and the Subcommittee continue to ask tough questions of the Pentagon, such as whether the military is doing an adequate job of providing quality health care for enlisted personnel. While Lee believes the military must meet the needs of enlisted personnel in peacetime, she acknowledges it is even more important that it be effective during periods of conflict.

Personal: born 11/25/58 in Long Branch, New Jersey. B.A. Duke Univ., 1979. M.I.A. Columbia Univ., 1981. 1981-1983, Presidential Management Intern, including positions in the Department of the Army and the National Security Council's Office of Legislative Affairs and Security Assistance. 1983-present, Professional Staff Member, House Committee on Armed Services.

Last year, while analyzing the question of medical readiness, the personnel subcommittee concluded that there was an imbalance in the various medical disciplines. For example, while there were an abundance of pediatricians in the military, the services were lacking in orthopedic surgeons. Thus, the subcommittee, with Lee's assistance, included a number of provisions in the FY 1988 defense authorization bill designed to recruit and retain wartime-critical medical personnel.

Lee is cautiously optimistic about the future of America's defense personnel. To be sure, she has witnessed steady improvements in this area, including increased numbers of high school graduates enlisting in the service. But she is quick to point out that the services must maintain both competitive levels of compensation and quality health care. Only that will ensure the quality and quantity of personnel necessary to meet U.S. defense requirements.

An area that continues to receive considerable attention in the international arena is the alliance defense, particularly NATO and Japan. This is also an area within Lee's purview and one in which she has clearly developed an expertise.

The issues of burden sharing and troop numbers are sensitive ones to many legislators, particularly because of the often widespread perception that U.S. allies are not doing enough to shoulder the common defense. Lee argues both sides of this issue very effectively. She claims that while America's friends can and should be more aggressive in their contributions to defense, she points out that our allies actually do more than is commonly believed. Lee adds that the U.S. will always have to play a much greater role simply because it has strategic interests that extend well beyond NATO and Japan.

Lee also maintains that pressuring or cajoling our allies to do more will have a limited impact at best. Nor is pulling out our troops the answer. Internal politics of the various European nations and Japan, says Lee, will determine how much they spend on defense.

No matter how difficult a day it has been on Capitol Hill, Lee knows it is only a short drive to Chevy Chase, where waiting for her is her favorite hobby—her two children.

Russell Murray II
Professional Staff Member
2117 Rayburn House Office Bldg.
225-5056

Personal: born 12/5/25 in Woodmere, New York. B.S. Massachusetts Institute of Technology, 1949. M.S. Massachusetts Institute of Technology, 1950. 1950-1962, guided missile flight test engineer and later assistant chief, operations analysis group, Grumman Aircraft and Engineering Corporation, Bethpage, NY. 1962-1969, principal deputy assistant secretary of defense for systems analysis, Department of Defense. 1969-1973, director of long range planning, Pfizer International, NY. 1973-1977, director of review, Center for Naval Analysis, Arlington, VA. 1977-1981, assistant secretary of defense, program analysis and evaluation. 1981-1984, principal, Systems Research and Applications Corp., Arlington, VA. 1985-present, special counselor, House Armed Services Committee.

Expertise: National security policy

In the mid-1960s, while working in the Pentagon's Systems Analysis Office, Russell Murray had under his supervision a recent Oxford graduate who had manifest talents. Two decades later, that same Oxford graduate would become chairman of the House Armed Services Committee and subsequently ask Murray to join the committee's staff. Chairman Les Aspin (D-WI) knew he had a gold mine in Murray.

One would be hard pressed to find a defense staffer with a more extensive and impressive background. Murray's experiences range from being a flight test engineer to advising three Chiefs of Naval Operations to being President Carter's assistant secretary of defense. When Murray decided to delve into the complex relationship between Congress and the Pentagon, he had a wealth of professional experience to guide him. That experience has served both him and the committee well.

Murray is most closely associated with the Defense Policy Panel, a non-legislative arm of the committee that analyzes U.S. national security policy and objectives. Murray's primary objective is to raise policy matters not usually addressed by the Congress. Last year, he and the Panel did this through a series of hearings designed to analyze several important policy issues including the defense of Europe, the Persian Gulf, the Far East, strategic nuclear matters, and various Navy-related issues. Some of the issues raised in these hearings included the reflagging of Kuwati tankers and the policy implications of the MX and Midgetman.

Also included among the Panel's agenda is an analysis of the budgetary implications of U.S. national security objectives. Murray's task is to help define the balance between ends and means—to relate U.S. defense policy alternatives to the military capabilities they would require and the effect that their cost would have on the U.S. economy.

The Defense Policy Panel is also concerned with the military balance between the United States and its adversaries. After careful and thorough review, the Panel submits its recommendations for the annual mark-up of the defense authorization bill to the full membership of the committee.

In general, Murray believes there is much more to America's defense than hardware and weapons systems. As he says: "If the man on the street knew how bad things really were in developing a sensible, coherent defense policy, he would be astounded." Yet Murray is also optimistic about the future. He maintains that if both the Congress and the White House address these problems with an eye toward solving them, great improvements are possible.

Douglas H. Necessary
Professional Staff Member
2342 Rayburn House Office Bldg.
225-6703

Expertise: Navy and Marine Corps procurement

The man who is responsible for seeing that the Marine Corps and the Navy get their allocations is Doug Necessary.

Necessary is a retired Army Lt. Col. with six years acquisition-related experience. He spent four years as a major weapons system staff officer in the Army's Office of the Deputy Chief of Staff for Research, Development and Acquisition. The last two years were with the Army Legislative Liaison where he was the procurement staff officer. Necessary also spent two combat tours in Vietnam where he was an infantry platoon leader and a rifle company commander.

Necessary's job is Navy and Marine Corps procurement, not including shipbuilding. Navy aircraft, missiles and other Naval and Marine matters fall under his $20 billion program allocations. He spends most of his time on airplane and missle matters because they are heavy users of technology and are the most expensive.

Personal: born 1944 in Los Angeles, California. B.S. Auburn Univ., Phi Kappa Phi. M.S. Florida Institute of Technology, Defense Systems Management Coll., program management course. 1964-1984, United States Army, Lt. Col. (Ret.). 1984-present, professional staff member, Procurement and Military Nuclear Systems Subcommittee.

When considering the programs, Necessary expects to hear from the Navy and Marine Corps first. He also affords them the opportunity to be heard from last. In between he is willing to hear from anybody, including contractors, lobbyists, the Pentagon, the White House and Congress. He acknowledges a tremendous amount of constituent motivated political pressure and copes with it by realizing that while their are many different agendas in Washington and all he has to do is listen to all sides and sort the good information from the bad. Once this is done he makes his recommendations and the Members do the rest.

In his quest for knowledge of programs, Necessary receives lots of information in forms that range from anonymous envelopes shoved under his office door to late night phone calls at his home. Necessary believes that the average man on the street wants a strong adequate defense but no more. He also feels strongly that both the taxpayer and the military should get what they pay for. Because of his military experience, he is sensitive to the needs of the combat soldiers. But he is probably more critical than most. He is fully expectant of the Pentagon's eternally optimistic budget. Necessary tries to take a realistic approach to it by "minimizing redundancies" and finding cost-effective programs that integrate successfully.

One program that Necessary has seen approved is the upgrade of an ASW (Anti-Submarine Warfare) helicopter.

When Necessary has some time on his hands, he will likely be found working on or racing his pride and joy, an Aston Martin DB4-GT. He has also been a part-owner in an interstate trucking firm that transported race cars and antique cars.

Warren L. Nelson
Professional Staff Member
2343 Rayburn House Office Bldg.
225-2191

Personal: born 12/29/40 in Philadelphia, Pennsylvania. B.A. American Univ., School of International Service, 1962. 1963-1966, Assistant Managing Editor,The Tehran Journal, Tehran, Iran. 1967-1969, UPI, Foreign Desk Editor, Washington, D.C.. 1969-1975, UPI, Pentagon Correspondent. 1975-1983, Legislative Assistant, Administrative Assistant, Rep. Les Aspin (D-WI). 1983-present, Professional Staff Member, House Armed Services Committee.

Expertise: Press relations, Middle East affairs

In 1975, when Rep. Les Aspin was looking for a Legislative Assistant with both Pentagon and journalism experience, Warren Nelson was the perfect candidate. And in 1983, when Aspin assumed the chairmanship of the Subcommittee on Military Personnel and Compensation, Nelson was asked to join its professional staff. Nelson subsequently developed an expertise in the area of military retirement.

As the only long-time staffer on the Armed Services Committee to have a newspaper background, Nelson has the most frequent contact with the press. This ranges from briefing reporters on various defense-related issues to writing the majority of the committee's press releases and official statements. Nelson takes considerable pride in maintaining an excellent relationship with the Washington press corps, which is not always an easy task. His frequent contact with the press, in fact, led his colleagues on the committee to label him the "Minister of External Relations." Both the *National Journal* and *Washingtonian* magazine consider Nelson one of Capitol Hill's most effective staffers.

If any single bill consumes the attention of Nelson and his committee colleagues, it is the yearly defense authorization bill. Among the provisions of last year's bill, Nelson worked closely on various personnel-related issues, including polygraph testing and the wearing of yarmulkes and turbans by military personnel. Also, Nelson's Middle East expertise resulted in his focusing closely on U.S. Persian Gulf policy. But as the staffer with the longest association with Aspin, Nelson's main duties are to get involved in whatever is consuming the chairman's interest and to execute his agenda.

While Nelson believes the committee plays an active and important role in U.S. defense requirements, he also thinks it needs to change its emphasis from concentrating on dollars and cents to establishing a long-term and effective defense policy. He is equally convinced the Committee must be more effective in communicating its work to the rest of the Congress, the defense community and the general public. While Nelson lauds the committee's legislative work, he feels it should make further strides in its investigative responsibilities. Nelson is particularly interested in this area. He has played a significant role in the investigation of the 1983 Marine bombing in Beirut, the U.S. sale of TOW missiles to Iran, and last year's investigation of the Marine guard espionage case in Moscow.

Away from Capitol Hill, for 15 years Nelson has edited the English-language section of the *Iran Times*, a weekly independent newspaper and the largest Persian paper in the country.

Colleen A. Preston
Assistant General Counsel
2117 Rayburn House Office Bldg.
225-4223

Expertise: DOD acquisition policy, defense contracting, and procurement

Colleen A. Preston managed to squeeze in one year with a law firm before her college ROTC commitment caught up with her. But it was no setback. Her four years in the Air Force made her, in her own words, "an instant expert in procurement." And since her discharge in 1983, the Armed Services Committee has been the beneficiary of that expertise.

While in the Air Force she was assigned to the general counsel's office. Her term of service was fairly routine, but it did acquaint her with her predecessor on the committee. When that predecessor left, Preston sold herself to committee members and staffers as the ideal replacement.

Focusing on the legal aspects of procurement and defense contracts on the House Armed Services Committee, Preston is relied upon to provide advice on this strictly nonpartisan, highly specialized, and highly centralized committee.

For nearly four years her duties were confined to the Investigations Subcommittee, which has jurisdiction over procurement reform. In January, 1987, she was given the added duties of assisting the committee's general counsel in such matters as the language of authorization bills.

Procurement reform, she explains, tends to run in cycles, one of which has coincided with her four years on the committee. This has made her a key player in drafting such legislation as the Competition in Contracting Act (1984), Defense Procurement Reform Act (1985), and Defense Procurement Improvement Acts of 1986 & 1987.

Personal: born 10/11/55 in Monterey, California. B.A. Univ. of Florida, 1975. J.D. Univ. of Florida Law School, 1978. LL.M. Georgetown Univ., 1985. 1978-1979, attorney, Akerman, Senterfitt & Eidson. 1979-1983, U.S. Air Force. 1989-present, Assistant General Counsel, Committee on Armed Services.

In this capacity Preston often finds herself assisting with the legal aspects of procurement and defense contracts and with member inquiries. Responding to the inquiries usually consists of making sure a constituent got a meaningful response, that the government acted properly, and so forth. Preston is available to give them a solid independent judgment.

But she still claims to be a pure technician, without an ideological bone in her body. She declines to categorize herself as anything other than "right in the middle of moderate," which in her committee would place her pretty much in the mainstream. She also hints that there is stiil much work to be done, such as streamlining the existing procurement process.

When she does take some time off she might be found on a golf course or a cross-country ski trail.

Armed Services

William D. "David" Price
Professional Staff Member
2340 Rayburn House Office Bldg.
225-1465

Expertise: Stockpile legislation on strategic and critical materials

David Price is your archetypical engineer/trouble-shooter, having spent an entire 43-year career solving unusual problems even before he began his present career on Capitol Hill.

He was just ending the first career when America was going through its great fuel crisis in 1974. There was a great clamor to open up this nation's naval petroleum reserves, first set up by President Teddy Roosevelt earlier in the century. Former Rep. F. Edward Hebert (D-LA) knew Price was ending his 28-year stint with Shell Oil, and that Price was no stranger to urgent crises. He brought Price aboard his Armed Services Committee. Price's first assignment was to monitor the parent bill which authorized opening those reserves. Price also found himself with a ringside seat in the turf battles attending that legislation.

That was just the start of eclectic assignments for Price. He spent six months investigating a rash of weapons thefts from military bases. He was involved in studying the "forward line of battle" involving our NATO allies against Warsaw Pact forces. The Construction Subcommittee borrowed him to work on an Air Force facility for testing engines under a variety of conditions. It was the biggest single line item on any construction authorization bill at that time.

Personal: born 8/17/09 in Blacksburg, Virginia . B.S. Virginia Polytechnic Institute & State Univ., 1930. M.S. Ohio State Univ., 1931. Univ. of Tennessee, 1937. 1931, Second Lieutenant, U.S. Army. 1971, released as Major General, U.S. Air Force. World War II, served with 58th Bomber Wing, 20th Air Force, and other commands. Recipient, Distinguished Service Medal. 1931-1936, Instructor in Engineering, Virginia Polytechnic Institute. 1936-1938, Engineering Draftsman, Tennessee Valley Authority. 1938-1939, Personnel Official, U.S. Housing Authority. 1939-1942, Executive Director, Tennessee State Planning Commission. 1946-1974, Personnel Official, aviation departments, Shell Oil Company. 1974-present, Professional Staff Member, House Committee on Armed Services

He now concerns himself with strategic and critical materials, especially in the area of stockpile legislation. He explains that there are always a number of strategic materials this country would use if it went to war. Perception of what needs to be stockpiled is always changing, he said. The problem, he explains, is a frequent impulse to sell off that stockpile to finance Great Society programs or to achieve a one-time reduction in the deficit. Price is not too fond of OMB-types he often finds more concerned with bottom-line budgetary priorities than the nation's defense needs.

Price should know something about defense. His advanced work in aeronautical engineering made him much in demand when America entered World War II. He was initially involved in getting the first crop of B-29s ready for combat. Next came service in the India-China theater and with the 58th Bomber Wing on Tinian (one of the Mariana Islands in the Western Pacific). Price's description of his wartime service reveals one logistical, procurement, recruiting, or planning challenge after another. After the war, it was an easy task for him to plan Shell Oil Company's 10-year projected needs in aviation lubricants and fuels. Assigned to Washington in 1949, he has been here ever since in a variety of tasks.

Nora Slatkin
Professional Staff Member
2343 Rayburn House Office Bldg.
225-6999

Expertise: Weapons systems

When, in 1985, the House Armed Services Committee needed an expert on weapons systems to help separate worthy programs from overrated ones, it found one at the Congressional Budget Office.

Nora Slatkin's interest in defense issues was sharpened by summer internships at the CIA and the NSC, and by an advanced degree from Georgetown's School of Foreign Service.

Six years at CBO—much of it writing reports on such topics as the costs of withdrawing ground forces and combat modernization—served as good preparation for Slatkin.

Slatkin's principal area of responsibility is Army weapons systems. The continuing controversy over the Bradley fighting vehicle has required Slatkin to devote attention to studying the issue and arranging hearings. Besides becoming well-acquainted with the Bradley, Slatkin is an expert on the DIVAD and chemical weapons systems.

When not at her desk, Slatkin can be found at home spending time with her husband and three children, or cultivating her garden. Slatkin also pursues her passion for travel when she gets the chance; her job has taken her to all of the active U.S. Army bases in the world.

Personal: born 5/5/55 in Massapequa, N.Y. B.A. Lehigh Univ. 1977. M.S. Georgetown School of Foreign Service, 1979 (Phi Beta Kappa). 1979-85, Principal Analyst, CBO. 1985-present, Professional Staff Member, Armed Services Committee.

Pete Steffes
Professional Staff Member
2117 Rayburn House Office Bldg.
225-6288

Expertise: Military construction, travel and environmental issues

When former Armed Services Chairman Mel Price (D-IL) needed a staff member to fill in as travel advisor and all-purpose man, it only made sense to hire a career military person who had served on all five continents. Air Force Liaison Pete Steffes was the man for the job. By the time Steffes retired from a life-long career in the Air Force in 1983 to join the Armed Services Committee, he had collected the Legion of Merit and the Meritorious Service Medal. But the greatest asset he brought to Armed Services was his first-hand knowledge of military airlift operation procedures. Steffes explains one of his strengths in his current position is "having been there, it is difficult for the Pentagon to snow me."

If Steffes sounds like a world-weary veteran, it's because he is. After reaching the Armed Services Committee, he only added to his already-long list of places visited—a list that even includes the South Pole. On a 1977 trip to the Middle East, led by Chairman Price, Steffes found his group carrying a message from Sadat to Begin. That communication helped pave the way for the two leaders to meet at Camp David.

Personal: born 11/12/43 in Detroit, MI. Univ. of Maryland (London, England campus) 1963-1965. U.S. Air Force 1961-1983, Chief Master Sergeant. 1975-1983, Air Force Congressional Liaison. 1983-present, Professional Staff Member, Committee on Armed Services.

When not on official travel, or assisting members and staffers form their own travel plans, Steffes devotes his time to work on Rep. Ron Dellums's Military Construction Subcommittee. Dellums's tenure has been marked by a special sensitivity to the quality of life for military families and by advocacy of better living and working conditions. Steffes has found himself hard-pressed to reconcile these improvements with funds that seem only to trickle in. As a result, Steffes explains that the Military Construction Committee—along with the rest of Congress—has been forced to "bite the bullet and forego some of the planned improvements."

In the environmental area, Steffes notes the increasing concern for environmental quality at military bases has caused the committee to form the Environmental Restoration Panel on which he serves. The first item of business for the panel was the Superfund amendments of 1985 which Steffes and another committee staffer worked on for over a year until its final passage.

Steffes and other staffers on Armed Services see his role as one of utility-man. His wide-ranging job includes finding more space for a growing Committee staff, a feat he once accomplished by convincing then-Speaker Tip O'Neill to convert departing member James Broyhill's Rayburn office to space for the Armed Services Committee.

James C. Waters
Professional Staff Member
2120 Rayburn House Office Bldg.
225-1463

Personal: born 11/8/30 in Woodside, New York. B.B.A. Hofstra Univ., 1958. 1948-1951, proof machine operator, credit dept. employee, cashier, Bank of Manhattan Co. and Florida State Bank. 1951-1955, U.S.A.F. 1958, accountant, Ernst and Ernst, New York City. 1958-1964, auditor, General Accounting Office, Kansas City regional office. 1964-1980, Audit and Project Manager, GAO Washington regional office. 1980-present, Professional Staff Member, House Committee on Armed Services.

Expertise: DOD inventory controls and investigations

Jim Waters has had broad experience as an investigator and auditor, dating back to probes of union corruption and the Billie Sol Estes frauds of the 1960's and ranging from investigating the 1983 attack on the Marines in Lebanon to probing inventory losses in armed forces supply centers and base commissaries.

While working with the General Accounting Office, he was detailed to help various congressional committees conduct investigations. It was in that capacity that he worked on union corruption and the Billie Sol Estes case. He served with the Senate Committee on Labor and Education, the House Committee on Agriculture, and the House Committee on Appropriations (Surveys and Investigative staff).

Waters has conducted studies and investigations for the Readiness and Investigations Subcommittees and had oversight responsibility for morale, welfare, and recreation activities. He is currently responsible for Air Force and Defense agencies operation and maintenance accounts.

As a member of the team which investigated the October 23, 1983, terrorist attack on Marine headquarters in Beirut, in which 241 servicemen died, Waters helped develop the committee report which was critical of the U.S. chain of command and Marine defensive procedures.

He also has investigated inventory losses at supply centers of all the armed services. Inadequate accounting controls, he says, made it possible for theft or losses to occur and the problems still exist. And he has investigated losses and buyer kickbacks at commissaries and exchanges, which have resulted in some companies being suspended from doing business with the Federal Government and a general tightening up of procedures by the armed services.

Waters also investigated the costs of evacuating former President Marcos and his party from Manila to Hawaii by members of the U.S. Armed Forces when Marcos was asked by President Reagan to step down as President of the Philippines in order to avoid bloodshed and ensure a peaceful transition to a new government.

In the field of legislation, Waters has worked on defense authorization bills, legislation setting standards for automated inventory control systems used by defense contractors, and legislation establishing a "whistle-blower" system for 200,000 civilians working on non-appropriated fund activities for the armed services such as bowling alleys, golf courses, and exchanges.

In his spare time, Waters enjoys reading, chiefly mysteries, as well as golf, fishing, jogging, and watching the Washington Redskins.

Dr. Michael West
Professional Staff Member
2343 Rayburn House Office Bldg.
225-6702

*Personal: born 7/22/46 in San
Francisco, California. B.A. San Jose
State Univ., 1970. M.A. Ohio State
Univ., 1972. Ph.D. Ohio State Univ.,
1980. 1981-present, Professional Staff
Member, House Armed Services
Committee.*

Expertise: Operations & maintenance, oversight, civilian personnel,
DOD commercial activities, environmental restoration.

 While in Washington, on a dissertation year fellowship in 1974,
West received assistance from the Armed Services Committee in
researching the activities of the House Naval Affairs Committee
during the 1930's. This association led to his subsequent
appointment to the committee staff that year.

While Armed Services Committee staff do not work for any
particular political party nor are they assigned exclusively to any
one subcommittee, West has spent the better part of his career
working in four areas: operation and maintenance budget
oversight, civilian personnel management, Department of Defense
commercial activities or contracting out programs, and
environmental restoration.

After spending two years as Executive Secretary and four years as
a research assistant, West became a professional staff member in
1981, and was assigned to the Subcommittee on Readiness. Prior
to that, he worked on the Special Subcommittee on NATO
Readiness, Standardization and Interoperability. West also served
on the Readinesss Panel of the Subcommittee on Procurement
and Military Nuclear Systems, which conducted a review of
readiness considerations in the development of the Defense
budget. This laid the foundation for the committee's subsequent
annual budget oversight of the operations and maintenance
accounts.

West served on the committee's Environmental Restoration Panel
in 1985 that was instrumental in developing the federal facilities
provisions of the Superfund Amendments and Reauthorization Act
and the establishing in law the Defense Environmental Restoration
Program and the Defense Environmental Restoration Account. He
continues to serve on the Environmental Restoration Panel of the
Subcommittee on Readiness which provides budget and policy
oversight for Department of Defense efforts to comply with
environmental laws and regulatory guidance.

West also worked closely with the late Congressman Dan Daniel
(D-VA) to provide authorization for Department of Defense to assist
the homeless by making available space at military facilities that
was not being utilized and providing support and blankets and
cots on a nonreimbursable basis.

G. Kim Wincup
Staff Director
2120 Rayburn House Office Bldg.
225-415B

Expertise: Defense issues

While in his junior year at DePauw University, Kim Wincup attended American University as an exchange student. Like many who hear Washington's siren song, Wincup was destined to return. And when he did, he commenced a career that would eventually place him in one of Capitol Hill's top staff roles. While still a staffer on the Subcommittee on Military Personnel and Compensation, Wincup played a key role in drafting the legislation which eventually became the Selective Service Registration Proclamation, which was signed into law in 1980.

Today, as Committee Staff Director, Wincup oversees a staff of over sixty, including some 42 professional staff members. According to Wincup, their goal is straightforward: providing timely, substantive and accurate information on the full range of national security issues to over 50 Members of the House.

The annual defense authorization bill is the greatest task before Wincup and the Committee staff. Last year's bill authorized $292 billion and it contained over one hundred floor amendments. Additionally, there were nearly five hundred legislative differences and literally thousands of programmatic differences between the House and Senate. These facts alone give considerable credence to Wincup's claim that the defense bill is the single most difficult piece of legislation the House must address each year. A portion of Wincup's work involves analyzing the Defense Department's "black" programs; those programs whose substance is highly secretive. Such programs include the Advanced Tactical Bomber (Stealth), the Advanced Tactical Fighter, and the Advanced Cruise Missile.

Personal: born 9/6/44 in St. Louis, Missouri. B.A. DePauw Univ., 1966. J.D. Univ. of Illinois, 1969. 1970-1973, United States Air Force. 1974-1983, counsel; 1983-1984, assistant General Counsel; and 1984-present, Staff Director, House Armed Services Committee.

Wincup anticipates a number of challenges throughout the remainder of the 100th Congress. Chief among the Committee's concerns will be interpretation of the ABM Treaty, the issue of nuclear testing, abiding by the unratified SALT II Treaty, and various issues related to SDI funding levels.

Yet Wincup's responsibilities extend well beyond the array of America's defense requirements. As a result of such a large staff, he must involve himself with the details of administration. Indeed, Wincup is responsible for recruitment of new staff, assignment of issues to the professional staffers, the budgeting process that the committee employs, the scheduling and coordination of committee and subcommittee hearings, and the issuance of committee reports.

No matter how difficult a particular situation, "When life here gets hectic and parochial, Kim emerges as an excellent arbiter. He is the essence of grace under pressure, one of his colleagues say."

HOUSE OF REPRESENTATIVES
COMMITTEE ON BANKING, FINANCE & URBAN AFFAIRS

Michael J. Bertelsen
Minority Counsel
Subcommittee on Economic
  Stabilization
517 House Office Bldg. Annex 2
226-7850

Personal: born 1/1/61 in Logan, Utah.
B.S. Univ. of Utah, 1982 (magna cum
laude). J.D. Univ. of Utah, 1985. 1985,
Staff Counsel, Representative Dean
Gallo (R-NJ). 1986, Staff Counsel,
Representative Jim Kolbe (R-AZ),
House Committee on Banking,
Finance & Urban Affairs. 1987-
present, Minority Counsel,
Subcommittee on Economic
Stabilization, House Committee on
Banking, Finance & Urban Affairs.

Expertise: Financial institutions, regulatory structure, banking reform

Mike Bertelsen had never been east of the Mississippi before graduating from law school in 1985. Bertelsen was the youngest person ever to graduate from the University of Utah law school.

After several months of job searching and waiting tables, Bertelsen realized his talents "might be utilized" in a congressional office. His previous experience in environmental law led to a position dealing with the Superfund issue for Representative Dean Gallo (R-NJ). He next served as staff counsel to Representative Jim Kolbe (R-AZ), a member of the House Banking Committee. When Kolbe was appointed to the Appropriations Committee at the start of the 100th Congress, Bertelsen chose to remain with banking issues. He looked for a new position and ultimately found his present job with the Minority Staff of the House Banking Committee. Appointed by Representative Norm Shumway, Bertelsen is now the minority counsel for the Subcommittee on Economic Stabilization.

Bertelsen keeps very busy as the only Republican staffer for the subcommittee. The Democrats have seven professional members on the same subcommittee.

Bertelsen's "first bill" was the Expedited Funds Availability Act, or the "check hold" bill. He also participated in the drafting of the Competitive Equality Banking Act.

Considered an expert on financial institutions' regulatory structure and reform, Bertelsen foresees a busy second session of the 100th Congress. He feels that radical change will occur in the industry in the near future, and that Congress needs to step in and legislate reform. An approachable man with a ready wit, Bertelsen's energy is apparent. Mixed amid the banking journals by his desk are outdoorsman magazines. Mike spends his free time hiking and hunting. Until he discovered the joys of summers at Dewey Beach, Bertelsen crewed on a sailing team in Annapolis.

Bertelsen expects to remain on Capitol Hill at least through the 101st Congress.

Anthony F. Cole
Minority Staff Director and General
  Counsel
B-301-C Rayburn House Office
  Bldg.
225-7502

Expertise: Financial services restructuring, banking supervision & regulation

As the Minority Staff Director for the Banking Committee, Cole plays a crucial role in all legislation that concerns the banking industry. In the 100th Congress, as a result of the evolution of the American financial system, the Committee has been forced to reexamine the country's depository financial institutions and their regulators. Cole has worked extensively on the Expedited Funds Availability Act, which limited the number of days a depository institution may restrict the availability of funds deposited into an account. The language in the bill was later included in the Competitive Equality Banking Act of 1987.

Cole also handles consumer legislation. He helped to draft the Credit Card Full Cost Disclosure Act. The Act requires that banks, department stores, and other companies that issue credit cards inform consumers well in advance of getting a card exactly what they will be paying for that credit. Passage was hailed as a victory over credit card issuers, which are currently required by Federal law to disclose interest rates, annual fees and other details only when a consumer actually receives a card. However, passage was also a victory for banks and national retailers, who had lobbied extensively against an amendment that would have imposed a nationwide, floating cap on credit card interest rates.

Cole helped put together a compromise version of the "Truth in Savings" bill. The bill requires that bank advertisements prominently display annual percentage rates, list deposit requirements, minimum balances, and time periods when advertised interest rates are in effect. Similar measures have passed twice in the past but died in the then Republican-controlled Senate. Lengthy negotiations with the financial services industry reduced its opposition to the measure.

Early in the 100th Congress, the Committee began drafting legislation to shore up the ailing Federal insurance fund for savings and loans. The crisis of the bankrupt Federal Savings and Loan Insurance Corporation (FSLIC) allowed Cole the opportunity to serve on the "working group" of staff appointed to rewrite the bill as instructed by the Conferees. Highly contentious debate separated the House, the Senate, and the White House. The working group's draft was integral to the passage of the legislation. The legislation was signed into law in August, 1987, allowing the FSLIC to borrow the money needed to reimburse depositors as bankrupt institutions are closed down. Among its scores of provisions, the bill froze the growth of "non-bank banks" and temporarily halted banks expansion into insurance, securities, and real estate.

Personal: born 7/31/47 in Hamilton, Ohio. B.A. Coll. of William and Mary, 1970 (Phi Beta Kappa). M.A. Rutgers State Univ., 1972. J.D. Coll. of William and Mary, 1975. 1975-1979, attorney, Federal Reserve Board. 1979-1981, Senior Attorney, Legal Division, Board of Governors of the Federal Reserve System. 1980-1981, Deputy General Counsel, Depository Institutions Deregulation Committee. 1981-1986, Special Assistant to the Board, Board of Governors of the Federal Reserve System. 1986, Minority Counsel, Subcommittee on Financial Institutions. 1987-present, Minority General Counsel, Committee on Banking, Finance and Urban Affairs. 1988-present, Minority Staff Director, Committee on Banking, Finance and Urban Affairs

Mary Martha Fortney
Staff Director
Subcommittee on General
  Oversight and Investigations
B304 Rayburn House Office Bldg.
225-2828

*Personal: born 12/8/47 in Jamestown,
New York. Attended Madison Coll. and
George Mason Univ.. 1973-76, Real
Estate Broker, Northern Virginia. 1977-
81, Agency Liaison Office of
Presidential Correspondence, White
House. 1981-82, Legislative Assistant;
1982-1985, Legislative Director, Rep.
Carroll Hubbard (D-KY). 1985, Staff
Director, Subcommittee on General
Oversight and Investigations,
Committee on Banking, Finance, &
Urban Affairs.*

Expertise: Banking and thrift institutions, FSLIC, and secondary
reserve of savings & loans.

The Subcommittee on General Oversight and Investigation has
the responsibility to review all programs under the jurisdiction of
the Committee on Banking, Finance and Urban Affairs. Chairman
Carroll Hubbard (D-KY) has not shown a great deal of interest in
partisanship in Congress. Hubbard has attempted to establish a
constructive relationship with all fourteen members of his
Subcommittee. Hubbard and Fortney concentrate their efforts on
the savings and loan issues that come under the jurisdiction of the
Committee. Hubbard's district in western Kentucky, as well as the
rest of rural America, has been of concern to the Chairman in
his Subcommittee work on the problems of rural and agricultural
borrowers, and the role and status of credit institutions servicing
rural areas.

In addition to Fortney's work on the Oversight Subcommittee, she
assists Hubbard on the other Banking Subcommittees he serves
on: Housing and Community Development, Domestic Monetary
Policy, and Financial Institutions Supervision, Regulation and
Insurance.

In the 99th Congress, the Subcommittee delved into various
banking issues. Hearings were held on the impact of Gramm-
Rudman-Hollings on the banking agencies; the Federal Home
Loan Bank Board (FHLBB), the Federal Savings and Loan
Insurance Corporation (FSLIC), the National Credit Union
Administration (NCUA), and the Office of the Comptroller of the
Currency. Oversight hearings were also held on the issue of high-
yield securities (junk bonds) and a perennial issue for the
Subcommittee, the reinstatement of the Renegotiation Act of
1951. The original Act was designed to prevent the realization of
excessive profits on defense contracts and subcontracts. The Act
expired in 1978. However, legislation has been introduced, the War
Profiteering Prohibition Act, to revise and reinstate the 1951 Act.

In 1987 the Subcommittee was immersed in controversy when it
held hearings on a critical study of the management of FHLBB and
FSLIC. The study, commissioned by the FHLBB, questioned
former FHLBB Chairman Edwin J. Gray's use of a special
entertainment fund.

In 1988 the Subcommittee will continue hearings, begun in 1987,
that address the need to attract capital to healthy thrift institutions.
With the majority of the country's thrifts not bankrupt or on the
verge of failure, it is important to determine the ways to keep them
well-capitalized and healthy. These hearings will work in
conjunction with the Subcommittee's continued interest in the
entire savings and loan industry.

John Heasley
Legislative Assistant
Representative Steve Bartlett (R-
  TX)
1709 Longworth House Office
  Bldg.
225-3168

Expertise: Banking, finance, housing

It's common knowledge that a Texan doesn't often stray far from his beloved state. It was an attractive offer that uprooted this native. Heasley moved to Washington after five years as an Assistant Criminal District Attorney in Dallas County where he was involved in cases involving white collar crime, felonies, robberies, and sexual assault. Steve Bartlett's (R-TX) reputation as a well informed Member of the House, willing to get involved with the intricate details of legislation, made Heasley's   decision to accept the post of Bartlett's legislative assistant an easy one.

Heasley has gained experience in the banking and finance areas and was a significant force in Bartlett's success in helping shape the FSLIC Recapitalization bill that was signed into law in August,1987. Bartlett had his own forebearance bill establishing certain accounting and regulatory procedures for Savings and Loans, and much of it was incorporated into the final FSLIC Recapitalization bill. The forebearance provision allows a weakened thrift institution to continue its operations if its problems result primarily from "economic conditions in an economically depressed region" and if it maintains a net worth of at least one-half of 1 percent.

Heasley was also involved in his boss's work on the Omnibus Housing bill. Heasley concurs with his boss in advocating that public housing should be deregulated, with control given to local authorities. He also favors rehabilitating public housing rather than constructing new units. Bartlett was successful in an amendment to the housing bill which prohibits the construction of most new public housing unless 85 percent or more of a community's public housing units meet certain minimum housing standards.

In his leisure time, Heasley loves to bird hunt, although he has yet to find the time or the place for such hunting in Washington or its surrounding area. He also enjoys athletics such as softball, football and squash. He is fluent in Spanish and has spent extensive time in Central and South America, travelling the countryside in a Jeep.

Personal: born 5/6/56 in El Paso, Texas. B.A. , Univ. of Texas, with honors. J.D., Univ.of Texas. 1980-1981, legislative aide, Texas State Legislature. 1981-1986, assistant criminal district attorney, Dallas County, TX. 1986-present, Legislative Assistant, Congressman Steve Bartlett (R-TX).

Steve Judge
Deputy Staff Director
2129 Rayburn House Office Bldg.
225-4547

Personal: born 9/27/53 in Pittsburgh, Pennsylvania. B.S. St. John's Univ., 1975. 1976-1977, Program Instructor, Portland Residence, a home for mentally retarded adults. 1977-1978, Legislative Assistant, Minnesota State Senate. 1978-1982, Legislative Assistant, and 1982-1987, Legislative Director to Representative Bruce F. Vento (D-MN). 1987, Professional Staff Member; 1987 to present, Deputy Staff Director, Committee on Banking,Finance and Urban Affairs.

Expertise: International banking, financial institutions, international trade, housing & community development

An easy-going manner combined with political savvy helped Steve Judge move from Professional Staff Member to the number two slot after only six months with the Committee in 1987. He has shown skill in negotiating with banking interests as well as with Committee members.

1987 was also the cumulation of five years of efforts on behalf of Vento's pet project, aid for the homeless. Championed by House Speaker Jim Wright, the Stewart B. McKinney Homeless Assistance Act of 1987 provides emergency assistance, shelters, training, mental health treatment, and other services for the homeless. From his new position on the Committee, Judge coordinated the consideration of the legislation by five committees and coordinated the Floor action.

He played a role in the handling of the Competitive Equality Banking Act of 1987, especially Title II, which places a moratorium on expansion of bank powers. The far-reaching ban expired March 1, 1988, and Judge is certain to be involved in the Committee's monumental task of restructuring the powers through a look at Glass-Steagall, the Bank Holding Company Act, the 4(c)(8) Amendments, and other areas.

As a professional staff member, Judge also had a major part in the farm credit bill, which establishes secondary markets for agricultural loans, and in ensuring that the international trade bill did not contain provisions in conflict with existing banking law.

Judge can't recall a time when he *wasn't* involved in politics, starting in kindergarten and going on to serve as president and vice president of his student body in both high school and college.

He came to Washington in 1978, a period he describes as "the post-Hubert Humphrey era of bigger, but less personal government." Not only does he love Capitol Hill politics, he also says he understands it. "It's taking care of business back home and being the best politician you can," Judge observes.

In his spare time, Judge goes flyfishing—his favorite spots being Alaska, where he caught a four-pound trout, Montana, and Shenandoah National Park. Each winter and spring, he volunteers his time at a church-sponsored clinic to help low-income persons prepare their tax returns.

Joseph C. Lewis
Professional Staff Member
B303 Rayburn House Office Bldg.
225-7141

Expertise: Banking, consumer protection

Prior to his service on the House Banking, Finance and Urban Affairs Committee, Joseph Lewis was exposed to several environments that have served to shape his "consumer-oriented" professional outlook in a significant way. First as a journalist for several "probing" Texas newspapers during major state and Federal investigations of political corruption in South Texas in the 1950s and subsequently heading a Committee investigative team probing the Watergate crisis, Lewis developed a keen sense of proper political and legislative behavior, which has had a lasting impact on his work.

Wright Patman (D-TX) was the first of three generations of Banking Committee chairmen whom Lewis has served. With individuals such as former staff director Paul Nelson, general counsel Richard Still and Curt Prins, staff director of the Consumer Affairs Subcommittee, Lewis helped guide hard fought battles for consumer milestones such as the Community Reinvestment Act, the Home Mortgage Disclosure Act and the Equal Credit Opportunity Act. He worked on the creation of the National Consumer Cooperative Bank in 1978, which chairman Fernand St Germain (D-RI) defended against attacks by the Reagan Administration by speeding its transition to private status, and was pivotal in the recent limits placed on the time that banks can hold checks. Lewis often presents a populist point of view and has been labeled the "consumer conscience" of the committee. Due to the close relationship of Patman with Ralph Nader, Lewis has understandably developed a long relationship with consumer advocates.

When Henry Reuss (D-WI) became chairman in 1975, Lewis became staff director of the Domestic Monetary Policy Subcommittee. He has also been staff director of the Joint Committee on Defense Production while maintaining his banking and speechwriting responsibilities. Lewis now serves St Germain as press liaison and director of a newly established investigative unit and enjoys assisting the chairman in developing consumer coalitions.

Lewis expects the banking agenda to be dominated by the debate over the extent to which banking and commerce should be mixed, and anticipates that many issues will take a back seat until there is some movement toward resolving this question. Lewis also notes considerable thought will be given to strengthening the community reinvestment criteria in evaluating banks. If banks are allowed to expand certain functions, he wants to see the preservation of traditional banking functions and neighborhood credit services. One way to do this is to rate banks on how well they've served their neighborhoods, and Lewis regards it as unfortunate that regulators have only been looking at safety and soundness issues and ignoring consumer protection. He favors a stronger regulatory posture which would assist in bringing banks to the table and demonstrate the benefit of working with neighborhood groups.

He anticipates the Committee, under St Germain, will place a greater emphasis on oversight, particularly of the rescue operations being carried out by the Federal Savings and Loan Insurance Corporation and the Federal Deposit Insurance Corporation.

Housing programs have not fared well under the current administration and the committee has engaged in efforts to "hold the line," trying to hang on to existing programs such as FHA. Lewis says St Germain is particularly effective when he "digs in his heels," to report out a major housing bill in 1983 by making it clear to the administration that the bill it sought for the International Monetary Fund was not going anywhere without housing concessions.

Lee Peckarsky
Staff Director
219 Rayburn House Office Bldg.
225-7057

Personal: born 3/30/51 in Milwaukee, Wisconsin. B.A. Univ. of Wisconsin, 1973. J.D. Univ. of Wisconsin, 1976. 1976-1985, Office of Legislative Counsel, U.S. House of Representatives. 1985-1987, Counsel; 1987-present, Staff Director, Committee on Banking, Finance, and Urban Affairs.

Expertise: Banking and legislative process and drafting

Filling the shoes of Dr. Paul Nelson, who retired after serving three chairmen as staff director of the House Banking, Finance and Urban Affairs Committee, is not an easy job. But Chairman Fernand J. St Germain, as well as many observers, is confident that his successor, Lee Peckarsky, can step in and continue where Nelson left off.

"Lee is one of the Hill staffers who brings both substantive and technical expertise in drafting banking law," says a well-respected banking industry observer. " He has the chairman's confidence and a close relationship with him."

Trade press reporters share this view. Says one congressional correspondent, "He's quiet, but very bright and well-respected, and he really knows banking law. Paul Nelson was known for putting together coalitions and being a master at floor procedures. Lee Peckarsky has got all the same abilities."

His first and only other employment outside of the committee was with the Office of the House Legislative Counsel. "At legislative counsel, I learned many of the skills I use today. They tried to achieve a high level of professionalism," Peckarsky recalls.

The crafting of banking legislation became his specialty, and he developed a long list of bills with which he is identified: The Chrysler Corporation Loan Guarantee Act of 1977, which created the federal government's bail-out package for the distressed Detroit auto manufacturer; the Depository Institutions Deregulation and Monetary Control Act of 1980, which restructured reserve requirements of the Federal Reserve and began to phase out controls on interest rates; the Garn-St Germain Depository Institutions Act of 1982, which provided new powers to savings and loan institutions and contained provisions to help federal regulators deal with troubled financial institutions; and the International Lending Supervision Act of 1983, which gave regulators more flexibility in helping large banks deal with Third World Loans.

As a committee counsel, Peckarsky played a major role in the Competitive Equality Banking Act of 1987 that recapitalized the Federal Savings and Loan Insurance Corporation. He is accorded high marks for his handling of the conference revisions of the over two hundred-page piece of legislation. He was also the chief committee staffer on the omnibus trade bill in 1987 and represented it during House consideration. Other areas in which Peckarsky has acquired expertise include economic stabilization, domestic monetary policy, the Export-Import Bank, and multilateral financial institutions.

Curtis Prins
Staff Director
Subcommittee on Consumer
   Affairs and Coinage
212 House Office Bldg. Annex 2
226-3280

*Personal: born 12/21/33 in Westport,
Connecticut. B.A. Univ. of Maryland,
1970. 1960-1964: Sports Editor,
Pocono Record, Stroudsburg, PA;
Editor, Golf Magazine, New York City;
Editor, Data Publications, Washington,
D.C. 1964-1974, Chief Investigator,
House Committee on Banking,
Finance and Urban Affairs. 1975-
present, Staff Director, House Banking
Subcommittee on Consumer Affairs
and Coinage.*

Expertise: Currency & consumer affairs

With the LBJ sweep of 1964 came an onslaught of new Members on the House Banking Committee. Its Chairman, Wright Patman (D-TX), had an organizational meeting during the first days of the Congress to get to know his new committeemen. During the gathering, Curt Prins was seated next to a new Member from Illinois named Frank Annunzio. The two men hit it off instantly and what was to become an enduring "father/son" relationship had begun. It was that year, 1964, that Curtis Prins began as the Chief Investigator for the Banking Committee, a position which he held for ten years. Prins investigated many of the issues which came before the Committee, becoming an expert on nearly all aspects of the banking industry. During the Watergate scandal, Prins spent two months tracing the money used to finance the Watergate break-in and also tracked the laundering of campaign contributions through Mexico.

In 1975 Prins became the staff director of Annunzio's subcommittee, where he has continued to serve as advisor to the Congressman and has been involved with drafting many landmark pieces of legislation, including the Fair Debt Collection Practices Act, the Truth in Leasing Act, and the Cash Discount Act. He was also closely involved with formulation of the Anti-Credit Card Surcharge Provisions of the Truth in Lending Act and the amendments to the Equal Credit Opportunity Act.

Regarding the recent deregulation trend in the banking industry, Prins is opposed to it, as is Annunzio. Prins quickly points out that his boss voted against the Conference Report, which accompanied the bill to authorize the deregulation of banks. Prins believes that deregulation has "never brought about the promised improvements for the consumer in this industry or any other that has been deregulated." As a solution, Prins advocates a reregulation of banks, an industry which he believes was never too tightly regulated.

Colleagues describe Prins as "a guy who's been around a long time and who knows what's really going on. He has political know-how." Prins tries to use this political acumen to help people, which to him, "is the biggest kick in life." He loves to play golf and to write. He's a "grinder on any subject" and loves to work under the pressures of a deadline.

Prins was a basketball player at Maryland, a memory which he recalls with a laugh. He summarizes himself as "the worst player in their history." Prins is also a member of the U.S. Olympic Fundraising Committee.

Frank Record
Minority Counsel
Subcommittee on International
  Finance, Trade and Monetary
  Policy
2222 Rayburn House Office Bldg.
225-1794

Expertise: Domestic and international banking and economics

Examining his highly diversified background, you may not automatically place Frank Record in the office of the Minority Counsel for the Banking Committee. But, in fact, Frank Record knew exactly where he was going.

With a strong background in international economic issues, Record went to work for the Worldwatch Institute, a private non-profit organization which concentrates on economic, energy and agricultural issues. While there, Record wrote an eighty-page manuscript with Erik Eckholm entitled *Two Faces of Malnutrition*, a study of both nourishment deficiency and excessiveness.

From there, Record moved to the bipartisan Arms Control and Foreign Policy Caucus, where he met Congressman Jim Leach, an active member. Record admired and got along well with Leach, and easily made the move to Subcommittee staff when Leach, now the ranking minority member, offered him the position.

Regarded by other staffers as "someone who definitely knows what he's talking about," Record has made a distinctive impression among his colleagues. During his four years on the staff, he has gained broad experience, participating in the formulation of the IMF Housing Authorization in 1983, the IDA Replenishment Program of 1985, the Export/Import Bank Reauthorization of 1986 and the recent FSLIC Banking Bill.

On the pressing subject of the deregulation of the banking industry today, Record believes "that there needs to be a more wholesale deregulation of the banks . . . product and functional deregulation" if consumers are to really experience its benefits. Record is fluent in both Spanish and French and loves to travel. He jokes about "all the wonderful junkets I'm supposed to be going on as a committee staffer" which, unfortunately, "don't exist." Although he does manage to travel with his family on occasion, he's usually in town, dreaming of court time at the Capitol Hill Squash Club.

Personal: born 7/29/50 in Boston, Massachusetts. B.A. Harvard Univ., 1972, cum laude. Certificate of Political Studies Institut D'Etudes Politiques, Paris, France, Junior Year Abroad, Sweetbriar Program, 1971. M.A. Johns Hopkins Univ. School of Advanced International Studies, 1975. 1972-1973, employment coordinator, Vista Riker's Island Project, Bronx, NY. 1974-1975, research assistant, International Bank For Reconstruction & Development, Washington, D.C. 1975-1977, researcher, Worldwatch Institute, Washington, D.C. 1978-1983, staff consultant, Arms Control & Foreign Policy Caucus, Washington, D.C. 1983-present, minority counsel, Subcommittee on International Finance, Trade and Monetary Policy.

Robert E. Ruddy
Minority Staff Director
B301-C Rayburn House Office
  Bldg.
225-7502

*Personal: born 06/08/36 in Aberdeen,
South Dakota. B.A. Univ. of South
Dakota, 1961. J.D. George
Washington Univ. Law School, 1961-
1964, J.D.. 1964-1965, Assistant
Attorney General, State of South
Dakota. 1965-1971, Legislative
Assistant, Sen. Karl Mundt (R-SD).
1971-1973, Special Assistant to
Secretary of Commerce. 1973-1976,
Deputy Under Secretary, Department
of Housing and Urban Development.
1976-1977, Assistant to Secretary for
Congressional Affairs, Department of
Interior. 1977-1983, Assistant Minority
Counsel, House Subcommittee on
Housing and Community
Development. 1983-1987, Minority
Counsel, Subcommittee on Housing
and Community Development. 1987-
present, Minority (Republican) Staff
Director, Committee on Banking,
Finance, and Urban Affairs.*

Expertise: Housing

Conceding a fondness for partisan wrangling, Robert Ruddy was a logical choice last March to fill the Republican Staff Director's slot on the House Committee on Banking, Finance, and Urban Affairs.

Ruddy's political background predates his working experience with the committee staff, the Department of Commerce, Housing and Urban Development, and the Department of the Interior. As a student at the University of South Dakota in 1960, Ruddy served as an intern for U.S. Sen. Karl Mundt. This led to campaign work for Mundt, who was being challenged for reelection by then Rep. George McGovern. Later, while working in Washington as a legislative assistant to Mundt, Ruddy made numerous contacts in the Nixon Administration. When Mundt suffered a debilitating stroke, Ruddy took a job with the Commerce Department as a special assistant to the Secretary. Ruddy then made contacts at HUD and soon became Deputy Under Secretary at the department.

In 1976, Ruddy moved over to the Department of the Interior as Assistant to the Secretary for Congressional Affairs, but he maintained his close contacts with HUD. The following year, Ruddy was offered the position of Assistant Minority Counsel with the House Subcommittee on Housing and Community Development. He served as Minority Counsel of the subcommittee until March, 1987, when he moved up to staff director of the full committee.

Ruddy's expertise in housing issues was put to quick use as Republicans on the banking committee crafted a substitute housing bill in an attempt to end a six-year dearth of comprehensive housing legislation. The substitute was intended to mollify White House opposition to the omnibus package. Ruddy also directed the housing subcommittee staff, which helped draft comprehensive homeless assistance legislation. The $923 million homeless aid bill represented Congress's first major foray into helping this growing segment of the population.

As banking committee staff director, Ruddy was also instrumental in leading efforts to draft legislation aimed at shoring up the Federal Savings and Loan Insurance Corporation, which guarantees deposits at thousands of financial institutions nationwide. The FSLIC recapitalization legislation was combined with other banking measures aimed at limiting the creation of new limited service banks to sell real estate, securities or insurance.

Richard L. Still
General Counsel
2129 Rayburn House Office Bldg.
225-3548

Expertise: Banking and housing, financial consumer protection

Anyone trying to approach Rep. Fernand J. St Germain (D-RI) in his capacity as Chairman of the House Committee on Banking, Finance and Urban Affairs, quickly encounters a formidable doorkeeper and buffer in General Counsel Richard Still.

St German's right-hand man has been staff director of the Subcommittee on Financial Institutions Supervision, Regulation and Insurance since 1973, and general counsel to the full committee since 1982. Still is proud of his work on consumer protection in the financial arena, including his efforts on behalf of the Home Mortgage Disclosure Act; the Community Reinvestment Act; the Fair Credit Reporting Act; the amendments to the Equal Credit Opportunity Act, which set the tone for legislation protecting women from discrimination; and the Check-Holding Bill, which took seven years to enact.

Given St German's hard-fought battles on behalf of consumers, Still thinks his boss is unfairly tagged by many as too accommodating to the financial sector. Such perceptions, he believes, are the result of St. Germain's old-fashioned political style and low-key public manner.

Personal: born 1928 in Newport, Rhode Island. B.S. U.S. Naval Academy, 1950. 1951-1953, Lt. Colonel, U.S. Marine Corps; First Marine Air Wing, Korea, (Five Battle Stars, Purple Heart), two years as a POW. Freedom Foundation Award, 1953. L.L.B., 1957, L.L.M., 1960, Georgetown Law School. 1960, advance man for John F. Kennedy. 1962, Commissioner and Chief Counsel, Community Facilities Administration, Housing and Home Finance Agency. 1966, Counsel to Joint Committee on Defense Production. 1971-1973, Director of Planning, Coastal Plans Regional Commission. Criminal Lawyer. House Government Operations. 1973, Staff Director, Subcommittee on Financial Institutions Supervision, Regulation and Insurance. 1982-present, General Counsel, House Committee Banking, Finance and Urban Affairs.

Still himself has come far from the experiences that shaped his entry into politics and government service in the era of John F. Kennedy and the New Frontier. He was the next-to-last American POW to be released from Korea in 1953, after two years of incarceration, attempted brainwashing and five failed escapes. While in the Marine Corps, he defended a black naval steward accused of assaulting a superior officer and instigated a controversial internal investigation into the steward system that ultimately led to its demise.

Attracted by Kennedy's charisma and idealism, Still became an advance man for the future president in Illinois, West Virginia and Maryland and later served as a commissioner in a public works agency. In the late 60s, he became a criminal attorney in Washington and found himself confronting the thought that many New Frontier programs were actually irrelevant to the needs of the disadvantaged.

When he joined the House Government Operations Committee in the early 1970s, Still participated in major national investigations of the Law Enforcement Assistance Administration and the "Inner City Scandals." The latter included a scheme in which mortgage bankers used the Federal Housing Administration as a screen while they moved welfare mothers into unaffordable housing. The greed he encountered left Still with a wariness of banking institutions which he took with him to the Committee on Banking, Finance and Urban Affairs in 1973

Today, Still sees the separation of banking from commerce as an important and continuing issue. Although he is not necessarily an advocate of antitrust laws, it is his view that there are no meaningful ones left on the books. Antitrust, he believes, must be clearly defined before the scope of banking can be defined. He is also involved in the debate over bank merger and acquisition statutes and a related definition of what serves the public interest. He recognizes changing circumstances in the financial arena and believes that matters of open competition should be systematically reviewed.

He views his job as educating committee members and his main concern is the role of institutions as providers of financial services. He is concerned that the economy will suffer if banking institutions continue to serve primarily the upwardly mobile and points to the growing underground economy as a reflection of this problem.

Still also deplores the low esteem in which the House as an institution, is held by the public. He considers it the most democratic group in the world, "reflecting the best, the worst and the average of us all." And although he fears he may have been "insufferable" as a young man, he now has a more mellow view of his role, he says, and disdains the egotism that often flows so abundantly in the halls of Congress. When he finally leaves the Hill, he says, he will concentrate on lecturing at banking workshops, teaching, and assisting his wife in her efforts to discover and promote old-time quilters in nearby mountain and farm communities.

HOUSE OF REPRESENTATIVES
COMMITTEE ON THE BUDGET

Budget

Nicholas A. Masters
Special Assistant to the Chairman
219-A House Office Bldg. Annex I
226-7218

Expertise: Budget

Nicholas Masters has the attention of the Speaker of the House, the ear of the members of the House Budget Committee and a wealth of experience that rivals anyone on the Hill. His fourteen years with the Budget Committee is but one valuable asset. Formerly a professor at Penn State and Southern Illinois Universities, he also directed a graduate public affairs program. He was a leading researcher for the Joint Committee on the Organization of Congress, and helped initiate the Standards and Conduct Committee for the House as well as the liberalization of House Rules. As research director of the Joint Committee on the Congress, he played a key part in developing the provisions of the Budget Act of 1974 which moved the fiscal year from July to October.

Masters' major influence has been in his work on the Budget Committee. After passage of the Budget Act of 1974, which created the Budget Committee, Masters acted as the liaison between the new Committee and its counterparts. He educated staffers and members about the purpose of the new Committee and acclimated them to its new procedures. Because the Budget Act of 1974 imposed a new budget process on the old, Masters also had to deal with "suspicion, skepticism, and the phenomenon of change itself" in his role as a liaison and educator. Despite the obstacles posed by the established hierarchy, Masters' work was so successful that he may have done himself out of a job. But this did not distress him, as he says, "If you do a good job, you'll end your job."

Personal: born February 8, 1928 in Carbondale, Illinois. Married with two children. B.A., M.A. Southern Illinois Univ. Ph.D., Univ. of Wisconsin. Assistant Professor, Wayne State Univ., 1955-1960. Staff Assistant to James Conant (past President of Harvard), 1961-1962. Professor, Pennsylvania State Univ., 1963-1968. Professor, Southern Illinois Univ., 1969-1971. Director, Public Affairs Graduate Program, Southern Illinois University, 1971-1975. Staff Director, Joint Committee on Congressional Operations, 1971. Director, Majority Associate Staff, Committee on the Budget, 1975-1981. Special Assistant to the Chairman, Committee on the Budget, 1981-present.

Masters says the most interesting aspect of his job is that the responsibilities are so varied and substantial. His opinion is frequently solicited by members who want a seasoned perspective on subjects ranging from the President's budget to the feasibility of a veto of line item appropriations. He has also advised members on implementing a freeze amendment. Masters uses his teaching skills to help him explain the budget process for freshman Members of Congress. He says his role is like that of a translator, "making esoteric language understandable."

Masters is not pleased by partisan antagonisms. "This (the Budget Committee) has been a divided committee since I got here." Partisan skirmishes arise over how to allocate scarce resources. Learning and adjustment characterize his job. As he says, the Budget Committee "is always dealing with scarcity" and "that's what politics is all about." Every year, his staff has said that because of partisanship, a budget resolution will not pass, but he adds "every year they've been wrong."

Van Doorn Ooms
Chief Economist
220 House Office Bldg. Annex 1
226-7210

Personal: born 10/29/34. La Grange, Illinois. B.A. Amherst Coll., 1956. 1956-1959, Rhodes Scholar, English language and literature, Oxford Univ. Ph.D. Economics, Yale Univ., 1965. 1965-1966, Planning Adviser, Government of Malaysia, Kuala Lumpur. 1965-1968, Assistant Professor of Economics, Yale University. 1968-1978, Professor of Economics, Swarthmore Coll. 1976-1977, Senior Staff Economist, Senate Budget Committee. 1977-1978, Chief Economist, Senate Budget Committee. 1978-1981, Assistant Director of Economic Policy, Office of Management and Budget. 1981-present, Chief Economist, House Committee on the Budget.

Expertise: Economics, budget

Political economy, like beauty, is much in the eye of the beholder. The political lens through which one views economic data largely depends upon the viewer, and the final translation of that view into policy is best left to the politicians, not to economists. At least, that's the way Van Doorn Ooms would like to keep it. "I see my job primarily as providing information and analyses to the budget committee. I'm a strong believer in a system in which the policy makers make the decisions, in which the staff is a source of information, not policy."

Ooms served in the Senate at the behest of then-Senate Budget Committee Chairman Edmund Muskie. Ooms was on a year's sabbatical from his academic obligations and was serving as a visiting economist with the Senate Budget Committee. Muskie asked him to stay for another year as Chief Economist, which led to his taking a permanent position on the Hill. He came to the House Budget Committee in 1981 at the request of Jim Jones, the chairman at the time.

Ooms and staff mostly deal with the larger issues of economic performance, the interaction of budget and economy, as opposed to targeting implications of specific programs. "This section tends to have a very broad, macro sort of perspective. We tend not to get into programmatic details except where those are large enough or important enough to have effects on the economy as a whole," he says. "My staff deals with the major issues of the economy, not only national but international. The trade issue, for example. We try to provide information on the relationship between the budget and fiscal policy and the trade deficit."

A further responsibility of serving as an information source means putting data into less technical terms. Ooms also defines his role as that of an interpreter. "In a way, I'm a translator. The time I spent teaching was a very good way of preparing for that. This means trying to take difficult, relatively complicated economic arguments and present them in terms accessible to members. Tracing through it, and trying to make it comprehensible to people who are very intelligent but have not had a lot of technical training."

Like most on the Hill, Ooms assumes he'll end up in the private sector eventually, but he's in no rush. "My rationale for being here, as opposed to someplace else, is a very strong commitment to providing balanced and accurate information to policy makers."

Budget

Martha Phillips
Minority Staff Director
278 House Office Bldg. Annex 2
226-7270

Expertise: Budget

"It's been a long haul," says Martha Phillips, whose tenure on the Hill now spans over twenty years. Phillips has become, according to *Roll Call*, one of "the most plugged-in non-Members on the Hill."

In 1969, the House Republican Research Committee was looking for someone with an advanced degree in education and her credentials got her the job. While at the committee she staffed a number of task forces (education, urban policy, international trade, population, energy, congressional reform) and served as staff director. The work there prepared her for her next assignment, director of the House Republican Policy Committee, where she assisted the committee's chairman, former Congressman Barber Conable, in identifying and articulating positions for Republicans on pending legislation.

In 1977, she followed Conable to the Ways and Means Committee, where she was asked to assess all federal programs for their impact on the family. "They had just discovered the 'family' issue, and so I was looking at not only what effect the tax code had on families but also such things as Social Security and welfare." Out of her work came repeal of the so-called marriage penalty as well as changes in the earned income tax credit and the child care credit. Over the next nine years she worked on a number of other issues, including taxation of fringe benefits, unemployment compensation, tax-exempt organizations and charitable contributions, federal debt collection, targeted job tax credit and various individual income tax items.

Personal: born in Washington, D.C. B.A. Univ. of Maryland, 1964. M.A. Columbia Univ. 1970. 1965-1966, aide to Congressman Melvin Laird. 1966-1967, Program Officer, U.S. Department of Education. 1969-1973, Staff Director, House Republican Research Committee. 1974-1976, Director, Republican Policy Committee. 1977-1985, Deputy Minority Chief of Staff, House Ways and Means Committee. 1986 to present, Minority Staff Director, House Budget Committee.

Today she helps Republican Members understand and manage what has become a thoroughly frustrating chore—passing an annual federal budget. "The problem around here is not the procedure," she observes, "but the fact that Members are facing enormously tough decisions. They want it all ways—they want to reduce the deficit, but not raise taxes or cut popular programs. It's a recipe for gridlock. Last year's 'budget summit' did achieve a political compromise, but it wasn't consummate budget statesmanship. It will just barely get us through the next round, then the next Administration will have to face the music."

When she's not buried in the budget, Phillips is active in a number of groups on and off the Hill. She has served as an officer and board member of The Tax Coalition, Women in Government Relations, Population Reference Bureau, Montgomery County Child Daycare Council and Montgomery Soccer, Inc.

Steve L. Pruitt
Executive Director
222 House Office Bldg. Annex 1
226-7234

Personal: born 10/23/49 in Columbus, Ohio. B.S. Ohio State Univ., 1972. M.A. Ohio State Univ., 1979. 1979-1981, assistant director of legislation, American Federation of State, County and Municipal Employees, Inc. 1981-1984, director of congressional affairs, Public Employee Department, AFL-CIO. 1984, staff director, House Post Office and Civil Service Committee, Subcommittee on Census and Population. 1985-present, executive director, Committee on the Budget.

Expertise: Congressional budget

When the House Committee on the Budget selected Steve L. Pruitt as its Executive Director, it selected a man with years of accumulated experience in the federal, state, and local legislative arena. A proven fund raiser with excellent political contacts, Pruitt has a solid understanding of legislative processes and government structures.

Pruitt's area of expertise covers a gamut of budget issues. Thorough and detail-oriented, he is the primary staff person responsible for working with Committee members, other House committees and the Senate Budget Committee to develop budget plans and to identify and resolve budget issues.

Pruitt has the managerial skills, knowledge and expertise to supervise a 118-member staff in overall budget analysis, special analysis, task forces, hearings, committee reports and managing the Committee's $8 million annual operating budget.

The politically attuned Pruitt considers his job to be threefold: "I am the eyes and the ears for the Chairman, a technician responsible for putting together budget documents and a manager for the people who serve under my leadership." He adds, "Understanding the political environment requires instinct, interpretive skills, the ability to communicate, establish priorities and to implement a budget that reflects those priorities."

Pruitt refers to his staff colleagues as hardworking: "The unelected people are committed to the process and often their work is unrecognized." Pruitt maintains a positive interaction with the press and is amazed with their detailed knowledge of the budget. His only concern is that those in the press who do not regularly cover the budget process sometimes write misleading stories. Therefore, "I try to educate and reeducate the public."

Pruitt's first participation in a political campaign was in 1968 for Humphrey. Since then he has worked on everything from local to federal to national campaigns. He also served on both the county and state Democratic Party Board.

Patricia Quealy
Chief Counsel
216 House Office Bldg. Annex 1
225-7233

Personal: born 7/23/55 in Chicago, Illinois. B.S. Univ. of South Carolina, 1976. J.D. Univ. of South Carolina Law School, 1979. LL.M., Georgetown Univ. Law Center, Anticipated degree in spring 1988. 1978 summer, Law Clerk, U.S. Tax Court. 1979-1980, Law Clerk, Morgan, Lewis, and Bockius. 1980-1981, Counsel; 1981-1985, Deputy Chief Counsel; 1986-present, Chief Counsel, Committee on the Budget.

Expertise: Budget process and policies, legislative procedures

Patricia Quealy is an ambitious and dynamic professional who is primary advisor to the Chairman and Budget Committee Members on the budget process and policies, legislative strategy, House rules, and parliamentary procedures.

Quealy is closely identified with the Balanced Budget and Emergency Deficit Control Act of 1985 and the Balanced Budget Reaffirmation Act of 1987, commonly known as the Gramm-Rudman-Hollings Act.

Considered a leading expert on the Budget, Quealy acts as a liaison with the House and Senate Leadership and with Members and senior staff of other committees on budget policy issues as well. She will participate in a review of the budget and appropriations process during the second session of the 100th Congress by the House Leadership for possible reforms to be implemented in the 101st Congress.

Quealy's opinion of the press is quite positive: "They do a good job covering the budget, which is an extremely complicated and never-ending issue."

"Both Democratic and Republican Budget Committee Members are among the best members in the House and they are extremely interested in budget policy issues." says Quealy. "I enjoy and work well with both the House and the Senate because there exists a very cooperative attitude."

Recently married, Patricia Quealy (Moore) describes herself as a golf fanatic. "I work as diligently to reduce my golf score as I do to reduce the budget deficit."

Shirley L. Ruhe
Director of Budget Priorities
203 House Office Bldg. Annex 1
226-7166

Expertise: Budget

To the Washington outsider, attempting to understand Shirley Ruhe's position on the Budget Committee might be akin to Alice peering through the wrong side of the looking glass. In fact, even to those inside the Washington Beltway, her responsibilities as Director of Budget Priorities may seem staggering. And they are.

When the House Budget Committee was established in June 1974, its primary task was to make reports and continuing studies of the federal budget and to report those studies regularly to the House. Today, with a staff of some 25 professionals, Ruhe takes great satisfaction in dissecting each year's federal budget, a document that is at once complex and vital to the congressional budget process.

Upon receipt of the budget each year, Ruhe and her staff work with the leadership of both parties to integrate and prioritize the entire document with the goal of developing a comprehensive budget plan for Congress. The committee does this by devising overall spending and revenue marks for the various standing committees.

While determining budget priorities is no easy task, Ruhe and her staff have at their disposal a veritable wealth of information and individual expertise to guide them. By combining such variables as five-year projections of needs, historical analyses, and political and various public policy considerations, Ruhe's staff develops alternatives for the committee to consider in crafting the budget blueprint for the House.

Personal: born 3/20/43 in Des Moines, Iowa. B.S. Iowa State Univ. 1965. M.S. Iowa State Univ., 1967 (Phi Kappa Phi, Ford Foundation Grant). 1967-1969, wire editor and photographer, Ames, IA, Daily Tribune. 1970-1972, Legislative Assistant, Rep. John Culver (D-IA). 1972-1975, Staff Assistant, Rep. John Blatnik (D-IA). 1975-1985, Associate Director and 1985-1987, Deputy Director, Budget Process and Operations, House Committee on the Budget.

Ruhe believes the congressional budget process has undergone monumental changes since the 93rd Congress, growing into an extraordinarily complex system. So complex that today Ruhe describes the original budget law as a child who through the years has grown into the present unruly teenager. As a participant in the evolution of the budget system now in use, Ruhe was administrator of the Budget Committee Task Force on the budget process as well as a key player in the reconciliation efforts since 1981 and the revision of Gramm-Rudman.

In light of these changes, Ruhe believes the process must be streamlined. She argues that there is simply too much overlap with the layers of required budget decisions. Just as importantly, Ruhe is convinced that Members of Congress need to summon the discipline and political will to make the system more effective.

Ruhe prides herself on the fact that, politics notwithstanding, her primary purpose is accurate, timely analyses. And as one who was there at the birth of the House Budget Committee and has risen through its ranks, her record speaks for itself.

Budget

Neil Strawser
Director of Communications
210A Cannon House Office Bldg.
225-7290

Expertise: Budget, media

Neil Strawser came to Washington in the early 1950s to study for his Master's degree in history and teach at George Washington University. During the second semester of his graduate work, he was drawn from his academic pursuits by an enticing offer from CBS. In 1956 he became Washington correspondent for the network; and one of the legendary voices of the airwaves.

Throughout the course of his career, Strawser covered a variety of assignments including the Justice Department (particularly during the eventful Bobby Kennedy days), the White House in the early 1980s, the Pentagon and Capitol Hill. He developed a special interest and, consequently, expertise in budget issues. Unlike other correspondents who tended to avoid this issue because of its complexity, the historian in Strawser was intrigued because the budget is the one document that most clearly reflects the nation's priorities. He enjoys the challenges of understanding the cumbersome subject, then getting a handle on the intricacies of congressional process around it, and making all of this understandable to a mass audience.

Personal: born 8/16/27 in Rittman, OH. B.A. Oberlin Coll., 1951. M.A. George Washington Univ., 1958. 1952-1986, Washington Correspondent, CBS. 1986-1987, Director, Public Affairs, Joint Economic Committee. 1987-present, House Committee on the Budget.

In his capacity as press secretary for the Budget Committee, Strawser is middle man between press and committee members. "After spending so many years outside the doors, it's fascinating to find myself on the inside looking at the guts of the process."

Strawser makes good use of his press experience and tries hard to keep clearly in mind the problems the press faces. Says one veteran newsman, "He knows what it takes to make a good story and he sees to it that we get it."

Allen T. Unsworth
Chief Economist
290A House Office Bldg. Annex 2
226-7270

Personal: born 6/16/38, Berkeley, California. B.A. Reed Coll., 1960. M.A. Univ. of Chicago, 1963. 1964-1967, Illinois Institute of Technology. 1967-1974, Pennsylvania State Univ. 1974-1976, Asst. Prof. of Economics, Stockton State Coll. 1977-present, economist, House Committee on Budget.

Expertise: Public Finance, economics, international trade

Allen Unsworth's background in economics has trained him to be an amiable skeptic. "Very often, when you're working on the Hill, you can't see the forest for the trees. I see my role as putting things in perspective," he says, and adds, "Part of my role is to throw cold water on things."

Unsworth's broad perspective on budget issues may come from the fact he has been with the thirteen-year old committee since 1977. He got a tip from some friends at the University of Chicago, and was hired by the then-staff director Bill Lilly, with final approval from Congressman Del Latta of Ohio, the ranking Republican Member. Unsworth says the creation of an alternative budget has changed over the years: "I think in the first few years our budget substitutes were more political documents than they are now." These days, "Generally, we try to come up with a substitute which at least has the potential of something we could use as a negotiating tool with the Democrats."

Unsworth's greatest impact so far has been in helping to prevent or restrict major tax increases. This fits in with his political ideology that he describes as conservative, but not rigidly so. "I tend to be conservative on economic issues, which means very market-oriented. I think there is a general bias against central government control when you've had training in economics. I would say economists generally, whether Democrat or Republican, tend to be more conservative than their non-economic colleagues. We tend to think in terms of "what are the unintended consequences of policies, what are the costs, what are the benefits'?"

The free market principle is a useful tool in judging what role, if any, the government should play in the provision of various types of goods and services to the public, according to Unsworth. "The primary responsibility of the federal government is to provide national defense, since it is probably the one activity that the market would be the least good at delivering." He continues, "After national defense, government does have important, if not all-inclusive, roles to play in ensuring a minimum standard of living for all, and in helping to provide adequate investment in both human and physical capital through expenditures on education and public works, as well as designing a tax code to encourage private investment."

Unsworth particularly enjoyed the budget battles during the early years of the Reagan presidency when the budgets he helped put together actually passed in the House with a coalition of Republican and conservative Democrats. He is successful in his current position perhaps because, as he puts it, "I'm not so committed to ideology that I can't see other points of view. My philosophy in terms of government is do things as efficiently and as fairly as possible, and I don't think those things are necessarily contradictory."

HOUSE OF REPRESENTATIVES
COMMITTEE ON DISTRICT OF COLUMBIA

District of Columbia

John Barnes
Senior Staff Counsel
1310 Longworth House Office
    Bldg.
225-8050

*Personal: born 6/26/47, Fort
Wayne, IN. B.A., cum laude, Central
State Univ. Wilberforce, OH, 1969. J.D.
Georgetown Univ. Law School, 1973.
1973, Adjunct Professor in legislative
and administrative law, Georgetown
University Law Center. 1977, staff
counsel, Representative Walter
Fauntroy (D-D.C.). 1981, staff counsel,
House Committee on District of
Columbia.*

Expertise: D.C. statehood, banking and trade

If the District of Columbia ever becomes the fifty-first state, John Barnes's name will be one of the first inscribed on any monument to its founders. From his early days as a professor at Georgetown Law school, he has been a leader in the D.C. Statehood movement, and he helped at that time to pass the home rule bill. In numerous public debates, he found himself on the podium, paired with Walter Fauntroy to argue the merits of D.C. home rule. Shortly after, he joined Fauntroy as staff counsel full-time.

One of his first tasks was to serve as liaison with the Select Committee on Assassinations, as a key participant in the independent congressional investigation on the Kennedy and King assassinations.

Since joining the committee, he has continued his efforts for the D.C. Statehood Bill. Barnes feels greater autonomy for the District is vital to its development. "Whether it's the 100th Congress, or the 101st, or beyond, we'll see it happen." He has also worked on numerous banking and trade issues involving the Committee, including debtor nation status and, closer to home, various consumer issues. He was especially active in efforts to cap credit card interest rates.

Barnes is a commissioned officer in the Army, with eight years in the reserves. His past political campaign experience includes the 1984 Democratic Convention, as the Jackson delegate with the highest number of votes in D.C.

Barnes takes a keen interest in sports, especially tennis and basketball with his three children. He plays on Representative Fauntroy's softball team, and is at work on several books.

Robert Brauer
Senior Assistant & Special Counsel
Representative Ron Dellums (D-
CA)
1310 Longworth House Office
Bldg.
225-2661

*Personal: born January 12, 1938,
Oakland, California. B.A. Univ. of
California at Berkeley, 1960,. M.A.
California State Univ. at Hayward,
1968. 1960, USAF, Captain. 1963,
Asst. Personnel Officer, Wells Fargo
Bank. 1965, Skill Bank Dir., Bay Area
Urban League. 1965, Dir. of Human
Rights Commission, Marin County.
1966, Dep. Dir. of the Office of Federal
Contract Compliance, Dept. of Labor.
1969, American Political Science
Assoc. Congressional Fellow. 1970,
Legislative Assistant; 1973,
Administrative Assistant; 1975,
Special Counsel, Rep. Ron Dellums
(D-CA).*

Expertise: D.C. Home Rule, foreign policy

Robert Brauer has worked for Rep. Ron Dellums for seventeen
years, sixteen of which he has staffed the Committee on the
District of Columbia. He also has assisted in all of Dellums'
campaigns since 1968. Brauer's responsibilities range widely, from
specific local issues affecting only D.C. to numerous foreign policy
concerns.

Brauer drafted the education portion of the D.C. Home Rule Bill,
as well as language for pension reform for D.C. firefighters,
teachers and police. Staff colleagues say: if you need to work with
Ron Dellums, talk to Bob Brauer.

Internationally, his activities reflect a "collective expression in our
office—really all our activities are centered around peace and
justice."

In 1975 and 1976, Brauer helped staff the Select Committee on
Intelligence hearings (the Pike Hearings). He has worked on
Dellums's alternate defense budgets and also helped draft
portions of the South African sanctions bill which passed the
House.

As Dellums' senior advisor for foreign affairs and intelligence,
Brauer has acted as political liaison between Dellums' office and
the international political community, "from Francois Mitterand to
Jesse Jackson." The major goal of his work: to establish a
"rational foreign policy," including reduced defense budgets and
changes in policy towards Central America and other parts of the
world.

Brauer is active in local politics back in Berkeley, California, and
enjoys jogging and backpacking with his six children.

HOUSE OF REPRESENTATIVES
COMMITTEE ON EDUCATION AND LABOR

Donald M. Baker
Counsel
2181 Rayburn House Office Bldg.
225-6808

Personal: born 6/7/25 in Beckley, WV. WW II, U.S. Army Air Corps. A.B. Univ. of Michigan, 1950. A.M. Univ. of Michigan, 1952. J.D. Univ. of Michigan, 1956. 1956-58, Attorney, Kramer, Morris, Stark, Rowland and Regan, Detroit, MI. 1959-63, Administrative Assistant, Rep. James G. O'Hara (D-MI). 1963-64, Counsel, Labor Subcommittee Senate Committee on Labor and Public Welfare. 1964-69, General Counsel, Office of Economic Opportunity, Executive Office of the President. 1969-71, Associate Counsel, Labor, Commerce, Education and Labor 1971-84, Staff Director, Committee on Education and Labor. 1985-present, Counsel, Committee on Education and Labor.

Expertise: Federal education and welfare programs, labor-management relations, employment, pensions, health and safety.

When a law school classmate of Don Baker's decided to run for Congress in 1958, Baker gambled on the relatively unknown Michigan Democrat and agreed to help in a tough campaign that ended in a recount giving O'Hara the lead by just five votes. It was Baker's ticket to Washington—a long way from the mining camps of his youth—and the beginning of thirty years of unparalleled leadership in shaping federal labor and welfare policy.

Serving first as O'Hara's administrative assistant, Baker quickly became an expert on education and labor, one of the committee assignments the new congressman was given. Baker gained valuable experience working on the Landrum-Griffin Act and various civil rights bills, and then, in 1963, went over to the Senate to become counsel to the Subcommittee on Labor. There, he helped shepherd President Johnson's poverty program through the Senate and worked on the Davis-Bacon fringe benefits amendments.

Baker's work at OEO came to a close in 1968 with the election of Richard Nixon, who promised to close down OEO. "Carl Perkins called me and told me Nixon would be after my job," Baker recalls. "The chairman invited me to come back to the Hill and work for him." Perkins (D-KY), who chaired the Education & Labor Committee until his death in 1984, gave Baker the job of labor counsel. There Baker assisted in the passage of the Occupational Safety and Health Act, The Federal Civil Mine Health and Safety Act, and Economic Opportunity Act. In 1971, Baker was elevated to staff director of the committee, supervising all of its activities and acting as liaison with the Rules and Appropriations Committees and the House leadership. It was during the 1970s, and under his direction, that the committee entered its last great activist phase before the "Reagan Revolution" led to a general retrenchment in social programs.

With the death of Perkins, Baker's power on the committee also waned. The new chairman, Gus Hawkins (D-CA), appointed his own assistant, Susan McGuire, to the top staff slot in 1985. But in deference to Baker's long tenure and service, Hawkins retained him as counsel to the committee. Although not as active as he once was, he remains a key resource for the committee—"our living memory chip," according to one committee professional.

Once cited by *Washingtonian* magazine as one of the "all-pros of Capitol Hill" and by *U.S. News & World Report* as a "key professional employee of Congress," Baker is not one to brag of his accomplishments or his influence. "I was just lucky enough to be in the right place at the right time," he says.

Phyllis Borzi
Counsel for Employee Benefits
Subcommittee on Labor-
  Management Relations
2451 Rayburn House Office Bldg.
225-5768

Personal: born 8/10/46 New York, NY. B.A. Ladycliff Coll., 1968. M.A. Syracuse Univ., 1970. J.D. Catholic Univ., 1978. Editor-in-Chief, Law Review. 1969-75, high school English teacher. 1978-79, associate, Hogan and Hartson. 1979-80, Maj. Leg. Assoc., House Task Force on Pension and Welfare Plans. 1981-present, Counsel for Pensions, Subcommittee on Labor-Management Relations. Published: "A National Retirement Income Policy: Problems and Policy Options, "19 U. Mich. J.L. Ref. 1987;" Prospects for 1984: What Plans Can Expect from the 98th Congress," Pension World, April 1984; "Statutory Visitation Rights of Grandparents: One Step Closer to the Best Interests of the Child, "26 Cath. U.L. Ref., 387 (1987); Past Pres., Women in Employee Benefits. 1986 recipient of Pension World Outstanding Achievement Award in public policy.

Expertise: Pension and Welfare Benefits Plans

Borzi is the consummate Hill professional—a bright attorney with a passionate interest in issues and a zeal for doing what's right for the American taxpayer. *Pension World* magazine has called her both pragmatic and principled, and colleagues on the Labor and Education Committee describe her as an unsurpassed expert on pension issues. A frequent public speaker on employee benefits, she remains accessible to interest groups yet detached enough to chart a legislative course that generally meets approval with both Democrats and Republicans.

A job on Capitol Hill was one of the last things on her mind when, while doing research for a law firm in 1979, she stumbled onto a description in the *Congressional Record* of a staff position being created to work on pension issues. Having specialized in employee benefits, she applied for the job and was soon hired by Congressman Frank Thompson, Jr. (D-NJ) to be the majority legislative associate for a new Task Force on Pension and Welfare Plans.

One of her first tasks was to help get through the House a major bill to tighten funding requirements and reduce government liability for multi-employer plans under the Employee Retirement Income Security Act (ERISA). With the decision to fold the task force into the Subcommittee on Labor-Management Relations in 1981, Borzi became the subcommittee's majority counsel for employee benefits. Since then, she has concentrated on helping the subcommittee address a growing array of pension and benefit issues. Recent legislation she has been active on includes the 1984 Retirement Equity Act, which clarified the rights of spouses and survivors under ERISA; "COBRA," which continues group health coverage for dependents of certain workers; and changes in pension and retirement plans, such as shortening investing periods, that were included in the 1986 Tax Reform Act.

Now under study by the subcommittee are proposals to bring state and local plans under ERISA, provide all U.S. workers access to health insurance, and address what Borzi terms the "retiree health crisis."

"I try to be as bipartisan as I can be, and I try to work with the private sector in a constructive way," Borzi says of her responsibilities as majority counsel. While at work, she puts aside her own politics, which she says lean to the left. "My job is to spot problems, to implement ideas and build consensus. People tell me I should be more partisan, but I leave that to my personal life, where no one could mistake me for a conservative Republican."

Beth B. Buehlmann
Education Staff Director/Minority
   (Republican)
2100 Rayburn House Office Bldg.
225-1743

Personal: born 4/19/47 in Chicago,
Illinois. B.S. Chicago State Univ.,
1966. M.S. Illinois State Univ., 1971.
Ph.D. Illinois State Univ., 1974. 1966-
1968, high school teacher, Maywood,
IL. 1973-1975, Assistant to the
President and Provost, Illinois State
Univ. 1975-1978, Executive Assistant
to the Commissioner of Education,
Nebraska Department of Education.
1978-1979, Policy Research Analyst,
National Institute of Education,
Department of Education. 1979-1985,
Senior Legislative Associate,
Republican Staff, Committee on
Education and Labor. 1985-present,
Education Staff Director/Minority
(Republican)

Expertise: Education and employment training

Colleagues and members on both sides of the aisle rely on
Buehlmann's expertise in education and employment training, and
with good reason. With a Ph.D. in education and an extensive
background in teaching and school administration, Buehlmann
can draw on both academic and practical experience to help the
committee solve education and training matters.

Buehlmann came to the Hill in 1979 when a spot opened up on the
Subcommittee on Employment Opportunities. Ranking Republican
James Jeffords (R-VT) wanted someone with an academic
background as well as agency experience to fill a legislative slot.
The job seemed tailor-made for Buehlmann, who had spent the
prior year at the Department of Education as a policy research
analyst. Six years later, when Jeffords became the ranking
Republican on the full committee, Buehlmann moved up with him,
assuming her current position as Education Staff Director for the
Minority.

Through the years, both she and Jeffords have developed
reputations as being straight shooters. Says Buehlmann, "He'll tell
you when he can't support you and why, and I'm brutally honest."

Jeffords and Chairman Gus Hawkins (D-CA) also have enjoyed a
good working relationship, which has made Buehlmann's job
easier. She and the majority staff work together closely, often
sharing in the writing of legislation and conference reports.

Buehlmann is best known for her work on the 1982 Job Training
Partnership Act (JTPA), a major bill that replaced the old CETA
"make-work" job program, emphasizing training for actual private
sector jobs. Since JTPA is still evolving, Buehlmann spends much
of her time monitoring its progress and working to see that it is
properly implemented by the Labor Department and state
agencies.

She also has had a hand in developing legislation on vocational
education, dropout prevention, drug education, bilingual
education, literacy, and student financial assistance. She was
instrumental in drafting education and training provisions for the
omnibus trade drug bills.

With Jeffords leaving the House after this year (1988) to run for the
Senate, Buehlmann's future is a little uncertain. But Jeffords has
made strong commitments to the education community, so if he
wins he may seek a spot on Labor and Human Resources. If that
happens, Buehlmann may have a chance to see how things work
on the other side of the Hill.

Maria Cuprill
Staff Director
Subcommittee on Select Education
518 House Office Bldg. Annex 1
226-7532

Personal: born 10/8/39 in Puerto Rico. B.A. Brooklyn Coll., 1962. 1968, Director for Programs, Williamsburg Community Corporation. 1969-1970, Program Director, Community Development Agency, City of New York. 1970-1971, Executive Director of an investment company attached to SBCC to develop MESBICS. 1974-1981, Legislative Aide, Rep.Major Owens (D-NY). 1982-1987, Administrative Assistant, Rep. Major Owens. 1987 to present, Staff Director, Subcommittee on Select Education, Committee on Education and Labor.

Expertise: Administration

A background in social work may seem like an odd preparation for handling administration for a House subcommittee but that background has worked well for Maria Cuprill, Staff Director of the Subcommittee on Select Education.

Cuprill's social work training and experience are in group work, which "gives me a knowledge of administration and of how groups function—what makes a group come together and work toward a common goal."

Cuprill began getting attention in community and political circles in 1970, when she was able to restructure successfully the finances of the South Bronx Community Corporation, placing the organization on a sound footing in only one year. She is considered responsible for organizing the largest election turnout ever in the Williamsburg section of New York, in 1968, as director of programs for the Williamsburg Community Corporation.

On the Hill, where "groups" translate into constituencies and lobbyists, Cuprill notes "one thing that comes through, loud and clear—there is always a well-organized advocacy group looking to better the situation for the people it represents."

Cuprill contributed to the drafting of the Child Abuse Bill (HR 1900), in which she has been "very involved." She has a strong commitment to serving the rehabilitation needs of disabled people, an area she sees the Subcommittee as being well-placed to aid. "One of the things people will recognize as I stay (on the Hill longer) is that I believe in maximum feasible involvement of people," she says. "People have the right to be the authors of their own destiny and personally advocate their needs through being involved in government."

Cuprill finds the long hours and working weekends a necessity, especially when her committee is involved in a bill mark-up. "I function best when I've had a harried day—I use the evening to catch up, do my (work-related) reading, hold staff conferences." Calling herself an "artsy" person in private life, Cuprill has been an antiques dealer and relaxes by translating classic artwork into fabric media—creating fabric versions of classic sculptures and paintings. She is fiercely proud of her origins in Siales, Puerto Rico—"The most beautiful place on the island."

Frederick L. Feinstein
Counsel/Staff Director
Subcommittee on Labor/
  Management
2451 Rayburn House Office Bldg.
225-5768

*Personal: born 6/27/47. B.A.
Swarthmore Coll., 1969. J.D. Rutgers
Univ. School of Law, Newark, NJ ,
1974. 1971, 3rd-6th grade teacher,
New York City public school system.
1975-1977, field attorney, National
Labor Relations Board, NC. 1977,
counsel, Subcommittee on Labor/
Management. 1980-present, staff
director and counsel, Subcommittee
on Labor/Management, Committee on
Education. Published articles in
professional journals, most co-
authored with Congressman William L.
Clay (D-MO), such as recent piece for
New York State School of Industrial
and Labor Relations on family and
medical leave issues.*

Expertise: Labor law

For Frederick Feinstein, committee work means handling several major pieces of legislation at once, a workload under which he thrives.

Feinstein's expertise in labor law has made him a key person in the drafting, committee work and passage of important bills such as the Labor Law Reform Act of 1977; the Plant Closing Bill; the Double-Breasting Bill (which restricts construction contractors from operating dual contracts with union and non-union workers); several pieces of pension reform legislation in past years; Minimum Medical and Health Benefits; and, perhaps most important, the Family and Medical Leave Bill.

Known for his expertise in labor law, Feinstein has worked tirelessly on the Family and Medical Leave Bill under Congressman William L. (Bill) Clay (D-MO), legislation which he sees as vital to fair treatment for workers and their families. His involvement has included legislative activity such as drafting language for the bill, as well as writing about the issue for publication in professional journals and for Clay's use in speeches.

Although Feinstein has never been a line worker, he is firmly committed to the needs and rights of working people. "I hope I am contributing to making sound, helpful, effective public policy in the interests of working people and better labor relations," he says of his goals with the committee. "I hope I would be seen by my colleagues as someone who listens to all points of view and is fair, trustworthy, and helps achieve those goals." According to Clay, Feinstein is viewed by every person connected with labor as "the preeminent, most knowledgeable labor person in the city."

A "pretty good" tennis player, Feinstein's favorite leisure-time activity is playing fiddle with the Hambone Sweets, an old-time string band; his wife also plays fiddle with the band. They have "two delightful children" who keep Feinstein entertained and active at home.

Adrienne Fields
Legislative Analyst
B-345 C Rayburn House Office
   Bldg.
225-9328

*Personal: born in Kensington, PA.
B.S., Pennsylvania State Univ., 1961.
Paralegal Degree, George Washington
Univ. 1961-1966, Special Assistant to
Chief Counsel for Labor, Committee
on Education and Labor. 1966-1977 ·
Administrative Assistant,
Subcommittee on Labor Standards.
1978-1981, Legislative Liaison Officer,
U.S. Department of Labor. 1981-1982,
Staff Director, Post Office and Civil
Service Subcommittee on
Investigations. 1982-present,
Legislative Analyst, Committee on
Education and Labor.*

Expertise: Labor, health and safety

Adrienne Fields has dedicated fifteen years to committee work as a legislative analyst, "the foot soldier," as she calls herself. Fields collects information, develops material to meet the policy objective of the chairman, develops amendments, and tracks a bill's progress on the floor.

One of the most obvious attributes of her success is her ability to readily adapt. She closely scrutinizes testimony, has her own "hot lines" into the Bureau of Labor Statistics, the Census Bureau and the Congressional Research Service, and covers a score of newspapers and journals in support of the committee's work. Fields also takes every opportunity to observe key people in the committee structure to expand her sources of information.

One of the most notable pieces of legislation she has worked on was the Coal Mine Act of 1969 which, Field points out, was very progressive legislation for its time. She believes she had an impact on this issue because of her childhood in Western Pennsylvania when coal miners were enduring hard times. Fields strongly believes that "success" on the Hill depends on people who have an even temper, a willingness to endure long hours, and dedication to legislative objectives. Fields claims that the institution is captivating in the sense that it can get the job done if it wants to. "It does not work when delays are caused for political reasons." Fields believes a committee becomes "political" depending on the issues and the ranking members of each committee. One of her favorite examples of bipartisanship is ERISA. "When it came down to the bottom line, both parties worked together because of the Act's crucial importance to the American people."

Fields spends a great deal of her personal time educating elementary children. Once a math tutor, she now devotes herself to the "Alley Library," a reading program for elementary school children in Washington, D.C. Fields has been on the Board of Directors for the last six years, in charge of fundraising and general oversight of the program.

Richard J. Fiesta
Counsel
Subcommittee on Labor Standards
B-346A Rayburn House Office
   Bldg.
225-1927

Expertise: Labor law

Although a relative newcomer to the Hill, Fiesta brings to it experience in labor law based on his background and current research at the University of Virginia where he is working on a Ph.D. in legal history. His specialty on the Subcommittee on Labor Standards has become occupational disease, worker's compensation and wage and hour laws.

Fiesta calls Chairman Austin Murphy's (D-PA) job offer at the beginning of the 99th Congress "a happy coincidence," but working for Murphy as a legislative aide in the late seventies and being a constituent didn't hurt either.

Fiesta handles Subcommittee issues on occupational disease and asbestos compensation, black lung benefits, agricultural labor and "industrial homework." Fiesta also had a hand in the Davis-Bacon amendments approved by the full committee last year (1987). The legislation would raise the "prevailing wage" threshold for federally funded construction from $2,000 to $50,000 for new projects, and from $2,000 to $15,000 for remodeling or repair work.

Personal: born 6/21/57 in Connellsville, Pennsylvania. A.B. Georgetown Univ., 1979 (magna cum laude). M.A., J.D. Georgetown Univ., 1982. Ph.D. candidate and graduate fellow, Univ. of Virginia, 1982-1985. 1980-1982, law clerk, U.S. Occupational Safety and Health Review Commission. 1983, attorney, Blum and Reiss, Mount Pleasant, PA. 1983-1985, Research and Projects Editor, Journal of Law and Politics, Univ. of Virginia. 1985-present, Counsel, Subcommittee on Labor Standards, Committee on Education and Labor.

Fiesta has recently been focusing his attention on migrant worker issues and expects to see more interest among members in farm labor as the new immigration reform law begins to have an impact on Western growers. He has already seen an interest in changes to the H-2A worker program, which allows foreign workers into the U.S. to do particular work for a specified period of time. "The U.S. work force is shrinking, and the supply of alien workers has been cut off, so there's a dynamic at work that will be making headlines," Fiesta says. "We've already seen claims of labor shortages in Washington and California. In the end, I think we're going to see some wage increases for these workers."

A Democrat, he doesn't give the Reagan Administration very high marks. "There's been no Reagan recovery in Pennsylvania. Unemployment is still high and the western part of the state is still economically depressed." He does give credit, though, to former Labor Secretary William Brock, who in Fiesta's book "was much better than Raymond Donovan, whose people didn't communicate often with Democrats."

In his spare time, Fiesta is trying to complete research on his Ph.D. thesis, which will analyze the rise of regulatory agencies, especially in the area of food and drug law. He also enjoys playing golf and softball.

S. Gray Garwood, Ph.D.
Staff Director
Subcommittee on Postsecondary
  Education
A-617 House Office Bldg. Annex 1
226-3681

Personal: born 10/28/39 in Blakely, Georgia. B.A. Clemson Univ., 1962. M.Sc. Univ. of Tennessee, 1966. Ph.D. Georgia State Univ., 1974. 1962-1964, Manager, Southern Bell Telephone Co. 1964-1975, various positions at universities and hospitals. Faculty, Center for Teacher Educ., Tulane Univ. 1977-1979, Project TEACH, Dir., New Orleans, LA. 1975-1984, Professor of Psychology, Tulane Univ. 1982-1983, Congressional Science Fellow in Child Development. 1984-1985, Legislative Assistant, Rep. Pat Williams (D-MT). 1986-1987, Professorial Lecturer, George Washington Univ. 1985-1987, Staff Director, Subcommittee on Select Education; 1987-present, Staff Director, Subcommittee on Postsecondary Education, Committee on Education and Labor.

Expertise: Education, handicapped infants & children

When Congressman Pat Williams (D-MT) left as chairman of the Subcommittee on Select Education to assume the chairmanship of the Subcommittee on Postsecondary Education, his decision to have Gray Garwood head the subcommittee staff was not a difficult one.

An accomplished educator and licensed psychologist, Garwood brought impressive credentials to the subcommittee. And now, with a team of seven professional staff members, Garwood and his staff are recognized as experts in the area of postsecondary education.

A top priority for Garwood this year is the contentious issue of college students defaulting on their government loans; a problem that involves about $2 billion yearly. Garwood argues that the stereotype of only "rich kids" defaulting on their loans is wholly unjustified. Rather, he suggests that the typical loan default involves mostly low-income minorities unable to secure employment. Further, Garwood says that Reagan Administration policies have precluded middle income students from participating in the financial aid process.

In response to this dilemma, the subcommittee will hear testimony from some twenty experts including educators, financial aid officers and students. Based on their recommendations, Williams intends to sponsor legislation designed to combat the student loan problem. In the meantime, Garwood would like to see the White House decrease its emphasis on fiscal matters and change its focus to include some of these vital social policy considerations.

A recognized expert in the area of handicapped children, Garwood is especially proud of two bills that were passed into law last Congress. In fact, he was one of the staff authors of the National Infant Intervention Initiative, legislation creating a system that encouraged states to provide assistance to disabled children up to two years old. A controversial bill because it meant new budget authority, this measure provides for education, therapy and family counseling where necessary.

Another bill, entitled the Handicapped Children's Protection Act, actually overruled a Supreme Court decision dealing with attorneys' fees. Essentially, this highly contested civil rights measure provided for reimbursement of attorneys' fees paid by parents of handicapped children.

Garwood is a well-respected writer, whose contributions include books, papers and articles dealing with handicapped infants and children.

Andrew J. Hartman
Senior Legislative Associate
1040 Longworth House Office
  Bldg.
225-7101

Personal: born 1953 in Buffalo, New York. B.A. Univ. of Notre Dame, 1975. M.A. SUNY Buffalo, 1979. Ph.D., Univ. of Illinois at Champaigne, 1983. 1983, Congressional Fellowship, Association for Advancement of Science. 1984-1986, Legislative Associate, Rep. James M. Jeffords (R-VT). 1986-present, Senior Legislative Associate, full committee and Subcommittee on Elementary and Secondary Education.

Expertise: Elementary and secondary education, bilingual education

As Senior Legislative Associate, Andrew Hartman works closely with two Congressmen in particular: James M. Jeffords (R-VT), the ranking Republican on the Education and Labor Committee, and Bill Goodling (R-PA), the ranking Republican on the Subcommittee on Elementary and Secondary Education. Most recently, Hartman helped draft significant portions of the reauthorized and rewritten Elementary and Secondary Education Act. The areas of greatest interest to him include compensatory education for economically disadvantaged children, vocational education and family-based literacy pre-school programs, among others.

Hartman wants to find new solutions to old problems—something comparable to welfare reform, but in the area of education. He has helped draft legislation for programs aimed at young families where the parents themselves have literacy problems. He worked on the Bilingual Education Act, passed in May, 1987, which promotes language acquisition models ranging from English as a Second Language programs to structured immersion techniques.

As a student, Hartman worked on research projects in developmental psychology on child abuse, on the effects of desegregation on children, and on self-image and self-esteem in school drop-outs (his dissertation topic). He has continued to write in this area, contributing chapters to various books and presenting papers at the American Educational Research Association and the Society for Research in Child Development. Hartman is especially interested in local efforts in educational reform: "A lot of exciting work is going on in state and local governments which the feds could learn from."

Hartman is an avid swimmer, bicyclist and backpacker.

Seymour Holzman
Deputy Staff Director
Subcommittee on Health and
  Safety
B-345A Rayburn
225-6876

Expertise: Occupational safety and health, labor, education.

After two decades of professional experience as a writer, editor and political consultant, it was only a matter of time before Seymour Holzman would hear Washington's siren song. Today, his wealth of experience serves him well as Deputy Staff Director of the Health and Safety Subcommittee of the Education and Labor Committee.

Holzman has been instrumental in conducting hearings and drafting reports on issues ranging from the potential hazards of video display terminals to industry health and safety to postsecondary education and issues affecting America's steel industry.

Last year, the Subcommittee took the lead on drafting a report which focused congressional attention on the potential hazards of occupations where video display terminals are common. Among other things, the report pointed to the need for employers to provide improved workplace surroundings.

Also, while there is not yet any empirical data to support the claim, the report concluded there may be reproductive hazards to people exposed to low-frequency radiation waves. And because the electronic age will doubtless lead to a proliferation of video display terminals, Holzman and the Subcommittee staff will continue to monitor this important issue.

Under Holzman's effective stewardship, the Subcommittee has also conducted hearings on various health, and safety-related issues. Last fall, for instance, they heard from the AFL/CIO which presented testimony suggesting the need for a Construction, Safety and Health Administration—an organization that would play a role similar to that of OSHA. Holzman believes OSHA could restructure its management to allow for the incorporation of such a program.

Because the Subcommittee on Health and Safety falls under the jurisdiction of the Education and Labor Committee, Holzman has also become involved in some postsecondary education issues. Of particular concern to Holzman is the Reagan Administration's proposal to limit funds to colleges and universities whose students have a high rate of default.

Holzman believes such institutions are at a severe disadvantage insofar as they are precluded from both the collection process and making the decisions over which students receive federal loans. While the Committee intends to hold hearings on this matter, Holzman believes such an initiative would penalize future students, those who have never even had the benefit of a college loan.

Personal: born 10/3/36, Orange, NJ. B.S. New York Univ., 1963. 1955-1958, U.S. Army, Korea. 1961-1963, Credit Analyst, Dun & Bradstreet. 1963-1967, newspaper editor and writer, The Record, Hackensack, N.J. 1967-1972, editor, Scholastic Magazine, New York City. 1972-1973, editor, Ogden (Utah) Standard-Examiner. 1973-1977, political editor, Tampa (Fla.) Times. 1977-1979, executive assistant, Florida Secretary of State. 1979-1982, self-employed lobbyist and political consultant. 1983-1984, Press Secretary, Rep. Michael Bilirakis (R-Fla.). 1984 to present, staff of Health and Safety Subcommittee, Committee on Education and Labor.

Education and Labor

John F. Jennings
Staff Director
Subcommittee on Elementary,
   Secondary & Vocational
   Education
Counsel for Education
B-346C Rayburn House Office
   Bldg.
225-4368

*Personal: B.A. in history, Loyola Univ.,
1964. J.D. Northwestern Univ., 1967.
1967-present, Staff Director,
Subcommittee on Elementary,
Secondary & Vocational Education.
1980-present, Counsel for Education,
House Committee on Education and
Labor.*

Expertise: Elementary, secondary and vocational education

Few major education decisions in recent years have been made in the House of Representatives without some input from John F. (Jack) Jennings, a stalwart on the House Education and Labor Committee for over two decades.

Jennings became counsel and staff director of the House Subcommittee on Elementary, Secondary & Vocational Education, in December, 1967. Since then he has counseled legislators on all aspects of elementary and secondary education, including school financing, busing and desegregation, and funding for education block grants and categorical programs. Jennings has earned a reputation as a skilled policymaker and efficient administrator.

A 1964 graduate of Loyola University, Jennings joined the Capitol Hill staff soon after graduating from Northwestern University's School of Law in 1967. He traces his interest in government back to 1960, when he was a volunteer in John F. Kennedy's presidential campaign and notes that involvement in politics was common for many young people who came of age when Kennedy was elected president.

On the subcommittee, Jennings first worked for Rep. Roman Pucinski of Illinois, then for Rep. Carl Perkins of Kentucky, and now he works for Rep. Augustus Hawkins of California. In 1980, Jennings became the counsel for education on the full committee, a post that gives him chief responsibility for coordinating the legislative activities of three subcommittees. That job also has given him input into higher education policy, humanities and the arts issues, and handicapped education legislation.

Jennings welcomes the recent resurgence of national interest in education but believes that there is still a long way to go. For the 1980's, he envisions greater interest in pre-school education, Head Start, student financial aid, educating disadvantaged children and increasing the number of minority teachers. Still he points out, it's going to take a number of years to get back to where we were in the late Seventies.

Jennings is a former member of the board of directors of the American Education Finance Association and the steering committee of the Educational Staff Seminar.

Richard E. Johnson
Senior Legislative Counsel
2181 Rayburn House Office Bldg.
225-4691

Expertise: Welfare, education, labor

From the time he went to law school, Richard Johnson wanted to enter the legislative arena. His career has included experience as a staffer on both House and Senate sides, and important roles in Democratic administrations and committees. He brings that varied knowledge of how the system works to his responsibilities as senior legislative counsel for the House Education and Labor Committee.

Johnson is the parliamentary authority for the committee, dealing with procedural questions, and coordinating with the parliamentarian of the House. As "staff negotiator," he also schedules legislation, negotiates arrangements for legislation drafted in subcommittees, and provides support in conference committees with the Senate.

He also becomes involved in the drafting of legislation in his areas of special concern, including occasional fast-track legislation dealt with at the full committee level. His specialization has been in job training, CETA, Legal Services, education and anti-poverty. He was a principal drafter of the education and labor components of the 1986 anti-drug abuse legislation, and of the worker adjustment portions of recent trade legislation.

In his early days in Congress, Johnson helped develop sections of Great Society education and labor programs. He has sought over the years to maintain continuity in the services offered by those programs. "We've reformulated most of the economic opportunity programs," he says. "But we've also sustained them. Most of those programs still remain."

Personal: Born 1936, Spartanburg, South Carolina. B.A. Univ. of Chicago, 1958. L.L.B. Yale Law School, 1961. 1961-1965, legislative attorney, Office of the General Inspector, HEW. 1965-1969, legislative specialist, Office of Legislation, Office of Education, HEW. 1969-1977, staff of Senator Gaylord Nelson (D-WI), Counsel to Subcommittee on Employment, Poverty and Migratory Labor, Senate Committee on Labor and Public Welfare. 1977-1982, Special Assistant to the Assistant Secretary of Policy, Evaluation and Research, Office of the Secretary, Department of Labor. 1982-1983, Counsel, House Administration Committee, staff of Rep. Augustus Hawkins (D-CA). 1983-1985, Counsel; 1985-present, Senior Legislative Counsel, House Education and Labor Committee.

Susan Grayson McGuire
Staff Director
2181 Rayburn House Office Bldg.
225-4527

Personal: born 9/20/40 in Portland, Oregon. B.A. Univ. of Michigan, 1962. 1962-1964, Staff, Central Intelligence Agency. 1965-1966, Assistant Finance Director, George Christopher for Governor Committee, San Francisco, CA. 1967-1968, Editorial Assistant, Appleton Century Crofts Publishing Company, Washington, DC. 1969-1970, Assistant to Campaign Director, Democratic National Committee, Washington, DC. 1970-1973, Legislative Assistant, Senate Select Committee on Equal Education Opportunity; Legislative Assistant to Sen. Walter F. Mondale on labor issues. 1973-1984, Staff Director, Subcommittee on Employment Opportunities of the Committee on Education and Labor. 1984-present, Staff Director, Committee on Education and Labor.

Expertise: Employment, education

Dedication to the concept of providing employment opportunities is the focal point of Susan McGuire's work. McGuire's career as a Congressional staff member began in 1970 as an assistant to the Senate Select Committee on Equal Educational Opportunity. She also kept Sen. Walter F. Mondale abreast of legislation under consideration by the Senate Labor Committee.

The primary role of the Staff Director, according to McGuire, is to ensure that the priorities and views of Chairman Augustus Hawkins are considered on legislation which is reported out of the committee. Chairman Hawkins and McGuire have worked together since she came over to the House side in 1973 to work on, and eventually direct, the staff of the old Subcommittee on Equal Employment Opportunities.

The broad scope of committee work not only utilizes McGuire's expertise in employment opportunities, but also requires knowledge of a wide range of education and labor issues. The decentralized nature of the committee allows for each subcommittee to be somewhat autonomous in terms of budget, staff, and agenda. McGuire follows the progress of legislation at the subcommittee level via full committee staff people who are assigned to work with each subcommittee. These employees represent Chairman Hawkins's interests at the subcommittee level so that any discrepancies may be addressed before the bill rises to the full committee. Thus, McGuire is responsible for promoting the Chairman's interests from the creation of the bill until it is reported out of the committee.

Chairman Hawkins and McGuire share a strong interest in the concept of expanding employment opportunities. McGuire is a proponent of giving people the tools necessary to allow them to help themselves obtain the highest possible levels of employment, not just full-time work. As a pragmatist and something of a populist, McGuire sees as a priority the goal of maximum employment for workers. Much of the legislation with which she has been involved reflects this philosophy.

McGuire has played a significant role in many major pieces of legislation providing educational and employment opportunities. Among these are the Age Discrimination in Employment Act Amendments of 1978, the Pregnancy Disability Act of 1978, the Comprehensive Employment and Training Act Amendments of 1978 (CETA), and CETA's replacement, the Job Training Partnership Act of 1982 (JTPA). Undoubtedly, McGuire's expertise will again come into play as the 100th Congress addresses the issue of welfare reform.

Mark Powden
Republican Labor Staff Director
2101 Rayburn House Office Bldg.
225-3725

Expertise: Labor and human resources

For a relative newcomer to Capitol Hill, Mark Powden holds an influential position. He attributes this to being in the right place at the right time. When Rep James Jeffords (R-VT) rose to ranking minority member on the House Education and Labor Committee in 1985, he looked to Powden—a personal staffer hired two years earlier whom Jeffords refers to as "my right arm"—to assume the duties of Labor Staff Director.

Raised in the small town of Peacham, Vermont, Powden was promoted to Jeffords' legislative director within one year after joining the staff. Working for an at-large representative exposed him to the large number of issues one state's concerns can encompass, ranging from Vermont wilderness cleanup legislation to energy assistance for the poor. Powden had also handled a varied agenda in an earlier position with the AFL-CIO's Food and Allied Service Trades group. There, he monitored labor legislation with a less obvious impact on union members—food stamps and immigration policy for example.

Powden's ability to deal with a wide range of issues prepared him well for the Education and Labor Committee's busy agenda, which has attracted widespread media attention in the 99th and 100th Congresses. Committee legislation is divided between Powden, who oversees labor and human resources matters, and Beth Buehlmann, responsible for education and job training issues. Powden also serves as the Committee's administrator, directing the entire staff of thirty professionals serving the Republican members of the full committee and its eight subcommittees. He is in constant contact with committee members, Administration representatives and other interested parties as labor policy is developed and considered.

Powden's issues include Davis-Bacon Act reform, minimum wage, family leave, occupational risk notification, plant closings and double breasting, among others. When asked about his political leanings, Powden responds simply: "As a staffer on a committee as diverse as this, I have no views." To Powden, the job entails getting a handle on the politics of each issue and a reading on the widely divergent views of the committee's Republicans. "I also try to remind people that districts are part of the whole equation," says Powden.

Personal: born 8/3/57 in Norfolk, Virginia. B.A. Harvard Univ., magna cum laude. 1980, research director, Schultz for Senate, Phoenix, AZ. 1981-1982, legislative representative, Food and Allied Services and Trades, AFL-CIO, Washington, DC. 1983, Legislative Assistant, Representative James Jeffords. 1985-present, Republican Labor Staff Director and Administrator, Committee on Education and Labor.

Education and Labor

Eugene F. Sofer
Budget Counsel
2181 Rayburn House Office Bldg.
225-4691

Expertise: Appropriations, budget

Since late 1984, Eugene Sofer has been the Budget Counsel for the House Committee on Education and Labor. In that role, he has helped to develop the Committee's response to the President's budget, acted as a liaison to other congressional committees on budget and appropriation issues, and worked with public interest groups to promote the Committee's priorities. In addition, Sofer has coordinated efforts at the staff level to participate in recent omnibus legislation on the issues of drugs, homelessness, and trade.

Sofer came to the House Committee on Education and Labor from the House Budget Committee, where he was an Associate Staff Member for Congressman Stephen J. Solarz (D-NY). He wrote speeches, testimony, and policy position papers in areas of the federal budget, taxes, and economic policy, in addition to drafting amendments to presidential budgets and congressional budget resolutions. Sofer was also responsible for developing and coordinating hearings for the Budget Committee Task Force on Transportation, Research and Development, and Capital Resources.

It was during this period in 1982 that Sofer's book, *From Pale to Pampa: A Social History of the Jews of Buenos Aires,* was published. The book is an analysis of Jewish occupational and residential mobility in Argentina during the twentieth century.

As Special Assistant to the Director of the Coalition of Northeastern Governors Policy Research Center, Sofer was responsible for issue development, liaison to other regional groups and governmental agencies, oversight of projects on defense expenditures, water resources, and economic development. He also developed positions on illegal immigration, infrastructure, and the federal budget.

Prior to this, Sofer worked as a Research Associate for the Latin American Program of the Woodrow Wilson Center for Scholars, where he developed the program's special activities and organized meetings and internship programs.

Personal: born 8/31/48 in New York, New York. New York Univ. 1968. Ph.D Univ. of California, Los Angeles, 1976. 1972-1973, 1974-1975, Teaching Fellow and recipient of dissertation Fellowships, Univ. of California, Los Angeles. 1977, Project Director, Anti-Defamation League of the B'nai B'rith, Washington, D.C. 1977-1978, Research Associate, Latin American Program, Woodrow Wilson International Center for Scholars, Washington, D.C. 1978-1980, Special Assistant to the Director, Coalition of Northeastern Governors Policy Research Center, Washington, D.C. 1980-1984, Associate Staff Member, House Committee on the Budget. 1985-present, Budget Counsel, Committee on Education and Labor. Publications: From Pale to Pampa: A Social History of the Jews of Buenos Aires, Holmes and Meier, 1982.

Dorothy L. Strunk
Senior Legislative Associate
2174 Rayburn House Office Bldg.
225-6910

Expertise: Worker's safety and health

Dottie Strunk liked the job as a secretary for the FBI and imagined if she were to ever leave that position, it would be to teach stenography. Once she was drafted to come to Capitol Hill, however, to help the Education and Labor Committee with their hearings, teaching stenography somehow fell by the wayside.

As clerk for the Committee, Strunk became familiar with the many issues within its jurisdiction and eventually developed her expertise in the area of occupational safety with a focus on mining issues. Having grown up in the heavy coal mining district of Northeast Pennsylvania, Strunk found the issue naturally appealing.

In her capacity as Senior Legislative Associate, Strunk develops strategy for legislative action, prepares questions and conducts briefings for hearings, mark-up sessions and floor action. She represents the Minority position in all negotiations with Majority staff and the Administration. Strunk has also initiated and organized a series of oversight hearings on the Occupational Safety and Health Administration.

Personal: born 1/2/48, Nanticoke, PA. Educated in the Public Schools of Pennsylvania. 1965-1967, Clerk-Stenographer, Federal Bureau of Investigation. 1967-1978, Minority Clerk, Committee on Education and Labor. 1978-1979, Office Manager, Committee on Ways and Means. 1979 to present, Senior Legislative Associate, Committee on Education and Labor.

During her near twenty-year stint with the Committee, Strunk has been involved with a long list of important legislative initiatives including the Migrant and Seasonal Agricultural Workers' Protection Act, Black Lung, the Service Contracts Act, the Fair Labor Standards Act, the Federal Employees' Compensation Act, and is presently working on the Workers' Notification Act. Regarding the Notification Act, Strunk believes it is a "luxury" bill. She states that the measure "is not a Hazard Notification Act but a 'Risk' Notification Act and industry cannot afford a bill like that at this point." Further, Strunk believes if there are problems with OSHA, "fix the particular problem areas, don't create an OSHA II which may run into the same problems."

The expertise she gained in the area of Mine Safety earned her a presidential nomination to the post of Assistant Secretary of Labor for Mine Safety and Health. Her nomination received considerable resistance from labor groups, however, particularly the United Mine Workers (UMW). The UMW had someone else in mind for the position, and let the members of the Senate Labor and Human Resources Committee know their stand on the matter. Thus, in a straight party-line vote, Strunk's nomination was killed by the panel. The display of strength by labor against Strunk's nomination was the subject of many articles in the nation's top newspapers and the office still remains vacant.

Away from the intense politics of the Hill, Strunk loves boating and is an officer of a yacht club.

Susan Wilhelm
Staff Director
Subcommittee on Human
    Resources
320 Cannon House Office Bldg.
225-1850

Expertise: Human service issues, including Head Start, child care & programs for senior citizens & the poor

Susan Wilhelm came to Washington, D.C., in 1977 with a political science degree from the University of Michigan and hopes of landing a full-time job. While surveying the local job market, she worked as an intern for her congressman, Rep. Dale E. Kildee, just elected in 1976 and himself a newcomer to Washington.

A self-described "intern who made good," Wilhelm soon joined Kildee's staff as a legislative correspondent and rose through the ranks to become Kildee's chief legislative aide. In 1985, when Kildee was named chairman of the House Subcommittee on Human Resources, Wilhelm became the subcommittee's staff director.

In her current post, Wilhelm handles a wide range of social service issues important to senior citizens, children and the poor—"what's left of the War on Poverty," she says. These include the Head Start program for disadvantaged children, juvenile justice, the Older Americans Act, low-income energy assistance and the Community Services Block Grant.

Working on behalf of these Great Society programs has been no easy task during the Reagan era, but Wilhelm takes pride in her work to reauthorize these programs and to target more help to the poor. The best thing about her job, she says, is "knowing that you might be able to make a difference."

Personal: born 9/3/55 in Flint, Michigan. B.A. Univ. of Michigan, 1976. 1977-1985, Legislative Aide, Rep. Dale E. Kildee (D-MI). 1985-present, Staff Director Subcommittee on Human Resources.

During debates in subcommittee and the full House Education and Labor Committee, Wilhelm often can be found at Kildee's side offering information and guidance. She says her boss deserves a lot of credit for maintaining a high-level of support for these social service programs. "It is easy to be director of this subcommittee because of Mr. Kildee. We work for a chairman who really believes in these programs. He considers himself a real advocate."

During the next few years, one of Wilhelm's—and Kildee's—top priorities will be improving early childhood services, chiefly through a national child care bill. Wilhelm also is optimistic about how her programs will fare in the 1980s. "We've had to fight a lot for these programs" during the Reagan era, she says, but the programs have enjoyed a lot of bipartisan support.

After 11 years in Washington, Wilhelm, who hails from Flint, Michigan, still expresses some surprise about her success on Capitol Hill. "If you would have told me 11 years ago that this is where I'd be, I wouldn't have believed it."

Dan Yager
Minority Counsel
Education and Labor Committee
2101 Rayburn House Office Bldg.
225-3725

Expertise: Family leave, dislocated workers, collective bargaining, plant closings, workers compensation

This Nebraska football fan is very comfortable in his position as Minority Counsel for the Education and Labor Committee. Dan Yager speaks as easily about the Parental Leave Act as he does about the annual Oklahoma-Nebraska game. His roots are in the Midwest, but Yager gained valuable experience in the problems of local government by coming to D.C. to monitor the effects of federal legislation on San Diego County. Yager's job was to keep an eye on legislation which would affect local issues.

Dan believes this experience with local government is instrumental in his understanding of legislation in the House Education and Labor Committee. He quickly points out that there is a huge difference between the goals of legislation at the federal level and at the local level. "Most folks in Washington know how to pass legislation, but rarely do they have hands-on experience with how to really implement that legislation."

These observations are central to Dan's specialty on the Committee labor issues. He notes that it is somewhat easy to come up with legislative ideas, but that "it is difficult to empathize with the day-to-day problems of putting the legislation into effect. "This is simply a frustrating reality in working to solve labor problems," Yager admits.

Personal: born 12/23/50 in Wichita, Kansas. B.S. Univ. of Nebraska, 1972. J.D. Univ. of Santa Clara, 1975 (cum laude). 1976-1980, Legislative Assistant, San Diego County Washington Office. 1980-1981, Legislative Assistant, Representative Lionel Van Deerlin (D-CA). 1981-1983, Legislative Staff Director, Representative Marge Roukema (R-NJ). 1983-1986, Associate Republican Counsel for Labor, House Committee on Education and Labor. 1986-present Minority (Republican) Counsel, House Committee on Education and Labor.

The most rewarding role so far for Yager has been his involvement in the issues of plant closings and dislocated workers. He values his excellent relationship with Committee members Jeffords and Roukema, who are very active on plant closings issue. While they both originally opposed the labor bill in 1985, Yager is pleased that they were able to shift the focus of the debate to "look beyond the contentious issues of plant-closing notification and consultation toward the whole problem of dislocated workers." These key players requested that the Secretary of Labor study the worker dislocation problem to seek a relationship where all the relevant parties worked together instead of at odds on this issue. He is particularly pleased to see that solid proposals are now coming back as a result of this agreement.

Despite the controversial nature of many labor issues, the good relationships between the minority and majority committee members have paid off in this year's labor section in the trade bill. Yager believes that the new dislocated worker provisions are more coherent than the current program, and the priorities for the program have strengthened the legislation as well. As Yager notes, there are going to be lay-offs; "the key is getting workers adapted for other job openings." He realizes that this task is not an easy one, but it is good for both the employer and employee involved.

HOUSE OF REPRESENTATIVES
COMMITTEE ON ENERGY AND COMMERCE

Michael F. Barrett, Jr.
Chief Counsel and Staff Director
Subcommittee on Oversight and
  Investigations
2323 Rayburn House Office Bldg.
225-4441

*Personal: born 2/2/36 in Glen Cove,
New York. B.A. St. John's Univ., NY,
1959, cum laude. LL.B. St. John's
Univ., 1962, dean's list. LL.M.
Georgetown Univ. Law School, 1964.
1966, attorney, Federal Trade
Commission. 1967-1970, trial attorney
and branch attorney, Securities and
Exchange Commission. 1970-1975,
staff counsel, Committee on Energy
and Commerce. 1975-1981, staff
counsel, Subcommittee on Oversight
and Investigations. 1981-present,
chief counsel and staff director,
Committee on Energy and Commerce,
Subcommittee on Oversight and
Investigations. Publications: 1962-
1966, articles in* Military Law Review.
1963-1964, monthly column, Federal
Bar News *.*

Expertise: Securities markets; corporations

When Democratic powerhouse John Dingell ascended to the chair of the House Energy and Commerce Committee in 1981, he appointed Michael Barrett Chief Counsel and Staff Director for the Subcommittee on Oversight and Investigations, his base of power on the committee. A cigar-smoking Irishman who relishes the role of investigator, Barrett brings impressive credentials to the job. The son of Irish immigrants, he graduated cum laude from St. John's Univ. where he also won a scholarship to law school. After obtaining his degree from Georgetown Univ., he served four years in the Judge Advocate General's office in the Pentagon, and has been practicing his craft in Washington, D.C. ever since—first with the Federal Trade Commission and then with the Securities and Exchange Commission.

While working at the SEC on the Penn Central case, Barrett met John Dingell, who had won election 15 years earlier to a House seat held by his late father. Barrett accepted a position on the staff of the Energy and Commerce Committee, moving to the Oversight and Investigations Subcommittee staff in 1975, where he was involved in the development of the National Energy Act of 1978, the Pipeline Safety Act of 1979 and the Energy Security Act of 1980. In 1981, he was named Chief Counsel and Staff Director of Oversight and Investigations, where he directed the subcommittee's investigations of Rita Lavelle at the EPA, unfair foreign trade practices, and professional accounting standards. Barrett is currently involved in a major investigation of the securities markets.

An able administrator, Barrett has overseen the growth of a staff which is now a potent force on the Hill, with jurisdiction over both security markets and energy. With his star hitched to one of the House's most influential members, he figures to be a key player among the Hill's unelected power-brokers in the 101st Congress.

Howard P. Bauleke
Staff Director
Rep. Jim Slattery (D-KS)
1440 Longworth House Office
  Bldg.
225-6601

Expertise: Telecommunications, taxation

Howard Bauleke's hobby is politics. The Staff Director for the Washington offices of Kansas Rep. Jim Slattery follows election news and governmental issues the way some people follow football scores.

A native Kansan himself, Bauleke, who is a lawyer, has worked for Jim Slattery since January of 1984, when he began his Capitol Hill career as a legislative assistant. In September of 1987 he took on his current role of Staff Director. As he describes it, his greatest responsibility lies in playing a "defensive strategy": he tries to anticipate potential legislative and political problems, crises, and disasters before they erupt.

His areas of legislative responsibility include energy, general business, telecommunications, transportation, judiciary and taxation. Because of Slattery's membership on the Energy and Commerce Committee, Bauleke has made the issues of this committee one of his primary concerns over the past three and a half years. Slattery is also on the Energy and Commerce Subcommittee on Telecommunications and Finance; so these policy issues also command Bauleke's study and attention. The brewing controversy over the regulation and control of the telecommunications industry, and recent decisions on the AT&T consent decree, are a few of the increasingly complex issues that Bauleke must stay updated on.

Personal: born 4/16/59 in Lawrence, Kansas. B.A. Univ. of Kansas (summa cum laude) (Phi Beta Kappa), 1981. W. Harold Otto National Merit Scholarship. J.D. Georgetown Univ. Law Center, 1984. Administrative Editor, Law Review: The Tax Lawyer. 1980, campaign co-coordinator, State Rep. John Solbach (D-KS). 1984-1987, Legislative Assistant, Rep. Jim Slattery (D-KS). 1987-present, Staff Director, Rep. Jim Slattery. Publications: "Just a Country Doctor: the Image Presented by Dr. Bill Roy in the 1974 Kansas U.S. Senate Race", Kansas Speech Journal, 1980. "Constitutionality of the Crude Oil Windfall Profit Tax, United States v. Ptasynski", The Tax Lawyer, 1984.

Among the more significant projects that Bauleke has been involved with is the Agriculture Shippers Protection Act, which was a part of the 1986 budget reconciliation bill. Constituent interest and concern over the tax reforms of 1986 required that Bauleke spend a great deal of his time on that issue during the 99th Congress. He foresees that the issues of corporate takeovers, product liability and railroad regulation will be heavy on his agenda in 1988.

Bauleke describes his political philosophy as a libertarian on social issues, a conservative on fiscal policy, and a believer in a strong central government to insure fairness in the market place and to protect public health and safety. He believes that the U.S. has been in an "Eisenhower cycle" that is now coming to a close, and that it will now have to deal with many problems it has basically been ignoring.

Glenda C. Booth
Legislative Director
Rep. Doug Walgren (D-PA)
Subcommittee on Health and the
    Environment
2241 Rayburn House Office Bldg.
225-2135

*Education: B.A. Longwood Coll.,
Farmville, VA., 1966. M.A. Univ. of Va.,
1967. 1967-1969, teacher, Madison
County Public Schools. 1969-1974,
National Audio Visual Association,
Assistant to the Vice President for
Legislation, Director of Public Affairs.
1974-1979, Senior legislative
assistant, Rep. Herbert E. Harris.
1979-1981, Executive Assistant to the
Assistant Secretary for Legislation,
U.S. Department of Education and
Assistant to the Deputy Assistant
Secretary for Education (HEW). 1981
to present, Legislative Director, Rep.
Doug Walgren (D-PA), House
Subcommittee on Health and the
Environment, Committee on Energy
and Commerce.*

Expertise: Health care, environment

Although most Legislative Directors on Capitol Hill would find a normal workload of supervising legislative staff enough to handle, Glenda Booth has responsibility for the Energy and Commerce committee and is personal staff liaison to the Science and Technology Committee. She is also Rep. Walgren's designee on the Health and the Environment Subcommittee.

Because Rep. Walgren has a particular interest in health care and aging issues, Booth says she has worked on numerous reforms and modifications to improve Medicare benefits, including a respite care amendment added to the catastrophic health care bill.

A significant amendment which she helped draft last year with Walgren would require nursing homes to have a registered nurse on duty twenty-four hours a day. Unfortunately the amendment failed on a tie vote in the committee. Booth indicates another topic of concern and priority is geriatric training for health professionals. Walgren feels the U.S. has a bias toward "youth and glamour" and neglects the health care of the elderly, she notes.

Another creative health care initiative which Booth has a role in promoting is an organ donor program intended to encourage hospitals to offer family members the opportunity to donate organs. In the Health Subcommittee, she has also worked extensively on the Clean Air Act reauthorization and is now developing an above ground oil tank storage bill, in response to the 4 million gallon oil spill near Pittsburgh.

When she is not devoting time to legislative endeavors, Booth spends it cheerleading for her two teenage sons at sporting events. She enjoys gardening and bird-watching.

William V. Corr
Counsel
Subcommittee on Health and
 Environment
512 House Office Bldg. Annex 1
226-7620

Expertise: Food and drug, HMO's, primary care & Medicare/Medicaid

William V. Corr works in Washington because he happened to be in the proverbial right place at the right time.

He spent his first four years after law school following what is still his first love, primary health care in rural Kentucky and Tennessee. His concern for the future of rural primary health care centers and other community-based activities entailed a good deal of political activism. It brought him to the attention of former Rep. Paul Rogers (D-FL), then Chairman of the House Subcommittee on Health and Environment. Rogers was thinking of expanding his committee staff. Corr was a natural selection.

Corr now works for Rogers' successor, Rep. Henry Waxman of California. He was Waxman's primary staffer during the passage of what he calls the most important drug legislation in the past 25 years. The Drug Price Competition and Patent Term Restoration Act opened up generic competition for all "off-patent" drugs and provided up to five years of patent extension for new drugs. This resulted, Corr notes, in hundreds of millions of dollars in savings to consumers and, at the same time, incentives for manufacturers to invest in new products. "It has changed the dynamics of the pharmaceutical industry tremendously," Corr says.

Corr points out that his subcommittee has had more success than many others in coping with recent budget cuts. Medicaid coverage has been expanded in every reconciliation bill, due to Waxman's leadership.

Personal: born 7/21/48 in Birmingham, Alabama. B.A. Univ. of Virginia, 1970. J.D. Vanderbilt, 1973. 1974-1977, Executive Director, United Health Services of Kentucky and Tennessee. 1977-present, Counsel, Subcommittee on Health and Environment.

Corr's present focus is the area of pesticides. He states that many of the pesticides approved in the 1950s are now known to be potent carcinogens and that the level of dangerous pesticides in the American food supply is still unknown.

The chief frustration for Corr is what he describes as the power of well-financed lobbyists "and the misleading statements and inaccuracies they employ that I have to deal with." He claims that there is an especially great amount of misinformation circulating about the cause of drug price rises and patent life loss.

But working for Waxman, he said, makes his job worthwhile. Waxman, he added, "treats us like colleagues." There is very little turnover on the subcommittee.

Corr prevents burnout by spending time with his two-year old daughter. He and his wife, Susan, were married in 1984. She was formerly on Rep. Ted Weiss's Government Operations Committee staff, and now works in the area of welfare reform for the non-profit Center on Budget and Policy Priorities.

Barbara A. Crapa
Legislative Director
Rep. John Bryant (D-TX)
412 Cannon House Office Bldg.
225-2231

Expertise: Energy and commerce, telecommunications, and finance

Rep. John Bryant (D-TX) has good reason to be grateful that a certain copper company would not let female employees work at the mouth of its mines. This particular policy sent chemistry graduate Barbara Crapa on the road to an advanced degree in the unrelated field of counseling, a decision that eventually brought her to her present position as Bryant's legislative director.

In those days, women were not only kept out of mines, but they were also expected to follow their husbands' career moves. But when Joseph Crapa finished his doctoral work in American literature at the Univ. of Arizona and considered taking a post in South Dakota, her reaction was clear: "No. Not on your life!"

Instead, through various connections both of them ended up in Washington, he as the first staff director of the 94th Caucus of "Watergate Babies," and she as a consultant to the Transport Workers Union. Between stints with the Union she worked as legislative assistant for Rep. James H. Scheuer (D-NY). She worked on the Bryant congressional race in 1982, joined him as chief legislative assistant the next year, and finally was promoted to legislative director in 1986, with supervisory responsibilities over the legislative counsel and legislative assistants.

A common word in her vocabulary is "fairness," especially in its applications to telephone users in the post-AT&T divestiture era. As far as she and Rep. Bryant are concerned, the $2.60 per month charge to interconnect with long-distance companies is a fixed cost, something already paid for. This has been, in her opinion, "a tremendous issue" recently. Other major issues for her have been Texas wilderness legislation, and the repeal of the Fuel Use Act of 1987.

Personal: born 7/28/46 in Brooklyn, New York. B.A. St. Joseph's Coll., 1967. M.A. Univ. of Arizona, 1974. 1968, quality control chemist, U.S. Customs Service, New York, NY. 1971-1975, counselor, Univ. of Arizona. 1975, consultant, Transport Workers Union. 1977-1982, assistant legislative director. 1976-1977, legislative assistant, Rep. James H. Scheuer. 1982, campaign worker, Rep. John Bryant. 1983-1986, chief legislative assistant. 1986-present, legislative director, Rep. Bryant.

Bryant is known as an "urban liberal" in a district gone increasingly conservative. His growing security might be attributed to an ability to convince his constituents that he is not, in Mrs. Crapa's words, a "pointyhead," and that he listens. Her contribution to that security is to follow up whenever Bryant makes inroads with conservative businessmen and industrialists. She shows them that Bryant cares about them, and Bryant gives her plenty of flexibility, sending her on field trips to Dallas from three to five times a year.

She is also allowed a great deal of latitude with the legislative staff, and she claims this helps defuse most of the tension that could arise.

She has well balanced the responsibilities of motherhood and Capitol staffer. Her son is now a college student. She relaxes on the bike trails near Mount Vernon, often with her husband, or by reading what she calls "class junk."

Jan M. Edelstein
Minority Counsel
564 House Office Bldg.Annex 2
226-3400

Personal: born 4/8/49, Asbury Park, New Jersey. B.A. Monmouth Coll., 1971. J.D., Seton Hall Univ., 1975. 1975-1979, attorney, private practice, New Jersey. 1980-1984, Hartford Steam Boiler Inspection and Insurance Company, Hartford CT. 1984, private consultant, pollution liability. 1985-present, Minority Counsel, Committee on Energy and Commerce.

Expertise: Environment

Like many on the inside of the labyrinthine congressional committee structure, Edelstein has several masters. She is one of approximately a dozen attorneys for the Energy and Commerce Committee's unified minority staff. Specifically, she works for all of the Republicans on the committee but spends most of her time working for the Republican leaders of two of the panel's subcommittees. The Commerce, Consumer Protection and Competitiveness subcommittee is led on the Republican side by Rep. William E. Dannemeyer (R-CA), its ranking member, and also Rep. Norman F. Lent, (R-NY), the full committee's ranking Republican, an ex-officio member of the subcommittee, and an active participant in its activities. In addition. Rep. Bob Whittaker (R-KS), the ranking member of the Transportation, Tourism, and Hazardous Materials Subcommittee, serves as Edelstein's part-time boss.

Under the umbrella of these various responsibilities, Edelstein is responsible for two general areas of legislation under the committee's jurisdiction: environment and liability. The genesis of her unique position on the committee staff was the expertise in environmental and pollution insurance that brought her to the committee in January, 1985.

After long and laborious legislative effort, the committee successfully extended Superfund for five years, although Edelstein remains skeptical of the program's status and direction. She views the Superfund reauthorization as "a victory for the environmental lobby, not the environment." She believes it has been made excessively complex and is the victim of gross politicization in Congress. Of the re-authorization effort, Edelstein says: "We were trying to make a mid-course correction without having reached mid-course."

Edelstein views her perspective on the committee staff as different for one reason–her experience outside of government as a lawyer in private practice, a manager of a pollution liability business for the Hartford Steam Boiler Company, and as a consultant. She has a special appreciation for the problems encountered by business in matters of liability and compliance with government regulation.

In the 100th Congress, Edelstein combines her scrutiny of Superfund and the Solid Waste Disposal Act with responsibility for a number of insurance-related issues and product liability.

Shelley N. Fidler
Assistant to the Chairman for
  Policy
Subcommittee on Energy and
  Power
331 House Annex 2
226-2500

*Personal: born 1/19/47 in Ryebrook,
N.Y. B.A. Brown University, Art History,
1968, . 1969, Coalition for Action,
Unity and Social Equality, Buffalo, N.Y.
1969-1973, executive director,
Massachusetts chapter, Americans for
Democratic Action. 1970, Kevin White
gubernatorial campaign,
Massachusetts. 1972, Barney Frank
state legislature campaign. 1973,
campaign director, Committee for Plan
3 (school board), Boston. 1874, Sylvia
Chaplain for Congress campaign.
1975-1980, legislative assistant, Rep.
Philip Sharp (D-IN). 1980-1987,
assistant to the chairman,
Subcommittee on Fossil and Synthetic
Fuels. 1987-present, assistant to the
chairman for policy, Subcommittee on
Energy and Power.*

Expertise: Fossil fuels, environment, legislative strategy, media

Though some Hill staffers might distance themselves from the political aspects of an issue, Shelley Fidler thrives on them.

Fidler says she was attracted to the legislative arena in large part because of her interest in politics. For 13 years, she has focused on coalition building and political strategy during her long association with Rep. Philip Sharp, a former professor who often takes an academic approach to issues.

A degree in art history might seem unlikely preparation for a career in Congress, but Fidler had extensive experience in politics before coming to the Hill. After graduating from Brown University in 1968, she directed a civic activist group in Buffalo, N.Y. and worked on numerous campaigns in New York, Massachusetts, and New Hampshire. "I found I could learn a lot simply by sitting and observing city council members, for example, arguing over some policy in Buffalo," she says. She also pushed for election law reform while working for the Massachusetts chapter of Americans for Democratic Action.

Migrating to Washington, D.C. in 1975, Fidler met Sharp, a freshman congressman and one of the "Watergate babies" who emerged from the 1974 elections. Fidler began supervising his legislative affairs, with an emphasis on energy issues.

That area brought Sharp to the Subcommittee on Energy and Power, which was created after the 1973-74 Arab oil embargo. When senior legislators chose other assignments over the new subcommittee, Sharp joined the panel and seized an early opportunity to become a key player on energy issues.

In 1980, When Sharp became chairman of the Fossil and Synthetic Fuels Subcommittee (re-created in the 100th Congress as the Energy and Power Subcommittee), Fidler became assistant to the chairman for policy, a position that gave her the flexibility to deal with legislative strategy, as well as substantive issues and media activity.

As a result, Fidler over the last decade has been involved in many major energy and environmental matters. In particular, she had a pivotal role in helping draft the original Automobile Fuel Economy legislation, which has improved U.S. auto fuel economy by 1000% since 1974. She participated in drafting the Natural Gas Policy Act (NGPA), the Public Utility Regulatory Act (PURPA) and parts of the energy program of the late 1970's.

Among environmental issues, she has focused more recently on acid rain, global warming and ozone non-attainment. She says she hopes to help Sharp achieve a middle-of-the-road compromise on these issues.

On the energy side, she has been looking at conservation measures, efforts to fund and stock the Strategic Petroleum Reserve, contract carriage for natural gas, competitive bidding for electric generation and the use of alternative fuels, such as methanol. Sharp does not oppose nuclear power, says Fidler, but wants to take measures that will increase safety and the industry's credibility.

Fidler says she considers herself fortunate to work for Sharp, describing him as a non-flashy member who "made up his mind long ago that he wants to be effective, focus on specific issues and work within the institution."

Rebecca M. Jill Gould
Minority Counsel
2322 Rayburn House Office Bldg.
226-3718

Expertise: International and domestic trade, transportation and insurance

A summer internship with Senator Robert Dole's office in 1979 provided "Becca" Gould her introduction to Washington life. This also provided the catalyst for her eventual return to the Hill upon completion of law school and the Kansas Bar.

Knocking on doors and making the rounds, Gould made her way to the Committee on Energy and Commerce and found her place as Minority Counsel responsible for the areas of international and domestic trade, transportation, sports-related issues, as well as back up on insurance and product liability.

With such a broad range of issues, Gould finds her position challenging.

When people think of Gould, it is usually in terms of H.R. 3, the Trade Bill. Her major concern over the past several months has been with the Bryant Amendment which places strict reporting procedures on foreign investors participating in American ventures. The Minority Members of the Committee are in strong opposition to this measure because of its anti-competitive nature.

Personal: born 6/19/60 in Wichita, Kansas. B.G.S. Univ. of Kansas, 1981. J.D. Washburn School of Law, 1982-1983. 1982-1983, Law Clerk, Gooddell, Stratton, Edmonds & Palmer, Topeka, Kansas. 1984-present, Minority Counsel House Committee on Energy and Commerce. Publications: "Procreation: A Choice for the Mentally Retarded", 23 Washburn, L.J. 359 (1984).

While most closely identified with international and domestic trade issues, Gould has spent a considerable portion of the last three years working with Representative Dan Coats (R-In.) in guiding the Luken-Coats's Railroad Unemployment Bill through the legislative maze. Among other things, this measure would set the railroad unemployment tax system on an experience-rated, rather than a flat tax system.

Gould has been spending much of her free time in pursuit of an LL.M. in International and Comparative Law from Georgetown University Law Center—expected in 1988.

Clarence L. (Larry) Irving, Jr.
Senior Counsel-Mass Media
Subcommittee on
  Telecommunications & Finance
316 House Office Bldg. Annex 2
226-2424

*Personal: Born 7/7/55 in Brooklyn,
N.Y. B.A. Northwestern Univ., 1976
(Dean's List 1974-1976; selected as
an outstanding senior, 1976). J.D.
Stanford Univ. School of Law, 1979
(President of class 1979). 1979-1983,
associate, Hogan & Hartson,
Washington, D.C. 1983-1987,
Legislative Director and Counsel, Rep.
Mickey Leland (D-TX). 1987-present,
Senior Counsel-Mass Media,
Subcommittee on Telecommunications
& Finance, Committee on Energy and
Commerce.*

Expertise: Broadcasting, cable and other electronic media

Communication, whether in the political arena of Capitol Hill or over television and radio airwaves, is a process Irving knows and understands. "Having been a personal staffer for four years, I understand the importance of keeping all members and their staffs apprised of what is going on," he says. "You can't call a staffer the day before markup or the day before a hearing and say, 'Here is what we've got to do.'" You've got to start talking to members, through their staffs, or to the members themselves as early in the process as possible. My job, as I see it, is basically to be a conduit of information, and to sit down with Members and staff to try to work out accomodations.

That approach has taken Irving to his current position, a job he calls "a watchdog on a watchdog committee of a watchdog agency." Translated, he is a monitor for a subcommittee that reviews the Federal Communications Commission (FCC), a panel that regulates the broadcast and cable industries.

Not that Irving doesn't have personal opinions on issues in which he is involved. "I'm a mainstream Democratic liberal, but I also know that the process requires give and take." And Irving has earned a reputation for his objectivity. "He has an ideology, but he's not an ideologue," says a lobbyist who deals with Irving. "Larry is always willing to listen."

Irving also has been lucky to be involved in legislation that follows his philosophy of providing opportunities for minorities and women. He was active in the 1984 Cable Telecommunications Act that strenghtened the FCC's power to enforce antidiscrimination regulations. Irving also helped shape the 1986 Conrail Privatization Act, which set a federal precedent requiring an opportunity for minority-owned or-controlled firms to participate in the stock sale.

Most recently, Irving was one of several staffers who played a significant role in drafting proposed Fairness Doctrine legislation maintaining a principle that requires broadcasters to cover and present all sides of issues of public importance, which President Reagan vetoed. Since the veto, the FCC has repealed the Fairness Doctrine which had been in practice since 1959. Irving expects to be involved in future attempts to recodify the fairness doctrine.

Irving believes that the key issue for the future of the broadcast, cable media technologies is High-Definition Television, which he says is "the most important technological development in broadcasting since the invention of television. High-Definition could cause a revolution in the electronic media and may be a $100 billion industry by the end of the century. I expect that the Subcommittee, under the leadership of Chairman Markey, will be very active in considering the technical, economic and trade implications of this new technology."

Irving didn't become involved in the communications industry by chance. There was a natural attraction from his years of interest in music, television and entertainment. During college, he worked as campus disc jockey at parties, and he is a self-proclaimed media junkie, with extensive record, compact disc and videotape collections.

William Michael Kitzmiller
Staff Director
2125 Rayburn House Office Bldg.
225-2927

Expertise: Administration, securities, environment, trade, health

Michael Kitzmiller has an interesting outlook on his position as Staff Director of the House Energy and Commerce Committee. To be sure, he compares his arrival at work each day to a compulsive gambler who finds an infinite number of slot machines into which he might put his token.

When considering the broad legislative jurisdiction of the committee and the seemingly limitless legislative causes it takes on, one realizes that Kitzmiller's comparison is altogether accurate.

As the committee's Staff director, Kitzmiller's responsibilities include preparing and implementing a committee budget that exceeded $4.5 million last year, supervising a staff of some 130 professionals, and playing an active role in a number of policy initiatives.

Kitzmiller's professional background in communications, public relations and writing also serves the committee well. He supervises the editing and publication of hearing records, and staff reports as well as relations with the press. Additionally, Kitzmiller is responsible for the scheduling of hearings, conferences with the Senate and committee-related appearances of the chairman, Rep. John D. Dingell (D-MI).

In terms of legislation, Kitzmiller and the committee are active in a number of different areas. For instance, the committee is studying last year's stock market crash with an eye toward possibly developing legislation which would address that problem. Also, the committee is interested in the product liability question as well as the U.S.-Canadian free trade agreement. Finally, the committee is in the process of reauthorizing several programs, including various hazardous waste laws and Amtrak.

The committee, under Kitzmiller's stewardship, has also focused congressional attention on the AIDS crisis and was instrumental in last year's House passage of legislation creating the AIDS commission. Further, the committee has addressed the uniform poll closing bill, several health-related measures and legislation involving imported automobiles.

While Kitzmiller originally came to Washington in 1965 for only a short time, he was smitten by both the city and the desire to contribute his wealth of talents. Ask him if he regrets the decision, and he is likely to tell you how much he enjoys playing the slot machine.

Personal: born 3/29/31 in Bryn Mawr, Pennsylvania. B.A. Yale Univ., 1954. Post-graduate study, 1956-1957. 1959-1965, account executive, Selvage & Lee, Inc., New York. 1965-1968, Legislative Assistant, Rep. Richard Ottinger (D-NY). 1968, Public Affairs Director, National Committee on Product Safety. 1968-1971, Executive Director, Grassroots, Inc. 1971-1974, Executive Secretary, Rep. Ogden R. Reid (D-NY). 1974-1975, freelance writer. 1975-1976, communications director, Westchester County, White Plains, NY. 1976-1984, Staff Coordinator; 1984-present, Staff Director, House Committee on Energy and Commerce. Publications: "United States Trade Relations with Japan and China", 1972 (2nd edition, 1983). Editor: "Energy and Helium: A Crisis in Future Energy Technology", 1979. "China's Economic Development and U.S. Trade Interests", 1985.

Jessica H. Laverty
Minority Counsel
2322 Rayburn House Office Bldg.
225-3641

Expertise: Electricity, nuclear, administrative and environmental law

Like many congressional staffers, Jessica Laverty came to Capitol Hill as a result of her experiences in the private sector. While an attorney in a downtown law firm, Laverty was summoned to the Hill by the Energy and Commerce Committee. At the time, the Committee sought her expertise in the area of nuclear power plant standardization.

Three years later, as a result of her knowledge and wide range of experiences both in and out of government, Laverty contributes substantially to the Committee's work on energy issues, from nuclear power to the generation of electricity.

While energy issues are no longer "sexy" by Washington standards, Laverty believes they are of extreme importance. Despite the public's perception that there is a surplus of electricity in this country, Laverty believes electricity will be in increasingly short supply in the years ahead. She also believes repeal of the Fuel Use Act was a major step forward for the country. That repeal permits utilities to build gas-fired electric plants.

Personal: born 9/28/53 in Winter Haven, Florida. B.A. Univ. of Maine, 1975 (magna cum laude). J.D. Coll. of William and Mary, 1978 (Law Review, Phi Beta Kappa). 1978-1980, Attorney, General Accounting Office. 1980-1981, Litigation Attorney, Nuclear Regulatory Commission. 1981-1983, Legal Advisor to Commissioner, Nuclear Regulatory Commission. 1983-1985, Conner & Wetterhahn. 1985 to present, Minority Counsel, Committee on Energy and Commerce.

Laverty is a proponent of nuclear power, citing studies that have found time and again that, if properly operated, nuclear power plants are one of the safest means of generating power. Further, while some talk of the dangers of nuclear plants, Laverty argues that oil and coal plants are more detrimental to air quality and the environment. Thus, she believes the passage of the Price-Anderson Act and defeat of the Emergency Planning Amendment in 1987 were very important.

Mark M. MacCarthy
Professional Staff Member
2125 Rayburn House Office Bldg.
225-2927

Expertise: Telecommunications

John Dingell is one of the most influential Members of Congress in the late 1980s, involved in a wide range of issues through his chairmanship of Energy and Commerce. Dingell is known for attracting able staff. One of them is Mark MacCarthy, a New York City native and a former government economist who follows telecommunications issues for the Michigan Democrat. He has worked for Dingell since he assumed the chairmanship in 1981.

"He's Dingell's eyes and ears on telecommunications," says a fellow staffer. "He runs the gamut of issues in that area and is an extremely important player on any of them."

MacCarthy serves as Dingell's and the committee's chief adviser for the wide-ranging field of telecommunications, which includes questions about the Fairness Doctrine, the role of the Federal Communications Commission, the breakup of AT&T and phone rates in general, and the growth of information services and other technological advances.

MacCarthy in 1987 worked on one of Dingell's foremost objectives, a bill to incorporate the Fairness Doctrine into law after the FCC repealed it. The legislation passed the House but eventually was deleted from the 1988 Continuing Resolution when the President threatened a veto if the provision as included.

Personal: born 3/9/48 in New York City. B.A. (cum laude), Fordham University, 1969, Phi Beta Kappa. M.A., Indiana University, 1974. Ph. D., Indiana University, 1975. M.A., University of Notre Dame, 1978. 1976-78, assistant professor, University of Notre Dame. 1978-81, economist, Occupational Safety and Health Administration, U.S. Department of Labor. 1981-present, Committee on Energy and Commerce.

MacCarthy is involved in legislation that would change the way AT&T and the local Bell companies are regulated, with an eye toward adjusting their rates, prices and marketing practices in an effort to make them more efficient. He also is working on a bill under which all telephones should be compatible with hearing-aid equipment.

The committee is looking at proposed access charges that the FCC wants to impose on heavy phone-using firms, such as information-service companies, which may damage their ability to be competitive. "Members of both parties are expressing concern over this, and Mark is examining the issue," says a Republican staffer.

Like other top committee aides, MacCarthy enjoys a close working relationship with Dingell. In 1984, he co-authored with the chairman and Timothy E. Nulty, an article on AT&T policies, titled ". . . on a Free Ride for AT&T?" in *Challenge* magazine.

And he is careful not to get out ahead of the chairman on an issue. "If Dingell doesn't want something to go through, it doesn't go through," says the Republican staffer. "Mark reflects what the chairman is thinking and what he wants."

Energy and Commerce

Karen Nelson
Staff Director
Subcommittee on Health and the
  Environment
2424 Rayburn House Office Bldg.
225-0130

Expertise: Medicaid, health programs

Where in the Congress would one find the institutional memory for the health programs initiated in the Great Society years? One of those places is the House Energy and Commerce's Subcommittee on Health and the Environment, chaired by Rep. Henry Waxman (D-CA). Waxman has proven to be a dynamic chairman who has resisted the Reagan Administration's efforts both to cut these programs as well as to underfund new needs such as AIDS research.

Waxman's staff director, Karen Nelson, is the epitome of the Hill committee staffer who has mastered her field in a way few on personal Congressional staffs or in the private sector ever do. In Nelson's case more than a decade of involvement in Congressional health policymaking is the reason.

The Illinois native received her education at the University of Illinois and Harvard before coming to Washington to work at the predecessor agency of the Health Care Financing Administration within what was then the Department of Health, Education and Welfare. Next she moved to the Senate Finance Committee in the mid 1970's where she handled health issues before coming to the House Energy and Commerce Committee in 1976 under then chairman of the health subcommittee, Rep. Paul Rogers (D-FL).

Nelson has dealt with a wide range of issues over the years but Medicaid has been one of the programs on which she has focused the most attention. One senior level official at HHS recently remarked "Karen Nelson knows more about Medicaid than anyone else in Washington."

As the staff director for Waxman's active subcommittee and its large and highly respected staff, Nelson oversees almost a score of professionals, each pursuing critical health issues, ranging from AIDS to Medicare to vaccines to laboratory standards to Clean Air. One observer of the subcommittee commented, "they may hold more hearings than any other subcommittee on the Hill."

Nelson, with her low profile and years of substantive involvement, seems to be the ideal staff director for this very active subcommittee and its high profile issues.

Nelson is an avid fan of the National Basketball Association's Washington Bullets and when the House is not in late session can frequently be found courtside at the Capital Centre.

John A. Riggs
Staff Director
Subcommittee on Energy and
Power
331 House Office Bldg. Annex 2
226-2500

Expertise: Energy

When it comes to issues of policy in the Subcommittee on Energy and Power, Jack Riggs is a key decision maker. Riggs's long and quasi-familial relationship with Subcommittee Chairman Sharp (D-IN) ensures he almost always knows where Sharp will stand on an issue before he presents it to the Congressman.

He and Representative Sharp "think alike," says Riggs, and work closely with each other. The two first met when they interned together on Capitol Hill in the early 1960s, and later Riggs managed Sharp's successful 1974 campaign.

With a history and public administration educational background, Riggs is the first to tell you he is not an energy "expert." But he knows the subject very well after six years of work as Staff Director. The Subcommittee staff does most all of the detailed energy work while Riggs oversees a broader range of policy and administrative questions.

Riggs has a moderate and pragmatic philosophy on energy policy, believing the country may soon face an energy problem if energy needs are not addressed. The ideal solutions, he feels, must be low cost, environmentally safe, and non-intrusive in order to pass political muster. Major areas in which Riggs has been involved include a 1983 bill to decontrol prices of specific categories of natural gas; an effort to give the President emergency authority to allocate oil supplies, which was opposed by the Reagan Administration; efforts to oversee and eventually abolish the Synthetic Fuels corporation; and a proposal to encourage the use of alternative transportation fuels.

According to his colleagues, Riggs is cautious, and looks at the issues thoroughly before making a move. He is neither flashy nor overly concerned with getting credit for legislative successes.

Literature and history are Riggs' favorite subjects for reading, which he does often in his spare time. He also spends time as a Scout leader with his son.

Personal: born 2/19/43 in Chicago, Illinois. B.A. Swarthmore Coll., 1964. M.P.A. Princeton Univ., 1966. 1966-1972, U.S. Agency for International Development, Vietnam and Brazil. 1972-1974 campaign aide/manager for two congressional campaigns of Philip R. Sharp (D-IN). 1975-1980, Administrative Assistant, Rep. Philip R. Sharp. 1981 to present, Staff Director, Subcommittee on Energy and Power, Committee on Energy and Commerce.

Ellen Riker
Minority Staff Associate
Subcommittee on Health and
  Environment
564 House Office Bldg. Annex 2
226-3400

Personal: born 2/17/57 in Columbus,
Ohio. B.A. Univ.of Cincinnati, 1980.
M.H.A., Xavier Univ.,1982. 1977-1979,
administrative intern, Saint Anthony
Hospital, Columbus, OH. 1980-1981,
management engineer, The Jewish
Hospital, Cincinnati. 1981-1982,
administrative resident, Bethesda
Hospital and Deaconess Association,
Cincinnati. 1983-present, Professional
Staff, Committee on Energy and
Commerce.

Expertise: Health, budget

Given her background, it is not surprising that Ellen Riker works almost exclusively with the Health and Environment Subcommittee and closely with its ranking minority member, Rep. Edward R. Madigan (R-IL). Riker and Mary McGrane, a committee counsel, team up to cover health issues for the Republican side.

Riker is responsible for a comprehensive array of public health issues. This includes researching issues, drafting important health care legislation and amendments, building strategies for passage in the House, and helping guide legislation from House-Senate conference committee to the President's desk for signature.

While Riker does not feel tied to one specific piece of legislation, she is recognized as the staffer responsible for the establishment of the nursing research center at the National Institutes of Health.

During her five years on the committee, she has made contributions to many public health service programs, the reauthorization of the National Institutes of Health, AIDS legislation, and the Nurse Training Act. Most recently, Riker was actively involved in fashioning the Republican substitute to the catastrophic health care bill.

Versatility in the arena of health policy is Riker's asset. She handles a heavy and varied workload, which she attributes in large part to Subcommittee Chairman Henry A. Waxman (D-CA). Riker feels that Representative Waxman maintains one of the most aggressive health agendas in the House of Representatives.

Riker is also aided in her work by her extensive experience and study of the health care field. She not only served in the administration of several hospitals, but also coauthored "Striking a Balance Between Competition and Regulation" in the May, 1986 edition of *Frontiers of Health Services Management.*

Riker has, in addition, delved into budget matters within the jurisdiction of the full Energy and Commerce Committee. This year she was heavily involved in preparing the Republican alternative budget, which included policy decisions for railroads and utilities, among other areas.

William J. Roberts
Counsel
Subcommittee on Commerce,
  Consumer Protection &
  Competitiveness
151 House Office Bldg. Annex 2
226-3160

Expertise: Product liability, hazardous & solid waste

Bill Roberts has held his current position as Counsel for the Subcommittee on Commerce, Consumer Protection & Competitiveness since 1985. When Subcommittee Chairman James J. Florio of New Jersey hired Roberts during the 99th Congress, the panel was known as the Subcommittee on Commerce, Transportation, and Tourism. The subcommittee oversees the Consumer Product Safety Commission and deals extensively with product liability, product safety, trade and insurance issues. Roberts, a versatile professional with legal and political experience, is articulate, knowledgeable and able to communicate complex ideas in an easily understood manner.

During the 99th Congress, Roberts devoted his time to legislation reauthorizing the "Superfund" hazardous waste clean-up program administered by the Environmental Protection Agency (EPA). Roberts focused on Title III of the legislation, the community right-to-know provisions. The right-to-know title requires those handling hazardous substances to notify the EPA and affected communities of the amount and type of toxic chemicals being released into the environment. Florio has a pro-consumer reputation, reflected in the work of his staff.

The reorganization of the Committee after the 99th Congress required Roberts to become involved with new issues. Product liability legislation now occupies much of his time. He worked extensively on the Uniform Product Safety Act of 1987 (HR 1115), the primary House bill dealing with product liability tort reform.

Personal: born 7/10/56 in Detroit, Michigan. B.A. (magna cum laude) and M.A. (with honors) in economics, Yale Univ., 1978. J.D. Univ. of Chicago Law School, 1981. 1981-83, attorney, Appellate Section, Antitrust Division, Dept. of Justice. 1983-85, Director of Special Projects, Democratic Senatorial Campaign Committee. 1985-present, Counsel, House Energy and Commerce Subcommittee on Commerce, Consumer Protection & Competitiveness.

Roberts likes to see what he calls a "creative" approach to addressing issues before the Subcommittee. Instead of relying solely on legislation and regulation which mandate a response to health and safety concerns, he supports efforts to provide economic and legal incentives for manufacturers to provide safe products and adopt safe practices. He cites the right-to-know title of the Superfund legislation as an example of "creative" legislation. This title provides incentives for companies to control dumping and emissions of toxic chemicals by bringing community pressure to bear, instead of imposing direct federal regulation.

Tom S. Runge
Counsel
Subcommittee on Energy and
    Power
131 House Office Bldg. Annex 2
226-2500

*Personal: born 8/7/45 in Sioux City, IA.
B.A. Univ. of Pennsylvania, 1967. J.D.
Univ. of Michigan Law School, 1973.
1974-1975, Assistant Editor, Antitrust
and Trade Regulation Report, Bureau
of National Affairs, Washington, D.C.
1975-1979, Counsel, House Judiciary
Subcommittee on Monopolies and
Commercial Law. 1979-1980, Deputy
Assistant General Counsel for
Legislation, Federal Energy
Regulatory Commission. 1980-1981,
Executive Assistant to the Chairman,
Supervisory Attorney, Federal Energy
Regulatory Commission. 1981-
present, Counsel, House Energy and
Commerce Subcommittee on Energy
and Power.*

Expertise: Energy policy, Federal Energy Regulatory Commission

Tom Runge first came to Capitol Hill as a counsel to the House
Judiciary Subcommittee on Monopolies and Commercial Law in
1975. The Subcommittee needed his legal skills to help with a
spate of antitrust legislation moving through Congress in the mid-
1970s. Hired by Chairman Peter Rodino of New Jersey, Runge
was responsible for the Subcommittee's antitrust legislation in the
94th and 95th Congresses and worked extensively on the Hart-
Scott-Rodino Act, a multifaceted piece of antitrust legislation.

Runge began building his expertise in energy policy when he left
Capitol Hill in April 1979 to work at the Federal Energy Regulatory
Commission (FERC). He joined FERC as a Deputy Assistant
General Counsel for Legislation, a position in which he developed
an extensive knowledge of legislation affecting FERC and rate
making in the electric utility, hydroelectric, petroleum and natural
gas industries. Later at FERC, Runge served as Assistant to the
Chairman in 1980.

Returning to Capitol Hill at the end of the Carter Administration,
Runge joined the Subcommittee on Fossil and Synthetic Fuels,
headed by Rep. Philip R. Sharp of Indiana. The panel
subsequently changed its name to the Subcommittee on Energy
and Power. The subcommittee oversees FERC and deals with oil,
gas, electric and nuclear energy policy. Runge's particular focus is
on policies affecting the oil, and natural gas industries. He is
responsible for issues such as import fees, energy taxes, gas
pipeline and gas producer regulation, energy trade, oil marketing
and pipeline regulation, energy mergers, Alaskan oil, and energy
security generally.

The Subcommittee's work on oil and gas issues is highly technical
in nature, affecting individual companies more than shaping large-
scale energy policy. Runge employs his legal background and
energy expertise to help oversee the myriad of regulations
governing the oil and natural gas industries and keep track of
energy bills before various House committees, such as Interior
and Appropriations. Alaskan oil leasing and the development of
"synfuels" and other alternate sources of energy also fall within
Runge's realm.

Another issue likely to command Runge's attention in the 100th
Congress and beyond is the Free Trade Agreement reached
between Canada and the United States, which Runge will monitor
due to the agreement's implications for the oil and gas industries.
Canada is this nation's primary supplier of oil and natural gas.
Runge will also be involved with the Alaskan oil provisions
contained in the massive Omnibus Trade Bill (HR3) as that
legislation moves through conference.

Lawrence E. Sabbath
Majority Staff Director
Subcommittee on Transportation,
   Tourism and Hazardous
   Materials
324 House Office Bldg. Annex 2
225-9304

Personal: born 3/7/48 in Washington, D.C. B.A. Univ. of Maryland, 1971. M.A. Univ. of Nevada, 1973. 1971-1973, teaching assistant, Univ.of Nevada. 1973-1975, instructor in political science, Clark County Community Coll., Nevada. 1975-1982, Rep. James Santini (D-NV). 1982-1983, Congressional Travel and Tourism Caucus. 1983-1985, Subcommittee on Antitrust and Restraint of Trade Activities Affecting Small Business. 1985-1987, Subcommittee on Tax, Access to Equity Capital, and Business Opportunities. 1987-present, Subcommittee on Transportation, Tourism and Hazardous Materials.

Expertise: Environment, energy, tourism

When the recently formed Subcommittee on Transportation, Tourism and Hazardous Materials needed a staff director to organize the agenda and staff for the new committee, Chairman Luken called on Larry Sabbath. Considered an expert in the areas of environment, energy and tourism issues, Sabbath found his new duties were to set strategies for the legislative program of this subcommittee which has jurisdiction over railroad legislation, hazardous waste materials and the Federal Trade Commission.

Noteworthy among the many pieces of legislation on which Sabbath has played a major role over the past eight years on Capitol Hill are the National Tourism Policy Act of 1980; the Resource Conservation Recovery Act of 1980; the Clean Air Act and National Energy Policy Act during the Carter Administration.

Through his work as Staff Director of the Subcommittee on Tax, Access to Equity Capital, and Business Opportunities, where he served from 1985-1987, he organized hearings for the Small Business Subcommittee, including hearings on the Tax Reform Act of 1986. He served as Staff Director of the Subcommittee on Antitrust and Restraint of Trade Activities Affecting Small Business from 1983-1985, where he organized its oversight hearings.

As a result of his work on tourism legislation while serving as Legislative Assistant to Congressman James Santini, Sabbath was appointed Executive Director of the Congressional Travel and Tourism Caucus from 1982-1983. He is widely known for his expertise in tourism policy.

While working on his Masters Degree in Political Science at the Univ. of Nevada, Sabbath taught American Government and Political Science at the university and later at Clark County Community Coll. He subsequently became involved in local Nevada politics, serving as staff member on several state and local races for Democratic candidates, which led him to become involved in the campaign of Rep. Jim Santini. He was appointed District Office Manager by the Congressman and eventually moved back to Washington, D.C. to serve as his Legislative Assistant.

Now living in Fairfax, Virginia, with his wife and two small children, Sabbath spends his free time pursuing family-oriented activities.

Michael S. Scrivner
Administrative Assistant
Representative Norman Lent (R-
  NY)
2408 Rayburn House Office Bldg.
225-7896

"There is a lot of competition among Members to gain a seat on the Energy and Commerce Committee. A member doesn't get on the Committee and get put up on a shelf. Things very frequently live or die by a very close vote. Everyone counts," says Mike Scrivner, Administrative Assistant to Congressman Norman Lent (R-NY). Lent became the Ranking Minority member of the House Energy and Commerce Committee in 1986 when Congressmen Broyhill (R-NC) was appointed to the Senate. Lent is also the Ranking Minority Member of the House Committee on Merchant Marine and Fisheries.

Scrivner, a soft-spoken native of Tennessee who joined Lent's staff as Legislative Director in 1981 and moved up to Chief of Staff in 1985, is more involved in the political aspects of his job than the substance of the issues themselves.

"I may come to regret this some day when I go to look for a job in the private sector, but I can't profess expertise in any one issue" says Scrivner.

But Scrivner admits he knows the Hill. And he is more involved in issues that have an impact on the state of New York (such as the Markey Amendment on nuclear power plant emergency evacuation).

"New Yorkers are concerned about clean air, acid rain and the environment, in general. They want us to look into what happened on Black Monday. These also happen to be two of the most important issues before the Energy and Commerce Committee," explains Scrivner.

Personal: born 10/18/54 in Knoxville, Tennessee. B.A. Univ.of Tennessee, 1976. Master of Public Administration, Univ. of Tennessee, 1978. 1978, Press Secretary and 1978-1981, Legislative Assistant, Rep. John Duncan (R-TN). 1981-1985, Legislative Director; 1985-present, Administrative Assistant to Rep. Norman Lent (R-NY).

With a solid block of 17 Republicans willing to take advantage of the splits between some very liberal subcommittee chairmen and a more moderate Chairman John Dingell, Scrivner delights in keeping up-to-speed on every issue and every angle.

"Lent is a consensus-builder and he is interested in exploiting the disharmony that exists on the other side. That kind of thing really interests me," says Scrivner.

"The staff is put in a position of referee. We play a broker's role. There is not a lot of red tape. We have to play loose and fast, stay vigilant and informed so our members can stay on top of the issues."

Scrivner, who works in close cooperation with a Committee staff that is "outmanned 6 or 7 to 1", is not shy of playing hardball when necessary. "Power breeds arrogance—we have to keep that in check. Our people are very good."

W. Edward (Ed) Senn
Legislative Director
Congressman Tom Tauke
2244 Rayburn
225-2911

Personal: born 12/12/56 in Rock Hill, South Carolina. B.A. Grinnell College, 1979. 1979-80, Unit Coordinator, Medical Intensive Care and Coronary Care Units, University Hospital, Boston, MA. 1979-80, Field Coordinator, National Unity Campaign for John Anderson, 1981-present, staff, Rep. Tom Tauke (R-IA).

Expertise: Telecommunications, energy, environment

W. Edward Senn came to Washington in 1981 with the idea of working for a Member from Iowa, because of his undergraduate work in biology at Grinnell College. But the only experience he had was one year of work at a Boston hospital and a volunteer job on John Anderson's ill-fated presidential campaign.

"It was a Cinderella beginning," he admits. "A legislative position was open in Congressman Tom Tauke's office, and his people were trying to get in touch with their first choice for the job. That person wasn't home, but I was there, and they offered it to me." Senn has worked for the moderate Iowa Republican for seven years and now serves as his Legislative Director.

Senn thought Washington would be "more rewarding and challenging" than the job he left in Boston, and his hunch has proven true. A major portion of Tauke's agenda centers on his activities as a member of the Energy and Commerce Committee, and Senn acts as principal advisor to Tauke on all telecommunications, energy and environmental issues. Senn shares Tauke's interest in these issues and is all the more active because of his boss's role as a moderate swing vote on the all-important Committee.

For example, on the controversial acid rain issue, Senn is quick to point out that Tauke worked with California Democrat Henry Waxman in the 99th Congress, to craft a compromise measure—the only major piece of acid rain legislation ever to make it out of a House subcommittee. "It was a moderate compromise which achieved significant reductions," says Senn.

While Tauke does not serve on the Budget Committee, last year Senn helped him spearhead a campaign with Rep. Tim Penny (D-MN) to push for reductions in House appropriations bills. "We called it the Tauke-Penny Appropriations Task Force, but some people likened our group to a *Meat Ax Budget Coalition*." The group tried to reduce total appropriations by $8 billion by suggesting less expensive program increases, but the coalition had limited success.

Senn also supervises Tauke's legislative staff and prepares speeches and floor statements for him.

"When I'm not working, I spend most of my time at the squash club," he says of his off hours. "It's a great release and helps to keep things in perspective."

Lawrence Sidman
Chief Counsel and Staff Director
Subcommittee on
  Telecommunications and
  Finance
316 House Office Bldg. Annex 2
226-2424

*Personal: born 9/25/48. B.A. Amherst
Coll. 1970 (magna cum laude, Phi
Beta Kappa). J.D. Boston Coll. Law
School 1973 (magna cum laude,
Order of the Coif, Law Review Editor).
1973-1974, law clerk to the Honorable
Christopher Armstrong,
Massachusetts Appeals Court. 1974-
1985, Associate and then Partner at
the firm of Fried, Frank, Harris, Shriver
and Kampelman. 1985-1986, Chief
Counsel and Staff Director,
Subcommittee on Energy
Conservation and Power. 1987-
present, Chief Counsel and Staff
Director, Subcommittee on
Telecommunications and Finance,
Committee on Energy and Commerce.*

Expertise: Litigation and administrative law

When Lawrence Sidman, Chief Counsel and Staff Director for the
Telecommunications and Finance Subcommittee, gets together
with his boss, Rep. Edward Markey (D-MA), Chairman of the
Subcommittee, it's as much a reunion as a meeting. Sidman
(Class of 1973) and Markey (Class of 1972) attended Boston
College Law School and were colleagues on the law review.
"Markey and Sidman go back a long way, and they have a very
close relationship," says a subcommittee staff member. "Larry
finds it very easy to reflect what Markey is thinking or doing on a
particular issue."

Sidman's subcommittee has jurisdiction over a wide range of
finance issues such as takeovers, insider trading, and oversight of
the securities markets generally and the Securities and Exchange
Commission; and telecommunications issues such as the Fairness
Doctrine, children's television, cable television, and the structure
and regulation of the telephone industry.

"It's real hot stuff, with a lot of money involved," says a former
subcommittee staff member. "It's exciting and challenging, but at
the same time it puts a lot of pressure on Larry."

In particular, the stock market plunge last October has brought
calls in Washington for changes in securities laws and regulation.
With the subcommittee's oversight authority on the SEC and on
the financial markets in general, the subcommittee is right in the
middle.

If Markey introduces legislation regarding the financial markets,
Sidman will play a key role, a subcommittee staff member says.
"There are a lot of ideas floating around now," he says. "Larry will
have a hand in developing any legislation."

Legislation moved by the Subcommittee and passed by the House
during the first session of the 100th Congress included several
long-overdue authorization bills for the Securities and Exchange
Commission, the Federal Communications Commission and the
National Telecommunications Information Administration.

The Subcommittee also passed legislation to codify the Fairness
Doctrine, which was repealed by the FCC in August, 1987.
Though passed overwhelmingly in both Houses of the Congress, it
was vetoed by President Reagan. An attempt to attach identical
language as an amendment to the Continuing Resolution was
ultimately unsuccessful.

In the first session of the 100th Congress, the subcommittee did
not rush to pass legislation dealing with a number of the extremely

complex securities issues such as tender offer reform. Markey and Sidman believed caution was in order because of the profound impact which legislation in this area could have on the nation's financial markets and on the economy in general. Instead, the subcommittee sought to lay the foundation for major legislative initiatives in 1988 through a series of hearings on takeovers, program trading, and globalization of the financial markets.

Other issues of prime interest and importance to Sidman include reinstating commercial guidelines for children's television, which also were repealed by the FCC under the Reagan Administration; and the development of the new technology of high-definition television, which greatly enhances the audio and visual qualities of television.

A former litigator, Sidman has surrounded himself with a high-powered staff with wide-ranging expertise since taking his post with the subcommittee. These include Larry Irving, former A.A. and Legislative Director for Rep. Mickey Leland (D-TX), who handles mass media issues; Gerard Salemme, formerly with U.S. Sprint and a longtime Markey aide, handling common carrier and other telecommunications issues; and Edward Leahy, formerly a partner with the Washington office of the firm of Steptoe and Johnson, handling the subcommittee's securities jurisdiction. "Larry employees a corporate style of leadership, setting general guidelines and delegating authority very well," says a former subcommittee staffer. "But everything comes through him."

Sidman, who left a lucrative partnership in a D.C. law firm to serve as the Chief Counsel and Staff Director for the subcommittee on Energy Conservation and Power, chaired by Markey from 1985 to 1986, played a key role in the successful passage of a number of important legislative initiatives during the 99th Congress. These included appliance efficiency standards legislation, amendments to the Low-Level Nuclear Waster Disposal Act, Low-Income Home Energy Assistance Reauthorization, Hydroelectric Licensing Reform, and the extension of Daylight Saving Time. All of these measures reflected compromises and passed largely on a consensus basis. That is Sidman's preferred way of dealing with controversial issues.

A native of Newton, Massachusetts, Sidman remains in close touch with the Boston area and spends as much time as possible with his wife, Hilda, and young son and daughter. He enjoys tennis and golf and lives in suburban Bethesda, Maryland

Paul C. Smith
Republican Chief Counsel
Staff Director
2322 Rayburn House Office Bldg.
225-3641

Expertise: Communications, legislative procedure

A sixteen-year veteran of the Hill, Paul Smith draws on that experience to help Republicans on the Energy and Commerce Committee tackle controversial and complex issues. Smith, as Republican Chief Counsel and Staff Director for the committee, has general legal and staff responsibility over twenty-three professional and support staff serving the Republican Members of the full committee and each of its six subcommittees.

Like many of his colleagues, Smith was trained as an attorney but never actually practiced law. He was recruited directly out of law school by the House Legislative Counsel's office in 1972. He worked there as an associate counsel for thirteen years, most of those on Energy and Commerce issues.

"Working on the Hill is less visible than having a law practice, but I felt the process was more fascinating," he says of his early years as Legislative Counsel, where he analyzed and drafted numerous bills. Some of the measures he has helped shape include the District's home rule bill, civil service reform, the 1976 tax reform bill, the Natural Gas Policy Act and a host of communications bills, including cable TV, AT&T divestiture and the ill-fated broadcasting reform bill.

Personal: born 2/6/44 in Schenectady, New York. B.A. Calif. State Univ., Long Beach, 1966. J.D. Univ. of Southern California, 1972. 1967-1968, Teacher, California School System. 1968-1969, Plant Manager, Celetron Corporation, San Fernando, CA. 1972-1985, Assistant Counsel, Office of the Legislative Counsel, U.S. House of Representatives. 1985-1987, Associate Minority Counsel, Committee on Energy and Commerce. 1987 to present, Republican Chief Counsel and Staff Director, Committee on Energy and Commerce.

In 1976 he began working exclusively on Energy and Commerce issues, helping to guide the committee staff through what often were thorny legal and constitutional issues. Then, in 1985, he joined the Energy and Commerce staff as Associate Minority Counsel and was responsible for common carrier and broadcast issues before the Subcommittee on Telecommunications, Consumer Protection and Finance.

Smith is also an associate professor of law at George Washington University, where he teaches an advanced course on the legislative process and legislative drafting. He has lectured at the Harvard orientation program for new Members of Congress and at American University.

According to Smith, the Committee has a full agenda in this final session of the 100th Congress. On its plate are clean air and acid rain legislation, product liability, trade reform, rail safety, as well as a thorough investigation of insider trading and the October 19 market collapse.

Active in local affairs, Smith has been chairman of the Law Enforcement Committee and a member of the Traffic Committee of the Town of Chevy Chase, MD. He has also served on the board of deacons of his church. Smith likes to sail and ski. He also restores old automobiles, his most recent challenge being a 1913 Maxwell.

Russell L. Smith
Minority Counsel
2322 Rayburn House Office Bldg.
225-3641

Personal: born 9/9/46 in Atlanta, Georgia. B.A. Vanderbilt Univ., 1968. J.D. (cum laude) Univ. of Georgia School of Law, 1972. 1972-1976, Attorney-Advisor, Office of the General Counsel, Department of Treasury. 1976, Federal Agency Liaison, Consolidated Rail Corporation (Conrail). 1976-1982, Washington Counsel (previously Associate General Counsel), Consolidated Rail corporation. 1982-1984, Special Advisor then Director of the Office of Automotive Industry Affairs, U.S. Department of Commerce. 1984 to present, Minority Counsel, Committee on Energy and Commerce.

Expertise: Law, research, rail and labor legislation

When House Republicans need answers to legal questions on defense contracting, nuclear weapons security and general oversight and investigations, they turn to Russell Smith.

Smith has provided Republican staffs with legal advice and assistance since 1984, when he became Minority Counsel for the Energy and Commerce Committee. He helps draft bills, legislative reports and committee statements on issues before the Subcommittee on Oversight and Investigations.

Smith has had considerable agency experience, serving stints not only at the Commerce Department but also at Treasury and the Consolidated Rail Corporation (Conrail). In fact, it was at the Commerce Department, while researching automobile issues, that he began working with the Energy and Commerce Committee staff. That led to his leaving the Commerce Department in 1984 for his current committee position.

Smith likes his duties on the Committee-especially his investigative responsibilities—better than some of the bureaucratic chores he handled while working in the executive branch. He recalls with amusement working on President Nixon's wage and price controls while at the Treasury Department. "We developed an entire bureaucracy that was massive and complex. I remember one year being involved in a big debate over whether we would allow an increase in the price of Christmas trees. We were micro-managing the economy—not the wisest thing in the world to do."

His transition to the Hill appears to have been a smooth one, and during the last two Congresses, Smith has proven himself in several areas. His work on unfair and illegal trade practices, for example, led to the preparation and adoption of the Trade Law Modernization Act. He also helped draft legislation enabling the federal government to sell Conrail.

His investigative assignments have ranged from the case of Michael Deaver to the problems associated with prescription drug diversion, which led to the Prescription Drug Marketing Act of 1986. Currently he is looking into the issue of insider trading as well as the October 19 market crash.

A notoriously hard worker, Smith carried the ball at the staff level for the Reagan Administration's opposition to further regulation of the automobile industry. For his work he received a U.S. Department of Commerce Meritorious Service Award in 1983.

Energy and Commerce

Consuela M. Washington
Counsel
2125 Rayburn House Office Bldg.
225-2927

Expertise: Stock market, financial issues, SEC

Like her boss, Committee Chairman John Dingell (D-MI), Consuela Washington is a shrewd and tough negotiator. Washington, a Harvard Law School graduate who spent several years in corporate law and at the Securities and Exchange Commission, came to the old Interstate and Foreign Commerce Committee in 1979. When Dingell assumed the chairmanship of the renamed Energy and Commerce Committee in 1981 from the retiring Harley Staggers, Washington stayed on board. She is now one of five counsels under the current staff director, William Kitzmiller (and is one of the most prominent black women on a congressional staff).

A Senate staffer who has worked with her called Washington "very sharp and very tough. She's a hard bargainer."

"She represents Dingell's interests very well," says a fellow staffer. "She knows a lot of what goes on and keeps him informed." A former staffer agrees, saying, "Consuela is very close to Dingell and has his ear."

In a recent profile, *The American Banker* said Washington is "little known, but much feared by bankers," because of John Dingell's "reluctance" to allow banks to enter the areas of insurance and securities.

Personal: born 9/30/48 in Chicago, IL. B.A. Upper Iowa Univ., 1970. J.D. Harvard Law School, 1973. 1970-1971, law clerk, Massachusetts Law Reform Institute; 1973-1974, associate, Kirkland & Ellis; 1975, counsel, corporate law department, Allis-Chalmers Corp.; 1976-1979, special counsel, attorney adviser in Office of Chief Counsel, Division of Corporate Finance, Securities and Exchange Commission; 1979-1981, staff member on Committee on Interstate and Foreign Commerce. 1981 to present, Counsel, Committee on Energy and Commerce.

Washington often worked on the Federal Trade Commission and related issues in the early and mid-1980s. During this time she also played an important role in legislation, authorization of appropriations and oversight of the Securities and Exchange Commission and the Consumer Product Safety Commission. More recently she has worked on the Committee's parts of the 1987 House Omnibus Trade Bill.

Noting her efforts on the FTC reauthorization bill in 1985 and 1986, an FTC staffer said that Washington "did a lot of hard work, and she really knew the issues. She was very impressive." The bill eventually died in conference.

These days, Washington spends a good deal of time monitoring the SEC, for which she once worked, and working on issues such as tender offer reform, insider trading, and stock market policies.

Ever vigilant over the Committee's turf, Washington refers to one of her major responsibilities as "jurisdictional patrol" over issues relating to the Commodity Futures Trading Commission and stock index futures; Farm Credit Bill referral and the Agriculture Committee; and Glass-Steagall issues and the Banking Committee. Her work in these areas has taken her away from FTC issues.

This has required Washington to work more closely with the Oversight and Investigations subcommittee, a focal point on financial issues, which Dingell also chairs. The Subcommittee, under staff director Mike Barrett, tends to focus on high profile probes, such as one into the Ivan Boesky affair, while Washington plays more of a role in legislative initiatives.

"The O&I subcommittee is heavily involved in those issues, and they like to take the lead," says a former staffer. "But her views are definitely respected."

In June, 1987, she was elected by members of the Harvard Alumni Association to serve a six-year term on the Harvard Board of Overseers. Washington received 12,635 votes. Away from the office, Washington enjoys music, theater, reading, writing and running.

Timothy Westmoreland
Counsel
Subcommittee on Health and the
  Environment
2415 Rayburn House Office Bldg.
225-4952

Expertise: Public health

Tim Westmoreland has become the leading Congressional staff expert on AIDS as the epidemic has demanded more attention and funding from the Congress over the past six years.

Westmoreland came to the subcommittee in 1979 out of Yale Law School and initially split his time between entitlement programs and public health; however he soon was devoting most his efforts to public health issues. In 1980 Westmoreland was involved in the consideration and passage of the Mental Health Systems Act, legislation in which Rosalynn Carter was deeply interested. In 1981 he helped chairman Henry Waxman and the subcommittee hold the line against the Reagan administration's attempts to consolidate numerous federal programs into block grants.

In 1982 Westmoreland staffed the subcommittee's first hearing on AIDS. At the time there were three hundred reported cases in the U.S. In the spring of 1988 the subcommittee held its twenty first hearing on the AIDS epidemic. By then Westmoreland's name was known to virtually all of the leading national players in AIDS policy and research.

In 1987 Westmoreland was involved in the Vaccine Liability and Copyright legislation, which created a trust fund for victims of vaccine mishaps, funded by an excise tax on the vaccines. He also handles family planning issues for Waxman, including the controversial "squeal rule" proposed by the Reagan administration.

Personal: B.A. Duke Univ. 1976. J.D. Yale Univ. 1979-present, Counsel, House Energy and Commerce Committee Subcommittee on Health and the Environment.

For the last six of his nine years with the Subcommittee on Health and the Environment, Tim Westmoreland has had the unique Congressional staff experience of daily leading the charge in a life-or-death struggle against the mushrooming AIDS epidemic. It would seem anything else he does in his professional career will be anticlimatic.

Denise Wilson
Legislative Director
2264 Rayburn House Office Bldg.
225-5006

Expertise: Telecommunications, broadcasting, finance

Denise Wilson came to the office of Rep. Cardiss Collins (D-IL) through a very ordinary channel: the House Placement Office. That was seven years ago, and since then Wilson has gained Collins's confidence and is now in charge of the Congresswoman's legislative staff.

Wilson works on issues that are a priority for Collins through her assignment on the Subcommittee on Telecommunications and Finance. She spearheads Collins's efforts toward equal employment in the communications industry, and is currently active with Collins's bill H.R. 1090, The Diversity in Media Ownership Act of 1987. Collins also introduced similar legislation in the 98th and 99th Congresses. Wilson is well versed in minority business ownership issues, and in fact, manned the field hearings in Chicago for the 99th Congress version of H.R. 1090. The legislation was broadened in 1987 to account for changes in the marketplace and new regulations.

Wilson has recently been working more closely on finance issues, especially those dealing with mergers and hostile takeovers.

Personal: born 12/9/54 in Washington, D.C. B.A. Howard Univ., 1977. 1977-1978, staff assistant, Reps. William Clay (D-MO), Jack Brooks (D-TX),and Herman Badillo (D-NY). 1978-1980, assistant marketing representative in data processing division, IBM. 1980-present, legislative assistant and legislative director, Rep. Cardiss Collins (D-IL).

Wilson takes time off from these matters by gardening and tending to her T-shirt and matchbook collections. She boasts over 400 T-shirts and over 1179 matchbooks from across the country. She uses the matchbooks as an occasional reference tool. Faced with a colleague or constituent planning on travel, she can give directions to the best restaurants in almost any town, U.S.A.

Energy and Commerce

Michael Woo
Professional Staff Member
2125 Rayburn House Office Bldg.
225-2927

Expertise: Energy

Michael Woo started his career on Capitol Hill as an intern on the Energy and Power Subcommittee in 1977, which was then under the leadership of Chairman John Dingell (D-MI). Woo began working for the Subcommittee full-time in 1978, and when Dingell became chairman of the Energy and Commerce Committee in 1981, Woo followed him and joined the staff of the full committee.

In his early days with the Committee, Woo concentrated on analyzing the economic impact of various energy-related initiatives, such as oil deregulation or the installation of the Alaskan natural gas transportation system. His responsibilities have since become more policy-oriented. He works chiefly with the Subcommittee on Energy and Power, but is also called upon to help other subcommittees under Energy and Commerce. He was involved with the sale of Conrail, and is active with aspects of the U.S.-Canada free trade agreement, and securities issues.

Woo has a long and stable history with the Energy and Commerce Committee, has worked for years on energy issues, and is now called upon to work on almost any legislation assigned to Energy and Commerce that would affect economic regulation within the context of the committee. He works hard and has a solid knowledge of his field. He is a devoted congressional employee and a strong player on energy-related issues.

Personal: born 5/7/53 in San Francisco, California. B.S. Univ. of California,Berkeley, 1975. M.A. Univ. of Chicago, 1977. M.S. Univ. of Chicago, 1978. 1978-1981, Staff Member, Subcommittee on Energy and Power. 1981 to present, Professional Staff Member, Committee on Energy and Commerce.

Emily Elizabeth Young
Legislative Director
Rep. Billy Tauzin (D-LA)
222 Cannon House Bldg.
225-4031

Expertise: Energy, environment, transportation, telecommunications, finance, health

Politically, Louisiana is one of the most colorful states in the Union, and through a variety of part and full-time jobs Emily Young has had the fortune of seeing Louisiana politics from all angles. Most recent was the Louisiana gubernatorial race in which her boss, Rep. Billy Tauzin (D-LA) was an unsuccessful candidate.

The preeminent problem facing Tauzin's south Louisiana district is the continued low price of oil. The economy of the area has been devastated and includes perhaps the highest unemployment in the nation. Needless to say, oil prices will be foremost on the minds of Tauzin and his key staff until they go back up.

Since Young joined his staff in 1985, Tauzin has been deeply involved in various energy and environmental issues before the House Energy and Commerce Committee. Among those are the reauthorization of Superfund, and revisions to the Clean Air Act. Tauzin has earned the nickname "High-tech Tauzin" in the bayous of Louisiana because of his extensive involvement in telecommunications issues and particularly the earth satellite station legislation.

Personal: born 3/25/61 in Shreveport, Louisiana. B.S. 1983, Louisiana State University. 1980, Congressional Intern, Congressman Gillis Long. 1981, College Intern, House Subcommittee on Energy Conservation and Power. 1981, College Intern, The Solar Lobby. 1982, State legislative lobbyist, Louisiana Chapter of the Sierra Club. 1982-83, Student Intern, Louisiana Department of Natural Resources, Coastal Zone Management Office. Campaign Aide, Edwin Edwards Gubernatorial, 1983-84. 1984-85, Legislative Aide, U.S. Senate Energy and Natural Resources Committee. 1985-86, Legislative Assistant; 1986-present, Legislative Director, Rep. Billy Tauzin (D-LA).

HOUSE OF REPRESENTATIVES
COMMITTEE ON FOREIGN AFFAIRS

Steven Kelly Berry
Minority Chief of Staff
B-360 Rayburn House Office Bldg.
225-6735

Personal: born 12/3/51 in Chilhowie, Virginia. Undergraduate courses at Wake Forest univ, 1970-1972. B.A., Political Science, Emory and Henry Coll., 1974. Graduate courses, Public Administration, East Tennessee State Univ., 1974. J.D. George Mason Univ., 1980. 1974-1977, manager, Division of Berry Enterprises, Supermarket, Chilhowie, VA. 1977-1978, Legal Staff Assistant, House Committee on Agriculture. 1978-1981, Special projects coordinator: 1981-1983, Administrative Assistant, Rep. William C. Wampler. 1983, Counsel; 1983-1986, Associate Counsel, Subcommittee on Legislation, House Permanent Select Committee on Intelligence. 1986-present, Minority Chief of Staff, House Committee on Foreign Affairs. Active Member, Virginia State Bar.

Expertise: Contra Aid

Foreign policy in the 1980's has sparked bitter controversy around the nation. Among the most divisive issues in which Congress has been embroiled is whether to aid the Contra resistance movement in Nicaragua. At virtually every stage of the effort in the House to provide assistance to the rebels, Steve Berry's presence has been felt.

Berry's career with Congress began when he came to Washington in 1977 to work for his hometown member of Congress, Rep. William C. Wampler of Smith County, VA. Rep. Wampler, who was the ranking minority member on the House Committee on Agriculture, asked Berry to work as an assistant on the committee during the summers while Berry attended law school. Berry would later become the special projects coordinator, and then the administrative assistant for Wampler's personal staff. Berry's work in Wampler's office included coordinating a $28 million development project which involved rerouting the Church River. He also concentrated on tobacco price-support programs and energy related activities.

After Wampler's defeat in 1982, Berry worked for a brief period with Wampler's consulting business, In March, 1983, Berry accepted a position as Counsel to the Subcommittee on Legislation of the House Permanent Select Committee on Intelligence. Soon Berry became the Associate Counsel to the full committee and began work on what he finds to be the most interesting part of his Capitol Hill career to date.

Aid to the Contras would become Berry's forte in his work with the Intelligence Committee. David Addington, Special Assistant to the President for Legislative Affairs, points out that Steve Berry played an integral role in gaining the support necessary to pass legislation providing $100 million in aid to the Contras. Berry's perseverance, Addington maintains, "helped to keep the Nicaragua program alive."

Berry has also acted as an associate counsel to the Select Committee to Investigate Covert Arms Transactions with Iran during the summer of 1987. He assisted Rep. William Broomfield in formulating statements and questions during the proceedings, and worked to ensure that the minority's interests were reflected in lines of questioning.

With the close of the 99th Congress, Berry took a new position as the minority chief of staff for the House Committee on Foreign Affairs. Berry views his role as minority chief of staff as one in which building coalitions is the "name of the game."

Robert K. Boyer
Senior Staff Consultant
2170 Rayburn House Office Bldg.
225-5021

Personal: born 3/31/41, in Marshall, Arizona. B.S. Eastern Illinois Univ. M.A. American Univ. 1966. 1965-1967, tutor, "Operation Reach". 1965-1969, teacher, Northwestern Senior High School, Hyattsville, Md. 1968 (summer), research aide, Rep. William V. Roth Jr.(R-DE). 1969-1971, special assistant, Rep. William S. Mailliard (D-CA). 1971 to present, Senior Staff Consultant, Committee on Foreign Affairs.

Expertise:

Counting all the areas Robert K. Boyer deals with, he might be considered a man for all issues. Boyer, who has spent almost two decades on the Foreign Affairs Committee, is one of two Senior Staff Consultants on the Foreign Affairs Committee. His position "automatically makes him a key player," says a staff member with the U.S. Agency for International Development.

"Boyer's portfolio is more wide-ranging than Ingram's," says a fellow committee staff member. "You won't find him focused in on a particular issue, at least not for any length of time." Boyer does pay particular attention to the State Department, terrorism and the budget and appropriations process. He also has been active on foreign aid programs and U.N. matters. Both consultants tend the hearings schedule and arrange for witnesses at hearings.

The forty-seven-year-old Boyer works quite a bit with budget issues. "He's the numbers man for the committee and gets into the real nuts and bolts of the budgeting process," says a State Department staffer. "He deals with the Budget and Appropriations committees and is the committee's liaison with the budget people in the State Department and other federal agencies."

Boyer works on the State Department's authorization bill every year and is involved in the funding process for foreign aid programs administered by the Agency for International Development.

Boyer takes a keen interest in terrorism issues. He played a key role in developing the Omnibus Diplomatic Security and International Terrorism Act, which was passed in 1985. The law authorized money for the State Department to beef up security at American embassies around the world, as well as at the State Department facilities in Washington, D.C. When concerns were raised last year about security at the U.S. Embassy in the Soviet Union and about problems with the new embassy building under construction, Boyer was part of the congressional delegation that went to Moscow for an investigation.

Boyer, who at one time was a Russian language teacher, helped in the probe, which was headed by Rep.Dan Mica(D-FL), chairman of the International Operations Subcommittee, and Rep.Olympia Snowe(R-ME), the ranking member. As a result of their probe, further construction has been put on hold until security concerns are satisfied.

Away from the office, Boyer is an enthusiastic tennis and squash player.

Foreign Affairs

John J. Brady
Chief of Staff
2170 Rayburn House Office Bldg.
225-5021

Expertise: International affairs

Dr. John J. Brady is twenty-year veteran of the House of Representatives Committee on Foreign Affairs and has been Chief of Staff for eleven years.

Brady brings a rich and varied background to the Committee. He was decorated for valor in combat in the European Theatre in World War II and was a Strategic Intelligence Officer in Washington and London after the war. Brady returned to Washington in 1967, after receiving a Ph.D. in International Relations from the London School of Economics. In 1967, Brady became a staff consultant with the Committee on Foreign Affairs. His first assignment was to do a special study on all aspects of the military assistance and arms sales programs. Since that time has also worked on all key foreign aid bills and written major legislation.

Two important early studies he worked on were on regional economic development in Southeast Asia (including the Philippines, Japan, Thailand, Malaysia, and Taiwan) and U.S. relations and troop levels in Europe. Because of his work on and knowledge of these issues, Brady became congressional advisor to the U.N. General Assembly in 1971.

In the 1970s, Brady researched and wrote extensively about the international narcotics problem, which led to legislation aimed at shutting down the international narcotics trade. Some of the studies he wrote on this problem include: 1971, *The World Heroin Problem*; 1972, *The U.S. Heroin Problem and Southeast Asia*; and 1973, *The World Narcotics Problem: The Latin American Perspective*

Personal: born 8/17/23 in Connellsville, Pennsylvania. B.S. St. Vincent Coll., 1948. M.A. Univ. of Notre Dame, 1959. Ph.D. London School of Economics, 1967. 1943-1945, 1948-1967,U.S. Army ; Military Decorations: Bronze Star Medal with Valour, device and one Oak Leaf Cluster, Purple Heart, Army Commendation Medal, and Combat Infantry Badge, Belgian Fourragere. 1967-1976, staff consultant, Committee on Foreign Affairs. 1976 to present, chief of staff, Committee on Foreign Affairs.

Brady also focused on the area of foreign military assistance and sales. He believes that the United States has a responsibility to have an effective foreign aid policy which includes economic and security assistance. Brady comments that George Washington's speech against the U.S. having foreign alliances was obsolete the day our first president gave it.

Brady views his position on the Foreign Affairs Committee as one of chief administrator, helping to facilitate compromise. He observes that reconciliation is always difficult, but his job is to advise a middle course.

The reputation Brady has with the House and with political leaders is that of being bipartisan, working for the national interest rather than for party interests.

When not trying to negotiate a foreign aid bill, Dr. Brady can be found playing golf.

Thomas Whitridge Bruce
Professional Staff Consultant
Subcommittee on International
  Operations
816 House Office Bldg. Annex 1
225-3424

Expertise: State Department, foreign relations

Thomas Bruce has a special commitment to doing everything he can "to insure that the foreign affairs infrastructure is healthy and effective." His responsibilities encompass any legislation in international relations.

Raised in the filmmaking and writing community in Paris, he possesses varying degrees of fluency in French, Spanish, Italian, Greek, and Arabic. His studies have included economics at the University of Paris and languages at the Institute of Oriental Languages. While still an undergraduate, he worked with international investors as an economic analyst for a firm in Cairo, Egypt. In 1978, he also helped start a travel incentive products company. In the summer of 1979, he joined the Carter campaign headquarters staff, in charge of coordinating all the advance teams.

Bruce joined the committee under Dante Fascell (D-FL) in March, 1981. He helped draft the Omnibus Diplomatic Security Act of 1986; the Foreign Relations Act of 1981, 1983, 1985 and 1987; the Foreign Missions Act of 1983; the Radio Broadcasting to Cuba Act of 1983; and other international communications legislation. His budget, authorization and oversight concerns include the State Department, USIA, and the Board for International Broadcasting. Of special interest are the areas of embassy security, and international communications.

Bruce and his wife have a young daughter. He's also very involved with the local community, as a member of the board of directors of Sasha Bruce Youthworks Inc., a non-profit organization that helps abused or delinquent children.

Bruce's first priority: "to make sure enough funds are available to help the people in State do their job."

Personal: born 6/24/56 in Midland, Texas. B.S.F.S School of Foreign Service, Georgetown Univ., 1978. 1975-1978, economic analyst, Cairo, Egypt. 1978-1979, staff assistant, Caucus for Foreign Policy & Defense. 1979-1980, advance coordinator, Carter presidential campaign. 1980-1981, staff assistant, White House scheduling office. 1981-1984, Staff Associate, Subcommittee on International Operations, House Committee on Foreign Affairs. 1985-present, Staff Consultant, Subcommittee on International Operations.

F. (Frances) Marian Chambers
Professional Staff Consultant
2170 Rayburn House Office Bldg.
225-5021

*Personal: born 8/25/54 in Wichita,
Kansas. B.A. Dartmouth, 1975 (Phi
Beta Kappa, Summa Cum Laude).
M.Sc. London School of Economics,
1976. 1977, Senior Foreign Policy
Analyst, Rep. Joe Skubitz (R-KS).
1978-present, Professional Staff
Consultant, House Committee on
Foreign Affairs.*

Expertise: International narcotics control, Micronesia, Central and South America

For the last four years, Chambers has traveled worldwide in her role as Staff Director of the Task Force on International Narcotics Control. Her career on the House Committee on Foreign Affairs has often taken her out of Washington for extensive travels.

When she began work with the Committee in the late seventies, her responsibilities included Micronesian and South Pacific affairs. Her work on oversight of the U.S. refugee processing system led to travel in Southeast Asia, Europe, Central America and Pakistan. She also worked as liaison to private voluntary organizations, such as CARE and the Catholic Relief Services.

More recently, Chambers handled oversight of the National Endowment for Democracy. As a member of the "economics team" for the committee, she has responsibility for monitoring the $4 billion worldwide economic support fund account, and has drafted legislation for various economic assistance programs.

Chambers also follows the budget process for the committee, tracking what is available in both authorized and appropriated funds for all U.S. foreign assistance programs. In fact, her "basic orientation" is trying to insure that these programs are well-run, and she closely follows audit reports in her areas.

Chambers has a special expertise in Central and South American affairs. Her languages include Spanish, French and Romanian (she spent three months in Romania working on trade policy issues). She returned to Eastern Europe in 1983 for a two-week horseback riding tour of Hungary. Chambers is a member of the DAR and the Business and Professional Women's Club, and the First Presbyterian Church of Wichita, Kansas. She is both a sky-diver and scuba-diver.

Susan Eckert
Professional Staff Consultant
Subcommittee on International
   Economic Policy and Trade
702 House Office Bldg. Annex 1
226-7820

Expertise: Export controls, economic sanctions

Initially hired on the Subcommittee by Rep. Jonathan Bingham (D-NY), Sue Eckert now works as staff consultant for Subcommittee Chairman Rep. Don Bonker (D-WA). Although her primary responsibility has been export controls, she also works on related issues: technology transfer, East-West trade, economic sanctions, foreign investment, export promotion, international telecommunications and foreign claims.

Eckert worked on the Export Administration Act Amendments of 1985, to streamline export licensing systems. Recently, she developed and managed Bonker's comprehensive export control reform legislation contained in the 1988 Omnibus Trade Bill, H.R. 3. She finds some irony in the Subcommittee's focus. "Our committee has jurisdiction over export promotion efforts as well as disincentives to exports, from sanctions to licensing requirements," she says. "At a time when much attention has been focused on foreign trade barriers, our efforts have been directed at removing our own self-imposed barriers to help U.S. exports."

She was active in developing amendments to the Export Trading Companies Act of 1982, to increase bank participation. Other issues that have received the Subcommittee's attention more recently include the Nicaragua trade embargo and South African sanctions. She participates as Bonker's representative to the President's Export Council, Subcommittee on Export Administration.

Personal: born June 3, 1958, in Warren, Pennsylvania. B.A. in history & political science, Pennsylvania State Univ., 1980 (magna cum laude). Course work for master's degree in international relations, Johns Hopkins School of Advanced International Studies. 1980-1981, Research Analyst, Discovery Analyst, Inc. 1981-1982, Legislative Assistant for Rep. Robert Edgar (D-PA). 1982-1985, Staff Assistant, Subcommittee on International Economic Policy and Trade. 1985-present, Professional Staff Consultant, Subcommittee on International Economic Policy and Trade.

Her international experience includes participation in numerous conferences, including a 1984 conference, "Forum for U.S.–Soviet Dialogue," held in the Soviet Union and a 1986 NATO conference, "High Technology, Western Security & Economic Growth". She has been a member of numerous Congressional delegations to Europe, the People's Republic of China and various countries in the Far East and South America. She also staffed delegations for the U.S. Congress-European Parliament Exchanges on economic and foreign policy issues.

Eckert's languages include some fluency in Russian and German. She has been active in the Washington Area Woman's Soccer League, and is an amateur sailor and avid gardener.

Robert M. Finley
Deputy Chief of Staff
2170 Rayburn House Office Bldg.
225-5021

*Personal: born in Miami, Florida.
B.S.F.S., Caitlin School of Foreign
Service, Georgetown Univ., 1964.
1965-70, executive assistant, Rep.
Dante B. Fascell (D-FL). 1970-71, staff
administrator, subcommittee on Legal
and Monetary Affairs, Government
Operations Committee. 1971-75, staff
director, Subcommittee on Inter-
American Affairs. 1975-76, staff
director, Subcommittee on Political
and Military Affairs. 1977-80, staff
director, Subcommittee on
International Operations. 1980-81,
Deputy Assistant Secretary of State
for the Caribbean. 1981-83, private
business. 1983-84, Staff Director,
Subcommittee on Human Rights.
1984-present, Deputy Chief of Staff,
House Foreign Affairs Committee.*

Expertise: Caribbean, Latin America, State Department, Foreign Service

On Capitol Hill, if one mentions staff identified with the House Foreign Affairs Committee chairman, Dante Fascell, the name of Robert M. Finley is usually not far behind.

Finley, a Miami native, served as Fascell's executive assistant for five years beginning in 1965. He then moved to the Government Operations Committee for a year before rejoining Fascell and the Foreign Affairs Committee. Except for a brief stint in private business from 1981-83, he has been on the panel since 1973 and has worked for three subcommittees, usually the same ones on which Fascell has served or has chaired.

"Finley and Spencer Oliver (the committee's counsel) are the two people closest to Fascell." says a State Department official. "That's understandable, since Mike and the chairman go back a long ways."'

Finley also is considered a strong possibility to replace Jack Brady when the longtime staff director decides to retire.

Finley is recognized as an authority on issues relating to the Caribbean and Central America, which is natural given the location of his boss's district and the importance of his hometown as America's gateway to Latin America.

Although the most recent request for aid to the Nicaraguan contras was rejected by the House, Fascell has been a consistent supporter of the rebels. Finley also follows the U.S. aid program to El Salvador and watches the progress of the Caribbean Basin Initiative, a Reagan Administration program to lower trade barriers and boost the economy of the many small countries in the Caribbean.

In addition, Finley for three years was staff director for the International Operations Subcommittee, which has jurisdiction over the State Department. He plays a key role in State Department authorization bills for the State Department and foreign aid, and Finley will spend time on both.

Fascell has indicated he will undertake a comprehensive review of America's foreign aid program, an endeavor in which Finley will play a key role.

Finley also tracks the United Nations, visiting New York frequently to observe U.N. agencies and to monitor issues in the General Assembly.

Carole A. Grunberg
Staff Director
Subcommittee on International
  Economic Policy and Trade
702 House Office Bldg. Annex 1
226-7820

Personal: born 5/8/54 in Washington, D.C. B.A. with Honors, Vassar College, 1976. Masters of International Affairs, Columbia Univ. School of International Affairs, 1978. 1978-1979, intern, office of Congressman Don Bonker (D-WA). 1979-1983, Staff Associate, House Foreign Affairs Subcommittee on Human Rights and International Organizations. 1983-1987, Staff Consultant, House Foreign Affairs Subcommittee on International Economic Policy and Trade. 1987-present, Staff Director, House Foreign Affairs Subcommittee on International Economic Policy and Trade.

Expertise: International trade and foreign affairs

Carole Grunberg clearly remembers the summer of 1978, pounding the pavement on Capitol Hill looking for a position in which she could use the knowledge she had gained at Columbia's School of International Affairs. She was offered a non-paying internship in Congressman Don Bonker's (D-WA) office handling foreign affairs issues. She took it. Now, almost ten years later, Grunberg is the Staff Director of Bonker's Subcommittee on International Economic Policy and Trade.

She was a staff player in the reauthorization of the Overseas Private Investment Corporation, and the Trade and Development Program. She was also involved in the South African Economic Sanctions, the China Nuclear Cooperation Agreement, and the Caribbean Basin Initiative. Grunberg is currently involved in congressional action on the Japan Nuclear Cooperation Agreement.

The Omnibus Trade Bill is now her major concern. The House has 17 sub-conferences on the bill and has conferees on 260 of the bill's provisions. Grunberg oversees the three that are chaired by the Foreign Affairs Committee: export controls, foreign policy, and export enhancement.

Grunberg is particularly interested in export promotion and market accessibility. It is her position that the U.S. should consider matching foreign subsidies so that businesses can compete on an equal footing with those from other nations. On the accessibility issue, she is specifically involved in the effort to prevent Brazil from shutting the U.S. out of its computer market.

Grunberg enjoys a challenging game of squash and often golfs with Bonker.

George Ingram
Senior Staff Consultant
2170 Rayburn House Office Bldg.
225-5021

Personal: born 9/1/44 in Knoxville, Tennessee. B.A. Univ. of North Carolina, 1966. M.A. Johns Hopkins School for Advanced International Studies, 1968. Ph.D. Univ. of Michigan, 1973. 1972-present, staff, House Foreign Affairs Committee. Publications: "The International Corporation: A New Challenge to the Discipline," 1970, SAIS Review.

Expertise: International economics, Western Hemisphere, trade

"I'm often a mediator," says George Ingram, a fifteen-year veteran of Hill policy wrangling. "I try to create understanding among the staff and the members, the majority and the minority, the Administration and Congress and all the parties who have an interest in foreign affairs."

Ingram is one of two senior consultants on the committee's staff, a position that includes the responsibility of directly advising members. Although that role requires him to keep abreast of all the committee's interests, the 43 year-old Ingram is primarily focused on Western issues and international economic affairs. He works most closely with the Western Hemisphere Affairs Subcommittee, chaired by liberal George Crockett of Michigan, and the International Economic Policy and Trade Subcommittee, chaired by the more moderate Don Bonker of Washington.

Ingram says he probably spends "a little more time" on economic issues. "George really heads up the economic team for the committee," says a State Department staffer who has worked with him. "He's their top guy on economic issues."

During the 100th Congress, Ingram has worked a lot on the committee's share of the Omnibus Trade Bill, particularly on national security and foreign policy aspects of export promotion and controls. He also has devoted his attention to the recent U.S.-Canada free trade agreement, which attracted considerable praise from many quarters.

Ingram also works on the foreign aid bill, legislation on which he has played a role for several years. That legislation is usually the subject of an annual tug-of-war, requiring staff to build a consensus if possible. Ingram is recognized as an advocate of private-sector initiatives in developing countries. He was instrumental in the "appropriate technology" legislation of the 1970s, which directed the government and the private sector in the United States to promote technology to the Third World countries consistent with their level of growth and sophistication. "It's a good program that makes a lot of sense," Ingram says. Policies to expand the private sector in developing countries also "are a useful focus of the foreign aid program," he feels.

"Ingram may be skeptical of some of the Reagan Administration policies on private sector development, but he is very supportive of the concept," says the State Department staff member. He further describes Ingram as a "political moderate who is very good to work with." Another department staff member seconds those views, calling Ingram, who holds a master's and a doctorate in international studies, "very bright and very capable."

Victor C. Johnson
Staff Director
Subcommittee on Western
  Hemisphere Affairs
709 House Office Bldg. Annex 1
226-7812

Expertise: Central America

Victor Johnson's long career with the House Foreign Affairs Committee began in 1975, when he became a staff associate on the Subcommittee on International Economic Policy and Trade, then chaired by Rep. Jonathan Bingham (D-NY). Johnson and Bingham later co-authored an article entitled "A Rational Approach to Export Controls," which was published in the Spring, 1979 *Foreign Affairs*.

In February, 1987, Johnson left his position as Staff Director of the Subcommittee on Western Hemisphere Affairs, thinking he had had enough of Capitol Hill. In his new position with the Inter-American Dialogue, he organized meetings among leading citizens of the U.S., Canada, Latin America, and the Caribbean to discuss issues in American relations. But when the new Chairman of the Subcommittee, Rep. George Crockett (D-MI), asked him to return to his former position, Johnson accepted readily. It seems, he says, that one can never have enough of the Hill.

Johnson believes that the most contentious issues that have surfaced under the current Administration involve Central America, and, much of his time and energy have consequently been focused on this part of the world. He was involved in formulating the much-publicized and controversial Boland Amendments, dealing with funding for the Nicaraguan Contras. Recently, Johnson wrote a chapter entitled "Congress and Contra Aid" to be included in Abraham F. Lowenthal, ed., *Latin America and Caribbean Contemporary Record*, Volume VI, (1986-87).

He was also active in drafting the Caribbean Basin Initiative, and the human rights conditions on aid to El Salvador and Guatemala. He has also been involved in issues relating to the Latin American debt problem, as well as the annual Foreign Aid bills.

Johnson continues to monitor the progress of the peace process in Central America. He is also involved with current issues in the Caribbean, including the situation in Haiti, and the organization of symposia with local government leaders.

His subcommittee has a small staff with a big jurisdiction, Johnson says, but he is gratified to be there at a time when Central America is on the nation's "front burner". And the subcommittee is likely to stay near the center of Congressional activity, as Latin America is likely to play an increasingly important role in U.S. foreign policy in the coming years.

Johnson often leaves the office with a briefcase full of work, but in his free time he enjoys softball, tennis, and listening to bluegrass and folk music.

Personal: born 7/24/41 in Pittsburgh, Pennsylvania. B.A. Whitworth Coll., 1963. M.A. San Francisco State Univ., 1971. Ph.D. Univ. of Wisconsin, 1975. 1963-1965, Peace Corps volunteer, Liberia. 1967-1969, Ford Foundation, Bogota, Colombia. 1975-1980, Staff Associate, House Foreign Affairs Committee, Subcommittee on International Economic Policy and Trade. 1981-1987, Staff Director, House Foreign Affairs Committee, Subcommittee on Western Hemisphere Affairs. 1987, Senior Associate, The Inter-American Dialogue. 1987-present, Staff Director, House Foreign Affairs Committee, Subcommittee on Western Hemisphere Affairs.

Stanley O. Roth
Staff Director
Subcommittee on Asian and Pacific
  Affairs
707 House Office Bldg. Annex 1
226-7802

Personal: born 3/1/54 in Brooklyn, N.Y. B.A. Brandeis Univ., 1975. M.A. Johns Hopkins School of Advanced International Studies, 1977, Phi Beta Kappa. 1975-1978, foreign affairs officer, Treasury Department. 1979-1982, Legislative Assistant, Rep. Stephen Solarz (D-NY). 1983-1985, staff consultant; 1985 to present, Staff Director, Subcommittee on Asian and Pacific Affairs, House Foreign Affairs Committee.

Expertise: South Pacific, Philippines, Korea, Middle East

With hot spots such as the Philippines, South Korea, Pakistan and Afghanistan under his Subcommittee's purview, Stanley Roth has his hands full. He joined Subcommittee chairman Steve Solarz' staff in 1979 as the congressman's legislative assistant for foreign affairs. Like Solarz, he is a Brooklyn native. Like Solarz, he graduated from Brandeis University. And like Solarz, he is interested in strategically important places such as the Philippines and South Korea. Roth shares other traits with the New York Democrat. "Solarz is very liberal, but he is sharp, always prepared and pragmatic," says a State Department official who has worked with the Subcommittee. "Stan reflects that. He's very liberal, too, but he's bright, competent and willing to listen." Roth sees an advantage in working for Solarz: "He's a very active member who has a lot of respect, so that comes over to me. When he's interested in something, people respond, and that helps me in obtaining information."

The Philippines, South Korea and Pakistan have occupied much of Roth's attention in the last two years. Solarz pushed an amendment to cut off all aid to the Marcos government, before Corazon Aquino took power.

Later that year, Roth worked on a proposal to provide $200 million in additional aid for the Aquino government, which was eventually approved. The Subcommittee is now exploring the idea of a "Marshall Plan" for the Philippines. The Subcommittee has been watching the continuing transition to democracy in South Korea as well. Solarz and Roth have visited the country twice in the last year. "The Subcommittee has really been involved more in an oversight capacity," he says. Roth worked on the 1985 Solarz amendment, which bars aid to countries without nuclear weapons that import material from the United States to be used in the production of nuclear explosives. The president can waive the provision on the grounds of national interest. Dante Fascell, the Florida Democrat who chairs the full committee, "gives the regional subcommittees like ours a lot of autonomy," says Roth. "Hearings are done at the subcommittee level, and we get a lot of leeway."

When not at the office, Roth enjoys traveling (his official duties require him to take several trips a year).

Ivo J. Spalatin
Staff Director
Subcommittee on Arms Control,
   International Security and
   Science
2401A Rayburn House Office Bldg.
225-8926

*Personal: born 2/10/46 in Rome, Italy.
B.A. Marquette Univ. 1967. B.F.T.
American Institute of Foreign Training,
1968. M.A. George Washington Univ.,
1970. 1967, market researcher,
Kimberly-Clark Corp. 1969, Assistant
to International Business Adviser, U.S.
Information Agency. 1970-1971,
international economic analyst,
Caterpillar Tractor Co. 1971-1976,
Administrative Assistant to Rep.
Clement Zablocki (D-WI). 1976-1984,
Staff Director, Subcommittee on
International Security and Scientific
Affairs. 1985-present, Staff Director,
Subcommittee on Arms Control,
International Security and Science.
Publication: "Political, Social and
Economic Effects of Western Tourism
in Yugoslavia and Bulgaria".*

Expertise: Arms control

It's a long way from Rome to Capitol Hill, but Ivo J. Spalatin has made the journey with a few detours along the way.

Staff director for the Subcommittee on Arms Control, International Security and Science, Spalatin was born in the Eternal City, after his Croatian parents moved there during World War II. Later, the family moved to Iowa, and Spalatin grew up mostly in Milwaukee.

After graduating from Marquette University he earned a degree in foreign trade from the American Institute of Foreign Training in Phoenix, Arizona, and a master's in international affairs from George Washington University. With experience as a market researcher at the Kimberly-Clark Corporation and as an assistant to the International Business Advisor at the U.S. Information Agency, Spalatin had impressive credentials for any employer.

In 1971, Rep. Clement Zablocki, a veteran Wisconsin congressman, needed an administrative assistant. Spalatin was only 25 when he became the Congressman's top aide. Zablocki later became chairman of the Foreign Affairs Committee. That, along with Spalatin's background in international affairs, made his eventual arrival there, after six years on Zablocki's staff, a natural one. He joined the International Security and Scientific Affairs Subcommittee (the forerunner of the subcommittee he now serves), which the full committee chairman traditionally chairs.

When Zablocki died in 1983, Rep. Dante Fascell (D-FL) assumed the reins and asked Spalatin to stay on as the subcommittee staff director.

The subcommittee's wide jurisdiction means Spalatin has no shortage of issues on which to work. His priority, however, is "promoting a more responsible, broad-based congressional perspective on foreign policy and getting away from micro-managing," he says. "Congress should be interested in policy and how much it spends overall. We need to look at the big picture."

Spalatin thinks he has had some success in that regard. He also thinks the subcommittee has done well in an area he calls fundamental to his efforts and one in which he spends the most time: arms control.

"We should keep the arms-control process moving," he says. "We may want to change the process somewhat or modify certain agreements, but to say agreements are fatally flawed"—which is how the Reagan Administration described SALT II—"and kill the process is not in our interests."

Michael H. Van Dusen
Staff Director
Subcommittee on Europe and the
    Middle East
B354 Rayburn House Office Bldg.
225-3345

Personal: born 10/13/42 in Philadelphia, Pennsylvania. B.A. Princeton, 1966. M.A. Johns Hopkins School of Advanced International Studies, 1968. Ph.D. Johns Hopkins Univ., 1971. 1964-65, summers of 1963 and 1966, studies in Middle East. 1967, Research Associate, Brookings Institution. 1967-71, Editorial Assistant, Middle East Journal. *1971-present, Staff Director, Subcommittee on Europe and the Middle East.*

Expertise: Middle Eastern affairs

Michael Van Dusen, Staff Director of the Subcommittee on Europe and the Middle East, can list a dozen or so issues with which his panel is involved or has jurisdiction, any one of which alone would be fascinating—and more than enough to handle.

"We look at U.S.-Soviet relations, arms control, regional issues, the Middle East peace process, the Persian Gulf, U.S. relations with Eastern Europe, NATO, problems with Southern Europe and U.S. economic and military assistance," he says.

"We move from issue to issue," he notes. "If something blows up in the Persian Gulf, we're on that issue. When the foreign aid bill comes up, we're on that. When Gorbachev is visiting, that becomes the topic."

When Van Dusen first came on the subcommittee in 1971, he was the lone staffer on the subcommittee and was called a consultant. It now has five staff members. "We work as a unit," says Van Dusen. "My job is to coordinate our efforts."

Van Dusen's entire career on the Hill has been under one chairman, the highly respected Lee Hamilton (D-IN).

"The ranking minority member has changed, but Hamilton has worked well with all of them," he says. "I consider him to be very fair and highly effective."

Van Dusen has definite ideas about the role of a congressional staff: "The staff has to remember that at a certain point our role stops and the members have to decide on an issue and fashion a compromise as needed with their colleagues. At that time, the staff fades into the background."

Staff members can present analyses of issues and offer recommendations, "but it's the members who make the laws," he notes. "We (staff) are here to provide expertise and advice. We're not here to promote an agenda."

Van Dusen has traveled extensively including several study missions to the Middle East and to Europe. In addition, he has been published in the *Middle East Journal, Current History* and the *International Journal of the Middle East and Foreign Affairs.* He also lectures frequently on the Middle East, the Persian Gulf and foreign policy.

In his free time, Van Dusen enjoys skiing, skating and tennis and adds, "My wife and I have three daughters, who also take up a lot of my time."

Toni G. Verstandig
Staff Consultant
2170 Rayburn House Office Bldg.
225-8926

Personal: born 1/15/53 in Pittsburgh, Pennsylvania. A.A. Stephens Coll., 1972. B.A. Boston Univ., 1974. 1974, intern, Mayor Kevin White of Boston. 1975-1976, Legislative Assistant, Rep. John Dent (D-PA). 1976-1978, Staff Director, Subcommittee on Accounts, House Administration Committee. 1978-1986, Staff Consultant, Arms Control Subcommittee, House Foreign Affairs Committee. 1986-present, Staff Consultant, House Foreign Affairs Committee.

Expertise: Terrorism, military aid & regional conflicts

Verstandig, a staff consultant on the House Foreign Affairs Committee, follows a number of issues, including the Persian Gulf, North Africa, Northern Ireland, international terrorism and the military aspects of foreign aid.

Covering such a wide range of subjects means a "degree of change that you probably don't have in other jobs," Verstandig says. It gives her the sense of having not one job, but many different ones.

Verstandig, 35, is one of 15 staff consultants on the full committee, each of whom focuses on specific issues. Like the others, her duties include developing legislation, setting up hearings, handling oversight and advising Members.

A Pittsburgh native, Verstandig graduated from Boston University in 1974 with a degree in political science. She worked briefly for Boston Mayor Kevin White before coming to Washington in 1975 as a legislative assistant to now-retired Rep. John Dent (D-PA).

After two years on Dent's personal staff, Verstandig took over as staff director of the House Administration Committee's Accounts Subcommittee, which Dent chaired.

Although she enjoyed being a subcommittee staff director at the age of 23, she was interested in foreign policy issues and had an eye on the Foreign Affairs Committee.

Rep. Clement Zablocki (D-WI), then committee chairman, invited her to join the committee staff and she accepted.

Verstandig came aboard the Arms Control Subcommittee as a consultant, remaining until 1986, when she moved to the full committee.

Verstandig's husband, Lee, is president of a Washington lobbying and consulting firm. In her spare time, she plays tennis and is active in fund-raising for charity.

Foreign Affairs

Stephen R. Weissman
Staff Director
Subcommittee on Africa
705 House Office Bldg. Annex 1
226-7807

Expertise: Africa, urban policy, development issues

If one's job involves looking at African issues and developing legislation on them, it would certainly be an advantage to have studied and taught on those issues and to have spent time in Africa. Stephen R. Weissman qualifies on both counts.

Weissman, staff director for the Africa Subcommittee, examined Africa's art, culture and politics a graduate student; his thesis was on American foreign policy in the Congo (now Zaire). He has written extensively on African issues, spent three years with the National University of Zaire and has traveled to the continent several times since. That experience and his nine years on the Hill gives Weissman a broad background as he approaches African issues.

Weissman's subcommittee is involved in a number of issues. He says Wolpe is trying to build a relationship with Marxist Mozambique, a policy in line with the State Department but opposed by conservatives.

Wolpe has been one of the major congressional advocates for tough sanctions against South Africa. Weissman says the subcommittee has worked to intensify trade and other impositions on the South African government and is trying to persuade other countries to do so.

Personal: born 4/10/41 in New York City. B.A., government, Cornell Univ., 1961. M.A., political science, Univ. of Chicago, 1965. Ph. D., political science, Univ. of Chicago, 1969. Falk Fellow in American Politics, Phi Beta Kappa, Phi Kappa Phi. 1966-69, instructor, assistant professor of political science, Fordham Univ.. 1969-71, associate professor of political science, National Univ. of Zaire. 1971-72, and 1973-75, assistant professor of political science, Jersey State City College. 1972-73, research associate in community development, Stanford Univ. 1975-79, associate professor of political economy, Univ. of Texas at Dallas. 1979-present, Staff Director, Subcommittee on Africa.

Weissman realized a goal with the inclusion in the 1988 Continuing Resolution of a provision earmarking $50 million to the Southern African Development Coordinating Conference, a group made up of nine countries that border or are near South Africa. The funding is intended to bolster the economy of those countries and reduce their dependency on Pretoria.

Weissman is an advocate of human-needs development, under which U.S. aid programs are geared toward specific projects that alleviate poverty in the Third World. He is less sympathetic to the Reagan Administration's view that policy changes in developing countries that encourage economic growth are more effective.

Wolpe and a fellow Michigan congressman on the subcommittee, George Crockett, are strong liberals. The ranking Republican, Dan Burton of Indiana, as well as Robert Dornan of California and Donald "Buzz" Lukens of Ohio are conservative. Thus, cooperation is difficult, and Weissman often has his hands full in negotiating on legislation.

Weissman, who is married and the father of one, is the author of numerous articles on U.S. foreign policy and urban and social policy. In his spare time he enjoys reading and bicycling.

HOUSE OF REPRESENTATIVES
COMMITTEE ON GOVERNMENT OPERATIONS

William M. Jones
General Counsel
2157 Rayburn House Office Bldg.
225-5051

Born 9/2/40 in Electra, Texas. B.A. Texas Christian Univ. 1961. J.D. George Washington Univ. 1964. Administrative Assistant, Rep. Jack Brooks (D-TX). 1973-1975, Staff Director, Subcommittee on Government Activities and Transportation, Committee on Government Operations. 1975-present, General Counsel, Committee on Government Operations.

The House Committee on Government Operations has jurisdiction over matters relating to budget and accounting, other than appropriations; the efficiency of government operations, including procurement; reorganization of the executive branch; relationships between the federal and state/local governments, including revenue sharing; and broad oversight of executive branch activities.

Other key staffers on the Committee on Government Operations include:

Peter Barash, Staff Director, Subcommittee on Commerce, Consumer, and Monetary Policy. B377 Rayburn House Office Bldg. 225-4407.

Richard Barnes, Staff Director, Subcommittee on Legislation and National Security, B373 Rayburn House Office Bldg., 225-5147.

Stephen M. Daniels, Minority Staff Director/Counsel, full committee. 2153 Rayburn House Office Bldg. 225-5074.

Donna Fossum, Professional Staff Member, full committee. 2157 Rayburn House Office Bldg. 225-5051.

John Galloway, Staff Director, Subcommittee on Government Activities and Transportation, B350-A&B Rayburn House Office Bldg. 225-7920.

Robert Gellman, Staff Director, Subcommittee on Government Information, Justice, and Agriculture. B349-B&C Rayburn House Office Bldg. 225-3741.

James Gotlieb, Staff Director, Subcommittee on Human Resources and Intergovernmental Relations. B372 Rayburn House Office Bldg. 225-2548.

W. Donald Gray, Staff Director, Subcommittee on Environment, Energy, and Natural Resources. B371-B&C Rayburn House Office Bldg. 225-6427.

Richard W. Peterson, Professional Staff Member, Subcommittee on Commerce, Consumer & Monetary Affairs. B377 Rayburn House Office Bldg. 225-4407.

Stuart E. Weisberg, Staff Director & Counsel, Subc. on Employment and Housing. B349-A Rayburn House Office Bldg. 225-6751.

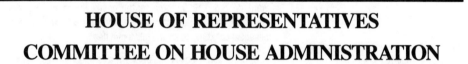

HOUSE OF REPRESENTATIVES
COMMITTEE ON HOUSE ADMINISTRATION

David C. Sharman
Staff Director
H-331 Capitol
225-2061

During World War II, David Sharman had to perform the jobs of bombardier, radio operator, and gunner aboard B-17 bombers. Today, Sharman demonstrates the same versatility in addressing the diverse issues the Committee on House Administration faces.

The Committee's primary goal is to support Members, Committees and officers of the House in the administration and funding of their operations. Sharman's Committee must sign off on all the House expenditures, from trash collections to the budget for the Library of Congress. The task of assuring each Member and committee enough office space and furniture is a tall order by anyone's standards. Additionally, Sharman must be ready to serve the Members on a day-to-day basis and always be accessible to the Committee, especially the Chairman.

Sharman considers a great deal of his job to be reacting to minor problems. But these "minor problems" can take on extreme importance to Members and their staff.

Given the nature of the Committee's responsibilities, political ideology has little impact on the performance of his job. Sharman is a Democrat and knows he would not be in this position if he were not. Since 1955, his career has been focused on Congress. His years with the Subcommittee on Accounts provided him with essential background for the full committee.

Personal: born 1/29/23 in Big Springs, Texas. B.A. Univ. of California, 1945-1949. Certificate, Stanford Univ. Institute for Organizational Management. U.S. Army Air Corps, World War II, Purple Heart. 1955-1967, Director of Washington Office and Assistant Administrative Director, American Optometric Association. 1967-1973, National Director, Car & Truck Renting & Leasing Association. 1973-1978, President and Proprietor, Sharman Associates. 1978-1984, Staff Director, Subcommittee on Accounts, Committee on House Administration. 1985 to present, Staff Director, Committee on House Administration.

Advanced technology is one of Sharman's major interests. His responsibilities as Staff Director include management control over House Information Systems, the computer center for the House, which consists of over two hundred employees. With ever-increasing use of information technology and state-of-the-art computer equipment in Member and Committee offices, the ability to "get things done" is happening sooner than anyone expected. But, it is the day-to-day matters which make Sharman proudest. A telephone system that works and oversight of the Capitol Police Force are issues that may not seem "earthshaking", but they are essential to the efficient operation of the Congress.

HOUSE OF REPRESENTATIVES
COMMITTEE ON INTERIOR AND INSULAR AFFAIRS

Daniel M. Adamson
Professional Staff Member
Subcommittee on General
  Oversight & Investigations
815 House Office Bldg., Annex 1
226-4085

Expertise: Energy and environmental issues

The excitement and responsibility of forging major legislation draws Dan Adamson to the Hill. Known for his unflagging energy and serious attention to the issues, Adamson helps the House Interior and Insular Affairs Committee formulate bills on groundwater contamination, irrigation subsidies, and nuclear power regulation.

Adamson first became familiar with energy issues during a brief stint at the Northeast-Midwest Institute, where he tracked Department of Energy issues.

Both before and after Chernobyl, Adamson played a role in providing Americans with protection from nuclear accident by pinpointing responsibility for malfunctions or mishaps under the Price-Anderson Amendments Act. "I think there needs to be more of an emphasis on safety in the nuclear industry." Adamson says he believes the days of the major federal public works projects are at an end, and in an era of fiscal austerity, Congress is reviewing government's role in water policy. "We need to stop wasteful spending on water projects," Adamson insists, since they cost the average taxpayer while supporting special interests.

Adamson also wants to eliminate irrigation subsidies to farmers who produce surplus crops. Doing so would reduce the cost of commodity support programs, he observes.

When not pouring over a government report or engaging in debate on committee issues, Adamson likes to relax by taking a spin on his bike. Day trips to the countryside are not uncommon.

Personal: Born 8/06/60, Cleveland, Ohio. B.P. Miami Univ., Oxford, OH, 1982. M.A., Univ. of California, Santa Barbara, 1984. 1985, consultant on energy policy, Northeast-Midwest Institute. 1985-1987, Legislative Assistant, Rep. Sam Gejdenson (D-CT). 1987-present, Professional Staff Member, Subcommittee on General Oversight.

Rick A. Agnew
Chief Minority Counsel
1329 Longworth House Office
   Bldg.
225-6065

Expertise: Energy, environmental, land use

As Chief Minority Counsel, Rick Agnew is respected among colleagues of both parties for being able to represent the minority viewpoint without sacrificing a good rapport with the majority.

After graduating from law school, Agnew worked as a legislative assistant for Rep. Don Young (R-AK). He aided in the drafting of the Alaskan Natural Gas Transportation Act of 1982 which made it possible to tap the unused natural gas potential of Prudhoe Bay. Agnew also applied his legal expertise to tax, environmental, Native American and land-use issues associated with the construction of a gas pipeline, and waivers that enable the gas to be marketed.

Work on the legislation gave Agnew a familiarity with the issues needed in drafting current proposals for oil prospecting in protected Alaskan wilderness. Agnew believes energy resources in the Arctic National Wildlife Refuge can be tapped without harming the environment.

The environmental impact of water use, and government involvement in water management projects are other key issues that cross Agnew's desk. While he continues to pursue the natural resource agenda of the Interior and Insular Affairs Committee, Agnew eventually hopes to pursue another of his interests— federal tax law. The Tax Reform Act of 1986 is a step in the right direction, he says, but he believes too many businesses still make decisions based on tax considerations: "A flat tax would be much more appropriate."

Agnew is an athlete, and in spare moments, likes to loosen up on the basketball court.

Personal: born 10/8/51 in New Bern, North Carolina. B.A. Univ. of Washington, 1973. J.D. Univ. of Puget Sound, Takoma, Washington, 1979. 1980, Legislative Assistant, Rep. Don Young (R-AK). 1980-1983, staff Counsel. 1983-1985, Counsel, National Parks and Public Lands Subcommittee, House Committee on Interior and Insular Affairs. 1985 to present, Chief Minority Counsel, Interior and Insular Affairs.

Daniel P. Beard
Staff Director
Subcommittee on Water and Power
  Resources
1522 Longworth House Office
  Bldg.
225-6042

Personal: born 4/14/43, Bellingham, Washington. B.A. Western Washington Univ., 1966. M.A. Univ. of Washington, 1970. Ph.D. 1973. 1970-1974, Congressional Research Service, Library of Congress. 1975-1976, Special Assistant, Rep. Sidney Yates (D-IL). 1977, Domestic Policy Staff, Carter White House. 1977-1980, Deputy Assistant Secretary for Land and Water Resources, Department of the Interior. 1981, independent lobbyist. 1982-1983, Administrative Assistant, Sen. Max Baucus (D-MT). 1984, lobbyist, Chambers Associates, Inc. 1985 to present, Staff Director, Subcommittee on Water and Power Resources.

Expertise: Environment, water and land management, energy

Seventeen years of broad experience on the Hill has earned Beard a reputation as a staffer with strong political instincts and an expertise on water policy issues. He is recognized as an authority in his field, and has contributed to many technical journals.

Beard came to Washington as an academic, and a doctorate in geography prepared him for a stint at the Congressional Research Bureau. Projects for Members of Congress led to a position as Special Assistant to Rep. Sidney Yates (D-IL.), who chairs the Interior Appropriations Subcommittee.

In 1977, as a member of President Carter's Domestic Policy staff, Beard picked up valuable experience on White House operations. He later became Deputy Assistant Secretary of the Interior, responsible for formulating and carrying out administration policies dealing with wildlife, water resources, land management and budgetary issues.

After the Carter years, he planned and coordinated the re-election campaign of Sen. Max Baucus as his Administrative Assistant. That, and several brief periods as a lobbyist, deepened his grasp of the internal workings of electoral politics and its influence on policy.

Now that the era of major water resource public works projects is coming to an end, Beard believes it is time to review the role of federal involvement. It is Beard's view the Bureau of Reclamation should assume a back stage position by assisting state and local government programs.

Beard unwinds by spending time with his wife and three children, keeping his suburban home in shape, and through his hobby, woodworking.

Deborah Ann Broken Rope
Staff Assistant
Office of Indian Affairs
522 House Office Bldg., Annex 1
226-7393

Personal: born 4/17/52 in Washington, D.C. 1971-1973, clerk, Indian Health Service. 1976-1978, secretary to the assistant secretary for Indian Affairs, Department of the Interior. 1978-1982, Clerk, Office of Indian affairs, Committee on Interior and Insular Affairs. 1983-present, Staff Assistant, Office of Indian Affairs, House Committee on Interior and Insular Affairs.

Expertise: Native Americans

Deborah Broken Rope's career in Indian affairs spans a decade and a half, beginning with a position at the Indian Health Service in 1971. She has spent most of that time on the Hill, exercising important influence over legislation to extend federal programs to Indian reservations.

As a member of the Oglala Sioux Tribe of South Dakota, Broken Rope's very personal concern for the plight of Native Americans is the driving force behind her work with the Indian Affairs Office. "As an Indian, I have a personal commitment to Indian communities," she notes.

Broken Rope can look back with satisfaction on legislation which took years to formulate and push through the myriad of authorizing committees. The Indian amendments to the Superfund and the Safe Water Drinking Act, and the Indian Youth Alcohol and Substance Abuse Prevention Act, count among the victories.

Not satisfied, Broken Rope wants to see federal funding of health care beyond the immediate attention given tribal citizens by the Indian Health Service. This would include funding of independent health services, preventative health care programs, and improvement in basic sanitation. "The status of health care should be at a parity with the rest of the American people, and it is not," she says. "Forty to fifty percent of Indians have inadequate sanitation systems."

Broad experience makes Broken Rope a trusted adviser on appropriations for Indian programs, which are usually adopted within budgetary constraints. She also prepares briefings for oversight and investigation of the Indian Health Service and the Bureau of Indian Affairs.

Women's rights is another issue Broken Rope cares deeply about: "Indian women have not really been promoted the way other minority and disadvantaged groups have been."

Broken Rope has served on the boards of the National Rural Housing Coalition and the OHOYO Indian Women's Organization. She is a sought-after speaker on Indian affairs at national conferences and workshops for government employees dealing with native American issues.

Dale Crane
Staff Director
Subcommittee on National Parks
  and Public Lands
812 House Office Bldg. Annex 1
226-7736

Expertise: Environmental planner

As a California park ranger, Dale Crane never imagined he would eventually end up in Washington and direct the staff of a House subcommittee. Yet Crane's responsibility for managing and patrolling some 11,000 acres and 100 campsites in California, combined with his three decades of experience in environmental and wildlife affairs, has made him a proven asset to the Subcommittee on National Parks and Public Lands.

As staff director for the subcommittee, Crane is responsible for the oversight of public parks ranging from the National Park System to the National Wild and Scenic Rivers System to the preservation of prehistoric grounds. Crane refers to the subcommittee as "the last outpost for trying to protect and preserve our cultural and natural resources."

He was the primary staff person on the Lake Tahoe Protection Act of 1980 and the creation of the Memorial and the Archeological Protection Act of 1979. His most recent project of note for the subcommittee has been his assistance in the creation of the Great National Park in Nevada, the first National Park to be created in 15 years.

Personal: born 9/15/31 in Tenino, Washington. B.S., Oregon State Univ., 1953. Management and graduate work, Univ. of California system; Univ. of Nebraska; Iowa State Univ.; U.S. Government; 1975-1979, faculty affiliate, Univ. of Montana. 1957-1961, park ranger, California State Parks. 1961-1962, recreation planner, California Dept. of Water Resources. 1962-1971, various management positions, including chief of Environmental Resources; and 1971-1979, chief of Natural Resources branch, U.S. Army Corps of Engineers. 1979-1984, professional staff member; 1984-present, staff director, Subcommittee on National Parks and Public Lands of the House Committee on Interior and Insular Affairs.

The 100th Congress has found Crane involved in two rather controversial issues. The first concerns legislation designed to establish a Park Service Review Board. Such a board, says Crane, could insulate our natural and cultural treasures from political micromanagement. Crane believes that a century of protecting our natural resources has been jeopardized as a result of only a decade of congressional micromanagement.

The other measure, authored by committee chairman Rep. Morris K. Udall (D-AZ), would guarantee certain levels of funding to the states for the maintenance of their forests and park services. Among its many responsibilities, the subcommittee and Crane have jurisdiction over wilderness designation, the Forest Service, Bureau of Land Management lands in eleven states, Wild and Scenic Rivers system, and battlefields.

Crane believes some of America's resources, including timber, oil and gas, mines, and grazing lands have been exploited by developers and others. Thus, a goal is the establishment of an effective, long-term plan to provide sustained utilization of resources on public lands.

Not surprisingly, Crane is an avid outdoorsman who prefers to spend his free time hunting and fishing. And if you happen to see his office walls, you will realize that he is an accomplished outdoor photographer.

Frank Ducheneaux
Counsel on Indian Affairs
House Office Bldg. Annex 1
226-7393

Expertise: Indian Affairs

A fifteen-year Interior Committee veteran, Frank Ducheneaux's low-profile demeanor belies a man whose personal imprint appears on virtually every American Indian policy decision made by the committee since 1973.

By the time he arrived on the Hill, Ducheneaux was already a recognized expert on Indian affairs and had experience with Capitol Hill. He served as legislative director at the Bureau of Indian Affairs, and after leaving the executive branch, he mapped out legislative strategy for the National Congress of American Indians.

In 1973, Ducheneaux was asked by Rep. Lloyd Meeds (D-WA) to serve as his principal advisor on the Subcommittee on Indian Affairs. In 1978, following a reorganization of the Interior Committee, the Indian Affairs Subcommittee was abolished. Ducheneaux was made counsel on Indian affairs for the full committee at the insistence of Chairman Mo Udall (D-AZ), a position he holds today.

Personal: born 1/30/40 in Cheyenne Agency, South Dakota. B.S. Univ. of South Dakota, 1963. J.D. Univ. Of South Dakota, 1965. 1965-1967, civil rights coordinator, Office of Economic Opportunity, Kansas City. 1968-1969, congressional fellowship program, American Political Science Association 1967-1970, director of legislative affairs, Bureau of Indian Affairs. 1970-1973, legislative relations, National Congress of American Indians. 1973-1976, counsel, House Subcommittee on Indian Affairs. 1976-present, counsel, House Committee on Interior and Insular Affairs

The span of Ducheneaux's Hill career has seen enormous changes in the congressional response to issues of Indian rights and sovereignty, in general as well as for specific tribes. Some of the most rewarding legislative victories for Ducheneaux include the Indian Child Welfare Act in 1978, which funded and established Indian child and family service programs, and the passage in 1982 of the Indian Mineral Development Act, a landmark bill that authorized Indian tribes to develop their own mineral resources.

At present, Ducheneaux is developing strengthening amendments to the Indian Health Care Improvement Act, a bill that originally passed in 1976 with his assistance.

Jeffrey Lloyd Farrow
Staff Director
Subcommittee on Insular and
    International Affairs
1626 Longworth House Office
    Bldg.
225-9297

*Personal: born 5/8/51. B.S. Boston
Univ., 1972. 1973, assistant to Rep.
Ron de Lugo (D-VI). 1976-1981,
Senior Adviser and Associate Director
on Carter White House Domestic
Affairs staff.*

Expertise: Insular affairs

Born in New York, educated in Boston, and working in
Washington, D.C., Jeff Farrow considers the Virgin Islands his
home. The son of a real estate developer, Farrow moved with his
family to St. Thomas as a young boy. It is there he spent his youth
and returned after college to work. Now he must settle for visiting
several times a year.

In his position as Staff Director of the House Subcommittee on
Insular and International Affairs, Farrow has the opportunity to
serve the people of his beloved islands as well as the over three
million residents of other islands (known as insular areas)
associated with the United States, including Puerto Rico,
Micronesia, the Republic of the Marshall Islands, Guam, American
Samoa, the Commonwealth of the Northern Mariana Islands, and
the Trust Territory of Palau.

The publisher and editor of the *Virgin Islands Post*, Farrow came to
Washington, D.C. to work as Rep. Ron de Lugo's (D-VI) press
secretary in 1973. His expertise in insular areas eventually gained
him a position in the Carter Administration serving as a Senior
Advisor, and later as the Associate Director, of Insular areas on the
Domestic Affairs staff. Disillusioned by the lack of interest to
insular areas shown by the Reagan Administration, Farrow left the
White House in 1981 making a conscious decision not to pursue
career opportunities on Capitol Hill. However, after consulting with
de Lugo in his efforts to form an insular areas caucus, Farrow
realized Congress needed to devise better policies to deal with the
political, social, and economic development of insular areas.

The Omnibus Insular Areas Act is one of the most important bills
Farrow deals with annually. However, his Subcommittee's
jurisdiction crosses that of almost every other committee in
Congress. For example, Farrow represents the concerns of insular
areas in tax legislation, such as the Tax Reform Act of 1986, and
bills considered by the Merchant Marine and Fisheries Committee.

According to Farrow, "The Constitution says states and the people
who live in them have certain rights. There are no similar
provisions for territories. Congress has a special responsibility to
these people, most of whom are Americans." Farrow's ultimate
goal and the focus of his career is to ensure the people of U.S.
associated insular areas are guaranteed those rights.

He expects to be involved in the 1988 Democratic presidential
campaign. In previous elections, he has worked as the offshore
areas coordinator and the liaison between the party and
Americans who live overseas.

Sam Fowler
General Counsel
Subcommittee on Energy and the
    Environment
1324 Longworth House Office
    Bldg.
225-8331

*Personal: born 2/2/52 in Washington,
D.C. B.S. Univ. of New Hampshire,
1974. J.D., George Washington Univ.,
1980. 1974-1977, Botany Dept.,
Smithsonian Institution. 1978 and
1979, Presidents Council on
Environmental Quality. 1980-1985,
associate, Fried, Frank, Harris, Shriver
and Kampelman. 1985-present,
Counsel, Subcommittee on Energy
and Environment, House Committee
on Interior and Insular Affairs.*

Expertise: Nuclear energy legislation

Sam Fowler had experience as both a botanist, studying
endangered species at the Smithsonian Institution, and a
corporate attorney specializing in nuclear energy, genetic
engineering and securities law when Chairman Morris Udall (D-
AZ) hired him as counsel to the House Subcommittee on Energy
and Environment in 1985.

Udall chairs the full Committee on Interior and Insular Affairs as
well as its Subcommittee on Energy and the Environment. The
Committee has primary jurisdiction in the House over the
regulation of domestic nuclear energy industry. Udall's permanent
nuclear staff consists of three people: Stanley Scoville, the staff
director of the full Committee; Dr. Henry Myers, the full
Committee's science advisor; and Fowler. Scoville focuses on
broad policy questions, Myers on technical oversight and Fowler
on legislation. Fowler focuses almost entirely on nuclear energy
issues, advising Udall in both the subcommittee and the full
Committee.

A major part of Fowler's time since he joined the subcommittee
staff has been devoted to the legislation amending the Price-
Anderson Act. The act, first passed in 1957, provides
compensation to the public for damages resulting from a nuclear
accident. Under Udall's leadership, the House passed legislation
in July 1987 to extend the act for an additional decade and to
increase the amount of compensation tenfold.

Fowler also advises Udall on nuclear waste management issues.
Udall was the "father" of the Nuclear Waste Policy Act of 1982,
which established a technical process for siting repositories for
high-level radioactive wastes. The Department of Energy's effort
to implement the 1982 law met with widespread public and
congressional opposition, however, because of the "feeling that
the Administration gave more consideration to politics than to
geology." As a result, Congress enacted a major restructuring of
the 1982 law in December 1987, with Udall again playing a major
role in shaping the final legislation.

Other issues on which Fowler advises Udall include: low-level
radioactive waste management, Nuclear Regulatory Commission
and Department of Energy budgets, Nuclear Regulatory
Commission reorganization, nuclear licensing reform, and nuclear
safety legislation. Measures to restrict uranium imports,
restructure the uranium enrichment enterprise, and clean up
uranium mill trailings wastes may also come before the
subcommittee in 1988.

Timothy W. Glidden
Minority Senior Legislative
    Counsel,
Nuclear Science Advisor
House Office Bldg. Annex 1
226-2311

*Personal: born, Sante Fe, New
Mexico. A.B. Middlebury Coll., 1961.
J.D. Univ. of New Mexico School of
Law, 1967. 1967-1970, Legislative
Assistant, Sen. Clinton P. Anderson
(NM). 1971-1975, Legislative Counsel,
Rep. Harold Runnels (NM). 1975-
1977, staff member, House Committee
on the Budget. 1977-1979, Staff
Director/Counsel, Special
Subcommittee on Investigations.
1979-1981, Staff Director/Counsel,
Subcommittee on Oversight and
Investigations. 1981-1985, Minority
Staff Director/Counsel, House
Committee on Interior and Insular
Affairs. 1985-present, Minority Senior
Legislative Counsel/Nuclear Science
Advisor. 1968, author, "An
Administrative Procedure Act for New
Mexico," Natural Resources Journal.*

Expertise: Nuclear Power, Indian Affairs, Micronesia, Wilderness
designations

Nuclear power has been a constant thread running through
Timothy Glidden's twenty years in Washington. Glidden began his
career in Washington as legislative assistant to Sen. Clinton P.
Anderson of New Mexico. Anderson chaired the Interior
Committee, the Space Committee and the former Joint Committee
on Nuclear Energy. The latter committee was dissolved in the
1970s, and in the reorganization that followed, the House Interior
Committee took over part of the former joint committee's
jurisdiction. That coincided with a move to the other side of the Hill
for Glidden, who found the scope of his own activities considerably
narrowed in the "lower" house.

Glidden describes as "mind-boggling" his stint as a House Budget
Committee staffer. He was charged with acquiring a complete
overview of the entire budget process and explaining it all to four
selected Congressmen with varying capacities of comprehension.
He was rescued when former Rep. Harold Runnels, hired him to
be the staff director/counsel of the Special Subcommittee on
Investigations.

Oversight and investigations, Glidden explains, is actually
preventative in nature. In his case, it involved keeping an eye on
the various agencies under the wing of the Interior Committee,
such as the Bureau of Indian Affairs, National Park Service, the
United States territories and any civilian involvement in nuclear
power. One such investigation was aimed on the construction of
the Alaska oil pipeline.

Glidden has also had some solid management responsibilities.
When he was the Interior Committee's minority staff director for
four years, he supervised a staff for each subcommittee which
changed with the shifts of power when Democrats and
Republicans took turns controlling the Senate. Throughout all the
changes of personnel, there has been no abatement of the
problems attending nuclear power or nuclear waste.

Glidden was heavily involved in the Nuclear Waste Policy Act of
1982, which set up an entire office in the Department of Energy.
That initial drive ground to a halt "because no member wanted the
stuff dumped in his district."

Glidden notes that from the very infancy of the nuclear industry in
the 1940s, high-level nuclear waste has been stored, not disposed
of. Despite the frustrations of the 1982 bill, Glidden is back at the
drawing board. Legislation for a safe nuclear industry, he believes,
"is do-able."

Meanwhile, another of his projects that hasn't gotten much publicity will, in his opinion, loom larger in importance in the future: the Compacts of Free Association drawn up with Micronesia. These agreements deal with the small island communities the U.S. acquired in the Pacific Ocean after World War II. Glidden worked on the legislative language, set up the appropriate funds, and helped plan funding for the new nation's infrastructure. Other projects such as the designation of numerous wilderness areas have also kept him busy.

A constant diet of drafting legislation, selling it to committee members, hearings, mark-ups, and bringing bills to life could result in a serious case of burnout. But Glidden says he doesn't have the time, and he enjoys the variety.

He has enormous respect for Congressmen Don Young of Alaska (technically, his boss), and Committee Chairman Morris K. Udall of Arizona, despite their differing personalities. "Just having known these two guys is an experience in itself."

Roy Jones Jr.
Associate Staff Director/Counsel
1324 Longworth House Office
  Bldg.
225-2761

Expertise: Alaska lands, public lands, territorial affairs

There was a time when Roy Jones entertained political ambitions of his own. With more than five years of the army and service in Vietnam behind him, and a political base in his Florida hometown, this West Point graduate thought his future might be in elected office. But he changed his mind. Jones opted to join the congressional staff and has not regretted the decision.

Jones has played an important role in the Alaska Lands Bill, the MX Missile Basing Report, the Big Cypress National Preserve, Florida, legislation, and the Compacts of Free Association with Micronesia.

Jones describes the Alaska Lands Bill, which preoccupied him from 1977 through 1980, as the landmark conservation bill of the century. In "one fell swoop," Congress doubled the National Park, Wilderness Preservation and Wildlife Systems, among other achievements. There was no conference activity on the Alaska Lands Act. It simply went from the Senate back to the House. At the time, Jones was on loan to Massachusetts Senator Paul Tsongas, who had asked House Interior Committee Chairman Morris K. Udall for the use of someone well-grounded in Alaska land issues. It was Jones's role to help hammer out the differences between the conflicting interests, and more specifically, to act as an advocate for the conservationist perspective.

Personal: born 2/16/42, Maxwell Field, Alabama. B.S. United States Military Academy, 1964. J.D. Univ. of Maryland, 1973. U.S. Army, 1964-1970, Resigned with the rank of major. Served in Germany and as an artillery officer with the 1st Infantry Division in Vietnam. Decorations: two Bronze Stars, Bronze Star with "v", Army Commendation Medal, and Vietnamese Cross of Gallantry with Silver Star. 1970-1975, Legislative Assistant, Rep. James Haley (FL). 1975-1977, 1979-1982, Counsel on Oversight, House Committee on Interior and Insular Affairs. 1977-1979, Counsel, Subcommittee on General Oversight and Alaska Lands (Interior). 1982-present, Associate Staff Director/Counsel, Committee on Interior and Insular Affairs.

Jones believes the MX Missile Basing Report, on which he worked in 1982, helped to deflect the Reagan Administration from its original "race track" concept for basing the missile. That concept would have carved millions of acres out of Utah and Nevada and, Jones believes, was proven to be strategically unsound. Jones tapped some of the best scientific and military minds available, and worked with the staffs of senators not likely to be accused of being anti-defense. By the time their information (and similar input from other sources) was digested at the White House, President Reagan "came to the same conclusion" about the proposal. Jones believes the U.S. saved itself from a mega-billion dollar mistake.

Jones's military background was useful in his involvement with the Compacts of Free Association with the U.S. trusteeships in the Pacific acquired after World War II. Jones feels the agreements have great, if unpublicized, significance and could serve to deny the Soviet Union strategic basing rights in a large area of the Pacific Ocean.

Some recent legislation and issues with which Jones has been involved include: oversight of proposed oil and gas product value regulations and draft legislation to make the territory of Guam a commonwealth.

Stanley Scoville
Staff Director and Counsel
1324 Longworth House Office
  Bldg.
225-2761

Expertise: Public lands, nuclear power

Stanley Scoville started his career with distinction. An article he co-authored for *The Arizona Law Review*, "Administration of Psychiatric Justice—Theory and Practice in Arizona," won the publication the American Psychiatric Association Award that year for outstanding contribution in forensic psychiatry.

After law school and clerkship for a United States District Court judge, he came to Washington to become, eventually, the right hand of one-time presidential candidate and longtime chairman of the House Committee on Interior and Insular Affairs, Rep. Morris Udall. In 1972 Scoville joined the Congressman's personal office as a legislative assistant. Within eight months he moved to the Subcommittee on the Environment as legislative counsel, and then worked his way up to his present position as Staff Director and Chief Counsel of the full committee.

In this position he sees himself as a generalist, with the responsibility of managing any issue that comes through the Committee. He has special strength, however, in the field of nuclear regulation. Scoville contributed to a major accomplishment in this area—the dissolution of the congressional Joint Committee on Atomic Energy (JCAE), which many Members of Congress felt was biased in favor of the nuclear industry. During the Democratic organizational caucus of 1977, Reps. Udall and Jonathan Bingham (D-NY) offered an amendment to the rules eliminating the JCAE's legislative power. The amendment passed, and without the authority to legislate, the JCAE was eventually dissolved.

Personal: born 2/20/46 in Phoenix, Arizona. B.A. Univ. of Arizona, 1968. J.D. Univ. of Arizona, 1971. 1971-1972, clerk for U.S. District Court Judge James A. Walsh. 1972, Legislative Assistant, Rep. Morris Udall (D-AZ). 1972-1973, Legislative Counsel, Subcommittee on Environment, House Committee on Interior and Insular Affairs. 1982-present, Staff Director and Counsel, Committee on Interior and Insular Affairs.

Scoville also was instrumental in achieving the passage of the Surface Mining Control and Reclamation Act of 1977 (SMACRA), legislation to regulate strip-mining of coal and acquisition and reclamation of abandoned mines. This was Scoville's first assignment as counsel for the Subcommittee on the Environment, and he worked for six years to see the bill passed.

Scoville's views on working on Capitol Hill are firm. "The best staff people don't have their own agenda," he says. "If they want to be philosophers they should write books. If they want to make a profound difference in public policy, they should run for office." His political philosophy, he says, is closely aligned with Udall's.

Scoville is a devoted runner, and likes to run on the Mall during lunch when things get hectic at the office.

Stan Sloss
Counsel
Subcommittee on National Parks &
   Public Lands
812 House Office Bldg. Annex 1
226-7736

Expertise: Public land law

The House Committee on Interior and Insular Affairs, where Stan Sloss has served for the last 12 years, remains one of the most active committees in the House. A large share of those Interior assignments are handed down to the Subcommittee on National Parks and Public Lands, where Sloss has labored since 1980. Among the many bills with which he has dealt in his tenure with Interior, Sloss counts two as the most significant.

The first in which he played a role was the most extensive land conservation bill in this century: "The Alaska Lands Bill" (The Alaska National Interest Lands Conservation Act) which became public law on December 2, 1980. This hard-fought struggle over some of Alaska's prime undeveloped land resulted in a conservation law which designated new national parks and wildlife refuges, expanded existing national parks, and tripled the national wilderness preservation system.

Sloss was also involved in the Compact of Free Association Act of 1985, which involved the U.S. relationship with the Federated State of Micronesia and the Marshall Islands. After World War II the United Nations assigned the islands to the U.S. as a trusteeship. This gave the U.S. certain rights on these lands, as well as certain responsibilities, including moving the islands toward self-government. The legislation opened a new relationship between the U.S. and these two Pacific governments.

Personal: born 3/8/42 in Glenwood Springs, Colorado. B.A. Amherst Coll., 1964. L.L.B. Harvard Law School, 1967. 1967-1972, Office of the General Counsel Counsel, U.S. Atomic Energy Commission. 1972-1975, private law practice. 1975-1977, Counsel, Subcommittee on Mines and Mining; 1977-1980, Counsel, Subcommittee on General Oversight and Alaska Lands; 1980-present, Counsel for Subcommittee on National Parks & Public Lands (formerly the Subcommittee on Public Lands), House Committee on Interior and Insular Affairs.

A similar bill was signed into law in 1986 involving the nation of Palau. However, the final settlement is still pending due to internal conflicts in Palau over the process of ratification. When the Palau legislature finally does ratify its own version of this free association compact, the U.S. Congress must pass a joint resolution agreeing with the updated Palau ratification. This could come up for consideration during the 100th Congress.

Sloss feels that it is most important for congressional staff to always keep in mind that they are there to serve the Members of Congress. He says, "I have always subscribed to the Washington cliche that there is no end to what you can accomplish if you do not worry about getting the credit. It is essential that the staff realize that nobody elected them to anything. It is their job to see that matters are presented to the Members in such a way that the Members can make informed decisions."

Mark F. Trautwein
Consultant on Environment,
  Energy and Public Lands
1328 Longworth House Office Bldg
225-8331

Expertise: Wildernesss, parks, public land management

Mark Trautwein came to Capitol Hill hoping to become involved in the kind of Western environmental issues in which he had developed a deep interest while attending school in California and working as a newspaper reporter there. When Congressman Mo Udall needed assistance with the Alaska National Interest Lands Conservation Act in 1979, he hired Trautwein away from the Environmental Study Conference. The Act created more than 100 million acres of new national parks and wildlife refuges and is considered one of the most important pieces of conservation legislation ever enacted.

Two major environmental issues currently before Congress have their roots in the Alaska Lands Act of 1980: the question of opening the Arctic National Wildlife Refuge to oil and gas development, and reform of the widely criticized timber management practices on the Tongass National Forest, the nation's largest. Udall has been at the forefront of both issues, and at the staff level they are Trautwein's responsibility.

Personal: born 8/14/49 in New York, New York. Georgetown Univ. 1967-69. B.A. Univ. of California at Berkeley, 1971 (Phi Beta Kappa). 1971-76, reporter, Berkeley Daily Gazette. 1977-79, writer, Environmental Study Conference. 1979-present, Consultant, House Interior and Insular Affairs Committee.

Trautwein has broad areas of responsibility as Consultant to the full Committee, which, staffers on that committee claim, reports more legislation to the Floor than any other. Many of the full Committee issues fall within his purview. Udall relies on Trautwein as his eyes and ears on the Committee for any issues involving public land management, wilderness and national parks. These issues have earned Udall a reputation as a national leader and the respect of his colleagues on both sides of the aisle. Other matters on Trautwein's desk include offshore oil and gas, historic preservation and many Arizona-related issues, such as the proposed exchange of Phoenix Indian School lands for conservation lands in Florida.

Trautwein counts the Arizona Wilderness Act of 1984 as one of his achievements for Udall. The law designated more than a million acres of wilderness on Forest Service and Bureau of Land Management roadless areas in the state. It is an example of the kind of delicate compromises between environmentalists, private industry and the federal government that are basic to the Committee's work.

In the 100th Congress, he is also handling Udall's major proposal to assure a much larger and reliable flow of money in perpetuity for federal, state and local acquisition of open space and recreation lands by making the Land and Water Conservation Fund a self-financing trust fund. Trautwein is proud of his long association with Udall and his work on the Committee.

James H. Zoia
Staff Director
Subcommittee on Mining and
   Natural Resources
819 Annex I
226-7761

*Personal: born 7/25/56 in Cleveland,
Ohio. B.S. (Journalism) Ohio Univ.,
1978 (Cum Laude). 1978-1979,
Managing Editor Athens News,
Athens, Ohio. 1979-1980, Executive
Editor; 1980-1981, Editor, Landmarc
Magazine. 1981-1983, Legislative
Assistant, Rep. Nick Rahall, (D-WV).
1983-1984, Legislative Director, Rep.
Nick Rahall. 1985 to present, Staff
Director, Subcommittee on Mining and
Natural Resources.*

Expertise: Energy and environment

The Subcommittee on Mining and Natural Resources produces a relatively small amount of legislation, but its omnibus bills are often large and controversial. The Subcommittee's primary jurisdiction covers coal-related issues, coal mining being the leading industry in Chairman Nick Rahall's (D-WV) district. From the Sierra Club to the American Mining Congress, Staff Director James Zoia appears to be both well-liked and respected.

Illustrative of Zoia's assistance is the Rahall bill to overhaul the system of leasing Federal lands for oil and gas drilling. Zoia helped engineer a compromise to reform the Mineral Leasing Act of 1920, which was not bringing adequate compensation to the United States Treasury. Contentious debate separated independent oil producers, the Bureau of Land Management (BLM), and environmental groups. Zoia and Rahall were able to put together an artful compromise on the legislation. Intense lobbying campaigns were mounted by all sides, but the Rahall bill prevailed. It was reported by the Committee and passed by the House as part of the Fiscal Year 1988 budget reconciliation package.

A related measure passed the House which would allow some onshore natural gas producers to get refunds on royalty payments to the Federal government. The bill required the Interior Department to undertake a case-by-case review of gas producers on Federal or Indian lands to determine if royalty payments were overpaid and if so, what refunds were due. Because of Rahall's insistence on a "highest reasonable standard" the bill would provide a net benefit to the Treasury.

One of the major Rahall initiatives with which Zoia has assisted is the passage of the West Virginia National Interest River Conservation Act of 1987. The bill protects several scenic rivers in West Virginia from development and makes those waterways the largest network of Federally protected rivers in the country.

The Administration is at loggerheads with full Committee Chairman Udall and Rahall over a "giveaway" of Federal oil shale lands. At issue are some 1,700 claims to Federal oil shale lands under the 1872 Mining Act, which allowed individuals and companies to claim title to such lands. The 1920 Mineral Lands Leasing Act put an end to that practice, reserving title for government and allowing mining companies only to lease the land. The Act "grandfathered" all valid claims made before 1920 if holders were actively developing the claims. In 1986, the Interior Department settled with oil companies, giving them title to some 82,000 acres of the land for $2.50 per acre. The bill would block similar action on about 260,000 acres still being claimed.

HOUSE OF REPRESENTATIVES
COMMITTEE ON THE JUDICIARY

David W. Beier
Assistant Counsel
Subcommittee on Courts, Civil
  Liberties, and the Administration
  of Justice
2137 Rayburn House Office Bldg.
225-3926

Expertise: Intellectual property rights, patent term restoration, trademark law, electronic communications

Having both a legal and an academic background has served David Beier well since he joined the House Judiciary Subcommittee on Crime in 1979. Beier has been immersed in a host of major issues: the creation a new bankruptcy court system, criminal justice and court reform, product liability, white collar crime and limitations on governmental investigative power.

The list does not end there. Beier has also been involved in the development of legislation to protect intellectual property rights, the Drug Price and Patent Term Restoration Act of 1984; Patent Law Amendments of 1984, the Trademark Law Reform Act of 1984; the Trademark Counterfeiting Act of 1984; and the Electronic Communications Privacy Act.

He is particularly proud of his work on the Electronic Communications Privacy Act, and the challenge of bringing together a broad coalition of diverse interest groups from the American Civil Liberties Union to AT&T. The effort was so successful that IBM took out a full page ad in *The Washington Post* to thank Congress for the Act.

Beier regrets only one lost battle, early in his career, on sentencing reform.

As evidenced by the list of published articles to his credit, Beier has been a prolific writer. Publications to his credit include: co-authored with Robert W. Kastenmeier: "Electronic Communications Privacy Act," *Harvard Journal of Legislation*, 1987. "Protection of United States Process Patents, Industrial Property," published by World Intellectual Property Organization, Geneva, Switzerland, May 1986, vol. 5, p. 228; "Bail Reform Revisited", 32 *Federal Bar Journal* 82 (1985); Co-author with Robert F. Drinan and Michael E. Ward, "The Federal Criminal Code: The Houses Are Divided", 18 *American Criminal Law Review* 509 (1981).

Personal: B.A. Colgate Univ., 1970. J.D. Union Univ., Albany Law School, 1973. 1974-1975, New York Civil Liberties Union. 1975-1978, Monroe County Legal Assistance Corporation, Rochester, NY. 1976, Adjunct Professor, School of Criminal Justice, Rochester Institute of Technology. 1978-1979, New York State Executive Advisory Committee on Sentencing. 1979, Adjunct Professor of Law, Brooklyn Law School. 1979-present, Committee on the Judiciary.

When not preoccupied with issues of the day or events on Capitol Hill, Beier manages to take time out to spend with his wife and their two-year-old daughter. He bicycles and has run the Marine Corps Marathon, finishing in the top half in 1983.

Alan F. Coffey, Jr.
Chief Minority Counsel
B-351C Rayburn House Office
  Bldg.
225-6906

Expertise: Antitrust, administrative law, civil rights

A fifteen-year veteran of Capitol Hill, Alan Coffey holds the top minority staff post on the House Committee on the Judiciary. Coffey, 43, started his career in the late 1960's at the Department of Housing and Urban Development and soon found his way to Capitol Hill with a four-year stint as legislative assistant on the personal staff of Rep. Hamilton "Ham" Fish, Jr., of New York. In 1974, he moved to the Judiciary Committee staff to serve as minority counsel for the Subcommittee on Administrative Law and Government Relations.

Although Coffey later returned to HUD for two years as a Reagan political appointee in 1982 as Deputy General Counsel, the bulk of his experience has been as a professional staffer with the House Judiciary Committee, headed by Rep. Peter W. Rodino, Jr. of New Jersey.

Coffey is the chief minority counsel to the seven subcommittees of the Judiciary Committee, running a shop of 10 lawyers and five clerical assistants for Fish. In addition, he is the principal minority counsel to the Subcommittee on Monopolies and Commercial Law.

Personal: born 11/08/44 in Syracuse, New York. B.A. Le Moyne Coll., 1966 (cum laude). M.A. American Univ., 1968. J.D. Georgetown Univ., 1972 (Pi Sigma Alpha, Pi Gamma Mu). 1967-1968, Program Analyst and 1969-1970, Assistant for Congressional Relations, Dept. of Housing and Urban Development. 1970-1974, Legislative Assistant to U.S. Rep. Hamilton Fish (R-NY). 1974-1981, Minority Counsel, Subcommittee on Administrative Law & Government Relations, House Committee on the Judiciary. 1981-1983, Deputy General Counsel, Dept. of Housing & Urban Development (Reagan political appointee). 1983-present, Chief Minority Counsel, House Committee on the Judiciary.

"Alan Coffey has a unique ability to absorb information and to explain the intricacies of legislation in plain English," says Fish of his aide. According to a recent *The National Journal* article, "The Hill People," (5/16/87), Coffey is considered by his colleagues to be "political—but a skilled lawyer, too." Coffey himself describes his job as a mixture of "politics and law", a combination of legal expertise and political sensitivity. His job, he says, is to "provide members with all of their options on a vote so they can make good decisions, and write the law fairly and clearly."

He spends 30-40 percent of his time working on antitrust issues. He was involved in the overhaul of the bankruptcy amendments in 1984, and recently worked on the U.S. Bankruptcy Trustees Program. He has received top marks from his colleagues on his efforts to draft a bill to shield local governments from antitrust lawsuits. The rest of Coffey's schedule is determined by the interests and agenda of Congressman Fish, such as the impeachment charges now being considered against a federal judge in the Subcommittee on Criminal Justice.

Judiciary subcommittee issues are a combination of commerce (antitrust) and social legislation (such as fair housing, Grove City, abortion, school prayer, balanced budget amendment, gun control) or procedural matters.

The committee is not particularly confrontational, Coffey says, but the issues are argued so thoroughly that the major issues usually develop a high profile long before they reach the floor—so there are few surprises.

Coffey notes that there is less deference to the "work product" of the committee today than 10 or 15 years ago, when a committee bill usually "weathered the storm." There is much more legislating on the floor than in the past, a change he views as generally positive.

His hobbies include tennis, basketball (coach, youth leagues) and reading.

Arthur P. Endres, Jr
Staff Director
Committee on the Judiciary
2137 Rayburn House Office Bldg.
225-7709

Expertise: Immigration legislation

Staff director, Arthur "Skip" Endres is an importance presence on the staff of the Judiciary Committee. In addition to administrative responsibilities, he handles several important areas, including immigration and refugees.

Endres is an integral player in developing the committee's immigration policy. He served as the chief immigration counsel under then-subcommittee Chairman Peter Rodino, where he developed an expertise that is widely respected in both the House and the Senate. These immigration issues are definitely where he has made his mark. As a colleague noted,"the committee relies on him for his institutional knowledge." and Endres is "very, very key" to any immigration legislation.

Endres worked at least ten years as the counsel for the Immigration Subcommittee, and he was the key staffer for the Immigration Reform and Control Act (IRCA) of 1986. Endres was well prepared to help direct the IRCA in the House in addition to working with the Senate on this legislation. He was central to the conference agreement on this legislation.

He has travelled extensively throughout Europe, working with the State Department in formulating U.S. refugee policies. In this capacity, he worked closely with the State Department consular affairs offices in Europe to develop comprehensive policies.

Personal: born 4/17/45 in Bethesda, Maryland. B.A. Univ. Of Maryland, 1967. J.D. Catholic Univ. Law School, 1970. Associate editor, Law Review.

More specifically, he worked extensively on the State Department authorization language, formulating the Thailand refugee language which was accepted by the Senate conferees and passed by both chambers last year. In addition, Endres is an expert on international law, working on immigration legislation such as the recent Extended Voluntary Departure bill and the on-going changes in immigration exclusion language.

Skip Endres's wealth of expertise has earned him the high regard of Chairman Peter Rodino and the current Immigration Subcommittee Chairman Romano Mazzoli, who share a deep concern and interest in immigration policies. These members often turn to Endres for guidance on important immigration questions.

Daniel Martin Freeman
Counsel
2140 Rayburn House Office Bldg.
225-4853

Personal: born 1946, Washington, D.C. A.B. Washington Univ., St. Louis, Missouri, 1968. J.D. Columbia Univ. School of Law, New York, New York, 1971. 1970, law clerk, Williams and Connolly, Washington, D.C. 1977-1978, attorney, Surrey, Karasik & Morse, Washington, D.C. 1973, Legislative Counsel, Executive Office of the President, Office of Emergency Preparedness. 1973-1977, Counsel, Committee on the District of Columbia. 1977-1978, attorney, Shea, Gould, Climenko & Casey, Washington, D.C. 1979, Special Legislative Counsel to the Assistant to the President, The White House, Office of Assistant to the President. 1979-present, Counsel, Committee Parliamentarian, Subcommittee on Monopolies and Commercial Law, Committee on the Judiciary.

Expertise: Parliamentary and procedural questions

Dan Freeman seems to know just about everyone in the Rayburn Building. It would be clear to even the most casual observer that Freeman's friendliness and good humor have served him well, winning him a large number of friends during his many years on Capitol Hill. Freeman takes his job seriously but maintains his sense of humor and staff members who work with him most often describe him as helpful and easy to work with.

The House Committee on the Judiciary is the only full committee with a parliamentarian. The job Freeman now holds was instituted during the Watergate hearings, when Chairman Rodino wanted a parliamentarian by his side. Comparing his job to that of an official in a football game, Freeman says, "If I do my job well, you don't see me."

Freeman chooses his words carefully, as only lawyers and parliamentarians can do. He takes particular pride in his professionalism and has worked hard to gain the respect of Members from both sides of the aisle, believing the application of the rules in the House Judiciary Committee is "pure and ultimately fair," allowing that "procedure can determine outcome." He spends his days advising the Chairman and the subcommittee chairman on parliamentary and procedural questions, and values the record he has built. No parliamentary ruling of the chairman based on his advice, has ever been challenged. He believes the rules live up to their purpose of protecting the rights of the minority and providing a rational method for considering legislation.

He recalls the most difficult parliamentary questions that have ever been brought before him were those from the conference committee sessions on the immigration reform legislation, which were complicated because five standing committees of the House held jurisdiction.

The Chairman refers to him as "chief cook and bottle washer" for the Committee. Freeman performs a wide variety of additional functions for the committee, including analyzing procedural and legislative strategy options and serving as liaison to Members' personal staffs. He must maintain a full working knowledge of the rules and precedents of the House, the Committee and its subcommittees.

Freeman takes and prints his own photographs, many of extensive travel in Europe. freeman met his British wife, ballet dancer Mimi Legat, when a mutual friend arranged for him to give her a tour of the Capitol. They enjoy ballet, theater, cooking, gardening, and spending weekends at their second home in the Shenandoah Valley of Virginia.

Hayden Gregory
Counsel
Subcommittee on Crime
207 Cannon House Office Bldg.
225-1695

Expertise: Administration, criminal legislation

Since Rep. William Hughes (D-NJ) assumed the chairmanship of the House Judiciary Subcommittee on Crime, 90% of the bills he has moved have become law. This phenomenal record is a result of not only picking his issues well, but also having Hayden Gregory as his Subcommittee Staff Director.

Gregory was first recruited from the Justice Department to work for the Crime Subcommittee when Rep. John Conyers (D-MI) was Chairman. When Conyers moved over to chair the Subcommittee on Criminal Justice, Hughes inherited the services of Hayden Gregory as staff counsel. The jurisdiction of the Subcommittee on Crime, in Gregory's view, has a dual focus: "To give the Justice Department the necessary legal tools to do their job, and to see that they use them properly." This Subcommittee has been active in providing these tools. In recent years Hayden has helped his boss with legislative victories in the House on banning cop-killer bullets, bringing international terrorists to justice, and curbing money laundering. The Comprehensive Crime Control Act of 1984, and the major drug bill of 1986, contained major provisions developed by the Subcommittee.

The other function of the Subcommittee, oversight of the Executive Branch, is Gregory's chief area of expertise. In 1985-86, he spearheaded the Committee's investigation of E.F. Hutton, and in the past year has focused on the investigation of U.S. government links to alleged Contra involvement in international drug trafficking.

Personal: born 6/6/35 in Washington, Indiana. B.A. Indiana Univ. 1956. J.D. Indiana Univ. 1958. 1958-1962, U.S. Army, Captain. 1962-1966, Liaison Officer, U.S. Forces, Heidelberg, Germany. 1967-1971, Staff attorney, HUD, San Francisco. 1971-1973, Justice Department, Community Relations Service Department. 1977 to present, Staff Director, House Judiciary Committee, Subcommittee on Crime.

Despite the demands of ongoing investigations, he has retained his skill in assisting Hughes put forth quality legislation. "He knows the system well" recounts a fellow Hill staffer. He is recognized as being able to quickly understand the substantive and political angle of legislation. Despite the fact this subcommittee is known for punching out more legislation than any of the other Judiciary subcommittees, those who have worked with Gregory agree that quality is his primary focus.

Warren S. Grimes
Chief Counsel
Subcommittee on Monopolies and
    Commercial Law
B-353 Rayburn House Office Bldg.
225-2825

Expertise: Antitrust and constitutional issues

Although he may describe himself as one of those individuals Garrison Keillor calls "the shy people," Warren Grimes has earned plenty of respect in 15 years as a government attorney.

In a period when antitrust law has been in a defensive posture, Grimes, according to *The National Journal*, "helped soothe tensions" between the Justice Department and Rep. Peter Rodino, Jr., chairman of both the Monopolies Subcommittee and the full Judiciary Committee. These duties were especially significant since much of the subcommittee's jurisdiction involves oversight of the Administration's enforcement of the law.

Efforts to strengthen the government's role in the 1980s wave of corporate mergers and acquisitions have been stymied by legal intricacies, economic uncertainties, and competing proposals from the Senate and other committees. Grimes and other key Rodino staffers have helped the Chairman successfully push tougher protections against vertical price-fixing, while negotiating bills to relax curbs on joint research and development, protect local governments from monetary damages in antitrust suits, and shift authority over airline mergers to the Department of Transportation, rather than Justice. Under the team-style operation at the Judiciary Committee, the subcommittee counsel is consulted on constitutional questions before the committee, such as proposed balanced budget amendments.

Personal: born 5/23/43 in St. Louis, Missouri. B.A. Stanford Univ., 1965. J.D. Univ. of Michigan Law School, 1968. 1968-69, associate, O'Melveny & Myers. 1969-72, fellowship, Volkswagon Foundation, studied in Heidelberg and Munich, West Germany. 1972-74, Office of Legal Counsel, U.S. Dept. of Justice. 1974-80, Office of General Counsel, Federal Trade Commission. 1980-present, Chief Counsel, Subcommittee on Monopolies and Commercial Law, House Judiciary Committee.

Grimes is "a low-key professional kind of guy," in the words of one fellow staff attorney. As an adjunct professor at Georgetown and Catholic Universities, Grimes has taught courses on antitrust and another of his specialties, comparative international law. While he was an attorney at the Federal Trade Commission, one of Grimes's chief duties was to represent the agency in negotiations among OECD countries (an association of developed, mostly free-market nations).

Grimes was married a year ago; he and his wife met as members of the Paul Hill Chorale, a group which has performed at the Kennedy Center and other local venues.

M. Elaine Mielke
General Counsel
2137 Rayburn House Office Bldg.
225-8088

Personal: born 7/16/51 in Easton, Maryland. B.A. Univ. of Santa Clara, 1973. Univ. of Paris (Sorbonne), 1972. J.D. Univ. of Santa Clara, 1976 (summa cum laude). Member, California Bar. 1977-1978, instructor, legal research and writing, Hastings College of Law, Univ. of California. 1976-1978, Judicial Attorney for California Court of Appeal, First Appellate District. 1978-1980, associate attorney, Pillsbury, Madison and Sutro, San Francisco. 1980-1981, Attorney Advisor for the Office of Legislative Affairs, U.S. Dept. of Justice. 1981-1984, Counsel, Subcommittee on Monopolies and Commercial Law, Committee on the Judiciary. 1984-present, General Counsel, Committee on the Judiciary

Expertise: Antitrust, bankruptcy, independent counsel law

As General Counsel to the House Judiciary Committee, where she must attend to the doings of 35 lawyer-Members and a similar number of lawyer-staffers, Elaine Mielke may frequently recall Shakespeare's oft-quoted words, "The first thing we do, let's kill all the lawyers." Or she might reflect more soberly on Thomas Jefferson's observations on Congress: "That one hundred and fifty lawyers should do business together ought not to be expected."

Mielke, however, is an experienced attorney herself, who relishes the arcane give-and-take of Judiciary Committee proceedings. Judiciary has one of the broadest jurisdictions of any committee on the Hill, and while Chairman Peter Rodino (D-NJ) relies heavily on seven very busy subcommittee chairmen, the Committee uses a unified staff team that minimizes the kind of turf battles seen on more decentralized panels, such as Energy and Commerce with its largely autonomous subcommittees. In such a situation, Mielke describes her job as "delegating everything, and reviewing everything."

Having served as a counsel to Rodino's Subcommittee on Monopolies and Commercial Law from 1981 to 1984, Mielke now concentrates on antitrust and bankruptcy law. According to *The National Journal*, Rodino chose her for the General Counsel slot over senior staffers with more legislative experience after her impressive work on the effort to overhaul the nation's bankruptcy laws during the 99th Congress.

During her service as General Counsel, Mielke has also developed an expert's knowledge of the hotly debated independent counsel law, and found herself at the center of three of the Committee's largest investigations ever.

In 1986, Mielke directed the collection of evidence by a precedent-setting special panel for the impeachment and Senate trial of U.S. District Judge Harry Claiborne of Nevada. Claiborne was the first federal official to be impeached in fifty years, on charges related to his 1984 conviction for tax fraud.

Finally, Mielke acted as Rodino's personal aide in the Iran-contra investigation. Even with these major inquiries occupying her time, Mielke has still managed to leave an imprint on such mega-issues as gun control, immigration, the anti-drug bill, and a myriad of other authorizations since 1984.

From her years in California, Mielke enjoys the outdoors and likes running, tennis, and sailing.

Thomas E. Mooney
Minority Counsel
2142 Rayburn House Office Bldg.
225-6504

Expertise: Patent, trademark and copyright law

When Rep. Carlos Moorehead (R-CA) pokes his head into Tom Mooney's office to ask for advice, you can assume Moorehead is listening, as he calls Mooney a "top professional".

A veteran Capitol Hill staff member, Mooney is best known for his work as the Chief Republican Counsel for the House Subcommittee on Patents and Copyrights, work which helped lead to the enactment of the landmark Copyright Act of 1976.

Today, he is still regarded as an expert in copyright and patent law. Mooney is a member of the Planning Committee for the Bicentennial Celebration of the Copyright and Patent Acts and a member of the Steering Committee, D.C. Bar Section of Patent, Trademark and Copyright Law.

Mooney has maintained a healthy sense of humor about life on Capitol Hill. It comes through when he tells a story about a photograph of himself and then Vice President Gerald Ford that hangs on his office wall. Ford, Mooney recounts, had requested a copy of a bill for a news interview. Naturally, Mooney rushed to provide a copy, only to discover he had brought the wrong bill. In the photograph taken to record the event, Mooney stands over Ford's shoulder as if conferring with the Vice President, while Ford inconspicuously covers the title of the bill with his hand.

Personal: born 2/8/43 in Lima, Ohio. B.A. Saint Joseph's Coll., Rensselaer, IN. A.Da. Ohio Northern Univ., 1968. J.D. Georgetown Univ. Law Center, 1967. 1970, Ohio State Bar. 1972, District of Columbia Bar. 1973, U.S. Supreme Court Bar. 1976, General Counsel to Rules Committee, Republican National Convention. 1980, Advisor to President Reagan's Congressional Task Force on Criminal Justice. 1969-present, Republican Counsel, Committee on the Judiciary.

Privately, Mooney serves as Chairman of the Board and co-owner of two Murphy's Restaurants, one in Washington and the other in Alexandria, VA. He sails when he can and is Vice Commodore of the West River Sailing Club near Annapolis, MD.

Janet S. Potts
Chief Counsel
Subcommittee on Administrative
  Law & Governmental Relations
B-351A Rayburn House Office
  Bldg.
225-5741

Expertise: Federal administrative & ethics law

Janet Potts, the Judiciary Committee's Administrative Law
Subcommittee Chief Counsel, has learned the intricacies of
administrative law in 10 years on Capitol Hill. Her principal
expertise and responsibilities are in the area of administrative law,
that vast body of law which regulates relationships among federal
agencies and between federal agencies and individual citizens.
Promoted in 1986 to Chief Counsel, Potts has devoted
considerable time and energy to several measures signed into law
in recent years, including the Superfund reauthorization, The Debt
Collection Act and The False Claims Act, among others. She
carefully observes the Judiciary Committee's low profile for staff,
working discreetly behind the scenes to complete the work of the
subcommittee.

The subcommittee was responsible for several major pieces of
post-Watergate legislation designed to ensure the integrity of U.S.
government officials. One of these landmark pieces of legislation
was the 1978 Ethics in Government Act, which imposed financial
disclosure requirements on government officials, provided for
independent counsel to investigate criminal charges against high-
level Executive Branch officials and established the Office of
Government Ethics, which advises Executive Branch officials on
ethical questions. The bill also tightened post-employment
restrictions imposed on federal government employees after they
leave government service—commonly known as the "revolving
door" provisions. The Lobbying Disclosure Act and the Federal
Tort Claims Act also fall under the jurisdiction of the

*Personal: born in Kansas City,
Missouri. B.A. California State Univ.
(magna cum laude) 1971. J.D. Univ. of
Santa Clara School of Law (magna
cum laude) 1978. 1978-1979,
Legislative Counsel, Rep. George
Danielson (D-CA). 1979-1986,
Counsel, House Judiciary
Subcommittee on Administrative Law
and Governmental Relations. 1986-
present, Chief Counsel, Subcommittee
on Administrative Law &
Governmental Relations, House
Committee on the Judiciary. Admitted
to bars of California, D.C., U.S.
Supreme Court, U.S. Court of Appeals
for the Federal Circuit, U.S. Claims
Court.*

subcommittee. Subcommittee staffers are also responsible for
oversight of agencies within their jurisdiction, including the Civil
Division of the Department of Justice and the Office of
Government Ethics and legislation regarding private claims
against the U.S. Government, filed only in those extraordinary
situations where all legal or administrative appeals for relief have
been exhausted.

In addition to several routine reauthorizations for which the
subcommittee is responsible, Potts is working on several major
legislative projects during this session, including a bill to enact into
law the provisions of the Hague Convention on International Child
Abduction, bills to strengthen the ethics laws applicable to current
and former federal employees, and the possible reorganization of
the current Administrative Law Judge system.

Judiciary

Eugene Pugliese
Chief Counsel
Subcommittee on Immigration,
  Refugees & International Law
2137 Rayburn House Office Bldg.
225-5727

Expertise: Immigration law, international refugees

Gene Pugliese is considered by many to be the leading expert in the House on U.S. immigration and refugee law. He is the person to whom Hill staffers turn when faced with the difficult and complicated questions of U.S. immigration law. He was one of the principal staff architects of the Immigration Reform and Control Act of 1986, legislation that occupied much of the Subcommittee's time during the past several years. Among the most important changes to the landmark 1952 Immigration and Nationality Act made by the 1986 Act were the imposition of sanctions against employers who knowingly hire illegal aliens and amnesty provisions to allow illegal aliens who had resided continuously in the U.S. since before January 1, 1982, to stay in the country legally.

The first staff person to whom Chairman Mazzoli turns in search of counsel and advice, Pugliese has earned a reputation during his committee tenure for thoroughness and care in the massive undertaking of developing and helping to move through the committee process the largest set of changes to U.S. immigration law in recent history.

The other major pieces of legislation on which Pugliese has worked are the 1986 Marriage Fraud Act and the amendments to the Refugee Act that passed the Congress in 1982 and 1985. The former, as the name implies, was designed to combat immigration marriage fraud; the latter amendments were designed to streamline resettlement of refugees in the United States. Pugliese also works closely with staffers on other committees, and serves as principal liaison to the full Judiciary Committee staff and Senate staff.

Like most Judiciary Committee staff, Pugliese has kept a low profile, working behind the scenes to make sure Committee members have the information they need to make important immigration policy decisions. During consideration of the Immigration bill, this kind of staff involvement was especially important, since it left members free to negotiate a final compromise package.

In his off-hours Pugliese is an amateur fiction writer who has produced several pieces of fiction, including a comedy screenplay. He describes himself as a bit of a homebody, who spends most of his time with his family—"a regular guy with two kids, a car, and a house in the suburbs," he says.

Personal: born 3/2/52 in Newark, New Jersey. B.A. Montclair State Coll., 1974 (cum laude). J.D. Univ. of Miami, 1977. 1977-1979, private law practice, Newark, NJ. 1979-present, Subcommittee on Immigration, Refugees & International Law, House Committee on the Judiciary. Admitted to bar in New Jersey and Florida.

Michael J. Remington
Chief Counsel
Subcommittee on Courts, Civil
Liberties, & the Administration of
Justice
2137 Rayburn House Office Bldg.
225-3926

Expertise: Federal judiciary & intellectual property

From a lawyer's perspective, Michael Remington can not think of a better subcommittee to work than the Subcommittee on Courts, Civil Liberties and the Administration of Justice, chaired by Rep. Robert Kastenmeier (D-WI). His extensive legal background both on and off Capitol Hill enables him to advise the Congressmen on the Subcommittee in a neutral manner about legal problems and the solutions to them.

Remington's career has spanned nearly 20 years of public service, reaching back to his early days as a Peace Corps volunteer working overseas in the Ivory Coast, where he served as a part-time teacher and a construction and architectural supervisor for government housing projects.

His primary areas of expertise on the subcommittee are two: the administration of the federal judiciary and courts, and intellectual property consisting of copyrights and patents. The latter area can be especially broad in today's rapidly changing technological society. Remington understands both the technical aspects and their impact on the legal rights of citizens, and it is his role to convey that understanding to the members of the subcommittee.

Remington is co-author, with subcommittee chairman Kastenmeier, of an article published in *The Minnesota Law Review* on the Semiconductor Chip Protection Act of 1984. This important piece of legislation was a major step forward in intellectual property rights, creating a State Justice Institute, federal courts improvements, and government research and patent policy.

Personal: born 6/5/45 in Madison, Wisconsin. B.S. Univ. of Wisconsin, 1967. J.D. Univ. of Wisconsin Law School, 1973 (cum laude). 1974-1975, Univ. of Paris (Sorbonne). 1975, Fulbright Scholar, France. 1973-1974, Law Clerk, Hon. John W. Reynolds, U.S. District Court, Wisconsin. 1975-1977, Honors Program Attorney, U.S. Dept. of Justice. 1977-1981, Counsel, Committee on the Judiciary. 1981-1983, Deputy Legislative Affairs Officer, Administrative Office of U.S. Courts. 1983-present, Chief Counsel, Subcommittee on Courts, Civil Liberties, & the Administration of Justice, House Committee on the Judiciary.

In 1979, Remington was recognized by the Carter Administration for his role in the reform of the U.S. Magistrate System. He was the Counsel of Record in 1980 at hearings on the Judicial Discipline and Disability Act of 1980. And in 1986, he was the in-house Counsel to Chairman Kastenmeier when the subcommittee drafted articles on the impeachment of Judge Harry Claiborne, later convicted and removed from office by the U.S. Senate.

A current project challenging Remington is the U.S. response to the Berne (Copyright) Convention. Remington is serving as counsel for the legislative proposal to allow the U.S. to adhere to the Berne Convention.

Remington and his wife are the adoptive parents of three children. Two were adopted from the Mother Theresa Orphanage in Delhi, India. Despite his extensive legal background and numerous career accomplishments, Remington proudly describes the adoption of his children and devotion to his family as his "greatest personal success."

Alan M. Slobodin
Associate Counsel
B-351C Rayburn House Office
  Bldg.
225-7195

Expertise: Civil and constitutional rights

As the sole minority counsel on the House Subcommittee on Civil and Constitutional Rights, where his colleagues on the majority side out rank him four to one, Alan Slobodin has his work cut out for him. In representing the minority members on the subcommittee, he sees his primary responsibility as that of enforcement and oversight of current civil laws and issues. This includes policing several federal agencies on major civil rights matters from fair housing to age discrimination.

But Slobodin is called upon to respond on various issues of concern to the Members and considers himself a generalist, who on occasion becomes a specialist on an issue. Because of the divisive and emotional nature of civil rights issues, Slobodin tries to bridge the partisan gap on the subcommittee by maintaining good relations with his Democratic colleagues.

Among his accomplishments, Slobodin lists his assistance to the ranking Subcommittee member James Sensenbrenner (R-WI) in accelerating impeachment proceedings against convicted Judge Harry Claiborne. He also was involved in the Children's Justice Act, which assists states in taking measures against child abuse.

Personal: born 5/4/57 in Neptune, New Jersey. B.B.A. Temple Univ., 1979 (magna cum laude). J.D. George Washington Univ. National Law Center, 1984 (Dean's List). 1984-1985, attorney, Ross, Dixon and Masback. 1985-1986, Assistant General Counsel, Washington Legal Foundation. 1986-present, Committee on the Judiciary.

Raymond V. Smietanka
Minority Associate Counsel
Subcommittee on Criminal Justice
111 Cannon House Office Bldg.
225-7087

Expertise: RICO & criminal law

In 1975, the lure of working in the Congress brought Raymond Smietanka from Michigan to Washington, D.C., in search of a career on Capitol Hill. He found it on the Criminal Justice Subcommittee of the House Judiciary Committee, where he has served for the last 12 years.

Smietanka is advisor to the Republican members of both the full Judiciary Committee and the Subcommittee on Criminal Justice, assisting them in dealing with issues in public hearings, in committee "mark-up" and on the floor of the House. Framing and researching issues, writing bills, and compiling statements for the members of the full committee and subcommittee are Smietanka's main responsibilities.

One of his areas of expertise is the controversial RICO (Racketeer Influenced Corrupt Organization Statute) reform measure of 1987. He was also instrumental in another controversial issue, the Criminal Code Revision, which attempted to codify federal criminal statutes and became an ongoing project for Smietanka from 1975 through 1980.

Personal: born 11/19/45 in Chicago, Illinois. B.A. DePaul Univ., 1967. M.S. Medill School of Journalism, 1968. J.D. John Marshall Law School, 1975. 1963-1965, sports correspondent, The Evening Press, Carthage, MO. 1968, Washington correspondent, Medill News Service. 1968-1969, 1971, reporter News-Palladium, Benton Harbor, MI. 1969-1971, U.S. Army, served in Vietnam as Army correspondent 1970-1971. 1973-1974, Special Assistant Prosecutor, Berrien County, MI. 1975-present, Minority Associate Counsel, Subcommittee on Criminal Justice, House Committee on the Judiciary.

In addition, he had significant input with a provision of the Omnibus Drug Bill of 1986. The amendment was a death penalty provision aimed at drug dealers convicted on murder charges. Smietanka was also instrumental in formulating legislation on crime victim compensation. The resulting federal act aids states in compensating victims for personal expenses incurred as the result of a crime committed against them.

A major success for the subcommittee and Smietanka was the Omnibus Crime Control Act of 1984. This major piece of legislation contained both an insanity defense reform measure and a sentencing reform provision. The latter set up a commission to establish sentencing guidelines for federal judges.

When he is able to find free time away from the office, Smietanka enjoys swimming and running. But time devoted to equine photography is perhaps his most enjoyable since it permits him an outlet for a continuing interest in sports journalism. His photos have appeared in the *Horseman's Journal, Spur* and *The Thoroughbred Racing*, but he is especially proud of his cover photo for the *Texas Thoroughbred* of Kentucky Derby winner Alysheba.

Eric E. Sterling
Assistant Counsel
Subcommittee on Crime
207 Cannon House Office Bldg.
225-1695

Personal: born 10/25/49 in New York, New York. B.A. Haverford Coll., 1973. J.D. Villanova Univ. Law School, 1976. 1976-1979, Public Defender, Delaware County, PA. 1979-1981, Assistant Counsel, Subcommittee on Criminal Justice, House Committee on the Judiciary. 1981-present, Counsel, Subcommittee on Crime, House Committee on the Judiciary.

Expertise: Drug enforcement, money laundering, pornography and gun control

Over the last five years, the House Judiciary Subcommittee on Crime has been hard at work rewriting the nation's criminal code. Under Chairman William Hughes (D-NJ), the committee produced the Comprehensive Crime Control Act of 1984, the drug bill in 1986, and last year focused on plastic guns, pornography, and synthetic drugs. The subcommittee and it staff have earned a reputation for thoroughness, vindicating Congressional prerogatives, and dogged attention to detail.

A former public defender, Sterling came to the Judiciary Committee to work for former Rep. Bob Drinan (D-MA) and the Subcommittee on Criminal Justice. Drinan did not run for reelection in 1980 after the Pope ordered priests, including Father Drinan, to extricate themselves from elective politics. In 1981, Sterling moved to the Subcommittee on Crime under Chairman Bill Hughes. He recalls that his years on Drinan's Subcommittee were "like working for a law professor," which taught him to pay attention to detail in legislation and analysis. Drinan, who introduced the resolution to impeach Richard Nixon, also conveyed to Sterling the important role that Congress, in its independence from the Executive, plays.

Sterling was one of the principal staffers behind the Comprehensive Crime Control Act of 1984, and the Anti-Drug Abuse Act of 1986. He also had the primary staff responsibility for the Child Protection Act during the 98th Congress and the Child Sexual Abuse and Pornography Act in the 99th Congress. He was the principal House staffer in resisting the National Rifle Association-sponsored McClure-Volkmer bill to weaken the 1968 Gun Control Act in the 99th Congress.

Other issues for which he is responsible include organized crime and racketeering, bank secrecy and gambling, terrorism, arson and explosives, military assistance to law enforcement, law enforcement powers, appropriations and coordination, prisons and corrections, and parental kidnapping.

Lobbyists praise his knowledge of the issues. Hill staffers familiar with Sterling note he is the quintessential loyal staff member. "He may be a bit more liberal than his boss," said one staffer, but his "loyalty to the agenda of the chairman is never in question." Sterling also receives high marks from colleagues for his amiable personality and accessibility to anyone on either side of the aisle.

Margaret L. Webber
Minority Counsel
Subcommittee on Immigration,
  Refugees and International Law
B351-C Rayburn House Office
  Bldg.
225-8338

Personal: born 1/28/55 in Salina, Kansas. B.A. in Political Science, Colorado State Univ., 1977. J.D. McGeorge School of Law, Univ., Pacific, Sacramento, California, 1981. LL.M. credits in International Law, McGeorge School of Law, Salzburg, Austria, 1981-1982 and Georgetown Law School, 1983. 1980-1981, fellowship, World Health Organization's Legal Counsel's Office, Geneve, Switzerland and Washington, D.C. 1982-1986, legislative assistant and counsel to Senator William L. Armstrong (R-CO). 1986-present, associate counsel for the House Subcommittee on Immigration, Refugees and International Law, Committee on the Judiciary.

Expertise: International law

Other than a brief fellowship after law school, Margaret Webber has spent her entire career working on Capitol Hill. When Webber came to the House Subcommittee on Immigration, Refugees and International Law, she became sole counsel for its Republican members.

Webber's primary responsibility on the Subcommittee is to oversee implementation of the 1986 Immigration Reform and Control Act (IRCA). Because of the Act's complexity, Webber works with the Departments of Labor, Agriculture, and Health and Human Services and the Office of Management and Budget. Through the oversight process, Webber identifies problems, presents them to the Members and helps clarify the Act's legislative history.

Webber has also been involved in the refugee consultation process, an annual dialogue between Congress and the Administration to determine refugee admissions levels. She has been instrumental in drafting and promoting the 1987 Temporary Safe Haven Act, a bipartisan bill which was introduced by Patrick Swindall (R-GA), Hamilton Fish (R-N.Y.) and Romano Mazzoli (D-KY). The Temporary Safe Haven Act is in Committee, but may be marked up in 1988, according to Webber.

In 1987, Webber attended a Consular Affairs Immigration Conference in Rome with Subcommittee members. Webber accompanied congressmen to Geneve in 1986 for an Intergovernment Committee for Migration Conference and has also traveled to Central America in conjunction with her responsibilities. At such conferences, Webber follows pending immigration issues, and researches and writes reports for the Subcommittee. Webber's proficiency in French and German is an asset in her work.

Currently, Webber is drafting provisions for a "Legal Immigration Bill," which will be a major issue before the Subcommittee in 1988. Webber plans to reexamine present law dealing with labor immigration, that is, the categories of individuals who come to the U.S. through work and business opportunities.

While working for Senator Bill Armstrong as his Legislative Assistant and Counsel, Webber worked to repeal the Walsh-Heley Act, which prevented private defense contractors from using flex-time work hours. According to Webber, the Act caused the government and private companies needless expense. She also worked on sentencing guidelines legislation which promoted the use of alternative prison for non-violent criminals. She was responsible for drafting a law review article on this subject and for the Immigration Reform and Control Act of 1986.

Jonathan R. Yarowsky
Majority Counsel
Subcommittee on Monopolies &
    Commercial Law
B-353 Rayburn House Office Bldg.
225-2825

*Personal: born 5/23/50 in Kansas City,
Missouri. A.B. Univ. of Michigan, 1971
(summa cum laude, Phi Beta Kappa).
M.S. Cornell Univ., 1974. J.D. UCLA
School of Law, 1977 (chief comment
editor, Law Review). 1972-1974,
teaching instructor, Cornell Univ. 1975,
summer associate, Federal Public
Defenders Office, Los Angeles, CA.
1976, summer associate, Rosenfeld,
Meyer and Susman, Beverly Hills, CA.
1977-1982, associate, Covington and
Burling. 1982-present, Majority
Counsel, House Committee on the
Judiciary.*

Expertise: Antitrust, constitutional law, product liability

When House Judiciary Committee Chairman Peter Rodino (D-NJ)
selected Jonathan Yarowsky as a counsel for his subcommittee,
he selected a professional with first-rate academic credentials.
Yarowsky's impressive education and work experience are
representative of the professional staff increasingly found on
Capitol Hill.

Yarowsky has been recognized for his contributions to legal
publications such as *Judicial Deference to Arbitral Determinations:
Continuing Problems of Power and Finality*. His area of primary
responsibility is antitrust legislation, and he was heavily involved in
working for passage and enactment of the research and
development joint venture bill and the municipal antitrust
legislation. He has continuing responsibility for developing all
antitrust merger legislation and legislation dealing with vertical
price-fixing.

Although a leading expert in antitrust and constitutional law,
Yarowsky rejects the notion that such a specialty should define his
interests and perspective. Instead he tends to be interested in
more than one area of the law, eschewing what he terms the
"pigeon-hole view".

An avid fan of modern art, Yarowsky follows art in both New York
and Washington. While he describes himself as post modernist in
his view of art, he does not take a post- modernist view of antitrust
law. In that area, he says he prefers the old-fashioned approach
. . . . enforcement of antitrust laws.

HOUSE OF REPRESENTATIVES
COMMITTEE ON MERCHANT MARINE AND FISHERIES

K.C. Bell
Minority Special Assistant
1337 Longworth House Office
  Bldg.
225-2650

Personal: born 7/12/54 in New York City. New York State Univ., 1972-1973. New School for Social Research, 1974-1975. 1978-1980, News Director, WUPY. 1980-1982, Assistant Press Secretary and Legislative Assistant, Rep. Robert W. Davis (R-MI). 1982-1985, Legislative Assistant and Special Projects Director, Rep. Davis. 1985-1987, Minority Professional Staff, Subcommittee on Coast Guard and Navigation. 1987 to present, Minority Special Assistant, Committee on Merchant Marine and Fisheries.

Expertise: Great Lakes

As a radio reporter in the 11th District of Michigan, K.C. Bell frequently interviewed Rep. Robert Davis (R-MI). When she moved to Washington in 1980, he offered her a job as his Assistant Press Secretary and Legislative Assistant.

For much of the past year, Bell's activities have centered on issues involving the Great Lakes, especially water levels. The high water levels of the lakes were an immediate concern because of the damage and danger they cause. "You could literally go up to Michigan and see houses falling into the water," said Bell. In addition to helping draft legislation to combat the problem, Bell was active in organizing the Congressional Lake Levels Network. Although the water levels and concern have dropped, Bell is keeping pressure on the International Joint Commission to issue its assessment of Lake regulation.

In addition to her administrative duties such as tracking Subcommittee staff activities, speech and news release writing and meeting with constituents, Bell has made a specialty of dealing with those issues which cannot be handled legislatively. An on-going concern is the Indian Fishing situation, which the state of Michigan and the Indian tribes ultimately settled in 1984. Bell works with the state and the parties involved to see that enforcement of the settlement and continuing disagreements are properly handled. Another recent problem is the closing off of a lock on the Michigan inland waterway by the Army Corps of Engineers. The closing of the lock cut off recreational boating traffic, and Bell has been instrumental in securing funding to keep the lock open for this year and is currently working on funding for the future. Bell also began an effort for authorization of a $240 million replacement lock at Sault Ste. Marie.

As a staff member on the Subcommittee on the Coast Guard and Navigation, Bell worked on Coast Guard Authorizations, Coast Guard Anti-drug legislation and recreational boating safety issues. The Great Lakes is her main focus today, and she is especially interested in those issues which directly affect constituents lives and livelihood.

Bell keeps her broadcasting skills in shape by conducting a weekly radio interview with Davis which is aired in his district. Her outside interests include music and cooking, and for a time she and a friend operated a small catering firm. Though still tempted by the thought of returning to the professional media, Bell concedes her eight years as a staffer are a stronger indication of her commitment and interest in the political and policy-making arena.

Gene Hammel
Staff Director
Subcommittee on Coast Guard and
  Navigation
547 House Office Bldg. Annex 2
226-3587

Expertise: Coast Guard

When Earl Hutto (D-FL) became ranking member of the Subcommittee on Coast Guard & Navigation of the Merchant Marine and Fisheries Committee, he sought out Gene Hammel, then Executive Assistant to Senator Lawton Chiles (D-FL), who had long worked with the Coast Guard on his state's massive drug interdiction problems. Today Hammel appreciatively notes he cannot think of another federal agency that has more different missions under its responsibility than the Coast Guard.

Hammel is a strong advocate of the Coast Guard and the vote it plays on important fronts such as the war on drugs. He will quickly tell you the Coast Guard was established in 1790, and has a long and distinguished record of service. It is Hammel's job to, first, ensure that the Coast Guard continues to enjoy adequate funding and, second, provide oversight of the Coast Guard's activities.

In addition, Hammel and his staff monitor legislation bearing on the Coast Guard in any one of its capacities including: search and rescue; military readiness; drug interdiction; ice operations in both polar regions; fisheries law enforcement; or marine pollution.

A sports enthusiast, Hammel played semi-professional baseball in Alaska for the pan Alaska Goldpanners. He also enjoys hunting and fishing and spending time with his family.

Personal: born 10/19/41 in Iowa. B.S. Univ. of Arizona, 1965. 1963-1970, Army National Guard, Arizona and California. 1965-1977, Supervisory Auditor/Management Analyst, U.S. General Accounting Office, Los Angeles and Washington, D.C. 1976-1977, Congressional Fellow in the office of Sen. Lawton Chiles (D-FL). 1977-1987, Executive Assistant, Sen. Chiles. 1987-1988, Staff Director, Subcommittee on Coast Guard and Navigation.

Thomas R. Kitsos
Senior Legislative Analyst
1339A Longworth House Office
  Bldg.
225-4047

*Personal: born October 8, 1941 in
Chicago, Illinois. B.S. Eastern Illinois
Univ., 1964. M.A. Univ. of Illinois,
1968. Ph.D. Univ. of Illinois, 1972.
1970-1974, Assistant Professor, Univ.
of Colorado. 1974-1975, Policy
Planner, National Oceanic and
Atmospheric Administration. 1975-
present, Legislative Analyst,
Committee on Merchant Marine and
Fisheries.*

Expertise: Environment, oceans

As senior legislative analyst on the House Committee on Merchant
Marine and Fisheries, Tom Kitsos works directly with the
Chairman, Walter Jones (D-NC), drafting bills and legislative
reports, writing speeches, and keeping Committee members
informed on issues in the areas of ocean and coastal policies,
offshore oil and gas development, and environmental protection.
Kitsos has had a hand in the enactment of several pieces of
legislation, including the Outer Continental Shelf Lands Act
Amendments of 1978, the Coastal Zone Management Act
Amendments of 1976, 1980, and 1985, the Deep Seabed Hard
Mineral Resources Act of 1980, and the Marine Science,
Technology, and Policy Development Act of 1987. Although these
measures are all instrumental in the protection of the world's
oceans, Kitsos is disappointed that aquatic environmental issues
have not received the same support today as in the 1970s.

"Instead of formulating policy", Kitsos says, "we spend the bulk of
our time preserving programs that are already in place." Kitsos
adds that there is "little time or political support" for new
programs and that during the 1980s, his Committee has largely
been delegated to "fighting budget battles with the Reagan
Administration." However, Kitsos believes that the Committee still
has a paramount role in overseeing and maintaining U.S. marine
programs: "We still play an important part in making certain that
the U.S. continues to be a leader in marine science and in
conserving our ocean and coastal resources—despite the fiscal
constraints within which the committee must work."

Kitsos is presently working on legislation to establish a new
administrative and environmental regime for the mining of ocean
minerals out to 200 miles from shore. An author of no less than 27
articles dealing with natural resources, coastal zone management
and land use planning, Kitsos has also participated as a
Committee staff representative to the Third United Nations Law of
the Sea Conference in Geneva and New York. He has been an
active participant in meetings of the Department of State Advisory
Committee on the Law of the Sea and advisory Committee on
Ocean Dumping.

Kitsos resides in the Washington suburb of Bethesda with his wife
and three children. Stating that his job takes the bulk of his time,
Kitsos claims his only hobby is "worrying about the Chicago
Bears."

Curt Marshall
Staff Director
Subcommittee on Oceanography
542 House Office Bldg. Annex 2
226-3508

Expertise: Fisheries, oceanography

Curt Marshall's recognition of the dependence of the Pacific Northwest on fisheries helps shape his actions as the Staff Director of the Subcommittee on Oceanography on the House Committee on Merchant Marine and Fisheries. Marshall first came to Capitol Hill in 1977 as a professional staffer on the Committee. In 1982 he left for a two-year stint at the Northwest Power Planning Council in Portland, Oregon, and then returned to Washington to serve in his present capacity.

It was his involvement in marine public policy and issues surrounding fisheries that brought Marshall back to the House. As staff director, Marshall now works closely with the chairman of the Subcommittee, Mike Lowry (D-WA) and other members of the Pacific Northwest delegation in developing legislation consistent with the needs of that region.

Marshall was instrumental in the passage of several measures that have had a tremendous impact on the oceanographic environment: the Deep Seabed Mineral Act of 1980, the Coastal Zone Management Act of 1980, and the US-Canada Pacific Salmon Treaty of 1985. In 1978, Marshall wrote an article that appeared in Ocean Development and International Law Journal which analyzed the effects of the Fishery Conservation and Management Act of 1976.

Personal: born December 17, 1948 in Richland Center, Wisconsin. B.A. Univ. of Wisconsin 1970. 1977-1982, professional staff, House Committee on Merchant Marine and Fisheries. 1982-1984, Northwest Planning Council, Portland, OR. 1984-present, Staff Director, Merchant Marine and Fisheries Subcommittee on Oceanography.

With his office located in House Annex 2, it could be easy for Marshall to develop a feeling that he has been banished to the "Siberia" of Capitol Hill. However, Marshall looks at his location as an advantage. "It seems like more work gets done", Marshall claims, "and the folks who do come out here to see me have a real interest in the agenda of the Subcommittee. It's not just people making courtesy call.

Marshall is a member of the American Association for the Advancement of Science.

Kurt R. Oxley
Assistant to the Chief Counsel
1334 Longworth House Office
   Bldg.
225-4O47

Expertise: Oil and gas policy

With six years of experience at Standard Oil of Ohio, Kurt Oxley came to Capitol Hill in 1985, ready to put his knowledge of oil and gas law to work. Serving on the House Merchant Marine and Fisheries Committee, Oxley has indeed utilized his expertise in oil and gas policy. Since joining the Committee, Oxley has had to wear several hats as Assistant to the Chief Counsel.

Oxley has been heavily involved in implementing many Coast Guard-related programs. The Coast Guard authorization bill is an annual ritual at Merchant Marine and Fisheries, and Oxley spends a good deal of time preparing proposals and pushing a finished product through the Committee. An advocate of strong boater safety policies, Oxley considers himself a watchdog, making sure no one slips a provision through the panel that would seriously jeopardize the boating safety responsibilities of the Coast Guard.

Perhaps the most controversial environmental issue Oxley will address has been the question of whether to open the Arctic National Wildlife Refuge (ANWR) to oil exploration. Merchant Marine and Fisheries, along with several other committees, has jurisdiction over this issue. Environmentalists and petroleum researchers are vehemently split on the subject, and it is Oxley who must assist in the crafting of legislation which will be mindful of both concerns. A proponent of opening up the region to drilling, Oxley believes it can be done, but only in a way that will permit the area's inhabitants and oilers to peacefully coexist.

Apolitical by nature, Oxley is especially proud the Merchant Marine and Fisheries Committee is one of the more bipartisan panels in the House. ANWR aside, politics rarely plays a part in the Committee's deliberations.

In his spare time, Oxley can be found scuba diving, or something better suited to a Wisconsin native–skiing.

Personal: born 9/5/54 in Beloit, Wisconsin. B.A. Carthage Coll., 1978 (cum laude). J.D. Golden Gate Univ., 1981. 1979-1985, Standard Oil of Ohio. 1985 to present, Assistant to the Chief Counsel, Committee on Merchant Marine and Fisheries.

George D. Pence
Minority Staff Director
1337 Longworth House Office
  Bldg.
225-2650

Personal: born April 9, 1940 in Fort Bragg, North Carolina. B.A. Carnegie Institute of Technology, 1962. M.S. Rutgers University, 1963. 1963-70 Federal Water Pollution Control Administration. 1970-83, Environmental Protection Agency. 1978-80, Member, Pennsylvania Public Power and Light Advisory Committee. 1983-84, Professional Staff, House Committee on Merchant Marine and Fisheries, Subcommittee on Fisheries and Wildlife Conservation and the Environment. 1985-present, Minority Staff Director, House of Representatives Committee on Merchant Marine and Fisheries.

Expertise: Wildlife programs, oceans, environment

When George Pence came to Capitol Hill in 1983, he brought twenty years of experience with the Environmental Protection Agency and other related federal agencies. His extensive background in environmental policy well prepared him for the post of Minority Staff Director of the House Committee on Merchant Marine and Fisheries, where he supervises and coordinates a staff of over twenty individuals.

As Republican staff director, Pence is involved with every facet of policy that falls under the jurisdiction of the Merchant Marine and Fisheries Committee. The Sport Fish Restoration Act of 1984, the Emergency Wetlands Resources Act of 1985, and the Superfund Reauthorization in 1986, are three measures in which Pence played a major role. Currently in the works in Pence's committee are various maritime development bills, in addition to measures to reauthorize the Endangered Species Act and to develop a comprehensive oil spill liability program.

Citing the environment as his forte, Pence is especially proud of legislation the Committee has enacted involving the expansion of monies available for various fish and wildlife programs and improvements in the management of resources and habitats of aquatic life.

Pence has co-authored ten publications dealing with the environment, ranging in topics from water pollution to dredging and disposal regulations. Many of Pence's articles have appeared in environmental journals and have been presented at major seminars. While the bulk of Pence's writing took place while he was with the EPA, he continues to draft legislation with much the same vigor as his earlier work.

A resident of the District of Columbia, Pence and his wife, Susan Sarason, have three children. Not surprisingly, Pence lists scuba-diving as a major hobby, along with hunting.

Jeffrey Pike
Senior Professional Staff Member
Subcommittee on Fisheries and
   Wildlife Conservation and the
   Environment
543 House Office Bldg. Annex 2
226-3533

*Personal: born 3/24/54 in East
Orange, New Jersey. B.A. Boston
Univ., 1976 (cum laude). M.P.A. Univ.
of Massachusetts, 1978. 1978-1980,
Staff Assistant, Subcommittee on
Oceanography. 1980-1983, Staff
Assistant, Subcommittee on Coast
Guard and Navigation. 1983,
commercial fisherman, Pike Fisheries,
Cape Cod, MA. 1984-1986,
Administrative Assistant for district
office, Rep. Gerry Studds (D-MA).
1987-present, Professional Staff
Member, Subcommittee on Fisheries
and Wildlife Conservation and the
Environment.*

Expertise: Fisheries

It is said there are only a handful of staff members on Capitol Hill
who "know fish" that is, who are experts in the law, history, and
future outlook of the fishing industry. Jeff Pike is one of them.

Pike's colleagues agree with this assessment. One "relies on him
as a resource because of his long experience as both a
commercial fisherman and legislative staff member." Another
colleague says Pike is an expert on fisheries and that "his
knowledge is widely appreciated—by Capitol Hill, the
Administration, citizens and industry concerned with fishing
issues.

Pike started his own fishing company in 1978, which his family still
operates today. The knowledge of the domestic and international
fishing industry that Pike gained while on the water has proven
vital to his work. He uses his experience to help frame public
policy.

Pike is involved in some way with every fisheries bill that passes
through the Subcommittee on Fisheries, which is chaired by Rep.
Gerry Studds (D-MA). Recently, these have included a bill to
improve fishing vessel safety and provide timely compensation to
seaman for fishing vessel injuries, as well as international fishing
agreements with Japan and Korea. Pike anticipates working on
seafood inspection reform, as Chairman Studds wants to take
legislative action in this area.

The key to the future success of the fishing industry, according to
Pike, is a clean coastal environment with a good fish product. In
addition, fish must be recognized as a "strategic resource," Pike
believes, and as a "worldwide commodity with a worldwide value."
Pike feels that this international perspective must replace the
traditional image of the family fisherman if U.S. fisheries are to
succeed in international trade.Pike seeks to become the most
knowledgeable individual in Washington when it comes to fishery
matters. He sees it as his job to be the number one expert, and he
focuses much of his time working toward this goal. Pike credits
Chairman Studds, an "internationalist who expects nothing but
the best from his staff," particularly in ocean-related matters, so
important to Studds's fishing oriented district, which includes
Cape Cod, New Bedford and the South Shore of Massachusetts.

Not surprisingly, one of Pike's hobbies is fishing. For recreation
outside of work, he also enjoys sports, especially downhill skiing
on his favorite slopes in Colorado, Wyoming, and Utah.

John Kip Robinson
Minority Counsel
Subcommittee on Merchant Marine
577 House Office Bldg. Annex 2
226-3492

Expertise: Merchant marine

John Kip Robinson's activity in maritime affairs dates back to his days as a Legislative Advisor at the National Oceanic and Atmospheric Administration (NOAA) where he was involved in some of the "ocean living resources" legislation of the 1970s. Such legislation included the Ocean Dumping Act (Marine Protection, Research, and Sanctuary Act) of 1972, the Marine Mammal Protection Act of 1972, the Coastal Zone Management Act, and the Fishery Conservation and Management Act of 1976. But his interest in the field dates back even further to his love for the outdoors. "That's really how I got started about 22 years ago. I came from Kansas to see how I could contribute to the protection of fish, wildlife, and the environment."

Robinson's interest in the environment served him well while at the predecessor of NOAA, the Department of the Interior's Bureau of Commercial Fisheries, Fish and Wildlife Service. Later at NOAA, Robinson had the opportunity to work with the House Merchant Marine and Fisheries Committee, and specifically with Congressman Edwin B. Forsythe (R-NJ). In 1983, when Forsythe became the Ranking Minority member of the full committee, he asked Robinson to come to the Hill to work on maritime affairs. Robinson made the transition to the Merchant Marine Committee and, after demonstrating his value to the committee, was kept on by the new Ranking Minority member after Forsythe passed away the following year.

Personal: born 10/15/41, Kansas City, MO. B.A. Kansas Univ., 1963. Kansas Univ. Law School, 1965. 1965-70, Resource Management Officer, Bureau of Commercial Fisheries. 1970-75, Legislative Advisor, National Marine Fisheries Service. 1975-83, Legislative Advisor, National Oceanic and Atmospheric Administration. Recipient, "Outstanding Performance Awards," 1978, 1980; author "Managing Aquatic Resources: Our Changing Fisheries, NOAA, 1970. 1983-present, Minority Counsel, Subcommittee on Merchant Marine.

In addition to the legislation which Robinson handled while at NOAA, after coming to the Hill he was very involved in the Shipping Act of 1984 (P.L. 98-237). "My current campaign is saving the merchant marine," says Robinson. He continues, "this is a 'people' process. One has to negotiate compromises between all involved–staffs, Members, lobbyists and all affected groups. The ultimate goal is getting beneficial legislation signed into law."

Looking back on his 22 years of government service, Robinson has no regrets. "I have been fortunate in being able to use my education in my professional career. I don't know that I'd do anything differently if I had it to do over again."

Gerald Seifert
General Counsel for Maritime
  Policy
1334 Longworth Office Bldg
225-6785

Personal: born 1/21/30, New York City,
New York. B.S. Rutgers Univ., 1951.
Univ. of Chicago 1953-54. J.D. Indiana
Law School, 1967. Master of Marine
Affairs, Univ.of Rhode Island, 1978.
1952-53, United States Army. 1967-68,
Chief Deputy Commissioner, Indiana
Public Service Commission. 1968-72,
General counsel, Indiana Municipal
League. 1970-72, Special Corporate
Counsel, City of Indianapolis, Model
Cities Program. 1972-76, vice
president, Aspen Systems Corp., and
director, Health Law Center. 1976-78,
attorney/consultant, private practice.
1978-present, House Committee on
Merchant Marine and Fisheries.

Expertise: Maritime issues

Prior to his current position, Gerald Seifert had worked as a regulator in state government, had practiced health law, and had been a lobbyist drafting legislation "on the outside." But his interests in transportation and governmental affairs gradually narrowed to maritime issues. It was this interest that drew him to the University of Rhode Island in 1977 where he studied marine affairs. "I was always interested in transportation," said Seifert. "I thought that the area of marine transportation had the most promise of change and 'modernization' of its regulations." In 1978, he graduated with his Master of Marine Affairs, set out for Washington, and was hired as General Counsel for Maritime Policy, Merchant Marine and Fisheries Committee.

In his words, the area of merchant marine affairs is "constantly refreshing because while the goals can be constant, there are issues and problems affecting many people that require attention. Congress is the 'court of last resort' for people wanting a change for the better. Our duty is to ensure that the necessary changes are implemented for the benefit of all involved'."

After 10 years, he has practically become the "institutional memory" of the Committee. While not all congressmen and lobbyists will agree with all of his conclusions, few doubt his integrity and dedication. Said one Hill staffer, "Gerri is not afraid of speaking his mind and letting all involved know his opinion. If I wasn't in agreement with him so often I might mistake his approach as being stubborn or blunt. I see it as neither. Those who know him and the issues, see it as conviction and dedication."

One of the pieces of legislation in which Gerald was most active was Public Law 98-237, The Shipping Act of 1984, which had as its purpose the improvement of the U.S. international ocean commerce transportation system through a clarification of legislation enacted in 1916. This legislation was the result of much compromise and negotiation, areas Seifert enjoys. "I like to think of myself as a superb negotiator."

William Watts Stelle, Jr.
Senior Counsel
Subcommittee on Fisheries and
   Wildlife Conservation and the
   Environment
543 House Office Bldg. Annex 2
226-3533

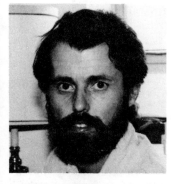

Personal: born 9/2/51 in Bedford Hills, New York. B.A. Boston Univ., 1974, magna cum laude. Dalhousie Univ. School of Law, Halifax, Nova Scotia, 1977. J.D. Univ. of Maine, 1978. LL.M. Univ. of Washington, 1981. 1978-1980, Attorney-advisor at the U.S. Environmental Protection Agency, Wash., D.C. 1981, Staff Counsel, Subcommittee on Oversight of Government Management, U.S. Senate. 1982, Staff Counsel for Select Committee on Indian Affairs. 1983-1986, Counsel, Committee on Merchant Marine and Fisheries. 1987 to present, Senior Counsel, Subcommittee on Fisheries and Wildlife Conservation and the Environment.

Expertise: Natural resource and environmental quality law

In 1983, Will Stelle joined the Committee on Merchant Marine and Fisheries with a legal background and considerable experience, and over the past four years has made extensive contributions to major environmental, fish and wildlife legislation.

Stelle was one of the principal House staff members who worked on the reauthorization of Superfund throughout the duration of the eight-month Conference committee. During the negotiations, he was able to rely on his legal education—a master's degree in natural resources law—as well as his work with toxic substance and hazardous waste regulations at the E.P.A. Stelle received the E.P.A.'s *Special Merit Award* in 1980. Since the start of the 100th Congress, Stelle has served as Senior Counsel for the Fisheries Subcommittee chaired by Rep. Gerry Studds (D-MA). Stelle is heavily involved with legislation to stop plastic pollution of the oceans, as well as the issue of reopening the Arctic National Wildlife Refuge for oil exploration.

In addition, Stelle is one of the principal authors of a comprehensive oil spill cleanup bill, which he refers to as the "Superfund equivalent for oil spills." His work reflects the high priority chairman Studds places on preserving the environment and ocean life in particular.

As co-manager of the Subcommittee with his colleague Jeff Pike, Stelle oversees most legislative areas under the Subcommittee's jurisdiction, including domestic and international fisheries and wildlife law, oceanography, and the National Environmental Policy Act. Managing a heavy workload with extraordinary energy is Stelle's trademark. According to one of his colleagues, Stelle's "only problem is that there are not more than twenty-four hours in a day for him." What Stelle enjoys most is mastering both the scientific and policy aspects of his work, a mix which he says is very complex; bringing these two sides together in order to offer "solid recommendations to the Members is the most stirring aspect of the job," Stelle says.

Stelle learned the tools of the trade of carpentry when he was young, rebuilding old farmhouses. These days, Stelle spends his free time doing renovation and plumbing jobs in the District, and quips that he can "hammer a nail better than he can write a sentence." On some weekends, Stelle can be found sailing off the New England coast.

Edmund B. Welch
Chief Counsel
1334 Longworth House Office
  Bldg.
225-4047

*Personal: born 10/6/50 in Vicksburg,
Mississippi. A.B. Univ. of North
Carolina, 1972. J.D. Univ. of North
Carolina, 1975. 1975-1981, Legislative
Assistant, Rep. Walter B. Jones (D-
NC). 1981-present, Chief Counsel,
House Committee on Merchant Marine
& Fisheries.*

Expertise: Administration

With his newly acquired law degree from the University of North
Carolina, Ed Welch came to Capitol Hill in 1975 to work as a
Legislative Assistant for Congressman Walter Jones (D-NC). As
soon as he came on board Welch took on a lot of responsibilities—
along with tracking all legislation which came before the House for
the Congressman, Welch concentrated particularly on legislation
before the House Agriculture Committee and its tobacco
subcommittee, which Jones chaired at the time.

After serving as Legislative Assistant and then moving to the
Committee for a short stint as Deputy Chief Counsel, Merchant
Marine and Fisheries, Welch gained the post of Chief Counsel in
May of 1981.

In this position, Welch is responsible for the oversight of all
legislation for the Committee, which Jones has chaired since
1981. Welch schedules hearings, writes committee reports,
oversees mark-up sessions, organizes debate and votes on the
floor, and arranges conference committee meetings with the
Senate.

Welch is also responsible for the administrative duties typically
handled by a Staff Director. In this capacity he supervises a staff of
85 people and prepares and administers a $1.7 million budget.

As Chief Counsel to the Chair of the full Committee, Welch also
makes policy recommendations to the other 41 members of the
Committee on all issues under its jurisdiction including merchant
marine, shipping, defense sealift, the Coast Guard, the Panama
Canal, outer continental shelf resource development, fisheries and
wildlife conservation and coastal protection.

During his thirteen years with Chairman Jones, Welch has
become an expert on most matters relating to marine resources.
He is instrumental in the formulation of legislation, including the
Shipping Act of 1984, and the Endangered Species Act. He will be
active in the upcoming debate surrounding proposed oil
exploration in the Arctic National Wildlife Refuge.

Cynthia M. Wilkinson
Chief Counsel
Subcommittee on Merchant Marine
531 House Office Bldg. Annex 2
226-3500

Personal: born 7/30/48 in Galveston, Texas. B.A. Lamar Univ., 1970. J.D. Potomac School of Law, 1981 (magna cum laude). 1970-1971, Staff Assistant, Rep. Jack Brooks (D-TX). 1971-1979, Executive Assistant, Rep. Mario Biaggi (D-NY). 1979-1981, Research Assistant, Merchant Marine & Fisheries Subcommittee on Coast Guard and Navigation. 1985-present, Chief Counsel, Subcommittee on Merchant Marine, Committee on Merchant Marine and Fisheries.

Expertise: Merchant Marine, admiralty matters

Cyndy Wilkinson came to Capitol Hill in 1970 as an LBJ intern for her congressman and "just never went home." Having worked her way through law school at night while working full time as the executive assistant for Rep. Mario Biaggi (D-NY), Wilkinson has found her way from intern to Chief Counsel for the Merchant Marine Subcommittee.

As Chief Counsel, Wilkinson organizes Subcommittee hearings, chooses panels to testify, and briefs Members on the issues to be discussed. Further, instead of using the services of Legislative Counsel, the Subcommittee drafts all of its own legislation. Wilkinson is consequently very much involved in the specific language of the Subcommittee's bills. Four other committee counsels work under her supervision and assist her in the formulation of legislative packages.

Having worked on the majority of the Committee's major bills, Wilkinson was closely involved with strengthening the cargo preference laws through passage of the Maritime-Agriculture Industry compromise of 1985, the Shipping Act of 1984, the Maritime Administration FMC Authorization bills and most recently, the U.S. citizenship manning requirement amendment to the Anti-Reflagging Act of 1987.

Wilkinson believes the most serious issue presently facing merchant marine is the stiff competition of foreign operators in international shipping. She emphasizes the need for reform of the Operation Differential Subsidy Program (ODS) which attempts to compensate American carriers for the higher cost of U.S. crews. Wilkinson believes the solution to this market inequity lies in a fiscally responsible combination of shipper subsidies and elimination of certain restrictions on U.S. operators. A major problem is non-tariff trade barriers imposed on U.S. operators in foreign countries. In addition, our shipyard mobilization base is rapidly declining, and legislation is necessary to reverse the decline.

Wilkinson attributes her success to "hard work and a good boss." When she's away from the Hill, Wilkinson is an active participant in a number of sports, including aerobics and tennis. She volunteers her time and counseling at a local shelter for runaways.

HOUSE OF REPRESENTATIVES
COMMITTEE ON POST OFFICE AND CIVIL
SERVICE

Louis Delgado
Staff Director
Subcommittee on Postal
　Operations & Services
209 Cannon House Office Bldg.
225-9124

Expertise: Postal Service

When Rep. Mickey Leland (D-TX) found himself lucky enough to land a mid-term chairmanship of the Postal Personnel and Modernization Subcommittee in 1981, his first move was to appoint a staff director he knew and trusted. Louis Delgado, experienced in the Texas State House and in the White House, found a new home: the U.S. House of Representatives and Leland's new subcommittee.

Delgado had gotten to know Leland, then a state representative, when he was a student columnist for the University of Texas *Daily Texan*, and working as a part-time press secretary for state representatives Gonzalo Barrientos and Ben T. Reyes. Through these men, Delgado met Leland, then a state representative, who would succeed the legendary Barbara Jordan in her inner-city Houston congressional district.

Delgado brought his administrative experience to the Post Office and Civil Service Committee, where he served notice that he favored practicality over gimmickry. When the Postal Service unveiled plans for a nine-digit zip code, Delgado immediately organized hearings. Delgado's instinct that the proposed system would prove unwieldy and expensive proved correct, and the longer zip code sees only limited use today.

Delgado also helped guide through Congress the only major postal legislation of the last decade. The Consumer Production Amendments sponsored by Leland streamlined the Postal Service's procedures for reacting to mail fraud and gave them the necessary authority to crack down on mail fraud schemes. The result has been a marked improvement in enforcement of the mail fraud statutes, particularly in cases involving schemes directed at the elderly, the infirm, the handicapped and disadvantaged persons.

Although issues and bills assigned to the Post Office and Civil Service Committee are not often burdened by partisan divisions, Delgado hopes to solidify the well-established pattern of cooperation and guide it toward achieving one primary goal: to create the office of Inspector General of the Postal Service—a position that Delgado is certain will help curtail the incidence of mail fraud and corruption within the Postal Service.

He also plans to move bills that would return the Postal Service to off budget status, reduce the amount that can be paid to outside consultants and curtail the Postal Service's contracting with foreign companies.

Personal: born 9/7/53 in Fort Worth, Texas. B.A. Univ. of Texas, 1975. 1975-1979, Press Assistant to Houston Comptroller Leonel Castillo. 1979-1982, Special Assistant to the Director, U.S. Census Bureau. 1982-1985, Staff Director, Subcommittee on Postal Personnel and Modernization, House Committee on Post Office and Civil Service. 1985-present, Staff Director, Subcommittee on Postal Operations & Services, House Committee on Post Office and Civil Service.

Thomas R. DeYulia
Staff Director
309 Cannon House Office Bldg.
225-4024

Expertise: Civil Service law and U.S. Postal Service

For Thomas DeYulia, the Postal Service and the federal personnel system, hold no mysteries. DeYulia, staff director of the House Committee on Post Office and Civil Service, is an expert on civil service law, federal pay, retirement policies, and benefit programs. Most recently, he has been involved in the most substantive reforms made to the federal retirement system in more than sixty years. "The system we designed has been cited as a model," DeYulia says of the new federal retirement system that will cover three million federal workers. "We have modernized the retirement system, integrating it with Social Security, and creating a new one for all federal and postal workers employed as of December 31, 1983."

The impetus for this mammoth effort came from Congress, which moved to cover new federal workers under Social Security, making the old civil service retirement system irrelevant. DeYulia's involvement was crucial to bringing together Administration and union officials. "There was fierce Administration pressure to reducing the value of federal retirement benefits, and the federal unions were determined to hang onto what they saw as a generous retirement plan. My role was to do the political work involved—get agreement from the unions and develop a bill that was acceptable to a Republican Senate, one that would be signed by President Reagan. It was a very difficult process."

Personal: born 9/14/39 in Syracuse, New York. B.S. LeMoyne Coll., 1961. M.A. Arizona State Univ., 1962. Ph.D. candidate, Univ. of Southern Illinois, 1963. Assistant to city manager, Phoenix, AZ. Executive assistant to Rep. James Hanley (D-NY). 1979-1981, Staff Director, Subcommittee on Investigations. 1981-1983, Staff Director, Subcommittee on Compensation & Employee Benefits, Committee on Post Office & Civil Service. 1983-present, staff director, Committee on Post Office and Civil service.

DeYulia is seen by colleagues as experienced and savvy about the political process. Rep. William L. Clay (D-MO), a member of the committee, refers to DeYulia as "an excellent legislative operative skilled in the arts of drafting legislation and of compromise needed to get legislation passed." DeYulia has worked his way up through the Democratic Party, running elections and raising funds. Asked about his hobbies, he will admit to running about twenty miles a week—"I'm no marathoner"—and playing a fair game of tennis, but says politics is his life.

Andrew A. Feinstein
Staff Director and Chief Counsel
Subcommittee on Civil Service
122 Cannon House Office Bldg.
225-4025

Expertise: Civil service, foreign service, whistle-blower protection, spouse equity

Andrew Feinstein is a strong government activist. Mounds of papers and books on his desk attest to his workload. He pushes for change in a quiet but concerted fashion and is effective at what he does.

He was a staff player in legislating "whistle-blower" protection and spouse equity. To Feinstein, working on issues such as these justifies his nine years with the Subcommittee. "There is no other place on earth you can have so much influence by being a staff person."

Although Feinstein is primarily concerned with civil service issues, he also works closely with Subcommittee Chairwoman Pat Schroeder in a number of other areas. He believes there is a role for generalists and specialists on the Subcommittee, as well as people with differing views on the issues.

In politics, however, Feinstein is a purist. He is a liberal Democrat and has worked on both the McGovern and Hart campaigns.

Personal: born 12/02/50 in Hartford, CT. B.A. Wesleyan University, 1971. J.D. New York Univ., 1975. 1973-1975, asst. to Bronx Borough President Robert Abrams. 1975-1978, attorney, Public Citizen Congress Watch. 1979 to present, Staff Director and Chief Counsel, House Post Office and Civil Service Subcommittee on Civil Service.

Joseph A. Fisher
Minority Staff Director
304A Cannon House Office Bldg.
225-0073

Personal: born 3/28/24 in Chicago, Illinois. 1943-1945, U.S. Army Air Corps. Recipient European Campaign ribbon, Distinguished Flying. B.S. Northwestern Univ., 1948. M.S. Northwestern Univ., 1949. 1949, reporter, Dubuque Telegraph-Herald. 1950-61, reporter, Rockford Morning Star. 1969-1970, Press Secretary, Senator Ralph T. Smith (R-IL). 1971-1974, Public Information Officer, U.S. Postal Rate Commission. 1974 to present, Minority Staff Director, House Post Office and Civil Service Committee.

Expertise: Employment and labor legislation for federal employees and retirees.

Though Joseph Fisher makes his current home in the Washington, D.C. metro area, he thinks of Chicago, where he was born, raised and educated, as his true home. His Illinois roots have served him well, taking him from the Midwest to Capitol Hill and into his current position as Minority Staff Director for the Post Office and Civil Service Committee.

Fisher's foray into the political world began as a reporter for the *Rockford Morning Star*. Fisher joined the newspaper in 1950 as a general-assignment reporter and later became the newspaper's first state-capital correspondent. Fisher's experience covering Illinois politics and the state's Congressional delegation provided a natural entree to a job on Capitol Hill. In 1969, he was named Press Secretary to Sen. Ralph T. Smith (R-IL), who was appointed to fill the seat of Senator Everett Dirksen. The stint was short-lived. Smith lost in a 1970 landslide to the popular Adlai Stevenson, Jr. Fisher found a new job when the Postal Service reorganization of 1971 resulted in the formation of the Postal Rate Commission. After four years on the Commission, Ed Derwinski (R-IL), an Illinois acquaintance, hired him to be his staffer on the Post Office and Civil Service Committee. When Gene Taylor of Missouri became Ranking Minority Member in 1982, he retained the experienced Fisher. He now leads a seventeen-member minority staff for a committee that deals with virtually every government agency, not the least of which is the Postal Service with more than 600,000 employees.

The Committee's jurisdiction is widespread, covering employment and labor related issues for the civil service, civilian military employees, and federal retirees. Fisher was instrumental in getting the Committee to support the President in his fight against the air traffic controllers' strike in 1981. The Committee wrestled over a majority proposal to require the President to rehire the thousands of fired controllers. The minority successfully blocked the rehiring and increased the employment benefits of those controllers who had remained on the job. More recently, Fisher participated in the creation of the new retirement system for the federal government, the Federal Employee Retirement System.

Fisher considers the American taxpayer to be as much a constituency of the Committee as are government employees and retirees. "The minority," Fisher says, "seeks to strike a balance between the needs of the public servant and the concerns of the taxpaying public."

Deborah A. Kendall
Staff Director
Subcommittee on Postal Personnel
    and Modernization
603-A House Office Bldg. Annex 1
226-7520

*Personal: born 1/29/55 in Taiwan.
B.S.W. George Mason Univ., 1977.
1979-1982, caseworker, Rep. Richard
Bolling (D-MO). 1982-1985, senior
caseworker, Rep. Alan Wheat (D-MO).
1985-1987, legislative director, Rep.
Frank McCloskey (D-ID). 1987-
present, staff director, Subcommittee
on Postal Personnel and
Modernization, Committee on Post
Office and Civil Service.*

Expertise: Labor management, personnel

With nearly a decade of Capitol Hill experience behind her, Deborah Kendall is widely recognized as a professional who is thoroughly familiar with the Congress and the legislative process.

Prior to 1985, Kendall handled casework for two House members until she was asked to join the staff of Rep. Frank McCloskey (D-IN), first as his legislative assistant and later as director of the office's legislative activities. She now is staff director of the Subcommittee on Postal Personnel and Modernization, of which McCloskey is the chairman.

Kendall's contributions to the subcommittee include developing and implementing the legislative agenda, particularly where it concerns labor-management relations of the U.S. Postal Service (USPS). She is also involved with monitoring mail transportation, modernization and automation of the USPS, along with various research and development initiatives.

Additionally, Kendall is responsible for the administrative functioning of the subcommittee, which includes planning and scheduling hearings, and the processing of subcommittee reports.

Among other things, the 100th Congress has found Kendall involved with legislation on deceptive mail. That measure would require mail to be identified as promotional, as opposed to the current system where such mail is designed to look like checks and other desirable items.

As a result of last December's budget reconciliation, considerable attention has been focused on the USPS. One of the reasons for this attention is the debate over the Reagan Administration's desire to "privatize" —to turn the postal services over to free enterprise.

Kendall sees the importance of making the USPS more efficient, but without taking the draconian step of privatizing mail service. "Sending a letter from New York City to Alaska cheaply and having it arrive in a matter of a few days is something we don't feel privatization could accomplish," says Kendall.

Robert F. Lockhart
General Counsel
309 Cannon House Office Bldg.
225-4054

Personal: born 12/16/37. B.A. Clark Univ., 1959. LL.B. Duke Univ. Law School, 1962. 1962-1968, U.S. Army Reserve. 1963-1971, Attorney, General Counsel's office, U.S. Government Accounting Office. 1971 to present, Attorney, General Counsel, House Committee on Post Office and Civil Service.

Expertise: Civil service legislation, parliamentary procedures

Robert Lockhart is an important part of the civil service system through his expertise on House parliamentary procedure and civil service employment matters such as pay, benefits and retirement programs for federal workers. His involvement in the Committee on Post Office and Civil Service spans more than fifteen years and includes key contributions to the smooth progress of major legislation through the House.

For Lockhart, parliamentary procedure is a unique system, critical to the smooth functioning of the House. "The House has its own unique parliamentary process, one that is not used anywhere else," he says. Lockhart's contributions to the legislative process focus on drafting and moving important bills through the parliamentary maze. In addition, Lockhart wrote much of the Federal Employees Retirement System Act of 1986, and was instrumental in drafting legislation for the Civil Service Reform Act of 1978.

When not knee-deep in parliamentary procedure, Lockhart enjoys tennis.

Alan Lopatin
Deputy General Counsel
309 Cannon House Office Bldg.
225-4054

Personal: born 5/25/56 in New Haven, Connecticut. B.A. Yale Univ.,1978. J.D. American Univ. Law School, 1981 (Phi Alpha Delta, law review). 1980-1981, law clerk, Federal Maritime Commission. 1981-1982, Counsel, Subcommittee on Civil Service, House Committee on Post Office and Civil Service. 1982-1985, Counsel; 1986-1987, Deputy Chief Counsel, House Committee on Budget. 1987-present, Deputy General Counsel, House Committee on Post Office and Civil Service.

Expertise: Budget process

Each year, as the House authorizing committees trudge through their budget proceedings, they often get tangled in the technicalities of the budget process. The Post Office and Civil Service Committee snagged a staffer with an eye for fine detail when it lured Alan Lopatin away from the Budget Committee and into the position of Deputy General Counsel.

After serving five years as Counsel to the Budget Committee, Lopatin had gained a reputation as an expert on the budget process. The House Parliamentarian still calls Lopatin for consultations on interpretations of the Budget Act. Now, besides overseeing such civil service issues as adjusting Federal pay, retirement annuities, employee benefits, or rehiring air traffic controllers, Lopatin reviews his committee's authorization legislation to avoid infraction of the budget process.

But it is the substance of the law, rather than the process, that convinced Lopatin to switch to the Post Office and Civil Service Committee.

During the first session of the 100th Congress, Lopatin immersed himself in the air-traffic controllers rehiring issue. His new expertise has helped yield some success: Rep. Guy Molinari's bill to rehire the controllers fired in 1981 was recently reported out of committee. Lopatin will continue to follow this issue and juggle several others throughout the Congress: civil service workers' retirement benefits, moving the Post Office off budget, and Hatch Act reform all promise to borrow much of Lopatin's time.

Lopatin's interest in the political process is understandable. At the age of 11, he started volunteering for his local New Haven representatives. While an undergraduate at Yale, Lopatin carried his expertise and interest in local politics further and founded The Organization of Democrats at Yale (TODAY). The group helped register 600 Yale students for a 1975 election which placed Democrat Frank Logue in the Mayor's office. Opponents linked the Logue's victory to the Yale vote.

Lopatin's work is aided by his willingness to compromise, accommodate and listen, and by a sense of humor, which he is ready to use even in tense legislative tussles. Lopatin finds these skills just as useful at home with his wife and two sons.

Dennis M. McGrann
Staff Director
Subcommittee on Human
   Resources
406 Cannon House Office Bldg.
225-2821

Personal: born 3/23/51 in Watertown, South Dakota. B.A. 1973; M.A. (Education) 1975; M.B.A. 1982, The College of St. Thomas, St. Paul, MN. 1974-1977, Secondary school social studies instructor in Rome, Italy; 1977-1978, Dover, Delaware. 1978-1983, Human Resources Manager, Control Data Corporation, Minneapolis. 1983 to present, Administrative Assistant, Rep. Gerry Sikorsky (D-MN). 1985-1987, Staff Director, Subcommittee on Investigations, Committee on Post Office and Civil Service. 1987 to present, Staff Director, Subcommittee on Human Resources, Committee on Post Office and Civil Service.

Expertise: Drug testing, contracting

Dennis McGrann wears two hats on Capitol Hill. He is the staff director of the Human Resources Subcommittee, as well as the Administrative Assistant in the personal office of Rep. Gerry Sikorsky (D-MN), the subcommittee chairman. His prior experience as a high school teacher and human resources manager seem to have well prepared him for juggling responsibilities.

As Staff Director of the Subcommittee on Human Resources, McGrann oversees such controversial issues as drug testing of federal employees.

He has been involved with the awareness campaign for National Youth Service. In conjunction with the office of the Governor of Minnesota, McGrann is trying to heighten the visibility of existing voluntary youth services and establish a legislative agenda for new and expanded programs.

McGrann considers Sikorsky's acid rain measure to be one of the most important pieces of legislation in which he has been involved. Originally introduced during the 98th Congress, McGrann believes the bill has had a substantial positive impact, focusing attention on the problem.

Politically active since 1968 when he was a student volunteer in "McCarthy's millions," the 36-year old McGrann thrives on Capitol Hill. McGrann emphasizes the importance of public service, whether it be in the National Youth Service or on Capitol Hill.

James Pierce Myers
Deputy General Counsel
306 Cannon House Office Bldg.
225-4054

Personal: born 1/5/47 in Kewanee, IL. B.A. (cum laude), Michigan State Univ. 1969. J.D. Univ.of Virginia Law School 1972. 1972-1974, Attorney, Office of General Counsel, U.S. Civil Service Commission. 1974-1975, Assistant City Attorney, City of Alexandria. 1975 to present, Deputy General Counsel, Committee on Post Office and Civil Service.

Expertise: Civil service law, postal service, House rules

James Pierce Myers left his position in city government in 1975 and came to the Hill where, as Deputy General Counsel to the Committee on Post Office and Civil Service, his turf suddenly included a significant share of the federal budget. The payroll of the federal civilian government ($71 billion), combined with the U.S. Postal Service annual budget and payroll ($36 billion), adds up to a healthy one-third of the total federal budget. While line-items tend to be determined by other committees, the Post Office Committee's legislative decisions can potentially have an enormous impact.

Colleagues say Myers combines two characteristics which uniquely qualify him for work on the Hill. Not only is he an excellent lawyer, but he is also a very savvy political analyst. Myers' political instincts give him an edge in working out solutions to conflicts, sometimes even before they actually surface.

Myers says, "It's like working on a giant puzzle; you've got to sort out lots of pieces together, pieces you swear will never fit. But if you keep working long enough and looking at the pieces from different perspectives, you get to see the whole thing come together and make a picture that satisfies everyone concerned."

For three years Myers focused his effort on the Federal Employees Retirement Act Congress passed in 1986. This legislation was not without its controversies, particularly in such a lean budget year. The Committee had to deal with such questions as how generous a retirement system could the government afford? How would funds be distributed within the salary levels and who would foot the bill? Myers worked through many complex aspects of the legislation to bring about a solution most agree is "about as good as it could be," given the circumstances of a very tight budget.

Myers worked on the Civil Service Reform Act of 1978, and the Foreign Service Act of 1980. Recently he assumed staff responsibility for matters involving the postal service. He also serves as the General Counsel of the House Commission on Congressional Mailing Standards.

Myers particularly appreciates Hill work because, unlike bureaucracies in which administrative layers obscure progress, "it's easy to see an immediate effect of the effort you make."

George A. Omas
Minority Staff Assistant
Subcommittee on Census &
  Population
B-27 Cannon House Office Bldg.
225-9370

Expertise: Federal statistical programs, commemorative legislation, redistricting & reapportionment, census & population

With the 1990 Census approaching, George Omas, Minority Staff Assistant on the Post Office and Civil Service's Subcommittee on Census and Population, is already at work studying the federal statistics on demographics. His expertise in redistricting and reapportionment is much in demand for strategies on drawing political boundaries.

Omas, a soft-spoken native of Mississippi, is also an expert on commemorative legislation. In the average legislative year, approximately 100 to 150 pieces of commemorative legislation are introduced in the House of Representatives, most of which cross Omas's desk.

Omas has a reputation as an excellent staff person who masters details. Colleagues, both on the Hill and off, cite his political "extra sense," knowing how to best play the political angle of an issue, as his most admired trait.

Omas's work played an important role in the 1978 Civil Service Reform Act. This measure, signed into law by President Carter, was the first major revision of the Civil Service system since it was established in 1883. Of some twenty attempts to revise the Civil Service system since 1937, this was the only one to succeed.

In 1982, Omas worked on legislation which granted retroactive pay to air traffic controllers who obeyed the government's back-to-work call and/or were able to show they stayed away from their jobs because they were harassed or intimidated by striking colleagues.

In his free time, Omas enjoys all types of cooking, a pleasure he often shares with his many friends.

Personal: born 7/28/40, Biloxi, Mississippi. B.A. Univ. of Mississippi, 1964. M.A. Univ. of Mississippi, 1965. Post graduate work, Florida State Univ., 1965-1966. 1964-1965, instructor of sociology at the Univ. of Mississippi. 1965-1967, social research worker. 1967-1968, community relations coordinator. 1968-1971, VISTA. 1971-1973, ACTION. 1973-1976, staff vice president, National Apartment Association. 1977-present Minority Staff Assistant, House Committee on Post Office and Civil Service.

Joseph H. Sisk
Staff Director
Subcommittee on Compensation
  and Employee Benefits
511 House Annex 1
226-7546

Personal: born 8/28/45, St. Louis, Missouri. B.A. St. Thomas College (MN), 1967. Doctoral work, Georgetown Univ. Graduate School, 1967-1970. 1973-1983, Administrative Assistant, Rep. Henry Reuss (D-WI). 1983-1985, Administrative Assistant, Rep. Gary L. Ackerman (D-NY). 1985-1986, Staff Director, House Human Resources Committee. 1987-present, Staff Director, Subcommittee on Compensation and Employee Benefits, Committee on Post Office and Civil Service.

Expertise: Federal compensation

Pinning down the expertise or legislative contributions of Joseph Sisk, Staff Director of the House Subcommittee on Post Office and Civil Service, means asking his colleagues, since he is too modest to speak for himself. Sisk was introduced recently by a union lobbyist as "one of your (federal employees') best friends on Capitol Hill." Sisk takes this kind of accolade in stride. In fact, he says, "I'm put off by staff who take themselves too seriously."

Sisk is firmly committed to improving working conditions for federal employees. "I can't present myself as an expert yet," Sisk says. "I hope to become an expert on federal compensation and the complex issues of federal pay, health, retirement programs, particularly pay reform."

Sisk cites his accomplishments in terms of the Subcommittee's successes. "In the last Congress," he said, "our Chairman (Ackerman) got federal flex-time authorized as a permanent program. This year, the Chairman is working on a bill to permit leave-sharing by Federal employees."

Sisk sees his role on the subcommittee as one of facilitating the overall activities of the subcommittee. "I do whatever a staff director does—help set our agenda, a lot of writing and speaking on issues, a lot of 'thought work.' I like the change from administrative assistant to staff director—I have a lot more time to read and think now."

On the personal side, Sisk is "a fanatic about crossword puzzles and Stephen King novels."

Steven Williams
Minority Staff Assistant
304-A Cannon House Office Bldg.
225-0073

Personal: born 4/1/54, Claremore, Oklahoma. B.A. Missouri Southern State Coll., 1977. 1975-1976, intern; 1977-1981, Legislative Assistant, Rep. Gene Taylor (R-MO). 1981-present, Professional Staff Member, House Committee on Post Office and Civil Service. Participated in Rep. Taylor's 1974 campaign.

Expertise: Civil Service retirement, air traffic controllers, postal service

For Steve Williams, detail is everything. His talent for researching the minutia is a great asset which has made him an expert on the complex issue of civil service retirement.

Williams was very involved with the 1986 reform of the civil service retirement system, the culmination of three years of work and six months in a House-Senate conference. The final law, which created a new pension system for federal employees, was necessary after the 1983 changes which brought new federal employees into the Social Security system.

Williams's main area of concentration is the air traffic control system. He travels to various airports once or twice a year to conduct investigations of the air traffic control systems. He has worked on all legislation involving the subject since the general air traffic controller strike in 1981, including the decision to allow air traffic controllers who had been fired for striking to apply for work in any federal department or agency other than the Federal Aviation Administration (FAA), as well as legislation selectively to rehire former controllers to the FAA, currently before the Congress in the form of HR 3396.

Williams's colleagues all note his thoroughness and attention to detail. "I like to know everything I possibly can before I begin an investigation," says Williams. "It is the best way I know to ensure we (the committee) get a 'feel' for what the real story is."

William does not claim expertise on any one issue, but regards himself as a "jack-of-all trades" because of the Post Office and Civil Service Committee's disparate jurisdiction.

An avid Civil War buff, Williams often spends his free time traveling to battle sites.

Thomas R. Wolanin
Staff Director
Subcommittee on Investigations
219 Cannon House Office Bldg.
225-6295

Personal: born 12/1/42. B.A. (magna cum laude) with highest honors in government, Oberlin College, 1965. Ph.D., Harvard Univ., 1972. 1975-1977, Staff Director, Subcommittee on Labor Management Relations. 1977-1978, Deputy Staff Director, Subcommittee on Select Education. 1978-1981, Staff Director, Subcommittee on Postsecondary Education, Committee on Education and Labor. 1981-1982, Executive Assistant to the President, New York Univ. 1982-1983, analyst, Senate Budget Committee. 1983-1985, Staff Director, Subcommittee on Investigations, Committee on Post Office & Civil Service. 1985-1987, Staff Director, Subcommittee on Postsecondary Education, Committee on Education and Labor. 1987-present, Staff Director, Subcommittee on Investigations, Post Office and Civil Service Committee.

Expertise: Education

To find Thomas R. Wolanin, one usually need look no further than long-time Michigan Rep. William Ford (D-MI).

Wolanin, in his second stint as Staff Director for the Subcommittee on Investigations, has spent more than a decade working for Ford in various capacities on the Post Office and Civil Service Committee and the Education and Labor Committee. Ford, first elected to Congress in 1964, chairs the former and has been subcommittee chairman and remains prominent on the latter.

"Tom has been very close to Ford for a long time and advises him on a number of issues," says a Post Office Committee staffer. "For example, even though he is now on the Post Office committee, he still consults with Ford on education bills."

Wolanin, a Detroit native, first came to Washington in 1975 as staff director for the Subcommittee on Labor Management Relations, of which Ford was a member. He worked on two other education subcommittees and then spent two years as an official at New York University.

He returned to the Hill in 1983, working briefly for the Senate Budget Committee before rejoining Ford in the House for his first stint as Staff Director for the Investigations subcommittee.

In the 99th Congress, he was Staff Director for the Postsecondary Education subcommittee, which Ford chaired at the time, and last year came back for a second tour of duty as Director of the Investigations staff.

Even after the latest switch, Wolanin keeps a close eye on education issues.

"I would say Tom is most interested in education matters," says a staff member on the full committee. "He has spent quite a bit of time on the Education & Labor Committee, and he has written a lot on education issues."

Wolanin worked extensively on the Overseas Teachers Act of 1987, which Ford introduced in the first session of the 100th Congress. The bill relates to schools abroad where dependents of U.S. military personnel attend.

The bill, which was assigned to the Post Office and the Education committees, would address issues regarding the recruitment and employment of Americans who teach at the schools, several of which Wolanin has visited.

In addition, Wolanin has been active on a bill that would permit some of the air traffic controllers fired by President Reagan in August, 1981 after an illegal strike to return to their old occupation. The bill passed the committee and the House and is pending in the Senate.

"If it comes out of the Senate this year, we'll be spending a lot of time on it," says the committee staffer, who notes that issues involving the controllers fall under the subcommittee's domain and that Wolanin has followed the situation closely since 1981.

Chairman Ford and the ranking Republican on the committee, Rep. Gene Taylor of Missouri (who will be retiring after 1988) hold the same positions on the Investigations subcommittees. Although the subcommittees reports no legislation, Ford uses the staff to carry out probes, perform research on various issues and assist in drafting bills. Legislation is then introduced at the full committee level.

"Because of that arrangement, Tom really has the freedom to get involved in a lot of different areas," says the committee staffer. "It gives him a lot more flexibility."

Wolanin is a member of Phi Delta Kappa, the National Democratic Club, the Polish American Congress and the Higher Education Group in Washington. He is the author of *Congress and the Colleges*, University of Wisconsin Press, 1975; and *Presidential Advisory Commissions: Truman to Nixon*, with Lawrence Gladeaux, D.C. Heath, 1976.

In his spare time, Wolanin enjoys playing squash and reading Polish literature and history, as well as military history.

HOUSE OF REPRESENTATIVES
COMMITTEE ON PUBLIC WORKS AND
TRANSPORTATION

Salvatore J. D'Amico
Special Counsel and Staff Director
2165 Rayburn House Office Bldg.
225-4472

Personal: born 2/11/14, New York City.
B.A., St. Francis Seminary, 1943.
Doctor of Law, Fordham Univ., 1948.
1951, Partner, D'Amico & Panagot,
New York. 1954-1961, Assistant
District Attorney to NY County D.A.
1961 to present, House Public Works
and Transportation Committee.

Expertise: Trucking and highways

Salvatore D'Amico is a seasoned veteran on Capitol Hill, having served for twenty-six years on the Public Works and Transportation Committee and worked with many influential chairmen including Jim Wright, Robert Roe and currently Rep. James J. Howard (D-NJ). D'Amico describes the Committee as one of unique bipartisanship that allows the members to work as a tight unit.

Highway and transportation legislation is D'Amico's specialty, and he has a long list of accomplishments, beginning in the sixties. He was instrumental in the legislation for honest appraisals of the right-of-way highway acquisitions, and in charge of the landmark hearings that established Americans' preference for a non-toll road system. D'Amico headed the investigation on the wide discrepancies in state traffic laws which resulted in the enactment of the Uniform Vehicle Code. D'Amico's work in the seventies was also extensive. He notes the Committee foresaw the energy crisis in l972 and held hearings which established the 55 mph speed limit, as well as energy efficiency standards for public buildings, before the oil embargo. He is proud of the hearings in the early seventies on the dangers of railroad crossings, which led to funding for improvements that substantially decreased accidents at crossings.

In the late seventies, D'Amico worked on hearings on the nation's aging bridges, which resulted in the enactment of a major federal aid program to the states for bridge rehabilitation and reconstruction. At the behest of then Subcommittee chairman Jim Wright, D'Amico also led an investigation into red tape in the highway program, which initiated efficiency reforms.

D'Amico staunchly supports the economic development program which provides grants and technical assistance to depressed areas of the country. Despite various administrations' attempts to eliminate the program, D'Amico feels that it addresses the major national problem of under-employment, as opposed to unemployment.

D'Amico's outside activities include membership in the National Committee on Uniform Traffic Laws and Ordinances, where he is an alternate member of its executive committee. He serves on the Board of Directors of the Fordham University Club of Washington, D.C.; and is a designated representative on the Board of Directors of the new National Building Museum.

Randolph W. Deitz
Counsel
Subcommittee on Investigations
and Oversight
B-376 Rayburn House Office Bldg.
225-3274

Personal: born 7/8/57 in Trenton, New Jersey. B.A. Univ.of South Florida, 1979. J.D. Nova Univ.Law Center, Fort Lauderdale, Florida, 1983. 1984-1985, trial lawyer, law Offices of Donald Kaltenbach, Newport Richey, Florida. 1985-1987, Assistant Counsel, Subcommittee on Water Resources, House Committee on Public Works and Transportation. 1987-present, Counsel, Subcommittee on Investigations and Oversight, House Committee on Public Works and Transportation.

Expertise: Water pollution control, hazardous waste regulation and cleanup, federal disaster relief

In 1985 the Subcommittee on Water Resources found itself vastly overworked with jurisdiction over three major five-year reauthorization bills. To help draft the bills, a lawyer and former intern, Randy Deitz, was recruited.

Deitz spent the next year drafting, redrafting and developing strategy on the Superfund Amendments and Reauthorization Act of 1986, the Water Quality Act of 1987, and the Water Resources Development Act of 1986. All three bills were enacted into law; the Water Quality Act was even passed over President Reagan's veto. After the passage of the three bills, Deitz moved over to work on the Subcommittee on Investigations and Oversight. As an actual author of legislation, and the only attorney on the Subcommittee, Deitz is often called upon to clarify the intent of the drafters. He keeps his eyes open for any mismanagement or failure to execute the law as passed by Congress that might be occurring in the many programs that come under the jurisdiction of the Public Works and Transportation Committee.

Both Subcommittee Chairman, Jim Oberstar, and the full Committee Chairman, James J. Howard, prefer oversight hearings designed to be the impetus for either legislative relief or forcing change in an administrative policy or ruling. Deitz and other members of the professional staff have the responsibility of doing the research, the investigation and related legwork in preparation for a hearing. Deitz enjoys having the opportunity to act as a watchdog on the legislation he has drafted.

An example of an oversight success story is the reevaluation of a proposed rule by the Federal Aviation Administration (FAA) to allow airplane manufacturers the option of eliminating "over-the-wing exits." The rule would have permitted an airline to add a number of seats to its planes. The Subcommittee's investigation determined that during a number of air disasters, lives were saved as a result of the extra exit. Two Subcommittee hearings were held and the evidence presented was powerful enough to convince the FAA Administrator, Donald Engen that the rule could cost lives, and he agreed to withdraw the proposal.

Deitz is an avid scuba diver and golfer who lately has been spending less time with his hobbies and more time with his wife and newborn daughter.

William T. Deitz
Associate Counsel
2188 Rayburn House Office Bldg.
225-4472

Expertise: Transportation systems

In addition to his position as Associate Counsel to the House Committee on Public Works and Transportation, William Deitz also serves as Administrative Assistant to its Chairman, James Howard (D-NJ). This Capitol Hill veteran wears two hats as a "problem solver" for both the committee and Chairman Howard.

As a former newspaper correspondent for the *Asbury Park Press* in New Jersey, Deitz was assigned to the state house in New Jersey, where he first wrote of the young Jim Howard's unsuccessful bid to obtain the Democratic nomination for Congress in 1962. Nearly 20 years later, Jim Howard was representing that district in Congress and William Deitz was an experienced professional staff member serving as Administrative Assistant to former Representative Frank Thompson. When Jim Howard became the Chairman of the Public Works Committee, he asked Deitz to join him as Associate Counsel. Deitz, a lawyer by profession, credits his experience as a newspaper correspondent in helping him to sort and arrange issues and problems and to act on them. He is a liaison between the committee, its chairman and the community. The Public Works and Transportation Committee is described by Deitz as a "nuts and bolts committee," working toward a common goal affecting the nation's infrastructure. Deitz's job is made easier due in part to the professional support staff of the committee, whom he describes as "superb." Also serving as Administrative Assistant to Representative Howard could be a position in most cases too difficult to undertake while being Associate Counsel, but his extensive experience on the committee and knowledge of the issues, personnel and structure enable him to take on both these important tasks.

Deitz's unique position on the committee makes the job, at times, very demanding. But he has always had a strong interest in public affairs and views himself as being very fortunate to be part of a committee that enjoys excellent bipartisan cooperation between both the majority and minority.

Personal: born 6/13/26 in Matawan, New Jersey. B.S. Rutgers Univ., 1953. J.D. George Washington Univ. School of Law, 1968. (Phi Beta Kappa, Kappa Tau Alpha). U.S. Navy, 1943-1949 (one battle star, Asiatic Pacific, 1946-1949). 1953-1963, newspaper correspondent, Asbury Park Press. 1963-1980, Administrative Assistant, Rep. Frank Thompson (D-NJ). 1980-present, Associate Counsel, House Committee on Public Works and Transportation.

Edward G. Feddeman
Professional Staff Member
Subcommittee on Investigations &
  Oversight
B-375 Rayburn House Office Bldg.
225-5504

Expertise: Economic development

Ten years of Capitol Hill experience and eight years working on
Western Pennsylvania's legislative and economic development
agenda have given Ed Feddeman the skills to pinpoint the
problems and find the solutions to programs implemented under
the jurisdiction of the House Committee on Public Works and
Transportation.

Feddeman is especially familiar with the ins and outs of local
government structure and the economies that govern smaller
communities. His earlier work with two consecutive
representatives for western Pennsylvania's 21st District made him
sensitive to the needs of smaller communities and their ability to
meet them, and landed him the position on the Committee.

On the Subcommittee on Investigations and Oversight, he works
primarily with the ranking minority member, Rep. William Clinger
(R-Pa.). Feddeman's main responsibilities with the Subcommittee
include conducting on-site investigations, researching program
weaknesses, setting priorities, and correcting faults by making
formal and informal proposals for legislation, rulemaking, or
procedural changes. His activities range across the spectrum of
the Committee's jurisdiction.

*Personal: born 5/23/52 in Lexington,
Virginia. B.A. Washington and Lee
Univ., 1975. 1975-1977, Legislative
Assistant, Representative Gladys
Spellman (D-MD). 1979-1982,
Legislative Assistant, Representative
Marc Lincoln Marks (R-PA). 1983-
1984, Legislative Assistant,
Representative Thomas Ridge (R-PA).
April 1985-present, Minority
Professional Staff Member, House
Committee on Public Works and
Transportation, Subcommittee on
Investigations & Oversight.*

Feddeman's major concentration is on infrastructure financing.
His expertise in that area, according to colleagues, is invaluable to
the committee. His recent investigation into how local
governments, saddled with increasing expenses, are able to meet
the expanding regulations and requirements mandated by the
Federal government led to a series of scheduled hearings on state
and local government infrastructure financing.

Feddeman says his expertise in local governments and
economies, combined with his knowledge of Capitol Hill and the
Federal agencies, allows him to "jump the gap between the
Congress and the Beltway" and help communities overcome the
economic obstacles facing them.

On weekends, Feddeman is involved with community
development projects of another kind. He has been active in the
National Capitol Area Council of Boys Scouts for the last fifteen
years.

Public Works and Transportation

Susan L. Fry
Assistant Minority Counsel
Subcommittee on Investigations &
  Oversight
B-375 Rayburn House Office Bldg.
225-5504

Expertise: Surface transportation

Susan Fry is valued by her colleagues on the staff of the Subcommittee as, in the words of one, a "problem solver who knows her way through the labyrinth of both Federal and local bureaucracies and can get results."

Surface transportation programs and related safety problems are Fry's special areas of expertise. She is highly familiar with the Department of Transportation and other Federal agencies that implement surface transportation programs. In addition, she has an in-depth knowledge of the workings of local government and understands Federal projects at a community level.

Her responsibilities with the Subcommittee include tracking and investigating both ongoing programs and proposed legislation. Her duties also include following up on program shortcomings by initiating investigations, suggesting issues for possible hearings, choosing and arranging witnesses, and developing pointed questioning designed to get at the heart of the problem.

Personal: born 6/29/58 in Longmont, Colorado. B.A. Transylvania Univ., 1980 (Phi Alpha Theta history honorary). J.D. Univ. of Louisville Law School, 1983. 1981-1983, part-time law clerk for Louisville, KY, law firm. 1983-1984, legal researcher for bank service consulting company. 1984-present, Assistant Minority Counsel for the Subcommittee on Investigations & Oversight, House Committee on Public Works and Transportation.

Fry has recently concentrated on problems in rural transit, and in particular on safe transportation for the elderly, handicapped and general public, in rural areas. The staff's on-site investigations led to the Subcommittee's hearings on "Needs in Rural and Specialized Transit" in May, 1985. Not satisfied with any one Federal agency addressing this problem, the Subcommittee helped to bring about the formation of the Joint Coordinating Council which combined the efforts of the Transportation Department and the Department of Health and Human Services to provide safe, coordinated transportation for the elderly and the handicapped in rural areas.

Fry is known for her concern not only for the success of a project, but for the well-being and safety of the people and communities affected by it. Her solutions to problems do not follow any strict pattern. "The most important thing is to look out for the people under the program", she says. "We work both formally and informally with legislative staff and administrative agencies to suggest alternatives and set priorities."

"Legislative changes are not always the best alternative. The Members often like to encourage changes without having to do it through legislation", she says. "If an agency knows that the Subcommittee is out investigating a program, questioning local authorities, or holding hearings, they may make changes or initiate new programs before the Subcommittee has to make any formal proposals."

John F. (Jack) Fryer
Counsel
Subcommittee on Surface
  Transportation
2165 Rayburn House Office Bldg.
225-4472

Expertise: Transportation safety and regulation

As counsel to the House Public Works and Transportation Subcommittee on Surface Transportation, Jack Fryer is a conduit for information. In negotiating legislative proposals, he addresses the interests of the Department of transportation, the Interstate Commerce Commission (where he worked previously for twelve years), industry representatives, unions, trade associations, and public interest/consumer groups. Fryer also taps these same resources for their expertise, to assist him in implementing the positions taken by the Subcommittee and its chairman.

The panel's jurisdiction is somewhat different than its Senate counterpart; it does not cover railroads. But this exception hardly narrows the Subcommittee's scope, which includes the economic structure of transportation systems, safety issues with respect to the trucking, bus and pipeline industries, and the transportation of hazardous materials.

During his thirteen years with the Subcommittee, Fryer has been involved in major regulatory reform and safety legislation: Motor Carrier Regulatory Reform Act of 1980, Household Goods Regulatory Reform Act of 1980, Bus Regulatory Reform Act of 1982, Surface Transportation Assistance Act of 1982, Motor Carrier Safety Act of 1984, and Commercial Motor Vehicle Safety Act of 1986.

Currently, Fryer is working on reauthorization of federal safety programs for pipelines that transport natural gas and hazardous liquids. As with his other assignments, Fryer did not rely solely on the experts to provide him with information on pipelines. He conducted his own on-site, fact-finding mission. "I go out and see what it [a particular industry] is, how safety controls are maintained, and how personnel are trained."

Personal: born 5/17/34 in Carbondale, Pennsylvania. B.S. Mount Saint Mary's Coll., 1956. LL.B. Georgetown Univ. Law School, 1959. 1960-1968, Air Force National Guard. 1960-1962, adjustor, State Automobile Insurance Company, Harrisburg, PA. 1962-1963 counsel, law firm of Thomas Lane, Esq.; concurrently, attorney, general counsel's office, Commonwealth of Pennsylvania. 1963-1975, Interstate Commerce Commission (1963-1967, attorney advisor; 1967-1970, legal counsel, congressional liaison office; 1970-1971, legal counsel, secretary's office; 1971-1975, legal counsel, general counsel's office.) 1975-present, Counsel, House Public Works and Transportation Subcommittee on Surface Transportation.

Although aviation is not under the Subcommittee's jurisdiction, Fryer is representing the panel's concerns regarding a Senate provision in an airline consumer bill. The proposal would require mandatory drug testing of airline pilots. Confined to aviation, this would affect only several thousand, but if applicable to other transportation "operators", Fryer is quick to point out, the provision could affect five million.

Fryer is frequently invited to address the many groups interested in congressional developments on transportation issues.

Caroline D. Gabel
Professional Staff Member
Subcommittee on Investigations
  and Oversight
B-376 Rayburn House Office Bldg.
225-3274

*Personal: born in Norristown,
Pennsylvania. B.A. Wellesley Coll.
M.A. Univ. of Pennsylvania. 1970-75,
Staff Assistant, Rep. John A. Blatnik
(D-MN). 1975-77, Staff Assistant, Rep.
James Oberstar, (D-MN). 1977-78,
Consultant, F. Robert Edman and
Associates. 1978-81, Liaison
Specialist, Congressional Affairs
Office, Environmental Protection
Agency. 1981-85, Professional Staff
Member, Subcommittee on Economic
Development; 1985-present,
Professional Staff Member,
Subcommittee on Investigations and
Oversight, Committee on Public Works
and Transportation.*

Expertise: Clean Water Act, Great Lakes water quality, navigation and economics

Gabel serves as Rep. James L. Oberstar's (D-MN) staff aide on the Public Works and Transportation Committee in his capacity as chairman of the Subcommittee on Investigations and Oversight. Her role is not limited to subcommittee issues: she handles all of Oberstar's work on the Public Works and Transportation Committee, as well as merchant marine and maritime issues.

Gabel generally concentrates her efforts on environmental matters. One of Gabel's major recent accomplishments was to assist Oberstar with the insertion of a provision in the Clean Water Act to eliminate the last remaining major cause of water pollution, contaminated runoff. The Clean Water Act was passed over President Reagan's veto in February, 1987 and the Environmental Protection Agency is in the process of implementing the provisions. One of Oberstar's current priorities is his legislation to eliminate the danger of pesticides in groundwater, which is likely to be adamantly opposed by all agriculture chemical companies. Gabel assisted with the bill, H.R. 3174, which is pending in Committee, and action is expected prior to the adjournment of the 100th Congress.

The oversight subcommittee has the jurisdiction to investigate all committee issues. Gabel believes "oversight is an important check on the process."

A longtime concern of Oberstar's has been the revitalization of the American infrastructure. In the 100th Congress he introduced two bills: H.R. 198 and H.R. 201. H.R. 198 is an emergency public works jobs bill designed to create jobs through short-term infrastructure repair projects. HR201 provides long-term infrastructure repair and rehabilitation. Gabel drafted both bills, but she believes the future of these costly bills is uncertain during these times of austerity.

Gabel was instrumental in having language inserted in the Water Resources Act of 1986 that protected and enhanced the wildlife habitat on the upper Mississippi River. She also helped organize the Subcommittee hearings on the Great Lakes Water Quality Agreement to determine whether the United States is following the required procedures to keep toxic pollutants out of the Great Lakes. The 1978 agreement between the United States and Canada was renegotiated and the new agreement was signed in November, 1987.

Gabel, like her boss, is an environmentalist. She enjoys travel and spends a majority of her leisure time raising and showing German warmblood horses.

Paul Christopher Goebel
Minority Counsel
Subcommittee on Investigations
and Oversight
B-375 Rayburn House Office Bldg.
225-5504

Personal: born 8/24/46 in Mendota, Illinois. B.A. Knox Coll., 1968. M.S. SUNY Coll. of Environmental Science and Forestry at Syracuse Univ., 1973. J.D. Salmon P. Chase Coll. of Law, Northern Kentucky Univ., 1981. 1970-1973, Natural Resources Planner/ Policy Analyst, Illinois Dept. of Business and Economic Development. 1973-1981, State Liaison/Public Participation Coordinator, Ohio River Basin Commission. 1981-1983, Committee on Merchant Marine and Fisheries. 1983-1984, Committee on Public Works and Transportation. 1984-1986, Committee on Merchant Marine and Fisheries. 1986-present, Minority Counsel, Subcommittee on Investigations and Oversight, of the House Committee on Public Works and Transportation.

Expertise: Aviation, Superfund, and water resources

The Subcommittee on Investigations and Oversight does not normally produce any legislation. However, it has the responsibility to review all programs that come under the jurisdiction of the Committee on Public Works and Transportation. The oversight subcommittee has delved into such issues as: clean water, Superfund, air traffic control, air carrier certification, mass transit, international aviation, infrastructure, and highways.

The Subcommittee, much like the full committee, rarely engages in bitter partisan battles. Goebel sees the Subcommittee's main role as providing the "groundwork and legwork" for the legislative subcommittees. The Subcommittee holds hearings on specific issues, often taking an in-depth look at problems, and then producing recommendations for legislative initiatives.

Goebel has worked on the controversial question of determining compensation for victims of hazardous waste. The Subcommittee found that it is "too early to put into Federal law any specific base or limit on compensation for victims of hazardous waste exposure." The recommendation is virtually identical to the position taken by the full committee during the reauthorization of Superfund.

The subcommittee's work also helped to encourage the Federal Emergency Management Agency (FEMA) to withdraw a proposed rule to change the Federal-State cost-sharing for emergency relief programs. According to Goebel, under the proposed rule, states and localities would be responsible for a greater share of the funding for relief programs. A number of Members were critical of the rule during the Subcommittee hearings and legislation was introduced in both Houses to prohibit its implementation. As a result FEMA decided to withdraw the proposal.

Pipeline safety has been an issue of concern to Goebel and the Subcommittee. The Subcommittee is working concurrently with the Subcommittee on Surface Transportation to assure that natural gas and hazardous liquid pipelines are receiving regular inspections to guard against leakage and any other potential hazard.

Former Congressman Gene Snyder originally brought Goebel to Washington to serve as the Assistant Minority Counsel on the Subcommittee on Coast Guard and Navigation of the House Committee on Merchant Marine and Fisheries. For relaxation, Goebel enjoys golf, running, reading and music. Married with two children, he enjoys the time he spends off the Hill on family-related activities.

Phyllis A. Guss
Professional Staff Member
Subcommittee on Aviation
2251 Rayburn House Office Bldg.
225-9161

Personal: born 3/10/50 in New York City. B.A. Wheaton Coll., Norton, Mass., 1970. 1970-1971, Urban Intern, U.S. Department of Housing & Urban Development. 1972-74, Director, Federal and State Policy Division, Office of Policy and Research, City of San Jose, Ca. 1975-78, Legislative Director, Rep. Norman Mineta (D-CA). 1978-1985, Senior Transportation Representative, Urban Mass Transportation Administration, San Francisco, Ca. 1985 to present, Professional Staff Member, Aviation Subcommittee, House Public Works and Transportation Committee.

Expertise: Transportation

Having dealt with transportation issues since the early 1970s, Phyllis Guss has the knowledge, experience, and connections to help shape and advance the aviation subcommittee's agenda.

Her close association with Subcommittee Chairman Norman Mineta dates back to 1972. At that time, she held an administrative post in the City of San Jose when Mineta was Mayor.

When Mineta was elected to the House, Guss became his legislative director. During the Congressman's first two terms, she helped analyze and draft significant highway, economic development, environmental, and public works legislation, while coordinating other legislative functions of Mineta's office, first in Washington and then in California.

Guss also established a close working relationship with state and local government officials in California.

In 1978, Guss left Mineta's staff for a post at the Urban Mass Transportation Administration's regional headquarters in San Francisco. As a Senior Transportation Representative, she became acquainted with the nuts and bolts of implementing federal grant programs on the local level. That included drafting regulations, identifying funding priorities, keeping an eye on performance objectives, and promoting comprehensive transportation planning. This experience with the interplay of federal, state and local interests has been valuable in implementing the Aviation Subcommittee's legislative programs.

Since assuming her present position in 1985, Guss worked on legislation to increase security at overseas airports. More recently, she helped develop the Airport and Airways Safety and Capacity Expansion Act of 1987. The act calls for $20 billion to be spent over five years on airport development and modernization of the air traffic control system. Guss coordinated hearings on the bill and worked to establish a consensus among divergent views in both the House and Senate.

The next hurdle the Subcommittee faces is to see that appropriations are sufficient to carry out the Act's mandate and to oversee the Federal Aviation Administration and DOT's actions to carry out their aviation safety, antitrust and regulatory mandates.

David A. Heymsfeld
Counsel
Subcommittee on Aviation
2251 Rayburn House Office Bldg.
225-9161

Expertise: Civil aviation and economic regulation of aviation

David Heymsfeld is most widely recognized for his work on the Airline Deregulation Act of 1978. He was the key staffer for the landmark legislation, deeply involved in writing the bill as well as resolving the debate surrounding its contentious issues.

Heymsfeld strongly defends deregulation, and calls it the "most radical departure in aviation regulation." He believes deregulation has been a "great success," resulting in low airfares and an explosion of air travel. Another benefit Heymsfeld sees is hub service, which allows air travel that would not be possible otherwise to small- and medium-sized towns. Airline accidents have decreased since deregulation, he points out.

But "near misses," flight delays and poor passenger service have kept Heymsfeld very busy of late. Heymsfeld assisted Subcommittee Chairman Norman Mineta (D-CA) in developing legislation which addresses these problems and is working with a wide array of concerned parties to help fashion compromises on these controversial aviation issues. The two major legislative efforts in which he has been involved—the Airline Passenger Protection Act and the Airport and Airways Improvement Amendments Act—recently passed the House.

Personal: born 1/2/38 in New York, New York. B.A. Columbia Coll., 1959 (cum laude). L.L.B. Harvard Law School, 1962. 1962-1963, Law Clerk for Bailey Aldrich, U.S. Court of Appeals, First District. 1963-1967, attorney, Civil Aeronautics Board. 1967-1968, law associate, Hale, Russell & Stenzel, Wash., D.C. 1968-1973, Chief of Legal Division, Bureau of Operating Rights, Civil Aeronautics Board. 1973-1975, Assistant General Counsel, Postal Rate Commission. 1975-present, Counsel, Subcommittee on Aviation, House Committee on Public Works and Transportation.

Heymsfeld attributes the present problems in the airline industry to the failure to rebuild the air traffic control system after the controllers's strike, and the impact of mergers, labor disputes, and inadequate inspection of airplanes.

Members heavily rely on Heymsfeld's knowledge because, according to one colleague, "he is generally regarded as one of the best aviation lawyers in town. He is very thorough, and he nails down the details."

Since his early thirties, Heymsfeld has grown to love endurance sports. He has competed in seven marathons, a number of l00-mile bicycle rides, and a triathalon. When he is not exercising, Heymsfeld reads non-fiction, particularly on World War II politics and military strategy.

Scot E. Imus
Staff Director
Subcommittee on Investigations
  and Oversight
B-376 Rayburn House Office Bldg.
225-3274

Personal: born 1/1/58 in Auburn, Indiana. B.A. Indiana Univ., 1980. Intern, 1981, Rep. Phil Sharp (D-IN). 1982-1986, Legislative Assistant, Rep. James J. Howard (D-NJ). 1986-present, Staff Director, Subcommittee on Investigations and Oversight, House Committee on Public Works and Transportation.

Expertise: Aviation safety, consumer/environmental safety

Scot Imus' job as Staff Director of the House Public Works Subcommittee on Investigations and Oversight is different than most subcommittee staff directors' jobs. Unlike most House and Senate subcommittees, this one has less to do with initiating legislation than it does with acting as a watchdog over the federal agencies that implement laws. Also the Subcommittee can set much of its own agenda—it can look into any agency's implementation of legislation under the full Committee's jurisdiction.

Imus, who has handled a wide range of issues on the Hill, oversees staff members assigned to specific issues, adding his expertise when needed and picking up new issues when he is reluctant to pull a staffer off his or her long-term projects. Imus and his staff have focused closely on aviation safety and plan to begin looking closely at the implementation of the Superfund and Clean Water laws in 1988.

In the fine art of preparing questions for witnesses and in attacking problems with how a law is being implemented, Imus says his journalism background—he worked during summers between college semesters for the *Auburn Evening Star* and graduated with a degree in journalism—has come in handy.

Imus, who classifies himself as "pro-consumer", says one of the reasons the Subcommittee is effective is its members and staff are united and bipartisan in their concern about safety issues. "I'd like to think that our persistence with the agencies under the Committee's jurisdiction has resulted in an increased commitment to safety." The subcommittee's approach to safety problems is to "try to avert a problem before it happens."

Imus lives in Washington, D.C. with his wife, and enjoys music, golf and other sports.

Carl J. Lorenz
Counsel/Staff Director
Subcommittee on Economic
    Development
B376-A Rayburn House Office
    Bldg.
225-6151

*Personal: born 10/21/27 in Baltimore,
MD. 1946-1947, Army. B.A. Univ. of
Maryland, 1953. LL.B. Univ. of
Maryland, 1957. 1960-1962, Assistant
U.S. Attorney in Baltimore. 1962-1967,
Investigator, Committee on Public
Works. 1967 to present, Counsel/Staff
Director, Subcommittee on Economic
Development, House Public Works
and Transportation Committee.*

Expertise: Economic development, infrastructure projects

When it comes to public works projects, Carl Lorenz is the
cornerstone of the Public Works and Transportation Committee.
He has worked on the Committee for more than twenty-five years.

Lorenz was at the Committee when the two major pieces of public
works legislation in the 1960s, the Public Works and Economic
Development Act of 1965 and the Appalachian Regional
Development Act of 1965, were passed and enacted. The former
also included creation of the Economic Development
Administration.

Since that heyday, Congress and, particularly, the executive
branch have taken a different view of such legislation, says
Lorenz. In contrast to the anti-recession public works projects that
were enacted in the 1970s, such as the Capital Investment Act of
1976, public works projects in recent years have been scaled back
as "everyone has become 'big-government' conscious," he notes.
Lorenz remains committed to the concept of projects such as
roads, buildings, dams and bridges. He calls such projects "the
underpinnings of business, and they promote economic
development." He says, "New water and wastewater systems
permit businesses to come into an area and create jobs." No
matter how prosperous the United States may be, certain areas
will need federal assistance to plan and accommodate economic
growth, says Lorenz. And many public works projects that create
jobs are cost-effective, he argues, in that "the country is paid back
in taxes from the new income." The Committee is working on
reauthorization of the two major bills from the 1960s, as well as
the EDA, which the Administration has been trying to kill since
1981.

In the 100th Congress, the Subcommittee has held hearings on
the concept of capital budgeting, by which the federal government
would create operating expenses and capital expenses accounts,
similar to a private business. "It might be a way to get a better
handle on the budget," he says. "Public works are a long-term
investment with a life expectancy of decades. But under the
current system, the spending is counted only in one year."

In addition, the Subcommittee is awaiting a report from the
National Infrastructure Council, which it helped to establish and
which has been studying the country's infrastructure for the last
three years. The council's report is due in 1988 and may help to
identify areas in which funding is needed.

Why has Lorenz stayed so long with the same subcommittee and
on the Hill? "I guess I'm kind of old-fashioned," he says. "I
thought I could make a contribution with a career in government."

Alan McConnell
Professional Staff Member
Subcommittee on Aviation
587 House Office Bldg. Annex 2
226-3220

Expertise: Aviation, environmental issues, media

Alan McConnell began his career on the Hill in Newt Gingrich's (R-GA) congressional office as Legislative Assistant/Press Secretary. In less than a year, he had become the Georgia representative's Legislative Director and his top advisor on aviation and environmental issues.

The North Carolina native continues to work with Gingrich, who is the ranking Republican on the Aviation Subcommittee of the House Public Works and Transportation Committee. Now, however, McConnell also advises other Republican members as a Subcommittee professional staff member.

McConnell has been involved in a number of important bills. Most recently, he worked on the Airport and Airways Improvement Bill, which was signed into law at the end of 1987. The legislation, which McConnell calls "the key bill out of our Subcommittee and the Committee as a whole last year," entails spending $22 billion over a five-year period to improve and upgrade airports around the country.

McConnell also worked extensively on the Air Passenger Protection Act, which has passed the House and is in conference. The bill is a "high-profile, controversial piece of legislation, providing consumers data on air carrier performance, and we had a number of long, drawn-out battles over it," he says.

Personal: born 8/6/58 in Gastonia, N.C. B.S. Univ. of Georgia, 1982. 1981, wildlife research assistant, Georgia Department of Natural Resources. 1982-1984, agricultural extension agent, Univ. of Georgia Cooperative Extension Service. 1984-1985, Press Secretary/Legislative Assistant, Rep. Newt Gingrich (R-GA). 1985-1986, Legislative Director, Rep. Newt Gingrich. 1986 to present, Professional Staff Member, Subcommittee on Aviation, Committee on Public Works and Transportation.

Included are provisions which establish airport capacity limits and new rules on baggage handling. The Senate version includes a mandate for drug testing of pilots and other aviation workers, he notes, which the House bill does not. Despite that and other differences, McConnell thinks a bill will eventually be hammered out.

McConnell also spent time in the 99th Congress on the drafting of a clean air/acid rain bill, which he says had 170 co-sponsors in the House and was designed as an amendment to the Clear Air Act. That bill failed to pass, but similar legislation has been introduced in both houses in the 100th Congress, and McConnell says some kind of legislation is likely to win approval.

McConnell's interest in environmental issues stems in part from his work as a wildlife research assistant in Georgia. He was captain of the 1981 and 1982 first-place Georgia Wildlife Competition Team and was honored as outstanding wildlife student in 1981.

Away from the office, McConnell continues to enjoy outdoors activities such as canoeing, backpacking and camping. He is attending George Washington University Law School at night. His goal is to become a lawyer specializing in environmental issues.

Gabor J. Rozsa
Minority Counsel
Subcommittee on Water Resources
2253 Rayburn House Office Bldg.
225-4360

Expertise: Environmental law

Rep. Arlan Stangeland (R-MN) knows an effective staffer when he sees one. As Ranking Minority Member of the Water Resources Subcommittee of the Public Works and Transportation Committee, Rep. Stangeland participated in one of the most successful periods in the Subcommittee's history, during which Gabor Rozsa, then Assistant Minority Counsel, played a key role.

Rozsa worked diligently with former Minority Counsel John Doyle on three major bills which came out of the Public Works Committee. One of those bills, the Army Corp of Engineers' water authorization bill, became a reality after ten years of hard political bargaining.

Rozsa, along with other key Hill staff, worked to develop a compromise between the Administration and Congress on a number of contentious issues. One of the most disputed subjects, developing cost-sharing formulas for hundreds of new water projects, was one that Rozsa had worked on while he was with the Corps of Engineers.

The 1986 Water Resources Development Act was the first major authorization bill in sixteen years to come out of the Subcommittee on Water Resources and become law.

Personal: born 10/23/49 in Gyor, Hungary. B.S. Univ. of Virginia, 1972. J.D. Washington Univ., St. Louis, 1975. LL.M. George Washington Univ., 1984. 1981-1985, Assistant Counsel for Legislation, Army Corp of Engineers. 1985-1986, Assistant Minority Counsel, Subcommittee on Water Resources, Public Works Committee. 1986-present, Minority Counsel, Subcommittee on Water Resources, Public Works Committee.

Rozsa has also contributed to the passage of the 1986 Superfund Amendments and the 1987 Amendments to the Clean Water Act by overseeing hearings and mark-ups as well as assisting in the drafting of the House bill and participating in the turbulent conference negotiations for both bills.

Part of Rozsa's success can be attributed to his tenure at the Army Corp of Engineers. As Assistant Counsel for Legislation, Rozsa was involved in most legislative initiatives that came from the Department of the Army, particularly those related to the Corps of Engineers' program. As a result, Rozsa was able to gain a keen understanding of the Administration's perspective on environmental legislation.

The 100th Congress holds a number of challenges for Rozsa. Ground water, oil spill liability, and disaster relief legislation are scheduled for consideration.

Jack Schenendorf
Chief Counsel for the Minority
2163 Rayburn House Office Bldg.
225-9446

Personal: born 5/29/44 in New York, New York. B.A. Union Coll., 1966. J.D. Georgetown Law School, 1975. 1967-1972, Officer in the U.S. Navy nuclear submarine program. 1975-1976, National Commission on Water Quality. 1976-1982, Assistant Minority Counsel, Surface Transportation Subcommittee and Minority Counsel, Investigations and Oversight Subcommittee. 1982-present, Chief Minority Counsel, Committee on Public Works and Transportation.

Expertise: Surface transportation, clean water

Jack Schenendorf serves as Chief Minority Counsel for the bipartisan Public Works and Transportation Committee. Schenendorf credits the committee's united front to observing that "people will always be for better highways, clean air, and clean water."

Schenendorf is a dedicated, soft-spoken attorney, who began working for the Committee eleven years ago. Schenendorf supervises a professional staff of twenty-seven, who all serve Republican members and their respective staffs. Schenendorf's responsibilities include overseeing the staff, drafting legislation, answering parliamentary law questions, and resolving jurisdiction crossovers concerning a particular bill. He also provides advice to members regarding policy decisions.

An expert on the complexities of highway appropriations, Schenendorf was a key staff player in the recent Surface Transportation Act of 1987. Other notable legislation he has worked on includes the Surface Transportation Act of 1982, Superfund, the Motor Carrier Act of 1980 which deregulated trucking, and the Clean Water Act of 1977.

According to Schenendorf, a major focus of the Committee's future work will include taking trust funds (accounts set up for the monies earned from taxes on highways, aviation, etc.) out of the unified budget. This, he believes, would ensure that trust fund monies are not being used for purposes other than those for which Congress intended. He will also continue to focus on motor carrier safety and oversight.

When not working on a legislative agenda, he enjoys running, tennis, movies, reading, and, most of all, spending time with his children.

Paul L. Schlesinger
Professional Staff Member
Subcommittee on Surface
  Transportation
2165 Rayburn House Office Bldg.
225-4472

Personal: born 12/28/54 in Washington, D.C. B.A. Univ. of Maryland 1976. Univ. of Maryland Graduate School, 1981. 1977-1981, Legislative Assistant, Rep. Glenn Anderson (D-CA). 1981-present, Professional Staff Member, Surface Transportation Subcommittee, House Committee on Public Works and Transportation.

Expertise: Surface transportation

When Representative Glenn Anderson (D-CA) became Chairman of the House Public Works Subcommittee on Surface Transportation in 1981, he asked Paul Schlesinger to take the helm as his professional staff member. Schlesinger was a four-year veteran of his personal staff and had a proven track record.

After seven years of dedicated service to the Surface Transportation Subcommittee, Schlesinger claims it has been a labor of love. One of the many personal rewards of this Subcommittee's endeavors, he says, are the visible results. Highways, mass transit systems, and subways comprise a portion of the jurisdiction of the subcommittee. Schlesinger feels proud driving down a highway or riding in a subway which transports hundreds of thousands of commuters to their destination and which was developed by the hard work of the Surface Transportation Subcommittee.

California, home of Chairman Glenn Anderson, is one of the prominent recipients of Surface Transportation aid. A recent addition to the freeway road system is the Glenn Anderson Freeway, which Anderson and Schlesinger helped steer through Congress. In April of 1987, the Highway/Transit bill was enacted over the President's veto. This culminated a tough five-year battle in which Schlesinger played a role.

Schlesinger exerts his straightforward, matter-of-fact character in sifting through the mountains of information associated with controversial bills like the Highway/ Transit bill. As a veteran professional staff member in constant contact with the Chairman, Schlesinger is adroit at separating the substantive from the unimportant.

Schlesinger combines his no-nonsense manner with an easy-going personality. He was educated in the Washington area and is a D.C. native. This combination has contributed to a fine-tuned appetite for politics.

John F. Smolko, Jr.
Professional Staff Member
Subcommittee on Economic
  Development
2165 Rayburn House Office Bldg.
225-3014

Personal: born 1/16/55 in Cleveland, Ohio. B.S. Florida State Univ., 1977. 1980-1982, Legislative Assistant, Rep. E. Clay Shaw, Jr. (R-FL). 1983-1987, Professional Staff Member, Subcommittee on Public Buildings and Grounds. 1987-present, Professional Staff Member, Subcommittee on Economic Development, and Legislative Director, Rep. Shaw.

Expertise: Economic development, infrastructure projects

If anyone has the confidence and trust of Congressman E. Clay Shaw, it is John Smolko. Smolko first allied himself with the Congressman in 1980 as a campaign volunteer. Seven years later, he is in a unique position. He is not only Shaw's point man on the Economic Development Subcommittee, where Shaw is the ranking Republican but he also keeps track of Shaw's and the Committee's Republican initiatives related to public buildings and grounds. In addition, he is the Congressman's legislative director, in charge of legislative initiatives as they relate to the committee and to other issues in the Congress.

As minority staff member for the Subcommittee, Smolko negotiates on water, wastewater, road, and other infrastructure projects with the Administration, Members of the Subcommittee and full Committee, minority and majority staffers, and their counterparts in the Senate. Compromise and persistence, he says, are the name of the game. Equally essential for all professional staff members on Public Works and its subcommittees, he says, is an intricate knowledge of the complex financing formulas that are part of nearly all public works projects and how to use those formulas to meet Members' needs.

In addition to shaping legislative policy, staffers on the Public Works and Transportation Committee and its subcommittees are geared toward "identifying what the problem points are for a project and coming up with ways to move around them," Smolko says. Smolko is good at doing just that. He also credits the committee's successes to the bipartisan, cooperative attitude of Members and staffers alike.

Smolko, like his boss, is politically conservative. Smolko lives in the Virginia suburbs. His hobbies include hunting and woodworking.

Richard J. Sullivan
Chief Counsel
2165 Rayburn House Office Bldg.
225-4472

Expertise: General committee legislation

As one of his colleagues says, Richard Sullivan is the "institutional memory of the place." After more than thirty years as Chief Counsel, Sullivan has seen it all when it comes to legislative issues before the Committee on Public Works and Transportation.

Sullivan's extraordinary experience is a vital asset to the committee. He delegates most of the detail work to other staff members on the committee, but his judgment on the broader issues has the force of decades of experience. "Because he has seen so much come and go," a colleague says, "he brings a unique institutional perspective" to overseeing the Committee's work.

Sullivan's political acumen, and his ability to interact with Members to work out political differences and trade-offs are central to his role.

For most staff members, two or three public works or transportation bills are a major part of their career. Sullivan, however, has been involved with a litany of legislation, including: the Federal Aid to Highways Act, the Appalachian Regional Commission Act, the Economic Development Act, the Water Pollution Act, the Civil Aviation Authorization Act, the Aviation Consumer Protection Act, and legislation on the Smithsonian Institution.

Personal: born 5/17/17 in the Bronx, New York. B.A. Fordham College, 1938. LL.B. Fordham Law School, 1948. WW II service with U.S. Army, 39the Infantry, 9the Infantry Division in North Africa, Sicily, ETO (8 battle stars, Combat Infantry Badge). 1957-present, Chief Counsel for Committee on Public Works and Transportation.

According to Sullivan, not much has changed over the years, but "with each Administration comes a new philosophy, which makes a difference in what type of legislation you can move." He holds strong beliefs, particularly about the proper role of staff, which is to support the Members when the occasion arises. In doing so, staff should carry out the Members' intent—nothing more; policy decisions belongs to the Members only.

Dorothy Beam, who has been an executive assistant to Sullivan for almost as long as he has been on Capitol Hill, says that in their years working together, "there has never been a dull moment," and "you learn something from him every day."

Sullivan is a theater buff. He also loves operas, ballet, and symphonies, which, as a native New Yorker, he has been attending since the age of eight. Exercise and sports are among his pastimes as well.

Why has Sullivan stayed with the Committee for so long? Because, he says, "I like the job and the people. I like the legislation. And I like the place."

Charles C. Ziegler
Minority Counsel
Subcommittee on Aviation
586 House Office Bldg. Annex 2
226-3220

Expertise: Aviation

An attorney with a strong background in transportation issues, Charles Ziegler is seen by fellow staffers as a key player in shaping aviation legislation.

As Minority Counsel for the Aviation Subcommittee–a position he has held for eight of his 12 years on the Hill–Ziegler applies his legal expertise and knowledge of aviation issues to crafting legislation at the direction of his members. He is often sought out by interest groups seeking to influence the minority viewpoint.

Ziegler sees his role as a facilitator of members' agendas, and not his own. "The views that I have are consistent with those of my members whose goal is to improve the safety and efficiency of the air transportation system," he says. "My job is to provide advice and counsel to the members of the policy issues confronting the Subcommittee".

A frustration of the subcommittee is its inability to apply the $6 billion surplus in the Airport and Airway Trust Fund to airport improvements. The surplus is being used as an accounting device to reduce the budget deficit."There is a backlog of projects out there that has not been funded, but the money has been paid by the users," Ziegler explains.

Personal: born 11/13/46, in Portsmouth, Ohio. B.A. Miami Univ. of Ohio, 1968. J.D. Ohio Northern Coll. of Law, 1972. 1972-1973, Counsel to Bluemont Corp. 1973-1976, Counsel and Staff Assistant, Rep. William Harsha (R-OH), National Commission on Water Quality. 1976-1981, Minority Counsel, Aviation Subcommittee, House Public Works and Transportation Committee. 1981-1983, Minority Counsel, Fisheries and Wildlife Subcommittee, House Merchant Marine and Fisheries Committee. 1983-1985, Minority Counsel, Investigations and Oversight, House Public Works and Transportation Committee. 1985-present, Minority Counsel, Aviation Subcommittee, House Public Works and Transportation Committee.

Some Subcommittee Members are also concerned by the growing use of the appropriations process to further legislative ends. Ziegler would like to see Congress steer clear of funding by continuing resolutions, and rely more on the traditional authorization and appropriation process.

Completion of the conference on the Airline Passenger Act will be a major focal point for the Second Session. After work on the consumer bill is finished, the Subcommittee is expected to take up proposals to restructure the Federal Aviation Administration or separate it from the Department of Transportation. Other issues likely to be addressed, according to Ziegler, include legislation to limit general aviation product liability and further scrutiny of airline maintenance and crew training practices and procedures.

When subcommittee work piles up, Ziegler brings work home. But he still manages to find time for hunting, fishing, and golf. For a while, he was able to combine his professional pursuits with his love for the outdoor life as Minority Counsel for the Fisheries and Wildlife Subcommittee.

HOUSE OF REPRESENTATIVES
COMMITTEE ON RULES

Leo Coco
Staff Director
Subcommittee on Legislative
  Process
H-133 Capitol Bldg.
225-1037

Personal: born 12/27/46, Marksville,
Louisiana. B.A. Centenary Coll. of
Louisiana, Shreveport, 1968. M.A. in
urban planning and education, Univ. of
New Orleans, 1977. 1968-1972,
Speech and English teacher,
Lafourche Parish School system,
Louisiana. 1972-1976, Planner, Senior
Editor, Comprehensive Planning
Associates, New Orleans. 1976-1977,
Public Relations Specialist, New
Orleans Historic Districts Landmark
Commission. 1977-1985, Special
Assistant, Rep. Gillis Long (D-LA).
1985-present, Staff Director,
Subcommittee on Legislative Process,
House Rules Committee

Expertise: Legislative process

Administrative Assistant to Congressman Butler Derrick (D-SC) and Staff Director of the Subcommittee on Legislative Process, Leo Coco works hard to maintain his reputation for always following through. Beginning his career as a high school teacher of mostly disadvantaged young people in the bayou country of Louisiana, Coco soon became interested in urban planning. He became a planner with a firm that specializes in planning architecture, and related disciplines and worked toward a master's degree in the subject.

His move from New Orleans to Capitol Hill began when he answered a blind newspaper ad in the *Times Picayune* seeking a good writer with a press background and an interest in politics. The job was for a special assistant to Congressman Gillis Long. Coco went for one interview with Long, who hired him that day. His responsibilities with Long included acting as a liaison among the Joint Economic Committee, the Democratic Caucus, the Rules Committee and subcommittees, the Capitol office and personal staff. Among his major accomplishments was managing Long's successful 1981 campaign for chairman of the Democratic Caucus. Coco is particularly proud of their subsequent work with the Democratic Caucus, working to "redirect Democratic policy, bringing more members into caucus activities."

After Long's death in January of 1985, Butler Derrick asked him to assume the duties of administrative assistant, as well as Staff Director of the Subcommittee on Legislative Process. Coco points to Derrick's 13 years on Capitol Hill and the fact he has served more years on the House Budget Committee than any other member except for Speaker Jim Wright.

Coco comments on the difficulty of conveying the work of the Rules Committee to a member's constituency, saying that it must be a constant process of education. Currently, Coco is directing the planning, staffing, and coordination of a six-phase subcommittee study on the historical and modern use of the continuing resolution, examining its effect on procedure in the House and the Senate and why its use has become more frequent in the past ten to twenty years. He also expresses interest in the issue of multiple referrals and the concept of biennial budgeting.

Coco spends most of his free time with his family and gardening at their home in Cleveland Park.

William Crosby
Minority Counsel
H-305 Capitol
225-9191

Personal: born 9/1/43, Louisville, Kentucky. B.S. political science, Yale Univ., 1965. LL.B. Columbia Univ. Law School, 1968. 1968-1971, enlisted as officer candidate, U.S. Navy. 1972-present, Minority Counsel, House Committee on Rules.

Expertise: House procedure

Stability appears to be part of William (Bill) Crosby's secret of success on Capitol Hill. Through the tenures of three ranking Republican members, he has served as minority counsel for the House Rules Committee since January, 1972.

Before taking on the responsibilities of his current position, Crosby joined the Navy in 1968 and was commissioned as an ensign with assignments both on an aircraft carrier and in the Naval Investigative Service Office in Washington, D.C..

After completing his naval assignment in 1971, Crosby began his career on Capitol Hill and his current position as House Rules minority counsel.

Though he lacked congressional experience when he became Rules minority counsel in what was then a two-person minority staff, Crosby has become a seasoned veteran with 16 years of dealing with a committee heavily dominated by Democrats. Currently there are four Republican congressmen on the thirteen member Rules Committee.

Crosby has the depth of experience to help Republican members respond on short notice to initiatives of the Rules Committee or the House Democratic leadership. Such response may involve researching information and briefing Members, preparing floor statements, drafting amendments and generally assisting Republican members.

Since 1970 Crosby has been involved at the local level in the Republican party. He was a member of the Alexandria (Virginia) Republican City Committee from 1972 to 1980 and has been a member of the Fairfax County (Virginia) Republican Committee from 1981 to the present.

John J. Dooling
Counsel
Subcommittee on Rules of the
House
H-152 Capitol Bldg.
225-9091

*Personal: born 2/7/47 in New York,
New York. Study in anthropology,
Columbia Univ., 1966-1969. 1970,
campaign secretary, Rep. John Dow.
1971-1973, Legislative Assistant, Rep.
John Dow. 1973-1975, Legislative
Assistant, Rep. Joe Moakley. 1975-
1979, Professional Staff Member,
House Rules Committee. 1979-
present, Counsel, House Rules
Subcommittee on Rules of the House.*

Expertise: History and parliamentary procedure of the Rules Committee

John J. Dooling describes the House Rules Committee as "the
best place in the world to work."

During his 12-year tenure with the Rules Committee, he has
observed and contributed to a number of important changes as
the House has adapted to modern times. Under the leadership of
Richard Bolling, the Rules Committee became more proactive in
reviewing and improving House procedures. During the era of
regulatory reform, the committee held exhaustive hearings on the
the legislative veto of regulations. It concluded that the practice
was unconstitutional, a decision later confirmed by the Supreme
Court. The Subcommittee is currently reviewing the recurring use
of continuing resolutions and budget reconciliations as catch-all
vehicles, as well as the impact of Gramm-Rudman-Hollings on
circumventing the committee process. Dooling is frustrated and
disappointed that no systematic approach has ever been devised
for Congress's role in over-sight. He says an effective solution is
needed to deal with a problem that happens "in most cases from
sheer overwork but sometimes by deliberate design of a
committee not to expose its programs to the violence of floor
amendments." Without routine reauthorization of agencies and
programs, Dooling says that no mechanism exists for Congress's
oversight function. He comments on the institution's "peculiar
ability" to spend hours debating a controversial, but low-cost item,
such as a Congressional pay raise, while much larger
authorization and appropriations' bill generate little interest.

While his job does not allow him to acquire in-depth knowledge in
any particular issue area, it does provide Dooling a broad
overview of the House. From that vantage he is exposed to all the
important legislation that will be considered by the House. He is
mindful of former Rep. John Anderson's observation that "the
Rules Committee sets the stage on Thursday for next Tuesday's
headlines."

A student of the history of parliamentary procedure and the Rules
Committee, Dooling believes most of the House traditions, while
arcane, have legitimate purposes. "The rules are horribly
inefficient, tremendous barriers to action, derived from the
philosophy that inaction produces less harm than precipitous
action. . . They are, in fact, Congress' great strength, because we
have every indication that they were designed to be that way," he
says.

Dooling believes that his understanding of parliamentary
precedents and their roots that reach back 200 years to England's
Parliament, are an asset in understanding the modern House of
Representatives.

Always an historian, Dooling is actively working to change the 50-year waiting period that the House observes before releasing its archived documents. As a result of increased access to executive branch documents and a 20-year waiting period recently adopted by the Senate, Dooling is concerned about a distortion of history, that the role of the House in World War II is not being adequately documented by historians. He hopes to develop a House rule that would balance the need for privacy against the legitimate needs of scholars and historians.

In 1975, Dooling sponsored a family of Cambodian refugees. Soon afterwards he began assisting more refugee families with housing, job training, education, employment and language training. Over the years, he developed a network that grew to include more than 80 Cambodian families. He is impressed that the longest period of welfare dependency among all of the families was only one year. Dooling says his reward has been seeing the families adjust and establish themselves in the United States.

David Pomerantz
Professional Staff Member
H-312 Capitol Bldg.
225-9486

Personal: born 2/22/52, Los Angeles, California. B.A., philosophy and economics, Dickinson Coll., 1974. Ph.D., philosophy, Vanderbilt Univ., 1979. Employed in the fiscal analysis division, Metro Nashville government. 1979-1982, professor, graduate and undergraduate philosophy, State University of New York at Stony Brook, Stony Brook, NY. 1982-1983, fellowship under Rep. Richard Gephardt (D-MO), American Association for the Advancement of Science/American Philoso-philosophical Association. 1983-present, Professional Staff Member, House Rules Committee.

Expertise: Budget process, developing rules for budget legislation

David Pomerantz took an unusual career path from a philosophy professor in the halls of academia to his current office, located in the Capitol adjacent to the House Rules Committee hearing room. As a professional staff member on the Rules Committee, he works on rules for all bills and resolutions originating from the Budget and Ways and Means Committees. An expert on budget process and developing rules for budget legislation, Pomerantz sees his staff role as one of providing information and advice, while the members and the committee's staff director decide on rules and devise strategy.

Pomerantz values his academic training as the means by which he gained the skills of careful reading, clear thinking and effectively conveying his ideas. However, he sees little direct application of the substance of his philosophical training to his current duties. Reflecting on the unique nature of his work, Pomerantz notes that the House Rules Committee is the only place to gain experience in formulating rules for consideration of legislation on the House floor. "There isn't really a background for this kind of work except to do it," he says.

Pomerantz's first professional exposure to budgeting came through employment in the fiscal analysis division of the Metro Nashville city government while he was earning his doctorate. Also during his academic work in Nashville, he became active in Steve Cobb's race for state representative. The interests in budgeting and politics would later merge and complement his work on Capitol Hill.

Pomerantz's dissertation at Vanderbilt University was a historical survey of thinkers including John Locke, Thomas Hobbes, John Rawls, and Robert Nozick on the concept of political equality and its effect on economic equality. He observes, "Scholars tend to go off by themselves, produce something, and then defend it against criticism. But on Capitol Hill, every product is a team product."

Rep. Claude Pepper (D-FL), Chairman of the House Rules Committee, then hired Pomerantz to staff the committee's task force on budget process, a bipartisan group that studied the Congress's budget problems, made legislative recommendations and reported a bill. Some of the task force's recommendations were adopted in the original Gramm-Rudman-Hollings legislation. Before his work in 1983, no staff member on the Rules Committee had full-time responsibility for budget issues and legislation. The committee will continue to consider options for budget process reform.

Thomas Spulak
Staff Director and General Counsel
H-312 Capitol Bldg.
225-9486

Personal: born 2/23/56, New York, New York. B.A., political science, Univ. of Miami (FL), 1977. J.D., Florida State Univ., 1982. 1977-1979, District Manager, Miami office, Rep. Claude Pepper. 1982-present, Staff Director and General Counsel, House Committee on Rules.

Expertise: Rules for floor consideration of bills and resolutions

As staff director and general counsel of the House Rules Committee, Tom Spulak says his goal is to help the Chairman bring bills and resolutions to the House floor under the best possible terms and procedures. From where Spulak sits, the hackneyed definition of the Rules Committee as only the "traffic cop" of the floor of the House of Representatives is a weak characterization of the function the committee performs for nearly every matter considered by the House.

The House Rules Committee continually walks a line. It is criticized for allowing too many amendments and producing "Christmas tree" bills; or it is criticized for permitting too few amendments and denying up-or-down votes on issues. In Spulak's view, the success of the vast majority of rules granted by the committee reflects long hours of commitment by Members and the staff.

Spulak finds the Rules Committee "dynamic, because there is a combination of strategies, substance, and personalities. It's never boring, much like the law in general, because it takes a combination of all those things—issues, people, and politics—in order to succeed."

Admiration for his boss is evident as Spulak describes (Senator) Claude Pepper as, "An excellent leader, one who leads by example. A hard worker who's always trying to accommodate both the needs of the Rules Committee and the needs of House members." (Although a member of the House of Representatives since 1963, Pepper is usually addressed as "Senator" as he served in the Senate from 1937-1951.)

In contrast to predecessor Chairman Richard Bolling, who held strong and clear opinions about what rules ought to be issued, Spulak sees the Committee in its most practical light, a way of managing, facilitating and streamlining the process of legislating, a process that would soon become impossibly tangled if not closely managed.

With ever-increasing use of continuing resolutions, omnibus authorizations and bills referred to several standing committees, Spulak believes the influence of the Rules Committee is on the rise. As a result of the nation's deficit and resultant crisis in budgeting, differences will have to be worked out increasingly in the Rules Committee.

Spulak views the Committee as an extension of the House leadership and works to make all rules consistent with the policies of the Democratic leadership. Although rules are sometimes singled out for defeat, few are rejected, an achievement Spulak says results from the Rules Committee being a "microcosm" of the House. Spulak observes, "The actions they (Rules Committee members) take are based on an excellent assessment of the House. Sometimes, the Rules Committee has the responsibility to make the tough choice and send out something that's unpopular. But if it's singled out, that gives us a stronger desire to make sure it's correct."

On the unique experience he is gaining, Spulak says "I may not be a mile deep in knowledge on any one issue before us, but I've been exposed to virtually every issue that is considered on the House floor...It makes me a better staff person and a better lawyer."

Kristi Walseth
Associate Staff
Representative Martin Frost (D-TX)
2459 Rayburn House Office Bldg.
225-3605

Expertise: House and Democratic Caucus procedure

After working for the Texas State Legislature four years and as a legislative aide to Rep. Bob Gammage for two, Kristi Walseth began her employment with freshman Representative Martin Frost of Dallas in 1979.

When Frost was appointed to the powerful Rules Committee as a freshman, he named Walseth his associate staff member. She has been immersed in House procedure for her boss and other Democratic members ever since.

The Democratic leadership takes an active position on some pieces of legislation, making its wishes known to Democrats on the Rules Committee; other bills are left totally to the discretion of the committee. Walseth's job is to assist Frost in addressing all of these bills and in determining what amendments should be made and in which order.

Personal: born 3/12/52, Riverside, California. B.S. Texas Women's Univ. 1971. Univ. of Texas 1974. 1971-1972, reporter Grand Prairie Daily News. 1973-1976, research assistant, Texas State Senator Oscar Mauzy. 1977-1978, Legislative Aide, Rep. Bob Gammage (D-TX). 1979-present, Associate Staff House Rules Committee, Representative Martin Frost (D-TX).

The Members of the Rules Committee and its staff help make decisions crucial to the outcome of legislation. Because of this Walseth points out it is important to look at the bills in larger, more general terms and know which forces are competing in order to make recommendations to her boss. "You must be a generalist legislatively, know where the bill stands politically, and understand procedure to know which procedure should be used."

One of Walseth's biggest challenges lies in her responsibility as sole professional staffer for the Committee on Organization, Study, and Review of the House Democratic Caucus. The rules changes in the Caucus can often affect both Caucus and House rules. Walseth was instrumental, for example, in the revised Caucus rule allowing Democratic representatives to be members of not more than five subcommittees. She observes, "Since the late 1970's there has been a move toward more formalized rules in the Democratic Caucus. These rules have had a big impact on House rules."

Walseth played a major role in changing a House rule which allowed for all riders to be attached to appropriation bills. She said, "Now, in order to offer, for example, an abortion amendment to an appropriations bill, the bill has to be worked all the way through, motion to rise has to be defeated and then the amendment can be offered."

Donald R. Wolfensberger
Minority Counsel
Subcommittee on the Legislative
  Process
421 Cannon House Office Bldg.
225-7985

*Personal: born 11/16/42, Freeport,
Illinois. B.A. North Central Coll., 1964.
Graduate studies, Univ. of Iowa, 1964-
1966. Reporter, Naperville Clarion;
newscaster, KXIC, Iowa City. 1967-
1968, Peace Corps, Tanzania, E.
Africa. 1969-1979, Legislative
Assistant and Rules Committee staff
assistant, Rep. John Anderson (R-IL).
1979-1980, Minority Counsel,
Subcommittee on Rules of the House.
1981-present, Minority Counsel,
Subcommittee on the Legislative
Process.*

Expertise: Congressional reform, budget process

Donald Wolfensberger came to Capitol Hill in 1969, after serving two years in the Peace Corp in Tanzania, East Africa as a secondary school teacher. Having served as a summer intern with Rep. John Anderson in 1965, he joined the Anderson staff full-time in January of 1969 as Anderson's Legislative Assistant. From the beginning, he also handled Anderson's Rules Committee staff work, and in 1975 was appointed as Anderson's associate staffer. In 1979, Anderson appointed him Minority Counsel to the Subcommittee on Rules of the House; and in 1981, he became Minority Counsel to the Subcommittee on the Legislative Process under the ranking subcommittee Republican Trent Lott of Mississippi.

Wolfensberger's duties differ a bit from the minority staff of the full Rules committee in that he deals mostly with original jurisdictional matters. Wolfensberger says, "I am tied in more with institutional reform."

Wolfensberger recognizes the minority team as a whole is at a procedural disadvantage and comments "Mr. Wright is more concerned on a day-to-day basis with House procedure than Tip O'Neill was. I keep a running count on how many restrictive rules there are: 42 percent of the rules in Congress today are restrictive while in the 95th Congress under O'Neill only 12 percent of the rules were restrictive."

Wolfensberger constantly watches for curtailments of minority rights. At the start of each Congress, he helps draft a Republican House rules package which the House Republican leadership presents as an alternative to the rules resolution offered by the Democrats. Although this is usually an exercise in futility, sometimes other efforts are more successful. Wolfensberger was instrumental, for example, in the passage of certain House procedural aspects of the Gramm-Rudman-Hollings law. As minority counsel Wolfensberger has also worked to develop the "legislative veto," which was recently included in a regulatory reform bill he helped draft.

"I try to help protect minority party rights in the House while devising procedures to advance our party's legislative goals and policies. Second, I try to make the House a more representative, better functioning institution, in the interest of all the people. Perhaps I am still a little bit of an idealist after all these years."

Wolfensberger has participated in a Capitol Hill league softball team, the Mastodons, as a coach and player since 1972.

HOUSE OF REPRESENTATIVES
COMMITTEE ON SCIENCE, SPACE AND TECHNOLOGY

Harold P. Hanson
Executive Director
2321 Rayburn House Office Bldg.
225-6375

Expertise: Physics, administration

"If you live long enough, everything will have happened to you," explains Harold Hanson, Executive Director of the Science, Space, and Technology Committee. In the realm of Science and Technology, that aphorism has nearly proven true in the five years that Hanson has directed the Committee. And considering the tasks that face the Committee over the coming session—helping to restore the Space Shuttle, placing a $30 billion space station in orbit, and overseeing developments in both superconductors and the supercollider—Hanson's prediction may further prove his prescience.

Working as an Academic Administrator at the University of Florida, Hanson got to know former Committee Chairman Don Fuqua (D-FL). In 1980, these ties led Hanson to accept Fuqua's offer as Executive Director of the Committee, where he was able to mesh his administrative experience with his expertise in physics.

Hanson gained valuable experience in inter-committee "turf" protection when he helped Fuqua fight back a 1982 attempt of the Appropriations Committee to cut back on funding for the National Science Foundation.

Personal: born 12/27/21 in Virginia, Minnesota. B.S. Superior State Coll., 1942. Ph.D. Univ. of Wisconsin, 1948. 1948-54, Professor, Univ. of Florida. 1954-1969, Professor, Univ. of Texas. 1969-1980, Academic Administrator & Professor, Univ. of Florida. 1980-1982, Executive Director, House Committee on Science and Technology. 1982-1984, Provost, Wayne State Univ. 1984-present, Executive Director, Committee on Science, Space and Technology.

Hanson describes his professional staff as being better scientists than many of the academicians with whom he has worked, which may partly explain his willingness to delegate to other committee staffers some leadership roles—whether on the House floor or in Committee. But another reason may lie in his firm belief in teamwork: in Hanson's view, subcommittee fine-tuning is best left to self-reliant subcommittee directors, while ultimate staff decision-making is best reserved for him.

As discussions in Congress turn toward "competitiveness," Hanson sees as a Committee goal the fortification of science education and technological developments. To help reach this end, he will oversee the doubling of the National Science Foundation budget over the next four years.

Hanson's modesty reflects his Northern Minnesota upbringing. He seems never to have lost the interest in Scandinavians he developed when growing up in a Norwegian-speaking home. Hanson spends most of his spare time translating Norwegian and Swedish poetry. Involvement with both Sweden and Norway throughout his long science career has brought him knighthood from both those countries, thereby earning him the title of "Sir". According to committee staff members, it is a fitting title.

Robert C. Ketcham
General Counsel
2321 Rayburn House Office Bldg.
225-6371

Personal: born 12/5/37 in Kansas City, Missouri. B.A. Washington and Lee Univ., 1959. J.D. Washington and Lee Univ., 1962. 1962-1966, military police officer, U.S. Army. 1967-1969 & 1971, Legislative Assistant, Rep. Bradford Morse. 1973-1975, Special Counsel, Committee on Committees. 1974-1978, Staff Director, Subcommittee on Fossil and Nuclear Energy Research, Development, and Demonstration of the House Committee on Science, Space, and Technology. 1981-present, General Counsel, Committee on Science, Space, and Technology

Expertise: Energy, legislative process and procedure

When Rep. Robert A. Roe (D-NJ) assumed the chairmanship of the House Committee on Science, Space, and Technology at the start of the 100th Congress, he retained the service of Rob Ketcham as general counsel. Ketcham previously served the Committee in the same capacity for then-chairman Don Fuqua (D-FL).

Described by *National Journal* as a career Capitol Hill staffer who thrives on politics and legislative strategy, Ketcham's bailiwick is helping guide legislation through the maze of House procedures and the committee process. Ketcham's previous experience as special counsel to the House Select Committee on Committees has aided him greatly with his present job; the Committee on Committees was responsible for revising and restructuring the House committee system.

During the mid-1970s, Ketcham directed the staff of the Subcommittee on Fossil and Nuclear Research, Development and Demonstration. That position was especially important in that the U.S. was in the midst of the Arab oil embargo. Consequently, Ketcham was suddenly thrust into the forefront of the debate on how best to fill that void in America's energy supply.

It was also Ketcham whom Chairman Roe appointed to direct the Committee's investigation of the 1986 Challenger accident.

As the Committee's general counsel, Ketcham is involved in virtually every issue the committee has under its purview. Specifically, Ketcham's primary responsibility is helping shepherd through the legislative process the bills that originate in the Committee on Science, Space, and Technology.

Currently, Ketcham's greatest focus concerns retaining the increases in the budget for various research initiatives. As he says, "research and competitiveness are inextricably linked." The competitiveness issue also has Ketcham involved in the omnibus trade bill.

Ketcham is married and a proud father of four children.

George S. Kopp
Professional Staff Member
388 House Office Bldg. Annex 2
226-6983

*Personal: born 6/22/44 in New Jersey.
B.S.E. Arkansas State Univ., 1967.
J.D. Univ. of Arkansas, 1971 (cum
laude). 1971-1977, attorney, Criminal
Division, Department of Justice 1977-
1978, Program Director, Franchising
and Business Opportunity Rulemaking
Proceeding, Federal Trade
Commission. 1978-1979, Deputy Asst.
Director, Division Professional
Services, Federal Trade Commission.
1979-1981, Counsel, Subcommittee
on Consumer Protection and Finance,
Committee on Energy and Commerce.
1981-present, Counsel and Staff
Director, Subcommittee on Natural
Resources, Committee on Science,
Space and Technology.*

Expertise: Environment

George Kopp is the Chief Counsel and Staff Director for the
Subcommittee on Natural Resources, Agriculture Research and
Environment. He first came to the Hill as a counsel on the House
Energy and Commerce Committee where he was responsible for
the Federal Trade Commission authorization and issues relating to
the insurance industry. In early 1983 Kopp was charged with
assisting members in the investigation of the Environmental
Protection Agency that was then under the direction of Ann
Burford. This investigation produced new leadership at EPA and
culminated efforts many saw as an attempt to weaken standards
to safeguard the public from hazardous materials. Looking back
over his career on the Hill, he finds this episode to be the most
gratifying. Kopp credits the congressional investigation with
getting the EPA "back on its feet and working again to protect the
environment from toxic chemicals."

Kopp is excited about his future work for the committee.
Chairman Robert A. Roe (D-NJ) has "reinvigorated" the
committee. Kopp hopes to see work progress in the area of
weather forecasting. Much of the equipment presently in use by
the National Oceanic and Atmospheric Administration is twenty or
thirty years old. Thus, the impact of the development and
introduction of new weather forecasting technologies could prove
to be dramatic. Efforts to improve weather prediction will have an
immediate impact on saving lives (i.e. advance warning of
tornadoes, guiding airplanes around areas of violent turbulence).

One of his most interesting stories concerns President Carter
during the Iran hostage crisis. Kopp was at a meeting with the
President on the day of the aborted Iranian hostage rescue
mission. At the time of the White House briefing with the
President, a public announcement about the rescue mission was
still hours away. Yet, President Carter was cheerful as he
conducted business and "was just shooting small talk with us after
the meeting." Never once did Carter's composure crack; yet the
President had to know that a successful end to this military effort
would probably save his foundering Presidency.

Kopp has recently moved into a "brand new" two hundred fifty
year old house. The house was moved 400 miles by barge from its
original site on the Eastern Shore.

Grace Laudon Ostenso
Staff Director
Subcommittee on Science,
 Research & Technology
2319 Rayburn House Office Bldg.
225-1060

Expertise: Scientific research and development, science policy

During her ten years on the Committee, Ostenso has noticed that Members have become more aware of the importance of basic research and its role in retaining a competitive position for the U.S. in the world marketplace.

She believes that the most important facet of her job is to assist Members in the development of a strong science policy for the nation and in understanding how science and technology can benefit the economic health and well-being of society. Ostenso believes that the frontiers of science cannot be advanced unless state-of-the-art technologies and instrumentation are available to researchers. One of her recent accomplishments was to work closely with Chairmen Robert A. Roe (D-NJ) and Doug Walgren (D-PA) to ensure that funds were authorized to provide university researchers access to supercomputers through the establishment of national supercomputer centers and networks.

Ostenso, a former professor, views herself as being rather apolitical. She emphasizes that her first duty to the Committee is to "examine the soundness of the scientific and technical aspects of a legislative proposal and then look at the political forces behind the bill."

Personal: born 9/15/32 in Tomah, Wisconsin. B.S. Univ. of Wisconsin-Stout, 1954. M.S., Ph.D. Univ. of Wisconsin-Madison, 1960, 1963, respectively. 1955-1959, Asst. Director of Dietetics, Peter Bent Brigham Hospital, Boston, MA. 1963-1967, Asst. Professor, Department of Foods and Nutrition, Univ. of Wisconsin-Madison. 1967-1970, Associate Editor for Technology, Encyclopedia Britannica. 1970-1978, Director, Nutrition and Technical Services Division, U.S. Dept. of Agriculture. 1978-1987, Science Consultant, House Committee on Science and Technology. 1987-present, Staff Director of the Subcommittee on Science, Research & Technology, House Committee on Science, Space, and Technology.

Robert E. Palmer
Staff Director
Subcommittee on International
  Scientific Cooperation
820 House Office Bldg. Annex 1
226-3636

*Personal: born 7/11/47 in Cleveland,
Ohio. B.A. Harvard Univ., 1970 (cum
laude). M.S. Northeastern Univ. 1976.
Ph.D. Univ. of Delaware, 1979. 1967-
1968, VISTA volunteer. 1976-1979,
researcher in marine biology, Univ. of
Delaware. 1979-1980, American
Association for the Advancement of
Science Congressional Science
Fellow, 1980-1986, Science
Consultant, Subcommittee on Natural
Resources, Agriculture Research &
the Environment; 1986-present, Staff
Director, Subcommittee on
International Scientific Cooperation,
House Science, Space, and
Technology Committee.*

Expertise: International space science, U.S. technological
competitiveness

In 1979 Robert Palmer enthusiastically greeted the news that he
had been selected one of twenty scientists to be named
Congressional Science Fellow of the American Association for the
Advancement of Science. At the beginning of the 100th Congress,
Congressman Bob Roe (D-NJ) became chairman of the committee
and initiated the formation of a new subcommittee dedicated to
the issue of international cooperation in science and technology.
Palmer's experience and interest combined to make him the
logical choice for Staff Director.

Roe's commitment to international scientific cooperation is
particularly appropriate given the advanced developments that
other nations are making and the tremendous costs of projects
requiring high technology. The space station which Japan, Europe,
Canada and the U.S. plan to launch is projected to cost nearly $30
billion. While acknowledging that international cooperative efforts
of this magnitude bring problems equally great, Palmer is clearly
excited by the prospect. Any international cooperative project
involves trade offs related to economic competitiveness and
national security. But the forces leading to cooperation will
ultimately overwhelm these concerns. In the case of the Space
Station, if we pull it off, it'll be the largest civilian internationally-
cooperative effort in history.

Palmer also worked on the 1984 Landsat legislation. This land
remote satellite system collects extraordinarily detailed
information about planet Earth, from pinpointing large mineral
deposits to monitoring the health of agricultural crops and
forestation. Inevitably potentially conflicting questions of market
competitiveness have arisen and Congress finds itself in the
middle, playing the role of arbiter. It must find a balance that will
maintain the country's economic competitiveness in the world
market while simultaneously protecting national security and
"brain resources."

Palmer considers himself particularly fortunate to be working on
major international issues, meeting and working with some of the
most notable leaders of the world's scientific community. "Initially
you sit down to negotiate with people representing every
conceivable side of an issue and think, no way this will ever go.
But it does and I love it."

But the real fun comes during lunch-hour basketball games with
other Hill staffers. "I secretly cherish dreams of being the first 50
year old drafted by an NBA team!"

Gregory C. Simon
Counsel and Acting Staff Director
Subcommittee on Investigations &
  Oversight
B-374 Rayburn House Office Bldg.
226-3645

Expertise: Investigation, biotechnology, ethics

When he heard of the opening for a counsel to the Subcommittee on Investigations and Oversight in 1985, Greg Simon, who was practicing law for a Seattle firm and was "tired of suing people for a living" jumped at the chance.

Simon, who had been bitten by the political bug long before arriving on the Hill, brought with him a diverse professional background. He had served as research assistant to then-Governor Winthrop Rockefeller of Arkansas, where he studied the changes in prison system from the Faubus administration. The burgeoning prison scandal and reform issues received national attention and formed the basis for the movie *Brubaker*.

After travelling the country for a few years with a music group, Simon wound up in Seattle where he attended the University of Washington Law School. He began school after a brief stint as press secretary to the Third Party Presidential Ticket of Barry Commoner and LaDonna Harris. Although he has served as Counsel for a little over two years and has been Acting Staff Director more recently, Simon has already begun to make his mark. He sees his job as involving two kinds of investigations. One entails monitoring agencies doing scientific research to make sure that laws are followed and executed. The other part of the job is to look ahead, identify and research new areas of interest for the committee.

Personal: born 11/18/51 in Blytheville, Arkansas. Univ. of Arkansas, 1973. B.A., J.D. Univ.of Washington, 1983. 1969-1970, Research Assistant to Governor Winthrop Rockefeller. 1975-1976, graduate assistant, Univ. of Arkansas. 1976-1979, President, Zambini Productions. 1980, Press Secretary to Presidential Candidate Barry Commoner. 1983-1985, attorney, Seattle, WA. 1985-present, Counsel, Subcommittee on Investigations & Oversight, Committee on Science, Space and Technology.

During the 99th Congress, biotechnology received a lot of attention because of the energies of Greg Simon and the subcommittee staff under then subcommittee chairman Representative Harold Volkmer. The culmination of these efforts was the Fuqua Biotechnology Bill of 1986 which Simon co-drafted, and a major report on federal regulation of biotechnology.

In the 100th Congress, the subcommittee—now chaired by full Committee Chairman Robert Roe (D-NJ)—has focused on agency investigations rather than hearings. Simon approaches his role as staffer with the belief that one must "serve the agenda of the elected representative, not one's personal agenda." Simon says he has escaped what he calls the jading process that sometimes accompanies Hill work and he's proud of the bipartisanship of the committee.

When off the Hill, Simon can be found playing softball or at the opera.

William S. Smith
Science Consultant
Subcommittee on Space Science &
 Applications
2324 Rayburn House Office Bldg.
225-8102

Expertise: Space science applications

Under the new leadership of Astronaut and Congressman Bill
Nelson (D-FL), the Subcommittee on Space Science &
Applications has set a course for the future of the US Space
Program that it hopes will rekindle the fire to reach out to new
frontiers. Mr. Nelson's principal advisor in space science is Bill
Smith, who finds the challenge in his work with the new science
and discoveries which the space program can bring back to earth.

Bill Smith began his government career working for the Federal
Aviation Administration studying the environmental effects of
supersonic aircraft on the ozone layer. As science consultant for
the subcommittee, Smith spends much of his time working on the
authorization, policy language and cost planning of the space
station.

For Smith, there are short and long-term goals involved in the
space program. The short-term goal is to recover from the
Challenger tragedy and get the space shuttle flying again. Long-
term it is necessary for the space agency and the space
community to focus on some long-term goal, such as a lunar
colony or Mars Mission. The latter is the other area where Smith
spends a good deal of his time. If the long-term goal is Mars, he
feels, then the US needs to make a commitment to getting the
preliminary science missions such as the Mars Observer launched
as soon as possible.

*Personal: born 10/3/47 in San
Antonio, Texas. B.S. and Ph.D. in
physical chemistry, Texas A&M Univ.,
1968 and 1974. Post doctoral
research fellowship, Univ. of
California, Irvine, 1974-1977. 1977-
1985, physical scientist, Federal
Aviation Administration. 1985-present,
Science Consultant, Subcommittee on
Space Science and Applications,
House Science Space and Technology
Committee.*

Smith understands space to be an investment in science and the
future. He sees himself as a scientist who understands and can
express what can be accomplished in the space program. Smith
feels that the intellectual stimulus available through space science
is a way to expand thinking and comprehend the universe. In other
ways, space science benefits the US in leadership and with
hardware spinoffs—from heart pacemakers to velcro.

Smith is a science buff right down to his hobby of photography,
which is directly related to his chemistry background. In his
darkroom, he often experiments with new technologies and ideas.

Anthony C. Taylor
Staff Director
Subcommittee on Transportation,
  Aviation & Materials
2321 Rayburn House Office Bldg.
225-9662

Expertise: Aviation, surface transportation, materials, communications and aviation weather

Anthony Taylor is a private man. What is public information is discussed freely. Anything else is top secret. Taylor served in the Air Force until 1975 and for the past thirteen years has worked on Capitol Hill. At present, he is the Staff Director of the Subcommittee on Transportation, Aviation, and Materials. His personal reticence is convincing and laudable. But his actions speak for themselves, and the United States listens.

In this high-tech age, federal government computers and communications largely owe their security to Anthony Taylor and his team for their role in assisting the Committee initiate the Computer Security Act of 1987. This act responded to growing concerns over the vulnerability of government computers to outside misuse and inside abuse. Taylor and his staff were also instrumental in initiating the National Critical Materials Act of 1984 which, according to Taylor, "created for the first time an executive office-level coordinator of policy related to critical materials research."

Like on most oversight committees, Taylor and his staff spend a lot of time on hearings which are not only a way to increase public awareness of an issue but also, as Taylor states, the "way to get things done in this country." The Subcommittee has held hearings on a variety of subjects ranging from the 55 mph speed limit to aircraft noise, the future of airport technology, and ways government can help the construction of airports. Under its communications jurisdiction, the Subcommittee will examine more closely the role of subliminal communications, first monitored in advertising, in modifying human behavior. The scope of the areas it covers leads Taylor to note that the Subcommittee has a "broad jurisdiction which enables some chairmen to use it imaginatively."

Colleagues of Taylor's comment on the magnitude of Taylor's jurisdiction. Taylor and his staff are "responsible for funding NASA, aviation and aeronautics research and development."

Anthony Taylor is a staffer's staffer. He provides support but attempts to divorce himself from making policy. Taylor prefers to remain anonymous.

Personal: B.E.E. Cornell Univ., 1964. M.S. Univ. of Southern California, 1974. Active duty, United States Air Force, 1967-1975. 1981-present, Staff Director, Subcommittee on Transportation, Aviation & Materials, Committee on Science, Space and Technology.

James H. Turner
Counsel
Subcommittee on Science,
  Research and Technology
2318 Rayburn House Office Bldg.
225-8128

Expertise: Science, research and technology

A quietly intense man, Jim Turner is one of the leading authorities on technology transfer, innovation and trade on the staff of the "Science and Tech" committee. He directs subcommittee staff work on matters related to technology, as opposed to science, and on how to make that technology available to the private sector.

Science Research and Technology oversees matters dealing with the National Bureau of Standards, National Science Foundation, Government Patent Policy, Technology Transfer, as well as several other areas, all of these, according to Turner, relating to the catchword "competitiveness".

As a new staff member of the Subcommittee in 1984, Turner worked on antitrust legislation, which permitted companies to work together on research, as opposed to production. He was also involved in federal patent policy which determines who owns the intellectual property that arises out of federal research. Much of Turner's recent activity has been on amendments to those laws and on legislation strengthening the National Bureau of Standards.

Turner has also been concentrating on the Federal Technology Transfer Act, trying to discover how federal laboratories can be available to the private sector, and trying to attract scientists and engineers to work in the Federal Government. Turner's most intense work, however, has been on the technology portions of the Omnibus Trade Bill, dealing with the government's role in advancing and expanding US competitiveness. This can be done, he believes, through industrial expansion and revitalization, helping small businesses, and restructuring the National Bureau of Standards and revitalization, as well as advancing semiconductors, superconductors and metric usage.

*Personal: born 10/31/46 in Chattanooga, Tennessee. B.S. Westminster Coll., 1968. Master of Divinity, Yale Univ., 1972. J.D. Georgetown Univ., 1975. 1973-1974, Budget Analyst, Federal Aviation Administration. 1974, Law Clerk, NASA.
1975-1977, Counsel, Rep. Gary Myers (R-PA). 1977-1981, Minority Energy Counsel, Committee on Science, Space and Technology. 1981-1984, Director of Government Affairs, International Coal Refining Co. 1984-present, Counsel, Subcommittee on Science, Research and Technology, House Committee on Science, Space and Technology.*

Turner sees his job as not just nursing one bill along, but seeing that the legislative agenda for the technology side of the committee moves forward. His oversight role is part of a team effort, to which Turner attributes the success of the subcommittee.

In his time off, Turner is highly active within his church, coaches youngsters in basketball, and works diligently on his family's genealogy.

R. Thomas Weimer
Minority Staff Director
2320 Rayburn House Office Bldg.
225-8772

Personal: born 8/18/49 in Laramie, Wyoming. B.S. and M.E. in engineering from Harvey Mudd Coll., 1972. M.E.E. in electrical engineering from the Univ. of Washington, 1976. 1976-1981, technical staff member at Sandia National Labs in Albuquerque, New Mexico. 1981-1985, Minority Nuclear Science Adviser to the Committee on Interior and Insular Affairs. 1985-1986, Minority Energy Coordinator, Committee on Science and Technology. 1986-present, Minority Staff Director, Committee on Science, Space and Technology.

Expertise: Energy, science and technology

R. Thomas Weimer has held three positions with two House committees since 1981. From 1981-85, he served as Minority Nuclear Science Advisor to the Committee on Interior and Insular Affairs. In that job, Weimer's responsibilities included oversight of federal regulation of commercial nuclear power. He worked on authorization legislation for the Nuclear Regulatory Commission and the Department of Energy's uranium enrichment and nuclear waste programs.

In 1985, Weimer became the Minority Energy Coordinator for the Committee on Science and Technology. As Coordinator, he dealt with the Department of Energy's Civilian Research and Development Programs, including nuclear, fossil, renewable (solar and wind), conservation and basic energy and science programs.

The Committee's jurisdiction includes most of the federal government's civilian research and development programs, including NASA, the Department of Energy, the National Science Foundation and parts of the National Oceanic and Atmospheric Administration (NOAA). Weimer has worked on annual authorization bills for these agencies and has oversight responsibilities for their actions. According to Weimer, hands-on engineering experience has been his most valuable asset in working for the Committee.

Weimer encourages Committee staff members to visit the major Department of Energy, NASA and other science facilities once every few years. He enjoys trips to these sites to "kick the tires" at least once a Congress. According to Weimer, the Committee will be hampered in its work if its staff and members do not appreciate what is actually happening "out in the field."

As Minority Staff Director, Weimer meets regularly with representatives of universities and private industries about Committee issues. He also makes annual visits on Lujan's behalf to the two New Mexico national laboratories: Los Alamos and Sandia.

According to Weimer, the Committee's main priority this session is the civilian space program. This includes three near-term goals: getting the space shuttle safely flying, commercializing space activities and constructing an orbiting space station. In 1987, legislation authorizing construction for the space station was passed. The next step, Weimer said, is "to actually get it built and launched." Stressing that science has "never been a partisan issue in American history," Weimer said that most debates in the Committee "focus more on pace rather than direction."

Ronald E. Williams
Chief Engineer
2321 Rayburn House Office Bldg.
225-1178

Expertise: Oversight for research and development, mechanical, structural, and environmental technologies

When Ron Williams accepted a technical consulting position with the Science, Space, and Technology Committee back in 1971, he fully expected that his Hill tenure would last no more than a couple of years. But, twelve years later, he is still with the Committee, serving now in the more senior capacity of chief engineer.

Williams's wide-ranging experience in the field of engineering has allowed him to provide the committee with an authoritative perspective in evaluating the effectiveness and quality of previously funded programs, and in his contribution to the authorization process as a whole.

Williams also serves as study director for the committee's technology policy study task force, chaired by Rep. Buddy MacKay (D-FL), which was initially launched to examine the premises of technology policies. Under Williams's direction, the task force is currently at work compiling and analyzing information for eventual publication on the impact of improving research infrastructure and performance of federal laboratories as well as making recommendations for improving technical education at the secondary school and university levels in an effort to advance U.S. technological competitiveness.

In the area of space technology, Williams recently participated in discussions on the re-design of the solid rocket motors for the space shuttle Challenger.

Williams feels that if the U.S. is to enhance its climate for technological innovation, Congress must continue to "ask the tough questions" of both federal agencies and the private sector, and remain vigilant in closely examining authorization requests for technical programs. "We have walked away from the basic understanding of quality," says Williams, but adds on a more hopeful note, "major problems will often shed light on new, better ways."

Some of Williams's empirical knowledge of the space and aviation technologies' applications derives from the fact that he is a licensed private pilot.

Personal: born 6/24/29 in Philadelphia, Pennsylvania. B.S. The Citadel, 1953. 1953-1956, U.S. Armed Forces, Korea. 1957-1959, resident engineer, McGuire Air Force Base, Wrightstown, NJ. 1959-1969, manager, RCA Principal Applied Information Industries, Morristown, NJ. 1970-1972, president, Eastern Management and Engineering, new technology, Medford. 1971-1976, consultant; 1976-present, chief engineer, House Committee on Science, Space, and Technology.

David D. Clement
Republican Counsel
2324 Rayburn House Office Bldg.
225-8152

Expertise: Space

As the Republican Counsel on the Space Science and Applications subcommittee, David Clement gives credit to a very experienced staff whom he says work in a bipartisan manner to enhance science and technology in the United States.

Clement usually handles the annual authorization for NASA, which is a yearly funding challenge. Since the end of the Apollo program NASA has been driven by the budget cycle, not long-range planning. Clement sees the role of Congress in space programs as visionary, as well as setting out programs and goals.

Clement has been involved in efforts important to the future of the space program. He helped secure funding for the Hubble Space telescope and worked diligently on the Congress' exhaustive Challenger investigation. This investigation led to major changes in the way NASA does business, and increased program safety. Clement believes that the future of the shuttle program is at a critical juncture in 1988.

Most recently, Clement has been working on the initial authorization to start full scale funding for the space station program. He does not see the station fully operational until 1996 or beyond. In the meantime, the Russians are already conducting experiments and collecting data on long duration space flight which will help them in the "race for Mars".

As a staff member of the Space subcommittee, Clement tries to make himself available to all members of the committee. He feels his should not be a partisan job. The Committee's duty is to provide the U.S. with the best possible science program.

To relax, Clement likes to scuba dive in West Palm Beach, not too far south of, you guessed it, Cape Canaveral.

Personal: born 12/15/40 in Vallejo, California. B.A. George WAshington Univ., 1969. M.S. George Washington Univ., 1972. J.D., George Mason Univ., 1980. 1970-1972, Asst. Chief, Office Equipment, U.S. House of Representatives. 1972-1973, Administrative Assistant, Rep. L. G. Williams (R-PA). 1974-1977, Staff Asst., House Committee on Appropriations. 1977-present, Republican Counsel, Science, Space, and Technology Committee, Subcommittee on Space Science and Applications.

Maryanne C. Bach
Minority Science Coordinator
2320 Rayburn House Office Bldg.
225-8123

Personal: born 11/21/56 in New York, NY. B.S. Providence Coll., RI. M.S. in botany and plant ecology, Iowa State Univ. 1981-1983. Minority Technical Consultant to the Subcommittee on Natural Resources, Agriculture Research and Environment. 1983-1986, Minority Consultant to the Subcommittee on Science, Research and Technology. 1986 to present, Minority Science Coordinator to the Committee on Science, Space, and Technology.

Expertise: Environmental science

The Committee on Science, Space, and Technology is both large and diversified. As Minority Science Coordinator, Maryanne Bach covers basic science and all of the technology issues. A substantial portion of her work has been on parts of the Omnibus Trade bill, including technology transfer, federal trademark and patent policy, federal laboratories and university research. Within the Trade Bill, Bach was most involved in provisions creating joint ventures of the federal government and the semiconductor industry to fund the production of new chip manufacturing capability. Bach worked on incentives in technological manufacturing and how to bring small and medium-sized businesses into the manufacturing mainstream.

Other bills Bach has worked on include the Federal Technology Transfer Act, which authorized federal research and development agencies to work with American companies to transfer property rights. The National Cooperative Research Act is another bill which took a good portion of Bach's time. This Act allows American companies to join together and pool their resources on research, within or across industries, without violating antitrust laws. Bach also worked on the Emergency Math and Science Act, which provided for immediate teacher training of current primary and secondary teachers.

Although Bach's expertise began in environmental sciences, her areas of concentration have grown to include basic sciences and engineering. To Bach, the Committee's most important work is to encourage U.S. competitiveness by strengthening the educational system, and investing in basic research.

Bach enjoys ballet as often as three nights a week. She is also in the midst of renovating her historical house in Annapolis.

HOUSE OF REPRESENTATIVES
COMMITTEE ON SMALL BUSINESS

John Drew Hiatt
Minority Staff Director
B-343C Rayburn House Office
 Bldg.
225-4038

Expertise: Appropriations, small business

Drew Hiatt brought a varied professional background to the Small Business Committee staff in January, 1987. After four years of working on the Hill, he had gained a broad legislative, communications and political experience that caught the eye of ranking Republican Joseph M. McDade, who was looking for a minority staff director at the convening of the 100th Congress. Hiatt became available when his previous employer, North Carolina Senator James T. Broyhill, lost the seat he had taken over after the death of John P. East.

As Broyhill's legislative assistant for appropriations, Hiatt handled all legislative matters pertaining to the thirteen appropriations subcommittees. He had begun developing an expertise in appropriations during three and a half years as an appropriations associate and legislative assistant for former Representative George M. O'Brien of Illinois. O'Brien, then ranking Republican on the Appropriations Subcommittee on Commerce, Justice, State, and Judiciary, charged Hiatt with the management of his Subcommittee issues.

Personal: born 03/06/57 in Elwood, Indiana. B.A. in political science and German, Western Maryland, 1979 (cum laude). Masters Program, Albert-Ludwigs Univ., Freiburg, West Germany. 1982, Deputy Director of Field Operations, Larry Hogan for U.S. Senate (MD). 1983, Assistant to the Director, Washington Office of Governor Robert D. Orr (IN). 1983, Legislative Aide and Assistant Press Secretary, Rep. Guy Vander Jagt (R-MI). 1983-1986, Appropriations Associate and Legislative Assistant, Rep. George M. O'Brien (R-IL). 1986, Legislative Assistant, Sen. James T. Broyhill (R-NC).

Hiatt's communications background is helpful in achieving that goal—his experience includes the role of assistant press secretary during his tenure with O'Brien, for whom he became acting press secretary when the position was temporarily vacant. He also doubled in legislative and press functions during his previous job with Representative Guy Vander Jagt of Michigan.

Hiatt considers the major legislative role of the minority staff as advocating free-market and free-enterprise principles in the development of committee initiatives, yet he underscores the bipartisan nature of the committee and its small-business constituency.

Colleagues familiar with his working style say that, although he does not compromise his fundamental Republican principles, he has cooperated with Democratic staff on key legislation. Hiatt's first major legislative involvement in his current position came in the development of the much-praised Small Business Title in the Omnibus Trade Bill.

His political background is as thoroughly Republican as are his beliefs. Before joining the staff of Republican National Campaign Committee Chairman, Guy Vander Jagt, Hiatt had served as assistant to the director of the Washington Office of Republican Governor Robert D. Orr of Indiana. Hiatt also worked for Republican candidates in U.S. Senate and state Senate campaigns in Maryland, as well as the 1984 Reagan-Bush campaign.

Donald F. Terry
Staff Director
2361 Rayburn House Office Bldg.
225-5821

Expertise: Small business

As staff director of the House Small Business Committee, Donald Terry has focused his efforts on one of the hottest topics of the day—international trade—and how to make American business more competitive in world markets.

With a resume seasoned with executive and legislative branch experience, Terry brings to his position knowledge of a variety of fields. In 1973 and 1975, he helped draft Nixon impeachment papers as an aide to the Judiciary Committee during Watergate. Later, he helped establish the position of special prosecutor.

Today Terry helps the Small Business Committee "bring small business into the public policy debate." He helped secure a small business title in the 1986 trade bill. He has also lobbied hard for more venture capital for business and for the creation of a government-sponsored venture capital entity. Another goal of the Committee is to "bring the Small Business Administration into the twentieth century."

Terry continues to emphasize trade issues, as he has done since he handled trade as a deputy to the Assistant Secretary for Legislative Affairs at the Department of the Treasury. He went on to work on trade issues at the Inter-American Development Bank, the Banking Committee, and the Joint Economic Committee, before being tapped in 1987 by Small Business Committee Chairman John LaFalce.

Personal: born 6/20/46 in Boston, Massachusetts. B.A. Yale Univ., 1968. J.D. Univ. Of California at Berkeley Law School, 1972. Program for Senior Managers of Government, Harvard Business School, summer 1978. 1972-1975, Administrative Assistant, Rep. Jerome R. Waldie (D-CA). 1975-1976, Counsel, House Subcommittee on Census and Population. 1976-1978, Staff Director and Counsel, House Select Committee on Ethics. 1978-1979, Executive Director, Federal Mine Safety and Health Review Commission. 1979-1981, U.S. Dept. of the Treasury. 1981-1983, Senior Advisor, Inter-American Development Bank. 1983-1985, Staff Director, House Subcommittee on Economic Stabilization. 1985-1987, Democratic staff director, Joint Economic Committee. 1987-present, Staff Director, House Small Business Committee.

On his wall hangs a portrait of John F. Kennedy, a personal hero of his, and next to that a framed impeachment document. On another wall are portraits of his four daughters, who, he notes, are the focus of life outside the office. However, he does play basketball, a game he played in college, and coaches a soccer team as well.

Terry is currently trying to impress upon the small business community the need for entrepreneurs to open their collective product lines to foreign markets. Like many sectors of the American economy, the approximately thirty thousand small businesses in this country "must figure out how they can become export trading companies," says Terry. "It's imperative that we focus the attention of everybody in the country on the challenge of the international marketplace."

HOUSE OF REPRESENTATIVES
COMMITTEE ON VETERANS' AFFAIRS

F. John Brizzi, Jr.
Counsel
337 Cannon House Office Bldg.
225-3569

Expertise: Compensation, pensions, insurance, education and vocational rehabilitation

Although he has been with the Veterans' Affairs Committee for just over a year, John Brizzi is no stranger to the subject or to Capitol Hill. In fact, he practically grew up in the halls of the Senate. His father, Frank J. Brizzi, had many years of experience on the Hill and, to a large degree, inspired John to want to follow in his footsteps. Coming to the Committee with eight years of legal experience at the VA, Brizzi knows the system well and asserts that "although it isn't perfect, the VA system is a very good one."

As Counsel for the Committee, Brizzi's particular areas of oversight are compensation, pension, and insurance issues. He briefs members on these issues, is charged with the preparation of Members for hearings, and is an instrumental staffer during mark-ups. He is always available to Members for advice on legal questions regarding benefit programs or to research matters for future Committee investigation.

Personal: born 3/1/54 in Washington, DC. B.S. West Virginia Univ., 1976. J.D. George Mason Univ., 1979. 1977-1978, pension benefit analyst, Office of Pension & Welfare Benefits Programs, U.S. Department of Labor. 1978-1986, staff attorney, Office of the General Counsel, VA. 1987-present, Counsel (Compensation, Pension & Insurance), House Veterans Affairs Committee.

During his short tenure, Brizzi has been involved with many of the issues which have come before the Committee including the VA Adjudication Procedure and Judicial Review Act, the Atomic Veterans Compensation Act, and legislation designed to address the penalization of veterans who concurrently receive VA compensation and retiree pay. He was a key staffer during consideration of the Veterans Compensation Act of 1987.

Regarding the Adjudication Procedure and Judicial Review Act, Brizzi is concerned with the effect such a measure would have on the VA compensation system and its relationship with the courts. He asserts that such judicial oversight might create an adversarial relationship where one of cooperation now exists and, ultimately, harm the veteran.

Brizzi would like to see the VA benefits delivery system improved, ensuring vets get the correct compensation and get it in a timely fashion. Although he would also like to see VA services expanded, he states that in light of current fiscal realities, the maintenance of current services is the Committee's first priority.

When away from matters of veterans policy, Brizzi can be found enjoying most any sport.

Jill Teague Cochran
Professional Staff Member
Subcommittee on Education,
   Training and Employment
337-A Cannon House Office Bldg.
225-9166

Expertise: Veterans' issues, especially education

Capitol Hill old-timers will note the maiden name of Jill Teague Cochran, top staffer on the House Veterans Affairs' Education, Labor and Training Subcommittee. For thirty-two years, Cochran's father, Congressman Olin Teague of Texas, served American veterans as a member and chairman of the Veterans' Affairs Committee. Cochran's father played a major role in writing the second GI Bill, which provided educational benefits to Korean War-era veterans.

Cochran herself played a major role in what could be the last GI Bill, first passed in 1984 and made permanent in 1987. It is named after its author and chief backer, Committee Chairman Sonny Montgomery of Mississippi.

The new bill "is a peace time bill. . . . God forbid we have another war. As a mother of an 18-year-old son, I really feel that," Cochran says.

Personal: born: 5/3/46 in Waco, Texas. B.A. Univ. of Texas, Austin, 1968. 1972-1974, medical illustrator's assistant, Univ. of Texas, San Antonio. 1974-1981, staff assistant, Veterans' Affairs Committee. 1981-present, professional staff member, Subcommittee on Education, Training and Employment, Committee on Veterans' Affairs.

Cochran has worked for Veterans' Affairs since 1974, but she first came to the Committee when she was only a few months old. Her father had been wounded in World War II. While recuperating in a Temple, Texas, hospital for two years he decided to go into politics. "I grew up here," Cochran said, in the "old days" when staffs were much smaller. In fact, the old committee room is now one of the several staff office suites. One thing her youth has given her is empathy for Members of Congress. "I know what a tough life it is if they are conscientious. It is difficult to balance congressional obligations and family responsibilities," she says.

Cochran is a real believer in the veterans programs the subcommittee covers— programs designed to make veterans more productive citizens. Cochran talks proudly about the job Chairman Montgomery and his committee did in getting the Montgomery GI Bill through, despite opposition from the OMB and, to a lesser extent, some members of the Armed Services committees. "It was a long, challenging process getting that enacted. But now I see that was the easy part. It was clear-cut. What is harder is implementing it. . . . But OMB can't stop the program now. They have already tried everything known to man."

Cochran says she gets along well with representatives of the bureaucracy, including the armed services. "The services played a big part in the development of the (GI) bill, and then supported it," she says.

In the employment area, Cochran finds it hard to measure the success of veterans programs. Veterans employment seems to do very well when the economy is strong, but drops below average during a downturn. "It's very disturbing to have a veteran on the phone who has had no job for years, and he has a wife and children," she says.

Charles Michael (Mike) Durishin
Professional Staff Member
Subcommittee on Oversight and
    Investigations
335 Cannon House Office Bldg.
225-3527

*Personal: born 11/7/47 in Memphis,
Tennessee. B.A. Birmingham
Southern Coll., 1969.1973-1978,
special assistant, director of field
operations, Sen. Jim Aburezk (D-SD).
1979-1984, legislative assistant, Rep.
Tom Daschle. 1985, subcommittee
staff, Subcommittee on Education,
Training and Employment; 1986,
professional staff member. 1987-
present, professional staff member,
Subcommittee on Oversight and
Investigations, Committee on
Veterans' Affairs.*

Expertise: Oversight

Charles Durishin is proud of his accomplishments, although he
tries not to make a big deal about them. The sheer size—240,000
employees and a $27 billion budget—of the VA makes his job as
significant and challenging as most any on the Hill. Next to the
Internal Revenue Service, the VA may touch more Americans lives
than any other federal agency—Durishin estimates about one-third
of the population, counting veterans and all other dependents. His
subcommittee checks the whole operation, acting as a watchdog.
"We look at whether veterans' services are being delivered
efficiently and effectively," Durishin says. That's a rather dry way
of putting what in the current budget-cutting climate has become a
key to keeping the cuts in the federally funded services from
slicing too deep. Responsibilities of federal agencies like the VA
have not shrunk. "When you're always looking, always wanting
more resources to do more, where you can, you try to identify
savings that can free up resources," Durishin says. The
Subcommittee on Oversight and Investigations holds no particular
portfolio of responsibilities, but does business with all the other
Veterans' Affairs subcommittees. Therefore, "my interests are a
little broader and more general than some of the other committee
staff," Durishin says.

In addition to watching the big picture, the subcommittee will focus
in on a particular area that seems ripe for oversight. In 1987, the
subcommittee conducted the first hearing of the VA Inspector
General's operations. No one had reported a problem with the
Inspector General, but no review had ever been conducted by
Congress, Durishin said. "We generally concluded the Inspector
General was effective, although a little slow to follow up. And
sometimes inflated savings were reported." The Subcommittee on
Oversight and Investigations also takes on issues that cut across
the areas of other subcommittees, such as a 1987 look at the
problems and concerns of women veterans.

Durishin came to Veterans' Affairs from the staff of former Rep.
Tom Daschle, (D-SD), who served on Veterans' Affairs until elected
to the Senate in 1986.

Durishin is a man who likes to feel he does some direct good
for the people. One example was an effort to provide disaster
relief to South Dakota farmers, which he began in 1984 while
working as a legislative assistant for Daschle. After a long fight
and court action, the Department of Agriculture was ordered in
January, 1988 to provide relief to 30,000 farmers.—"I have pride in
that. We were able to make the system work."

Mack G.Fleming
Chief Counsel and Staff Director
335 Cannon House Office Bldg.
225-3527

Personal: born 5/3/32 in Hartwell, Georgia. B.S. Clemson Univ., 1956. J.D. American Univ., 1966. 1956-1958, U.S. Army. 1960-1965, administrative assistant, Rep. W.J. Bryan Dorn. 1965-1968, special assistant, VA. 1969, counsel, Rep. W.J. Bryan Dorn. 1970-1974, private practice. 1974-1981, chief counsel, House Veterans' Affairs Committee. 1981 to present, chief counsel and staff director, House Veterans' Affairs Committee.

Expertise: Veterans' Administration

In 1974, the Veterans' Affairs Committee needed an experienced veterans' advocate to fill the slot of Chief Counsel. What the Committee got was a man seasoned by Hill experience and by working for President Lyndon Johnson and knowledgeable in veterans' affairs through a stint with the Veterans' Administration. The new Chief Counsel came in the form of Mack Fleming.

After serving with the Army, Fleming headed for Washington without much work experience, and with no political experience or contacts. Nevertheless, that limited neither Fleming nor his job chances. Subscribing to the view "you don't get it if you don't ask for it," Fleming walked into his Representative's office—Democrat William Jennings Bryan Dorn of South Carolina—and asked for a job as administrative assistant. To everyone's surprise, including his own, Fleming landed the job.

Through his experience with Dorn, who was a member of the Veterans' Affairs Committee, Fleming found a job with the Veterans' Administration. Although he acted primarily as a liaison between the White House and Congress, Fleming also took several trips as President Johnson's advance man. It was from Johnson that Fleming found his two-pronged key to success: work relentlessly and pay attention to the smallest of details.

When one meets Fleming, it is evident the years with Johnson left their mark. Favoring cowboy boots and speaking with an easy Southern accent, Fleming is a Southerner through and through. But he does not have the rough edges of the old Commander-in-Chief. Instead, Fleming is seen by many of his colleagues as affable and easy to work with—a trait that might smooth the way for passage of the legislation that lies ahead for the second session of the 100th Congress.

As in past Congresses, one of the Veterans' Affairs Committee's foremost chores will be passing its authorization bill. Fleming is quick to point out that with an annual budget of nearly $30 billion, the VA is not an easy program for Congress to oversee. In the second session of the 100th Congress, the Committee will also continue on its mission to upgrade the VA to cabinet level. Although this promises to be no simple chore, Fleming reminds anyone who is willing to listen that with a little hard work, anything might happen.

Jack McDonell
Professional Staff Member
Subcommittee on Hospitals and
   Health Care
338 Cannon House Office Bldg.
225-9154

Expertise: Data systems, veterans' health benefits

After 36 years in the Navy and more than a decade on the Hlll, Jack McDonell knows a thing or two about veterans' affairs.

McDonell, concentrates on health care, data processing systems and on improving the efficiency of the Veterans' Administration. McDonell also works on the budget for veterans' programs for which the committee is responsible.

McDonell also advises the committee chairman, Rep. G.V. "Sonny" Montgomery of Mississippi, on automated data processing systems in the VA and is overseeing the implementation of a new, decentralized computer system. "I had a lot of experience working with data processing systems while I was in the service, which really helps me in my committee job," he notes.

In looking at his Hill career, McDonell says he is particularly proud of P.L. 99-272, which mandated the VA to provide in-patient care for certain veterans as part of the VA's benefits, rather than on the VA's discretion. More recently, McDonell, has been working on H.R.2616, the Omnibus Health Care Bill, which would make out-patient care for certain veterans a mandatory rather than a discretionary benefit as well.

One of the primary reasons the committee wanted to change the system from discretionary to mandatory was to assist VA planers in better defining the population that the agency serves, in part to determine future health care needs of the veterans. McDonell says the committee's efforts have paid off. The VA's planning has improved over the last 10 years with the assistance of Congress," he says. Although he is now on the Hospitals and Health Care Subcommittee, McDonell has served occasionally on the Oversights and Investigations Subcommittee.

In his last few years in the service, McDonell was stationed in the Pentagon and worked in congressional affairs. "That really got me interested in the legislative process, and I decided to come to the Hlll after my military career was over," he says.

Away from the office, McDonell continues what he did for more than three decades, sailing. "I have a boat and enjoy sailing in the Chesapeake Bay," says McDonell, who lives in the old port town of Alexandria.

Personal: born 6/16/23 in North Dakota. B.S. State Univ. of New York. 1942, enlisted as seaman; 1977, retired as captain, U.S. Navy. 1977-1978, legislative assistant, Rep. David Satterfield. 1978-present, professional staff member, Subcommittee on Hospitals and Health Care.

Gloria Royce
Professional Staff Member
337 Cannon House Office Bldg.
225-3569

*Personal: born 7/19/51 in Berlin, NH.
A.S. Champlain Coll., 1971. 1971-
1973, secretary/French interpreter,
Vermont Law Firm. 1973-1974, staff
assistant, Rep. Richard Mallory (D-
VT). 1974-1975, personal secretary/
office manager, Rep. Ray Roberts (D-
TX). 1975-1983, staff assistant,
Veterans Affair Committee. 1983-
present, professional staff member,
Veterans' Affairs Committee.*

Expertise: Housing, memorial affairs

"Gloria Royce knows housing issues like no one does," declares a colleague. With thirteen years of Veterans' Affairs Committee staff experience to her credit, and a long list of legislative issues which she has followed through Congress, it is easy to understand how Royce has developed a special expertise in her field.

As the professional staff member charged with oversight of Housing and Memorial affairs, Royce organizes all hearings on theses issues and is very much involved with mark-ups and floor action. She travels regularly to field sites to see first-hand how new housing policies are working or to ascertain any problems that may have developed.

During her tenure, Royce has worked on many of the major bills under the Committee's jurisdiction, including pension reform measures, service-connected compensation bills and all the major housing bills of the last five years. Royce also works on issues affecting the memorials under the jurisdiction of the American Battle Monuments, coordinating efforts to improve and maintain the National Cemetery System.

Royce is obviously very enthusiastic about housing issues and expresses her fascination with the many facets of the economy and the community affected by them. "An unbelievably big part of the nation's GNP is dependent upon the state of housing in this country," she asserts.

Patrick E. Ryan
Deputy Chief Counsel
335 Cannon House Office Bldg.
225-3527

Personal: B.A. Univ. of Maryland. J.D. Georgetown Univ. Law Center. 1974-1977, veterans' benefit counselor and veterans' representative on campus, VA Regional Office. 1977-1978, budget analyst, Office of Comptroller, VA. 1978-1983, staff attorney, Office of General Counsel, VA. 1983-present, deputy chief counsel, House Veterans Affairs Committee.

Expertise: Budget, VA programs

Patrick Ryan enjoys serving veterans and has done so since college days at the University of Maryland.

Although he had ambitions to work for a Congressional committee, it was not until he began working with veterans that he realized "what a special constituency" he served. "If you're going to work in a federal agency you can't do better," Ryan says of the VA.

Apparently, the VA felt the same about Ryan. When Mack Fleming, staff director of the committee, called his friend Guy McMichael, general counsel of the VA (and former staff director of the Senate Veterans' Affairs Committee) in search of a young attorney to fill a vacancy in the committee staff, Ryan's name was among those highly recommended.

Ryan has worked on numerous pieces of Veterans legislation including the Health Care Reform bill of 1986 and the Home Loan bill. However, he enjoys working on less cumbersome matters such as an amendment for Chairman Montgomery for the 1987 Supplemental Appropriations bill which provided funds for the veterans domiciliary program to house homeless veterans.

Ryan is diligent in his routine which involves all subcommittee legislation, oversight of all Veterans programs and budgetary work.

Rufus H. Wilson
Minority Staff Director/Chief
  Counsel
333 Cannon House Office Bldg.
225-3551

Personal: Wayne State Univ.,1945-46. American Univ., 1946. LL.B. Univ. of Baltimore, 1969. Enlisted Private, U.S. Marine Corps, 1943; released as Corporal, 1945, after WW II; Purple Heart, Presidential Unit Citation, 2 Battle Stars. 1947-54, AMVETS National Headquarters. 1954-55, National Commander. AMVETS, 1958-65, Regional Mgr., FL; 1965, Regional Mgr., NE; 1965-69, Regional Mgr., MD; 1969-1970, Chief Benefits Dir. in Central Office; 1970-1973, Assoc. Dep. Admin.; 1973-1974, Dir. of National Cemetery Service; 1974-1977, Chief Benefits Dir.; 1979-1981, Dep. Adm. and 1981, Acting Adm., Veterans Administration. 1981-present, Minority Staff Director/Chief Counsel, Committee on Veterans Affairs.

Expertise: Veterans issues

Rufus Wilson, the Minority Staff Director of the House Veterans' Affairs Committee, enjoys an outstanding reputation among Members.

No doubt part of Wilson's ability to get things done derives from his influence and deeply personal commitment to veterans' issues. Wilson is himself a disabled veteran of World War II. His outstanding reputation is also the result of his service in the Veterans Administration. Even now, seven years after his departure from the Veterans Administration, Wilson still maintains excellent relations at the VA. "I love them all," he says of his former colleagues.

Although he spent most of his career with the VA and received the Exceptional Service Award from the Veterans Administration, Wilson does not feel he is missing anything. "I enjoy the legislative process,. . . and enjoy being involved," he says. It is a chance to make a contribution on matters that he feels "very deeply" about.

Wilson is also very complimentary of his majority counterpart on the committee, Mack Fleming, saying that because the committee is virtually non-partisan in nature ("our bosses think alike") they work very well together. This committee would be "hell on wheels" if that was not the case, according to Wilson.

Wilson says the primary goal and concern of the Committee involves oversight and maintenance of health and benefits programs for veterans.

HOUSE OF REPRESENTATIVES
COMMITTEE ON WAYS AND MEANS

Thelma Askey
Minority Trade Counsel
1106 Longworth House Office
  Bldg.
225-4021

*Personal: born Lakehurst, New Jersey.
B.A. Tennessee Technological Univ.,
1970. Graduate work in history and
economics at George Washington
Univ. and American Univ. 1972-1974,
Press Assistant, Rep. John Duncan.
1974-1976, Editor, The National
Research Council Marine Board.
1976-1979, Assistant Minority Counsel
for Trade. 1979-present, Minority Trade
Counsel, House Committee on Ways
and Means.*

Expertise: Countervailing duties, intellectual property, unfair trade
practices, trade negotiations

Thelma Askey was at "the right place at the right time." This
Tennessee native took a general interest in government and
wound up on a committee with many of today's premier issues. As
Minority Trade Counsel for the Committee on Ways and Means,
Askey advises Republican members, prepares legislation for
introduction and handles mark-ups, trade conference committees
and a myriad of other areas. She also travels to Geneva, Tokyo
and other areas around the world to monitor trade issues for the
Members.

At this time the main priority for Askey is the trade bill. She spent
considerable time helping Republican Members draft
amendments. She is also staffing the massive conference working
out the differences between the House and Senate trade bills. She
enjoys working with such a large group to work out a consensus.
The most important part of the negotiations is to "finalize the
proposals for enactment, and cut out the controversial provisions
as well as non-trade provisions that are not needed or intrusive." If
Askey seems rather "business-as-usual" about the entire process,
it is because she works on a new trade bill about every other year.

The trade bill conference committee is especially important since
"we need a consensus at home to negotiate abroad."

Contrary to many perceptions about trade, Askey points out that
her experience has illustrated the consistency in trade policy
between differing Administrations. Referring to the Carter and
Reagan Administrations, she has found that the "trade policy has
been consistent even with different parties." "There is, however, a
more competitive environment for U.S. industries both at home
and abroad and the trade bill should reflect a greater emphasis on
competitiveness."

Askey's other major priority is the current Uruguay Round of the
General Agreement on Tariffs and Trade (GATT). This ten-to-
fifteen-year trade cycle pulls countries together because
"increased world competition and hard budget and monetary
realities have made countries want to come to the table." Askey
monitors these GATT negotiations so that she can advise
members on the implications of various trade agreements. It is in
the areas that Askey uses her expertise in countervailing
duties (government subsidies) and anti-dumping laws, unfair trade
practices statutes and intellectual property/services issues.

Brian Biles
Staff Director
Subcommittee on Health
1114 Longworth House Office
Bldg.
225-7785

Expertise: Health

Brian Biles would be on anyone's list for the most influential health policy professionals in Washington. Biles has seen health policymaking from a diversity of perspectives.

Out of medical school he worked for Kansas congressman/physician Bill Roy who was an influential member of the House Subcommittee on Health and the Environment. In 1974 Roy ran for the Senate, challenging incumbent Robert Dole. In a bitter contest, in which Roy was pilloried for his pro "baby killing" abortion stance, Dole won a narrow victory.

Biles then went to work for the Senate Committee on Labor and Public Welfare, the forerunner of the Committee on Labor and Human Resources. Then in the Carter Administration, Biles went to the Department of Health, Education and Welfare on the senior staff in the Office of the Deputy Assistant Secretary for Planning and Evaluation/Health.

After stints with the House Energy and Commerce Committee's Subcommittee on Health and the Environment and as Deputy Secretary of Health and Mental Hygiene for the state of Maryland, Biles came to the House Ways and Means Committee in 1986. Specifically Biles became staff director of the Subcommittee on Health, chaired by Rep. Fortney (Pete) Stark (D-CA).

In that capacity Biles oversees one of the two key House subcommittees in the health field. The other is Rep. Henry Waxman's health subcommittee on Energy and Commerce, where Biles once worked. The Ways and Means subcommittee has jurisdiction over much of Medicare. This includes programs which provide payments for health care, health delivery systems, or health research; health care programs relative to the Social Security Act (including Medicare Part B); and tax credits and deduction provisions of the tax code dealing with health insurance and health care costs.

Personal: B.A. Univ. of Kansas, 1966. Rotary International Fellow, Univ. of Edinburgh, 1967. M.D. Univ. of Kansas, 1971. M.P.H. Johns Hopkins Univ. 1980. 1970-1974, Legislative Assistant, Rep. William Roy (D-KS). 1975-1976, Professional Staff Member, Senate Labor and Public Welfare Committee Subcommittee on Health. 1977-1978, Senior Staff, Office of the Deputy Asst. Sec., HEW. 1980-1983, Senior Staff Associate, House Energy and Commerce Committee Subcommittee on Health and the Environment. 1983-1986, Deputy Secretary, Dept. of Health & Mental Hygiene, State of Maryland. 1986-present, Staff Director, House Ways and Means Committee Subcommittee on Health.

In 1988 two of the major issues before Biles and the subcommittee will be the final passage of the Catastrophic Health Insurance Bill and the annual debate over Medicare savings. With full committee chairman Dan Rostenkowski concerned primarily with tax and trade policies, health issues are left largely to the domain of subcommittee chairman Stark and his staff.

M. Kenneth Bowler
Staff Director
1102 Longworth House Office
   Bldg.
225-3625

*Personal: born 9/16/42 in St. George,
UT. B.A. Stanford Univ. 1967. Ph.D.
Univ. of Wisconsin, 1970. 1971-74,
Asst. Professor of Political Science,
University of Maryland, Baltimore
County. 1974-75, Legislative
Consultant to Rep. James Corman.
1975-84, Professional Staff,
Committee on Ways and Means.
1984-85, Legislative Consultant,
James C. Corman Law Offices. 1985-
87, Deputy Chief of Staff, Committee
on Ways and Means. 1987-present,
Staff Director, Committee on Ways and
Means.*

Expertise: Medicare, Social Security, welfare

When one thinks of the Ways and Means Committee, visions of tax reform come to mind. But a large area over which the Committee holds sway is social welfare—Medicare, Social Security, and Welfare. Ways and Means plays the role of a modern Robin Hood: a portion of the Committee sets taxes and another portion allocates these revenues for the elderly and poor. Jurisdiction over these two functions is equally divided between Chief Counsel Robert Leonard who oversees matters of finance, and Bowler, who has a long resume of political and Committee experience.

After receiving his Ph.D. in political science from the University of Wisconsin, Bowler taught political science at the University of Maryland. Bowler sharpened his interest in politics—and put his foot in the Ways and Means door—by taking a job with the Subcommittee on Unemployment Compensation. Soon afterward, Bowler gained a reputation as helpful and hardworking. As a reward, he moved up to Deputy Chief of Staff for the full committee.

Despite a reputation for being low-key, Bowler is not without a sense of humor. When C-Span televised the last night of the tax bill conference, one camera caught a shot of Bowler, standing behind conferee Charles Rangel, telling a joke to a fellow staffer. A viewer with the mistaken notion that Bowler was Rangel's aide fired an angry letter off to Rangel asking that he fire aides who do not take their jobs more seriously.

But after the tax conference, Bowler was not fired; he was promoted to Staff Director, a perch from which he will oversee Committee activities in the Medicare catastrophic health bill conference and welfare reform conference during the second session of the 100th Congress.

Charles M. Brain
Assistant Staff Director
1102 Longworth House Office
Bldg.
225-3625

Expertise: Administration/tax

Legislative assistants value committee staffers for filling them in on technical information, helping them find useful publications and keeping them abreast of committee plans and action. But L.A.s voice one complaint: committee staffers are often inaccessible or unwilling to spend much time on updating non-committee staffers. Charles Brain, Assistant Staff Director of the Ways and Means Committee is widely seen as an exception.

During the 1986 tax reform scramble, the Ways and Means Committee held a lunch during which L.A.s were given the chance to ask any tax questions that came to mind. With committee tax experts Rob Leonard and Janice Mays on hand, the L.A.s all thrust their hands up when questions began. The first question was "What does Chuck Brain really do?" Despite its incongruity with the discussion topic, the question drew an appreciative roar from the audience which, apparently, also wondered what Brain's primary job was.

It might be hard to pin down Brain's job with a single explanation, but it's not hard to see his worth. As a utility-man for the Committee, Brain has helped in all areas—from filling in as a subcommittee staff director, to organizing meetings for Ways and Means L.A.s. In his nearly seven years with the Ways and Means Committee, Brain has pinch-hit in the Social Security Subcommittee, acted as trouble-shooter for the chairman and staff director of the Committee, and become, at one point, designated expert on railroad retirement systems. In short, Brain is everyone's man Friday.

Personal: B.A. Univ. of Pittsburgh, 1972. M.A. Univ. of Pittsburgh, 1974. 1977-79, Legislative Assistant to Rep. Doug Walgren (D-PA). 1979-81, Chief Legislative Aide to Rep. James Shannon (D-MA). 1981-84, Prof. Asst., Committee on Ways and Means. 1985-present, Assistant Staff Director, Committee on Ways and Means.

After having worked as an L.A. for Reps. Doug Walgren and James Shannon, Brain has developed a sensitivity to the needs of staffers. That, in part, explains Brain's popularity among L.A.'s. He is widely viewed as good natured and is as wiling to answer substantive questions as he is to find a tax summary sheet for a desperate staffer.

During Ways and Means 1986 tax-reform preparations, two Members' L.A.s were pregnant and working at home. In an area where possible bill content changes daily, the two staffers were hard-put to feed their bosses accurate information. But Brain regularly called both of them to keep them updated on committee proceedings—a chore that bolstered Brain's reputation as a reliable and versatile staffer of unusual thoughtfulness.

Donald G. Carlson
Legislative Director
Representative Bill Archer (R-TX)
1135 Longworth Office Bldg.
225-2571

Expertise: Tax, trade and social security

A young Hill veteran, Don Carlson has made a career of working for Congress since his college years at American University.

In 1971, Carlson was hired as Rep. Bill Archer's (R-TX) Legislative Assistant. Carlson stayed in that position until 1978 when he was promoted to Archer's Chief Legislative Director. As Legislative Director, Carlson has become an expert on tax, trade and social security issues through Archer's participation on the House Ways and Means Committee. In his current position, Carlson is responsible for the entire range of legislative issues that Archer covers and for supervising constituent contacts for those issues.

As Chief Legislative Director, Carlson has been involved in every major tax, social security and trade bill that has come before Congress since 1978. In 1983, he worked to incorporate many needed Social Security changes into the 1983 Social Security Act, as well as identifying and solving problems in the Social Security system.

Carlson has worked to promote free trade and the reduction of international trade barriers. He is presently concentrating on the trade bill conference and the U.S.-Canada Free Trade Agreement. With respect to social security, Carlson has helped draft legislation to ensure the financial stability of the system, to reform the current disability process and to eliminate the current earnings limitations.

Personal: born 12/27/48 in Bridgeport, Connecticut. B.A. American Univ., 1970. 1967, Legislative Aide, Rep. Don Riegle (D-MI). 1967-1970, Legislative Aide, Rep. Jim Harvey (R-MI). 1970-1976, Marine Corps Reserves. 1971-present, Legislative Director, Rep. Bill Archer (R-TX).

Carlson has helped draft pending tax legislation, specifically, provisions that relate to energy taxation, tax indexing and capital gains taxation.

As Chief Legislative Director, his responsibilities also include serving as Archer's liaison with interest groups and political groups in Texas. Carlson travels to the Congressman's district several times each year to meet with various groups on the full range of issues Archer covers.

A soft-spoken man, Carlson works quietly and steadily behind the scenes to effect changes on issues Archer believes are important. While a minority staffer has a more difficult time influencing legislation on any committee, Carlson's experience on Ways and Means Committee issues has given him an edge. Carlson notes he has seen significant change in the attitude of the Ways and Means Committee over the years. While it is still possible to get things done, the Committee has become much more partisan than in past years.

James Dale Clark
Minority Tax Counsel
1106 Longworth House Office
  Bldg.
225-4021

Expertise: Tax

Jim Clark is an unassuming man with a serious nature. In 1971, he took two years off from college to serve as a voluntary representative of the Church of Jesus Christ of Latter Day Saints in London and its environs.

Clark worked his way through Brigham Young University. Upon graduation, he was turned down for a Rhodes scholarship, but so impressed a member of the review board, that he was granted a foundation scholarship and studied law for two years at Oxford University.

At the University of Virginia Law school, he was senior editor of the Virginia Journal of International Law. Upon graduation, he set up his own law offices and supported himself and his family as a tax consultant.

With his education, expertise, and drive, it is no wonder that Clark was singled out for the position of Minority Tax Counsel to the Ways and Means Committee.

In his current position, Clark's guiding principle is to carry out the wishes of the thirteen Republican members of the committee. He does so by advising them of the desirability of particular pieces of legislation and by framing an approach for implementation. In lieu of their absence of input, Clark does "what makes proper tax policy sense." Clark believes that most people don't realize that it is easy to draft a bill, but hard to get it enacted.

Personal: born 3/3/52 in Washington, D.C. B.A. Brigham Young Univ., 1976 (summa cum laude). M.A. in Jurisprudence, Oxford Univ., 1978 (graduated with honors). J.D. Univ. of Virginia, 1980. 1983, attorney advisor, Judge Richard C. Wilbur, U.S. Tax Court, Washington, D.C. 1983-1985, self employed tax consultant. 1985-present, Minority Tax Counsel, Committee on Ways and Means.

As an insider with a good grasp of the legislative process, Clark states that if you have a large rock and everyone pushing against it, the rock will eventually begin to roll. In the scheme of things, Clark is one of the people who sees it as his job to get things rolling on the Hill.

In his role as Minority Tax Counsel, Clark has had an impact on two of the most publicized bills ever to reach the floor of Congress: the Tax Reform Act of 1986 and the Omnibus Reconciliation Act of 1987.

Much of Clark's spare time as well as work hours is spent cogitating on the U.S. Tax code. Clark is often invited to speak to a host of groups across the country on tax-related issues.

A folk music enthusiast, Clark gets away from tax code issues to play his banjo and to spend time with his wife and two children.

Ways and Means

Janice A. Mays
Tax Counsel & Staff Director
Subcommittee on Select Revenue
  Measures
1111 Longworth House Office
  Bldg.
225-9170

Expertise: Tax

Janice Mays is known for always being willing to help other Hill staffers. Even though she deals with taxation and the intense, contentious debate which often accompanies tax issues, her colleagues emphasize that Mays is like the eye of the storm, listening and seeking to help everyone work through his or her particular problem.

As staff director of the Subcommittee on Select Revenue Measures, the panel to which Chairman Rostenkowski refers many revenue-related bills which are to come before the full committee, Mays is one of the most important staff players in the House on tax matters.

Often the lower profile tax issues of concern only to a particular industry or even a particular segment or corporation within an industry are addressed in this subcommittee. The sweeping tax issues, such as those embodied in the 1986 reform legislation are usually addressed at the full committee level. However, Mays is Tax Counsel to the full committee as well and would be found intimately involved in tax legislation regardless of whether it emanates from the subcommittee or is initiated by Rostenkowki at the full committee level.

The Tax Reform Act of 1986 and the Reconciliation Act of 1987 are two of the most significant bills in which Mays has been involved recently. Mays is certain to be at the center of any tax initiatives which the committee undertakes in the foreseeable future.

Personal: B.A. Wesleyan Coll., 1973 (cum laude). J.D. Univ. of Georgia 1975. M.L.T. Georgetown Univ.Law School 1981.

Algernon Johnson Cooper, Jr. (Jay)
Administrative Assistant/Tax Counsel
Representative Harold Ford (D-TN)
2305 Rayburn House Office Bldg.
225-3265

Expertise: Nonprofit organizations, tax-exempt status

Jay Cooper's Tennessee campaign work in 1970 ultimately landed him on Capitol Hill. While working on Albert Gore, Sr.'s senatorial campaign, Cooper formed a friendship with Harold Ford, the future Congressman from Memphis. Many years and a few jobs later, Cooper joined Ford's staff as Administrative Assistant and Tax Counsel.

Jay Cooper has had an active career in several areas–private law practice, the federal government and local government. His position with Harold Ford is his first in the legislative branch. The breadth and diversity of his background has certainly been an asset to Cooper in his work on the Hill.

As Ford's Administrative Assistant and Ways and Means point man, Cooper brings a background of dealing with constituent groups which serves him well in dealing with the forces that go into developing a legislative package, especially in such matters as tax. His years as mayor of Prichard, Alabama, and positions in the District of Columbia government, and at HUD have also aided in his ability to "know how much or how little" to ask for and also the importance of timing.

As a Ways and Means professional staffer, he was intensely involved in the working of the Tax Reform Act of 1986, especially in the area of nonprofit organizations. Cooper worked closely on tax-exempt status provisions for hospitals and educational institutions as well as for Memphis-based businesses and corporations. During the 100th Congress, he has continued to monitor tax-exempt regulations and regulations affecting lobbying by various organizations throughout the Budget Reconciliation process.

Cooper considers his knowledge of taxation to be conceptual in nature, as opposed to transactional and mechanical. A meditative man, Cooper explains that as Tax Counsel he must have a thorough, working knowledge of the tax code, as well as the ability to respond to the desires of his Member or a constituent group and to form a workable legislative proposal.

Outside of his hectic work schedule, Cooper finds refuge in his family. His wife and three children are a "relief from the cynicism" he encounters so often. He is active in neighborhood politics, the Knights of Columbus and the Washington International School.

Personal: born 5/30/44 in Mobile, Alabama. A.B. Univ.of Notre Dame, 1966. J.D. New York Univ., 1969. 1969-1970, NAACP Legal Defense Fund. 1969-1970, private law practice, Mobile. 1972-1980, Mayor, Prichard, AL. 1980-1981, HUD, Washington. 1981, Government of the District of Columbia. 1981-1982, Executive Director, Congressional Black Caucus Foundation, Washington. 1981-1982, Senior Policy Advisor to the Commissioner on Social Services, Government of the District of Columbia. 1982-1983, Director of Executive Services, Match Foundation, Washington. 1983-present, Administrative Assistant and Tax Counsel, Representative Harold Ford (D-TN).

Sharon H. Cranford
Budget Associate/Legislative
  Director/Tax Counsel
Representative Frank Guarini (D-
  NJ)
2458 Rayburn House Office Bldg.
225-2765

*Personal: born 4/7/46 in Washington,
D.C. B.A. in English Literature, Trinity
Coll., 1968. J.D. New England School
of Law, 1978. 1975-1978, Legislative
Aide, Rep. Yvonne Brathwaite Burke
(D-CA). 1979-present, Director/Tax
Counsel, Representative Frank Guarini
(D-NJ).*

Expertise: Tax, Social Security, health

Sharon Cranford is a "lifer." After twelve years of legislative experience on Capitol Hill, Cranford continues to thrive on the challenges and satisfactions that come with the position learned from her parents (both Hill people) that there is a special honor and privilege attached to public service. Her success stems from this philosophy, and her ability to immerse herself in every project she takes on.

In 1979 Cranford took a chance with Representative Frank Guarini and accepted a Legislative Aide position without knowing what his committee assignments would be. When the freshman legislator was assigned to the influential House Ways and Means Committee, Cranford was pleasantly surprised.

As Guarini's Tax Counsel, Cranford has worked on amendments to every major tax bill since 1981, including the Tax Reform Act of 1986, Surface Transportation Act of 1982, and the Social Security Amendments of 1983. Foreign Tax, minimum tax, housing and life insurance, are Cranford's major areas of responsibility. Her boss is the only member from New Jersey on the influential Ways and Means Committee, so Cranford has to stay abreast not only of the national legislation, but be sensitive to the special concerns of New Jersey as well.

A few of her most successful legislative initiatives include the Displaced Homeworkers Assistance Act (part of CETA), the Federal Employees' Part-time Career Employment Act, Opportunities for Adoption Act, and the National Commission on Neighborhoods. These projects took Cranford approximately three year to complete, during which she was also finishing her law degree part-time.

When asked why she stays on year after year, Cranford reflects on the fact that every time she thinks of leaving she gets involved in another project and the next thing she knows, another two years have passed.

Despite all of this, Cranford's priority is her family. Many weekends are spent with her sons. The boys—one is three, one is two months old—campaign with Mom in Montgomery County, where she is a Democratic Precinct Chairwoman.

Rob Hartwell
Legislative Director
Representative Richard Schulze
  (R-PA)
2369 Rayburn House Office Bldg.
225-5761

Expertise: Energy, budget, trade, taxes

Rob Hartwell started his career on Capitol Hill hoping to use the knowledge of foreign affairs he acquired at Virginia Wesleyan College. Instead, he has become something of an expert in such diverse areas as energy, taxation and trade.

A six-month stint with Congressman Bill Whitehurst (R-VA) started him in his political career. A lifelong resident of Fairfax, Virginia, Hartwell seemed always to know that a political life was in store for him. Just to make sure, however, he spent one year away from political life, working in the private sector.

While he considers himself a strong Republican, Hartwell is a bipartisan conservative. He spent several months working for the election of Democratic Governor Charles Robb of Virginia. Back in the Republican fold, he became a legislative assistant for Congressman Mike Oxley (R-OH) where for three years he worked on issues in the Energy and Commerce Committee and became an expert on Superfund during the 1984 reauthorization process. After a short period as a legislative assistant for Congressman Mac Sweeney (R-TX), Hartwell found his current home as a legislative assistant to Congressman Dick Schulze. Hartwell quickly moved up to become senior L.A. and was made Legislative Director in 1987.

Since working for Schulze, Hartwell has made a name for himself on the Ways and Means Committee as a hardworking staffer with a keen eye for tax reform issues. He was instrumental in helping add an amendment to the 1987 Tax Reform Act which increased the availability of simplified accounting procedures for small businesses. In addition, he played a key role in the 1987 pension reform legislation.

Personal: born 9/23/56 in Fairfax, Virginia. B.A. in political science, Virginia Wesleyan, 1978. 1978, Legislative Assistant, Rep. Bill Whitehurst (R-VA). 1980-1983, Legislative Assistant, Rep. Mike Oxley (R-OH). 1984-present, Legislative Assistant, now Legislative Director, Rep. Richard Schulze.

Hartwell's dedication to a bipartisan working relationship with other members and staff of the Ways and Means Committee has helped his boss achieve the passage of numerous amendments and broad support for a pending bill to allow deductions for interest on student loans.

Hartwell worked on the unsuccessful campaign to reelect Jack Herrity as Chairman of the Fairfax (VA) County Board of Supervisors and is also a district chairman of that county's Republican Committee. He is a member of the Southeast Fairfax Development Corporation which seeks to improve economic development in Fairfax and is a member of the Mount Vernon-Lee Chamber of Commerce. While he has been approached to run for political office himself, Rob prefers the behind-the-scenes role and intends to stay where he is for several years.

Charles N. (Chip) Kahn III
Minority Health Counsel
1106 Longworth House Office
  Bldg.
225-4021

Expertise: Health

Chip Kahn believes he has the best of both worlds. He has worked in both Houses of Congress and now, as Minority Health Counsel to the Health Subcommittee, he has the unique opportunity of combining his interests in public policy and the health care field.

Kahn's expertise in health matters is extensive. His rolodex is jammed with contacts from every corner of the health care spectrum, and the respect he receives from these different corners is considerable. Says one professor from a prominent West Coast medical school: "Chip is extremely knowledgeable, thoughtful and perceptive. He is a problem solver." Capitol Hill colleagues speak of Kahn's thorough understanding of the unique relationship between public policy and health policy.

Kahn has played an integral role in several major bills, including annual budget reconciliations, the Medicare fraud and abuse bill and catastrophic health care legislation, two proposals of which Kahn helped draft–the Stark Gradison Medicare catastrophic bill and the House Republican substitute. Kahn seems to thrive on such challenges.

Kahn has been in the midst of legislative reform of Medicare payments for hospitals and physicians services based on sound economic incentives. He feels such reforms are critical for both deficit reduction and improvement in the quality and efficiency of care for Medicare beneficiaries.

Personal: born 1/4/52 in New Orleans, Louisiana. B.A. The Johns Hopkins Univ., 1974. M.P.H. Tulane Univ. School of Public Health and Tropical Medicine, 1980. 1979-1980, Administrative Resident, Association of American Medical Colleges, Washington, D.C. 1980-1983, Director, Office of Financial Management Education of the Association of University Programs in Health Administrations, Washington, D.C. 1983-1984, Legislative Assistant to Sen. Dan Quayle (R-IN). 1984-1986, Legislative Assistant to Sen. David Durenberger (R-MN). 1986-present, Minority Health Counsel, House Committee on Ways and Means.

Kahn also holds firm to the philosophy that all Americans should have health insurance coverage. He sees the federal role evolving to encourage the private sector and state and local governments to provide coverage for the 37 million Americans presently without health coverage.

The demand for knowledgeable people in the health care field brings Kahn to make some fifty speeches per year to medical societies, hospital associations and various business groups on issues ranging from Medicare payment reform to retiree health benefits. This expertise also extends into the classrooms, where Kahn has taught seminars at his alma mater, Tulane University and George Washington University. He has edited several books on health care finance and book reviews for the other publications including the *New England Journal of Medicine*.

Prior to entering graduate school at Tulane, Kahn cut his political teeth by managing Rep. Newt Gingrich's (R-GA) first two campaigns for Congress in 1974 and 1976.

Joel D. Kassiday
Administrative Assistant to
Rep. Hank Brown (R-CO)
1424 Longworth House Office
Bldg.
225-4676

Personal: born 9/1/52 in Chicago, Illinois. B.A. Colorado State Univ., 1974. 1974-1979, staff writer, associate editor, managing editor, Triangle Review newspaper, Fort Collins, Colo. 1979-1981, Legislative-Press Assistant, Rep. Jim Johnson (R-CO). 1981-1982, Legislative Assistant, Rep. Hank Brown (R-CO). 1982-present, Administrative Assistant, Rep. Hank Brown.

Expertise: Colorado issues, energy, foreign affairs, welfare reform

Although born in Chicago and raised in the Washington, D.C. area, Joel Kassiday calls Colorado home. He is one Washingtonian equally at ease wearing a suit in a congressional office or settling back in his cowboy boots at a barbecue.

The 35-year-old Kassiday is the Administrative Assistant to Rep. Hank Brown, a four-term Colorado Republican who is gaining influence rapidly as a member of the powerful Ways and Means Committee.

Although he enjoys his role as Brown's top aide, Kassiday misses the Centennial State's rugged beauty. Fortunately, his position enables him to visit his adopted home.

After graduating from Colorado State University in Fort Collins, Kassiday spent several years at a weekly newspaper, focusing on local and regional issues and politics. That background was an asset when he decided to trade his editor's pen for the halls of Congress.

Kassiday actually began his congressional career with Brown's predecessor, the iconoclastic Jim Johnson, who held the seat for eight years. When Johnson grew tired of Washington and decided to retire in 1980, Brown, a businessman and lawyer and a respected member of the Colorado Senate, was a natural and popular choice to succeed him.

Kassiday also serves as Brown's press secretary, where his journalistic background is useful, particularly since the congressman's work on welfare reform has brought him more national media attention.

Brown's district covers the rural eastern half of Colorado, the small cities of Greeley and Fort Collins and parts of Denver's northern and eastern suburbs. It ranks in the top 20 of all congressional districts in geographic area, and Brown maintains five district offices.

Having so large a district with many different elements "can be a mixed blessing," Kassiday says, but it regularly returns Brown to office with more than 70 percent of the vote.

Robert J. Leonard
Chief Counsel
1102 Longworth House Office
  Bldg.
225-3628

*Personal: born 4/24/46 in Hoboken,
New Jersey. B.A. Univ. of
Pennsylvania 1968. J.D. Vanderbilt
Univ. Law School 1971. M.B.A.
Wharton School of Finance, Univ. of
Pennsylvania 1972. 1974-1980, tax
staff; 1981-1986, Chief Tax Counsel;
1987-present, Chief Counsel,
Committee on Ways and Means.*

Expertise: Taxation

By outside measure, Rob Leonard holds one of the very top staff positions on the Hill. Insiders, however, consider his dominance of tax policy and the trust he enjoys from individual politicians of both sides of the aisle virtually without equal. Since being formally named Chairman Dan Rostenkowski's chief tax advisor seven years ago, Leonard has emerged as both thinker and conscience for the committee. His present title of Chief Counsel gives him reach over the largest jurisdiction in the House, including taxes, Medicare, Social Security, international trade, public assistance and unemployment compensation.

From the first meeting with then Secretary of the Treasury Regan on the outlines of the 1981 tax bill to the final selection of transition rules in the 1986 Tax Reform Act, Leonard has been at Rostenkowski's side. *The New York Times* described him as playing "Tonto to Rostenkowski's Lone Ranger—a loyal, savvy, tireless companion, never in the forefront but always at hand to provide sage advice and protection against the wild."

Through it all he has remained the House's most sensitive arbitrator of conflicting tax interests. He has managed to give intricate shape to Rostenkowski's legislative outlines—and also to negotiate artfully with those whose philosophies and politics don't naturally coincide. Leonard was roundly considered the chief strategist in the final days of the 1986 tax conference when Rostenkowski and Sen. Bob Packwood (R-OR) settled their differences behind closed doors.

Most lobbyists consider him as fair as he is accessible. A match for the most aggressive corporate tax specialist, Leonard is a good listener and an astute judge as to where compromise ultimately lies. His availability and directness have won high praise from the national press covering the Committee. He has emerged as the most articulate and one of the best informed spokesmen on taxes in both Houses. He has become the anonymous voice on a variety of issues—with quotes more accurate than colorful.

While many of his former colleagues on Ways and Means have accepted top money offers downtown, Leonard has chosen to defer. Instead he accepted Rostenkowski's invitation to take the Committee's top job—and its largest office.

Leonard's administrative style is as good natured as it is guarded, according to his colleagues. His background in committee issues, along with constant feedback from one of the best staffs on the Hill, gives him enormous reach as a strategist. But, it is Rostenkowski who is the initial benefactor of his inner thinking. The two understand one another's patterns very well.

Until he was elevated by Rostenkowski, Leonard worked anonymously in the corners of the small committee tax office. He was hired during the last year of Wilbur Mills' reign when staff was rarely seen, and never heard. Under Chairman Al Ullman, he gained the trust and experience, if not the recognition, as a draftsman of great promise. The true advisory power on taxation still lay with the Joint Committee on Taxation at that time. But that was to dramatically change with the emergence of Rostenkowski and Sen. Bob Dole (R-KS) who took over Congressional tax policy in 1981.

Leonard is married to his former fellow law student Jane Evins. They have four children, and live in Washington. When he's not playing ball with his boys, he puts his feet up with a good book.

Barbara Pate
Legislative Director & Tax Counsel
Representative Jake Pickle (D-TX)
242 Cannon House Office Bldg.
225-4865

Expertise: Tax

During the legislative whirlwind of tax reform, if anyone wanted to find Rep. J.J. Pickle's legislative director, Barbara Pate, he only had to look in Pickle's office—the spot where, for the last three years, she has spent seven days a week.

Pate is used to hard work. When her husband came to Washington to work for Senator Lloyd Bentsen, Pate followed and landed a job with Pickle, a Ways and Means Subcommittee Chairman.

As soon as she was assigned a desk, Pate worked on Congress's first reconciliation bill. Each year since, a tax bill of some form has been considered. Often, Pickle—and therefore Pate—has spent time in Ways and Means ensuring that private bonds do not crowd out public purpose bonds. During both the 1984 and 1986 tax bills, Pate helped Pickle curb the proliferation of private bonds in favor of bonds traditionally used for the construction of roads, schools, and sewers.

A visitor to Pickle's legislative director might be left with the first impression that Pate is a soft-spoken pushover, not given to digging her feet in for uncomfortable squabbles. First impressions can be deceiving. Pate does not lack any ardor, and the source is her boss, to whom she is intensely loyal, and for whom she is always willing to fight. During the 1986 tax bill scramble, a haggard lobbyist for an oil and natural gas producer wandered into Pickle's office and aggressively suggested that Pickle had been no friend of the industry. The loyal Pate bridled at the suggestion. After she recited a litany of Pickle's oil-friendly legislative accomplishments, the lobbyist quickly retreated.

Personal: born 11/16/52 in Lubbock, Texas. B.A. Univ. of Texas, 1975 (high honors). J.D. Univ.of Texas School of Law, 1978 (Phi Beta Kappa, Phi Kappa Phi, Omicron Delta Kappa, Friar Society, Mortar Board, Alpha Lambda Delta). 1978-1979, administrative assistant, Texas State Rep. Gerald Hill. 1980-1981, Legislative Assistant; 1981- present, Legislative Director and Tax Counsel, Rep. J.J. Pickle (D-TX).

Among her colleagues and most other lobbyists, Pate is recognized as friendly, hard-working and thorough. The latter trait she lists as one of her most useful: "I try to be as tenacious a staff member as Mr. Pickle is a member. I try never to leave anything unturned."

Legislation Pate is likely to be working on in 1988 includes an extension of the research and development tax credit, a fight Pickle successfully led in 1986. That credit expires in 1988, so Pickle again will lead the push for renewal. In the 99th Congress, the legislation had over 240 co-sponsors and it should have wide support this year.

Pickle is also likely to push a bill to allow "out-of-pocket" cash expenses to be deducted by taxpayers who were severely restricted from doing so by the 1986 tax reform bill. Pickle's bill is designed to give relief against the passive loss provisions of the 1986 act. Pate will coordinate these initiatives.

Nancy Powers Perry
Tax Counsel/Legislative Director
Representative Mike Andrews
(D-TX)
322 Cannon House Office Bldg.
225-7508

Personal: Born 4/5/59, Philadelphia, Pennsylvania. B.S. Duke Univ., 1981. J.D. Catholic Univ., 1986 (American Jurisprudence Awards in Tort Law and Constitutional Law). 1981-1983, legislative analyst, Aetna Life and Casualty. 1983-1985, lobbyist, Equitable Life Insurance. 1985-1986, lobbyist, Household International. 1986-present, Tax Counsel/Legislative Director, Rep. Michael A. Andrews (D-TX).

Expertise: Tax (master limited partnerships)

When Congressman Michael Andrews (D-TX) was appointed to the House Ways and Means Committee in 1986, he recognized the need to hire someone to help shape the direction of his new work. He found that person in Nancy Powers Perry, a young woman who has a keen sense of the political process.

As Legislative Director, Perry oversees a staff of three other legislative assistants. In maintaining general oversight of the office's legislative activities, she is responsible among other things for devising current and long-term legislative strategies, reviewing statements and speeches, and planning official mailings.

Apart from these duties, Perry also assists Andrews with his two subcommittee assignments—the Subcommittee on Select Revenue Measures and the Subcommittee on Trade.

As Andrews's key staffer on trade issues, Perry has focused considerable attention on this year's Omnibus Trade Bill. Of particular concern was the repeal of the windfall profits tax. During the Carter Administration, a tax was imposed on the oil and gas industry because of rising profits. But times have changed and windfall profits are now a thing of the past. While repeal language was not included in the House bill, it was included in the Senate measure and Perry is cautiously optimistic that such language will survive a House-Senate conference.

Perry has also gained an expertise in the taxation of master limited partnerships (MLPs). Last year, as the Ways and Means Committee addressed the budget reconciliation bill, these limited partnerships became an issue of contention. The controversy centered around the question of whether such partnerships ought to be taxed as corporations. And since most MLP's concern the oil and real estate industries, Andrews had a particular interest.

It was eventually resolved—in no small part through the diligent efforts of Perry—that the oil and gas industry as well as the real estate industry would retain tax-exempt status. Perry views this accomplishment as especially significant since these industries are prevalent in Andrews's Houston District, as well as the State of Texas.

The ability to grasp the intricacies of a complex issue distinguishes Perry on Capitol Hill. Yet, rather than securing kudos for her hard work and dedication, Perry's goal is simple and straightforward: improving the quality of life for the half-million people Andrews represents in Congress.

Franklin C. Phifer
Professional Staff Member and
  Counsel
Subcommittee on Trade
1136 Longworth House Office
  Bldg.
225-7604

Personal: born 1/23/50 in Orange, New Jersey. B.A. Lafayette College, 1972. J.D. Cumberland Law School, 1976. LL.M. Georgetown Univ. Law School, 1986. 1976, National Advance Staff, Udall for President Campaign. 1977-1978, The White House Presidential Personnel Office. 1978-1979, Attorney, Department of Justice. 1979-1981, Associate Counsel to Vice President Walter Mondale. 1981 to present, Professional Staff Member and Counsel to the Chair, Subcommittee on Trade, Ways and Means Committee.

Expertise: International trade policy

When Frank Phifer came to the Ways and Means Trade Subcommittee from the executive branch at the end of the Carter-Mondale Administration, he brought with him a great deal of experience and an equal amount of enthusiasm for his new position. As the political advance organizer for the Udall for President campaign in 1976 and through subsequent work on Vice President Mondale's staff, Phifer developed his considerable talent for dealing with people of different cultures. He put this skill to good use in the new job which brought him into contact with major political figures from all over the world.

Trade legislation combining domestic politics with international economics particularly attracted Phifer to the Ways and Means Trade Subcommittee. In 1981, when he joined the staff, the international trade issue was important but few could imagine the proportions it would later assume in the national consciousness. The negative balance of trade together with the enormous budget deficit became a campaign issue in 1982 and suddenly U.S. competitiveness in the international marketplace became a hot topic. Phifer found himself in the middle of a very active and exciting field. "All of a sudden people all around the country began to see that a well-considered trade policy and expansion of U.S. markets abroad are critical to the health of the U.S. economy."

Phifer's international orientation pairs nicely with the demands of his position which include extensive worldwide travel. He organizes and directs foreign trade missions in Asia, Europe and South America for the Subcommittee and participates in bilateral trade talks with foreign ministries and heads of state.

Phifer finds great differences between the White House work environment and that of Congress. "In Congress the excitement is centered around issues and strategy. It's more people-oriented in a sense and I'm fascinated watching some of the most unlikely coalitions form, across party lines if necessary, to get things done."

Wendell E. Primus
Chief Economist
1104 Longworth House Office
  Bldg.
225-2747

Expertise: Budget, Gramm/Rudman, health, welfare

For a solid source of information on the provisions and implications of the Gramm/Rudman Deficit Control Act, go no further than Wendell Primus. In his role as the Chief Economist for the House Ways and Means Committee, Primus was one of the leading staffers working on the original Gramm/Rudman Act, as well as the revised version.

Primus describes Gramm/Rudman as a "necessary evil" to bring the Administration and Congress to the table on budget matters, in pursuit of real reduction.

With the burden of the federal deficit upon the economy, Primus comments, "The federal deficit must certainly become more manageable and we need to work toward a zero-deficit, a balanced budget. Gramm/Rudman will work as long as reduction targets are reasonably set and the nation avoids a recession."

Primus's ten year stint on the Committee has earned him a reputation as an honest, fair and highly professional staff member. He has been heavily involved with drafting the welfare reform legislation of the late seventies and was a key staffer during consideration of the Social Security Amendments of 1983. Primus also works closely on Medicare and catastrophic health care legislation. His expertise is heavily relied upon during deliberation over reconciliation measures.

Spending long hours on the Hill is commonplace to Primus, but when he does manage to get away, he divides his extra time between his family, church activities and enjoying almost any sporting event. Primus mentions he is not able to garden as often as he would like.

Personal: born 12/9/46 in Eldora, Iowa. Education: B.S. Iowa State Univ., 1968. Ph.D., Iowa State Univ., 1975, Economics. 1975-1976, part-time Staff Assistant, Committee on Agriculture. 1977-1986, Economist, Committee on Ways and Means. 1987-present, Chief Economist, Committee on Ways and Means.

Michael J. Prucker
Administrative Asst./Legislative
  Director
Representative Barbara Kennelly
  (D-CT)
1230 Longworth House Office
  Bldg.
225-2265

*Personal: born 12/5/49, Stafford
Springs, Connecticut. B.A. Univ. of
San Francisco, 1972. M.A. State Univ.
of New York (SUNY), Binghamton,
1978; Ph.D., 1982. 1973-1976,
teacher of political science, SUNY
Binghamton. 1978, House of
Representatives Post Office. 1978-
1982, Legislative Assistant, Rep.
William Cotter (D-CT). 1982-present,
Administrative Assistant/Legislative
Director, Rep. Barbara Kennelly (D-CT)*

Expertise: Insurance industry taxation, health insurance risk pools

Rep. Barbara Kennelly (D-CT) represents Connecticut's capital city of Hartford, home to a number of major insurance corporations, yet ranked the fourth poorest city in the nation. Kennelly's even-handed work on the House Ways and Means Committee representing the contrasting interests of her constituents is backed up by the expertise of staffer Michael Prucker.

As Administrative Assistant and Legislative Director in Kennelly's office, Prucker often has to wear many hats—a task he does well after nearly ten years on the Hill. Prucker arrived in the area in 1978 to work on his doctoral dissertation at the Library of Congress. "Sidetracked" by his jobs with the House Post Office and then with Rep. William Cotter, Kennelly's predecessor, Prucker didn't complete his dissertation until 1982 but in the intervening years grew to love his work on the Hill.

Prucker's knowledge of the insurance industry made him a major player in overhauling tax policy for insurance companies. This first major rewrite of the code since 1959 was included in the 1984 tax bill. Again in the 1986 Tax Reform Act, Prucker helped revamp the complex portions of the Internal Revenue Code affecting property and casualty insurance companies. Although insurance industry taxes rose in both cases, Prucker notes the goal was reached: more "reasonable" rates of taxation.

Prucker has also worked diligently since his tenure with Rep. Cotter on historic preservation tax credits, used widely in the Hartford area. Most recently, Prucker was involved in the successful 1986 fight to maintain the credit at twenty percent rather than going with the Administration's proposal to eliminate it. Prucker also staffed Kennelly in her work on the six-person Low-Income Housing Task Force, commissioned in 1986 to study how tax policy can encourage the building of low income housing.

On Prucker's agenda is a Kennelly legislative initiative to provide investors with relief from the passive loss provisions of the 1986 tax act, which have adversely affected historic preservation and low income housing projects. Prucker will also be working on another run at state health insurance risk pools to cover the uninsured and hard-to-insure populations. Kennelly has been pushing this idea since 1985, reflecting Connecticut's successful experience in running the U.S.'s first state risk pool.

Without hesitation, Prucker labels himself a liberal Democrat. In his free time, he enjoys motorcycle touring and hopes to make a cross-country trip someday.

James W. Rock
Legislative Assistant
Representative Ed Jenkins (D-GA)
203 Cannon House Office Bldg.
225-5211

Personal: born 2/15/54 in Port Isabel, Texas. B.A. in history, Univ. of Texas at Austin, 1978 (graduated with Honors). M.A. in public affairs, Univ. of Texas, Lyndon B. Johnson School of Public Affairs, 1980 (graduated first in class and received Lyndon B. Johnson Award for Academic Excellence). 1979, intern, office of Sen. Lloyd Bentsen (D-TX). 1980-1985, Legislative Director/Ways and Means Assistant, Rep. Kent Hance (D-TX). 1980-present, Legislative Assistant, Rep. Ed Jenkins (D-GA). Publications: "The Impact of Mexican Immigration on the Texas Public School System." Master's Professional Report, University of Texas at Austin, May, 1980.

Expertise: Taxes and the budget

Jim Rock grew up in the South Texas town of Port Isabel where, like his father, he worked on shrimp boats. When he went to the University of Texas, he was determined not to be burdened with student loans he would have to repay after he graduated. So he worked his way through undergraduate school by running the university movie theater.

His film-watching career did not interfere with his academic studies, because he graduated with honors and received a full fellowship for his graduate work at the Lyndon B. Johnson School of Public Affairs. He was selected for a graduate internship in the office of Senator Lloyd Bentsen of Texas, where he worked on legislation before the Senate Environment and Public Works Committee, writing committee and floor statements.

After he finished requirements for his master's degree in Austin (first in his class at the LBJ school), friends in Senator Bentsen's office steered him toward a vacancy on the staff of Texas Congressman Kent Hance, one of the Democratic "Boll Weevils" who supported President Reagan's economic programs in the early 1980s. Rock has remained on Capitol Hill ever since.

For Hance, he worked on a number of major pieces of legislation, much of it involving taxes and trade. Among the bills he helped staff were the Economic Recovery Act of 1981, the Social Security Amendments of 1983, the Tax Equity and Fiscal Responsibility Act of 1982, the Surface Transportation Act of 1983, the Deficit Reduction Act of 1984, the Trade Remedies Reform Act of 1984, and the Superfund Expansion and Protection Act of 1984.

After Hance ran unsuccessfully for the Democratic nomination for the U.S. Senate in 1984, Rock went to work for Rep. Ed Jenkins of Georgia. There, he specializes in budget and tax legislation, working on the Consolidated Omnibus Budget Reconciliation Act of 1985, the Omnibus Budget Reconciliation Acts of 1986 and 1987, the Tax Reform Act of 1986, and the tax provisions in the 1988 reconciliation bill.

Rock's wife works for the Senate Budget Committee. His sports interests include skiing, tennis, racquetball, and softball.

Jon Sheiner
Legislative Counsel
Representative Charles Rangel
   (D-NY)
2330 Rayburn House Office Bldg.
225-4365

Expertise: Tax

With mark-up of the Tax Reform Act approaching the Ways and Means Committee, Rep. Charles Rangel (D-NY) had to fill a legislative counsel opening with someone who could go toe-to-toe with the many competing groups seeking to influence tax reform, as well as the Finance and Ways and Means staff, and protect the interests of one of the nation's poorest districts. For this task, which promised plenty of bruises, Rangel selected New Yorker Jon Sheiner.

After spending six years as the Washington lobbyist for Consolidated Edison, Sheiner was no newcomer to either the Hill or its tax battles. But a sweeping tax reform bill was different. Sheiner, considered by his colleagues to be open-minded and easy to work with, knew only that he would be jumping into a maelstrom of harried tax Legislative Assistants and frenzied lobbyists.

Sheiner's immediate chore was to ignore the pleas of most of the lobbyists who sought special tax breaks and, instead, focus on lessening the tax burden of the poor. At a time when tax "L.A.s" were in high demand with corporate representatives, Sheiner's strategy was simply "not to let the sudden attention distort the view of who your friends are." Maybe his tactics worked: the poor ended up with a lighter tax load and incentives for building low-income housing were not greatly reduced, despite the predictions of many.

Personal: born 06/24/50 in Brooklyn, New York. B.A. George Washington Univ., 1971. J.D. New York Univ. School of Law, 1974. 1974-1977, attorney, Consolidated Edison Co. of N.Y. 1977-1978, associate, Lowenstein, Newman, Reis and Axelford. 1978-1979, assistant general counsel, Washington Metropolitan Area Transit Authority. 1979-1985, assistant to the vice president, Consolidated Edison Co. of N.Y. 1985-present, Legislative Counsel, Rep. Charles Rangel.

Representing the predominantly Puerto Rican neighborhoods of Washington Heights and East Harlem, Rangel also sought to preserve the deductions for American businesses in Puerto Rico. Again, Sheiner did not let down his boss: the deduction for businesses working in U.S. territories was not rescinded.

After the tax battle ended, Sheiner felt that he had stuck to his task of keeping focused on his immediate needs—but not because special interests with very different agendas did not try to sway him. At one point, Sheiner found himself meeting with a representative of Rolls Royce who sought support for a special exemption from the "gas guzzler" tax. Sheiner wondered what might lead a Rolls Royce representative to try to find a sympathetic ear in the offices of a Harlem Congressman. Then, putting aside his wonder for a moment, Sheiner quickly dispatched the misled lobbyist. Even so, Sheiner is patient and willing to listen to anyone who has done his homework and who might have a good idea.

Arthur L. (Pete) Singleton
Minority Chief of Staff
1106 Longworth House Office
  Bldg.
225-4021

Expertise: Trade

Since 1970, "Pete" Singleton has served in various capacities as Ways and Means staff. Most recently, he heads up the entire Republican staff.

As the first non-lawyer to hold the job, Singleton prefers the title "Chief of Staff" to "Chief Counsel". He describes his job informally as that of a "traffic cop." Daily he is busy anticipating committee action, assigning legislative areas and monitoring work progress, with his principal role to serve the needs of the 13 Republican Members on the Ways and Means Committee.

Singleton has had the opportunity to work on several significant and highly publicized pieces of tax legislation, including the 1971 Revenue Act and the Tax Reform Act of 1986. Singleton feels that the role of government in this area should be to tax only to the extent necessary for effective federal operation.

A trade specialist, but not an intractable free trader, Singleton believes in the unfettered flow of goods between nations and considers the Trade Act of 1974 to be one of the most important bills on which he has worked.

Personal: born 1/26/26 in Richmond, Virginia. A.B. Univ. of Richmond, 1949. M.A. George Washington Univ., 1965. Additional graduate work, 1966-1969. 1950-1954, Associate Editor, Petersburg, VA Progress Index. 1954-1956, Political Reporter, The Baltimore News American. 1956-1960, Reporter and Feature Writer, The Washington Star. 1960-1970, Public Relations Officer, U.S. Steel Corp. 1970-1975, Assistant Minority Counsel; 1975-1981, Deputy Minority Counsel; 1981-present, Minority Chief of Staff, House Committee on Ways and Means.

Although he may have his own opinions and philosophies on the different pieces of legislation he has helped shape, Singleton says his longevity on the minority staff of the Ways and Means Committee may be partly attributed to his practice of never permitting himself to be quoted on professional matters by the press. "I do not believe I can do an effective job if I seek the limelight," says Singleton. "Peer respect is much more important to me."

Although he enjoys public speaking and lectured for a number of years at the University of Maryland and George Washington University, he avoids situations leading to media coverage. More often that not, he can be found spending his leisure time at his Virginia river house fishing, boating or writing for his own entertainment.

J. Francis (Frank) Toohey
Administrative Assistant
Representative Ronnie G. Flippo
(D-AL)
2334 Rayburn House Office Bldg.
225-4801

Expertise: Taxes, finance

As the first financial advisor for the Alabama legislature, Toohey struck up a working relationship in 1973 with a young legislator known for his interest in budget reform. Three years later Ronnie G. Flippo was elected to Congress and convinced the business-minded Toohey to join him in Washington as a legislative assistant.

In 1982, Toohey's interest in finance and expertise in funding federal programs paid off when Flippo gained a coveted seat on the powerful Ways and Means Committee. He made Toohey his chief tax aide, a role Toohey continues in addition to his new duties as administrative assistant.

Toohey has a reputation for diligence, thoroughness and an easy-going manner.

He worked a grueling schedule for 18 months during the committee's review of tax reform beginning in 1985, focusing especially on the reduction of individual tax rates. Flippo, a C.P.A , takes a very active role in the Committee and as a Southern Democrat occasionally follows a different path from Ways and Means Committee Chairman Dan Rostenkowski. Toohey can point to a significant list of Ways and Means initiatives in which he has assisted Flippo, including reforms in Social Security, trade, welfare and federal health programs.

But the adopted Alabama resident also understands the needs and diversity of Flippo's 5th District. When he first arrived in Washington, Toohey served as the congressman's aide on the Public Works and Transportation Committee and the Science and Technology Committee, and helped Flippo gain federal commitments and funding for research and development of the space and rocket program in Huntsville. Because of Flippo's concern for the rural poor in the western half of the district, Toohey expects to spend more time looking at federal health programs aimed at the poor.

With Flippo mentioned as a likely candidate for Alabama governor in 1990, Toohey and the rest of the congressman's longtime staff are not against a run. In the meantime, Toohey and his wife, an associate counsel for the House Committee on Energy and Commerce, are comfortably settled on Capitol Hill.

Personal: born, Philadelphia, Pennsylvania. B.A. Roanoke Coll., 1963. M.A. Economics, Univ. of Alabama 1969. Ph.D. Business Administration, 1971. 1963-1966, bank security analyst. 1971-1973, assistant director, Graduate School of Business, Univ. of Alabama. 1973-1975, appointed first fiscal officer for Alabama legislature. 1975-1976, assistant to President, Univ. of Alabama. 1976-1987, Legislative Aide, Rep. Ronnie G. Flippo. 1987-present, Administrative Assistant.

Beth Kuntz Vance
Staff Director
Subcommittee on Oversight
1105 Longworth House Office
  Bldg.
225-2753

Expertise: Tax, IRS operations

When Beth Vance came to the Ways and Means Subcommittee on Oversight, she was hired by then-Chairman Sam Gibbons (D-FL).

Vance served as assistant counsel under Gibbons and later under Rep. Charles Rangel (D-NY), and presently serves under Rep. J.J. Pickle (D-TX). When she first joined the Committee, Rep. Al Ullman (D-OR) was Chairman of the full Committee, upon whose retirement, Dan Rostenkowski (D-IL) inherited the top spot. Vance has remained with the Subcommittee during all of these Committee shifts, when a new Chairman can mean a complete change of staff. Thus, Vance has been a key staff member during the formulation and implementation of the Economic Recovery Tax Act of 1981 (ERTA), the Tax Equity & Fiscal Responsibility Act of 1982 (TEFRA), the Deficit Reduction Act of 1984 and the Tax Reform Act of 1986.

The subcommittee coordinates the oversight of changes in the tax code, monitors the effects of new policy, addresses problem areas, amends possible errors and reviews IRS activities. Eventually, the Oversight Committee makes recommendations to the full Committee, which nearly always heeds its advice.

Legislatively, she coordinates the efforts of each of the Ways and Means Subcommittess as well as those of the Joint Committee on Taxation, the Senate Committee on Finance, the Congressional Budget Office and the General Accounting Office. She also works extensively with the Treasury and Justice Departments on legislative and tax policy issues, and with IRS officials on administrative, compliance and taxpayer-related matters.

Personal: born 7/29/53 in Rockford, Illinois. B.A. Univ. of Florida, 1975. J.D. Univ. of Florida, 1978. 1978-1985, Assistant Counsel, Ways and Means Oversight Subcommittee. 1985-present, Staff Director, Ways and Means Oversight Subcommittee

Rufus H. Yerxa
Assistant Chief Counsel and Staff
  Director
Subcommittee on Trade
1136 Longworth House Office
  Bldg.
225-3943

Personal: born 5/6/51 in White Plains,
New York. B.A. Univ. of Washington,
1973. J.D. Univ. of Puget Sound,
1976. M.A. in International Law,
Cambridge Univ., 1977. 1973-1976,
Campaign Coordinator and Staffer,
Representative Brock Adams (D-WA).
1977-1981, Legal Advisor to Chairman
of International Trade Commission.
1984-present, Staff Director,
Subcommittee on Trade. 1987-
present, Assistant Chief Counsel,
Committee on Ways and Means.

Expertise: U.S. trade law & policy, international trade agreement

During the 100th Congress, Rufus Yerxa coordinated the sorting and the appointment of the 200 conferees for the Omnibus Trade Bill. No small undertaking, this task is evidence of Yerxa's negotiating strength which has received praise from both sides of the aisle.

Though a consummate negotiator, when it comes to trade policy, Yerxa doesn't compromise his expertise. According to Pete Robinson, Deputy Staff Director of the Democratic Steering and Policy Committee, Rufus Yerxa "knows more about trade than anyone else around here."

In addition to being the Staff Director of the Subcommittee on Trade since 1984, Yerxa has more recently been appointed Assistant Chief Counsel to the Committee on Ways and Means by its Chairman, Representative Dan Rostenkowski (D-IL). Yerxa brought to the Staff Director position, as he put it, "a certain receptivity to new ideas–to modernizing trade laws. "Legislation like the Trade and Tariff Act of 1984 attests to Yerxa's commitment to trade reform. Describing himself as a pragmatic free-trader, Yerxa confirms what even his closest Republican friends say about him—that he's "just plain realistic" and is a "good, loyal Democrat who doesn't let partisanship get in the way," so says Claude Gingrich, former General Counsel to the United States Trade Representative.

Yerxa's realistic approach to trade policy serves as his hallmark on legislation like the Omnibus Trade Bill which in part addresses the need to reduce Japan's trade surplus with the U.S. Yerxa sees results already from the United States' challenge to what he calls Japan's "subtle barriers to trade." Stating that retaliatory measures have been working and that "where we've played hardball, we've gotten results," Yerxa corroborates his "forceful but fair" approach to U.S. trade policy.

Yerxa is well aware that 1988 has brought with it the need for dealing with the Omnibus Trade Bill, the Canadian Free Trade Accord, a new Prime Minister of Japan, and the Soviet Union's hope for access into western financial organizations. But as a seasoned Washingtonian and the proud father of a newborn son, it is clear that Rufus Yerxa has things in perspective.

Anne D. Zeppenfeld
Tax Counsel
Representative Fortney "Pete"
  Stark (D-CA)
1125 Longworth House Office
  Bldg.
225-5065

Expertise: Tax

Anne Zeppenfeld never considered working on Capitol Hill, although she had lived in the Washington, D.C. area for a longtime. After graduating from Washington College of Law at the American University in 1983, Zeppenfeld planned to study for the bar exam and then take the rest of the summer off for a much needed rest. A friend suggested she talk with Congressman Pete Stark, since a counsel position on his staff was opening in the fall. Stark offered her the job and she decided to give it a try. It appears to have been a good decision.

From day one, Zeppenfeld has been involved in markups and conferences on significant tax legislation. Stark, a senior member of the House Ways and Means Committee, chairs the Subcommittee on Health. During her first week on the job, Zeppenfeld was faced with subcommittee mark-up of life insurance provisions to be included in the Deficit Reduction Act of 1984.

Stark has been chosen as a conferee for conference committees on each of the major tax bills of recent years. This has provided Zeppenfeld with an opportunity to become a staff player and develop expertise in tax policy. She was quite active in all aspects of the Tax Reform Act of 1986, especially accounting and insurance provisions.

Zeppenfeld had no previous experience in accounting or insurance but has gained her knowledge from on-the-job training. Prior to law school, she was on the "carpool, nursery school circuit." A mother of two, Zeppenfeld postponed law school and her career until her children were older. Outside of her Hill duties, her children and home-oriented activities now occupy her time.

Personal: born 10/4/50 in Norwalk, Connecticut. B.A. Rosemont Coll., 1980. J.D. American Univ., 1983. 1983–present, Tax Counsel, Rep. Fortney "Pete" Stark.

HOUSE OF REPRESENTATIVES
SELECT COMMITTEES

Joseph A. Fredericks
Minority Deputy Staff Director
Select Committee on Aging
606 House Annex 1
226-3393

Personal: born 10/21/56 in Springfield, Missouri. B.G.S. Univ. of Iowa, 1980. 1979-1980, advance man, Baker for President Committee. 1980, campaign press aide, Iowans for Jim Leach Committee. 1980, campaign press secretary, Cooper Evans for Congress Committee. 1981-1986, Legislative Assistant, Rep. Cooper Evans. 1984-1985, assistant director, security and inventory control, Committee for the 50th American Presidential Inaugural. 1986-present, Minority Deputy Staff Director, House Select Committee on Aging.

Expertise: Oversight and aging issues

When he came to Capitol Hill seven years ago to work as a legislative assistant to Congressman Cooper Evans and, as he puts it, "to have something to do between elections," little did Joe Fredericks realize that he'd ward off the campaign spirits long enough to become the Minority Deputy Staff Director to the Select Committee on Aging.

As the Minority Deputy Staff Director, Fredericks heads up a team that monitors older adults' programs and analyzes the quality of life for various groups of these older Americans. His job, like any, has its pros and cons. The advantage of being a staffer on a Select Committee is the opportunity to investigate issues. But, the Select Committee can only pose questions and hold hearings; it has no legislative authority.

Some of Fredericks emphasis has been on the role of private insurance in long-term care for older adults. He drafted titles two and three of the minority substitute to the Catastrophic Illness Bill. This substitute advocated tax code changes which provided incentives for insurance companies to market long-term care insurance.

During his eight-year tenure on the Hill, Fredericks has been involved in other legislative areas. While a legislative assistant in Rep. Cooper Evans's office, Fredericks developed background in aging issues through his work on the Senior Environment Employment Program—an EPA pilot project using older workers to inspect environmental problems.

A former colleague remembers Fredericks as "a worker, not doctrinaire, not a hard-liner." Fredericks also was a participant in the 1985 Farm Bill Conference which he says, "was the most fun he's had on Capitol Hill."

Fredericks is a moderate conservative. He eyes the Republican Party's so-called non-negotiating contingency with slight disdain saying that "because some Republicans have been so ideologically rigid, instead of negotiating on certain issues, they end up rolling over dead." He views himself as a participant in government, not a voice in the wilderness.

When Fredericks gets home after a long day in House Annex 1, he might pursue his interest in parliamentary procedure—coupled with his love of election campaigns, a keen dual interest—or make plans for the current renovation of an historic house he is working on in southern Virginia. Other interests include reading political fiction, tennis and classical music.

Kathleen Gardner-Cravedi
Staff Director
Subcommittee on Health and Long-Term Care
Select Committee on Aging
377 House Office Bldg. Annex 2
226-3381

Personal: born 4/1/49 in Billings, Montana. B.A. Univ. of Montana, 1971. M.S. American Univ., 1977. 1975-1976, Legislative Asst., Rep. Claude Pepper (D-FL). 1976-1982, Professional Staff Member, House Select Committee on Aging. 1983-1985, Deputy Staff Director; 1985 to present, Staff Director, Subcommittee on Health and Long-Term Care, Select Committee on Aging.

Expertise: Health, aging issues

"She's one of the best at what she does." That comment could just as easily come from Kathleen Gardner-Cravedi's political opponents as her allies. Both sides agree she has been instrumental in helping Rep. Claude Pepper bring the problems of senior citizens to the forefront of the nation's political agenda. Gardner-Cravedi has been at Pepper's right hand on the Aging Committee since it was first established in 1976.

Gardner-Cravedi came to Washington, D.C. from Harvard University, where she was doing graduate work in Education and Art History. She also did course work at the Harvard Center for Advancement of Criminal Justice at Harvard Law School. She was deeply interested and involved with the problems of juvenile delinquency and crime. At the Harvard Center, she learned about Pepper and the House Crime Committee he was chairing. She applied for a position on his staff and was hired, beating out Connie Chung, now with NBC News. Gardener-Cravedi took on her new job with the enthusiasm that has characterized her career. Within months she helped get legislation passed that would assist juvenile delinquents with learning disabilities.

When Pepper became Chairman of the House Aging Committee, Gardner-Cravedi moved from his personal staff to become a professional investigative staff member on the Committee. One of her most memorable assignments was in 1978, when she went undercover to investigate the sale of Medigap insurance to the elderly. Her investigations became the basis for a 3-part ABC News segment and resulted in the passing of a law setting minimum standards for the sale of life insurance policies. A lawsuit was filed against her and ABC News by the insurance company that eventually tested and upheld the investigative authority of Congress.

Gardner-Cravedi has been responsible for directing congressional inquiries, hearings and reports on such issues as the sale of over-the-counter drugs, the elimination of the mandatory retirement age, Alzheimer's Disease, catastrophic health insurance, and other health care issues. Gardner-Cravedi was the Co-Director of the National Conference on Mental Health and the Elderly, and a congressional delegate to the last White House Conference on Aging. Gardner-Cravedi was also responsible for organizing the International Conference on Cancer and Aging.

Gardener-Cravedi enjoys spending time with her family, and participating in such outdoor activities as horseback riding, biking and swimming. She also maintains her life-long enjoyment of travelling and studying art.

Dr. Manual Miranda
Staff Director
Select Committee on Aging
712 House Office Bldg. Annex 1
226-3375

Personal: born 10/14/39. B.S. San Jose State Univ., 1962. Ph.D. clinical psychology, Univ.of Washington, 1971. 1973 to present, Professor, UCLA School of Social Welfare. 1983-85, Distinguished Visiting Professor, National Institute of Mental Health. 1987 to present, Staff Director, House Select Committee on Aging. Author of five books on mental health and special populations with an emphasis on Hispanic older adults.

Expertise: Mental health service delivery systems, aging and mental health problems.

Although Dr. Manuel Miranda is new to his position as Staff Director of the House Select Committee on Aging, he is well known from his work at the National Institute of Mental Health in Washington, D.C. where he served as distinguished visiting professor.

Even though Miranda will only serve two years as Staff Director, he has a hefty legislative agenda he is already pursuing. He is pushing for the Mental Health and the Elderly bill which would improve benefits under Medicare and Medicaid and would include mental health services in addition to physical health services. He is also a proponent of a long-term health care bill for senior citizens in nursing homes and institutions.

An area of specific concern for Miranda is the development of legislation to identify key needs and solutions in meeting mental health needs of ethnic elderly Americans. Miranda plans to hold hearings on this subject.

Dr. Martha Sotomayor, Director of the National Hispanic Council on Aging, says that Miranda is "unusual in that he is not limited to the ivory tower of academia." According to Sotomayor, Miranda enjoys not only the respect of his peers but also the respect of a broad policy-making constituency. Sotomayor sees Miranda's strength both as a scientist and a researcher. She expects Miranda's work on the Select Committee will manifest itself in an increasing emphasis on public policy studies in the curricula at UCLA's School of Social Welfare when Miranda rejoins the faculty.

Miranda enjoys the outdoors and has a particular penchant for wildlife photography. Avocations aside, Miranda enjoys his work. He says he "loves the human drama—that's why I'm a clinical psychologist."

Ann Rosewater
Staff Director
Select Committee on Children,
    Youth & Families
385 House Office Bldg. Annex 2
226-7660

Personal: born 7/30/45 in Philadelphia, PA. B.A. Wellesley Coll., 1967. M.A. Columbia Univ., 1969. 1970-73, program & policy assoc., National Urban Coalition. 1973-76, national education staff, Children's Defense Fund of Washington Research Project, Inc. 1977, freelance consultant on education. 1978, assoc. producer public TV series, WETA-TV. 1979-83, Senior Legislative Assistant to Rep.George Miller (D-CA). 1983-87, Deputy Director, 1987-present, Staff Director, House Select Committee on Children, Youth, and Families.

Expertise: Family issues

In 1983, Congressman George Miller (D-CA) and others felt the unique needs of children, youth, and families required special attention on Capitol Hill. Thus, the House Select Committee on Children, Youth and Families was created to provide an ongoing assessment of the conditions of American children and families, and to make recommendations to Congress and the public about how to improve public and private sector policies.

Miller was chosen Chairman and he, in turn, chose Ann Rosewater, his senior legislative assistant with a strong background in family issues, as deputy director.

Rosewater has been there since the beginning and knows how the committee functions inside and out. She is driven by an intense love of her work and a belief her committee can really make a difference to those whose interests it represents in Congress. She possesses the legal, administrative, and political skills that make her a tough advocate for her issues.

In a committee with a large jurisdiction ranging from AIDS to childcare, from nutrition and prenatal care to medicaid and race relations, Rosewater has the unique ability to see how everything relates and fits together and is adept at demonstrating for others the inter-relationships between health, education, and family support issues. Although her committee is not a legislative one, Rosewater knows how to affect legislative policies to the benefit of children, youth and families, by providing good information to those committees with legislative jurisdiction.

Due to Rosewater's leadership, the Committee has been instrumental in influencing policy to expand medicaid coverage for low-income pregnant women and children, and in enabling the Women, Infants and Children (WIC) program to reach more eligible pregnant women and infants who are at nutritional risk.

Improving public policy concerning child care is one of Rosewater's priorities and she feels her committee has played a strong role in this area, having offered a series of proposals that have been adopted. She helped organize hearings for the committees considering the Welfare Reform Act on the importance childcare in the transition from living at home on welfare to getting a job, particularly for low-income families with nowhere else to turn. She feels strongly the federal government has a responsibility to make a significant investment in safe and affordable childcare.

Rosewater's convictions keep her working at a frenetic pace: the committee has held twenty hearings across the country and issued four reports in 1987 alone.

Miranda G. Katsoyannis
Chief of Staff
Select Committee on Hunger
507 House Office Bldg. Annex II
226-5470

Personal: born 3/16/56 in Brooklyn,
New York. B.A. Clark Univ. 1978. M.A.
American Univ. School of International
Service, 1980. 1981, fellowship with
Congressional Research Service.
1981-1982 researcher, Rep. Hamilton
Fish, Jr. (R-NY). 1983-1984,
Legislative Assistant, Rep. Mickey
Leland (D-TX). 1984-1985, Deputy
Staff Director, House Select
Committee on Hunger. 1985-present,
Chief of Staff, House Select
Committee on Hunger.

Expertise: Social issues and international development

When Congressman Mickey Leland (D-TX) started looking for staffers for his newly created Select Committee on Hunger in 1984, his then legislative assistant, Miranda Katsoyannis, was a natural choice. She had helped Leland gain both congressional and private voluntary support for creation of the committee. Katsoyannis handled social programs, among other issues, in his personal office and received her undergraduate and master's degrees in international development. She also had hands-on experience as a volunteer for ACTION—an umbrella agency which includes VISTA and the Peace Corps—and had helped resettle Asian refugees.

As the Chief of Staff of a committee with no jurisdiction over legislation, Katsoyannis faces unique challenges. Instead of simply drafting legislation to address a problem, she must channel the committee's efforts into identifying important issues, publicizing them through hearings and reports, and working with standing committees on issues that may result in specific legislation.

Katsoyannis indicates that the most satisfying aspect of her work is being told by people who are dedicated to working with the hungry that the committee is making a real difference.

Katsoyannis is a believer in the team approach to overseeing the Hunger Committee. A colleague of hers says of Katsoyannis's style of management: "She lets people own their issues and have a stake in them." The staffer added: "She's wonderful at mobilizing public opinion, and she has a real vision for the committee."

Katsoyannis is a movie buff and likes to read and travel.

Elliot A. Brown
Minority Staff Director
Select Committee on Narcotics
   Abuse & Control
234 House Office Bldg. Annex 2
226-3040

Personal: born 12/15/36 Glens Falls, New York. B.A. Univ. of Vermont, 1959. M.A. Columbia Univ. Department of Public Law and Government, 1965. 1965-1966, Instructor, Government and Research Associate, Univ. of South Dakota. 1967-1968, Contract Performance Reviewer, National Association of Blue Shield Plans, Inc. 1968-1975, Faculty Member, Political Science Department, Park College, Kansas City, Missouri. 1975, Visiting Fellow, Princeton University, Department of Politics. 1975-1977, Chief Legislative Assistant, Benjamin A. Gilman (R-NY). 1977-1983, Special Assistant to the Chief Counsel, and Professional Staff Member for the Select Committee on Narcotics Abuse and Control. 1983 to present, Minority Staff Director, Select Committee on Narcotics Abuse and Control.

Expertise: Narcotics control and interdiction, international drug trafficking

"It's a cause, a movement to control drug trafficking," Elliot Brown says of the "mission" he shares with the ten Republican members of the Select Committee on Narcotics Abuse and Control. The Committee's work to control the production, trafficking, and consumption of drugs is a constant battle, and includes prevention and public education efforts.

Brown says much of his work is devoted to "raising the consciousness" of the international community. He has participated in study missions to eighteen nations around the world, and was a member of the first congressional delegation to evaluate linking economic aid with drug control efforts in Peru. Brown also worked closely with Colombia on the capture and extradition of one of the world's largest cocaine drug kings.

Whether working with foreign governments, U.S. government agencies, the military, private corporations, public service organizations or Congress, Brown feels his job is always exciting. In the past, "Congress and the Executive Branch have been fragmented in their study of the broad range of issues which are affected by drug problems," Brown explains. Since the oversight committee was created in 1977, it has been "very instrumental in getting legislation through Congress by using the select committee to mobilize the standing committees."

Brown's workload includes briefing and counselling the ten Republican committee members for hearings, and directing the preparation of their questions, statements and reports. He works closely with numerous other committees and key federal agencies, and also manages all of the drug-related initiatives of Rep. Benjamim A. Gilman.

In 1977, he took on the additional duties of developing the Select Committee's initiatives and budget as Special Assistant to the Chief Counsel. Prior to his Hill career, Brown was a political science professor at the University of South Dakota, Park College in Missouri and Rider College in New Jersey. He continues to work in academia, serving as an adjunct professor of government and public administration at American University since 1977.

Brown is a member of the National Social Science Honorary Society at Princeton. He manages to maintain current membership and involvement with eight educational and professional associations, including the International Narcotic Enforcement Officers Association, the American Political Science Association, and the American Society of International Law.

Edward H. Jurith
Staff Director
Committee on Narcotics Abuse &
   Control
H2-234 House Office Bldg. Annex
   2
226-3040

*Personal: born 9/11/51 in Brooklyn,
New York. B.A. American Univ., 1973.
J.D. Brooklyn Law School, 1976.
1971-1974, Legislative Aide,
Representative Frank J. Brasco (D-
NY). 1976-1981, associate, Lyon &
Erlbaum, Esq., Kew Gardens, NY.
1981-1987, Counsel; 1987-present,
Staff Director, House Select
Committee on Narcotics Abuse &
Control.*

Expertise: Drug enforcement

Ed Jurith traces his interest in drug enforcement to the days when he was a criminal defense attorney in New York and saw the problems caused by rampant drug abuse and governmental neglect of the problem.

Intrigued by the way we go about processing drug crimes through the criminal justice system, he decided to work for the Select Committee on Narcotics Abuse and Control, with his focus on facilitating an effective partnership between federal, state, and local efforts to combat drug abuse. His vantage point has changed from the courtroom to the committee room, but he still is convinced government must do more to right substance abuse.

Jurith has closely monitored the drug abuse policies of the Reagan Administration over the last seven years and is critical of what he regards as a refusal by the Administration to make narcotics control a major objective. To that end, he advocates a number of measures geared toward increasing the effectiveness of state and local narcotics enforcement efforts.

Jurith worked on the Anti-Drug Abuse Act of 1986, advocating state and local assistance for drug treatment, prevention and law enforcement efforts. More recently, Jurith proposed the creation of an Assistant Attorney General for State and Local Law Enforcement, who would be solely responsible for regional drug enforcement.

Jurith also lobbies the State Department to expand its drug interdiction and control measures, arguing especially for linkage of debt renegotiation and economic development aid to a country's cooperation with U.S. efforts to fight narcotics exports. His other areas of expertise include domestic treatment and prevention programs and education.

Jurith summarizes the thrust of his work as a nonpartisan effort: instead of characterizing narcotics control as a political problem, he sees it as one of leadership and coordination. As staff director of a select committee, Jurith works with a number of standing committees and agencies and emphasizes the necessity of a bipartisan approach.

Jurith's colleagues on other committees comment that he understands the need for coordination. They respect his good political sense, including a refusal to become a political ideologue—an inclination that has plagued the Committee in the past according to some Hill staffers. "Unlike his predecessors, he is not partisan and he is not an ideologue; he has a balanced perspective," says one colleague. Jurith agrees: "I'll work with anyone. We're committed to finding solutions."

HOUSE OF REPRESENTATIVES
OTHER KEY STAFF

Other Key Staff

Richard Bates
Executive Director
Democratic Congressional
  Campaign Committee
430 S. Capitol Street
485-3414

Expertise: Congressional campaigns

When Rep. Beryl Anthony (D-AR) was named Chairman of the Democratic Congressional Campaign Committee (DCCC) by Speaker Jim Wright after the 1986 elections, it was logical he would choose his Ways and Means staffer and trusted aide Richard Bates as head of the campaign committee.

Following the tenure of Rep. Tony Coehlo (D-CA) who moved from campaign committee chairman to House Majority Whip, Anthony inherited a rejuvenated organization on which he quickly put his own stamp. Anthony, who has travelled tirelessly to raise money for the committee in preparation for the 1988 elections, is well liked by his colleagues.

Bates, who was a veteran Hill staffer before joining Anthony in the early 1980's, has maintained a low profile as executive director of the committee.

Administrative Assistant
M. F. "Buddy" Bishop
Rep. Jamie Whitten (D-MS)
2314 Rayburn HOB
225-4306

Personal: Born 2/24/28, Drew, Mississippi. B.A. Univ. of Mississippi, 1950. Served for two years as a Captain in the U.S. Army (infantry officer) during the Korean War. Bishop was a House member of the Mississippi state legislature from 1956-1960. From 1958 to 1961, he was a Mississippi farmer and merchant. 1962-present, Administrative Assistant, Rep. Jamie Whitten (D-MS).

Expertise: Mississippi politics, administration

The expression "Southern gentlemen" is the best way to describe Buddy Bishop, Administrative Assistant to Rep. Jamie Whitten. Bishop has been with Whitten, Chairman of the House Appropriations Committee, for 26 years and is the Chairman's "catch-all man," by his own description.

Bishop's career philosophy, "kill 'em with kindness," is what he says makes Whitten's office run. As the main conduit to Chairman Whitten, Bishop does everything with an eye toward making the work of the Chairman and his office effective. He states that the smooth operation of the office is essential to Whitten. And, after 46 years as a member of the House of Representatives, Whitten has a track record not only for longevity but for being a major player in the House.

When asked what his area of expertise is, Bishop replies "whatever Rep. Whitten wants." His loyalty to Whitten is further described by an ex-colleague, Paris Fisher.

"Buddy is a great caretaker of Whitten's domain. Buddy is a confidante and extension of Whitten himself. He is always candid with you, if you are a close friend or merely an acquaintance. He means what he says and he will let you know if you are coming out of left field."

Fisher also cites Bishop's strength of never forgetting his roots as another of his assets. "Like Rep. Whitten, Buddy is a Mississippian and he knows his district. Both Bishop and Rep. Whitten think and act with the home district in mind."

What strikes you most about Bishop is his sincere interest in constituent matters, which often become mundane after years on Capitol Hill. He states, "It is very important to me to let people know you are working for them when they come to you for assistance. Even if I know the answer to their question, I never respond with an off-hand remark. I look into it just a bit further so I can let the person know I am concerned with his issue and that I have put some effort into learning more about it and how we can best aid them. It is human nature to want to help someone else out and I never let anything get in the way of that."

Bishop is an avid golfer who says he golfs, "wherever I'm invited. If you want to get to me or the Chairman, the golf course is the best temptation."

Other Key Staff

William H. Brown
Parliamentarian
House of Representatives
H-209 Capitol
225-7373

Expertise: Rules and procedures of the House of Representatives

Bill Brown was appointed to the position of Parliamentarian by Speaker Carl Albert when his predecessor, Lewis Deschler, resigned in 1974 after a half-century of House service. The Parliamentarian is appointed without political consideration by the Speaker in his constitutional role. As a nonpartisan employee of the House, he serves both parties, working with all Members, Members' staffs, and committee staff. In addition to the Parliamentarian, the Office of the Parliamentarian consists on one Deputy Parliamentarian, and two Assistant Parliamentarians. Every effort is made by the Office to give impartial and fair procedural advice, anticipating possible parliamentary problems on the introduction, consideration, and passage of legislation. While some earlier parliamentarians may have been close to speakers of the House (Deschler was close to Speaker Sam Rayburn), House customs have long since changed. Brown's role is more that of an objective arbiter than of the speaker's ally. In fact, Brown is widely recognized as scrupulously fair in interpreting and applying House rules—sometimes to the leadership's advantage and sometimes to its disadvantage. In that vein, the Office of the Parliamentarian makes a point of striving to maintain neutrality on political issues. The Office makes itself available for personal consultation with respect to rules either by phone or by visitation to the Office.

When the House is in session, the Parliamentarian, or one of his assistants, is stationed to the right of the Speaker where his function is to advise, in a quiet way, the presiding officer and other Members with respect to parliamentary questions. The Speaker, in applying the rules, follows precedent (that is, he follows prior rulings of other Speakers, much as a court follows judicial precedent). Therefore, the Parliamentarian's job is to find the applicable precedents quickly. His sources include the published precedents of the House, a compilation of the thousands of decisions of Speakers and Chairmen of the Committees of the Whole that have been recorded since 1789. Part of the Parliamentarian's job is to compile and publish all the rulings of the Chair which result from the application of House rules and to edit and update the House Rules and Manual for each Congress.

Personal: born 9/3/29 in Huntington, West Virginia. B.S. Swarthmore Coll., 1951. J.D. Univ. of Chicago Law School, 1954. (Delta Upsilon). 1954-1957, U.S. Naval Reserves. 1958-1974, Assistant Parliamentarian. 1974-present, Parliamentarian of the House of Representatives.

After thirty years in the Parliamentarian's Office, Brown still finds each day a distinct challenge. "Every day a new parliamentary question comes up that requires research and analysis."

Virginia C. Fletcher
Administrative Assistant
Rep. Dan Rostenkowski (D-IL)
2111 Rayburn House Office Bldg.
225-4061

Expertise: Administration

Virginia Fletcher has served long-time Chicago ward politician and Ways and Means Chairman Dan Rostenkowski in various capacities for her entire career. She joined the staff of the young Congressman from Illinois's 8th district in 1963, shortly before the death of one of her greatest heroes in public life, John F. Kennedy. Fletcher has remained on the staff for twenty-five years, holding every job in the office at one time or another. She has handled immigration, Social Security, and Medicare casework as well as a variety of other issues. She has worked her way into the position of Administrative Assistant for one of the most powerful members of Congress by learning on the job. "As Rostenkowski grew in stature and became interested in a wider variety of issues, I grew in knowledge." Fletcher is a jack-of-all-trades administrator whose role is district oversight. Fletcher has a reputation for deferring to committee technicians on questions of substantive policy but she has played an important role in the development of committee legislation, particularly the 1981 and 1986 tax bills.

Fletcher's principal responsibility is to ensure the Chairman of the Ways and Means Committee is meeting the needs of his diverse and changing district—a goal which often competes with the persistent pull of committee responsibilities. "This is a new era, with new personalities and new issues to which the Chairman has had to adjust." Since joining Rostenkowski, programs like Medicare, Social Security, and pensions have developed and grown beyond expectation, and Fletcher is pleased she's been able to be a part of these developments.

Personal: born 11/17/44 in Norton, Virginia. 1963-present, various staff positions in the personal office of Rep. Dan Rostenkowski.

"The Chairman is the kind of member who likes to make every corn beef and cabbage dinner in his District. We as a staff are constantly trying to make sure his schedule is such that he can make important *local* affairs as well as oversee the Ways and Means Committee and its broad jurisdiction," Fletcher observed.

During 1986, considerable speculation surfaced about Chairman Rostenkowski's ambitions for the Speakership. However, Fletcher notes the most significant moment of decision for Rostenkowski was in 1980 when he decided to pursue the Chairmanship of Ways and Means rather than attempting to climb from Chief Deputy to Majority Whip.

Fletcher is known on Capitol Hill as a master duplicate bridge player. As former president of the Hill Staff duplicate bridge club, she has earned the title of "Bridge Master," and has competed nationally in the game.

Joseph R. Gaylord
Executive Director
National Republican Congressional
  Committee
320 1st Street, S.E.
479-7000

*Personal: born 12/21/45, in Elgin, IL.
B.A. Univ. of Iowa, 1967. In 1967,
various administrative posts in the
Republican Party of Iowa. 1973,
Executive Director, Iowa State Central
Committee. 1975, Director of Special
Voter Groups, Republican National
Committee. 1976, Director, Special
Projects, Republican National
Committee (including Director of the
1976 Campaign Management
College). 1977-1978, Eastern Director,
Local Elections Campaign Division,
Republican National Committee. 1979-
80, Director, Local Elections (for the
nation), Republican National
Committee. 1981, Campaign Director,
National Republican Congressional
Committee. 1982 to present, Executive
Director, National Republican
Congressional Committee.*

Expertise: Congressional campaigns

When it comes to running a campaign, Joe Gaylord, Executive Director of the National Republican Congressional Committee (NRCC), is a walking encyclopedia of "how-tos."

His experience in politics began in Iowa where, after graduating from college, he supervised the Iowa Party's record door-to-door canvass of 524,000 households, using 44,000 volunteers to register 75,000 new voters.

This outstanding performance was followed by a series of high-level positions with the Republican National Committee (RNC), including direction of the Local Elections Campaign Division. Under his leadership, this Division held more than 300 campaign seminars and schools and trained more than 13,000 candidates, campaign managers, and party activists.

Gaylord says, ". . . my expertise, my love, is in organizing volunteers and campaigns." Gaylord describes himself as a "groomer" of candidates who reminds people that "politics should be fun."

Gaylord's work is admired by colleagues and associates. Rep. Guy Vander Jagt (R-MI), NRCC Chairman, says: "The best thing that has happened to the NRCC in the last five years was to obtain the services of Joe. And, this is something that not just I am saying, but something the political community throughout the country tells me continuously."

When not working, Gaylord enjoys playing bridge and sailing off Maryland's Eastern Shore where he and his wife, director of the RNC's Political Education Department, spend "too few" weekends.

David Geiss
Administrative Assistant
Representative William D. Ford (D-MI)
239 Cannon House Office Bldg.
225-6261

Expertise: Administration

In 1982, when Rep. Bill Ford needed an administrative assistant, he turned to a long-time ally in local politics and hired Wayne County councilman David Geiss.

Before coming to the Hill, Geiss divided his time between two jobs: financial secretary for United Auto Workers Local 189, and Taylor city councilman. Geiss was therefore better equipped than most to be Ford's administrative assistant since it combines the two jobs of Washington Administrative Assistant and District Manager. As a result, Geiss finds that he must spend almost half his time in the district.

His position with the union, where he negotiated contracts, carried grievances to the boss, and took care of the books, provided good training for his present position. Geiss is as much a team player as is his boss. In 1983, he formed a monthly working group of Michigan Democratic Administrative Assistants in order to alert one another to emerging issues and trouble spots. But Geiss is also just as willing to work with conservative Republicans: "If they have trouble with their farmers and it's an issue that can help Michigan, we'll help them out."

Personal: born 9/26/42 in Philadelphia, PA. Henry Ford Community College, 1961-62. 1962-68, U.S. Army Service. 1965-75, Michigan Rivet Corp. 1975-82, Sec'y Treas., United Auto Workers Local 189. 1973-79, councilman, City of Taylor, MI. 1980-81, Wayne County Charter Commissioner. 1982-present, Administrative Assistant, Rep. William Ford.

Michigan's 15th district is packed with auto plants; each of the major American manufacturers operates a plant within its boundaries. Geiss's UAW experience therefore serves him, and Ford, well. After he became Ford's Administrative Assistant the district was plagued with an unemployment rate that was among the nation's highest. Since much of the joblessness was due to a decline in American auto sales, Geiss proved to be an effective liaison, calming most of his former colleagues' concerns and winning points for Ford.

Although he confesses a love for politics—to the point that it might be easy to confuse his vocation with his avocation—Geiss finds time to relax at home with his three children, read, and bowl.

G. Harris Jordan
Legislative Director
Representative Philip Crane (R-IL)
1035 Longworth House Office
  Bldg.
225-3711

*Personal: born 1/6/46, Duluth,
Minnesota. B.A. George Washington
Univ., 1986 (deferred). 1969-1970,
U.S. Army Engineer Officer in Vietnam.
1970, Staff Assistant, Sen. Stephen
Young (D-OH). 1975-1977,
Management Consultant, Analyst,
Intrec, Inc., Santa Monica, CA. 1978
to present, Legislative Director, Rep.
Philip M. Crane (R-IL).*

Expertise: Tax and trade

As Rep. Phil Crane's "broker/ideas guy/negotiator," and Legislative Director, Jordan hones in on issues where Crane can play a pivotal role, especially in the areas of tax and trade .

Crane is "stalwart in his interests," Jordan says, and in advancing Crane's agenda Jordan has found himself embroiled in his share of legislative battles. But he isn't one to shy away from a fight, according to a former colleague: "The weak and timid get left in the trenches on the Hill. Harris is an intelligent man who is not afraid to get fairly aggressive." And yet, Jordan is "definitely not someone unwilling to bend," says a staffer for the Democratic majority on Ways and Means.

Jordan played a role in the enactment of the Economic Recovery Tax Act of 1981. Identified as President Reagan's first major legislative push, the ERTA is quite unlike most Democratic tax-cut proposals, which generally favor the lower end of the economic spectrum. The ERTA was designed to put over $700 billion back into the hands of business and individual tax payers via various methods, including across-the-board tax cuts and investment incentives. Says Jordan of the experience: "Working with a Republican, you don't have that many opportunities to turn the deck over on the Democrats."

As the Reagan Administration enters its final days, however, promoting Crane's agenda may prove more difficult. Jordan is critical of legislation that would impose sanctions against countries engaged in so-called unfair trade practices. Part of the Omnibus Trade Reform bill, this proposal, he says, "is trying to correct problems of competition when the real problems for business are in the tax code."

Recounting the hectic days working on the 1986 Tax Reform Act, Jordan acknowledges: "The bill did not go far enough. We didn't get as much into it as we'd have liked."

Although Jordan has evolved into one of the top legislative aides for one of the most conservative members of Congress, his first job on Capitol Hill was in 1970 with Sen. Stephen Young (D-OH). Jordan got the job as staff assistant because Young was "a family friend and neighbor." But eight months later, Jordan was gone "for philosophical reasons."

"It took Crane to show me I was more of a conservative than I originally thought," Jordan says. He admits to occasional philosophical differences with Crane, but adds he sees great value in "playing the devil's advocate."

John Orlando
Administrative Assistant
Rep. John Dingell (D-MI)
2221 Rayburn Home Office Bldg.
225-4071

Expertise: Politics, administration

John Orlando has served the Chairman of the powerful House Energy and Commerce Committee since 1986, when he moved over from a position as the Deputy Director of the Democratic Congressional Campaign Committee. During the course of his stint as a DCCC staffer, Orlando played a role in countless campaigns; fundraising, advising, and providing political assistance and support to candidates.He was also Executive Director of the Democratic Congressional Dinner.

His position as Administrative Assistant to Chairman Dingell places him at the crossroads of many important jurisdictional and political battles in the House. Dingell has a reputation for being a tough, sometimes stubborn chairman who uses his committee post to ensure that the interests of his district's most important industry—autos—are protected. Orlando's job is to coordinate district, committee, and larger House politics—in that order. He is also responsible for staffing Dingell in his Steering and Policy capacity.

Orlando takes an active interest in all of the significant legislative issues over which Energy and Commerce has jurisdiction. While he relies on committee staff on most technical questions which come before the committee, he acts as a political advisor to Dingell on committee politics and procedural strategies. Dingell's reputation as a legislative strategist is well-known. As he observed before the Rules Committee in 1982: "If you let me write procedure and I let you write substance, I'll screw you every time."

Personal: born 5/29/56 in Detroit, Michigan. B.A. with honors in Political Science, San Diego State Univ., 1978. 1978, Deputy Campaign Manager, Rep. Mike Blouin (2nd District, IA). 1979-1986, various staff positions with the Democratic Congressional Campaign Committee. Left DCCC as Deputy Director in 1986. 1986-present, Administrative Assistant to John Dingell.

Orlando's experience as a political advisor has put him in good stead to serve Dingell as chief political aide, helping to manage the political relationships between his boss and other committee members, and the membership of the House itself.

In addition to his political responsibilities, Orlando manages the Washington office and district offices in Dearborn (home of Ford Motor Co.'s world headquarters) and Monroe. Even with redistricting in 1982, Orlando has observed few changes in the political complexion of the district other than the addition of a large area of agricultural land. The district is composed largely of working-class whites: auto and steelworkers, tool and die manufacturers, and chemical workers.

Recently married, Orlando is a father of a baby girl who sits quietly in her infant seat on the couch while her father carries on the business of the day. He is an avid sports enthusiast, and enjoy playing golf, basketball, and softball. Other interests include photography, furniture restoration and antiques.

Other Key Staff

Charles Scalera
Administrative Assistant
Rep. Peter Rodino (D-NJ)
2462 Rayburn House Office Bldg.
225-3436

Expertise: Judiciary, tax, New Jersey politics

When Charles Scalera came to the Hill in 1979 and was offered a staff position, he was one of the fortunate few able to start at the top. Prior to this, Scalera was employed at the I.R.S. as a tax attorney. When he heard Congressman Peter Rodino, Chairman of the House Judiciary Committee, was looking for a new administrative assistant, Scalera sought out and was offered the job. In his words, "Mr. Rodino set three criteria for hiring a new A.A. : he or she should have extensive political experience, should know the state and district, and should be an attorney. Fortunately for me, I grew up in the district, had been involved in many state and local elections as well as Eugene McCarthy's in '68, and was a lawyer. It worked out well."

As A.A. to Rodino, Scalera is in a unique position as confidant and advisor to one of the most powerful Members of Congress. Since taking over as A.A. in 1979, Scalera has helped Rodino review such legislation in his committee as the Extension of the Voting Rights Act of 1965 (as passed in 1982), the Immigration Reform and Control Act of 1986, and other initiatives involving bankruptcy laws, school prayer and school busing, where Rodino has often established himself as a leading opponent. According to Scalera, however, "Mr. Rodino's and my biggest concern is constituent service."

When asked about his career goals, Scalera responded by saying he wants to continue in politics. "I like to consider myself as someone who tries to help people." Scalera would like to continue to practice law and to stay involved on the Hill. By way of example, he was a senior political advisor to the Joe Biden for President campaign. At this point, however, it is definitely premature to speak of life after Rodino. The New Jersey 10th District Democrat has served in Congress since 1948. Despite the growing minority population in his district and the active campaigning of Jesse Jackson against him in 1986, Rodino seems likely to seek his seat in Congress again.

Personal: born 9/22/42 in Newark, New Jersey. B.A. in Economics, Windham Coll., Putney, Vermont, 1967. J.D. (Magna Cum Laude) Massey Law Coll., Atlanta, Ga., 1970. 1969-1970, law instructor, Massey Law College. 1973-1975, Vice President and General Counsel, Guernsey Petroleum Corp. 1976-1979, attorney, Internal Revenue Service. 1979, attorney, Dept. of Labor. 1979 to present, Administrative Assistant, Rep. Peter Rodino (D-NJ).

In addition to his role as A.A. to Rodino, Scalera finds time to preside as president of the Burro Club, a staff club founded by Lyndon Johnson when he was in the House; and to practice one of his more enjoyable, nonwork-related activities—cooking. "Being from an Italian-Irish background, I tended to focus on these ethnic foods but have lately branched out. Cooking and enjoying foods is one of the better ways to celebrate life with friends."

James M. Sparling, Jr.
Administrative Assistant
Rep. Guy Vander Jagt (R-MI)
2409 Rayburn House Office Bldg.
225-3511

Expertise: Administrative, politics

With the revolving door of many congressional offices, it is not surprising that anyone with five to ten years experience is considered a Hill "veteran." But when it comes to sheer longevity, few can match the record of Jim Sparling, Administrative Assistant to Rep. Guy Vander Jagt, and 27-year veteran of Capitol Hill.

To what does Sparling attribute his 27-year record of public service? According to him, "there's nothing glamorous about it. Just old-fashioned common sense and one hell of a lot of hard work." A record made all the more noteworthy by the fact that Sparling did not complete his college studies. While some might view that as a handicap, Sparling disagrees, noting "I've always considered it an asset, because it forced me to work that extra bit harder than the next guy, and the results speak for themselves."

Indeed they do. Since his arrival on Capitol Hill in 1961, Sparling has been noted for his professionalism and prowess as an administrator and political confidant. Working first as an A.A. to former Representative James Harvey for 12 years, he subsequently held positions as Assistant to the President for Legislative Affairs, and Assistant to the Secretary of Commerce as Congressional Affairs Liaison before landing with one of the House's best known Republican members, Guy Vander Jagt, in 1975.

Personal: born 6/30/28 in Saginaw, Michigan. 1946-1948, U.S. Navy. Attended Alma College, Alma, Michigan, 1948-49. 1961-1974, Administrative Assistant, Rep. James Harvey. 1975 to present, Administrative Assistant, Rep. Guy Vander Jagt.

Over the past two decades, Sparling notes that he has seen significant changes come about, both positive and negative. He is encouraged by the rising caliber of legislators sent to the Hill by their constituents, replacing "the old boy network" with its emphasis on personal connections, with legislative know-how. Conversely, he is troubled by the proliferation of committees and subcommittees. His feeling is that "these committees must hold hearings to justify their existence, and the result is often poor legislation drafted into bad public policy."

Sparling twice attempted to win election to Michigan's Eight District Congressional seat. Following the resignation of Harvey in February, 1974, whom he served as AA, Sparling won the Republican nomination in the special election only to lose an extremely close race. Later that fall during the general election, Sparling fell victim to the Democratic incumbent by a margin of 55% to 45%. In the wake of Nixon's resignation the previous August, it was an election result repeated often around the country for many Republican candidates.

Wendy Strong
Administrative Assistant
Rep. E. Clay Shaw, Jr.
440 Cannon House Office Bldg.
225-3026

Expertise: Hill operations

Wendy Strong became interested in politics in high school, when she volunteered for local campaigns in Mercer Country, New Jersey. In 1972 she helped to organize a local chapter of "Young Voters for Nixon." While attending American University, in 1973, she volunteered to work in Senator William Brock's office and shortly after was hired on staff. Brock did not have a filing system, so Strong organized his files into a highly efficient operation.

In 1976, Strong moved to the National Republican Congressional Committee, where she became an Assistant Director in the research division, tracking Republican campaign efforts. She was poised for her return to the Hill after the Republican comeback year of 1980, when she joined the staff of newly elected Florida Congressman E. Clay Shaw, Jr., of Fort Lauderdale.

As Shaw's Legislative Director, Strong covered the Public Works and Transportation Committee, and specialized in immigration issues. The Mariel boat lift refugees from Cuba was a focus for Strong. The location of Shaw's district made the problem of illegal aliens a top priority.

In 1985, Strong switched gears to become Shaw's Administrative Assistant, and now keeps abreast of the whole gamut of his political activities in the course of running his office. Strong maintains a very close daily working relationship with Shaw's district office, briefing them on congressional operations and consulting on district issues.

Personal: born 2/15/55, Teaneck, New Jersey. B.A. Political Science, American Univ. 1976. 1973-76, Part-time Assistant to Sen. William Brock (R-TN). 1976-80, Assistant Director of Research Division, National Republican Congressional Committee. 1981-85, Legislative Director; 1985-present, Administrative Assistant, Rep. E. Clay Shaw, Jr. Vice President for Social Activities, Administrative Assistants Association, Capitol Hill.

Her colleagues attest to Strong's drive and enthusiasm. "I let each person know that they are making a contribution, and exactly why the boss needs them to work on a certain project," she states. Strong attributes much of her successful managerial style to getting a staff that is bright and aggressive.

In her free time, Strong works at Children's Hospital in its Child Life Program. She is also a "hugger" for the Special Olympics, and recently finished a two-year program with the Northern Virginia Hotline as a "crisis listener." Strong is an avid reader (especially of classics), and a movie buff. She runs twenty to sixty miles per week and is captain of the Florida Power Softball team.

Ruth M. (Tina) Tate
Superintendent
House Radio and Television Gallery
H-320 U.S. Capitol Bldg.
225-5214

Personal: born 9/5/44 in Atlanta, Georgia. B.A. Emory Univ., 1966. 1967-1969, staff assistant, library of the Univ.of Georgia at Athens. 1970-1972, staff assistant, Cox Broadcasting Company, Washington, D.C.. 1972-present, Staff Assistant and, since 1981, Superintendent, House Radio and Television Gallery.

Expertise: Broadcast liaison

On April 20, 1939, a one-sentence provision was adopted and made part of the official Rules of the House of Representatives. This clause mandated that a portion of the House Press Gallery be set aside to accommodate radio and television reporters for the purpose of reporting the debates and proceedings in the House. A half century later, the House Radio and Television Gallery remains a viable and indispensable function of the people's house.

After her tenure with Cox Broadcasting, Tina Tate became the first woman to be hired as a member of the Gallery's staff. And, in 1981, after nearly a decade on the staff, Tate became the third Superintendent in the Gallery's 49-year history.

Needless to say, Tate and her staff of five serve an important role on Capitol Hill. And chief among the Gallery's responsibilities is serving as the broadcast liaison between broadcast journalists and Member's offices and congressional committees.

Because Tate and the Gallery are there to accommodate the broadcast media, they are responsible for preparing statistical lists and other information for correspondents and providing logistical support for press conferences and committee hearings. In this last respect, Tate was responsible for organizing on the House side the television and radio coverage of last year's Iran-Contra joint hearings.

The Gallery also keeps a running log of the proceedings of the House—a blessing for correspondents. Now, instead of having to wait for the *Congressional Record* the following day, reporters are able to remain informed of the House's activities on a minute-by-minute basis.

Although the Republican and Democratic conventions will take place this summer, Tate and the Gallery began preparing for them early last year. The Gallery will handle everything from planning the physical set-ups for the broadcast media to laying out the floor plans to credential the various broadcasters. According to Tate, one of the greatest challenges for the Gallery is providing some 30 anchor booths for as many independent networks.

If anyone thinks the Gallery is at all partisan in its daily activities, consider this: The Gallery staff is under the guidance and direction of the Speaker's Office; the Doorkeeper of the House pays them; and employees of the Gallery are essentially hired by the broadcasters. This rather complicated procedure insulates the staff from political interests and consequently ensures nonpartisanship.

Tate makes a convincing case that hers is the ideal job. "I don't necessarily want to be a journalist nor do I have any desire to be a politician," says Tate. "But I do like having a front row seat." And a front row seat she has.

Herbert Wadsworth
Administrative Assistant
Rep. Bill Grant (D-FL)
1331 Longworth House Office
   Bldg.
225-5235

Expertise: Management of political campaigns and congressional offi

Herb Wadsworth embodies the tradition of the Hill professional. In 1975 he was named Congressional Staffer of the year by *Roll Call*. For twenty-four years Wadsworth was the Administrative Assistant and political advisor to his close friend, Rep. Don Fuqua of Florida. On Fuqua's retirement in 1986, Wadsworth became the Administrative Assistant for successor Rep. Bill Grant, another old friend, and oversaw the assembling of a new staff.

Wadsworth credits his success on the Hill to his relationships with Reps. Fuqua and Grant, and a developed managerial ability. "Herb has always had a sixth sense when it comes to communicating with political workers, and making sure all operations are running smoothly," says one colleague. Wadsworth himself declares, "I always make sure that my boss can concentrate on the committee he is chairing and does not have to worry about the day-to-day operations of the office." Also, he adds, it is important to remember that "no one is indispensable," including oneself.

This modesty belies a fighting spirit. Part of Wadsworth's life was spent on crutches, and in high school he was told that he could not become an Eagle Scout because he would not be able to make long hikes. In response, Wadsworth not only walked a ten-mile hike on crutches, but ran a fourteen-mile hike to boot.

Personal: born 6/15/31 in Live Oak, Florida. B.S. in Journalism Univ. of Florida, 1953. 1953-1961, Editor, Suwannee Democrat. 1962-1986, Administrative Assistant, Rep. Don Fuqua (D-FL). 1986-present, Administrative Assistant, Rep. Bill Grant (D-FL).

When Wadsworth was twenty-three, he became Florida State Vice-President of the Jaycees and a member of their national board of directors. From 1953-1961, he worked as editor on *the Suwannee Democrat* in Live Oak, FL, before teaming up in 1962 with the newly elected Rep. Don Fuqua.

As Chairman of the Science and Technology Committee, Fuqua was a key player in the development of the American space program, from the Apollo moon shots to the shuttle program. Wadsworth's assistance provided Fuqua with the time to concentrate on his legislative programs, and Wadsworth's political counsel helped in Fuqua's reelection campaigns. Currently, as Grant focuses on economy and energy issues, Wadsworth provides the same indispensable administrative support for him.

Kirk E. Walder
Administrative Assistant
Representative Olympia Snowe (R-ME)
2464 Rayburn House Office Bldg.
225-6306

Personal: born 6/30/53 in Dixon, Illinois. Attended Coe College, 1971-1972. Illinois State Univ., 1975. 1975-1976, Research Assistant with Legislative Digest. 1977-1979, Chief Research assistant for the House Republican Conference. 1979-1980, Political Director, John Anderson for President. 1983-1985, Legislative Assistant, Rep. Olympia Snowe. 1986-present, Administrative Assistant, Rep. Olympia Snowe.

Expertise: Administration, campaigns

As Kirk Walder candidly admits, "some people are just born to be Republicans," referring to the political affiliation he shares with another more famous native of his hometown Dixon, Illinois—President Reagan. A self-proclaimed "political junkie," he first became hooked in college after interning in the office of then Republican Congressman John Anderson from Illinois. His internship with Anderson came during the "Watergate summer" of 1974, a time he recalls as being one of the most politically explosive and exciting he has witnessed since his arrival on the Hill.

Soon after graduating from Illinois State University, Walder found himself drawn back to the Hill. Following two year stints with *Legislative Digest*, and the House Republican Conference as chief legislative assistant, he was enlisted to serve in the post of Political Director for the presidential campaign of his former boss, John Anderson, an opportunity he refers back to as "the chance of a lifetime." Though Anderson's ill-fated bid on the Independent ticket failed to upset the two major parties, it captured national headlines and provided Walder with invaluable campaign and political experience.

His move to Rep. Snowe's office as legislative assistant in 1983 for two years proved prophetic. Attracted by the congresswoman's pragmatic approach to complex issues and political savvy (the youngest Republican woman ever elected to Congress), Walder rose quickly, becoming her Administrative Assistant in 1985 at the age of 32. Though Walder's political views are virtually a mirror image of Rep. Snowe's, their working relationship is a study in contrasts. While the congresswoman prides herself on being aggressive and outfront on the issues, Walder's style is characterized more by compromise and behind the scenes work. As he enters his third year as Snowe's AA, it's apparent that it's a match that works.

Walder defines his managerial approach as one of "quiet authority," preferring to work closely with the staff on all aspects of office operations.

Snowe is virtually unbeatable in her district (winning 76% of the vote in 1984 and 77% in 1986), owing in part to the extraordinary attention she has her staff, Walder included, devote to casework and constituent service. While Walder is very interested in campaign finance reform, spawned by his work on the Anderson campaign, he works most closely on issues relating to the budget.

SENATE

SENATE
LEADERSHIP

Sheila P. Burke
Chief of Staff
Office of the Republican Leader
S-230 Capitol Bldg.
224-31351

Personal: born 1/10/51, San Francisco, California. B.Sc. Univ. of San Francisco, 1973. M.P.A. John F. Kennedy School of Government, Harvard Univ., 1982. 1973-1974, staff nurse, Alta Bates Hospital, Berkeley, CA. 1974-1977, Director of Program and Field Services, National Student Nurses Assn. 1975-1977, staff nurse, Doctor's Hospital, NY. 1977-1978, Legislative Assistant, Sen. Robert Dole (R-KS). 1979-1982, Professional Staff Member, Senate Committee on Finance. 1978-1980, visiting lecturer, Univ. of Michigan School of Nursing, Ann Arbor, MI. 1980-1981, Research Assistant, Center for Health Policy and Management, John F. Kennedy School of Government, Harvard Univ. 1982-1983, visiting lecturer, Marymount Coll. Graduate School of Business Administration. 1982-present, Adjunct Lecturer, Univ. of Pennsylvania, School of Nursing. 1985-present, Adjunct Faculty, Georgetown Univ. School of Nursing. 1982-1984, Deputy

Expertise: Health care, welfare and social security

To the untrained eye, there are few similarities between a registered nurse and a successful Senate aide.

On closer observation, however, many of the same "tools of the trade" employed by health care professionals are used by those who work for the country's top politicians. Nurses develop many skills working with doctors, patients and hospital bureaucrats which are transferable to the political world, including learning to communicate with patients, determining proper treatment, teaching and negotiating. While these talents might not result in the political equivalent of Clara Barton, Sheila Burke says that "a nurse's ability to work with people is an important component for anyone's success on Capitol Hill."

To Burke—who has practiced and taught nursing since 1973—combining the "people skills" of a registered nurse with the political instincts of a Hill veteran is much more than mixing metaphors. It's an important reason why, in 1986, Senate Majority Leader Robert Dole (R-KS) named her as his chief of staff—the first woman ever to hold the job.

Burke was first attracted to nursing because "it was a profession that cared about people, and there were a lot of challenging jobs available. It just made a lot of sense to me at the time."

Her gravitation towards politics made sense, too.

Burke remembers thinking in the mid-1970's that, with the increasing federal and state intervention into health policy, "it was clear that the process would need people who understood the health care delivery system, how it worked and what was involved in patient care. I thought my practical experience as a nurse could make a big difference in working to reconcile a broad spectrum of issues and views about health care."

Burke admits that she has been "blessed to work for someone who understands what a health care delivery system can and cannot do. Because of his lengthy hospitalization after World War II for war wounds, the Senator has an awful lot of sensitivity and understanding about these issues." Over the years Burke has had ample opportunity to bring her own sensitivity and caring to the legislative process. She has worked on a wide range of domestic-related legislation including the social security bailout, drugs, the homeless, AIDS, Medicare, Medicaid, and maternal and child health.

Burke lost the luxury of concentrating on specific issues, however, when she became Dole's chief of staff.

Now she is a jack-of-all trades. Working with a staff of 16 and a budget in excess of $900,000, Burke does what has to be done—whether it's working with committee staff directors, keeping Dole

Staff Director, Senate Committee on Finance. 1985-1986, Deputy Chief of Staff, Office of the Majority (Republican) Leader. 1986, Chief of Staff, Office of the Majority (Republican) Leader. 1987-present, Chief of Staff, Office of the Minority (Republican) Leader.

informed, writing statements, following legislation, managing the many resources available to the office and keeping in touch with federal agencies.

While Burke has come a long way since nursing school, she hasn't forgotten how she got where she is today. That's why she tries to make it easier for others who might like to pursue careers on Capitol Hill, and makes sure that health care professionals have opportunities to work as interns in Dole's office.

"Throughout my career I've met and worked with people who were very important role models for me. And I think that if we care enough about our own careers and professions, we should try to give a little of it back in some way," she says.

Today, despite the demands of the job, Burke still finds time to serve as member of the nursing faculty at Georgetown University and the University of Pennsylvania, was elected to the American Academy of Nurses, is active in the American Nurses Association and chairs the Harvard Alumni Council.

Leadership

Henry Kuualoha Giugni
Sergeant at Arms and Doorkeeper
S-321 Capitol Bldg.
224-2341

Expertise: Administration

On January 6, 1987, Henry Giugni was appointed Sergeant at Arms and Doorkeeper, one of six officers elected by Members of the United States Senate. The office of Doorkeeper was established in 1789, one of the first items of business taken up by the new Congress. The position was created to address the single most pressing problem confronting the Senate at its birth—its inability to keep a majority of Senators in the Capitol long enough to conduct business.

Today, the Sergeant at Arms serves as chief law enforcement and protocol officer and is the principal manager of most of the support services in the Senate. As administrator of the largest office in the Senate, Giugni oversees more than 1400 employees and a budget of over $100 million.

Some of Giugni's responsibilities include: presidential inaugurations, maintaining security at the Capitol and all Senate buildings and all Senate support services including mail and telecommunications.

Sen. Daniel Inouye (D-HI) has been Giugni's friend and mentor since 1957, when Inouye was in the Territorial House of Representatives before Hawaii was granted statehood. Inouye brought Giugni to the U.S. Senate in 1963, and Giugni served as his administrative assistant until appointed to his current position in January, 1987. After 25 years with the Senate, Giugni knows most of the Senators well enough to understand their personalities and address their needs. However, he feels he learned more about the Senate as an institution in his first 10 months as Sergeant at Arms than he had in all the previous years, and remains stimulated by his variety of tasks.

Personal: born 1/11/25 in Honolulu, Hawaii. Iolani School, Univ. of Hawaii. U.S. Army, 1942-1945. Officer, Honolulu Police Dept. Inspector, Liquor Commission, City and County of Honolulu. Former member of the State Central Committee, Democratic Party of Hawaii. Delegate to the Democratic National Convention 1964, 1968, 1972, 1976, 1980. Board of Directors, Rehabilitation Hospital of the Pacific, Honolulu. Member Hawaii State Society. 1963-1986, Administrative Assistant, Sen. Daniel K. Inouye (D-HI). 1987-present, Sergeant at Arms and Doorkeeper, U.S. Senate.

Giugni appreciates solutions that are simple and direct. As a former street and vice-squad police officer in Honolulu, he is unflappable and well-suited to a job that requires him to be prepared for any contingency. He is a world traveler who looks forward to returning eventually to his beloved Hawaii, and when it's time to leave his job, he will do so with no regrets about his career. He is as colorful as the bold art in his office and his ostrich cowboy boots, and takes pride in being as accessible to his varied employees as he is to the Senators he serves.

Howard O. Greene, Jr.
Secretary for the Minority
Officer of the Senate
S 337 Capitol Bldg.
224-3835

Expertise: Management and procedures of the Senate floor

Since 1981, Howard Greene has served as the Senate Republicans' legislative traffic cop. Every day the Senate is in session he can usually be found on the floor working closely with his eight-person staff to keep Minority Leader Robert Dole (R-KS) on top of—and sometimes ahead of—the legislative plans and actions of the Democrats.

Greene is only one of four people in the history of the Senate to serve as Secretary for the Minority, a post first created in the 1930s. The Secretary is elected by Senate Members every two years at the start of each Congress.

Greene became Secretary thanks to a combination of skill and seniority. His intimate knowledge of how the Senate works was gained through years of toiling in a succession of key staff posts often ignored or overlooked by congressional outsiders.

Personal: born 6/1/41, Lewes, Delaware. A.A., Wesley College, 1963. 1963-66, Univ. of Maryland. 1968-69, Door Messenger, U.S. Senate. 1969-71, Secretary for the Minority in the Senate Cloakroom. 1972-81, Assistant Secretary for the Minority. 1981-87, Secretary for the Majority, U.S. Senate. 1987 to present, Secretary for the Minority, U.S. Senate.

Greene's first job—as a doorman outside of the Senate's third floor visitors gallery—led to a stint answering phones inside the Republican Cloakroom off the Senate floor. He later went on to assume responsibility for the operations of the Republican page service, the legislative information service, and coordinating legislative and floor schedules. When Republicans gained control of the Senate in 1981, Greene was named Secretary for the Majority. He worked closely with Majority Leaders Howard Baker and Robert Dole to help clear bills for consideration on the Senate floor, schedule votes and oversee the party's patronage system.

When the Democrats regained control in 1987, Greene's job became more defensive in nature as he tried to discern Democratic tactics and strategies so Republicans can respond accordingly. Now he also serves as a legislative watchdog for Dole, keeping an eye on the floor when the Republican leader and his whips are tied up in their offices or in committee meetings. Greene spends at least 90 percent of his time on the Senate floor or in the Republican Cloakroom. "You have to be on the floor constantly to pick up what's going on, figure out what the Democrats are going to do next, and answer the two most often-asked questions I get: when is the next vote and how many votes will there be at the start and end of each week."

Greene has grown adept at "reading the floor"; that is, figuring out what the Democrats might be up to based on which Senators are huddled together in conversation, who is still in town, and which committees are holding hearings.

Roy F. Greenaway
Chief of Staff to Senate Democratic
Whip
S-148 Capitol Bldg.
224-2158

Personal: born in 1929 in Takoma Park, Maryland. American Legion national oratorical contest winner, 1947. Big Ten Debate Champion, 1950. Univ.of Chicago, 1951. Fresno State Coll., Masters in Linguistics, 1956. Teaching certificate, 1955. 1952-1954, U.S. Army in Japan. 1955-1959, high school teacher in Fresno, CA. 1959-1967, Inheritance Tax Appraiser, Fresno County. 1967-1968, instructor at Fresno State College. 1968-1969, Expert Witness in Condemnation Cases. 1956, 1960, California Delegation to Democratic National Convention. 1957-1960, Regional Vice President of California Democratic Council. 1965-1967, Northern California Vice President. 1969-1970, Chief Legislative Aide to Senator Alan Cranston. 1971-present, Administrative Assistant to Senator Alan Cranston.

Expertise: Administration, environment, domestic issues

Roy Greenaway is an accomplished orator who has been a force in California Democratic politics for 33 years. He has been a colleague of Senator Alan Cranston (D-CA) since 1954, when they served on the California Democratic Council, which Cranston chaired. Through reapportionment and other measures, they helped revitalize the California Democratic Party and reversed the political devastation that accompanied Eisenhower's landslide.

When Cranston became California State Controller, he appointed Greenaway as Inheritance Tax Appraiser in Fresno County. Cranston brought Greenaway to the Senate to be his chief legislative advisor in 1969 and made him his administrative assistant in 1971. Greenaway's prowess on domestic issues continues to complement Cranston's interests in arms control and foreign policy.

Greenaway's major interests are wildlife protection and the environment. He was instrumental in creating the Channel Islands National Park, and is seeking additional protection for the California desert, endangered species, and the world's rain forests. He is proud of his role in legislation that established earthquake prediction and paramedical training for emergency personnel.

California's nation-like and trend-setting elements allow politicians to often reject conventional wisdom. As an example, Greenaway offers the rejection of school prayer by the devout, who want religion taught in church and not by the government. He feels there is validity to California's "Yuppie" image of being liberal on social issues and conservative on economic issues, a total reversal from twenty years ago.

Although he welcomes lobbyists and is willing to hear their arguments, his debating background prompts him to take up the merits of opposing viewpoints to insure they are not overlooked.

One of Greenaway's concerns is that society might become less democratic in the pursuit of efficiency. While he admits the Senate often seems inefficient, he views it as a small price to pay for protecting minority views and unlimited debate. He avoids the burnout problem, which he feels many on the Hill fail to recognize, by constantly changing the nature of his job, delegating duties, trying to learn something new every day, and accepting that the right answers are apt to change. His eclectic outside interests include evolutionary biology, tropical fish, South American travel, wood-working, coin collecting and writing poetry.

Kent H. Hughes
Chief Economist
Democratic Policy Committee
619 Hart Senate Office Bldg.
224-3232

Personal: born 2/23/41, in Portland, Oregon. B.A. Yale Univ., 1962. LL.B. Harvard Law School, 1965. Ph.D. Washington Univ., 1976. 1967-1969, Poverty Law Project, Brazil. 1970-1971, Urban Law Institute. 1973-1976, C.R.S. International Trade and Financial Analysis. 1977-1982, Joint Economic Committee. 1983-1984, Legislative Director, Sen. Gary Hart (D-CO). 1985, Senior Economist and Special Counsel, Joint Economic Committee. 1985-1987, Staff Director, House Foreign Affairs Subcommittee on International Economic Policy and Trade. 1987-present, Senate Democratic Policy Committee. Admitted to D.C. Bar. Author, "DISC and its Effect on U.S. Foreign Trade and Employment," CRS, 1976. "The Escalator in Brazil," House Subcommittee on Housing, April 1976. "U.S. Policy Toward Developing Countries," Joint Committee on Economics.

Expertise: International trade, banking, finance, budget

Kent Hughes is a difficult man to categorize. Trained in law, he has become one of the Congress' leading economic policy advisers. His chosen problem areas seem to be those that are of international scope and pose a long-term economic challenge to the country.

After completing his qualifying exams for a Ph.D. in economics, Hughes worked for two years in Brazil on a project to reform Brazilian legal education. He first worked in Washington for the Urban Law Institute, a poverty law firm established to work with group and national clients.

His work since that time has been on a more macroeconomic level. At the Joint Economic Committee, he focused his efforts on the international aspects of long-term downturn in U.S. productivity growth. Studying the theory behind this problem and the range of macroeconomic options available to Congress proved to be of lasting value for Hughes. He had helped to elaborate the Joint Economic Committee's vision of the economy's future. Moreover, he worked in this capacity shortly before the advent of "Reaganomics," and was able to contribute to the Democratic dialogue on economics both before and after 1981.

At this point, he assisted the House Democratic Caucus, where he helped author *Rebuilding the Road to Opportunity*, which elaborated a Democratic framework for long-term economic growth based on steady demand, low interest rates, public investment and incentives to boost private investment and savings.

He left the Joint Economic Committee to work as Senator Gary Hart's legislative director. During this time, he oversaw not only Senate policy, but led the issues staff for the presidential campaign as well.

After the 1984 Democratic Convention, Hughes served as a Senior Economist to the J.E.C., and then became Staff Director of the House Subcommittee on International Economic Policy and Trade. He has now moved to the Democratic Policy Committee as chief economist.

Asked what he likes most about his job, he pointed to the challenge of proposing policy in a political environment. He is currently working on trade bill conference, long-term outlook for U.S. high technology industries, U.S.-Japanese economic relations and the prospects for the restructuring of the Soviet economy. He speaks Portugese, Spanish and some Russian.

Once interviewed by the Wall Street Journal about the "Rugby Connection" on Capitol Hill, he stated "politics was my chance to play rugby in real life."

Charles L. Kinney
Counsel
Senate Democratic Policy
    Committee
S-118 Capitol
224-5551

Personal: born 5/31/52 in Parkersburg, West Virginia. B.S.F.S. Georgetown Univ., May 1974. J.D. Georgetown Univ. Law Center, 1979. 1974-1977, Special Assistant, Senate Majority Whip in Democratic Cloakroom. 1977-1979, Chief Clerk, Senate Democratic Cloakroom. 1979-present, Counsel, Senate Democratic Policy Committee and Staff Representative for Sen Robert Byrd (D-WV) on the Senate Judiciary Committee.

Expertise: Legislative analysis and process

Charles Kinney first came to Washington from West Virginia to attend Georgetown University and, after graduating *cum laude* in 1974, he was selected by his home-state Senator to work in the Senate Democratic Cloakroom. The position gave Kinney a unique view of and solid basic-training in the Senate legislative process. His duties–first as Special Assistant then as Chief Clerk–were to analyze and follow legislation and to advise Democratic senators of the content and timing of the legislation as it approached a Floor vote. Kinney describes the Cloakrooms as "the nerve centers" for Senators off the Floor. These positions, which he held while attending Georgetown Law Center at night, gave him a clear view of his career path.

He earned his law degree in 1979 and was promoted to the positions he holds today: Counsel to the Senate Democratic Policy Committee and Staff Representative for Senator Robert C. Byrd (D-W. Va.) to the Senate Judiciary Committee.

As Judiciary Committee Staff Representative Kinney works closely with the Senator, "briefing him and making recommendations on the major legislation and nominations on which the Committee has acted." Kinney's primary interest among issues before the Committee includes business and civil matters.

Most of his time and attention are taken by his duties as Counsel to the Senate Democratic Policy Committee. Explaining that although "Democratic" signifies the party in the majority, Kinney emphasized that the policy committee works with *every* Senator on *every* piece of legislation. As the cloakrooms are "nerve centers," the Policy Committee serves as "the legislative gears of the Senate."

As counsel to the policy committee, Kinney is in direct touch with legislation, analyzing its wording, its legal aspects, its relations to issues and policy. He also schedules legislation and negotiates time-agreements for Floor action. He has "gained a skilled knowledge of Senate Rules and Procedure," the intricate and tradition-hewn protocol for the Senate legislative process. Since the policy committee sees every piece of legislation taken up by the Senate, he must be knowledgeable with every bill coming to the Floor. Describing himself as a "moderate liberal," he says most legislation is "too complex to be easily key-holed."

Kinney lives near Washington with his wife and two small children. He also enjoys classical music and plays it at the piano.

Thomas J. Sliter
Staff Director
Democratic Policy Committee
619 Hart Senate Office Bldg.
224-3232

Expertise: Budget

Perhaps no committee mirrors better the ups and downs of the Senate's legislative cadence than the Democratic Policy. In addition, the chairman is one of the Senate's most demanding taskmasters, Majority Leader Robert Byrd. Enter Tom Sliter, a mild-mannered former civil engineer, who, after being elevated from the second-in-command slot to staff director for domestic policy, has brought a sense of stability and reliability to a difficult job.

Sliter's early engineering career fostered an enduring interest in environmental issues, which eventually brought him to Washington, D.C. from his native California. In 1979, he accepted a position as senior environmental analyst with the Senate Budget Committee under the tutelage of then-Chairman Ed Muskie. His legislative responsibilities were substantially broadened in 1981, and two years later he joined Democratic Policy as deputy staff director for domestic policy.

While Sliter's primary issue emphasis remains the budget, he also has the responsibility of coordinating the development and tempo of every majority domestic policy initiative from committee to floor conference. At the beginning of each session, Sliter must gain an insider's knowledge of each committee's domestic agenda and assess the answers to: what has been reported out; what remains to be done; what action can be expected by the House on compromise legislation and when it will occur; what is the level of Administration interest in any given bill; which bills are interrelated and how does the timing of action on one bill impact on the consideration of another. Responses to these queries assist Sliter in fashioning an overall Democratic agenda that serves as Byrd's legislative blueprint for the entire session.

Personal: born 7/16/48 in California. B.S. University of California, Berkeley. 1971-1973, associate engineer, Brown & Caldwell, San Francisco, CA. 1973-1974, senior editor, Water Pollution Control Federation, Washington, D.C. 1974-1978, senior analyst, Government Research Corporation, Washington, D.C. 1979-1981, senior environmental analyst, Senate Budget Committee. 1981-1983, special assistant to the minority staff director, Senate Budget Committee. 1983-1987, deputy staff director, domestic policy, Senate Democratic Policy Committee. 1987-present, staff director domestic policy, Senate Democratic Policy Committee.

Sliter also serves as the majority leader's principal advisor on the budget. While both the House and the Senate have enacted substantial changes this Congress affecting the budget process, Sliter observes that during the past few years, "the budget process has substituted activity for achievement. Activity is up and achievement is down."

During the few spare moments when he is not plotting legislative strategy or striking budget compromises, Sliter enjoys sailboat racing in Annapolis.

Walter J. "Joe" Stewart
Secretary of the Senate
S-208 Capitol Bldg.
224-2115

Personal: born 5/11/35 in Waycross, Georgia. LL.B. American Univ., 1963. 1963-1971, Counsel, Senate Committee on Appropriations. 1971-1977, Legislative Assistant, Senate Majority Whip. 1977-1979, Assistant to the Majority Leader for Senate Floor Operations. 1979-1981, Secretary for the Majority of the Senate. 1981-1986, Vice President of Government Affairs, Sonat, Inc., Birmingham, AL. 1987-present, Secretary of the Senate. Chairman, Developmental Committee and Member, Dean's Advisory Council, American University Law School; 1986 Distinguished Alumni, American University; 1987 Distinguished Fellow of the John Sherman Myers Society, American University Law School.

Expertise: Senate operations and floor procedure

Joe Stewart and the U.S. Senate have become synonymous in Democratic circles—partly because of his long association with Majority Leader Robert Byrd (D-WV) but mostly because of his strong devotion to the institution he has worked for nearly all of his adult life. Except for a six-year hiatus when he headed the Washington office of Sonat, Inc., he has worked for the Senate since age 14. He came to Washington in 1951 as a Senate page, became president of his page school class and then stayed to study at George Washington University and American University. Even during his college days he worked part-time on the Senate floor.

Upon earning a law degree in 1963, Stewart landed a job as counsel to the Senate Appropriations Committee and began cutting his teeth on agriculture and transportation issues. "I can't think of a better training ground in legislative craftsmanship than the Appropriations Committee," he says of his eight years there. "I learned how the executive agencies operate, what their needs are and how a smart legislator can accommodate them without cramming something down their throats."

In 1971, he began working for Sen. Byrd, who had just become Majority Whip. He and Byrd first met in law school, and he felt comfortable with Byrd's style and admired the senator's diligence, thoroughness and attention to detail. Stewart assisted Byrd with his legislative responsibilities and then, with Byrd's elevation to Majority Leader, was appointed Assistant to the Majority Leader for Floor Operations and later elected Secretary for the Majority. In those positions, he attended to the details of floor debate and the scheduling of upcoming votes, conveying the leadership's voting instructions to members, and also serving as executive secretary to the Democratic Conference and Steering Committee.

Stewart left the Senate in 1981 when the Republicans became the majority party. During those years he ran the Washington office of a major Southern energy production and distribution corporation, Sonat, Inc. But with the Democrats back in control after the 1986 elections, Stewart was asked by the new majority leader, Byrd, to return to the Senate—this time as its secretary. As Secretary of the Senate, Stewart is the chamber's principal administrative and financial officer, overseeing all of its disbursements.

Stewart has also taken an active interest in efforts to preserve and restore the U.S. Capitol. "Compared to what's been done at the White House and State Department, our restoration efforts have been pitiful," he says. Among his goals is to acquire more original and period furniture, artwork and lighting fixtures for the Capitol's public spaces and offices.

SENATE
COMMITTEE ON AGRICULTURE, NUTRITION, AND FORESTRY

Edward Barron
Deputy Chief Counsel
164 Russell Senate Office Bldg.
224-2035

Expertise: Nutrition, food safety

Ed Barron's responsibilities on the Committee staff center on programs such as food stamps, school lunch and school breakfast, the Child Care Feeding Program, the food distribution program on Indian reservations, the Temporary Emergency Food Assistance Program and others.

In the food safety area, his mandate includes meat and poultry inspection. He also handles farm credit, including the Farm Credit System and the Farmers Home Administration.

Before joining the Committee staff, Barron worked 11 years as an attorney for the Office of the General Counsel in USDA. He was a hearing officer on cases that fell under the jurisdiction of the Perishable Agriculture Commodities Act, handled food and nutrition legislation, and litigation dealing with nutrition programs such as food stamps and food distribution on Indian reservations.

In recognition for his work on revising the Food Stamp Program, Barron received a certificate of merit and a cash award from the Department's general counsel.

Personal: born 10/25/48 in Cortland, New York. B.A. Syracuse Univ., 1970. J.D. State Univ. of New York, 1975. 1975-1987, Attorney, Office of the General Counsel, U.S. Department of Agriculture. 1987-present, Deputy Chief Counsel, Senate Committee on Agriculture, Nutrition, and Forestry.

Since joining the Agriculture Committee staff, Barron has been able to continue his work on national nutrition and agriculture related programs, including the Stewart B. McKinney Homeless Assistance Act, the Commodities Distribution Reform Act and WIC Amendments of 1987, the Charitable Assistance and Food Bank Act of 1987, and the Agricultural Credit Act of 1987.

Janet Breslin
Deputy Staff Director
647 Dirksen Senate Office Bldg.
224-5207

Personal: born 11/16/45 in St. Louis, MO. B.A. Univ. of Southern California, 1967. M.A. UCLA, 1970. Ph.D. UCLA, 1975 (Phi Beta Kappa). 1975-76, Professional Staff Member, Commission on the Operation of the Senate. 1976-78, Executive Assistant to Sen. Bentsen (D-TX). 1978-80, Legislative Assistant to Sen. Leahy (D-VT). 1983-87, Legislative Director to Sen. Leahy. 1987-Present, Deputy Staff Director, Committee on Agriculture, Nutrition and Forestry.

Expertise: Dairy legislation, nutrition appropriations, international development

When Senator Patrick Leahy (D-VT) became Chairman of the Agriculture, Nutrition, and Forestry Committee in January, 1987, he asked Janet Breslin, his Legislative Director of the past three years, to join the Committee as Deputy Staff Director. Breslin, who had handled dairy legislation in her previous position, welcomed the chance to delve more deeply into specific policy issues. Today, her areas of expertise include dairy legislation, nutrition, appropriations and international development.

Breslin, a Phi Beta Kappa from the University of Southern California, first came to Capitol Hill in 1975 almost as a natural extension of her dissertation topic which concerned the role of Senate staff.

Deeply committed "to the support of the legislative branch in the policy formation process," Breslin is currently concerned with the Dairy Farm Protection Act introduced in 1987 by Sen. Leahy. She shares Leahy's concern that dairy farming be protected where it is currently practiced as opposed to its increased concentration in certain geographic areas, especially California.

Breslin's personal commitment to human rights stems from traumatic first-hand experience. As a student, she was living in Chile in 1973 when the military coup took place. As she recalls, witnessing random violence in a society without recourse to law was "truly terrifying." Her observation fifteen years ago of "shooting, looting, and burning books" has made her "very supportive and protective of the democratic process."

A Democrat, Breslin did advance work briefly for Sargent Shriver in his 1972 bid for the presidency.

The executive director of a public interest group dealing with food issues describes Breslin as "a terrific person to work with . . ." and notes "she does her job well with a soft edge so she gets along with people."

Agriculture, Nutrition, and Forestry

Carolyn W. Brickey
Majority Counsel
638 Dirksen Senate Office Bldg.
224-5207

Expertise: Commodities, FIFRA

Carolyn Brickey is an excellent example of the Capitol Hill staffer who develops expertise outside of the Congress and brings the benefit of that knowledge to the committee for which she works. In Brickey's case, the training ground was a public interest group and state government.

On the Senate Agriculture Committee, two of Brickey's main concerns are commodity programs and pesticides. She oversees virtually every commodity with the exception of sugar, and is also involved in the reauthorization of the FIFRA legislation.

The difficulties facing family farms is another area of concern to Brickey. Last year she was involved in both disaster relief legislation and modification of the law mandating which farmers qualify for government assistance.

Having grown up in a rural community with family members involved in farming gives Brickey added insight into the day-to-day realities of American farming.

Personal: born 1/12/52 in Grundy, Virginia. B.A. East Tennessee State Univ., 1973. J.D. Georgetown Univ., 1979. 1976, co-authored Almanac of Virginia Politics. 1979-1981, staff attorney, Public Citizen's Congress Watch. 1981-1983, staff attorney, Food Research and Action Center, Washington, D.C. 1983-1987, agricultural coordinator, Office of State-Federal Relations, State of Texas, Washington, D.C. 1987-present, Majority Counsel, Senate Committee on Agriculture, Nutrition, and Forestry.

John Campbell
Legislative Assistant
Senator Rudy Boschwitz (R-MN)
506 Hart Senate Office Bldg.
224-5641

Personal: born 06/08/57 in Rawlins, Wyoming. B.A. Univ. of Nebraska, 1979. Post Graduate Diploma Univ. of Sydney, Australia, 1986. 1979-1980, ranch manager, San Angelo, Texas. 1980-1982, legislative assistant, Rep. Virginia Smith (R-NE). 1982-1984, House Agriculture Appropriations Subcommittee. 1984-1986, Senate Committee on Agriculture, Nutrition, and Forestry. 1987-Present, legislative assistant, Sen. Rudy Boschwitz (R-MN).

Expertise: Agriculture

John Campbell spent the 1986 academic year pursuing a post graduate degree in agriculture economics in Australia. "It was a good experience to see America through another country's eyes," and broadened his perspective to serve as an agriculture legislative assistant for Senator Rudy Boschwitz.

Campbell specializes in agricultural policy, and likes to emphasize the technical aspects while recommending policies consistent with economic realities.

Like many of his colleagues who have worked on the Hill for several years, Campbell was involved with the most important agricultural legislation in recent history, the 1985 Farm Bill. It was a two year process for Campbell, who worked on committee staff at the time, and handled the major commodities and the commercial trade provisions of the measure.

Campbell says there are two unique things about agriculture and the people who work with the issue. First, besides the banking committee it is the only sector specific committee. "When you work on the committee or with the issue, you effect the everyday livelihood of farmers."

Campbell notes that his favorite part of his job is getting farmers to understand the world that they're doing business in rather than reacting to the world as they wished it existed.

Campbell also observes that many of the agriculture committee staff legislative assistants come from agriculture backgrounds and are actively engaged in the industry.

Originally from North Platte, Nebraska, Campbell is personally involved in the cattle industry. He grew up working on farms and ranches in the area. His father is a livestock researcher with the University of Nebraska.

Campbell is at his best working face to face with farmers. He believes that, for right or wrong, the farm sector has been built by government intervention, and that it has become necessary to tailor policy that does not disrupt the system too much, but moves it in a direction of less government intervention. Campbell advocates a policy consistent with the economic realities of a global marketplace. Campbell plans to spend 1987 working on rural development and legislation as well as continuing to advance the concept of "decoupling" farm income supports from planting decisions on a national as well as global level.

He describes himself as, "someone who is very attracted to public policy, but who would rather be living a more rural and isolated life in the off hours."

Dan Cassidy
Legislative Assistant
Senator Christopher Bond (R-MO)
293 Russell Senate Office Bldg.
224-5721

Expertise: Agricultural issues

Dan Cassidy is new to Capitol Hill having joined the staff of freshman Senator "Kit" Bond of Missouri.

"This first year," said Cassidy, "will be low-key for us." We are available to talk to anyone about agriculture issues. The buzz words in the office are "available" and "learn."

While he was born in Chicago, Albuquerque, New Mexico is his home. Raised on a cattle ranch, Cassidy grew up showing horses and participating in rodeos. He also came up through the ranks of the 4H and Future Farmers of America institutions.

Since coming to Washington, Cassidy has worked on such diverse areas as food safety, Farm Credit restructuring, the trade bill, budget reconciliation, and Commodity Credit Corporation funding.

In the area of food safety, Cassidy has worked on, and Senator Bond has introduced, legislation that promotes research in the field. The bill, specifically, authorizes the USDA to fund competitive research grants to universities for research in the area of microbiological and chemical contaminants.

Personal: born 05/01/62 in Chicago, Illinois. B.S. New Mexico State Univ. 1984. M.S. Univ.of Missouri-Columbia, 1986. 1986-1987, Manager of Strategic Planning and Export Programs, National Dairy Promotion and Research Board. 1987 to present, Legislative Assistant for Agriculture, Senator Christopher Bond (R-MO).

Like all legislative assistants in agriculture, Cassidy is acquainted with the 1985 Farm Bill. He is currently working to emphasize agricultural trade—working within the bill. Cassidy believes it is necessary to become more competitive in the world market. But Cassidy will not be working on legislation to change the 1985 Farm Bill, unless the changes will ease regulations for the farmers.

When he is not caught up in the Farm Bill or food safety, Cassidy enjoys fishing and hunting. He also takes a swim each day during the lunch hour.

Fred Clark
Legislative Assistant
Senator Howell Heflin (D-AL)
728 Hart Senate Office Bldg.
224-4124

Expertise: Agricultural finance

Fred Clark, the son of a farmer and small-town Alabama banker, was drawn to Washington by a keen interest in Senator Heflin's role in the Senate Agriculture, Nutrition and Forestry Committee. Clark feels his experience and upbringing have helped him bring practical, first-hand knowledge and informed opinion to Senator Heflin's staff.

Senator Heflin serves on three Senate Agriculture subcommittees keeping Clark busy indeed on such legislation as the Farm Credit Bill, where Clark can leverage his knowledge gained from working in rural Alabama for the Farm Credit System.

Senator Heflin is chairman of the Rural Electrification and Rural Development Subcommittee, and relies on Clark to help develop legislation to champion incentives for rural development. Clark has a particular interest in promoting legislation which will help revitalize depressed agricultural areas. Incentives Clark supports include loan assistance, promoting new businesses in rural areas and job training programs. Clark also assists Heflin with specific Alabama agricultural concerns such as a recent assistance package for Alabama farmers hard-hit by drought.

Although well-adjusted to Washington, Clark says he misses good Southern football and food. Clark plans to someday return to Alabama and Auburn University to complete a master's in agricultural economics.

Personal: born 3/5/60 in Enterprise, Alabama. B.A. Auburn Univ., 1983. 1983-86, Federal Land Bank. 1986, Post-Graduate work at Auburn Univ. 1987 to present, Legislative Assistant, Sen. Howell Heflin.

Thomas R. Clark
Minority Counsel
328A Russell Senate Office Bldg.
224-2035

Expertise: Agriculture

Tom Clark came to Washington in 1973 with an interest in agriculture. He views himself as a generalist but does have expertise in produce marketing programs from a regulatory perspective. During his first "tour of duty" on the Hill he worked on the 1981 Farm Bill and key legislation on food safety regulation, federal pesticide laws and agricultural foreign trade. As Deputy Director the Agricultural Marketing Service, he oversaw the marketing ordering system.

Clark returned to the Senate Agriculture, Nutrition, and Forestry Committee in May of 1987. Looking for more of an opportunity to help shape agricultural policy, rather than carry out policies since then, he has worked on the Farm Credit bill and has had the opportunity to influence the basic structure of the legislation.

Clark feels the farm credit system needs discipline rather than appropriations, and has advocated a disciplinary board as part of the banking system. He believes the credit system should be self-monitoring and less burdensome to the budget.

Clark has a reputation as a perfectionist. A majority staff member, while working with Clark, threw up his hands and stated "The trouble with you is you are just too thorough".

Personal: born 1/13/48 in Quantico, Virginia. B.S. Pennsylvania State Univ., 1970. J.D. Univ. of Akron School of Law, 1973. 1970-1972, reliability engineer, private industry. 1973-1981, staff attorney, Office of the General Council, U.S. Department of Agriculture. 1981-1984, Deputy Counsel, Senate Committee on Agriculture, Nutrition and Forestry. 1984-1987, Deputy Director for Agricultural Marketing Service, Department of Agriculture. 1987-present, Minority Counsel, Senate Agriculture, Nutrition, and Forestry Committee.

Although he has little time for sports these days, Clark was a gymnast and attended Penn State on an sports athletic scholarship. He describes gymnastics as a perfectionist's sport, one which helped him learn commitment to achieve goals he set for himself.

Charles Conner
Minority Staff Director
328 Russell Senate Office Bldg.
224-6901

Expertise: Conservation, farm programs

When Sen. Richard Lugar was looking for someone to fill a spot on his legislative staff in 1980, he specifically wanted a Purdue graduate who had worked on a farm.

Chuck Conner fit the bill perfectly. A recent graduate with no political aspirations, he had roots firmly planted on the family farm in LaFayette, Indiana. That farm experience gave Conner the understanding and expertise needed to propel him to the Minority leadership position of the Agriculture Committee staff before his thirtieth birthday.

Conner took over the reins of his family's 11,000-acre soybean and grain farm during college because of his father's illness. This experience has helped shape his work in Washington. "You have to work with commodities and policies at the farm level, to see how the policy actually affects the farmer. Unless you've had that experience, you just can't know." Conner has collected an eight-person staff, most of whom also have rural backgrounds.

Though many of his peers were lured back to the farm with the high incomes of the 1970's, Conner opted for college, realizing that the high returns could not last forever. Starting out as a trainee at the Federal Land Bank in Louisville after graduating from Purdue, he heard about the legislative position from a friend and thought it sounded intriguing. Conner spent time at the district office as well as in Washington as a member of Lugar's staff.

Personal: born 12/30/57 in LaFayette, Indiana. B.S. Agricultural Economics, Purdue Univ., 1980. 1980, loan officer trainee, Federal Land Bank, Louisville, KY. 1980-1985, Agricultural Legislative Assistant to Sen. Richard Lugar (R-IN). 1985-1987, Staff Member, Senate Committee on Agriculture, Nutrition, and Forestry. 1987-present, Minority Staff Director, Senate Committee on Agriculture, Nutrition, and Forestry.

While the land in his hometown is blessed with rich soil and solid markets, Conner's instincts lie with those less fortunate, and his sensibilities turn to ways to help them.

With the farm credit issue strengthened with the fairly comprehensive 1987 legislative package, the committee hopes to work on such issues as pesticides and other environmental concerns, areas relatively new to their jurisdiction. Conner, who considers the environment one of his specialties, is more moderate in these areas than in fiscal matters, on which he is more conservative.

While he misses the open spaces and the farm work, he continues to do woodworking in his spare time, and has found trees and green space out in Alexandria, where he lives with his wife and children.

James Cubie
Senior Counsel
647 Dirksen Senate Office Bldg.
224-5207

Expertise: Environment, energy, budget

Cubie's grasp of environmental issues and experience with the budget process offer a substantial contribution to the majority staff of the Senate Agriculture Committee.

Cubie began his Hill career in 1979 working for another New Englander, Sen. Edward Kennedy (D-MA). In Kennedy's office he served as chief energy advisor and majority counsel to the Energy Subcommittee of the Joint Economic Committee. The next two years found Cubie developing far-reaching energy conservation legislation and shaping Kennedy's alternative energy program to the legislative package supported by the Carter Administration. Cubie also served in an unofficial capacity in Kennedy's 1980 presidential bid as speechwriter and advisor to the candidate on energy and environmental issues.

In 1981, Cubie began his long association with Sen. Patrick Leahy (D-VT) when he was appointed minority clerk of the District of Columbia Subcommittee. While his official duties related to federal funding for the District, the bulk of his work was directed once again toward energy and the environment. Cubie led the successful effort to prevent the Environmental Protection Agency's budget from being slashed by 50%.

Since leaving the D.C. Subcommittee staff, Cubie has served as senior counsel to two Senate Appropriations subcommittees—HUD and Independent Agencies, and Foreign Operations. In the past four years his legislative responsibilities have expanded considerably, with greater emphasis on environmental protection, science policy, and foreign affairs.

Personal: born 11/4/46 in Haverhill, Massachusetts. B.A. East Nazarene Coll., 1968. Princeton Theological Seminary, 1968-1970. J.D. Univ. of Maryland Law School, 1974. 1974-75, Congress Watch. 1975-76, Union of Concerned Scientists. 1979-81, majority counsel, Subcommittee on Energy, Joint Economic Committee. 1981-84, minority clerk, Senate Subcommittee on the District of Columbia. 1985-86, minority clerk, Senate Subcommittee on HUD and Independent Agencies; 1987, counsel, Senate Subcommittee on Foreign Operations, Senate Appropriations Committee. 1987-present, senior counsel, Senate Committee on Agriculture, Nutrition, and Forestry

In his relatively new position as senior counsel to the Senate Agriculture Committee, Cubie wears two hats. He coordinates all committee press activities and oversees natural resources legislation, including such programs as the forest Service and Soil Conservation Service.

Cubie is an avid tennis player and an enthusiastic fisherman.

Michael V. Dunn
Professional Staff Member
164 Russell Senate Office Bldg.
224-5207

*Personal: born 9/19/44 in Keokuk,
Iowa. B.A. Univ. of New Mexico, 1971.
M.A. Univ. of New Mexico, 1972.
1964-68, secret control officer,
Nuclear Testing Task Force, U.S. Air
Force. 1972-73, administrative aide to
mayor of Keokuk. 1973-77, executive
director, Southeast Iowa Regional
Planning Commission and Chairman
of the City Development Board. 1977-
81, Midwest area director, Farmers
Home Administration, U.S.
Department of Agriculture. 1977-81,
Chairman, Midwest Federal Rural
Development Task Force. 1981-82,
vice president for marketing and
management, Conrad Industries.
1981-84, commissioner, Iowa
Development Commission. 1982-84,
vice president, government relations,
Farm Credit Banks of Omaha. 1987-
present, Committee on Agriculture,
Nutrition, and Forestry.*

Expertise: Farm credit, rural development

Mike Dunn, who grew up on a Iowa farm and has held a number of agricultural-related positions, spent almost all of 1987 helping to draft legislation to revitalize the farm credit system.

Incoming committee Chairman Patrick Leahy of Vermont hired Dunn at the start of the 100th Congress, and the Iowa native was immediately thrust into the middle of the wrangling over the farm credit bill. Over the first session, Dunn attended or presided at more than two dozen meetings, working with other staff members in forging the legislation.

The result was the Agricultural Credit Act of 1987, which passed the Congress late last year and was signed into law on Jan. 6. The legislation creates a three-member board within the Farm Credit Administration that is authorized to raise up to $4 billion in government-guaranteed bonds to inject into the farm credit system.

One particularly contentious issue centered on whether new money should be provided in the form of a direct loan from the Treasury or from a guaranteed bond authority, with Dunn helping to choose the latter.

Even though the farm credit legislation is now law, Dunn's work on it is not finished. In 1988, he and the Committee will be monitoring the system to determine how effective it is.

Dunn says the committee also may consider establishing "Farmer Mac," a secondary market for long-term agricultural loans, similar to "Freddie Mac" (Federal Home Loan Mortgage Corporation).

Dunn is looking at the Farmers Home Administration, a federal agency that is part of the Agriculture Department with an eye toward pushing for changes in the way the agency operates. He is also spending time on rural development issues and would like to develop legislation to promote economic growth in rural areas.

In particular, Dunn is examining the role and the policies of the Rural Electric Administration, which provides low-cost electricity to rural households and which for years has been a prime target of budget-cutters, and the Rural Telephone Bank, which is a part of REA and which provides phone service to rural areas.

Despite his recent arrival in Washington, Dunn is no newcomer to politics. He served as a county chairman for John Glenn during the Ohio senator's presidential campaign in 1984. Before that, Dunn was a member of the Iowa State Democratic Party Platform Committee and Chairman of the State Party's Finance Committee. He also served on the party's Central Committee.

Mark Fleming
Legislative Assistant
Senator Jesse Helms (R-NC)
403 Dirksen Senate Office Bldg.
224-6342

Personal: born 5/28/60 in Forsythe County, North Carolina. B.S. North Carolina State Univ., 1982. 1983-present, Legislative Assistant, Sen. Jesse Helms (R-NC).

Expertise: Tobacco, peanuts

Although raising turkeys in North Carolina is a distant cry from working on legislation, that experience did nothing to impede Mark Fleming's ability to reach Capitol Hill. In fact, his hands-on experience with the Goldsborough Milling Company, a North Carolina turkey farm, brought Fleming highly recommended to Sen. Jesse Helms.

As the former chairman of the Senate Agriculture Committee, Helms recognized the need to secure an aide with proven ability in agribusiness and the commodities market. And while Fleming is relatively youthful by Washington standards, his background clearly met the needs of the North Carolina senator.

While Fleming's responsibilities have included helping craft the 1985 farm bill and last year's farm credit legislation, his main focus is the three subcommittees on which Helms sits. On one of these, the Subcommittee on Agriculture Production, Helms is the ranking Republican.

Two commodities common through out North Carolina are peanuts and tobacco. But because these products are limited to a particular geographic area, they are often the source of debate in Congress.

Fleming argues that because peanuts have a long shelf life, industry has in the past purchased peanuts at low prices, there by causing some farmers to suffer losses. In response to this problem, Helms has initiated supply and demand controls that would raise their prices. Fleming makes a convincing argument that such artificial controls are necessary to the peanut farmer and create no additional burden to the taxpayer.

The tobacco commodity is another contentious issue, partly as a result of the efforts of various Washington lobbying groups. Yet Helms, with Fleming's assistance, has been successful in defeating proposals designed to cripple that industry.

As a North Carolina native whose family owns tobacco fields, Fleming understands why tobacco is referred to as the "golden leaf." As he says, "When the tobacco industry is doing well, so too do the automobile and construction industries. "Indeed, increased levels of tobacco production can well spark North Carolina's entire economy.

By all accounts, Fleming is likely to remain on the frontlines, defending these agricultural interests on behalf of Helms and North Carolina.

William A. Gillon
Counsel
647 Dirksen Senate Office Bldg.
224-5207

*Personal: born 11/18/58 in Memphis,
Tennessee. B.A. Mississippi State
Univ., 1980. J.D. Univ. of Georgia
School of Law, 1983. 1983-1987,
Office of the General Counsel, United
States Department of Agriculture,
Attorney. Published: Georgia Journal
international and Comparative Law,
"Extraterritorial Criminal Jurisdiction
Under the Proposed Federal Criminal
Codes," (1982).*

Expertise: Agricultural law

Agriculture has been a life-long interest and responsibility for the twenty-nine year old counsel to the Senate Agriculture Committee, Bill Gillon. Working on the family farm in Gore Springs, Mississippi, during summer vacations was the genesis of his interest in agricultural law.

Upon graduating from law school, Gillon began working for the United States Department of Agriculture in the Office of the General Counsel. His major areas of responsibilities included domestic commodity programs, international trade, and conservation programs. After three years with the USDA, he moved on to the legislative branch of government, in his present position where he is primarily responsible for legislation dealing in international trade and commodity programs.

While working for the USDA, Gillon helped draft the final proposal for the Conservation Reserve Program which was included in the Food Security Act of 1985. He also worked on this program in its initial stages of implementation. Another important legislative involvement for Gillon was the consideration of the Omnibus Trade Bill, in which he worked on several components.

As for the future, Bill Gillon sees negotiations under the General Agreement on Tariffs and Trade (GATT) as a major emphasis. He would like the Agriculture Committee to work on improvements of the rules governing international agricultural trade.

Colleagues of Gillon give him high marks. It was noted by a couple of his colleagues that it is a tribute to Gillon that he worked for the USDA under a Republican Administration and is now representing the Democratic majority on the Senate Committee on Agriculture, Nutrition, and Forestry.

As a husband and father, Gillon plays the guitar at area churches for Sunday school children every Sunday morning. Joining in the weekly sing-along is his five-year-old son.

Alex Mathews
Legislative Assistant
Senator Pete Wilson (R-CA)
720 Hart Senate Office Bldg.
224-3841

Personal: born 10/13/54 in Greenwich, CT. B.A. Dartmouth Coll., 1976. J.D. Univ. of Miami (Florida), 1979. 1979-1984, law firm of Curtis, Mallet-Provost, Colt and Mosle, New York City. 1984, Chase Manhattan Bank, New York City. 1985-1986 Deputy General Counsel, Senate Committee on Agriculture, Nutrition, and Forestry. 1986 to present, Legislative Assistant, Sen. Pete Wilson (R-CA).

Expertise: Agriculture, trade

California leads the nation in terms of the dollar value of its agriculture and the sheer variety of agricultural commodities produced and exported by the state. A seat on the Senate Agriculture Committee is important to Sen. Pete Wilson and to the state of California.

Alex Mathews is Wilson's legislative assistant for the Agriculture Committee and handles the many varied agricultural issues affecting the state which come before the Committee.

As a lawyer with the law firm of Curtis, Mallet-Provost, Colt, and Molse, Mathews worked primarily on international trade and investment matters. Subsequent to his tenure with this law firm, he joined Chase Manhattan Bank in New York to work on commercial lending matters.

Mathews then accepted a position as Deputy General Counsel to the Senate Committee on Agriculture, Nutrition, and Forestry, where in 1985, he helped to draft the 1985 farm bill with primary emphasis on the trade and commodity provisions. In 1986 he joined Wilson's staff as legislative assistant for agricultural and trade matters.

John D. Podesta
Chief Counsel
228-A Russell Senate Office Bldg.
224-5207

Expertise: Agriculture

After eight years serving the Senate Judiciary Committee, functioning as counsel for Sen. Patrick Leahy (D-VT) on the Committee, John Podesta has found it fascinating to learn a new policy area. He jokes that his on-the-job training on the Agriculture Committee makes him a "jail house economist." But Podesta offers no apologies for being city-rather than farm-bred, believing that it is the quality of the job done, not background, that is important when it comes to working for the Agriculture Committee, or any other committee.

During his service on the Judiciary Committee staff, Podesta made a significant contribution to the Regulatory Reform Act of 1980, which passed the Senate but not the House; the Semiconductor Chip Protection Act, enacted in 1984; and the Electronic Communications Privacy Act, enacted in 1986. He also played a key staff role in preventing the weakening of the Freedom of Information Act, especially in the area of information policy, and was involved in other open government issues.

In the current Congress, Podesta had a hand in the agriculture portion of the trade bill.

Podesta has been active in a number of political campaigns, including serving as field organizer in the McCarthy and Muskie presidential campaigns, running the speakers' bureau for the McGovern campaign, and working as campaign manager in Sam Brown's campaign for Colorado State Treasurer. More recently, he worked for Peter Hart Associates, analyzing survey information for the Mondale presidential campaign.

Podesta, who sums up his professional and campaign experience by saying that he is "amazingly uncynical" and that "government does matter," enjoys cooking for his family in his spare time and claims to be a "great cook" with a special forte in Italian cuisine.

Personal: born 1/8/49 in Chicago, Illinois. B.A. Knox Coll., 1971 (magna cum laude). J.D., Georgetown Univ. Law Center, 1976 (Editor, Case and Notes, Georgetown Law Journal). 1976-77, trial attorney, Dept. of Justice. 1978-79, Special Assistant to the Director, ACTION. 1979-80, Counsel, Subcommittee on Administrative Practices and Procedures; 1981-82, Chief Minority Counsel, Subcommittee on Regulatory Reform; 1983-84, Chief Minority Counsel, Subcommittee on Security and Terrorism; 1985-86, Chief Minority Counsel, Subcommittee on Patents, Copyrights and Trademarks, Senate Judiciary Committee. 1987-present, Chief Counsel, Senate Committee on Agriculture, Nutrition, and Forestry.

Stephen Raby
Administrative Assistant
Senator Howell Heflin (D-AL)
728 Hart Senate Office Bldg.
224-4124

Expertise: Agriculture issues

Agriculture is not only his specialty but also had a direct influence on Steve Raby's involvement in politics. He comes from a farm family and actually farmed himself while attending Calhoun Community College in Northern Alabama. But Raby decided he could not make a living farming, which was what he wanted to do. Instead, he went to Auburn University so that he could stay involved in agriculture in a different way.

At Auburn, Raby heard about a job with Senator Howell Heflin (D-AL) as an assistant dealing with agricultural issues. He moved his family from Alabama to Washington and started work in January of 1984. In his position with Heflin, Raby works on rural development and public works for an area "sensitive to my part of the world," the Tennessee Valley Authority.

Raby was very involved in the 1985 Food and Security Act, especially in sections dealing with rural development and commodities. "Its strange to see something you've drafted become public law," Raby said. Initially, his incentive on this legislation was to get not only the best program for southern agriculture, but a good overall agricultural policy and agricultural commodity programs. He received an education, Raby says, and had to separate his personal feelings about many issues and amendments from the votes.

Personal: born 4/3/58 in Huntsville, Alabama. B.S. Agriculture Economics, Auburn Univ. 1982. M.S. Economics, Auburn Univ. 1984. 1976-1980, farming. 1982, staff, Federal Reserve Bank in Atlanta. 1983-1984, graduate research and teaching. 1984-1987, Legislative Assistant for Agriculture; 1987-present, Administrative Assistant, Sen. Howell Heflin (D-AL).

Raby's first involvement in Alabama politics was Albert McDonald's race for Commissioner of Agriculture and Industries in 1982. Raby continued his political involvement during college in various student activities, including several honor societies.

As a member of the agricultural professional society at Auburn, he was instrumental in bringing together students, faculty, alumni and businesses in the state to work on issues of critical importance to all. While at Auburn, Raby also researched the impact of property taxation on land use decisions for business and private individuals, as well as foreign ownership of agricultural lands. Some of his research was later published by the Alabama Cooperative Extension Service. "If I can get back to Alabama, I feel like I'm at home, no matter what part of the state I'm in," Raby says.

Administrative Assistant to Senator Heflin since February of 1987, Raby says that he thinks he wants eventually to return to Alabama. A major goal is to see Senator Heflin reelected in 1990. Since he has been in Washington Raby has been back to the state almost every break, and is so busy that he has only visited one Smithsonian museum. He is now even busier with a new son.

Bob Redding
Executive Assistant
Sen. Wyche Fowler (D-GA)
204 Russell Senate Office Bldg.
224-3643

Personal: born 12/27/56 in Blakely GA. B.A. Mercer Univ., 1978. J.D. George Washington Univ., 1981. 1981-1986, Administrative Assistant, Rep. Charles Hatcher (D-GA). 1987 to present, Chief Counsel, Sen. Wyche Fowler (D-GA).

Expertise: Rural development, farm issues

Bob Redding has successfully made the adjustment from the House to the Senate, and has carried over to Sen. Wyche Fowler's staff his personal expertise in rural development and farm legislation issues.

As Rep. Charles Hatcher's administrative assistant, Redding worked on farming and rural development issues—two important staples of southern politics. His efforts helped Hatcher become recognized as one of the leaders in special legislation for peanut farming programs. During this time Redding also began to learn and work on rural development issues to help bring economic vitality to outlying, depressed agricultural areas.

In the Senate, Redding's work as Executive Assistant to Sen. Wyche Fowler is focused primarily on rural development legislation. In 1987, he worked on legislation that provided matching federal funds for towns of 20,000 or less, to form coalitions to attract some of the commerce which has been migrating to larger southern cities. The legislation marked an important foray into rural issues for Fowler who is from urban Atlanta.

Redding sees rural development as one of the most serious challenges facing the new South. He notes that within two hours of a major city like Atlanta there are unlimited facilities for commerce, with the necessary infrastructure. However, he says, just outside that zone, land prices plummet, farmers are burdened with debt, and there are no alternative industries in sight.

Redding is from a small town himself. He grew up in a Georgia town of fifteen hundred people, where he witnessed new cities developing, drawing people and resources from the agricultural communities. "You just see these towns drying up," he says.

In addition to his work on rural development, Redding also handles legal issues for the staff, monitors the Judiciary Committee, and handles some ethics issues. He is the Senator's designated campaign contact on the Washington staff, having worked as treasurer and campaign manager for his former boss in the House.

When he is not on Capitol Hill, Redding enjoys the outdoors, including golf and bird hunting.

Charles H. Riemenschneider
Staff Director
328-A Russell Senate Office Bldg.
224-2035

Expertise: Agriculture policy development, resource economics

Charles Riemenschneider grew up on a dairy farm about 75 miles north of Washington, D.C. His family's dairy herd was sold about the time he went to college and he turned his eye toward farming on a broader scale, studying agriculture and resource economics.

He was a graduate student and served on the faculty at Michigan State and as a consultant to the U.S. Department of Agriculture.

When a position opened up on the Senate Budget Committee in 1978, his name was recommended to the chairman, Edmund Muskie (D-ME). Riemenschneider was appointed analyst for agriculture and science and, later, senior analyst for physical resources.

Personal: born 5/13/52 in Baltimore, Maryland. B.S. Rutgers Univ., 1974. M.S. Michigan State Univ., 1976. Ph.D. Michigan State Univ., 1978. 1978-1982, Professional Staff Member, Senate Committee on Budget. 1982-1985, Senior Agricultural Economist, Economic Research, Chemical Bank. 1985-1987, Vice President Global Portfolio Management, Chemical Bank. 1987-present, Staff Director, Senate Committee on Agriculture, Nutrition, and Forestry.

The position offered the opportunity to "go from the academic world to a place where I could practice what I taught." In 1981, when Republicans took over the Senate majority, Senator Peter Domenici (R-NM), the newly appointed chairman of the Committee, asked Riemenschneider to stay to pursue a smooth transition.

A Democrat, Riemenschneider did not work too long for Republicans. In 1982, he took a job as a Senior Agricultural Economist in Chemical Bank's Economic Research Department, a position that involved economic analysis of agribusiness and other industries. In 1985, he moved within Chemical Bank to the Credit Division working in the area of portfolio management.

After the Democrats won back the Senate, Riemenschneider was offered the position of Staff Director of the Senate Committee on Agriculture, Nutrition and Forestry. In the meantime, he had served as a member of the President's Agricultural Task Force to Zaire and the Democratic Platform Committee Working Group on Agriculture. He was also Chairman of the Industry Committee of the American Agricultural Economics Association.

It is the opportunity to have policy input into the Committee's legislation that brought Riemenschneider back to the Hill. He has been involved in every major bill before the committee since 1987, and has been closely tied to farm programs and farm credit legislation. For Riemenschneider, the challenge is to adapt farm policy to a constantly changing agriculture system.

Riemenschneider also has worked to broaden the Committee's agenda. Issues like rural economic development, biotechnology, and the environment—which the committee rarely heard in 1986—are now getting greater attention.

Dennis Robertson
Legislative Assistant, Agriculture
Senator David Pryor (D-AR.)
264 Russell Senate Office Bldg.
224-2353

Expertise: Agriculture, marketing loans

Dennis Robertson's background is pure agriculture—from summers spent baling hay on his family's registered Angus farm in southwest Missouri to his ten-plus years of work with the Arkansas Farm Bureau Federation. Robertson's ties to Sen. David Pryor (D-AR) date to 1974, when his statehouse lobbying allowed him to work on a number of agriculture projects with then-Governor Pryor. Once elected to the Senate, Pryor became the first U.S. senator to move agriculture operations to his state office. In 1981, he tapped Robertson to head up these operations. In 1983, Robertson moved into the number one staff spot in Pryor's Little Rock office. It wasn't until the 1985 Farm Bill reauthorization that Robertson joined Sen. Pryor's Washington staff.

Robertson's main contribution to the 1985 Farm Bill was the creation of a innovative "marketing loan" program for cotton and rice. Along with a member of Sen. Thad Cochran's staff, Robertson drafted the details of this new competitive program that allows farmers to repay loans at world market prices rather than default if prices don't rise above the loan rates set by Congress. "We've got to recognize conditions in international markets and give American farmers the tools to compete," he says. The program has yielded results: between 1985 and 1987, farmer surpluses in these crops have decreased to almost nothing and prices have nearly quadrupled. Next on Robertson's agenda is bringing soybeans and corn under the marketing loan program.

Personal: born 11/11/47 in Tulsa, OK. B.S. Univ. of Arkansas, 1971. 1971-1974, safety director, Arkansas Farm Bureau Federation. 1974-1976, Director, Blue Cross-Blue Shield program, Arkansas Farm Bureau Federation. 1966-1977, Field Services Director, Northwest District, Arkansas Farm Bureau Federation. 1978-1981, Asst. Director, Legislative Affairs, Arkansas Farm Bureau Federation. 1981-1982, Agriculture Asst., Sen. David Pryor, Little Rock, AR. 1982-1983, Legislative Director, Arkansas Farm Bureau Federation, Little Rock, AR. 1983-1985, Administrative Asst., Sen. David Pryor, Little Rock, AR. 1985 to present, Legislative Asst., Agriculture, Sen.Pryor.

Pryor's role as chairman of the Senate Agriculture Subcommittee on Domestic and Foreign Marketing and Product Promotion has given Robertson a chance for both national and international exposure. He helped draft the agriculture section of 1987's Omnibus Trade Bill, which beefs up the U.S. export enhancement program and the U.S.'s ability to compete against subsidies for European exports. His approach is aggressive. "European exporting communities don't respect you until your economic programs get their attention," Robertson notes.

With Arkansas being the largest chicken broiler-producing state in the country, Robertson has also been involved in meat and poultry inspection issues and the furor over salmonella contamination. Like his boss, Robertson is enthusiastic. "We like to shake things up, to make things happen—even, some would say, at the expense of going overboard," he adds.

Robertson is an avid golfer always looking for an opportunity to play, and often carries his clubs with him to speaking engagements across the country.

Mark K. Scanlan
Legislative Assistant
Senator Robert Dole (R-KS)
141 Hart Senate Office Building
224-6521

Personal: born 8/9/57 in Abilene, Kansas. B.S., Kansas State Univ., 1979. 1979-1982, advertising sales representative, Drovers Journal, Kansas City, MO. 1982-1986, Research Assistant; and 1986-present, Legislative Assistant, Sen. Robert Dole.

Expertise: Agriculture

Growing up on a registered Holstein dairy farm in Abilene, Kansas, coupled with his study of agronomy at Kansas State University, has made Mark Scanlan a welcome addition to the office of Sen. Robert Dole (R-KS).

Scanlan regards his role as agriculture adviser to Sen. Dole as especially challenging particularly because of Dole's key position on the Agriculture Committee. As a member of that committee for 27 years, Dole is currently its senior Republican.

Scanlan's role in the development of the 1985 farm bill afforded him the opportunity to garner a greater understanding of the legislative process where it relates to agriculture legislation. In terms of that particular measure, Scanlan sees merit in advancing a market-oriented approach to American farmers. And his own experiences on a family farm only serve to bolster that feeling.

As Dole's principal agriculture aide, Scanlan monitors the plethora of issues addressed each year by the committee. And like most staffers, he focuses on those issues that are most relative to the members' interests and those of his Kansas constituents.

Two issues that will continue to be a priority to Dole and his aide are rural development and environmental conservation. In fact, Dole has authored legislation designed to focus congressional attention on these important areas.

The first initiative, entitled the Rural Revitalization Act, would establish a $1 billion fund over the next three fiscal years with the goal of stimulating small business development. Scanlan feels such a program would foster better coordination between state and local interests where they concern the promotion of rural development.

The other bill, called the Environmental Conservation Acreage Reserve Program, would set up a separate reserve similar to the Conservation Reserve Program. Such a measure would target environmental programs ranging from ground water to pesticide contamination.

It is clear that the expertise Scanlan has developed under Dole will serve him well in his long-term pursuit of a career in the agribusiness industry.

Mark E. Ulven
Press Secretary
Sen. Thomas A. Daschle (D-SD)
317 Hart Senate Office Bldg.
224-2321

Personal: born 3/23/54 in Sioux City, Iowa. B.A., Univ. of South Dakota, 1976. M.A., Univ. of Missouri, 1982. 1981-1982, journalism instructor, Univ. of Missouri. 1982-1983, assistant city editor, Texarkana Gazette. 1983-1986, legislative director/press secretary, Rep. Berkeley Bedell (D-IA). 1986, press secretary, Harriet Woods for Senate Campaign. 1987, legislative assistant, Sen. Quentin N. Burdick (D-ND). 1987-present, Press Secretary, Sen. Thomas A. Daschle (D-SD).

Expertise: Agriculture

Mark Ulven is quick to point out that, though only a freshman, Sen. Tom Daschle has established himself as a player in helping shape America's agriculture policy. Indeed, Daschle was instrumental in the creation of an assistance board to oversee the bailout of the Farm Credit System.

While it is still two years in the offing, Daschle and his aide have begun the process of shaping the contours of the 1990 farm bill. One area of particular importance is that of targeting farm program payments to family-owned farms. At the present time, Ulven believes such payments are made indiscriminately to all farmers, no matter their economic circumstances. The goal of keeping farmers competitive in the world market will be an important component of Ulven's work as the next farm bill nears.

One way to modify the current system may be to define differently persons eligible for payments. In that regard, Daschle was successful through last year's budget reconciliation bill in modifying this area. Another way, says Ulven, is to shift the emphasis away from payments based on a per/acreage or per/unit basis.

One of Daschle's chief legislative priorities on the committee is substantially improving the U.S. farm economy. Daschle and his aide are studying ways to do just that, which includes attempting to find additional markets and changing price support mechanisms to increase price supports.

While Ulven will continue to focus on the committee's legislative agenda, he will also follow Daschle's guidance in monitoring both the conservation and the rural development provisions of the 1985 farm bill. In this latter regard, the emphasis will be on possibly making adjustments to farm program payments, thereby stimulating economic growth in rural communities.

Ulven will also continue monitoring last year's Agricultural Credit Act. By talking to farmers, attorneys, and others involved in this area, Ulven has developed a strong working knowledge of the Farm Credit System. Further, as Daschle sits on the Subcommittee on Agricultural Credit, Ulven will undoubtedly continue to hone his expertise in this area.

Formerly a cartoonist, Ulven has changed his artistic emphasis so that now he paints reproductions of prints he purchases from the National Gallery of Art. He also attends a class in painting still-lifes.

David K. Voight
Special Assistant
Sen. John Melcher (D-MT)
730 Hart Senate Office Bldg.
224-2644

Expertise: Agriculture

When Sen. John Melcher was looking for a Montanan to handle small business issues for him in 1981, David Voight, who had been a Carter Administration appointee at the Small Business Administration, met all requirements.

Although it was Voight's business-related experience that initially got him the job, his willingness to explore unfamiliar territory has led him to represent Melcher's interests in agriculture—a formidable task, since Melcher is the second- ranking Democrat on the Senate Agriculture, Nutrition and Forestry Committee.

"When I was working for Sen. James Abourezk, who was from South Dakota, agriculture was a very important issue" to his constituency, Voight explains. Therefore, as legislative director, Voight took the initiative to monitor legislation and conduct research in that area, gaining enough knowledge during his four-year tenure with Abourezk to become something of an expert.

Personal: born 9/3/41, Billings, Montana. B.A. Univ. of Montana, 1963. M.A. Univ. of Montana, 1965. 1966-1971, Political Science Instructor, Black Hills State Coll., Spearfish, SD. 1971-1975, Legislative Director, Senator James Abourezk (D-SD) (Representative 1971-73; Senator 1973-79). 1975-1978, Legislative Representative, National Federation of Independent Business. 1978-1981, Deputy Chief Counsel for Advocacy, Small Business Administration. 1981 to present, Special Assistant, Sen. John Melcher (D-MT).

Today, Voight is proud of his steadfast and vigorous efforts toward enactment of the Agricultural Aid and Trade Missions Act. An innovative program applauded for its humanist approach, the Act establishes U.S. offices in eligible countries to encourage development of mutually beneficial, coordinated packages of aid and trade.

The legislative route of this proposal spans three Congresses and exemplifies one of Voight's strengths—the ability to think strategically. Previously passed by the Senate three times and by the House twice, the proposal last year was included in the Omnibus Trade Reform bill, which, due to its high visibility, seemed destined for enactment. After four months of relatively little action, however, the bipartisan proposal was pulled from the trade bill and attached to the fiscal year 1988 continuing resolution—once adopted, enactment was inevitable.

Melcher solicits Voight's assistance on other issues. Melcher is chair of the Senate Special Committee on Aging, and a member of the Committee on Energy and Natural Resources, the Select Committee on Indian Affairs, and the Joint Economic Committee.

Raised in a small town (population 800), Voight has a genuine affinity for the rural communities he left behind seventeen years ago when he relocated to D.C. "But I have the good fortune," he admits, "to travel back to Montana with the Senator."

In his spare time, Voight enjoys antiquing and travelling. He also is an enthusiastic bridge player.

Robert Young
Majority Economist
649 Dirksen Senate Office Bldg.
224-5207

Expertise: Agriculture, economic modeling, budget issues, livestock and commodity programs

Robert Young's colleagues on the Agriculture Committee describe him as the consummate practitioner. While still a graduate student, he worked as a consultant developing applied weather/crop yield models for the world's major grain-producing regions. During a seven year stint as a consultant, he built agricultural models for and provided analysis to bodies such as the Government Accounting Office, the NATO Strategic Planning Committee in Canada, and the American Farm Bureau Federation.

Young also served as Director of Operations of the University of Missouri's Food and Agricultural Policy Research Institute. In that post, he built an econometric model of U.S. agriculture, generated commodity forecasts and produced several semi-annual ten-year econometric forecasts of world agriculture.

When the Agriculture Committee needed an economist it looked to Young. In his current position as Majority Economist, Young analyzes the impact of proposed policies. He also oversees budget reconciliation measures, commodity programs and livestock issues.

While he has been closely connected with the Trade Bill and the Disaster Relief Bill, Young is involved with all committee legislation and studies as an economist. While believing that agricultural income needs to be protected, he feels that in tight budgets this can only be done through properly managed programs. These are programs which keep stocks under control, but allow a farmer to produce as much as possible while still being able compete in world markets. Young expects to continue work on commodity programs this year, as well as being active on the Trade Bill, the Canadian Free Trade agreement and GATT negotiations.

Personal: born 10/16/52 in Gulfport, Mississippi. B.S. Univ.of Missouri, 1974. M.S. Univ. of Missouri, 1982. Ph.D. Univ.of Missouri, 1986. 1981-1987, Director of Operations, Food and Agricultural Policy Research Institute, University of Missouri. 1987-present, Majority Economist, Senate Committee on Agriculture, Nutrition, and Forestry.

SENATE
COMMITTEE ON APPROPRIATIONS

Appropriations

Jerry L. Bonham
Professional Staff Member
156 Dirksen Senate Office Bldg.
224-7245

Personal: B.A. Southwest Missouri State College, 1962. M.A. University of Illinois, 1968. Ph.D. University of Illinois, 1975. 1965-77, taught Public Administration, Public Policy and Budget at Western Carolina College, Indiana State, Purdue (Visiting Lecturer) and Northern Iowa universities. 1978-85, Legislative Assistant to Sens. Dennis DeConcini (D-AZ) and Frank Lautenberg (D-NJ). 1985-86, minority staff member, Subcommittee on the District of Columbia; 1987-present, Staff Director, Subcommittee on Transportation.

Expertise: Appropriations, transportation, aviation

When the Democrats regained control of the Senate in 1986, Bonham was catapulted from minority status on the Subcommittee for the District of Columbia to a more eminent position on the staff of the Appropriations Committee. With the backing of two former Senate bosses, committee members DeConcini and Lautenberg, he moved up to direct operations of the Transportation Subcommittee.

Considered by colleagues as "responsive" in providing his legislative and budgeting expertise, Bonham is regarded for his knowledge of the issues and his clarity in pleading them.

Bonham specializes in the Federal Aviation Administration and the Coast Guard. He also serves as liaison with the House Appropriations and Budget committees in all transportation areas.

While serving in four positions in his 10 years in the Senate, Bonham has carved out a singular reputation in budget and appropriations matters. As a senior member of DeConcini's personal staff for six years, he was the senator's principal contact with the appropriations committee, specializing in budget analysis and drafting of committee amendments and reports.

This background has served him well in his present duties of analyzing agency and federal budgets and liaison with other key committees, members and their staffs.

Bonham, who considers himself a moderate Democrat, cut his political teeth in state and party politics in Iowa and Indiana during his college teaching years. Besides serving on a number of state and local Democratic Party committees in Iowa, he was a consultant to Cedar Falls during the reorganization of its city government in the mid-1970s.

An active outdoorsman, Bonham jogs and plays tennis and an "occasional" round of golf. But his favorite activity when Senate duties permit is backpacking with his wife in the nearby Virginia and Maryland mountains.

Jeff Cilek
Professional Staff Member
Subcommittee on the Interior
153 Dirksen Senate Office Bldg.
224-7262

Personal: born 6/5/54 in Iowa City, Iowa. B.B.A. Univ. of Iowa, 1980. 1981-1984, legislative staff, Sen. James A. McClure (R-ID): 1984, Legislative Director. 1985-present, Professional Staff Member, Senate Appropriations Committee, Subcommittee on the Interior.

Expertise: Interior appropriations

Managing Republican interests for the Senate Appropriations Subcommittee on Interior, Jeff Cilek is the only staffer assigned to work with the minority members of the panel

It wasn't always such a lonely job. When he joined the subcommittee staff in 1985, the Republicans had control of the Senate and Cilek worked with three other subcommittee staffers in the Majority. But the 1986 elections shifted that balance of power and now Cilek is the only Republican staff member of the subcommittee.

The Subcommittee on the Interior is one of the thirteen subcommittees of the Committee on Appropriations with the responsibility of funding thirty federal agencies with approximately $10 billion. The agencies range in diversity from the Smithsonian Institution to the Bureau of Land Management and include most of the Department of the Interior, the non-nuclear side of the Department of Energy, the Forest Service, various Indian agencies, the National Endowment for the Humanities, etc. The dollar size of the Interior Subcommittee is small compared to other Appropriations subcommittees, but it does consider 900 requests totalling $2 billion made by various senators each year.

Born in Iowa City, IA, and raised in Twin Falls, ID, Cilek sees his job as monitoring the resources managed by the these agencies. "If the government is going to be a landowner, we should be responsible in providing the services necessary to protect the resources. This has required some creative work in the last few years since the subcommittee's allocation of funds has remained relatively static since 1980."

On site inspections are an important part of the job and Cilek is pleased that the subcommittee's jurisdiction encompasses some of America's most interesting sites. Touring national parks, national wildlife refuges and the Smithsonian museums is not hardship duty, says Cilek.

W. David Gwaltney
Professional Staff Member
Subcommittee on Energy and
    Water Development
131 Dirksen Senate Office Bldg.
224-7260

Expertise: Water resource development and energy research

Unlike many Hill staffers, David Gwaltney had no political contacts when he joined the Senate Appropriations Committee's subcommittee on Energy and Water Development in 1973. Acting on a friend's suggestion, Gwaltney applied to the Committee at a time when many of its staff were nearing retirement, and the Committee was recruiting new professionals.

Gwaltney's background is with the military. He served in the U.S. Air Force following his graduation from Virginia Military Institute in 1967. He worked on budgeting and programming for construction projects nationwide. His military career took him to Taiwan for 15 months and to the Pentagon for three years. Ready to put down roots, and seeing that the Air Force's top-heavy management promised little immediate advancement, Gwaltney then accepted an Appropriations subcommittee position in order to remain in his native Virginia.

Personal: born 2/12/45 in Washington, D.C. B.S. Virginia Military Institute, 1967. 1967-1972, U.S. Air Force. 1973-present, Professional Staff Member, Subcommittee on Energy and Water Development, Senate Appropriations Committee.

During his fifteen years with the subcommittee, Gwaltney has developed significant expertise in water resource development—Army Corps of Engineers water projects, Bureau of Reclamation western water programs and economic development work with the Tennessee Valley Authority and the Appalachian Regional Commission. He has also been involved with power marketing and other activities within the Department of Energy. In these areas, it takes years to develop the institutional memory and background knowledge of the programs to be effective.

During his tenure Gwaltney has developed a reputation for being someone who "really does his homework," says a subcommittee colleague. A tribute to Gwaltney's competence is the fact that he has always served with the subcommittee's majority. In 1980, when Sen. Mark Hatfield (R-OR) took over the Appropriations Committee's chairmanship, Gwaltney remained with the majority staff at Hatfield's request.

A civil engineer who has opted not to go into hands-on engineering, Gwaltney nonetheless believes his engineering training provided the discipline necessary to meet the demands of his current position. In comparison to his days with the executive branch, Gwaltney appreciates the flexibility and autonomy his job affords, noting that the Energy and Water Development subcommittee members value the staff's experience and judgment.

Besides a daily lunch-hour run, Gwaltney's main out-of-the-office devotion is to his wife and two children. "I try not to do what I've seen too many people up here do—lose sight of their ability to use time wisely and spend more time at work than necessary."

J. Michael Hall
Staff Director
Subcommittee on Labor, Health
and Human Services
186 Dirksen Senate Office Bldg.
224-7288

For over ten years, J. Michael Hall has helped negotiate the $600 billion budget of the nation's largest employer—the federal government.

Currently, Hall is Staff Director for the Senate Appropriations Subcommittee on Labor, Health and Human Services, and Education. Since 1976, when he first joined the Committee staff, he has worked for the Subcommittees on the District of Columbia; Treasury, Postal Service and General Government; and Transportation.

Hall's responsibilities have always been focused—on the numbers. In 1970, after he returned from two years in Thailand as a Peace Corps volunteer, Hall joined the Office of Management and Budget as a budget examiner.

The Subcommittee on Labor–HHS oversees more than 1/10 of the federal budget. The fiscal year 1988 continuing resolution included $127 billion for programs under that Subcommittee's jurisdiction. Every appropriations measure is a major piece of legislation, and Hall must balance the various interests involved.

On the personal side, Hall participates in budget matters on a somewhat smaller scale, as vice chairman of the Arlington County (VA) Planning Commission. A sportsman, Hall enjoys bird hunting and bird watching.

Personal: born 11/9/43, Carbondale, Illinois. B.A. Univ. of Illinois, 1967. M.A. Univ. of Illinois, 1970. 1967-1969, Peace Corps Volunteer, Thailand. 1979-1975, Budget examiner, Office of Management and Budget. 1976 to present, Professional Staff Member, Appropriations Committee.

Irma I. Hanneman
Minority Clerk
Subcommittee on Agriculture,
   Rural Development, and Related
   Agencies
150 Dirksen Senate Office Bldg.
224-7337

Personal: born 7/28/37 in Worland, Wyoming. B.A. Univ.of Wyoming, 1958. 1958-1962, high school teacher, Casper, WY. 1962-1977, Research Assistant/Caseworker, Sen. Gale McGee (D-WY). 1977-1983, Assistant Majority Clerk; 1983-1987, Majority Clerk, Appropriations Subcommittee on Agriculture, Rural Development, and Related Agencies. 1987-present, Minority Clerk, Appropriations Subcommittee on Agriculture, Rural Development and Related Agencies.

Expertise: Agriculture, rural development, domestic food programs

Professional career opportunities for women on Capitol Hill were nearly nonexistent when Hanneman came to Washington in 1962 to take a summer job with former Sen. Gale McGee (D-WY). But loyalty, perseverance and hard work led her to successively more responsible positions, and today she holds an important position on one of Congress's most powerful committees.

Her 15-year stint with Sen. McGee ended in 1976 when he lost a reelection bid to Republican challenger Malcolm Wallop. She joined the Appropriations Agriculture Subcommittee the next year, serving first as secretary to the Subcommittee, then Assistant Majority clerk (assistant staff director) and then during Sen. Thad Cochran (R-MS) chairmanship, as Majority Clerk (staff director). When the Republicans lost the majority in 1986, she stayed with ranking Republican Thad Cochran as minority clerk for the subcommittee.

The Subcommittee produces one of the most important and perennially controversial of Congress's 13 appropriations bills, and Hanneman says the process is "anything but routine." Working closely with her counterpart on the Democratic side, Hanneman helps subcommittee members establish the funding levels for a wide array of federal programs, mostly in the U.S. Department of Agriculture. These programs include agricultural research and extension activities, conservation programs, farm income and commodity price support programs, marketing and inspection activities, domestic food programs, as well as the Farmers Home Administration, the Food and Drug Administration and the Commodity Futures Trading Commission.

Emergency supplemental appropriations for the Commodity Credit Corporation, restoration of funding for research and conservation programs that the Administration slated for elimination, and expansion of the Farmers Home Administration to help solve the "farm crisis"—these are just some of the issues that have consumed her time in recent years.

After 25 years of working on the Hill, Hanneman understandably counts as one of her proudest accomplishments "starting almost at the bottom and working my way to the top." She remembers when almost no women held top staff positions, and even today, she is one of the few women at Appropriations to have held a staff directorship.

In her spare time, Hanneman has taken an active role in Senate staff activities, serving on the Credit Union's board of directors and as an officer of the Senate Staff Club. She is also a collector of antiques and enjoys horseback riding.

W. Proctor Jones

Deputy Staff Director of Committee
& Staff Director of Subcommittee
on Energy and Water
Development
131 Dirksen Senate Office Bldg.
224-0335

Personal: born 7/5/41 in Twin City, Georgia. Univ.of Georgia, 1959-1960. B.A. George Washington Univ., 1965. 1966-1968, U.S. Marine Corps. 1960-1965 & 1968-1970, Special Assistant, Sen. Richard Russell (D-GA). 1971-present, Senate Committee on Appropriations.

Expertise: Appropriations

Proctor Jones began his career in the Senate in 1961 earning just $2700 a year. According to Jones, though, that sum covered the essentials—"my living expenses and some left over to take a girl out on weekends."

Since those days, the Senate as an institution has changed dramatically and along with it Jones's role. In subsequent years, Jones has risen to become one of the senior staffers on the Appropriations Committee. His experience in the Senate and knowledge of the institution is widely recognized.

Jones left Georgia in 1960 to work for Senator Richard Russell (D-GA) under what was then the "patronage program." It was the forerunner of today's internship program for college students. When Jones took a year's leave of absence from the University of Georgia, he had every intention of returning to Athens for the following term. As it turned out, he never went back.

Except for a brief stint in the military, Jones stayed with Russell until the Senator died in 1971. A year earlier, he moved from Russell's personal staff to the Appropriations Committee, which Russell chaired at the time. For a brief time, he served as a staff assistant on what was then the Labor-HEW Subcommittee, but soon moved over to the Public Works Subcommittee, renamed the Energy and Water Subcommittee during the 1970s energy crisis.

During his years with the Appropriations Committee, Jones has served under a number of Democratic Chairmen—Senators Russell, Ellender, Magnuson, McClellan, and now Stennis—in almost every capacity.

Today, as Deputy Staff Director of the full committee, he works closely with Senate staff director, Frank Sullivan, in breaking down the Committee's annual allocation from the Budget Committee into its thirteen component parts—one for each of the thirteen Appropriations subcommittees.

Following Senator Russell's advice to "always stay close to the issues," Jones continues to split his time between the full committee and the Energy and Water Development Subcommittee. On the Subcommittee, he has served under Senators Stennis, and now Bennett Johnston (D-LA). Although no relationship to an individual Senator will equal the one he had with Russell, his relationship with Stennis is also very close.

His primary Subcommittee responsibility is assembling an Energy and Water bill that will pass once it goes to the floor; no easy task. It requires knowing the controversial issues, understanding the parochial pressures that influence a Senator's actions—particular in this area—and working out suitable compromises.

Half of Jones's time organizing the Energy and Water bill is spent on defense issues. The other half is on energy R & D programs and Corps of Engineers projects. On the defense issues, the Department of Energy has jurisdiction over research, development, engineering, testing, production, maintenance and ultimate disposal of all nuclear weapons. In the past year, these appropriations reached nearly $8 billion.

Proctor Jones's typical work day is long. When the Senate stays in session until the early hours of the morning to complete consideration of a Supplemental Appropriations measure or a Continuing Resolution, he will be on the floor. When there is a filibuster on an appropriations measure, as there was on the fiscal 1988 Energy and Water bill, he will be there from start to finish.

"I was infected early and its been in my blood ever since," he says about the Senate's effect on him. He has grown up with it, has become a valuable part of it, and in the process, has come to love it.

Warren Kane
Clerk
Subcommittee on Commerce,
   Justice, State, and the Judiciary
S-146A Capitol Bldg.
224-7282

Personal: born 2/9/35 in Long Island City, New York. B.A. Hope Coll., 1957. 1958-1960 management analyst, Bureau of the Census. 1960-1965, budget analyst, Dept. of Commerce. 1965-1968, budget officer, Dept. of Commerce. 1969-1971, budget officer, regional development programs, Dept. of Commerce. 1971-1973, legislative assistant, Sen. Norris Cotton. 1973-1974, minority staff; 1974-1981, professional staff; 1981-1986, minority staff; 1986-present, professional staff, Senate Committee on Appropriations

Expertise: Commerce, justice and state appropriations

Warren W. Kane is a seventeen-year Hill veteran with considerable experience in appropriations for the Departments of State, Justice and Commerce the Judiciary, and some twenty-two related agencies and he has some very definite opinions about the process.

Kane believes that current budget process is simply not working. He emphasizes he does not want to endure another two weeks like those at the end of the last session of Congress. Kane believes the accelerated budget calendar under Gramm-Rudman-Hollings does not work and that the old calendar under the Budget Reform and Control Act was far more practical. He is unhappy about what he sees as a "bottom-line mentality" and the fact that the budget is used more and more for political posturing by both the Executive and Legislative branches. Exasperating is the fact that appropriations bills frequently end up with unrelated issues like abortion and everything else tied on. When a congressman is unable to get his bill passed through the normal committee channels, all too often the tendency is to attach that bill to the appropriations bills to ensure passage. Kane strongly believes that there is a definite need to preclude all extraneous amendments from appropriations. This in turn would reduce the growing politicization of what should be a simple budget bill. Kane also thinks that authorization should be for no less than three years— one year to get the authorized program off the ground, one year to see how it works, and one year to evaluate.

Kane has had no personal experience in political campaigns. He believes that the staffs of the Appropriations and Finance Committees tend to be less political due to the traditionally bi-partisan nature of their responsibilities. Kane finds divisions more along the lines of urban interests versus rural interests as opposed to Democrats versus Republicans.

J. Keith Kennedy
Minority Staff Director
119 Dirksen Senate Office Bldg.
224-7335

Expertise: Appropriations

Keith Kennedy first worked on Capitol Hill as an intern in 1972 and in the classic Capitol Hill progression climbed the ladder to staff director. When the Democrats regained control of the Senate in 1986, Kennedy moved from majority to minority staff director.

As Minority Staff Director on Appropriations, Kennedy acts as liaison with the Democrats and oversees the Committee's relationship with the Office of Management and Budget, the House and the Leadership in the Senate. He also coordinates for the Republicans the interaction of the thirteen Appropriations Subcommittees, making sure they adhere to scorekeeping and procedural rules.

Any full committee bill, such as a supplemental or a continuing resolution, comes under Kennedy's scrutiny, and he is responsible for the Republicans' interests on the District of Columbia and Legislative Branch Subcommittees, the latter in which he has extensive experience.

Personal: born 4/29/48. in Charlotte, North Carolina. B.A. Duke Univ., 1970. M.A. Divinity Duke Univ., 1974. 1974-77, Legislative Assistant to Senator Mark Hatfield (R-OR). 1977-79, Minority staff member, Select Committee on Indian Affairs. 1979-81, Minority staff member, Energy and Water Subcommittee; 1981-86, Staff Director; 1987-present, Minority Staff Director, Appropriations Committee.

Kennedy's philosophy as a veteran of the Appropriations Committee is: "Is this expenditure justified?" Despite public perception, he says the Committee is very frugal and has "an ingrained bias against spending money." In his view, federal agencies must make a very good case before the Committee to justify their requests for additional funds.

Kennedy says the best part of his job is dealing with the professional staff of the Senate and House Appropriations Committees and the good working relationship which exists between them. The worst part is the "constant frustration of dealing with the misperception that we are the big spenders on the block," and "constantly being the focal point of all the attacks on federal spending." He is also aggravated by what he calls the "intellectual dishonesty" of those who blame the deficit problem on non-defense discretionary spending.

Kennedy attributes his career successes to the fact the he "doesn't take himself too seriously." Steve Bell, formerly the Staff Director for the Budget Committee and now with Salomon Brothers Inc., says Kennedy is "one of the best" on the Hill. According to Bell, Kennedy's success can be attributed to the fact that "Keith's not in it as a stepping stone to some big job. He's in it because he believes in public policy, and he's very good at it."

Kennedy is also good at sailing, enjoys movies, and polishes off political biographies with relish.

Robert E. Mills
Professional Staff Member
190 Dirksen Senate Office Bldg.
224-6208

Expertise: Appropriations, budget, policy administration

Bob Mills knew that a career involving public policy would be far more satisfying than managing a local drug store. So in 1973, he tried his luck by sending 40 resumes to Capitol Hill. Several interviews and six job offers later, Mills accepted a position on the staff of Rep. Gillis Long (D-LA). That long shot launched what would become a Capitol Hill career spanning some 15 years.

The Senate Appropriations Committee, which last year had jurisdiction over approximately $129 billion of the federal budget, has 13 subcommittees and is viewed as one of the most powerful committees in the Senate.

As a professional staffer of that committee, Mills has played an active role in a string of legislative initiatives. In fact, staff colleagues on both sides of the aisle praise his effectiveness.

Mills is currently Majority Staff Director of the Subcommittee on Treasury, Postal Service, and General Government. Earlier in his career, Mills was instrumental in crafting Selective Service draft legislation and Section 503 of the Supplemental Appropriations Act of 1987, which established procedures for the drug testing of federal employees. Mills regards that measure as especially significant since it passed despite strong ideological resistance and with strong bipartisan support.

Personal: born 6/26/46 in Washington, D.C. B.A. Univ. of Maryland, 1971. M.A. George Washington Univ., 1979. Georgetown Univ. Law School, J.D. expected in May, 1988. 1973-1974, Legislative Assistant, Rep. Gillis Long (D-LA). 1974-1975, Legislative Assistant, Sen. William Proxmire (D-WI). 1975-present, Professional Staff Member, Senate Committee on Appropriations.

One of Mills's major accomplishments has been his involvement with the Anti-Drug Abuse Act of 1986. Recognizing his expertise in that area, senior staffers of Senators Byrd, Biden and Chiles requested his assistance in drafting Title 3, an integral portion of that bill. Title 3, dealing with drug interdiction assets, contained provisions involving U.S. intelligence considerations; various command-and-control efforts; agency roles in drug interdiction; and the effective use of the military in assisting civilian drug enforcement agencies.

As the coordinator of the House-Senate effort of this important provision, Mills worked with the leadership of both houses in drafting the bill and planning and scheduling floor consideration. That coordination was so successful that this bill became the first crime measure in congressional history without a formal conference between the two chambers. Finally, the importance of this provision is evidenced by the fact that it involved the largest level of federal appropriations.

Mills's efforts have also extended to the international trade arena. At the present time, Mills is working with Sen. Dennis DeConcini (D-AZ) on measures that would have a positive effect on U.S.-Mexico trade relations.

He is also working with DeConcini and other key border state senators in establishing a U.S.-Mexico Border Business Council—a group designed to bring the border business community together with key members of Congress with the goal of focusing legislative attention on U.S.-Mexico trade problems.

A counselor in the United Methodist Youth Program, Mills tried out as a wide receiver with the 1974 Washington Redskins. While he fell short of that goal, Mills has more than compensated with his first-string duties on the Senate Appropriations Committee.

Michael J. Russell
Legislative Director
Senator Arlen Specter (R-PA)
303 Hart Senate Office Bldg.
224-4254

Expertise: Foreign affairs, crime, appropriations

A longtime interest in foreign affairs has this past year turned into Mike Russell's bread and butter—he has become Senator Arlen Specter's leading legislative aide on foreign affairs and foreign assistance (Senate Appropriations Subcommittee on Foreign Operations).

Russell is well-known among Hill staffers and lobbyists for the key staff role he played during the 99th Congress in oversight of, and work on, continued funding for the Justice Department's Office of Juvenile Justice and Delinquency Prevention in light of Administration attempts to eliminate the program. He also was involved in implementation of the 1984 Armed Career Criminal Act, which mandates minimum sentences for career criminals who have three prior convictions and who are caught with a firearm. After that bill passed, Russell helped in drafting several amendments which expanded the Act to include all serious violent crimes and drug offenses. Russell staffed the Senator's trade bill and floor amendments to provide a private right of action in federal court to enforce existing trade laws. He is also the Senate contact for the Congressional Crime Caucus, which meets informally to consider issues relating to crime.

After spending over two years on the Judiciary Committee, concentrating on juvenile justice and judiciary issues, Russell was asked to be Specter's legislative director, and assumed responsibility for supervising a ten-person legislative staff and for advising him on foreign affairs and other issues before the Subcommittee on Foreign Operations. In addition, he continues to handle certain Judiciary Committee matters, such as the career criminal program, as well as state issues for the Senator.

Personal: born 5/19/58 in Northampton, MA. B.A. Gettysburg College, 1980. M.A. Vanderbilt University, 1984. J.D. Vanderbilt Univ. School of Law, 1984. LL.M. (candidate) Georgetown Univ. Law Center. 1984-1985, Attorney, Office of the General Counsel, U.S. Department of Agriculture. 1985-1986, Counsel, Subcommittee on Juvenile Justice, U.S. Senate Judiciary Committee. 1987, Minority General Counsel, Subcommittee on the Constitution, U.S. Senate Judiciary Committee. 1987 to present, Legislative Director, Sen.Arlen Specter. Publications: "The War Powers Resolution: An Act Facing 'Imminent Hostilities' a Decade Later," Vanderbilt Journal of Transnational Law, Fall 1983.

Russell works extensively as Specter's liaison with embassies and law firms that represent foreign governments who are seeking military and/or economic assistance from the U.S. He includes the following as key areas of concern for him during the 100th Congress: ratification of the Intermediate-range Nuclear Forces treaty; interpretation of the Anti-Ballistic Missile Agreement; international trade; human rights; and War Powers Act issues, especially as the Act relates to U.S. activities in the Persian Gulf.

Francis J. Sullivan
Staff Director
133 Dirksen Senate Office Bldg.
224-7254

Personal: born 10/8/32/ in Boston, Massachusetts. B.A. Boston Coll., 1953. Lincoln Lab M.I.T., 1956-1957. Master of Commerce Univ. of Richmond, 1956. Industrial Coll. of the Armed Forces, 1972-1973. 1953-1956, Lieutenant, U.S. Army. 1956-1964, Engineering Supervisor, Western Electric Company . 1964-1966, Senior Operations Research Analyst, Army Logistics Mgmnt Ctr. 1966-1972, Director of Manpower Requirements Office of the Secretary of Defense. 1973-1983, Staff Director (majority and minority, respectively) Senate Armed Services Committee. 1983-present, Staff Director (minority and majority, respectively) Senate Appropriations Committee.

Expertise: Defense

Francis J. "Frank" Sullivan is the epitome of the self effacing but effective and loyal staffer. For years he has shyed away from interviews and attributes his own accomplishments to his boss, Sen. John Stennis (D-MS). Recently when a magazine asked Sullivan to pose for a photograph, he declined and offered a picture of Stennis.

Sullivan's primary expertise is in defense, stemming from his active and post active duty involvement with the U.S. Army. After graduating from Boston College with a degree in mathematics in 1953, Sullivan entered the Army. He spent three years as a second and first lieutenant before taking his experience to Western Electric Company in 1956. He returned to the Armed Forces in 1964 as a senior operations research analyst at the Pentagon, specializing in logistics, transportation and distribution systems. He quickly moved to the office of the Secretary of Defense where he spent six years as director of manpower requirements.

It was a natural next step for Sullivan to come to the Senate Armed Services Committee with his military experience. He became staff director for the committee in 1973, beginning his long relationship with (then Armed Services Committee Chairman) Stennis. Sullivan worked almost exclusively on military authorizations during those years, working with the Department of Defense and individual senators on a yearly military appropriations package. He became an expert on both U.S. military hardware and the congressional appropriations process. *Legal Times* has called him, "one of the Hills top defense experts." And he has long been an informal advisor to current Armed Services Committee Chairman Sen. Sam Nunn (D-GA).

He moved to the Appropriations Committee with Stennis in 1983 serving as minority staff director until he assumed his current position when the Democrats regained control in 1986. On the Appropriations Committee, he has continued his involvement with the defense authorization process. He doubles as clerk for the Defense Subcommittee that Stennis also chairs.

The 13 Appropriations subcommittees are the real centers of committee activity. Sullivan mediates among the various subcommittee chairmen and plans strategy to steer their through the Senate. He also is known for being bi-partisan, both because of Stennis' style and because party barriers often break down at the technical level of appropriations.

SENATE
COMMITTEE ON ARMED SERVICES

Mark Jennings Albrecht
Legislative Assistant
Senator Pete Wilson (R-CA)
720 Hart Senate Office Bldg.
224-5422

Expertise: Defense, arms control, foreign policy, intelligence

Mark Albrecht majored in the history of the Middle Ages in college, but moved into the highly technical field of national security public policy analysis. The Middle Ages intrigued him because they represent the coming together of economic, social, political and technological forces on an unprecedented scale. And to Albrecht, the nuclear era is a similarly critical period.

In his position as a Senior Analyst in the intelligence community, he participated in national security working groups, analyzed the resource productivity of manpower and high-technology intelligence systems, and conducted risk analysis in connection with the resource allocation.

Moving into consulting at Science Applications, he continued his role in strategic analysis, which soon carried him to the U.S. Senate. He was chosen by Wilson to advise him on national security issues, an area in which Albrecht has specialized. He has since assumed the position of National Security Legislative Assistant. In this capacity he oversees a defense and foreign policy office staff coordinating the Senator's work on the Armed Services Committee, defense constituent services and national security policy formulation.

Personal: born 3/10/50 in St. Louis, Missouri. B.A. History, UCLA, 1972. California State Scholar, 1972. Phi Beta Kappa, 1972. M.A. UCLA, 1973. Departmental Scholar, UCLA History Department, 1973. Ph.D in Policy Analysis, Rand Graduate Institute, 1978. 1975-1978, Research Associate, Rand Corporation; Member, Rand Advisory Board. 1978-1981, Senior Analyst, Resource Management Staff, Director of Central Intelligence. 1981-1983, Senior Policy Analyst, Science Applications, Inc., McLean, VA. 1983 to present, Legislative Assistant for National Security Affairs, Senator Pete Wilson (R-CA).

The issues on which he has worked hardest and longest on Wilson's foreign policy agenda have centered on the Strategic Defense Initiative, as well as Strategic Forces and Arms Control. Additionally, he has handled U.S.- Mexico relations, primarily in the areas of immigration and drug-control, for the Senator.

He took a leading role clarifying the early objectives and goals of the SDI changing them from an early focus on feasibility to an articulation of a phased architecture, thereby putting the program on a strong footing over the near as well as the long term. He has also led the emerging debate on the future of nuclear defense strategic stability. Albrecht says he is proud to have helped define a national strategy that includes SDI and Start, as opposed to SDI or arms control. Albrecht believes these efforts have shifted the U.S. perspective on arms control toward credible negotiation and away from arms control as an end in itself. He thinks the world is a safer place now that arms control is actually reducing totals, rather than managing their increase. Albrecht foresees that Senator Wilson will take a very active role in the ratification of the INF treaty. He will work very hard to ensure the treaty's implications for weapons systems not proscribed are not misinterpreted, and to guarantee the adequacy of the verification, compliance and safeguard provisions.

Kent Bankus
Professional Staff Member
Subcommittee on Defense Industry
and Technology
222 Russell Senate Office Bldg.
224-3871

Personal: born 10/11/42 in Milan, Missouri. B.S. Univ. of Missouri, 1964. M.B.A. Auburn Univ., 1974. 1968, USAF Squadron Office School. 1974, Air Command and Staff College. 1975, Industrial College of Armed Forces. 1964-1969, Flight Officer, USAF. 1970-1974, Test Pilot and Chief of Operations and Training at Armament Development and Test Center. 1974, Flight Officer. 1975-1977, Chief of Test and Evaluation for the Pacific Air Forces Weapon System Evaluation Program. 1977-1979, Air Operations Officer, Directorate of Plans, Pacific East Asia Division. 1979-1981, Program Manager, Advanced Technology Bomber. 1982-1984, Deputy Commander for Operations, 388th Tactical Fighter Wing. 1984-1985, USAF Tactical Division Deputy Chief. 1985-1987, Special Assistant to Undersecretary of Defense for Research and Engineering/Acquisition.

Expertise: Procurement, defense industry

Kent Bankus joined the Senate Armed Services Committee staff with two decades of military development, testing, evaluation and management experience under his belt. He was program manager for the Advanced Technology Bomber and responsible for Special Access for minority contractors programs in the Office of the Secretary of Defense (OSD), before being recruited by the Committee. Since February of 1987, the former Air Force pilot has dealt with issues before the Subcommittee on Defense Industry and Technology, and legislation involving minority programs.

The desire to fly lured Bankus to the Air Force. Bankus has flown in four generations of fighter aircraft, from the F-100 to the F-16. He has witnessed great leaps in technology through the years, but he admits, "The F-100 was my favorite aircraft—no radar, no autopilot, it was just you and the aircraft."

Bankus survived a year of combat in Vietnam, during which he was shot down by ground fire. The Missourian later became a test pilot, a position he found "most enjoyable" because of the variety of aircraft he flew and its relative lack of structure. Through several testing, evaluation and operations positions, the Purple Heart recipient broadened his knowledge of weapons systems and aircraft. He also had the unique opportunity of helping to re-negotiate the U.S. military base rights agreement with the Philippines government in the late 1970's.

Because of his broad experience, Bankus was chosen to serve in the Low Observables Technology Office, during which time he initiated and managed the Advanced Technology Bomber program. Asked about matching his fighter background with a bomber program, Bankus remarks, "It was very useful because I think we got a synthesis, perhaps, the best of both the fighter and the bomber." Later he returned to his roots, validating and advocating the Air Force's newest fighters, including the Advanced Tactical Fighter. As a retired colonel, Bankus topped off his experiences in developing, evaluating and managing technology as head of OSD's "minority programs."

Bankus came to the Committee at a low point in government-defense industry relations. Responsible for industry and technology issues, he has assisted the Committee in trying "to remove the adversarial attitudes and try to end up with a very business-like arm's length arrangement." To help achieve this, Bankus helped form an ad-hoc defense industry advisory group made up of prominent CEOs and senior executives. The group discusses in private various problems facing DOD and the defense industry. "Because everything is private they have been saying things they probably couldn't say on the record, and have been helpful in making suggestions," Bankus says.

While he has promoted a more constructive relationship with industry, Bankus focuses on the University Research Initiative, the Defense Manufacturing Initiative, and procurement reform. "We are seeking to increase spending for the technology and industrial base despite budget cuts." Bankus says he is most concerned about "the subcontractors on the second and third tier levels" because "they don't have the resilience of big companies . . . and are hurt most" by protectionism. Bankus describes himself as a "free trader". He has assisted members in opposing protectionist legislation for the defense industry, believing "in the long run it hurts everyone."

With the flurry of procurement reform legislation, Bankus observes, "We need to sit back and see where things are bad and where they are working." Once this reform legislation is evaluated, Bankus believes the Committee will consider a comprehensive package of proposals.

Promoting superconductor research, the Defense Industrial Base Preservation Act and developing proposals for a career service for program managers, are also future priorities for the Committee, according to Bankus. Describing proposals on these programs, Bankus asserts, "There are a lot of little things but together they all add up." Bankus's career achievements from earning "Top Gun" in his F-100 training class to directing Special Access Programs have helped him to know that doing a lot of little things can have a big impact.

Robert E. Bayer
Professional Staff Member
303 Dirksen Senate Office Bldg.
224-3521

Personal: Born 10/26/41 in Cleveland, Ohio. B.S. John Carroll Univ. 1962 (magna cum laude). National Defense Fellow, Loyola Univ. (1962-1963). 1963-1983, U.S. Air Force, retired as Lt. Col. 1983 to present, Professional Staff Member, Armed Services Committee

Expertise: Military construction

Considered an expert in the area of military construction, Robert Bayer was called on by Chairman Sam Nunn (D-GA) to join his personal staff in 1983 and serve as professional staff member for the Committee. Bayer's unique background includes twenty years of military experience, management of Air Force installations, and congressional affairs liaison for the Secretary of the Air Force. These positions have enabled Bayer to take on the challenge of maximizing creativity and productivity in the 1980s era of budget cuts and military spending reform.

Bayer oversees the Committee's $10 billion dollar budget for military facilities construction, land acquisition and family housing. When the Committee was reorganized with the 100th Congress, Bayer was charged with developing policy for military operations and military construction maintenance, and served as the Committee's liaison with the Pentagon and the Appropriations Subcommittee on Military Construction. In addition, he serves as staff member on the Subcommittee on Readiness, Sustainability and Support. In earlier budgets, operations and maintenance were separate items from new construction costs. When they were combined it became Bayer's responsibility to coordinate input for the authorization bill.

Bayer's priorities include promoting a higher quality of life in military housing and completion of construction projects that have near-term readiness capability.

When he first came to work for Sen. Nunn as a defense and foreign policy specialist, Bayer served as liaison with defense industry constituents and tracked veterans' and immigration policy. The work brought him into daily contact with all levels of government and the private sector dealing with sensitive defense, socio-economic, and environmental issues—with special focus on the impact of federal resource decisions on local communities.

Bayer has authored successful proposals for federal and private grants to initiate nonprofit housing cooperatives for low- and moderate-income tenants; and developed and effectively defended five controversial installation realignments which netted an annual savings in excess of $50 million.

Bob Bayer has travelled extensively and lived all over the world.

Milton Beach
Legislative Assistant
Senator John Glenn (D-OH)
503 Hart Senate Office Bldg.
224-3353

Expertise: Defense acquisition, weapons systems testing

Milton Beach came to Senator Glenn's personal staff after a distinguished career in the U.S. Navy and five years in the private sector as a defense consultant. He serves as the Senator's expert on military weapons' systems acquisitions and testing, after performing those same duties at the Pentagon where he became familiar with the DOD, OMB, Congressional Armed Services and Appropriations Committee's budget process.

Beach managed several major acquisition programs for military combat aircraft and weapons systems and produced comprehensive studies on conventional and nuclear warfare planning; and military hardware and personnel requirements.

In his role as Defense Legislative Assistant, Beach serves as the Senator's liaison with the defense industry in Ohio and arranged over five defense acquisition seminars to guide local companies through the complex negotiations necessary to do business with the government.

He participates in the writing and development of the annual Senate Armed Services Defense Authorization bill and works with the Subcommittee on Conventional Forces and Alliance Defense, and the Subcommittee on Strategic Forces and Nuclear Deterrence on which the Senator serves.

Personal: born 11/9/33 in Houston, Texas. B.A. Univ. of Houston. Currently working toward M.A., Legislative Affairs, George Washington Univ. 1955-1976, U.S. Navy, career officer, serving in Europe, Vietnam and 1977-80, Pentagon. 1980-1981, taught U.S. history and government, high school level. 1981-1985, defense consultant to private industry. 1985 to present, Legislative Assistant, Senator John Glenn. Beach's awards and honors include the U.S. Navy Legion of Merit; Distinguished Flying Cross (three times) and Joint Service Commendation.

Prior to joining Glenn's staff, Beach worked as a defense consultant initiating and directing a public relations and media policy for an industry client and also served as senior spokesman for that organization.

His naval career covered a wide range of defense and geopolitical staff positions in Washington and overseas. He served as Commanding Officer of a carrier-based aircraft squadron during combat operations in Vietnam— where he completed three tours of duty. He was an Operations and Tactical Officer for conventional and nuclear-powered aircraft carriers, including the Nimitz; Weapons System Research and Development test director for the Navy's independent test agency; and Intelligence Specialist for Europe serving in France and England directing operations for the U.S./NATO Electronic Intelligence Center. While based in England, he served one year in the Royal Air Force. During his career in the U.S. Navy he also served in a joint service capacity covering Army, Navy, Air Force, and Marine Corps issues where he became familiar with the complexities of inter-service functions.

He has two sons who are Navy pilots. Hobbies include golf, handball and flying.

Robert Gregory Bell
Professional Staff Member
222 Russell Senate Office Bldg.
224-9339

Expertise: Arms control, strategic weapons and policy, NATO

With Robert Bell's background and expertise in military and foreign affairs, it is understandable why Senator Sam Nunn, Chairman of the Senate Armed Services Committee, chose Bell as his principal staff assistant on arms control matters. Bell's additional responsibilities include strategic policy and alliance security issues. Finally, Bell serves as Senator Nunn's staff aide on the Senate Arms Control Observers Group (ACOG).

The Arms Control Observers Group was founded by the Senate leadership in January, 1985. Established as an ad hoc organization, this group's primary purpose is monitoring ongoing arms negotiations in Geneva.

The group travels to Geneva approximately four times a year to observe the Nuclear and Space Talks (NST) and received frequent briefings from the Administration and weekly reports on the progress of the negotiations.

"The group has been very successful", says Bell. "The administration sees it as a positive development. As a result of the group's activities, senators are more informed than in the past on arms control negotiations, and receive more information on key issues before votes are made."

The Arms Control Observers Group has also helped to reinforce to the Soviets the idea that certain Soviet actions are not acceptable. Bell believes this approach, which is bipartisan in nature, is an essential factor in ensuring U.S. national security interests.

Personal: born 8/26/47 in Birmingham, Alabama. B.S. Intl. Affairs, U.S. Air Force Academy, 1965-1969. M.A. Intl. Security Studies, Tufts Univ., Fletcher School of Law and Diplomacy, 1969-1970. Graduate course work in defense policy and Soviet foreign policy, Johns Hopkins Univ. School of Advanced International Studies, 1971-1972. 1969-1975, Squadron Commander, U.S. Air Force. 1979, Staff Director, Military Committee, North Atlantic Assembly. 1975-1979 and 1980, Defense Analyst, Assistant Division Chief for Research, Principal CRS Analyst on SALT II for the Congressional Research Service. 1981-1984, Professional Staff Member, Senate Committee on Foreign Relations. 1984-present, Professional Staff Member, Senate Committee on Armed Services.

Yet Bell's work with the committee extends well beyond the ACOG. Indeed, Bell considers his primary function as advancing and implementing various policy initiatives originated by Sen. Nunn. Two recent initiatives include Sen. Nunn's arguments on the interpretation of the 1972 Anti-Ballistic Missile Treaty, and the Senator's successful effort to establish—together with Sen. John Warner (R-VA)—Nuclear Risk Reduction Centers in Washington and Moscow.

The yearly defense authorization bill is another area where Bell has proven to be effective. In particular, Bell was instrumental in assisting Sen. Nunn with several arms control matters that were contained in the bill. And while those issues were contentious, Bell's able assistance helped Sen. Nunn pass them out of the Senate and to the President's desk for signature.

Bell's extensive background with the military is clearly an asset to both the Senator and the Committee.

Bob Bott
Professional Staff Member
232A Russell Senate Office Bldg.
224-8636

Personal: born 2/1/45 in Logansport, Indiana. B.A. Holy Cross Coll., 1967. M.S. in administration of science and technology, George Washington Univ. 1977. 1967-1972, Flight Officer, US Navy. 1972-1975, program analyst, Strategic Systems Project Office, Navy Department. 1975-1981, staff member, Office of Secretary of Defense (OSD), Program Analysis and Evaluation (PA&E). 1984-present, Professional Staff Member, Senate Committee on Armed Services.

Expertise: Nuclear and space systems

Bob Bott's extensive experience in offensive strategic nuclear systems made him a natural selection for handling strategic and theater nuclear systems for the Senate Armed Services Committee. Bott brings a pragmatic, consensus-seeking approach to the issues of nuclear and chemical weapons, missiles, aircraft, submarines, SDI and space systems.

While completing the Navy's ROTC program at Holy Cross, the American history major decided he wanted to fly P-3 Anti-Submarine Warfare aircraft. Says Bott of his 5 years flying P-3s: "Operating out of Iceland was very interesting because there was a lot of exposure to Soviet submarine activity. My most exciting experience was continuing a fairly important operation while the computers and electronics went down." Bott and fellow crewman won the Navy Commendation for their performance.

Bott left the Navy and joined the Navy's Strategic Systems Project Office because, he says, it had the most interesting intern program. While there, he dealt with many facets of the Trident, Poseidon and Polaris weapons systems.

Bott's experience landed him a job in Office of Secretary of Defense's Program, Analysis & Evaluation office to evaluate land-based missile and basing options, conduct targeting research and assess strategic balance and arms control issues. "It was an interesting transition from program analyst to options research analyst. The MX, trench basing, SALT II negotiations and Soviet deployments made for interesting work." The work included a year and a half study of the ICBM modernization issue which led to Secretary of Defense Brown's endorsement of the ICBM Modernization program.

In 1981 Bott was promoted to Director of the Strategic Offensive Forces Division, a Senior Executive Service position in OSD. He recalls the excitement of helping implement the Strategic Modernization program early in an administration committed to rebuilding the U.S. nuclear deterrent.

Handling strategic and theater nuclear systems on the Senate Armed Services Committee staff, Bott has added space systems, SDI, chemical weapons, theater nuclear weapons and the Department of Energy production complex to his plate. Describing his philosophy, Bott says, "My job is not primarily to set agendas or be an advocate–it is to collect and analyze data as objectively as possible and make these data available to our members and let them make the political choices." He has been involved over the last few years in bridging substantial differences in arms control matters regarding SDI and the ABM Treaty, nuclear weapons testing and adherence to the SALT II agreement.

Bott highlights the close vote in favor of the MX, the Navy Strategic Communications System, chemical weapons modernization and SDI when asked about important issues he has dealt with on the Committee. In addition, he has been involved in the Committee's anticipation of the space-launch problem resulting from the Challenger tragedy.

Future priorities in the "sleeper" category include modernizing the aging nuclear weapons production complex. We have to face up to this substantial investment." A second important sleeper issue is space-launch support: "We are billions of dollars behind in our, ability to support our space program."

Summing up his role on a committee handling high-stakes issues, Bott remarks, "Listening and being honest with people makes all the difference in the world."

R. Les Brownlee

Professional Staff Member
232-A Senate Russell Office Bldg.
224-3871

Expertise: Military

Les Brownlee became Deputy Staff Director of the minority staff in January, 1987, and assumed responsibility for issues involving ground warfare and associated tactical air power. Brownlee's twenty-two year Army career and three-year tour on Senator Warner's personal staff have provided him the in-depth experience to deal with the Defense Department's bureaucratic maze.

The retired colonel's infantry experience, including two tours in Vietnam and a three-year tour in Europe, has provided him with intimate knowledge of the environment under which service personnel and weapons must operate. Brownlee notes being an infantry commander, "was quite an experience . . . taking a bunch of guys and equipment, getting them all trained the way you want them trained, and then go out and be severely tested . . . and having them perform very well."

Ensuing assignments enabled Brownlee to utilize his combat experiences in finding solutions to military problems. As Chief of the Doctrine and Systems Integration Division at HQDA, Brownlee developed long-range planning and budgetary guidance for the Army's financial program development. He also assisted the Undersecretary of the Army in developing, directing, and managing procurement programs in excess of $17 billion and R&D programs exceeding $4 billion.

Personal: born 7/11/39 in Pampa, Texas. B.S. Univ. of Wyoming, 1962. M.B.A. Univ. of Alabama, 1969. 1962-1965, rifle platoon leader and company commander in 173rd airborne brigade in Vietnam. 1966-1967, attended Infantry Officers Advanced Course. 1969-70, battalion senior advisor to Republic of Vietnam Army airborne division. 1970-1971, graduate of Army Command and General Staff College. 1971-1973, chief of management division, Office of Management and Budget, Fort Benning. 1973-1975, executive officer of TRADOC Command. 1976-1978, commander, 3rd Battalion, 36th Infantry in Europe. 1978-1979, U.S. Army War College. 1980-1981, chief, doctrine and systems integration division, Requirements Directorate, HQDA. 1981-1983, executive officer to undersecretary of the Army. 1983-1987, national security assistant, Sen. John Warner (R-VA). 1987-present, Deputy Minority Staff Director. Senate Armed Services Committee

Brownlee's path from a rifle platoon leader in Vietnam to the upper echelons of the Army has provided him with unique insight into military issues.

Brownlee has worked on a wide array of issues since coming to the Hill in 1983. During that year, Senators Warner and Nunn surfaced a proposal to establish Nuclear Risk Reduction Centers in both the U.S. and the Soviet Union to help reduce the risk of nuclear war. With the help of Brownlee and others, the Senators' idea is slowly being realized. In September 1987, both nations signed an agreement to build the centers, and Brownlee is currently involved in implementing the agreement.

In 1986, the massive task of passing legislation to reorganize DOD was completed. Brownlee helped Warner gain acceptance of 38 amendments to the Senate's version of the bill.

Brownlee was involved in the National Strategy Act, an initiative to improve Congress's understanding of America's foreign and defense policy strategy so that resources will be better distributed. The legislation, which became law in 1986, dealt with sensitive turf issues between DOD, the State Department, the NSC, and the Commerce Department.

In another effort to promote teamwork, Brownlee assisted Warner in encouraging inter-service cooperation in command, control, and communications programs, big priorities during the Reagan Administration.

In the personnel area, Brownlee helped Senator Warner in his efforts to protect tax benefits in military housing allowances and gain approval of the Overseas Military Personnel Absentee Voting Registration Act.

Brownlee says his job as minority Deputy Staff Director, "is to support the minority Staff Director in any way that he sees as helpful." Doubling as the minority staff person for ground warfare issues, the retired colonel was involved in the House-Senate debate over competition for the next generation of Army heavy trucks, as well as funding for the Anti-Tactical Ballistic Missile program. Implementation of the DOD Reorganization Act and the Nuclear Risk Reduction Centers Agreement also have been, and will continue to be, high priority issues.

The former University of Wyoming football player says future priorities will include the Army Air Defense System, as well as the Army Command and Control System program.

Lorne W. Craner
Legislative Assistant
Senator John McCain (R-AZ)
111 Russell Senate Office Bldg.
224-2235

Expertise: Foreign affairs

In his first job as a staff assistant, Lorne Craner spent a lot of time stuffing envelopes. Now, he is one of the Senate's most knowledgeable staffers on Central America.

Most recently, he was appointed to the Senate Central America Negotiations Observer Group as the minority staffer. The Group originated August 7, 1987, the night of the introduction of the Arias Peace Plan, with the objective of observing and monitoring progress on the negotiations and implementations of any Central America peace plan.

While the focus of his foreign affairs work has been on Central America, Craner terms Asia his real interest in international geopolitics. His international focus may have been shaped by his many travels. Being an Air Force brat, Craner moved frequently while growing up. He still considers traveling one of his favorite pastimes, along with playing squash and reading.

Diversity is one of the characteristics of Crane's Hill career. Aside from his work in foreign affairs, he considers one of his most significant accomplishments to be in the domestic sphere. While he was working for McCain in the House of Representatives, the Administration attempted to cut WIC (Women, Infants and Children) funding, a move that would have affected nutrition for some 300,000 individuals. McCain played an important role in drafting a bill to force the Administration to spend the appropriated funds and backed the Administration down before the cuts were even introduced. Craner is particularly proud of that accomplishment, because of the number of people affected, and because funding for social programs is not typically an issue identified with Republicans.

These accomplishments seem consistent with what Craner regards as his and McCain's management styles—working behind the scenes, focusing on amendments rather than the introduction of bills.

Personal: born 4/16/59 in Bitburg, Germany on U.S. Air Force Base. B.A. in international relations, Reed Coll., 1982. M.A. in national security studies, Georgetown Univ., 1986, with honors. 1983-1984, staff assistant, U.S. Rep. John McCain (R-AZ). 1985, Legislative Assistant, Rep. Jim Kolbe (R-AZ). 1986 to present, Legislative Assistant, Sen. McCain.

Brian D. Dailey
Professional Staff Member
232-A Russell Senate Office Bldg.
224-8630

Expertise: Arms control, strategic issues

Dr. Brian Dailey is relatively new to Washington but not unknown in the Capitol. Before becoming a professional staff member for arms control on the Senate Armed Services Committee, Dailey was an adjunct professor at the Naval Postgraduate School in Monterey, California. He came to the attention there of national security analysts in the U.S. and Europe through his teaching and writing.

Dailey taught courses at the Naval Postgraduate School in nuclear strategy and deterrence, revolution and terrorism, intelligence and strategic deception. This latter issue–strategic deception–and its implications for arms control and military planning has especially caught his interest and later resulted in a 1985 conference on strategic deception which he organized and chaired, and a book, *Soviet Strategic Deception* which he edited.

His work at Monterey allowed him to achieve certain near-term goals before coming to Washington. He says, "My original idea after leaving U.S.C. was to find a place where I could teach, research various issues of interest, and to write my dissertation. After three years at the Naval Postgraduate School, I heard about the position on the Armed Services Committee and applied for it. I have a strong arms control portfolio and felt well-qualified for the job." The professional committee staff, as well as Senators Warner and Thurmond, agreed and Dailey started work on the committee one week before the INF hearings commenced.

Personal: born 8/12/51, Pittsburgh, CA. M.F.A. Otis Art Institute of Los Angeles. B.A. in International Relations, Univ. of Southern California, 1982. M.A. in International Relations (National Security Adviser), 1984. Ph.D. in International Relations (National Security Affairs, Soviet Studies, Foreign Policy Analysis), 1987. 1981-83 Research Assistant, Defense and Strategic Studies Program (DSSP), U.S.C. 1983, Visiting Research Scholar, Hoover Institution on War, Revolution, and Peace, Stanford Univ. 1983-84, Program Teaching Assistant, DSSP, U.S.C. 1984, Acting Assistant Director for Chemical Warfare Negotiations, OSD/ ISP. 1985-88, Adjunct Professor of National Security Affairs, U.S. Naval Postgraduate School, Monterey, California; 1988-present, Professional Staff Member, Armed Services Committee.

Dailey's personal philosophy is best summed up by his comment, "I want to ensure that arms control has a positive impact on supporting U.S. national security. It must maintain the integrity of the U.S. deterrence and defense capability. I want to help put arms control in the proper perspective; it should supplement rather than supplant national security."

Andrew S. Effron
Counsel
222 Russell Senate Office Bldg.
224-8631

Personal: born 9/18/48 In Stamford, Connecticut. B.A., in government, Harvard Coll., 1970. J.D. Harvard Law School, 1975. 1970-1975, Legislative Aide, Rep. William A. Steiger (R-WI). 1976-1977, military attorney, Office of Staff Judge Advocate, Fort McClellan, AL. 1977-1987, attorney, Office of General Counsel, Department of Defense. 1987-present, Counsel, Senate Armed Services Committee.

Expertise: Legislative issues

One of the Hill's most self-effacing staff members, Andrew (Andy) Effron sees his contributions to the legislative process from a strictly professional viewpoint. "My expertise and contributions are in the full range of legal and legislative issues related to national security," he says simply. Asked about his specific contributions or personal activities, Effron clams up. "In my spare time, I read Armed Services Committee hearing transcripts," he says with a laugh.

Effron's colleagues, however, are not so reticent. One Senate defense specialist describes Effron's considerable legal expertise in the acquisitions area as "remarkable. In the relatively short time he has been with the committee, he has covered an awful lot of territory." A case in point was Effron's skillful handling of the National Defense Authorization Act, which was signed into law in December 1987.

As congressional debate continues to focus on the many competing demands to maintain and upgrade U.S. military and defense capabilities in the face of limited resources, so to will Effron's deft approach in helping the Armed Services Committee strike effective and acceptable legislative balances.

Jonathan L. Etherton
Professional Staff Member
232-A Russell Senate Office Bldg.
224-3871

Expertise: Defense acquisition, industry, technology

Jonathan Etherton is considered one of the most knowledgeable staff members on the Hill in the area of defense acquisition policy. Prior to the November, 1986 elections, Etherton was the principal staffer on the Senate Armed Services Committee's Subcommittee on Defense Acquisition Policy. The Subcommittee was chaired by Senator Dan Quayle (R-IN) while the ranking minority member was Senator Carl Levin (D-MI). Following the 1986 elections, the Armed Services Committee was reshuffled and many of the duties previously under the jurisdiction of the Defense Acquisition Policy Subcommittee fell to the newly formed Subcommittee on Defense Industry and Technology, now chaired by Senator Jeff Bingaman (D-NM) with the ranking minority member being Senator Phil Gramm (R-TX). As one of the staffers on this subcommittee, Etherton oversees such issues as the industrial base and procurement policies affecting the defense industry.

According to former colleagues, Etherton is "a hard-working individual who does his homework on defense procurement. He is a key guy in the area of the defense industry and the congressional agenda regarding acquisition policy."

When he finds time to get away from his work on the Senate Armed Services Committee staff, Etherton spends time with one of his other interests—philosophy. During the winter of 1987-1988, he took graduate courses in philosophy at Georgetown University.

Lori Beth Feld
Legislative Director
Senator Paul Trible (R-Va)
517 Hart Senate Office Bldg.
224-4024

Expertise: Civil Service, governmental affairs, defense

Just graduated from the University of Virginia in 1982, Lori Beth Feld thought to herself: "Since the car's paid for and I don't have any major obligations, there is no reason why I can't work for free as an intern for Congressman Trible." Six years later Feld is the Legislative Director for Paul Trible, now the junior Republican Senator from Virginia.

As Legislative Director, Feld oversees all of Senator Trible's legislative initiatives, but has direct responsibility for defense and governmental affairs issues.

Being an "army brat" has helped her to overcome traditional Pentagon wariness of young Hill staffers. She is also comfortable with the Armed Services Committee staff, many of whom are retired from the military. According to Les Brownlee, the Deputy Minority Staff Director for the Armed Services Committee, "Lori Beth is very competent and well organized. She has a good sense of what's going on, and understands the issues."

Feld has extensive knowledge of Virginia's military installations and shares Trible's support for his defense initiatives and his enthusiasm for encouraging the federal government to use the expertise of the defense industry located in Virginia.

Personal: born 8/13/60 in Spokane, Washington. B.A. Univ. of Virginia, 1982. Catholic Univ. Law School 1985-1988. 1982-1983, Staff Assistant, Rep. Paul Trible. 1983-1986, Legislative Assistant; 1987-present, Legislative Director, Sen. Paul Trible.

Feld admits she derives the most satisfaction from legislation which "makes a positive difference in people's lives." A longtime resident of Virginia, Feld is well aware of the state's high proportion of federal employees and has been active in Trible's efforts to improve their benefits, including base pay, merit bonuses, retirement annuities, and day care.

Feld played an important role in a Trible amendment to improve benefits for former spouses of members of the military. Attached to the Department of Defense Authorization in 1985, the amendment "was the only one opposed by the Armed Services Committee that made it," Feld recalls. "It was something we felt very strongly about, and we got it through despite the opposition."

As a full-time law student and Legislative Director, Feld has little spare time for the many sports she once enjoyed. She likes running and reading anything by Ayn Rand.

George K. Johnson, Jr.
Professional Staff Member
232A Russell Senate Office Bldg.
224-8629

Personal: born 5/14/53 in Spartanburg, S.C. B.A. The Citadel, 1975. 1975-1979, Instructor, Army basic training. 1979-1982, Army special forces. 1982 to present, Professional Staff Member (Readiness, Sustainability and Support), Senate Armed Services Committee.

Expertise: Counterterrorism, low intensity conflict, military construction

With his considerable military experience, Ken Johnson has had plenty of training for the position he now holds.

Johnson was hired in 1982 by Sen.John Tower, the former Texas Republican who chaired the committee from 1981-85. He is one of two minority staffers on the Readiness, Sustainability and Support Subcommittee. Johnson also advises Sen. Strom Thurmond, a fellow South Carolinian and a senior member of the Committee, on defense issues and legislation.

On the Subcommittee, Johnson's responsibilities include military construction accounts and defense department reprogramming activities. Johnson also is knowledgeable about counterterrorism and low-intensity conflicts and is one of the committee's experts on special operations forces.

Johnson has responsibility for policy and program oversight for all special operations forces procurement, research and development, and intelligence. He advises Republican members on counterterrorism policies and related defense programs that support those policies. In addition, Johnson reviews Defense Department requests to transfer money between various military construction accounts to cover changes in programs.

Johnson works on the annual defense authorization bill and played a key role in drafting the Cohen-Nunn Special Operations Reorganization Amendment to the 1987 Defense Authorization bill. The amendment requires the establishment of a unified command structure within the military for all special operations forces, as well as the creation of a new position, assistant secretary for special operations forces, within the Defense Department. Unlike its House counterpart, the Senate Armed Services Committee staff has a majority and a minority staff. Nonetheless, Johnson says he maintains an apolitical viewpoint which gives him credibility with members of both sides.

Johnson says his military background is helpful in his job, particularly in dealing with the Pentagon and in advising members, and adds that a majority of staff members have served in the armed forces.

In the Army Special Forces, he served as a brigade-level operations officer and commanded a 250-man Special Forces Operational Detachment and served as a general staff officer responsible for special forces training and deployment around the world. He also was responsible for operational preparation of the Mobile Training Team deployment in support of the U.S. Foreign Military Sales Program.

Ron Kelly
Professional Staff Member
Subcommittee on Readiness,
    Sustainability and Support
232A Russell Senate Office Bldg.
224-8639

Expertise: Readiness, maintenance & operations

After years of dealing with the Congress and its staff, weary of bureaucratic warfare in the Air Force, Ron Kelly decided to take his experience to Capitol Hill. The retired colonel's love for "analytical challenge" and "getting people to talk to each other" suits his position on the Senate Armed Services Committee. After two years working defense and foreign affairs issues for Senator Gordon Humphrey, Kelly moved to the Armed Services Committee to handle the largest portion of the defense budget—readiness, operations, and maintenance—always the target of cuts to pay for more glamorous programs.

While attending the University of North Carolina, Kelly was told he could not obtain an accounting C.P.A. degree and play football at the same time. He chose accounting because he "loved to figure things out." To replace football he joined the Air Force ROTC program. "As it turned out, I liked the Air Force and flying more than accounting, so I made it a career."

Kelly navigated B-52s for the Strategic Air Command (SAC) during a time when strategic missions were one-way trips to the Soviet Union. He also flew many sorties over Vietnam. Early in his career, he earned the responsibility to evaluate and instruct B-52 crews.

Personal: born 7/29/38 in Statesville, North Carolina. B.S. in Accounting, Univ. of North Carolina, 1960. M.B.A. in Accounting, and M.B.A. in Business Management, Florida State Univ., 1972. 1960-1973, navigator and staff assignments, Strategic Air Command (SAC), USAF. 1973-1975, Staff Officer, HQ SAC, responsible for future concepts development. 1975-1981, HQ USAF Program Manager, B-52. 1981, Cost and Performance Analyst, DOD Strategic Bomber Study. 1981, retired from Air Force. 1981-1982, Consultant. 1982-1984, Military and Foreign Affairs Legislative Assistant, Sen.Gordon Humphrey (R-NH). 1984-present, Professional Staff Member, Senate Armed Services Committee.

His eleven years experience in navigator, evaluator and staff assignments provided Kelly with a list of problems to solve when he became an avionics integrator. Says Kelly, "It's a pilot's Air Force, so all improvements went in the pilot's compartment. The rest of the crew was using 20- to 30-year-old equipment and that had to change." Kelly viewed himself as an "interpreter." "You had crews who had problems, and engineers who tried to solve the problems, but because they couldn't understand each other, problems were not really solved. I tried to get them around the table, lock the door and referee until they came up with genuine solutions." With this philosophy, Kelly successfully developed new targeting and strike tactics, including the concept of arming bombers with cruise missiles, and led efforts to enhance B-52 avionics.

On the Committee, Kelly is using his accounting and analytical skills to help Senator Humphrey devise a system in which the true ramifications of cutting readiness, operations and maintenance budget can be understood, and clearly explained. Kelly exclaims, "You don't see articles in the Washington Post when a billion dollars is cut from Operations & Maintenance, but they'll write a full-page article when an aircraft account is stretched out." Because the Operations & Maintenance accounts are lump sum funded, Kelly says, "it is very difficult to precisely explain the consequences of budget decisions."

To accomplish this task Kelly spends a lot of time outside the Washington Beltway. "You cannot legislate this kind of system—

you have to go out in the field and listen to the troops' problems, get the right amount of money to the right people in headquarters, and facilitate their solving the problem. I'm doing now what I did in the Air Force—acting as an interpreter."

Kelly is also helping the Committee to develop better operating cost factors in planning, continue the push for higher ammunition budgets, and get weapons procurers to think about support costs when they purchase weapons systems. Kelly points out that without funding for readiness and Operations & Maintenance, weapons systems could not function.

Because of the complexity of the task, Kelly says it will take a long time to achieve results. He exudes optimism in accomplishing his objective as he relates a story about a recent trip to a SAC base in Grand Forks. A crew member was describing the life of the B-52 to the delegation and said, "A while ago a guy named Ron Kelly fathered the modifications that have kept these aircraft flying." Reflecting on that remark Kelly says, "I hope to stay around that long again."

David S. Lyles
Professional Staff Member
Subcommittee on Readiness,
    Sustainability, and Support
222 Russell Senate Office Bldg.
224-3871

Expertise: Defense, budget, military personnel

As a professional staff member on the Readiness, Sustainability and Support Subcommittee, David Lyles is responsible for one-third of the defense budget. It takes a considerable expertise to oversee the operating and maintenance costs of the military. These funds are for such things as repairs, training, and operating fleets and aircraft of the military services.

In the Air Force, Lyles had experience in analyzing defense expenditures. As a staff member on the Senate Appropriations Committee, he has basically these same budgetary responsibilities. While working for the Secretary of Defense, he worked on the Intergovernmental Affairs Military Manpower Task Force which was established and organized by President Reagan.

"Those who work on the defense and the budget itself have a great deal of influence on those people in uniform," says Lyles.

Personal: born 3/8/51 in Spartanburg, South Carolina. B.A. Oberlin Coll., 1973. M.A., in History, Univ. of Wisconsin, 1976. 1976-1977, budget analyst, U.S. Air Force Budget Office. 1977-1981, Senate Appropriations Committee staff. 1981, Program Analyst, Office of the Secretary of Defense. 1981-present, Professional Staff Member, Senate Armed Services Committee.

Terence M. Lynch
Sen. Richard Shelby (D-AL)
Legislative Assistant
313 Hart Senate Office Bldg.
224-5744

Expertise: Defense/military affairs

Defense analyst and foreign policy advisor Terry Lynch's Congressional career had included just about every job in a Congressional office prior to his joining the legislative staff of Senator Richard C. Shelby. Although Lynch's major focus is the military, he also maintains a fair degree of responsibility in the areas of foreign affairs, budget, and labor issues.

At Shelby's direction, Lynch has directed much of his energy the past few years toward the process of improving U.S. conventional force capability and closing the NATO/Warsaw Pact forces gap.

With respect to strategic forces, Lynch labors diligently to insure Shelby's high profile in protecting the SDI (Strategic Defense Initiative) program from funding cuts, particularly since Huntsville, Alabama, is home to the Army facility from which SDI is managed and overseen.

These issues and a multitude of others, however, will more than likely take a backseat for several months, as Lynch juggles the more immediate demands presented by Senate hearings on the ratification of the intermediate-range nuclear missile treaty (INF) signed by General Secretary Gorbachev and President Reagan in December (1987).

Although Lynch does not have a military background, he has quickly established himself on a committee whose staff is reknowned for its expertise and exacting standards.

An involved civic activist, Lynch lends a good deal of his precious off-Hill time to the Virginia Jaycees as well as other charitable and community services.

Personal: born 9/5/52 in Youngstown, Ohio. B.A. History, Youngstown State Univ., 1975. M.A. History, Youngstown State Univ., 1978. 1979-1981, Legislative Correspondent, Rep. Charles Carney (D-OH). 1981-83, Computer Systems Manager/ Legislative Assistant, Rep. Albert Lee Smith (R-AL). 1983-1987, Legislative Assistant, Rep. Richard Shelby. 1987-present, Legislative Assistant, Senator Richard C. Shelby (D-AL).

William J. Lynn
Legislative Counsel
Senator Edward M. Kennedy (D-MA)
315 Russell Office Bldg.
224-4543

Personal: born 1/1/54 in Key West, Florida. M.P.A. Woodrow Wilson School, Princeton Univ., 1982. J.D. Cornell Univ., 1980. B.A. Dartmouth Coll., 1976. 1976-1977, Assistant Professor of English, Kashan Institute of Science, Kashan, Iran. 1982-1985, Executive Director, Defense Organization Project, Center for Strategic and International Studies. 1985-1986, Professional Staff Member, Institute for Defense Analyses. 1986, Senior Fellow, Strategic Concepts Development Center, National Defense University. 1987-present, Legislative Counsel for defense issues, Senator Edward M. Kennedy (D-MA).

Expertise: Defense organization, arms control, strategic nuclear force

As a member of the Senate Armed Services Committee, Edward M. Kennedy (D-MA), in 1987, sought an individual who had a keen understanding of the U.S. military as well as the needs of the NATO nuclear arsenal. Bill Lynn, with exceptional credentials in these areas, filled this position on Kennedy's staff.

Described as a hard worker concerned with details, Lynn has earned the respect of his colleagues by demonstrating an impressive knowledge of the current state of the United States military.

Lynn's extensive ties to defense-related organizations has enabled him to consider the U.S. military establishment from various viewpoints, ranging from budgetary analyses to political feasibility. He devoted a considerable amount of research to the structure of this country's military forces as it relates to the effectiveness and overall efficiency of the armed forces.

Lynn's contributions to the Defense Organization project at the Center for Strategic and International Studies included a detailed analysis of U.S. Defense structure. The study was a forerunner to the Goldwater-Nichols Defense Reorganization Act of 1986. The study involved a critical assessment of the Joint Chiefs of Staff, as well as recommendations to improve the coordination between the four branches of the U.S. military.

Although with Kennedy only a year, Lynn has been involved in two major overseas trips for his boss. He represented the Senator on a three-day trip to Greenland and the Arctic ice cap. More recently, Lynn and another staff member accompanied Kennedy to the Persian Gulf. The trip provided first-hand experience of the regional conflict, thereby illuminating the ramifications of increased U.S. involvement.

Additionally, Bill Lynn has published works exploring U.S. defense policy, American-Soviet crisis-management, as well as nuclear arms control. These include his book entitled *Toward a More Effective Defense*, and various articles and book reviews which display his grasp of current security issues.

An avid tennis player, Lynn's expertise on defense matters and Hill experience have made him an invaluable member of the Kennedy staff and the Armed Services Committee, as well as a sought after tennis partner.

Norman G. Mosher
Professional Staff Member
Subcommittee on Projection
  Forces and Regional Defense
222 Russell Senate Office Bldg.
224-3871

Personal: born 10/2/35, Glens Falls, New York. B.A. Boston Univ., 1957. MA/MALD Fletcher School of Law and Diplomacy, 1958. Officers' Candidate School, Newport, R.I., 1958. 1958-1984, U.S. Navy. 1984-1985, president of a hi-tech start-up company, Washington, D.C. 1985-1987 Fruehauf Corporation, Detroit. 1987-present, Professional staff member, Senate Committee on Armed Services.

Expertise: Naval force structure issues

Norman Mosher came to the Senate Armed Services Committee earlier this year after a successful 27-year Naval career, commanding ships in both the Atlantic and the Pacific. He also served in Washington, D.C., and at the Pentagon, gaining the experience that now makes him valuable to the Armed Services Committee.

Naval force structure is Mosher's area of expertise and responsibility. He says this means deciding "what, when, how, and for what reasons to build." He is also in charge of the Subcommittee on Projection Forces and Regional Defense, as well as the budget-oversight of the Navy shipbuilding program, including ASW aircraft.

Other areas of responsibility include the U.S. Marine Corps' aviation equipment; military transportation command, both airlift and sealift; and all special operations forces. He also influences related issues affecting procurement and research and development.

Mosher feels the United States needs a strong defense behind which the "greatest social experiment ever can continue to grow and prosper." The problem, according to Mosher, is affordability within a constrained defense budget.

The Department of Defense Authorization Act has occupied most of Mosher's attention since he joined the Committee. He has been involved in resolving program issues and tailoring the budget. In 1987, the DOD budget had to be reduced over $30 billion in response to the budget request from Congress, and Mosher was involved in picking the strategies and making the choices that accomplished this goal.

When the Committee starts hearings in preparation for defense authorizations in 1989, Mosher, who prefers to remain apolitical where Naval defense issues are concerned, will be involved in deciding how to fill the gaps in defense left by budget reductions.

Mosher and his wife are the parents of six children and have raised Portuguese Water dogs for the past four years. They also enjoy sailing and skiing.

Frederick F. Y. Pang
Professional Staff Member
Subcommittee on Manpower &
  Personnel
222 Russell Senate Office Bldg.
224-3871

Personal: born 11/16/36 in Honolulu, Hawaii. B.A. in Education, Univ. of Hawaii, 1958. M.B.A. Univ. of Hawaii, 1972. 1959-1986, United States Air Force, including: 1974-1977, Chief, Total Officer Force Programs, USAF headquarters; 1977-1980, Assistant Director, Officer Force Structures; 1980-1982, Director of Officer Personnel Management; 1982-1984, Director of Officer and Enlisted Personnel Management, Office of the Secretary of Defense; 1984-1986, Director of Compensation, Office of the Secretary of Defense. 1986-1987, management consultant, Research Consultants, Inc., Tysons Corner, VA. 1987-present, Professional Staff Member, Senate Committee on Armed Services.

Expertise: Manpower and personnel

Fred Pang is a retired Air Force Colonel who spent 27 years in the service. His interest in manpower and personnel issues began at the base level. As he defines it, "manpower" means meeting the demand for people in the armed services while taking force structure, doctrine and emerging technology into consideration. "Personnel" means how you bring people into the military, and educate, train, assign, develop, and serve them and their families.

Pang's competence and his love of his work eventually landed him in the Office of the Secretary of Defense, where he was entrusted with the job of formulating and overseeing Defense policy on manpower and personnel issues for the entire military.

Pang, who was actively recruited for a position on the Senate Armed Services Committee by the Democrats when they regained control, finds himself working the other side of the issue. Instead of formulating the policy, he is now in charge of analyzing, weighing, recommending, and tailoring proposals from the Department of Defense to fit the newly constrained Defense budget.

Pang works closely with Senator John Glenn (D-OH), the chairman of the Senate Armed Services Subcommittee on Manpower and Personnel. Senator Glenn describes Pang as "extremely knowledgeable and experienced in manpower issues." This is almost an understatement, for Pang has consistently demonstrated that he is one of the Hill experts in his field. He has concentrated on what he calls the "human" side of the military: providing for the well-being of the military member, whether active, in the reserves or retired, and their families.

Since Pang began his work at the Committee, his main chore has been to oversee the manpower and personnel section of the DOD Authorization Act for Fiscal Years 1988 and 1989. This work includes authorizing certain strength levels, spending and new entitlements. His work has been guided by Senator Glenn's philosophy that our number one priority should be combat readiness—making sure that our fighting forces are ready to go, and trained well enough to be able to return safely. Pang's other responsibilities include "support" programs that help improve the quality of military life.

One of Pang's priorities is helping to insure the readiness of our reserve forces. He feels there is a great need to correct training and manpower problems. Pang is particularly concerned with how the reserve forces, which constitute one-half of the army, will integrate under the total force. He is most skeptical about the capabilities of the medical reserve personnel. He hopes to be able to work with DOD on this problem.

He will also be working with the Defense Department on the CHAMPUS Reform Initiative. The costs of CHAMPUS, which provides peace time medical care for dependents, families, and retirees, have soared in recent years. Pang hopes that reform will help CHAMPUS to contain costs and become more efficient, and provide better service. Pang sees this as a major undertaking.

Pang will continue to push DOD toward a more coherent policy on manpower and personnel budget issues.

Pang credits the "brilliance" of Glenn and Senate Armed Services Chairman Sam Nunn (D-GA) as the attraction for him to leave the private sector and come work on Capitol Hill. He firmly believes the work the committee does is a priority for the nation.

Pang enjoys tennis and gardening. He has also competed in the Marine Corps marathon and the Virginia Beach and Honolulu marathons. He and Brenda, his wife of 23 years, have two children.

Al Ptak
National Security Legislative
  Assistant
Senator Phil Gramm (R-TX)
370 Russell Senate Office Bldg.
224-2934

Personal: born 8/25/49 in Cleveland, Ohio. B.S. U.S. Naval Academy, 1971. 1971-1975, Anti-Submarine Warfare Officer and Weapons Officer, U.S.S. Calcaterra. 1973-1975, Anti-Submarine Warfare Officer and Weapons Officer, U.S.S. Pratt. 1975-1977, Congressional Committee Liaison Officer under the Secretary of the Navy. 1978-1980, Weapons Officer, U.S.S. Manley. 1980-1981, Assistant Legislative Counsel, CIA. 1981-1985, Senior Legislative Liaison Officer, Intelligence Community Staff. 1985 to present, National Security Legislative Assistant, Sen. Phil Gramm (R-TX).

Expertise: Intelligence, naval weapons systems

In 1985, when Sen. Gramm needed a national security assistant with military experience, he called on Al Ptak, a naval officer with an in-depth knowledge of the military, the intelligence community, the budget process, and the workings of Capitol Hill.

Ptak, a former Anti-Submarine Warfare and Weapons Officer, has unique hands-on experience with naval strategies, tactics, operations, weapons systems and intelligence gathering.

His expertise in intelligence matters helped land him a job as Assistant Legislative Counsel to the Director of Central Intelligence. He worked closely with the Congress in gaining approval of the CIA's budget and provided information on significant intelligence developments. Ptak's interaction with the Armed Services, Budget, Appropriations, and Judiciary Committees in the Senate and the House Appropriations Committee was enhanced when he was promoted to Senior Legislative Liaison on the Intelligence Community staff. Reflecting on his military background and involvement with the budget process and major intelligence programs, Ptak says he "has a sense of how the military and intelligence community interact in support of our defense and foreign policy."

As a member of Gramm's staff, Ptak has worked on the Conventional Defense and Balanced Technology Initiatives—offspring of the SDI program designed to bolster U.S. leadership in conventional defense technologies.

Ptak believes the U.S. must continue to lead the world in developing conventional weapons and would like to see greater emphasis placed on their development and deployment. "What keeps us ahead of the Soviets is our technological base," he says.

Ptak is helping Sen. Gramm explore more efficient procurement procedures. One idea under consideration is the creation of a career service for defense contracting officers.

Ptak says he is excited about opportunities to develop and implement technological breakthroughs so that they can be made part of the nation's defense effort. As a Commander in the Naval Reserves, Ptak also is "enthusiastic about the transformation of pride in the military" in recent years. "Quietly, twenty-four hours a day, three hundred sixty-five days a year, excellent people are working to defend the country."

Arnold L. Punaro
Staff Director
222 Russell Senate Office Bldg.
224-9337

Expertise: National security affairs

When one considers the fact that the Senate Armed Services Committee has nearly two dozen Members, fifty staff people and jurisdiction of over thirty percent of the federal budget, one can appreciate the magnitude of Arnold Punaro's responsibilities as that committee's staff director. The Staff Director is responsible for directing the Committee's staff in support of the members' review of the defense budget and related activities.

Punaro must oversee the work of the full committee and its six subcommittees. Because he is the Committee's top staffer, his involvement with the subcommittees includes both defense policy and administrative responsibilities. In other words, he keeps a watchful eye on virtually everything associated with the Committee.

Punaro views the Senate Armed Services Committee much like a business: it must be run efficiently. According to Punaro, one of the best ways to do that is by effective management. Thus, when Senator Nunn became the Committee's chairman early last year, he initiated, with Punaro's assistance, numerous procedures that have improved the Committee's operations.

Personal: born 8/10/46 in Augusta, Georgia. B.S. Spring Hill Coll., 1968. M.A. Univ. of Georgia, 1973. M.A. Georgetown Univ., 1979. Entered active duty as Private, U.S. Marine Corps, 1969; released as 1st Lt. in 1972 after service in Vietnam. 1973-1977, Press & Legislative Assistant, Sen. Sam Nunn. 1977-1983, Director of National Security Affairs, Sen. Sam Nunn. 1983-1987, Minority Staff Director; 1987-present, Staff Director, Senate Armed Services Committee.

These reforms include regulations on running hearings, the printing of transcripts, two-year budgeting, foreign travel, security classification procedures and the processing of nominations. Most importantly, the Committee has shifted its focus to a more mission-orientation, with a particular emphasis on the major requirements of defense such as nuclear deterrence and NATO defense.

Punaro also believes that Senator Nunn's stewardship has given the Committee a different focus on America's defense establishment. By moving the Committee and hopefully the rest of the defense community away from the minutia of line-item defense budgets, Punaro believes that Nunn has correctly refocused the decisions to broad national security policy.

Over his many years on the Senate staff, Punaro has been involved in many complex and controversial issues. In 1985 he was involved with the reorganization of the Defense Department including the reform of the Joint Chiefs of Staff. He has also worked on widely diverse security issues ranging from draft registration to the MX Missile to the NATO alliance.

A Vietnam veteran who served as a Infantry Platoon Commander, Punaro was awarded both the Bronze Star for valor and the Purple Heart. He is currently a lieutenant colonel in the U.S. Marine Corps Reserves.

Pat Putignano
Military Assistant
Senator John McCain (R-AZ)
111 Russell Senate Office Bldg.
224-2235

Personal: born 8/10/51 in San Angelo, Texas. B.S. U.S. Military Academy, 1973. M.A. Woodrow Wilson School of Public and International Affairs, 1981. 1972, Supreme Headquarters Allied Powers Europe, staff member. 1973, Assistant to Commissioner, Mayor's Office for Veterans Action, New York City. 1974-1975, Supervisor and Personnel Manager, U.S. Army unit. 1978-1979, Training Manager and Coordinator, Army Division Staff, Germany. 1980, Assistant to the President's Principal Aide on Iran, Middle East Office, NSC. 1983, Assistant to Special Assistant to the President, Near East and South Asia Office, NSC. 1981-1984, Assistant Professor, U.S. Military Academy. 1984-1985, White House Fellow. 1985-1987, War-gamer, Center for Army Tactics, Fort Leavenworth, Kansas. 1987 to present, Military Assistant, Senator John McCain (R-AZ).

Expertise: Army personnel, war-gaming, policy analysis

When Sen. McCain arrived in Washington in January, 1987, the former Navy Captain brought with him vast knowledge of defense affairs from a naval perspective. Pat Putignano complements his boss with considerable knowledge and broad experience in military affairs from the outlook of a former Army officer. In-depth knowledge of Army personnel, training, management, and war-gaming, coupled with positions involving intelligence and policy analysis provide Putignano breadth and insight when considering military issues on Capitol Hill.

Although Putignano is not responsible for foreign affairs for McCain, he has gained expertise and understanding about the context in which the U.S. military must operate. Two stints at the NSC under both Presidents Carter and Reagan afforded Putignano valuable experience in intelligence affairs covering the Middle East.

Putignano's position as a war-gamer at the Center for Army Tactics rounded out the in-depth military experience McCain required in a military assistant. Responsible for Senate Armed Services Committee issues, particularly those under the Force Projection, Manpower, and Readiness and Sustainability Subcommittees, Putignano has staked out a balanced approach to the nation's defense.

"We are a maritime *and* a continental nation . . . I won't favor either a maritime strategy or a continental strategy over one another." On complementing McCain's Navy background he says, "What I bring to this party is a little bit of ground experience."

Putignano helped McCain and his allies gain authorization of funds for the AH-64 attack helicopter, a program for which the Administration requested no FY 89 funds. "Having flown the AH-64 and its predecessor . . . I say bravo for the AH-64." Putignano expects McCain will play an important role in shaping the next generation of helicopters, the LHX.

As a strong supporter of the Navy's Forward Deployment strategy, Putignano also took great interest in authorization of two new aircraft carriers. "They are just amazing weapons platforms."

Personnel issues have also been a focus for Sen. McCain, particularly pay increases and officer reduction. While Putignano stated the services' arguments against reducing the Officer Corps, the former officer and personnel manager concludes that, "the ratio of officers to enlisted is just too high."

Samuel J. Routson
Administrative Assistant/Legislative
    Director
Sen. Steve Symms (R-ID)
509 Hart Senate Office Bldg.
224-6142

Expertise: Defense and office administration

Sam Routson is not your average congressional staffer. He has an unusual first-hand approach to research, as noted by *The New York Times* (January 23, 1984): "The chief administrative assistant to a Republican Senator from Idaho said today that he made a secret trip into the Nicaraguan jungle last month to meet with Eden Pastora Gomez, the leader of one of two main rebel factions seeking the overthrow of the Nicaraguan Government."

The *Times* continued "A congressional official who was informed about the trip after the aide's return. . .said the aide carried a rifle at times while inside Nicaragua. The aide to Senator Steven Symms, Samuel T. Routson, is a 34-year old former Marine officer who commanded a rifle company in Vietnam and now holds the rank of major in the Marine Corps reserves."

Lately Routson has settled for doing battle in Washington as Administrative Assistant and Legislative Director for Senator Steve Symms. With his military service and master's in national security studies, Routson is Symms's advisor on defense and armed services issues.

"I come from a work ethic based on a family farm background," notes Routson. "Because of this, I consider myself a loyal, conscientious worker used to long, hard hours. I believe I approach problems and challenges in a logical, common sense fashion."

Personal: born 11/26/49 in Weiser, Idaho. B.S. in forestry, Univ. of Idaho, 1972. B.A. in political science Brigham Young Univ., 1977. J.D. Brigham Young Univ. 1980. M.A. in National Security Studies, Georgetown Univ., 1986. Military Service: United States Marine Corps, 1972-1976, served in Southeast Asia; currently a Major in the USMC Reserves. White House military aide to President Gerald Ford. 1980, area and field representative for "Symms for Senate" campaign. 1981-1983, Legislative Assistant and Counsel; 1983-present, Administrative Assistant/Legislative Director, Sen. Steve Symms (R-ID).

Sam Routson believes in the need to maintain a strong national security in order to deter aggression throughout the world. He has traveled extensively and, in addition to Nicaragua, has visited many of the world's other trouble spots to see first-hand the conflicts affecting issues before the Armed Services Committee. Some of these include traveling throughout the Far East, Southeast Asia, Africa, and the Middle East and meeting with rebel forces in Angola, as well as Nicaragua. He has also been an observer to the presidential elections in El Salvador, Guatemala and Nicaragua.

Routson is married and has six children.

Charles C. Smith, Jr
Legislative Assistant
Senator Alan Dixon (D-IL)
331 Hart Senate Office Bldg.
224-2854

Personal: born 10/12/44 in Chicago, IL. B.S. in Political Science, Loyola Univ., 1966. M.A. in Business and Public Administration, Sangamon State Univ., Springfield, Illinois, 1972. 1966-71, U.S. Army Intelligence Command, Special Agent and Intelligence Officer. Joint Commendation Award for Service in Vietnam. 1972-73, Administrative Assistant to Illinois Secretary of State. 1973-77, Assistant to President and CEO of Aries Limited. 1977-81, Illinois Assistant Deputy Secretary of State. 1981-present, Legislative Assistant to Senator Dixon.

Expertise: Defense, small business, communications, shipping

One might assume the staff of the Senate Armed Service Committee with its multifaceted expertise would leave little for personal staff of Senators on the Committee to contribute. That is not the case.

Charles Smith is recognized by both committee and personal staff as an example of the personal staff legislative assistant who, in carrying out his Senator's responsibilities, has an impact within the Committee.

By his own admission, Smith is sensitive to both the congressional and defense establishment perspectives, an orientation which means a less confrontational approach. He also clearly benefits from Chairman Nunn's insistence that committee and personal staffs work closely together.

Smith considers his most significant achievement with the Armed Service Committee to be his role in helping to draft, while in the minority, the Small Business amendments to the 1985 Defense Authorization Act. He also was involved in the legislation which created the position of an Under Secretary of Defense for Acquisition and the Amendments on Technical Data Rights and Special Tooling in the 1988 bill.

Smith views the amendments addressing technical data rights and special tooling in the 1988 bill to be of considerable significance.

Versatility is one of the requirements of Smith's position. In addition to his work with the Armed Services Committee, he has been deeply involved with small business and protection of Great Lakes shipping. In fact, he considers his work with Industrial Base legislation his greatest strength. Moreover, of all the bills he has been involved with, he believes he would most like to be identified with the Small Business Competition Enhancement Act of 1985.

Smith views his role as that of an intermediary between the Senator and the staff of the Armed Service Committee.

Smith is a Chicago Cubs and Notre Dame Irish fan and will always be found rooting for the Chicago Bears. He also enjoys golf and bridge.

Jeffrey H. Smith
General Counsel
222 Russell Senate Office Bldg.
224-3871

Personal: born 10/24/44 in Salina, Kansas. B.S. United States Military Academy, West Point, New York, 1966. U.S. Army Infantry, 1966-1968. J.D. Univ. of Michigan, 1971. 1971-1973, Office of International Affairs, Office of the Judge Advocate General, Pentagon. 1973-1975, Legal Adviser to the Deputy Undersecretary of the Army, member of the U.S. delegation to the Panama Canal Treaty negotiations, 1975-1984, Office of the Legal Adviser, Dept. of State. 1981-1984, Assistant Legal Adviser for Law Enforcement and Intelligence, 1984-present, General Counsel, Senate Armed Services Committee.

Expertise: Intelligence & foreign policy matters

Jeff Smith has been on the frontlines of U.S. foreign policy in the 1970s and 80s—helping negotiate the transfer of the Panama Canal, involved with the Church and Pike Committee investigations of the intelligence community and negotiating for the U.S. in an incident at JFK Airport in New York City regarding a Soviet ballerina who attempted to defect to this country. In 1980, he was sent to South Korea to be the U.S. trial observer at the trial of Kim Dae Jung, the South Korean opposition leader. At the State Department, Smith negotiated several extradition treaties and also negotiated and conducted several exchanges, in Berlin and Cuba, of imprisoned intelligence agents.

In 1981, he was promoted to the position of Assistant Legal Adviser for Law Enforcement and Intelligence. He was responsible for directing the office that provides legal advice and operational assistance to the Secretary of State and other top officials on intelligence activities; and criminal law matters, such as extradition treaties, terrorism, and narcotics.

When the powerful ranking member of the Senate Armed Services Committee, Senator Henry M. Jackson of Washington, died and was replaced by Senator Sam Nunn of Georgia, Smith was offered in 1984 the job of Minority Counsel to the Armed Services Committee. Since he was not a career Foreign Service officer, or a political appointee, and therefore had risen as high as he could in the State Department, Smith seized the opportunity to continue his work on intelligence and foreign policy matters. When the Democrats regained control of the Senate in 1986, Smith became the General Counsel to the Committee.

As such, he oversees ethical questions, technical legal questions on legislation, and parliamentary procedure on the Senate floor. He also is the senior staff member for foreign policy matters, Nunn's designee to the Senate Select Intelligence Committee, and was Nunn's designee to the Iran/Contra Committee. He also was one of the main staff people who worked with Nunn on the reinterpretation of the ABM treaty in 1987 when Nunn challenged the Reagan Administration's views on the legal interpretation of that treaty.

According to Smith, the top two priorities for the Committee for the second session of the 100th Congress will be the INF treaty with the Soviets and the defense authorization bill.

Henry David Sokolski
Legislative Assistant
Sen. Dan Quayle (R-IN)
524 Senate Hart Office Bldg.
224-5623

Expertise: Military/foreign affairs

When Senator Gordon Humphrey (R-NH) was in search of a professional staff member to aid him in his opposition to Tennessee's Clinch River Breeder Reactor, Henry Sokolski left the Heritage Foundation and the Hoover Institute and directed his energy toward providing the Senator with fuel for his fire.

Uniting an unlikely coalition of fiscal conservatives, environmental leaders and antinuclear groups, Sokolski focused on the economics of the issue, arguing that the Clinch River breeder could not be justified on economic grounds. He calculated that a majority of Congress, once properly educated, would come to the same conclusion. He was right.

The $4 billion plus project, designed in the early 1970s appealed nationwide to those who forecasted uranium shortages and increased electricity demands. To them, Clinch River was a major energy breakthrough. But eleven years and a couple of billion dollars later, the controversial project became the victim of changing economic and environmental times. Uranium supplies had soared while electric demands dropped. Humphrey fired the fatal shot in the form of a four-hour Senate debate against the bill. Sokolski said his ideologically diverse allies "proved that if you have the arguments, you can reverse people's views. It requires a lot of work and it may only happen every ten years, but it's those once-in-a decade events that define why people come to this city."

Personal: born 7/10/51 in San Francisco, California. B.A. Pomona Coll., 1972 (cum laude). A.B.D. Univ. of Chicago. M.A. Univ. of Chicago, 1980. 1981, Public Affairs Fellow, The Hoover Institute. 1982, Visiting Scholar, The Heritage Foundation. 1983 (summer), consultant, National Intelligence Council. 1982-1984, Legislative Assistant, Senator Gordon Humphrey (R-NH). 1984-present, Military Legislative Assistant, Senator Dan Quayle (R-IN).

Foreign affairs and related funding controversies have become Sokolski's focus over the past four years with Senator Dan Quayle (R-IN).

The areas of primary importance to Quayle and his aide are near-term applications of strategic defense technologies (Sokolski has particular expertise in this area); critiquing the recently-signed INF Treaty; and offering improvements to anti-tactical ballistic missile defenses, or drawing attention to the value and importance of cruise missile technology. In addition, Quayle has been very active with NATO arms cooperation issues.

Sokolski once had his own bicycle business—with exclusive rights to rent to the Holiday Inns of America. He still enjoys high performance bikes. He spends free time tinkering with a rebuilt 1970 Cutlass and 1972 Corvette.

Karl Henry Stegenga
Legislative Assistant
Senator Dan Quayle (R-IN)
524 Hart Senate Office Bldg.
224-5623

Expertise: Defense

As a senior Republican member and frequent conferee on the Armed Services Committee, Senator Dan Quayle (R-IN) plays a key role in the formulation of national defense and appropriations issues. One of his Legislative Assistants for defense issues is Karl Stegenga. Stegenga prepares research, written materials and policy advice for the Senator about upcoming legislation in these areas.

Stegenga chose to intern for Senator Quayle as a part of the "Washington Honors" program at Hope College during his senior year. His academic focus was defense policy, so he elected to serve his internship with a member of the Armed Services Committee. Stegenga continued to work for Quayle as a legislative correspondent while he completed his master's degree in international security affairs and was promoted to legislative assistant.

Providing support for the Senator's "corporate constituency" is one of Stegenga's major duties, particularly in helping Indiana companies deal with the Department of Defense. Working with Senator Levin's (D-MI) staff, Stegenga arranged meetings with Indiana subcontractors and national associations to successfully amend the Prompt Payment Act of 1986. He is also involved with veteran's issues and defense procurement. The focus of his work is fairly narrow concerning appropriations. "I look at budget issues at the program level as opposed to worrying about the INF treaty. I keep an eye on the dollars in the bill which will go to DOD programs in Indiana."

Stegenga says he will continue to work on his usual programmatic issues, such as the demilitarization proposal by the Army of chemical weapons stocks. Stegenga prefers to keep a very low profile in his contributions to the work of the Committee.

His extracurricular interests include skiing and record collecting, and he's an avid ice hockey fan. However, his primary interest is job-related: defense policy theory.

Personal: born 11/13/57 in Holland, MI. B.S. Hope Coll., 1981. M.S. Georgetown Univ., 1984. 1981-1983, Legislative Correspondent, Office of Senator Dan Quayle (R-IN). 1983 to present, Legislative Assistant, Senator Dan Quayle.

Jeffrey Bernard Subko
Legislative Assistant
Senator J. James Exon (D-NE)
330 Hart Office Bldg.
224-4224

*Personal: born 4/4/56 in Chicago,
Illinois. B.A. International Affairs, Univ.
of Southern California, 1978. M.A.
National Security Studies, Georgetown
Univ., 1985. 1978-1982, Lieutenant,
U.S. Navy, Surface Warfare–Destroyer.
1982-1983, Professional Analyst–
Naval Tactics, Delex Systems. 1983-
present, Legislative Assistant, Sen. J.
James Exon. 1982-present, Lieutenant
Commander, U.S. Naval Reserve,
Intelligence.*

Expertise: Defense, foreign policy, intelligence, veterans affairs

Jeffrey Subko has successfully blended two public service careers: first, as a military professional and second, as a congressional staffer. The majority of Subko's time is allocated to the annual $300 billion Armed Services Authorization Bill. He is specifically responsible for covering the subcommittees on Strategic Forces and Nuclear Deterrence, Projections Forces and Regional Defense, and Manpower and Personnel.

While Exon is committed to a strong defense and capable military, he is also a fiscal conservative and feels that the military needs to deal with the nation's budget realities. "Hopefully," he states, "the Pentagon will be starting to make some hard choices. While a proper defense is critical, DOD can't have everything. Decisions need to be made on the proper share of the defense budget that will be allocated to nuclear versus conventional forces, future research and development versus current equipment among the various branches of the military. Some programs will have to be killed."

Subko aided Senator Exon during the arduous consideration of the Goldwater-Nickles Department of Defense Reorganization Bill of 1986. "Streamlining the chain of command within DOD and reducing costly duplication," he explained, "were the paramount objectives of this bill." The intent of the bill was to instill a new attitude among Pentagon bureaucrats, so that overseas troops will get more support.

Subko was also involved in Exon's response to the MX. He built the case for Exon's view that the MX can only be a valuable and cost-effective system if it is a mobile system. He rejected the Air Force's proposal to base the missiles in silos; however he feels that their new railroad basing proposal has merit. Similarly, he views the Midgetman system as extravagant. While potentially useful, according to Subko, the Midgetman is too light and ultimately will cost $30 billion more than the MX.

For Jeffrey Subko, future defense issues include funding for SDI, ICBM modernization, space defenses, navy ship building and arms control. He feels that the INF Treaty, which is likely to be passed, should not reduce troop levels or weapons. In fact, the treaty may result in higher budgets for conventional forces, since the threat to NATO remains, ". . . unless we lapse into a false sense of security and bring the troops home."

Unsurprisingly, Subko is a military history buff. When he is not on Capitol Hill, one can often find him walking the battlegrounds at Gettysburg or Chancellorsville.

Patrick A. Tucker
Minority Counsel
232-A Senate Russell Office Bldg.
224-3871

Personal: born 3/17/47 in Beckley, West Virginia. B.S. in public administration, Virginia Polytechnic Inst., 1969. J.D. Honors, George Washington Univ., 1972. 1972-1974, Assistant Staff Judge Advocate, USAF. 1974-1975, Area Defense Counsel, USAF. 1975-1978, Staff Judge Advocate, USAF. 1978-1980, Associate Appellate Defense Counsel, USAF. 1980-1983, Attorney-Advisor, Office of Judge Advocate General, Department of the Air Force. 1983-1985, Counsel; 1985-87, General Counsel; 1987-present, Minority Counsel, Senate Armed Services Committee.

Expertise: Legal affairs, legislative process, manpower and personnel programs

Eight years of legal experience as a judge advocate and three years as a civilian attorney-advisor on legislation with the Air Force prepared Patrick Tucker well for his current position as minority counsel.

Of his legal career in the Air Force, Tucker observes "There are a lot of opportunities as a judge advocate." During his first tour as Assistant Staff Judge Advocate, he tried and defended criminal cases, was legal advisor to various administrative board proceedings, and also handled environmental and labor law issues, and claims against the government. Tucker decided he enjoyed trying criminal cases the most, and volunteered to go to Thailand as a defense counsel for his second tour where drug and AWOL cases proved to be standard fare.

Tucker broadened his experience during his third tour as Staff Judge Advocate at Fort Lee AFB, Virginia. The assignment required extensive travel to Air Force installations throughout the Southeast and, for his efforts, he earned the honor of Aerospace Defense Command Outstanding Judge Advocate of the Year.

Tucker finished his active-duty arguing criminal appeals as lead defense counsel before the Courts of Military Review and the U.S. Court of Military Appeals. Tucker says of this tour, "I had done most everything I had wanted to do in the Air Force as Judge Advocate . . . when the opportunity arose to work as a civilian for the Air Force Office of the Judge Advocate General doing legislation." Tucker reviewed large numbers of legislative proposals arising within the Defense Department and helped draft several major bills, including the Defense Officer Personnel Management Act, and the Uniformed Services Pay and Benefits Act of 1983, both of which became public law. While there, the Air Force reservist earned honors as the USAF Judiciary Outstanding Reserve Judge Advocate of the Year.

As minority counsel to the Committee, Tucker provides all legal advice, and handles nominations, parliamentary procedure, and interpretation of legislation.

One important legal issue he has worked on involves interpretation of the 1972 ABM Treaty. "The question of interpretation of the Treaty has certainly been presented in legal terms; although in my view, it is more of a policy issue than a legal issue . . . There is a good legal argument to be made on both sides, so the issue is which side is better from a policy point of view . . . if it is not clear the Soviets are bound to a narrow interpretation of the Treaty, then we should not be so bound." Tucker is now working on similar issues arising from the ratification process of the INF Treaty.

Tucker also dealt with the nomination procedures of the Marine Corps' general officer promotion board, a sensitive issue with implications for the civilian-military relationship in the Department of Defense. In addition, he has an ongoing interest in the military's criminal justice system, and is studying the issue of the status of the Court of Military Appeals.

Tucker has helped push through major reforms of large military programs. Reform of the retirement system was a decade-old debate until the Committee reformed the system in 1986. Observes Tucker, "I had been on active-duty during this time and . . . the continued debate . . . was causing a lot more morale problems than a slight retirement benefits reduction for personnel who join the service after the law was implemented." 1987 "was the first year there had been no debate on retirement reform in many years. Hopefully, the issue is settled for a while."

Tucker is also actively involved in urging the reform of the military health care system. With his help, the DOD designed, and the Congress approved, a new system that is currently being tested for implementation.

Other issues Tucker is involved in include military pay and personnel retention, particularly with pilots, medical personnel, and nuclear engineers.

Phillip P. Upschulte
Chief of Staff
Senator John Glenn (D-OH)
503 Hart Senate Office Bldg.
224-3353

Personal: born 9/16/32 in Quincy, Illinois. B.A. Univ. of Chicago, 1952. M.B.A. George Washington Univ., 1981. Ph.D. Nova Univ., 1978. 1952-1983, U.S. Marine Corps. 1983-1984, Defense Legislative Assistant; 1985-1986, Director of Foreign Policy and Defense; 1985, Legislative Director; 1986-present, Chief of Staff, Senator John Glenn (D-OH).

Expertise: Defense, foreign policy

As a Marine Down Range Recovery Officer for NASA's Project Mercury in the 1960s, Phil Upschulte piloted the helicopter that rescued astronaut Gus Grissom from his sinking capsule in the Atlantic Ocean. He was there, too, for the recoveries of astronauts Shepherd, Cooper and Schirra on their more normal re-entries from space. But as luck and the schedule would have it, he was not close at hand for the recovery of John Glenn. However when Upschulte retired from the Marine Corps in 1983, Glenn, now a Democratic Senator from Ohio, hired him as his legislative assistant for defense.

As one of the Hill's few Chiefs of Staff who also is a Legislative Director, Upschulte runs Glenn's staff both administratively and legislatively, concentrating on issues of defense and foreign policy, areas with which the Senator is profoundly concerned. Issues affecting the Armed Services Subcommittee on Manpower and Personnel, which Glenn chairs, are a particular priority.

In his foreign policy and defense role, Upschulte's own long experience in the Marine Corps provides him with his best reference on military realities. He was executive assistant to the Marine Corps Deputy Chief of Staff for Aviation, Chief of Staff for the First Marine Aircraft Wing in Okinawa, Chairman of the Department of Military Strategy at the National War College, Director for General Plans for NATO's Adm. Isaac C. Kidd, and Air Force Operations Officer for the Fleet Marine Force Atlantic. He was a helicopter pilot in Vietnam and served as Air Operations Officer of the USS Valley Forge from 1965-1967. He also has extensive experience in weapons testing and supervised the introduction of the Bronco aircraft into the Marine Corps.

In the halls of Congress, Upschulte promotes Glenn's position on matter such as retaining the land-based small ICBM system rather than the MX missile (which Glenn regards as a target with less survivability and deterrence capability), support for the Triad and military budget controls such as those Glenn advocated for the B-1 bomber, which resulted in bringing the plane in under budget and ahead of schedule.

Believing that nuclear arms control will not result in a major cutback in costs because of the resulting upgrade in conventional systems, Upschulte advocates closer coordination of nuclear and conventional arms control discussions. He also favors having Japan underwrite a percentage of U.S. defense costs—particularly those relating to protection of oil coming from the Persian Gulf—by measures such as reimbursing the U.S. for some Navy shipyard costs in the Pacific, rather than building up its own forces. Similarly, he thinks other U.S. allies should spend a higher percentage of their GNPs on their own and allied defense.

In Korea and the Philippines, echoing his chief's views, Upschulte urges patience. "The development of foreign democracies is on a rheostat, not a light switch," he says, advocating continued support for Corazon Aquino, the president of the Philippines.

Other issues looming on the Glenn agenda include START and INF negotiations, tactical weapons programs, and a new tilt-rotor aircraft that has both military and commercial applications. Glenn is also concerned about the lack of readiness in military combat medical care, an issue he calls a potential "warstopper". Opposed to contra aid, the senator and his staff are exploring alternative proposals for resolving the Central America conflict and are reviewing the War Powers Act. They will also assess the current viability of the "total force concept," which has put increased emphasis on the National Guard and Reserve Forces for "round-out" and immediate combat functions.

In the non-foreign policy area, Upschulte is seeking innovations to the budget process that would reduce the use of continuing resolutions and related amendments. He hopes Glenn's concept of compressing the budget, authorization and appropriations processes into a two-step system will be examined seriously. He also is actively pursuing Glenn's emphasis on revitalization of technologies (including bio-degradable plastics), and on problems of the aging.

Off the Hill and away from the arduous task of running a 50-person staff, this former Marine still does not let up in the search for excellence. In the evenings, Upschulte attends law school at Georgetown University.

Greg Weaver
Legislative Assistant for Defense
  Policy
Sen. Carl Levin (D-MI)
459 Russell Senate Office Bldg.
224-6221

Expertise: National security affairs, defense policy

Career: Legislative Assistant for Defense, Rep. Fortney H. Stark (D-CA), 1983 to 1986; current position, 1986 to present.

As the legislative assistant for defense policy to Senator Carl Levin, member of the Senate Armed Services Committee, Greg Weaver assists Levin in wielding considerable influence in the outcome of decisions on strategic issues and arms control. Levin's strength on the Committee springs from his ability and hard work as well as subcommittee assignments. In addition to being a member of the Subcommittees on Strategic Forces and Nuclear Deterrence, and the Subcommittee on Readiness, Sustainability and Support, Levin is also the chairman of the Subcommittee on Conventional Forces and Alliance Defense. This places Weaver at the center of debates on national security in general, and arms control policy in particular.

For that reason, the media and many analysts in the defense community took notice of a report that Weaver helped his boss draft that countered much of the logic used by military planners and the administration to calculate the balance of power in Europe. This 67-page report entitled, "Beyond the Bean Count: Realistically Assessing the Conventional Military Balance in Europe," was released by Levin one week prior to the hearings on the INF Treaty. The report has been used to counter arguments that the Treaty in eliminating intermediate-range ground-launched nuclear missiles will give a conventional advantage to the Warsaw Pact. It challenges the traditional "bean counting" approach to the East-West conventional balance in Europe.

According to *The Washington Post* (January 1, 1988), the report was the work of "Levin and staff aide Greg Weaver [who] calculated the relative quality of NATO and Warsaw Pact forces, their readiness for war, ability to fight over a long period, loyalty, and other factors."

The Levin report is rebutted, however, by those who see a serious imbalance resulting from the treaty. For instance, Levin and staff are challenged by Senator Jesse Helms (R-NC) who argues that, "with the removal of INF missiles, we would have to be willing to spend billions—billions we don't have—for a major expansion in conventional forces."

In addition to working on the report "Beyond the Bean Count," Weaver tracks other legislation of particular concern to Levin and advises him on general defense issues facing the Congress.

William Wight
National Security Assistant
Senator John Warner (R-VA)
421 Russell Office Bldg.
224-2023

Expertise: National security affairs

Bill Wight first came to work on Capitol Hill as a Congressional Fellow through the American Political Science Association. He was selected in 1983 to take part in this program for one year. This led to a series of positions related to legislative affairs work that eventually has brought him full circle back to a Congressional office—that of Senator John Warner.

Wight was well-prepared for his position as national security assistant to the Senate Armed Service committee's ranking minority member. Upon graduation from West Point, Bill was commissioned a Second Lieutenant in the Air Defense Artillery. While in the military, his education included Airborne and Ranger schools, U.S. Army Aviation school, and the Armed Forces Staff College. More recently, he has served as the Deputy Director of External Affairs for the Strategic Defense Initiative and, subsequently, as Director of Legislative Affairs for the SDI. Although much of his background is in air defense and strategic defense, Wight tries not to be parochial in his outlook. "I like this job for the variety of issues and challenges facing me every day. Here I have an opportunity to have an effect on national security issues, to have a meaningful input on the legislative process. In fact, as a former serviceman, much satisfaction has come from addressing certain discrepancies in previous legislation pertaining to veterans and active service personnel."

In addition to defense issues in general, some of the other national security issues Wight has been most active in recently include the FY 88/89 defense budget request for two replacement aircraft carriers, and such strategic programs as the perennial MX/ICBM debate, as well as a host of acquisition issues.

Personal: born 4/8/44, Chehnalis, Washington. B.S. United States Military Academy. M.B.A. Univ. of Washington, 1966. 1975, Defense Systems Management College. Military service: United States Army. 1966-1987, Airborne and Ranger Schools, Senior Army Aviator; Viet Nam veteran; awards: Bronze Star Medal, Meritorious Service Medal (two Oak Leaf clusters), Air Medal (26 Awards), Army Commendation Medal. 1984-1985 Programs Analyst (Missile, Air Defense, Strategic Programs), Office of the Chief of Staff of the Army. 1985-1987 Deputy Director of External Affairs, Director of Legislative Affairs, S.D.I. January 1987-present, National Security Assistant, Senator John Warner (R-VA).

D. John Wildfong
Professional Staff Member
Subcommittee on Conventional
   Forces and Alliance
232-A Russell Senate Office Bldg.
224-8636

Personal: born 8/20/53 in Bethesda, Maryland. B.S.S.E. United States Naval Academy, 1975. Navy Test Pilot Graduate School, 1982. 1975-1986, United States Naval Officer, attaining the rank of Lieutenant Commander. Positions included Naval Aviator, Top Gun Instructor and Navy Test Pilot. Currently in Naval Reserves. 1986-present, Professional Staff Member, Senate Armed Services Committee.

Expertise: Tactical aircraft, conventional weapons

A Navy pilot with over 2700 hours of flight time in Tactical Jet Aircraft, Wildfong has displayed proudly on his office wall a plaque stating that he was a member of the squadron "Top Gun." At San Diego's Miramar Naval Air Base, Wildfong taught young pilots the exciting but exceedingly dangerous art of dog fighting.

Wildfong's eleven years in the Navy included flying multiple types of aircraft. As a Naval Aviator, he flew F-14A Tomcats and later became a test pilot for both that plane and the A4M aircraft. He has flown the B-1 Bomber and the U-2 reconnaissance plane since becoming a member of the Committee staff and is currently in the Naval Reserves, where he flies the A-4 adversary aircraft.

Two years ago, Sen. Barry Goldwater (R-AZ) and the Senate Armed Services Committee set out to find a former serviceman with extensive flight time in various military aircraft who was preferably a test pilot. John Wildfong seemed perfect for the job.

The Conventional Forces and Alliance Defense Subcommittee is now Wildfong's focus. He reviews all issues related to the procurement and development of various tactical aircraft and conventional weapons systems. He is also responsible for tactical communications, spare parts procurement and multi-year contracting.

When the Congress is not in session, Wildfong often travels to various defense contractors and military installations. This interaction, says Wildfong, is indispensable for developing an "information network." Such a network allows those outside the Washington Beltway to garner a greater understanding of how the Congress operates. Wildfong is able to glean important information about how the U.S. defense establishment does business.

One of Wildfong's greatest challenges is balancing the interests of the Pentagon with those of the defense industry. By keeping the interests of both sides in mind, Wildfong believes the American taxpayer gets the most for the dollar.

Wildfong gives credit to the Reagan Administration for making vast improvements in military hardware, particularly block upgrades to existing missiles and aircraft. His Navy experience certainly lends credibility to his arguments. Wildfong says that as a Navy fighter pilot, he wanted to feel confident about the quality of his equipment: "You can have one hundred missiles at your disposal, but if they don't work they won't do you much good." He adds "over the last few years all services have been receiving more reliable hardware which has significantly enhanced the U.S. war fighting capability."

SENATE
COMMITTEE ON BANKING, HOUSING AND URBAN AFFAIRS

Wayne A. Abernathy
Legislative Assistant
Senator Phil Gramm (D-TX)
370 Russell Senate Office Bldg.
224-2934

Expertise: trade, economics, banking

An economist by trade, Wayne Abernathy is the point man for Texas' activist junior Sen. Phil Gramm on issues before the Banking Committee. In addition, Abernathy's legislative portfolio includes a wide range of issues, including trade, exchange rates, export controls, East-West trade and South Africa.

Abernathy's understanding of export controls is rare on Capitol Hill, and his support for strengthening export control laws even more so. With the East-West confrontation increasingly fought on economic grounds, Abernathy believes the United States should work toward "a marriage of our security and economic interests." Toward this goal, he was one of the principal staffers in the 1985 rewrite of the export control act, also known as the Export Administration Act Amendments of 1985.

His other major legislative accomplishments include work on the Export-Import Bank legislation and the Gramm-Kemp trade bill. Elements of the Gramm-Kemp trade legislation were included in the trade legislation passed by the Senate in 1987. Abernathy discusses his views on strategic trade in the Heritage Foundation's book, *Mandate Two.*

Abernathy's close relationship with the Heritage Foundation is underscored by a senior policy analyst at that conservative think-tank, who describes him as her first source on any question on East-West trade. She claims Abernathy is the most knowledgeable, efficient and principled staffer on the issue of East-West trade.

Personal: born 6/1/56 in Colorado Springs, Colorado. B.A. Johns Hopkins Univ., 1978. M.A. School for Advanced International Studies, 1980. 1979, assistant to Republican staff director, Senate Banking, Housing, and Urban Affairs Committee. 1981-1986, economist, Subcommittee on International Finance and Monetary Policy, Senate Committee on Banking, Housing and Urban Affairs. 1986 to present, Legislative Assistant, Sen. Phil Gramm (D-TX).

In the 1970 campaign of former Sen. James Buckley of New York, Abernathy cut his political teeth. Buckley was elected that year on the Conservative Party ticket and served in the U.S. Senate until his defeat by Daniel Patrick Moynihan in 1976. In 1972, Abernathy served as the County Youth Coordinator for the Committee to Reelect the President. As a volunteer, he lent a hand to the Senate campaigns of Republicans J. Glenn Beall in Maryland in 1976 and Paul Trible in Virginia in 1982.

Outside the office, Abernathy devotes a lot of hours to his church. In fact, he once spent two years as a missionary in Spain.

W. Donald Campbell
Staff Director
Subcommittee on Housing and
  Urban Affairs
535 Dirksen Senate Office Bldg.
224-9204

Expertise: Housing, finance, urban affairs

Upon graduation from Colby College with a degree in German language and literature, Campbell entered Harvard Divinity School to prepare for the ministry. At Harvard Divinity, he received the Danforth Internship, was assistant chaplain at Dickinson College, in Pennsylvania, and performed field work in Massachusetts at a housing project and mental hospital.

Upon ordination in 1965, he served as pastor of Saint Andrew's United Methodist Church in Boston, where he founded an organization of seven local Roman Catholic and Protestant churches to operate youth centers, an elderly center, and housing rehab projects. Campbell was twice elected Jamaica Plain's representative to Boston's Model Cities Board, serving as its vice-chairman.

Beginning in 1976 as a Senate Budget Committee staff specialist on housing, community development, federal credit programs and intergovernmental relations, Campbell analyzed agency budgets, prepared sections of the congressional budget, and developed legislative strategy. He developed a framework for analyzing the budgetary impact of federal credit guarantees.

Campbell represented Sen. Donald Riegle (D-MI), on the Budget Committee and led the staff team that developed legislative strategy for the Chrysler Loan Guarantee Act, organized the successful effort to avoid the collapse of McClouth Steel Corporation, and implemented other projects related to housing and industrial development in Michigan. From 1982 through 1986 he was Minority Staff Director of the Housing and Urban Affairs Subcommittee.

As staff director of the Housing and Urban Affairs Subcommittee since January, 1987, Campbell has worked with Chairman Sen. Alan Cranston (D-CA) to plan legislative strategy for enactment of the Homeless Assistance Act, the Urban Mass Transportation Act, the Housing and Community Development Act of 1987 and other housing legislation. He is leading staff support for Cranston's effort to draft legislation and build a national consensus for a new national housing policy for the 1990s. He has introduced a system for computer-based analysis in committee.

Campbell most recently worked on the Housing Act of 1987. With passage of the Chrysler loan guarantee, and the Stewart McKinney Homeless Assistance Act, these three are the accomplishments of which he is most proud.

The Senate has published three of Campbell's writings, *Federal Energy Financing*, 1976; *Off-Budget Agencies Government Sponsored Corporations*, 1977; and *Budget Impact of the Emerging Urban Policy*, 1978.

Personal: born 2/24/39 in Boston, Mass. B.A. Colby College, 1961. M. Div. Harvard Divinity School, 1965. M.B.A. Harvard Business School, 1975. Completed graduate course work in Urban Studies and Planning, Massachusetts Institute of Technology. Casewriting and consulting with Harvard Business School and Boston Univ. School of Management; Teaching assistant, Management of Urban Systems and Municipal Finance. 1976-1982, Senate Budget Committee. 1982-present, Senate Banking, Housing and Urban Affairs Committee.

John C. Dugan
Minority General Counsel
547 Senate Dirksen Office Bldg.
224-7391

Expertise: banking, trade

John Dugan's inauguration as General Counsel to the Republican staff of the Senate Banking, Housing, and Urban Affairs Committee was a tumultuous event: he assumed the helm at the height of the unusually partisan negotiations over the Competitive Equality Banking Act of 1987.

Often cast in the role of legislative "deal maker," Dugan enjoys negotiating and forging alliances. He also finds appealing the normally non-partisan working environment of the Senate Banking Committee.

Dugan brings to his position on the committee a technical background from his law practice at the Washington firm of Miller and Chevalier, where he worked primarily on banking, trade, and litigation matters. Equally important, Dugan understudied for his current role, serving as both Senate Banking Committee majority and minority counsels, as control of the Senate shifted.

His most significant legislative accomplishment is probably his work in drafting the Garn banking bill. However, the bill died a slow death at the end of the 99th Congress. But Dugan's work on the Competitive Equality Banking Act led to a more favorable result. He was the Senate minority staff lawyer working with the conference committee to craft the final legislative package on its way to becoming law. In addition, when the Senate considered the Omnibus Trade bill, Dugan works with Committee Republicans on several critical provisions with Banking Committee jurisdiction.

Personal: born 6/03/55 in Washington, D.C. B.A. Univ. of Michigan, English Literature, 1977, magna cum laude. J.D. Harvard Law School, 1981, cum laude. 1981-1985, attorney, Miller & Chevalier, Washington, D.C. 1985-1987, Counsel, Senate Banking, Housing, and Urban Affairs Committee. 1987 to present, Minority General Counsel, Committee on Banking, Housing, and Urban Affairs.

As one would expect, much of Dugan's work centers around staying one step ahead on legislation referred to the Committee and preparing senators for upcoming hearings before the Committee. As a key staffer on a committee which is lobbied intensely, Dugan stresses that a crucial part of his job is to listen to the opinions of interested parties on all sides of the issue.

Jim Boland, currently Chief of Staff at the Federal Home Loan Bank Board and the previous Minority General Counsel, describes Dugan as "strong both substantively and in understanding the politics of issues." Boland says of Dugan, "He is the kind of guy who you can expect to return your phone call. He is straightforward and candid."

Dugan, a former competitor in the Boston Marathon, still runs several times a week.

Steven Brown Harris
Staff Director
Subcommittee on Securities
534 Dirksen Senate Office Bldg.
224-7391

Personal: born 10/23/47 in New York, New York. B.A. Dartmouth Coll., 1969 (with honors). LL.B. George Washington Univ. Law School, 1973. 1969-70, Time, Inc. 1973-1975, Office of General Counsel, Office of Economic Opportunity. 1975-1977, Staff Attorney, Legal Services Corporation. 1975-1978, Asst. General Counsel, Municipal Securities Rulemaking Board. 1978-1979, Staff Representative to the National Commission for the Review of Antitrust Laws and Procedures. Counsel, Rep. Barbara Jordan (D-TX). 1979-1981, Legislative Counsel, Sen. Donald Riegle, Jr.(D-MI). Counsel, Senate Banking, Housing and Urban Affairs Committee. 1981-present, Staff Director, Subcommittee on Securities, Senate Committee on Banking, Housing and Urban Affairs.

Expertise: Deregulation, securities industry reform

For some people who deal in the complex world of securities industry issues, economic issues are often abstractions that include little consideration of long-term impacts on real life people. Though he grew up in New York City in a family deeply involved in high finance, Steve Harris cannot be accused of a narrow focus that ends with computer readouts on stock shifts. He deviated from the financial ladder long enough to earn the Office of Economic Opportunity Certificate for Dedicated Service to the Disadvantaged of the Nation in 1975, and participated in the creation of the Legal Services Corporation.

Being a counsel for the brand new Legal Services Corporation taught Harris more about the best and worst of politics than any other experience. He was at the "focal point of every single controversial issue coming down the pike, in a highly charged political environment that was hotter than anything since."

After a stint with the Municipal Securities Rulemaking Board, Harris represented former Congresswoman Barbara Jordan (D-TX) on the National Commission for the Review of Antitrust Laws and Procedures. Senator Donald Riegle (D-Mich) was interested in many of the issues dealt with by the commission, and Harris became the legislative counsel on Riegle's personal staff in 1979. Harris joined the staff of the Banking Committee at the end of 1981, and was directly involved in the deregulation of financial institutions, export administration, energy financing and loan guarantees for Chrysler. While on the personal staff of Riegle, he also covered the Commerce Committee and worked intensively on issues related to the Communications Act of 1934, broadcast and cable deregulation, trucking and airline deregulation, the Federal Communications Commission, and Federal Trade Commission.

Harris regards much of the way regulation has been handled in past years as a failure of balance. In the seventies, he observed what often seemed excessive regulation that "made it as clear as the day is long that someone like President Reagan would pick up on the backlash and swing the pendulum very hard." His involvement in the deregulation process has shown Harris that issues become progressively more difficult as you go from "trucks with relatively easy market entry, to airlines with somewhat more complex entry, to communications with quasi-monopolies, to banks and profound economic issues." He believes "insider trading, the crash, and other problems are not totally unrelated to deregulation excess."

Black Monday is getting a great deal of scrutiny from the committee, which also seeks to define what "insider trading" actually is, a definition Harris feels will solve part of the problem. As Harris handles securities matters for both the full committee and the subcommittee, he was very involved in the Tender Offer, Disclosure, and Fairness Act of '87, and will continue work on similar issues, including corporate takeovers.

The committee will also focus on coordinating regulatory policies toward stock options and stock indexes, which are increasingly viewed as one market; and on "circuit breakers," margin requirements and consolidation of clearing organizations. The Brady Report, which Harris thinks deserves a lot of serious thought, may guide some legislation on market mechanisms resulting from the October crash. The pervasive question of the consolidation of commerce and banking will continue to dominate the committee, perhaps for another half dozen years. Harris points out that many states are loosening past divisions, and that if Congress doesn't react to proposals to expand banking activities, the Federal Reserve is likely to loosen things for it through the regulatory process.

Harris believes in a pragmatic approach and in achieving the "do-able" with respect to the legislative process when neither party controls both the executive and legislative branches. He thinks legislative accomplishments in the financial services sector have been limited since 1980 because people keep going for the "Hail Mary pass" with limited successful completions.

John R. Hauge
Legislative Assistant
Senator John H. Chafee (R-RI)
567 Dirksen Senate Office Bldg.
224-2921

Personal: born 3/30/51 in New York, New York. B.A. Dartmouth Coll., 1973. M.A. Oxford Univ., 1975. M.B.A. Harvard Business School, 1977. 1977-1981, Vice President, Corporate Finance, Lehman Brothers Kuhn Loeb, New York, NY. 1981-1982, Manager, Financial Strategy Development, GTE Corporation, Stamford, CT. 1982-1986, Director of Finance (Chief Financial Officer), The GHK Companies, Oklahoma City, OK. 1987-present, Legislative Assistant, Sen. John H. Chafee (R-RI).

Expertise: Banking, small business

John Hauge, Senator John Chafee's senior banking advisor, may be relatively new to the Hill but he is no stranger to the complexities of banking and financial institutions. A 1977 graduate of Harvard Business School, Hauge began his career in corporate finance at Lehman Brothers and joined the GTE Corporation four years later as Manager for Financial Strategy Development.

In July of 1982, Hauge arrived in Oklahoma City to accept a position as Director of Finance for the GHK Companies amidst the confusion and chaos wrought by that city's Penn Square Bank failure. Once a great booster of the Penn Square Bank, GHK was particularly hard hit and accumulated staggering debts. Over the next few years, Hauge performed some fancy financial footwork in helping to map out GHK's massive non-bankruptcy restructuring with numerous lenders, investors, and the FDIC while at the same time serving as financial advisor to the "magnetic and irrepressible" Chairman of GHK, Robert A. Hefner, III.

A self-described "moderate Republican," Hauge joined Chafee's staff, a welcome opportunity to shift professional gears and possibly translate some of his considerable expertise into public policy development.

The agenda of the Banking Committee is quite active under Proxmire's chairmanship, as evidenced by the passage of the Competitive Equality Banking Act of 1987, Chafee is a force on the Committee, as his support is considered essential to Democrats in their efforts to press ahead with financial services reforms, including insider trading and corporate takeover legislation. Hauge especially appreciates Chafee's pivotal role on Banking, which affords the Senator a "wider latitude," and increases the likelihood of generating "positive compromise."

Hauge's primary concerns include the rewrite of laws affecting financial institutions; he also takes note of the procedural maneuvers which can "take some getting used to." He observes that "the process can be as important as the product in shaping legislation."

Robert W. Hickmott
Deputy Administrative Assistant
Senator Tim Wirth
380 Russell House Office Bldg.
224-5852

Expertise: Fundraising and banking

An expert in fundraising, Bob Hickmott's first experience was with the Carter campaign of 1980. In 1981 he became the Executive Director for the Democratic Business Counsel of the Democratic National Committee, responsible for the fund raising at the corporate level, and also from Political Action Committees. His most effective fund-raising venture was the Senate campaign of Timothy E. Wirth, for which he raised $4.2 million. Wirth won a close race with a margin of only 16,179 votes.

Hickmott joined Sen. Wirth's personal staff in January, 1987 and continues to do campaign work. Each senator is allowed to have two individuals doing political work on his/her staff. Hickmott enjoys the fund-raising aspect of his job because it allows him to work with the corporate world in a political environment.

Among his other tasks, Hickmott does the staffing for the Banking Committee. He works primarily on mergers, takeovers and financial restructuring. Sen. Wirth recently co-sponsored a bill to establish a Financial Services Oversight Commission, which Hickmott co-drafted. "Bob has worked diligently in helping me to launch a major new banking bill," Sen. Wirth stated. Recent hearings on the measure were held in the Committee on Banking, Housing and Urban Affairs.

Personal: born 6/19/54 in Needham, Massachusetts. B.A. Boston Univ., communications, 1976, summa cum laude. Georgetown Law School, 1984, 1986. 1976-1980, speech writer, public affairs, DuPont Company, Wilmington, DE. 1980-1981, associate finance director, fund raising, Carter campaign. 1981-1983, executive director Democratic Business Counsel, Democratic National Committee. 1984, director political affairs, Congoleum Corporation. 1985, national finance director, Tim Wirth Senate campaign. 1987-present, deputy administrative assistant, Sen. Tim Wirth.

Sen. Wirth plays a unique role in the Banking Committee, because he previously chaired the House Subcommittee on Telecommunications, Consumer Protection and Finance. Wirth's experience makes Hickmott's job much easier. "I know the players and the issues, Sen. Wirth knows the specifics." Hickmott says. The senator and Hickmott work closely together to create Wirth's respected position on the committee.

Hickmott has been attending Georgetown Law School for the past three years. Working full-time and attending classes at night keeps him extremely busy. If he had time to do anything other than study and work, he would like to read and travel. Hickmott has travelled extensively throughout the United States, China and Russia, and is anxious to broaden his travelling experiences.

Hickmott is married to Diane Dewhurst, Press Secretary for Sen. George Mitchell (D-ME). Though they have been married for two and a half years, and work in the same building, they have only seen each other a few times at work. "We had lunch in the Senate cafeteria one day, it was quite strange."

Jennifer A. Hillman
Legislative Assistant and Counsel
Senator Terry Sanford (D-NC)
716 Hart Senate Office Bldg.
224-3154

Personal: born 1/29/59 in Toledo, Ohio. A.B. 1978 and M.Ed. 1979, Duke Univ. J.D. Harvard Law School, 1983. 1976-1980, Member, Duke Univ. Board of Trustees, Durham, NC. 1983-1986, Attorney, Patton, Boggs & Blow, Washington, D.C. 1986 to present, Legislative Assistant and Counsel, Sen. Terry Sanford (D-NC)

Expertise: Banking, international trade

The day after his election to the Senate, Terry Sanford phoned Jennifer Hillman and invited her to join his legislative staff. The invitation was not exactly a surprise. She and Sanford had forged a harmonious working relationship during their respective tenures at Duke University while he was President and she was a full member of the Board of Trustees. Hillman also served as a campaign advisor to Sanford in the last month of his Senate race.

After completing a B.A. and M.Ed. at Duke, Hillman attended Harvard Law School and graduated in 1983. She joined the prestigious Washington law firm of Patton, Boggs & Blow, where she represented various industries in trade actions, prepared for international commercial arbitration, and took on legislative projects related to trade and education.

Although Hillman's area of expertise includes banking and international trade, Sanford relies heavily on her judgment on most issues, and Hillman maintains considerable influence in spearheading his legislative initiatives.

Hillman admits to feeling somewhat overwhelmed when she first arrived on the Hill in December, 1986, but readily followed Sanford's lead and immersed herself in the job. As if familiarizing herself with the issues, the legislative process, Senate colleagues and industry lobbyists were not enough, she had to prepare for the Banking Committee's quick start. Under the energetic chairmanship of Senator Proxmire, the Banking Committee and the Senate passed a broad banking bill in the early months of the 100th Congress.

To Hillman, the expeditious passage of the competitive Equality Banking Act of 1987, a surprise to many industry experts, is certainly a highlight of her legislative career. In looking ahead, she will endeavor to help Sanford expand his role in shaping financial services reforms, particularly as a coalition builder among junior committee members in the areas of insider trading and corporate takeover legislation. On other fronts, Sanford has a long held interest in housing legislation and international economic development in Central America. Hillman expects to become increasingly involved in these issues.

A runner and one-time Boston Marathon participant during her Harvard days, Hillman is now so busy the only time she can find to run is on her way to work.

Peter Kinzler
Staff Director
Subcommittee on Consumer
    Affairs Subcommittee
Senate Committee on Banking,
    Housing, and Urban Affairs
541 Dirksen Senate Office Building
224-7391

Expertise: Consumer banking issues

Peter Kinzler is a veteran Capitol Hill policymaker. In 1985, Kinzler shaped the first legislation introduced in Congress to provide a quicker and more efficient way to compensate those injured by defective products. This innovative approach, which for the first time focused on victims as well as manufacturers, helped change the whole product liability tort reform debate. During the height of the 1970s consumer activism, Kinzler spearheaded the drive in the U.S. House of Representatives for no-fault automobile insurance. Although the national measure was not enacted, such laws are now on the books in many states.

Most recently, consumer banking issues are on his plate. In 1987, he helped shepherd through the Congress legislation to shorten the amount of time a bank may hold a deposited check, and early 1988 will see enactment of a law he worked on to require credit card issuers to give consumers basic cost information in all solicitations.

Kinzler's Senate career began in 1981 when be became Counsel for Consumer Subcommittee Ranking Member (now Chairman) Christopher Dodd (D-CT). As a staff member in the U.S. House of Representatives, the consumer expert guided into enactment in 1980 legislation to reauthorize funding for the Federal Trade Commission—an accomplishment that has not since been repeated. The first Super Fund public law, enacted in 1980 to clean-up toxic waste, was influenced greatly by a House Commerce Committee report on Hazardous Waste Disposal and a subsequent bill to implement the report, both of which were drafted by Mr. Kinzler.

Personal: born 4/18/43 in New York City. B.A. Trinity Coll., 1964. J.D. Columbia Univ., l967. 1967-1969, Attorney, National Labor Relations Board. 1969-1974, Counsel, Rep. Lud Ashley (D-OH). 1975, General Counsel's Office of Legislation, Federal Trade Commission. 1976-1981, Counsel, Consumer Protection and Finance Subcommittee, House Committee on Interstate and Foreign Commerce. 1981-present, Consumer Affairs Subcommittee, Senate Committee on Banking, Housing and Urban Affairs.

From 1967 until 1969, Kinzler worked as an attorney for the Appellate Division of the National Labor Relations Board. He then joined the staff of Congressman Lud Ashley, where he worked until 1974. Following that, for one year he worked in the General Counsel's Office of Legislation at the Federal Trade Commission. Returning to the Hill, he joined the staff of the Consumer Protection and Finance Subcommittee of the House Committee on Interstate and Foreign Commerce. He served on that Subcommitee under four Chairmen before moving over to that Committee's Oversight Subcommittee.

A folk music fan, Peter Kinzler also appreciates the workmanship and charm of hand-made crafts. He and his wife Ginny often spends weekends scouring craft fairs and galleries.

Thomas J. Lykos, Jr.
Minority Counsel
534 Dirksen Senate Office Bldg.
224-1561

Personal: born 7/1/56 in Houston, Texas. B.A. Harvard Univ., 1978 (cum laude). J.D. Univ. of Texas, School of Law, 1981 (cum laude). Admitted to State Bar of Texas and District of Columbia Bar. 1981-1982, associate, Bracewell & Patterson. 1982-1983, attorney, Securities and Exchange Commission. 1983-1985, Minority Counsel, Subcommittees on Telecommunications and Finance, and Oversight and Investigations, House Committee on Energy and Commerce. 1985-1987, Majority (Republican) Counsel; 1987-present, Minority (Republican) Counsel, Senate Committee on Banking, Housing and Urban Affairs and Chief Minority (Republican) Counsel, Subcommittee on Securities.

Expertise: Securities, white collar crime, banking

Thomas Lykos has been an active participant in the debate regarding tender offer reform. This role stems from his membership on the tender offer task force while at the SEC's enforcement division. At present, he questions whether the inclusion of some provisions of the legislation recently approved by the Senate Banking Committee tips the balance between bidders and targets established by the Williams Act in favor of target managements and the absence of provisions which provide for enhanced shareholder participation in contests for corporate control.

"Unfortunately the debate over corporate takeovers which has occurred in Congress is often dominated by hype, hysteria and myth. Too little emphasis has been placed on the empirical evidence which demonstrates the positive gains of takeover activity and too much emphasis has been placed upon the anecdotal evidence offered by opponents of takeover activity. Public policy is not best served by undue reliance upon anecdotes," notes Lykos.

A member of the "Pitt Commission," an *ad hoc* group of securities attorneys and legal scholars charged by Senators D'Amato (R-NY) and Reigle (D-MI) with the task of drafting a statutory definition of insider trading, Tom Lykos believes we need to "explore the pervasiveness of insider trading." According to Lykos, the gray areas and unspoken understanding of insider trading need to be defined so that clearer legal standards can be imposed on market participants. To this end, Lykos has been working doggedly to conduct hearings and to draft legislation in the Banking committee to "define the parameters of insider trading."

Lykos has faith in the ability of the securities market to weather heavy financial storms. Despite "Black Monday 1987," Lykos believes that the financial system has been endowed since the 1930s with certain intrinsic safeguards so that the devastation wrecked on the market in the 1929 crash should never reoccur. Those safeguards, developed and strengthened over the years, will keep the financial system "relatively stable."

Nevertheless, Lykos sees some reforms to the securities industry as necessary to curb abuses and increase stability on Wall Street. "The impact of the increased globalization of the securities markets, new trading techniques such as program trading and the interplay between the commodities and equities markets require a careful examination of the adequacy of the current regulatory structure." Lykos also serves as Special Counsel to the Administrative Conference of the United States.

He has also worked on other significant banking legislation. Recently, he has directly participated in the drafting and enactment of the Government Securities Act of 1986, the FSLIC Recapitalization provisions of the Competitive Equality Banking Act of 1987, the Conrail Privatization Act of 1986, and the Shareholder Communications Act of 1985.

"Tom is known for flexibility; he is no rigid ideologue and people know he gets a lot accomplished," said one House colleague. His profound knowledge of the securities industry is highly respected on the Hill.

Having spent two years on the House Energy and Commerce Committee before coming to the Senate Banking Committee, Lykos comments that House Committees have a much broader range of legislation to review, whereas the Senate Banking Committee concentrates its energies on only a few bills. "The House Energy and Commerce has a more rough and tumble atmosphere, but the Senate allows for much greater responsibility," said Lykos.

Kenneth A. McLean
Staff Director
534 Dirksen Senate Office Bldg.
224-7391

Expertise: Banking

Ken McLean had worked in the executive branch when he came to Capitol Hill as a Congressional Fellow to work for Sen. Paul Douglas (D-IL). When Douglas lost his reelection bid to Charles Percy, McLean went to work for another Democrat, one from the adjoining state of Wisconsin, Sen. William Proxmire.

McLean immediately went to work on banking issues for the maverick Proxmire. Over the years McLean was intimately involved in numerous landmark bills in the financial services field. These included Truth in Lending, Fair Credit, and others.

McLean's colleagues note his low profile, but emphasize his intelligence. One called him "without a doubt the brightest staffer I ever dealt with on the Hill."

In addition the colleague said "Since Proxmire does not like to wheel and deal on issues, that is left to McLean and it is a role he handles well." Others point out McLean always seem to know exactly what the Chairman wants on a particular issue and is not likely to waffle during legislative debate.

In 1987 *The New York Times* described McLean as "a 53-year old former Commerce Department bureaucrat who has been with the Senator for 20 years and is highly regarded by many lobbyists and industry experts as a cagey, calculating strategist who can play political hardball."

As the Congress addresses the twin issues of modification of federal banking laws and reform of the scandal-ridden securities industry, McLean will remain at the core of the Senate debate during the second session of the 100th Congress.

Patrick A. Mulloy
General Counsel
544 Dirksen Senate Office Bldg.
224-7391

*Personal: born 9/14/41 in Dallas,
Pennsylvania. B.A. Kings Coll., 1963.
M.A. Univ. of Notre Dame, 1965. J.D.
George Washington Univ., 1971.
L.L.M. Harvard Law School, 1978.
1965, State Department Foreign
Service. 1973-1977, Lands Div., Dept.
of Justice. 1978-1982, Antitrust Div.,
Dept. of Justice. 1982-1983, Am.
Political Science Assoc.
Congressional Fellow from Justice
Dept. with House Ways and Means
Committee and Senate Banking
Committee. 1984, Minority Counsel;
1984-1987, Minority General Counsel;
1987-present, General Counsel, Senate
Committee on Banking, Housing and
Urban Affairs.*

Expertise: International trade, finance, banking

In 1960, Mulloy was smitten by Camelot. Working as a Student for Kennedy was his first exposure to politics. Mulloy liked the work and decided to dedicate himself to public service.

"I'm proud and happy to be in a position where I can help top elected political leaders deal with pressing problems in finance and international trade."

Mulloy's public service began as a Foreign Service officer. He was posted as a vice consul to Montreal. Then he served as executive secretary of the group which put together the U.S./Canadian agreement to clean up the Great Lakes. In 1973 he moved to the Department of Justice where he first litigated environmental law cases and then became a senior attorney working on international antitrust matters which involved much international travel and negotiations.

An interest in the inner workings of the Hill motivated him to work for one of the Justice Department's Congressional Fellowships in Political Science.

Senator William Proxmire (D-WI) took notice of Mulloy's successes as a fellow and when the position of minority counsel opened on the Senate Banking Committee, the call went his way.

One of his first assignments was the sanctions legislation on banking relations with South Africa. The legislation banned new bank loans and investments in South Africa. It also stopped the sale of the South African gold coins in the United States. "It was a clear signal from the U.S. that South Africa should move toward government based on the consent of the governed."

Mulloy also worked on export controls legislation, the Export-Import Bank, and the U.S. contribution to the IMF's quota increase. General Counsel since 1987, Mulloy has worked on the Committee's banking, trade and anti-takeover bills.
An Expert in international trade and finance, Mulloy believes U.S. trade problems are directly related to budget deficits. Trade deficits, he believes, are leading to the new problem of foreign ownership of U.S. assets. Helping to develop legislation that will integrate the U.S. into an increasingly competitive world economy occupies a major portion of Mulloy's time on the Banking Committee.

Mulloy has no ambition to become an elected official. "My job is to help elected officials carry out what they were elected to do."

Mulloy enjoys playing tennis, reading history and politics and "rough-housing" with his three children.

Clifford Reed Northup
Legislative Assistant
Senator William Armstrong (R-CO)
528 Hart Senate Office Bldg.
224-5941

Personal: born 7/7/50 in Washington, D.C. U.S. Navy 1973-1975. B.A. Univ. of North Carolina at Chapel Hill, 1976. 1979-1984 Credit Union National Association. 1984-1985, American Banker's Association. 1985-present, Legislative Assistant, Sen. William Armstrong (R-CO).

Expertise: Tax, finance, banking

When "Black Monday" produced a 508-point drop in the Dow Jones Industrial Average, Cliff Northup, legislative assistant for tax and banking to Senator William Armstrong (R-CO), ranking member on the Securities Subcommittee, knew he would be called upon to analyze what events led to the drop and consider changes in regulation of the securities markets. Northup was right, As Armstrong's aide, he had covered much of this area on proposed legislation to alter federal takeover laws and their impact on companies and shareholders.

Handling tax, banking and securities issues, Northup has been a valuable assistant to Senator Armstrong for the last three years. Since joining the Armstrong staff in 1985, Northup assisted the Senator in his role in the passage of the Tax Reform Act of 1986.

Northup has participated in the formulation of a number of major bills during his nine-year career. In 1979, he worked for the enactment of a banking deregulation bill that legalized interest-bearing checking accounts and for the first federal tax incentive for saving. Two years later that initiative resulted in the expansion of IRA's to all wage earners.

Northup is a rarity on the Hill, a native Washingtonian. He enjoys golf, tennis and opportunities to hike in the Blue Ridge.

Anne K. Scully
Legislative Assistant
Senator John Heinz (R-PA)
293 Russell Senate Office Bldg.
224-6324

Personal: born 7/25/54 in El Paso, Texas. B.A. Univ. of Virginia, 1976. J.D. George Mason Univ. School of Law, 1980. 1976-1979, Paralegal, Sheridan, Grimaldi & Shevlin. 1980, Legal Intern, U.S. Regulatory Council. 1981-1982, Attorney, National Credit Union Administration. 1982-1984, Attorney, Federal Home Loan Bank Board. 1984-1986, Chief Legislative Aide to Rep. Norman Shumway (R-CA) and Minority Counsel, Committee on Banking, Housing and Urban Affairs. 1986 to present, Legislative Assistant, Sen. John Heinz (R-PA).

Expertise: Banking, securities

Anne Scully's first exposure to Capitol Hill came in 1981 as an attorney in the legislative division of the Federal Home Loan Bank Board. This experience, together with her two years as Rep. Norman Shumway's (R-CA) aide on banking and tax matters, brought Scully highly recommended to Sen. John Heinz. As the second-ranking Republican on the Banking, Housing, and Urban Affairs Committee, Heinz is involved with a panoply of issues in which Scully is well-versed.

Scully assisted her boss in considering and developing legislative responses to the 1987 insider-trading scandals and aftermath of the Boesky case. Similarly, she has worked diligently on legislation that would help restrict or limit hostile corporate takeovers, while protecting the rights of workers and local communities.

Scully believes corporate raiders should be prevented from attempting to manipulate markets. Furthermore, she favors strengthened SEC disclosure requirements. This is an intensely personal issue to Heinz since hostile corporate takeover activity has dramatically affected the lives of Pennsylvania workers.

Another issue that has captured Scully's and her boss's attention concerns the restructuring of the banking and financial services industries. In particular, Scully and the Banking Committee are attempting to determine the degree of flexibility—as dictated by state and federal law—banks should be permitted when expanding their lines of business particularly in the area of insurance underwriting.

As an attorney, Scully is also responsible for handling the wide range of issues taken up by the Senate Judiciary Committee.

Although her responsibilities on Capitol Hill are considerable, Scully does find time to pursue her first love—racing sailboats.

Kristin Siglin
Legislative Assistant
Senator Kit Bond (R-MO)
293 Russell Senate Office Bldg
224-5721

Personal: born 2/17/61 in San Francisco, California. B.A. Brown Univ., 1983, magna cum laude. 1983-1985, Legislative Assistant, Rep. Jim Leach (R-IA). 1985-1987, Legislative Assistant, Sen. Charles Grassley (R-IA). 1987 to present, Legislative Assistant, Sen. Christopher (Kit) Bond (R-MO).

Expertise: Banking

Four years ago, Kristin Siglin took the Foreign Service exam. While waiting for the results she took a temporary job as a receptionist with Rep. Jim Leach (R-IA). After a few months, she was promoted to Legislative Assistant in the area of banking. When she learned that she had passed the exam, she had to decide whether she wanted to move to another country to work or remain in the United States. She chose to continue working on Capitol Hill, and hasn't tired of it yet.

Working for freshman Sen. Kit Bond, Siglin has so far been primarily concerned with laying a foundation for the Senator's work on the Banking, Housing and Urban Affairs Committee. Bond is a moderate member, occasionally serving as a pivotal vote on issues. As a freshman last year, he and his staff found the initial settling into the job took up much of their time. Siglin expects to be busy this year working more extensively on new legislation.

Yet even in her short time working with the Banking, Housing and Urban Affairs Committee, Siglin has already made a name for herself. She has extensive experience in Banking issues, having worked on them on both the House and Senate side. While on Sen. Charles Grassley's (R-IA) staff, she was a key worker on the Farm Credit System Central Reserve Act of 1985, a bill that amended the Farm Credit Act of 1971 to provide additional farm credit. She joined Grassley's staff after two years in Rep. Jim Leach's office.

In her hours off, Siglin relaxes in her garden, planting flowers and trees and practicing the landscaping she'd like to make a career of someday—if she ever tires of the Hill.

W. Lamar Smith
Minority Staff Director
545 Dirksen Senate Office Bldg.
224-7391

Personal: born 5/31/43 in Oklahoma City. B.A. Princeton Univ. (cum laude), 1966. M.A., 1970, and Ph.D., 1975, Univ. of Texas. 1975-1981, Senior Vice President, Texas Commerce Bancshares, Houston. 1981-1987, Economist, Senate Committee on Banking, Housing and Urban Affairs. 1987, Chief Economist, American Bankers Association, Washington. 1987 to present, Republican Staff Director and Economist, Senate Committee on Banking, Housing and Urban Affairs.

Expertise: Finance

Last spring, when President Reagan appointed Danny Wall as Chairman of the Federal Home Loan Bank Board, the Senate Banking Committee found itself without a Republican staff director. The selection of Wall's replacement was not a difficult task. Sen. Jake Garn (R-UT), the ranking Republican on the committee, summoned his erstwhile aide back to the committee, and Lamar Smith gladly returned.

The Committee has played an increasingly important role as the issues of banking and securities reform have moved to the top of the congressional agenda. The wide ranging jurisdiction of the committee not only includes banks and financial institutions, but also: financial aide to commerce and industry; deposit insurance; housing (public, private and veterans' housing); deposit insurance; issuance and redemption of notes; federal monetary policy and the Federal Reserve System; price controls on commodities, rents and services; urban mass transit and development, promotion and controls of foreign trade and exports; construction of nursing homes; renegotiation of government contracts. The committee is also responsible for studying and periodically reporting on the matters concerning international economic policy as they affect the domain within the committees jurisdiction.

Smith brings an impressive background to Capitol Hill. An Ivy League graduate with a Ph.D. in finance and economics, Smith has also held senior positions in the private sector, including a six year stint at Texas Commerce Bank in Houston.

This combination of education and professional experience led one Washington insider to label him a "Washington treasure." Others point to his abundance of energy and intellect as sufficient reason to label him one of the Committee's key people.

Finance, monetary theory, and financial institutions are Smith's bailiwick. And because the Banking Committee is familiar territory to Smith, he has played an active role in several pieces of important legislation, including the trade bill, measures dealing with insider trading, and initiatives to restructure deposit insurance.

Additionally, as the Committee has rather wide legislative jurisdiction, Smith has also been involved with the foreign debt issue, U.S. monetary policy, regulatory reform, the International Monetary Fund and housing legislation.

While he admits that some of these issues are not "sexy" by Washington standards, Smith is genuinely fascinated with his work, especially in the restructuring of the financial services industry.

Smith believes American financial institutions are at a severe disadvantage since they are by law prohibited from offering the full-range of financial services, including brokerage services and insurance underwriting. Japanese and European institutions are not burdened with similar regulations.

Smith is optimistic the Congress will eventually address this dilemma and amend the laws that determine the structure of individual institutions. Such changes, says Smith, will allow U.S. firms to become more competitive internationally.

Gordon Stoddard
Legislative Assistant
Senator Jim Sasser(D-TN)
363 Russell Senate Office Building
224-3344

Expertise: Banking Reform

Gordon Stoddard's technical grasp of banking issues has made him a player in legislation reforming the financial services industry.

After experience in banking regulation in the private sector, Stoddard began working for Senator Jim Sasser (D-TN) in March of 1987. He immediately became involved in drafting the Corporate Takeover bill, which passed both houses of Congress that same year. He wrote major portions of the committee report language as well as some of the "additional views" found at the end of the report. The Omnibus Trade Bill also kept Stoddard busy in 1987, particularly the provisions on regulation of foreign investments.

Stoddard's work with the Banking Committee has involved him in a number of other regulation issues. He participated in the drafting of the Community Impact bill a measure that seeks to slow down or curb takeover abuses. He worked on the Comprehensive Equitable Banking Act which deals with safety in banking, and was part of the effort on the Committee to examine whether banks should be allowed to deal in securities and businesses permitted to diversify into banking.

Although Stoddard's stint with Sasser is just beginning, he appears to be off to a good start. Committee staff recognize his ability to handle banking issues and Sasser has come to trust his judgement and initiative. According to a Banking Committee staffer, "Gordon is the kind of person you would definitely want on your side."

Personal: born 4/18/55 in Providence, RI. B.A. Georgetown Univ., 1978. 1986, Dept. of HUD. 1978, Representative, National Association of Homebuilders. 1983, Associate with Trubin Sillcocks, New York. 1984, Henry, Gager, Narkis Conn. 1985-86, Naegele and Associates. 1985, Georgetown Law School.

John Walsh
Minority Economist
534 Dirksen Senate Office Bldg.
224-7391

Expertise: International trade and finance

John Walsh has pursued his career in international affairs from a humid high school physics lab in Ghana to the frenetic halls of Capitol Hill. During his years at the Office of Management and Budget, Walsh continued to follow the Peace Corps with interest while immersing himself in export credit programs, multilateral development banks and the international debt crisis.

At the Treasury, Walsh explored solutions for the debt problems of developing nations like Ghana and worked on other international finance programs.

From his current position as economist and chief minority staff member on the Banking Subcommittee on International Finance and Monetary Policy, Walsh can still keep an eye on the problems of developing countries. He spent many hours on the massive omnibus trade bill, including export control, exchange rate and foreign investment legislation and other issues affecting international debt and the trade deficit. The small size of the subcommittee staff has required Walsh to handle all major international finance legislation for the Republican minority.

Walsh came to the subcommittee to tackle the Herculean task of analyzing "all elements of the trade bill." Recently, he has been particularly active in advancing legislation for import sanctions against Toshiba for their sale of sensitive technology to the Soviet Union.

Personal: born 9/6/50 in Baltimore, Maryland. B.S. in mechanical engineering and B.A. in liberal studies, Univ. of Notre Dame, 1973. M.P.P. John F. Kennedy School of Government, Harvard Univ., 1978. 1973-1975, Peace Corps Volunteer in Ghana, Africa, teaching high school physics. 1975-1976, directed management information program for Mutual Broadcasting Systems. 1978-1984, International Program Analyst, Office of Management and Budget. 1984-1985, International Economist, Dept. of Treasury, Office of the Assistant Secretary for International Affairs. 1986-present, Professional Staff Member, Senate Banking, Housing and Urban Affairs Committee.

Sen. John Heinz (R-PA), was responsible for bringing Walsh to the subcommittee, which he chaired in 1986. Heinz and Sen. Jake Garn (R-UT), who is former chairman of the Banking Committee and ranking minority member, both have come to rely on Walsh to advise them on all issues concerning international trade and finance.

With a wife and three young children, Walsh admits he has little time for activities or hobbies outside the office. "Living in a suburb of Baltimore makes commuting my only hobby," Walsh said. Recently, however, he has become intrigued with woodworking and furniture making. He is an avid "house fixer-upper".

Leslie Woolley
Legislative Director
Senator Bob Graham (D-FL)
241 Dirksen Senate Office Bldg.
224-3041

*Personal: born 4/7/53 Ada, Oklahoma.
B.A. Oklahoma State Univ. 1975.
M.B.A. Oklahoma State Univ. 1976.
1977-1981, Legislative Assistant, Rep.
Wes Watkins (D-OK). 1981-1984,
Legislative Assistant, Rep. Bill
McCollum (R-FL). 1984-1986,
Assistant Vice President, Chemical
New York, Inc., affiliate of Chemical
Bank. 1984-1985, President, Woman
in Housing and Finance. 1986-1987,
Legislative Assistant, Rep. Norm
Shumway (R-CA). 1987-present,
Legislative Assistant, Legislative
Director, Sen. Bob Graham (D-FL).*

Expertise: Banking

Leslie Woolley has been involved in most of the major banking legislation of the last decade. She worked on such bills as the 1978 Banking-Financial Institution Restructuring Act, the 1982 Monetary Control Act, and the 1987 Competitive Quality Banking Act.

Today, the widely respected Woolley, is Legislative Director to Florida's freshman senator and Senate Banking Committee member, Bob Graham. Her ten years of experience are serving her well as Graham addresses the intense interest of the financial services community not only in national issues, but in his home state. As Florida has become a major attraction for national financial services companies, local bankers have stepped up their efforts to protect their interests and they view Bob Graham, their popular former governor, as one of their first lines of defense.

Having worked as a banking lobbyist, as well as for members of the House Banking Committee, Woolley knows most of the players in Washington in the financial services field. Her colleagues have respect both for her in-depth knowledge of banking laws, as well as the savvy she has demonstrated in furthering Bob Graham's interests on the committee.

In her previous work on the House side, as Legislative Assistant to Rep. Norm Shumway (R-CA), Woolley's responsibilities included all activities of the Economic Stabilization Subcommittee, as well as handling all full House Banking Committee activities.

She was involved in efforts to seek expanded securities powers for the banking industry. In 1987, she was responsible for helping to draft the amendment giving Employee Stock Ownership Plans an opportunity to participate in the bidding during corporate takeovers.

While working as a lobbyist for Chemical Bank New York, Woolley advised the bank on legislation and issues pending before Congress, and was liaison with various federal agencies, other trade associations, industry groups and interested parties.

Woolley's versatile career has led her into all facets of banking from the corporate to the legislative arenas. According to one colleague, she has been able to bring to her position, "exceptional insight and an ability to obtain timely information."

SENATE
COMMITTEE ON THE BUDGET

Richard N. Brandon
Staff Director
Dirksen Senate Office Bldg.
224-0836

Expertise: Health services

The Senate Budget Committee have given Rick Brandon the opportunity to marry his interests in politics with those in human services public policy. He brings to the committee first-hand knowledge of the challenges of the human services provider. This work experience overlays his impressive academic credentials as a doctoral student and researcher. While at Harvard University, he was both a lecturer and post doctoral researcher on health services planning. He has a no-nonsense, "real world" perspective gained from his work as director of the New York City Department of Mental Health.

When Brandon joined the Senate Budget Committee as a professional staff member in 1975, he focused his attention on nutrition, children's programs, social security, housing, education and job training. In 1980, he played a lead role in helping develop the budget reconciliation process.

Since becoming Democratic staff director in 1983, Brandon has seen his role broaden to the point where he now supervises over 40 people and is responsible for coordinating the entire budget package. During Sen. Lawton Chiles's tenure as chairman, the budget bills have been uniformly supported by Democratic senators. Brandon has worked with staff and committee members to produce legislation all Democrats could support.

Personal: born 1/8/45 in New York City. A.B. Government, Cornell Univ., 1966. 1973-1975, Post Graduate Research, Urban Planning and Social Policy, Harvard University. Ph.D. University of Pennsylvania, 1975. 1969-1972, Director/Systems Analyst, New York City Department of Mental Health. 1973-1975, Lecturer, Harvard University. 1975-1983, Professional Staff Member; 1983-1987, Minority Staff Director; 1987-present, Staff Director, Senate Budget Committee.

While Brandon covers all issues, he has paid special attention to a number of controversial bills, including Gramm-Rudman-Hollings I and II, and working to set realistic budget limits on defense programs. He helped with Chiles's proposal on the MX missile, effectively reducing the scope of the program and its funding level.

Brandon says that the huge federal deficit is the nation's major immediate and future challenge. He devoted much of his energies last fall to the "budget summit" between the Administration and Congress. He feels that ". . .one of the thorns in the process to reduce the deficit is the uncooperative attitude of many Republican members." Nevertheless, he sees this as another political challenge and opportunity.

James Hudson Carr
Group Leader
Tax policy, Housing and Credit
624 Dirksen Senate Office Bldg.
224-0852

Expertise: Urban policy, tax policy, federal credit budget

In addition to his responsibilities involving tax policy and federal credit matters, Jim Carr coordinates committee activities involving housing, transportation and community development programs. In this coordinating capacity, Carr not only reviews housing and transportation budget recommendations at the program account level, but also analyzes the aggregate impact of federal budget policies on the fiscal heath of state and local governments.

Of the many areas for which Carr is responsible, he views credit reform as a major issue looming before Congress. Present accounting rules for federal credit programs, according to Carr, fail to reflect accurately the total costs of those activities to government. Carr assisted in preparing credit reform legislation and shepherding it through the Senate in the last session. The debate over the accounting rules incorporated in that amendment have helped to draw needed attention to an often overlooked aspect of federal spending, says Carr. Also related to federal credit activities, Carr has served in an oversight capacity, for the Budget Committee, for the federal government's multi-billion dollar pilot loan sales program currently underway.

While tax reform, deficit reduction, and credit reform make working on the Senate Budget Committee a job and a half, Carr has found time to continue his writing, and is co-author of a forthcoming book on industrial America.

Personal: born 2/13/53 in Hampton, Virginia. B.A. Hampton Univ., 1977. M.S. Columbia Univ., 1979. Currently, doctoral candidate Univ. of Pennsylvania, Dept. of City and Regional Planning. 1983-1986, Senior Analyst for tax policy, housing and federal credit, Senate Budget Committee. 1980-1983, Research Associate, Center for Urban Policy Research, Rutgers Univ. 1983, visiting lecturer, urban policy, Rutgers Univ. 1979, director, Neighborhood Resource Center of Bedford-Stuyvesant Restoration Corporation. Publications: The New Reality in Municipal Finance, (co-author), 1984. Crisis and Constraints in Municipal Finance, (editor), 1984. Land Use Issues of the 1980s, (co-editor), 1983. Plant Closings in the United States, (co-author), forthcoming.

Barbara Ann Chow
Group Leader
Physical Resources and General
  Government
621 Dirksen Senate Office Bldg.
224-0548

Personal: B.A. Pomona College, 1977. M.A. Univ. of California, Berkeley, 1980. 1980-1985, budget examiner, Office of Management and Budget. 1985-1987, senior analyst, Energy, Natural Resources and Agriculture. 1987 to present, Group Leader, physical resources and general government, Budget Committee.

Expertise: Energy, environment, national resources, agriculture

While Barbara Chow's early experience as a volunteer for the George McGovern presidential bid in 1972 is far removed from her present duties on the Senate Budget Committee, it did introduce her to many aspects of the political process.

She developed an initial interest in environmental programs while in graduate school at the Univ. of California at Berkeley, and later spent five years at the Office of Management and Budget as a budget examiner for EPA programs. When she moved over to the Senate Budget Committee in 1985, Chow continued her work in environmental issues, and took on added responsibilities in agriculture, energy and natural resources.

She defines her role on the Senate Budget Committee as the coordinator and monitor of all appropriations and authorization bills within her budget function, responsible for developing deficit reduction options, and for reviewing legislation to ensure compliance with the governing budget bill.

Chow feels that farming has emerged as one of her most important concerns. In 1985, she worked on many of the revisions to that year's farm bill, including overall federal expenditures, and encouraging greater efficiencies in the industry. The plight of the small farmer is one of Chow's primary areas of focus.

Chow has also been involved in a number of energy issues. In 1987, she developed proposals to reduce energy and natural resource subsidies for domestic oil production. While many of these proposals failed to gain Senate approval, Chow is confident some of the same ideas will surface again.

In the past couple of years, Superfund legislation has been on the front burner. Chow took a lead in assisting with many of the budget increases proposed by Sen. Lawton Chiles (D-FL), the committee chairman.

Doug Cook
Group Leader for National Security
612 Dirksen Senate Office Bldg.
224-0572

*Personal: born in 4/13/49 in
Annapolis, Maryland. B.A. North
Carolina Wesleyan Coll., 1971. M.A.
East Carolina Univ., 1973. M.P.A. Univ.
of Southern California, 1980, with
honors. 1973-1980, infantry officer,
rifle platoon and company
commander, U.S.M.C. 1980-1983,
presidential management intern,
budget analyst, naval sea systems
command. 1983, special assistant to
deputy assistant Secretary of Defense.
1983-1986, Senior Defense Analyst,
Budget Committee. 1986 to present,
Group Leader, Budget Committee.
Publications: Strategic Defense
Initiative: Progress and Challenges,
co-author, 1987.*

Expertise: National security, defense

Douglas Cook feels that one of his strongest points is his ability to work compromises on contentious issues. He feels fortunate to work for Sen. Lawton Chiles (D-FL), whom he sees as a paramount consensus builder.

His spot on the Senate Budget Committee gives Cook the opportunity to combine his interests in policy formulation with his specialty in national security. Cook is an acknowledged expert in defense. In addition to writing articles for *Arms Control Today*, he is often called upon to give presentations on national security and budget issues before such forums as the Air Force War College and the National War College. Cook recently co-authored a book on the Strategic Defense Initiative.

Maintaining realistic limits on defense spending has been the guideline for his efforts on the Budget Committee. He assisted Sen. Chiles in devising a bipartisan compromise on the MX missile program that resulted in the reduction of the total number of missiles. Recently, he has played a key role in the debate on appropriate levels of SDI funding.

Cook's interest in politics has led him to participate in local and state politics as well. In the 1986 elections, he lent a hand in Terry Sanford's campaign for a Senate seat from North Carolina. Cook is also active in Virginia politics.

He has been a member of the Fairfax County, Virginia, Democratic Committee for the past four years and in 1986, worked on Virginia Gov. Gerald L. Baliles's campaign. Thinking about the 1988 elections, he anticipates volunteering to work for Chuck Robb's bid for U.S. senator. Cook is a member of the American Society for Public Administration, Armed Services Controllers and the Capitol Hill Marines.

An athlete, Cook has participated in several marathons, including the Marine Corps Marathon in Washington, D.C. Because marathons are too exhausting, he promises his family to give it up. He has switched to the triathlon instead.

William G. Dauster
Chief Counsel
Committee on the Budget
621 Dirksen Senate Office Bldg.
224-3961

Expertise: Budget procedures, parliamentary procedures, budget law, security law

After a two-year stint in private practice with a New York city law firm, William Dauster altered his career path to pursue his interests in policy formulation, federal legislation and ethical issues. Although active in the New York Bar Association and the New York County Lawyer Association's Committee on Federal Legislation, the schedule of an associate in a busy firm did not allow much time to indulge other interests.

Dauster serves as the procedural advisor to the committee. It's a role that enables him to have a hand in drafting all legislation that comes before the panel, and to monitor its progress of all spending legislation through the Senate.

Dauster says that reviewing and writing budget resolutions and coordinating reconciliation give him a true sense of participation in national affairs. He assisted in drafting a budget resolution adopted in June, 1987 which made increases in defense spending contingent on increased revenue, and was involved in redrafting the budgetary procedures for Gramm- Rudman-Hollings II.

Dauster says he would like to spend more of his free time reading, but the arrival of a new son has reordered many of his priorities.

Personal: born 11/25/57 in Sacramento, California. B.A. Univ. of Southern California, 1978 (Phi Beta Kappa).M.A. Univ. of Southern California, 1981. J.D. Columbia Univ., 1984 (Stone Scholar, Editor-in-Chief, Columbia Journal of Law and Social Problems). 1972, Volunteer, Henry "Scoop" Jackson Presidential Campaign. 1984-1986, associate, Cravath, Swaine and Moore, New York, NY., securities law and commercial litigation. 1986-present, Chief Counsel, Budget Committee.

Kathleen M. Deignan
Group Leader, Human Resources
615 Dirksen Senate Office Building
Washington, D.C. 20510
224-9284

Personal: Born 6/6/44 in Walworth County, Wisconsin. B.A. Sociology, Psychology, Howard Univ., 1971 (magna cum laude). 1964-65, Peace Corps Volunteer, Gabon, French West Africa. 1966-69, Recruiter/Evaluator, U.S. Peace Corps. 1969-72, Research Assistant/Director of Issues Research, Democratic National Committee. 1972, Regional Hearings Editor, Staff Member, National Democratic Platform Committee; 1972, Research Director, 1972 Democratic Convention. 1973-74, Social Worker, Wisconsin Dept. of Health and Social Services. 1974-75, Research Assistant/Training Officer, Inter Study, Minneapolis, MN. 1975-76, Consultant, Virginia Polytechnical Inst. and State Univ., Blacksburg, VA. 1976-82, Professional Staff Member/ Research Director, Senate Special Committee on Aging. 1983-present, Senate Budget Committee

Expertise: Health financing and services, biomedical research, veterans program.

Politics and public service highlight Kathleen Deignan's background—from serving as a Peace Corps volunteer in Gabon, as a Democratic Party operative, and a respected Capitol Hill staffer, she has had an active and varied role in the formulation and implementation of public policy.

She served in a number of leadership positions within the Democratic Party, including issues research director for the 1972 Democratic National Convention.

Today Deignan is a respected analyst on health services and aging issues. While modest about her accomplishments, she is often called upon as an expert on these issues. Her perspective is based on a wide range of experiences that mixes practical, hands-on experience at all levels of government. As a consultant and training professional, she has worked with a number of state and local health and human services providers. Her tenure on the Senate Special Committee on Aging and now, the Senate Budget Committee, allows her the advantage of viewing issues on a larger scale.

In her current position as Group Leader for Human Resources, Deignan has overall coordination responsibility for human resources, education, welfare, medicare, medicaid, biomedical research, veteran programs and other health services. She has been involved in recent changes in Medicaid and Medicare programs, especially those that expanded programs for children and pregnant women, catastrophic health care, and hospital cost containment. She feels that while budget constraints are real and need to be factored into any decision or policy, health concerns are of paramount importance for a vital society, the goal being to work within a balance.

When Deignan has the opportunity, she enjoys outdoor activities such as camping and canoeing, and is active in photography and painting. Her Peace Corps days sparked a taste for travel. After her assignment was completed in Gabon, she traveled home through Senegal, the Ivory Coast and other parts of Africa. Deignan has also visited Europe and Mexico and Central America.

George William Hoagland
Minority Staff Director
634 Dirksen Senate Office Bldg.
224-0769

Expertise: Agriculture, income security, food and nutrition policy, mac budgeting

An interest in budget and fiscal policy issues, combined with a background in agriculture and food policy, has led Bill Hoagland to a number of key positions in the Department of Agriculture and the Congress. As Minority Staff Director of the Senate Budget Committee, he is responsible for evaluating budgetary impact of legislation before the Senate, and coordinating budget and fiscal policy actions for Republican committee members.

Hoagland's expertise in budget issues and food policy is well known. In 1986, he assisted various Republican Senatorial candidates in their campaigns, and is frequently called upon to make presentations on federal budget issues. He continues to research and write on agriculture and nutrition. The Senate Budget Committee and the American Enterprise Institute have published a number of his writings and edited works.

In his role first as Majority and then Minority Staff Director, Hoagland was a key player in drafting the 1986 Omnibus Budget Reconciliation Act, and the 1985 Gramm-Rudman-Hollings Budget Deficit Reduction Act. He led the staff effort to write provisions covering agricultural programs, and program exemptions for low income families.

Personal: born 10/15/47 in Danville, IL. 1965-67, Marine Engineering, U.S. Maritime Academy. B.S. Purdue Univ., 1969. M.S. Penn State Univ., 1972. 1972, Research Associate, PA Health Research Inst.. 1973-74, Assoc. Dir., Comprehensive Health Planning Agency, Fort Wayne, IN. 1974-75, Economist, Food and Nutrition Service, Dept. of Agriculture. 1975-79, Economist, Human Resources and Community Development Division, CBO. 1979-81, Chief, Income Security and Employment Unit, CBO. 1981, Administrator, Food and Nutrition Service, Dept. of Agriculture. 1981-82, Special Asst. to the Secretary, Dept. of Agriculture. 1982-84, Group Leader, Agriculture and Natural Resources; 1984-86, Deputy Majority Staff Director; 1986, Majority Staff Director; 1987 to present, Minority Staff Director, Committee on Budget.

Edward Bentley Lipscomb
Deputy Staff Director
250 Senate Russell Office Bldg.
224-5274

Expertise: Aging

Bentley Lipscomb has long worked in politics and public service. He volunteered for the political campaigns of Pug Ravenal, who ran unsuccessfully for the governorship of South Carolina, and for Richard Reilly, who later won. He also worked for Bob Graham's Florida campaigns for governor and senator.

Lipscomb's professional background is in social and human services programs. He gained administrative experience managing state programs in South Carolina and Florida and later joined the U.S. Senate Committees on Aging and the Budget.

Lipscomb feels his work as Deputy Staff Director of the Budget Committee has given him the opportunity to work on major social service issues, especially Social Security and Medicare.

He says that the "budget neutrality of any new program is essential," an attitude reflected in his work on Catastrophic Health Care and Medicare. Lipscomb views his role as ensuring that policy is affordable, and that programs will not depend on the Federal treasury.

Lipscomb is an avid photographer and enjoys deep-sea fishing.

Personal: born 11/24/36 in Gaffney, S.C. B.A. Univ. of Georgia, 1958. M.A., Gerontology, Florida State Univ., 1966. 1970-1975, Post Graduate, Public Administration, Univ.of Georgia. 1983-1986, Deputy Minority Staff Director, Senate Budget Committee. 1981–1983, Minority Staff Director, Senate Special Committee on Aging. 1979-1981, Majority Staff Director, Aging Programs, State of Florida. 1975-1977, Commissioner, SC Department of Social Services. 1970-1975, Associate Director, Regional Institute For Social Welfare Research.

SENATE
COMMITTEE ON COMMERCE, SCIENCE AND TRANSPORTATION

Marguerite (Macky) Dixon Ayers
Republican Director of
   Administration
554 Dirksen Senate Office Bldg.
224-7535

Personal: born 7/1/50 in Washington, D.C. B.A. Univ. of North Carolina at Chapel Hill, 1972. A.A. St. Mary's College, Raleigh, North Carolina, 1970. The American School of Tangier, Morocco, graduated 1968. 1973-present, Senate Committee on Commerce, Science, and Transportation, Republican Director of Administration.

Expertise: Presidential nominations

A Senate staffer since 1973, Macky Ayers is a longtime staffer for the Senate Commerce Committee. As Director of Administration for the Commerce Committee's Republican staff, Ayers is responsible for reviewing all Presidential appointments within the Committee's jurisdiction. She maintains contact with regulatory agencies and briefs Committee Republicans.

While evaluating a nominee's credentials are among the most important tasks assigned to her, familiarizing the nominee with key players prior to a confirmation hearing is her special talent.

Ayers also manages all administrative operations of a Senate committee that has a very diverse jurisdiction—communications, regulation of consumer products, science and technology, transportation, international trade, and tourism. Her responsibilities include hiring, training and supervising staff, and developing office policies and procedures.

As the daughter of a Foreign Service officer, she spent her elementary and secondary education abroad. She is conversant in seven languages and graduated from high school in Tangier, Morocco.

A gourmet cook, Ayers supervised of the production of a well-received cookbook to benefit a nonprofit community organization in her hometown of Baltimore. She manages to fit into her schedule extensive and varied volunteer work, though she's a working mother with a two-hour commute to her Senate office. Her colleagues are amazed at her ability to juggle work, community, and family. Her secret: a kind of portable filing cabinet—a gigantic canvas bag in which she carries everything she needs to get through the day!

Timothy Barnicle
Legislative Director
Senator John F. Kerry (D-MA)
362 Russell Senate Office Bldg.
224-2742

Expertise: Employment policy

When asked about any particular hobbies he might have, Tim Barnicle replied wryly that he is "too busy working." Indeed he's a political junkie, as his resume clearly shows.

A staunch Democrat, Barnicle has been involved in several political campaigns over the years, including Hubert Humphrey's Senate campaign in 1976, and his present boss-John Kerry's Senate campaign in 1984. He also pitched in to help re-elect Mike Dukakis as Governor of Massachusetts in 1986, after his term away from the seat. He continues to stick by "the Duke", helping out with his current presidential campaign when his busy schedule on Capitol Hill gives him a chance.

Though Barnicle's return engagement on Capitol Hill is quite recent, his experience over the years in a variety of politically related jobs has rendered him a depth of background in issues of interest to Kerry. Barnicle's personality also serves him well. In an effort at self-description, Barnicle quips that he is "often confused with Robert Redford. . .witty and charming." Though the former may be a bit far-fetched, the latter is not far off the mark.

Personal: born 6/2/44 in Worcester, Massachusetts. B.A. Assumption Coll., 1966. M.P.A. Maxwell School, Syracuse Univ., 1967. 1967-1972, State Department. 1972-1973, Congressional Fellow. 1973-1977, Legislative Assistant/Legislative Director, Sens. Hubert and Muriel Humphrey. 1978-1983, Regional Administrator/Director of Youth Programs, Dept. of Labor, New England. 1983-1986, Director of Federal Relations, Commonwealth of Massachusetts. 1986-present, Legislative Director, Senator John F. Kerry.

Amy Berger
Legislative Assistant
Senator John D. Rockefeller IV (D-WV)
724 Hart Senate Office Bldg.
224-6472

Personal: born 5/14/56. B.A. Wellesley Coll., 1977. LL.B. National Law Center, George Washington Univ., 1980. 1980-1984, lobbyist, American Association of University Women. 1984-1985, deputy director of Congressional Caucus on Women's Issues. 1985-present, legislative assistant, Sen. John D. Rockefeller IV.

Expertise: Science and technology, tourism, product liability, aviation

Amy Berger has seen the Hill from several sides and covered a wide range of issues in her career, from lobbyist to deputy director in the House to legislative assistant in the Senate. A self-described "generalist with a law degree," Berger now focuses primarily on science and technology topics on Sen. Jay Rockefeller's personal staff.

In 1985, Berger moved to the other side of the Hill when she joined the small staff of the newly elected Rockefeller as his legislative assistant. Rockefeller became a member of the Senate Commerce Committee where he deals with a wide range of issues, including aviation, science and technology, tourism, product liability, and telecommunications. Berger spends a great deal of time assisting Rockefeller on these issues.

Having lived in Japan as a student, Rockefeller has a keen interest in U.S.-Japanese technology exchange and economic relations. Berger has aided the senator greatly in this area. She monitors the work of the Japanese translation office (created in 1987) for important technical documents at the Department of Commerce and is currently following the U.S.-Japan science and technology agreement now under negotiation. Rockefeller is concerned with the U.S. lag, compared to Japan, of the transfer of laboratory innovations to commercial use. Berger is pursuing federal efforts to expedite this process.

Assigned to the Foreign Commerce and Tourism Subcommittee, chaired by Rockefeller, Berger is also active in the promotion of international tourism to the U.S. (and West Virginia) through the little-known U.S. Travel and Tourism Association of the Department of Commerce.

In the area of science, she follows the development of the advanced materials industry. Berger is also beginning to cover NASA and telecommunications issues for Rockefeller.

In addition to commerce and science issues, Berger covers a multitude of domestic issues, including civil rights, banking, and the socially controversial areas of gun control, abortion, and school prayer.

Mary Pat Bierle
Minority Legislative Planning
  Director
554 Dirksen Senate Office Bldg.
224-1251

*Personal: born 7/31/51 in South
Dakota. B.A. Catholic Univ., 1973.
1974-1978, Teacher, Bishop
McNamara High School, Forestville,
Maryland. 1979-1984, Legislative
Assistant, Sen. Larry Pressler (R-SD).
1985-present, Republican Legislative
Planning Director, Senate Committee
on Commerce, Science and
Transportation.*

Expertise: parliamentary procedure, legislative strategy

Mary Pat Bierle is best known at the Senate Commerce Committee as a guiding light. As the expert on the arcane parliamentary maze faced by staff and Members every day, Bierle leads the way through the federal budget, Senate procedure, legislative strategy, and the English language.

Bierle began her career as a high-school teacher. After four years of teaching English, speech, and drama to the students of Bishop McNamara High School in Forestville, Maryland, she joined the staff of Senator Larry Pressler (R-SD) in 1979.

Bierle was responsible for all issues relating to the Senator's assignment on the Senate Commerce Committee. Communications and transportation were areas of special focus.

Over five years on Senator Pressler's staff afforded her many opportunities to help citizens of her home state—South Dakota. For example, as the Senator's liaison with South Dakota's telephone co-ops during the turbulent days of the AT&T divestiture, she championed Pressler's support of adequate telephone service for rural communities.

She joined the staff of the Senate Commerce Committee in 1985, serving the Chairman, Senator Jack Danforth (R-MO). Bierle coordinated staff work on the committee's portion of the trade bill in the l00th Congress. In 1987, she worked on floor strategy for Senate passage of Danforth bills to require testing transportation professionals for substance abuse, to improve the commercial airline system, and to provide a safer railroad system.

In 1986, she played an important role in bringing to the Senate floor Danforth legislation on transportation safety; and in Senate passage of Commerce Committee bills to provide for the Conrail sale, and to transfer National and Dulles airports to local authorities.

In short, Bierle is the "backroom manager" of the Commerce Committee's Republican staff and Committee legislation. She left South Dakota to attend Catholic University in Washington, D.C. Bierle has completed course work for a Master's degree in American Literature.

A dedicated theatre-goer, Bierle also enjoys spending time in libraries, and playing golf. She is best known for devising a way to play a solitary contract bridge hand while awaiting the committee's legislative turn on the Senate floor.

James C. Brenner
Legislative Assistant
Senator John F. Kerry (D-MA)
362 Russell Senate Office Bldg.
224-2742

*Personal: B.A., Wesleyan Univ. 1979.
Thomas J. Watson Fellowship for
independent study and travel in South
and East Asia, 1979-1980. Masters of
public policy John F. Kennedy School
of Government, Harvard Univ., 1982.
1982, issues staff, The Dukakis
Committee, Boston, MA. 1983-1984,
special assistant for policy and the
budget, Executive Office of Consumer
Affairs and Business Regulations,
Commonwealth of Massachusetts,
Boston. 1984, Federal-State Liaison,
Office of Lt. Governor John F. Kerry.
1985-present, Legislative Assistant,
Sen. John F. Kerry.*

Expertise: Tax, trade, banking, transportation, housing

Jim Brenner, economic advisor to Sen. John Kerry, has the
reputation of being open-minded and bright. Added one well-
known lobbyist, "he's managed to cover a lot of territory over a
relatively short period of time. He knows his stuff—procedurally
and substantively." His four years on the Hill were preceded by his
graduate work in public policy, his campaign experience, and his
assignments in state government, providing ample training for his
Senate work.

Although Brenner's boss has used his Foreign Relations
Committee assignment as a forum for much of his legislative
activity, Kerry has placed considerable emphasis on "being well
positioned on the issues of broad impact to the economy," with a
steady eye on the future implications of such policy.

Brenner was heavily involved on Kerry's behalf during the
Senate's lengthy deliberations on the 1986 tax bill and the 1987
trade bill. In addition to tax and trade policies, Brenner deals with
a host of regulatory reform issues, the result of Kerry's
Commerce, Science, and Transportation, Subcommittee on
Communications assignment. During the next session of the 100th
Congress, Brenner expects to stay busy as the Senate takes up
financial services reform, alternative housing legislation, and
continues consideration of the pending omnibus trade bill.

Brenner usually welcomes the opportunity to share information
with association and industry representatives, as well as with
public interest groups on a regular basis. For Brenner, maintaining
such informational ties serves to widen his and Kerry's "resources
and expands their opportunity to use timely information as
effectively as possible."

Wallace D. Burnett
Legislative Director
Sen. Ted Stevens (R-AK)
522 Hart Senate Office Bldg.
224-3004

Personal: born 1958 in Fairbanks, Alaska. B.A. in Economics, Stanford, Univ., 1980. J.D. Univ of Michigan, 1983.

Expertise: Arms Control, defense, foreign affairs

Of all the individuals who have come to Capitol Hill from around the country to work, Wally Burnett is among those who have travelled the farthest. Born and raised in Fairbanks, Alaska, he attended college in California and Michigan. After receiving his J.D., he began full-time legislative responsibilities for Sen. Ted Stevens.

Before assuming his present position, Burnett served as staff attorney and legislative assistant to Stevens. One of his primary responsibilities in his current position as legislative director is serving as counsel to Stevens for his work as chairman of the Senate Arms Control Observer Group.

Burnett is actively involved in speech writing, as well as drafting and analyzing legislation. In recent years, his areas of responsibility have not only included foreign affairs, but also trade, banking, transportation, commerce, and consumer protection. He often represents Stevens in Washington and Alaska and has traveled to Geneva for nuclear and space arms control negotiations.

A sports lover, Burnett spent the summer of 1986 as an assistant coach of an American Legion baseball team in Anchorage. He also enjoys hiking, running, basketball, and swimming. With his interests in sports, it is no surprise that Burnett has taken a special interest in the Amateur Athletics Act and the U.S. Olympic movement. Since Alaska is bidding for the 1994 Winter Games, he is actively involved in working to make that a reality for his home state.

Thomas W. Cohen
Senior Counsel
227 Hart Senate Office Bldg.
224-9340

Personal: born 11/23/50. B.S. Univ. of Michigan, School of Engineering, 1972. J.D. Univ.. of California, Los Angeles, School of Law, 1975. Master in City Planning, Univ. of California, Berkeley School of City and Regional Planning, 1977. 1976-1977, attorney, Environmental Defense Fund, Berkeley, CA. 1977-1979, attorney, Common Cause. 1979-1981, Assistant General Counsel for Legislation and attorney, Common Carrier Bureau, Federal Communications Commission. 1981-1986, Minority Counsel, Senate Committee on Commerce, Science, and Transportation. 1987-present, Senior Counsel, Senate Committee on Commerce, Science, and Transportation.

Expertise: Communications

As an attorney with the FCC, Tom Cohen prided himself on skillfully working both sides of the Hill. When the Reagan Administration rose to power in 1981, Congressional Democrats sought professionals with expertise as well as an understanding of Hill politics to staff the committees. Cohen, not surprisingly, was among them.

Senator Fritz Hollings of South Carolina, then ranking minority member of the Commerce Committee, recruited Cohen on the basis of his outstanding record in the communications field. Since then, he has worked closely with Hollings, as well as with Hawaii's Senator Daniel Inouye, who became Chairman of the Subcommittee on Communications when the Democrats regained the Senate in 1986.

Cohen's particular areas of expertise are broad and include telephones, broadcasting, cable legislation, private radio and satellite monitoring. Cohen is credited particularly with expertise in the telephone industry. According to his peers in his field, once he had mastered the telephone industry, understanding the broadcast and cable industries was easier.

During his first year with the Committee in 1981, Cohen worked on important legislation such as the television provisions of the Communications Act, lengthening license terms for broadcasters, and instituting the lottery. He also played a major role in the Cable Communications Policy Act in 1984, and he is currently embroiled in the battle over the controversial Fairness Doctrine. He keeps in close contact with the U.S. Telephone Association, the National Association of Broadcasters, the Cable Association, and the major networks.

Cohen is known for working long hours and avoiding evening Hill receptions. He likes to spend his free time with his wife and three children and playing a number of sports. His trademark is his bow ties, which he wears everyday—and he insists that he started the trend well before Illinois Senator Paul Simon made it famous.

Glenn R. Delaney
Legislative Assistant
Senator John Breaux (D-La)
516 Hart Senate Office Bldg.
224-9325

Personal: born 9/23/55 in Toledo, Ohio. B.S. in Biology, Union Coll., 1977. Masters in Marine Science and Ocean Policy, Coll. of William and Mary, 1986. 1977-1982, Commercial Fisherman. 1982-1986, Professional Staff, House of Representatives Merchant Marines and Fisheries Subcommittee on Fisheries and Wildlife Conservation and Environment. 1986-present, Legislative Assistant, Senator John Breaux (D-LA).

Expertise: Merchant marine, commerce, trade, aviation

Glenn Delaney grew up on the banks of the Long Island Sound where he developed his love for marine biology. His fascination with the water encouraged him to work as a professional fisherman throughout college and graduate school. He came to Washington committed to promoting sound policies on fishery issues that concerned him.

When Delaney was awarded a fellowship during his graduate program, he worked on the staff of the Subcommittee on Fisheries and Wildlife Conservation and Environment, chaired by then Congressman John Breaux. After Delaney earned his degree, he continued his work with the Subcommittee, moving into his current position of legislative assistant when Breaux won his Senate bid in 1986.

During his years with the Subcommittee, he was involved with legislation on water pollution coastal zone management, oil and gas development, and mineral development. Delaney primarily has focused on developing dealing with domestic and foreign fishing in US waters. He works closely with the State Department and Japanese officials along with US and Japanese leaders in the fishing industry.

Delaney cites the 1976 Fishery Conservation and Management Act as a landmark domestic fishing legislation that has given rise to all subsequent policy. The Act established large-scale domestic and international fishery management guidelines. Delaney has been active in legislation born out of the 1976 Act, such as the National Fishing and Enhancement Act in 1984 that established a program to enhance the marine environment through placement or artificial reefs and other structures on the ocean floor. In 1983, Delaney was involved in the Fish and Seafood Marketing and Promotion Act, that established a national seafood marketing council to promote seafood consumption and market competitiveness.

Delaney considers his post as a legislative assistant to Senator Breaux as more "reactive" than his work on the Subcommittee which he finds "more intellectually gratifying." He is responsible not only for merchant marine, but also commerce, trade, and aviation issues.

Delaney considers his work on the Hill to be of great value to those who make their living off of a boat. He still considers himself a fisherman first, and tries to return to the water at any free moment.

Loretta L. Dunn
Senior Trade Counsel
428 Hart Senate Office Bldg.
224-9325

Personal: born 12/3/55 in Owensboro, KY. B.A. Univ. of Kentucky, 1976 (Phi Beta Kappa). J.D. Univ. of Kentucky Law School, 1979. LL.M., Georgetown Univ. Law Center, 1983. 1979-1983, Staff Counsel, Senate Committee on Commerce, Science and Technology. 1983-present, Senior Trade Counsel, Senate Committee on Commerce, Science and Transportation.

Expertise: Foreign commerce

As a Senior Counsel on the Senate Commerce, Science and Transportation Committee, Dunn is the person Chairman Ernest F. Hollings (D-SC) turns to for help with trade issues. Dunn is responsible for all trade and investment matters within the committee's jurisdiction. Dunn serves as the committee's liaison to the Commerce Department, the International Trade Commission and the Office of the U.S. Trade Representative.

Dunn is acknowledged as one of the Hill's experts on textile issues. In the 100th Congress, she has been closely identified with S.549, a trade bill introduced by Hollings that would provide for orderly growth of textile, apparel and footwear imports into the United States. Dunn also had a hand in the development of S.891, an alternative trade bill introduced in March 1987 by Hollings—portions of which found their way into HR 3, the 1987 Omnibus Trade Bill.

Dunn joined the Commerce Committee immediately after her 1979 graduation from the University of Kentucky law school. She was recruited by Senator Wendell Ford (D-KY), who brought her to Washington as a staff counsel for transportation on the consumer subcommittee, which he chaired. In that position, Dunn oversaw automobile, regulatory reform and product safety legislation, and served as the panel's liaison to the Transportation Department and the Consumer Product Safety Commission.

Dunn participates frequently in trade forums and symposiums, both at home and abroad, and is often asked to speak on textile and trade issues. In 1984, Dunn wrote an article analyzing the Transportation Department's decision-making process regarding the placement of collision air-bags in automobiles, which was published in the *Chase Law Review*. She is a member of the Washington International Trade Association, and Women in International Trade.

In her free time Dunn relaxes with her husband, and their young son, in their suburban Maryland home. She likes to read, swim and travel.

Robert Eisenbud
Professional Staff Member
566 Dirksen Senate Office Bldg.
224-8170

Expertise: Maritime and ocean policy

On paper, Robert Eisenbud is a legislative expert on maritime issues. As the Senate Commerce Committee's Chief Counsel for the Republican staff (for what he calls "all the wet stuff"), Eisenbud has proved to be much more.

Since joining the Committee as a professional staff member in 1985, Eisenbud has earned a reputation as a consensus-maker. He typically produces legislative initiatives which are unanimously approved by majority and minority members. Legislative efforts in the subcommittees are often "very smooth, thanks to Bob's guidance", says a colleague.

Eisenbud's role as counsel is highly specialized—centering around issues to which the shipping and fishing worlds pay close attention.

Eisenbud is concerned with matters within the framework of the National Ocean Policy Study and the Subcommittee on Merchant Marine. He has contributed to legislation on ocean shipping, foreign trade issues and conservation efforts. Eisenbud says that while he considers himself a conservationist, he works to meet the interests of both commercial enterprises and conservation groups.

His legislative priorities include "finding solutions to problems facing the U.S. Merchant Marine (specifically, the decline in the Merchant Marine and its effect on national security), and continuing efforts to conserve living marine resources. Eisenbud enjoys the outdoors, especially fly fishing.

Personal: born in New York, New York. B.A., Washington Coll., 1965. J.D., George Washington Univ. Law School, 1969. J.D., LL.M. in Ocean Law, Univ. of Miami School of Law, 1972. 1971-1973, Counsel and Special Assistant to the President, National Parks & Conservation Association, Washington, D.C. 1974-1983, General Counsel, Marine Mammal Commission. 1984-1985, Consultant, Special Counsel, Environmental Defense Fund. 1984-1985, Consultant, National Oceanic and Atmospheric Administration. 1985-present, Minority Chief Counsel for Maritime and Ocean. Most recent publication: "Problems and Prospects for the Pelagic Driftnet", Boston College Environmental Affairs Law Review, 1985.

Ralph B. Everett
Staff Director and Chief Counsel
254 Russell Senate Office Bldg.
224-0427

Personal: born 6/13/51 in Orangeburg, South Carolina. B.A. Morehouse Coll., 1973 (Phi Beta Kappa). J.D. Duke Univ. Law School, 1976. 1976-1977, Associate Attorney General for state of North Carolina and administrative assistant for legal affairs, North Carolina Department of Labor. 1977-1982, Legislative and Special Assistant to Senator Ernest F. Hollings (D-SC). 1982-1986, Minority Chief Counsel and Staff Director, Senate Commerce, Science and Transportation Committee. 1986-present, Majority Chief Counsel and Staff Director, Senate Commerce, Science and Transportation Committee.

Expertise: Commerce, space, science and technology

Ralph Everett, chief counsel and majority staff director at the Senate Commerce, Science and Transportation Committee, is the first black in the history of the Senate to head a committee staff. After his 1976 graduation from Duke University Law School, he quickly made a name for himself as an up-and-coming Associate Attorney General for the State of North Carolina. His success in that position drew the attention of Senator Fritz Hollings (D-SC), who recruited Everett for his staff in March, 1977.

Everett's main responsibility is to serve as liaison between Hollings, the committee staff, and the other Members on the panel. In addition, he oversees the workings of the panel's seven subcommittees.

In the past, Everett has been closely identified with product liability reform, which Hollings strongly opposes. In both the 98th and 99th Congresses, Hollings successfully blocked the legislation, introduced by then-chairman Sen. John Danforth (R-Mo), by threatening to filibuster—and it seems likely product liability reform will go nowhere in the 100th Congress.

But on the Commerce Committee, this sort of partisanship is rare. All markups are done in full committee, and Hollings and his staff have taken care to avoid party bickering. Everett helps smooth the bumps between the majority and minority. An admiring lobbyist recently told the *National Journal* that Everett was "the best politician on the Commerce staff."

Early in the 100th Congress, Everett took an active role in ensuring passage of the Fairness Doctrine, which passed the House and Senate last spring and was subsequently vetoed by President Reagan. After the legislation was sent back to the Commerce Committee, Everett expected to move swiftly to get the legislation attached to another bill.

Aviation safety and airline re-regulation also loom large on his agenda, as does the space program, which is undergoing re-evaluation in the wake of the 1986 Challenger space shuttle explosion.

Another major initiative, and a pet project of Hollings, is a provision attached to the 1987 trade bill that would create a National Institute of Technology. As the trade bill went to conference committee, Everett remained confident the measure would be included in the final package.

When he has time, Everett likes to fish, travel, read, and spend time with his wife and their ten-year-old son. Everett is an active member of his local Baptist Church.

Ira H. Goldman
Legislative Assistant and Counsel
Senator Pete Wilson (R-CA)
720 Hart Senate Office Bldg.
224-5422

Personal: born 12/21/52 in Philadelphia, Pennsylvania. B.S. (summa cum laude), Boston Univ., 1974. J.D. Temple Univ. School of Law, 1977. 1972-1973, studio cameraman/news assistant, KHOU-TV (Houston) and WCAU-TV (Philadelphia). 1976-1977, law clerk, Office of the United States Attorney Eastern District of Pennsylvania. 1977-1978, Legislative Assistant and Counsel, Rep. Robert McClory (R-IL). 1978-1983, Counsel, House Permanent Select Committee on Intelligence. 1983-present, Legislative Assistant and Counsel, Sen. Pete Wilson (R-CA).

Expertise: Foreign trade, communications, tax, crime

Ira Goldman is where he is today thanks to two people he never met: columnist George F. Will and former CBS News law correspondent Fred Graham. Goldman decided to attend law school with the intention of becoming a journalist after admiring the work of Fred Graham, as well as documentary filmmaker Frederick Wiseman. "There's not much difference between a journalist and what I do here," Goldman observes. Both jobs require the quick marshalling of facts, coming to a conclusion and trying to present the story in a clear way. "The difference is that, in the Senate, we want to take the extra step and set policy based on those facts."

Goldman first learned about Pete Wilson after reading a column Will wrote about the mayor of San Diego in 1982. The focus of the piece was Wilson's political philosophy and management style, which Goldman admired.

"He sounded like an interesting guy, and it turned out that we had a lot in common. Will's column turned out to be fairly accurate," Goldman recalls. Impressed by what he read, he later volunteered to do research in Wilson's Senate campaign.

In the legislative arena, Goldman was instrumental in efforts to successfully slow down congressional "micro-management" of the nation's intelligence community. "Intelligence is inherently something that can only be managed by the President and the Executive Branch. It simply can't be done by statutes." Goldman is most proud of his efforts to convince the Federal Communications Commission to provide more radio frequency channels for law enforcement agencies. Because of a national limit on radio frequencies, sheriffs in Los Angeles County could not use walkie-talkies, a basic item in law enforcement.

But just as important as his involvement with legislation is Goldman's work for Wilson in the appointment of federal district court judges. Goldman has been involved in the appointment of more than a dozen district court justices.

When one of the coveted seats on the five member Federal Communications Commission came open in 1987, Goldman was one of a handful of candidates considered by the White House for appointment. During the intense lobbying campaign on behalf of the different candidates, it is alleged by insiders in the Washington telecommunications industry, the President himself reportedly received a call from his agent of 25 years ago, Lew Wasserman, urging that Ira Goldman be appointed. Although Goldman was not selected, he obviously is in good standing with his boss' all-important constituency—the Hollywood community.

John E. Graykowski
Professional Staff Member
427 Senate Hart Office Bldg.
224-9360

Personal: born 8/17/53 in Colorado Springs, Colorado. B.S. State Univ. of New York at Brockport, 1975 (magna cum laude). M.A. Legislative Affairs, George Washington Univ., 1980. Senior Managers in Government Program, Harvard Univ., 1985. Columbus School of Law, Catholic Univ., J.D. degree expected in December of 1988. 1975-1976, Legislative Assistant, Rep. John L. Burton (D-CA). 1977-1979, Legislative Assistant, Rep. Fortney Stark (D-CA), House Ways and Means Committee. 1979-1987, Legislative Assistant, Sen. Donald W. Riegle, Jr. (D-MI). 1987-present, Professional Staff Member, Science, Technology and Space Subcommittee, Senate Commerce Committee

Expertise: Energy, agriculture

Throughout his Senate career, John Graykowski can be classified as more of a generalist than most. He has dealt with a very wide range of issues. Originally, when he worked as a legislative assistant for Representative John Burton (D-CA), he was responsible for such subjects as agriculture, military contracts, banking, as well as other general legislative issues. Later at Electronic Data Systems he represented EDS to both the state legislatures and Congress on matters of health care policies and government contracts with EDS. Less than two years after graduating from college he was Representative Fortney Stark's (D-CA) legislative assistant for the House Ways and Means Committee.

In February of 1979, Senator Donald Riegle of Michigan was looking for a legislative assistant for the Senate Commerce Committee. When Graykowski accepted the position, some of his major areas of legislative concern became oil and natural gas legislation along with his prior agriculture concerns and other legislation within the Commerce Committee.

At the beginning of the 100th Congress (January, 1987), Senator Riegle became Chairman of the Science, Technology, and Space Subcommittee. Graykowski joined Riegle's subcommittee as a Professional Staff Member while retaining his Commerce Committee legislative assistant position. As Graykowski puts it, he has been associated with, "almost every issue in the Senate." He has worked with many different issues including a $400 million farm disaster relief bill for Michigan farmers in 1982, the sale of Conrail, product liability, maritime concerns, space commercialization, and all other Commerce Committee legislation.

Patricia A. Hahn
Minority Counsel
Subcommittee on Aviation
516 Dirksen Senate Office Bldg.
224-4852

Personal: born 1/2/53 in Boston, MA.
B.A. Univ. of Michigan, 1974. J.D.
Columbia Univ. School of Law, 1977.
Admitted to Maryland State Bar, 1977.
Admitted to District of Columbia Bar,
1980. 1977-80, Staff, Civil Aeronautics
Board. 1980-82, Attorney-Advisor,
Interstate Commerce Commission.
1982-83, Assistant State Attorney
General, Antitrust Division, Office of
the Maryland State Attorney General.
1983-86, Associate Attorney,
Beckman & Kirstein, Washington, D.C.
1986, Contract Associate, Wald,
Harkrader & Ross, Washington, D.C.
1986-present, Minority Counsel,
Aviation Subcommittee.

Expertise: Aviation, administrative law, antitrust

In comparing her experiences as a litigator and as a congressional staff member, Patricia Hahn summarizes the difference between practicing and making law this way: "While the procedures in litigation are more or less predictable, in Congress you're faced with endless surprises. It's the frequency of unexpected events that makes life here interesting."

Satisfying the varied demands of work as staff to the Aviation Subcommittee presents a constant challenge. The subject area involves everything from airline fares to airport grants to prevention of mid-air collisions. Among Hahn's responsibilities are development of legislation, briefing Committee members, maintaining liaison with the Federal Aviation Administration, and staffing House-Senate conferences on pending legislation.

The 1987 Aviation Reauthorization bill was one of Hahn's first major assignments on the Subcommittee. She helped develop a Commerce Committee consensus on the legislation, and worked to see the bill through final passage of the conference report.

Meeting with the representatives of special interest groups is a part of Hahn's job as she researches issues related to specific legislation.

Though she doubts it will have a practical relevance to her work with the Aviation Subcommittee, Hahn is considering learning to fly and obtaining a pilot's license.

Gerri L. Hall
Professional Staff Member
516 Dirksen Senate Office Bldg.
224-4852

Personal: born 4/6/54 in Aberdeen, South Dakota. B.Sc. Univ. of South Dakota, 1975. M.P.A. Univ. of Winnipeg/Univ. of Manitoba, 1982. 1976-79, Legislative Assistant/ Caseworker for Sen. Larry Pressler (R-SD). 1981, Research Consultant to Manitoba (Canada) Department of Northern Affairs. 1982-83, Policy Analyst/Program Planning Consultant, Canadian Department of Indian Affairs and Northern Development, Manitoba Region. 1983-84, Program Analyst/ Auditor. Manitoba Department of Labor and Employment Services. 1984-85, Policy Analyst, Economic Resource Investment Committee of Manitoba Provincial Cabinet. 1986-present, Professional Staff Member, Senate Commerce, Science and Transportation Committee.

Expertise: Railroad safety, random drug & alcohol testing, hazardous materials transportation

If Henry Clay were alive today, chances are he'd want Gerri Hall on his Senate staff to help maintain his reputation as the "Great Compromiser."

Hall is a professional staff member of the Senate Commerce, Science and Transportation Committee, one of two minority staff members of the Subcommittee on Surface Transportation, and the sole minority staff member for the Subcommittee on Foreign Commerce and Tourism.

Hall is responsible for railroad safety issues, mandatory drug testing for train and airline crews and bus and truck drivers, transportation of hazardous materials and pipeline safety legislation. According to Hall, the two most "compelling issues" she will work in 1988 are rail safety and drug testing. She is working on legislation to prevent drug-related accidents such as the 1987 Conrail-Amtrak train crash that killed 16 people and injured dozens more. The Rail Safety Act of 1987, which would grant the Federal Railroad Administration the authority to penalize rail employees who violate safety rules, was one of Hall's priorities last year. Hall also worked on a transportation industry drug and alcohol testing amendment that was incorporated last year by the Senate into the Air Passenger Protection Act.

Hall's responsibilities include two other safety issues—the transportation of hazardous materials and pipeline safety. She is currently in the process of drafting bills related to both issues.

As a staff member of the Senate Subcommittee on Foreign Commerce and Tourism, Hall works with groups that promote U.S. tourism overseas, including the U.S. Travel and Tourism Administration within the Department of Commerce. In 1986, Hall organized meetings for the U.S. Senate Travel and Tourism Council, a 20-member body created by the Senate Commerce Committee.

She is probably one of the few people at work on Capitol Hill who has legislative experience in both democratic and parliamentarian forms of government. After a three-year stint with Senator Larry Pressler, Hall moved to Canada and worked as the equivalent of legislative consultant to a succession of cabinet ministers in various cabinet departments in the Province of Manitoba.

When Hall is able to find the time, she enjoys singing with The National Singers, a swing/jazz group that makes occasional appearances in the Washington area.

Charles Harwood
Minority Professional Staff Member
554 Dirksen Senate Office Bldg.
224-1251

Personal: Born 4/11/58 in Portland, Oregon. B.A. Whitman Coll., Walla Walla, WA, 1980. J.D. Willamette Univ. Coll. of Law, Salem, OR, 1983 (published several articles in Law Review). 1983-1984,Law Fellow under Senator Packwood of Oregon for the Senate Commerce Committee. 1984-present, Professional Staff Member, Senate Committee on Commerce, Science, and Transportation.

Expertise: Consumerism

Chuck Harwood believes consumer relationships are the essence of commerce.

"The laws and regulations must be fair to all parties, to the consumer as well as to business or there can be a break-down in commerce," he states. "All parties must have equal protection and they must have confidence in the market place." Harwood's duties include drafting legislation, organizing committee hearings, shepherding legislation through Congress, and briefing Senators on issues before the Committee.

He was involved in the drafting of legislation to direct the activities of the FTC, addressing the issues of advertising, deception and competition. Harwood also assisted in the drafting of legislation which directs the activities of the Consumer Product Safety Commission in areas such as product safety and recall. He also participated in drafting product liability legislation defining circumstances under which businesses are liable for product-related injuries and the amount of compensation for which they are properly liable.

He has been active in defining the rights a consumer has in dealing with a business and also the rights a given business entity has when dealing with other businesses.

Harwood worked extensively on legislation which regulates the relocation of sports teams (football, baseball, hockey, etc.) from one city to another.

Insurance is another area of interest. Harwood was instrumental in helping draft Risk Retention Act amendments which were enacted in 1986. These amendments makes it easier for businesses to self-insure or to jointly purchase insurance.

Among his colleagues, Harwood has a reputation of being helpful and accessible to answer questions and to offer advice in the area of consumerism. He is known to be fair, and recognizes and understands both sides of a consumer question or problem.

Harwood lives in Washington and enjoys hiking, back-packing, and traveling.

Robert W. Holleyman II
Subcommittee on Surface
  Transportation
428 Senate Hart Office Bldg.
224-9350

*Personal: born 2/4/55 in New Orleans,
Louisiana. B.A. Trinity Univ., 1976.
J.D. Louisiana State Univ. Law Center,
1979. member, Louisiana State Bar,
Texas State Bar. 1979-1981, law clerk
for U.S. District Judge Jack M.
Gordon, New Orleans, LA. 1982,
attorney, Hargraves, Schueler, Parker
Law Firm, Houston, TX. 1982-1985,
Legislative Assistant, Sen. Russell B.
Long (D-LA). 1985-1986, Legislative
Director, Sen. Russell B. Long (D-LA).
1986-present, Senior Staff Member,
Senate Committee on Commerce,
Science, and Transportation.*

Expertise: Surface transportation

Riding in a car, bus, train or truck is an activity taken for granted by most Americans—but not by Robert Holleyman, whose responsibilities concern the regulations that rule the roads and railways.

Holleyman is senior staff members for the Senate Commerce, Science and Transportation Subcommittee on Surface Transportation, where he works with committee members to "make consistent, sound policy" governing the railroad, bus, truck, barge, pipeline and automobile industries.

Safety is at the core of Holleyman 's legislative endeavors. Last year his subcommittee drafted the Railroad Safety Act of 1987 after careful negotiations with the Federal Railroad Administration and labor organizations. In addition to reauthorizing the Federal Rail Safety Program, the measure would close a loophole in current law by providing for penalties against individuals who violate federal rail safety regulations. Holleyman emphasizes that this provision applies to "both labor and management."

The proposal also would increase current penalties against rail carriers and ensure training and qualifications for train operators. Subsequently passed unanimously by the full Senate, the bill is now in conference.

Holleyman's next project, presently in the research stage, will review the principle piece of legislation responsible for deregulating the railroad industry—the Staggers Railroad Act of 1980. Hearings are anticipated to examine possible amendments to the Act. The impact, Holleyman says, will be significant in the areas of competition, shipping and pricing.

Also under scrutiny is the Motor Carrier Act of 1980, which deregulated the trucking industry. And inevitably, Holleyman has been drawn into the debate over another issue related to transportation safety—alcohol and drug testing.

Holleyman began working in the area of surface transportation several years ago under the auspices of Sen. Russell Long (D-LA), "as the need arose and my interest grew." That specialization became more focused when Holleyman joined the Commerce staff in 1986.

America's four-million miles of highways and 200,000 miles of railroad tracks aren't enough to keep Holleyman in the U.S.—he loves to travel and has toured Europe more than once. Back home, however, Holleyman tries to maintain a personal, as well as professional, rapport with the road, enthusiastically participating in the sport of running.

Richard Jerome
Legislative Assistant
Senator Brock Adams (D-WA)
513 Hart Senate Office Bldg.
224-2621

Expertise: Transportation, judiciary

Richard Jerome plays a different sort of role than most legislative assistants who staff committees for members of Congress. Because Jerome covers transportation issues for a former Secretary of Transportation, Sen. Brock Adams (D-WA), he can play a pivotal role.

Adams's experience "allows us to be inside players on mediation between different interests, for example, labor and management," Jerome says. "And it means the contacts I can develop are a lot more extensive because everyone is an old friend of Brock's from the DOT days."

Although with the Senator's office only since July, 1987, Jerome has already contributed to legislation on various transportation issues: airline deregulation, truck safety and labor relations in the railroad industry. He contributed substantially to the labor protection provisions in the Air Passenger Protection Act, a legislative response to the recent influx of airline mergers.

Jerome also contributed to the Truck Safety Bill, which calls for the elimination of commercial zones currently exempt from federal safety regulations, and charges the DOT with investigating the need for anti-lock brakes.

Personal: born 11/28/58 in White Plains, New York. B.A. Brown Univ., 1980 (magna cum laude, Phi Beta Kappa). J.D. Harvard Law School, 1984 (cum laude). 1984-1987, associate, Verner, Liipfert, Bernhard, McPherson and Hand, Washington, D.C. 1987 to present, Legislative Assistant, Senator Brock Adams (D-Wash).

Jerome also serves as Senator Adams's expert on the Judiciary. In that capacity, he assisted Adams with covering and lobbying against controversial Supreme Court nominee Robert Bork.

Before coming to Capitol Hill, Jerome was an associate with the law firm of Verner, Liipfert, Bernhard, McPherson and Hand, where he was part of a legal team which won a voting rights case in Springfield, Ill. The case was brought against the municipality by its black community, which sought and won single-member voting districts instead of the at-large districts which had kept the Springfield City Council all-white for seventy-five years.

Jerome's previous political activities took him to Mississippi, where he campaigned for Congressman Mike Espy, the first black from Mississippi elected to the House of Representatives.

Regina Markey Keeney
Minority Counsel
Subcommittee on Communications
554 Dirksen Senate Office Bldg.
224-1251

Expertise: Communications

As Minority Counsel to the Senate Commerce Subcommittee on Communications, Keeney reaches out and touches a lot of people in the complex world of American communications, and she knows a lot about phones.

Keeney has been working in communications since the divestiture of AT&T was announced—and she is seeing divestiture through its maturation. The intertwining of different types of communications technologies has not made her job any easier. "Computers and telephones . . . are harder and harder to distinguish," she points out. All these interconnections make for a vast constituency.

The Subcommittee has addressed the legalities of such thorny issues as the restrictions on the activities of Bell operating companies, broadcasting requirements such as the Fairness Doctrine, the regulation of cable television and international telecommunications. Keeney steers away from voicing personal opinions on any communications issues stating she is "just the lawyer." But, she notes most of the Senators on the Committee get passionately involved one way or the other in communications issues.

Her objectivity comes from years of experience: when she joined the committee staff in June of 1985, she brought solid communications law credentials with her. She had "fallen into" a job as a lawyer with the FCC, where she stayed for two years. Prior to the FCC, she had worked for three years in the Washington firm of Hamel and Park. A longtime resident of the Washington, D.C. area, Keeney did her undergraduate work in Business Administration at Georgetown University.

Personal: born 8/20/55 Sumter, South Carolina. B.S. Georgetown Univ. 1977 (magna cum laude). J.D. Harvard Law School 1980. 1980-1983, attorney, Hamel & Park, Washington, D.C. 1983-1985, attorney, Federal Communications Commission, Common Carrier Bureau. 1985-present. Minority (Republican) Counsel, Senate Committee on Commerce, Science and Transportation, Subcommittee on Communications.

Martin P. Kress
Professional Staff Member
427 Hart Senate Office Bldg.
224-9360

Personal: born 11/2/48 in Syracuse, New York. B.A. Univ. of Notre Dame, 1970. MPA, Northeastern Univ., 1974. Ph.D. coursework in Political Science at Georgetown University. 1975-1977, Legislative liaison for Governor and Lt. Governor of Massachusetts, Office of Federal-State Relations, Washington, D.C. 1978-1979, Associate Director, T.E.A.M., Inc. Springfield, VA. 1979, Budget Liaison Specialist, U.S. Department of Energy. 1979-1980, Majority Senior Energy Analyst, Senate Budget Committee. 1981-1982, Minority Staff Analyst for Energy, Agriculture and International Affairs, Senate Budget Committee. 1983-1984, Professional Staff Member, Science, Technology and Space Subcommittee. 1986 to present, Senior Professional Staff Member, Science, Technology and Space Subcommittee.

Expertise: Space and space policy, energy

Martin Kress came to Capitol Hill in 1979 as the Senior Analyst for Senator Edmund Muskie (D-ME), Chairman of the Senate Budget Committee. He was sought for his previous experience as a budget specialist for the Department of Energy and as an energy consultant.

As Senior Energy Analyst, he was responsible for formulating and interpreting the federal budget for energy programs and policy.

Nine years later, he is the Senior Professional Staff Member of the Science, Technology, and Space Subcommittee where he is responsible for all space-related issues and oversight of NASA. Kress now works for Sen. Ernest F. Hollings (D-SC), Chairman of the Senate Commerce Committee.

Best known as the staff person for the NASA Authorization Bill, Kress also drafted the Commercial Space Launch Act and the Land Remote Sensing Commercialization Act, two key elements of President Reagan's space commercialization plan.

The largest part of his days are spent on NASA, particularly "the safe return to flight of the space shuttle" which the Subcommittee has set as its principal goal. On a broader scale, he also is working to help form a consensus on the goals of the civil space program.

When he joined the Commerce Committee in 1983, Kress was responsible for formulating legislation and policy on energy issues which included coal slurry pipelines, oil pipeline deregulation, natural gas pipeline safety, and hazardous materials transportation. In that capacity, he contributed to the Nuclear Waste Disposal Act.

Kress has close ties to presidential candidate Mike Dukakis. Governor Dukakis employed Kress as his liaison to Congress for two years, beginning in 1975.

"Marty" to his colleagues, Kress is clearly a family man—almost every inch of wall space in his office is lined with pictures and drawings made by his three children. A self-described "jock," Kress was a member of Notre Dame University's basketball and baseball teams. When it comes to sports, "you name it and I love it," he says.

Jill M. Luckett
Legislative Assistant
Senator Bob Packwood (R-OR)
259 Russell Senate Office Bldg.
224-5244

Personal: born 9/23/58 in Buffalo, New York. B.A. Bucknell Univ., 1980 (magna cum laude). 1980-1981, Legislative Correspondent for Sen.Packwood. 1982-1984, Legislative Assistant (Foreign Policy, Defense, Banking, Housing, and Small Business), Sen.Packwood. 1985-1986, Associate at Aycock Associates, Inc., government relations consulting firm. 1986 to present, Legislative Assistant (Commerce, Science and Transportation issues), Sen. Bob Packwood.

Expertise: Commerce, science and transportation

During Senator Packwood's fourth run for a Senate seat—and as the campaign started heating up—a legislative position suddenly became available which needed to be filled quickly. Senator Packwood required an individual who could jump right into the work; be familiar with his office operation; and, know his preferences on how to do things. It didn't take any amount of time to think of a former staff member, Jill Luckett, as the one who could fit all the above criteria.

Among the many issues she follows, Luckett is especially interested in the area of communications and deregulation. Because Senator Packwood is a senior member of the Senate Commerce Committee which has jurisdiction over communication and transportation issues, Luckett can actively pursue this interest and others on the Commerce Committee agenda.

During 1978, Luckett spent much of her time on behalf of Senator Packwood fending off congressional attempts to make the Fairness Doctrine a federal law. Abolished by the Federal Communications Commission on August 4, the Doctrine required broadcasters to air opposing views on controversial issues of public concern. Opposed by the Reagan Administration and subject to a veto once in 1987, the highly controversial Fairness Doctrine became tied to a couple of major pieces of must-pass legislation. Luckett was instrumental in working to secure the necessary Senate votes to sustain a presidential veto. Senator Packwood said of Luckett. "I was glad to have her on my side and fighting in the trenches. She is quite a formidable opponent."

A strong proponent of the First Amendment, Luckett would like to continue efforts to protect and expand these rights. In addition, Luckett supports continued efforts made in the deregulation area, particularly in transportation and communications. She views continued transportation deregulation as good for consumers resulting in improved service and rates.

In her spare time, Luckett focuses her attention on a different communications medium—the piano. Although she doesn't have much time to devote to it, her love for the piano and music in general is a preferred escape from Capitol Hill.

Robert L. Mallett
Legal Counsel
Senator Lloyd Bentsen (D-TX)
703 Hart Senate Office Bldg.
224-5922

Personal: born 4/1/57 in Houston, Texas. B.A. Morehouse Coll., 1979 (magna cum laude). J.D. Harvard Law School, 1982. 1982-1983, Judicial Clerk for the Hon. John R. Brown, U.S. Court of Appeals for the Fifth Circuit. 1983-1986, associate attorney for Kaye, Scholer, Fierman, Hays & Handler, Washington, D.C. Member, American Bar Association. Commission on Advertising; Section on Minority Rights & Equal Opportunity.

Expertise: Environment, commerce

Robert L. Mallett came to work as legal counsel for Sen. Lloyd Bentsen (D-TX) the way many people find jobs in Washington. An acquaintance knew Mallets's background. He knew he hailed from Texas and knew the Senator was looking for an attorney to handle environment and commerce issues and generally serve as a sounding board for many of the legal issues which arise in the context of legislation, agency regulation or ethics rules. Before long, another Washington job match was made.

Mallett began serving as Bentsen's legal counsel in January, 1987. It was his first job on the Hill and much of the first year was spent learning how things work.

Essentially, Mallett spent the year monitoring. His bailiwick includes dealing with such federal agencies as the FTC, EPA, FCC, FAA, DOT and a host of others. A number of issues demanded Mallett's close scrutiny: airline safety, the Clean Water Act, the Clean Air Act, private ownership of satellite dishes as well as the authorizations of the Departments of Commerce and Transportation and appropriations legislation. Mallett also has worked on nuclear waste disposal legislation.

Mallett describes himself as an avid reader with a particular weakness for biography and fiction. Like many voracious readers, he demurs when asked to name a favorite author, but says he is partial to the essays of James Baldwin and the fiction of Toni Morrison and Nadine Gordimer.

Alan D. Maness
Minority Counsel
Subcommittee on Surface
    Transportation

Expertise: Transportation economic and consumer issues

After nearly four years at the Justice Department and a number of clerkships, Alan Maness was named Majority Counsel for the Surface Transportation Subcommittee of the Senate Commerce, Science and Transportation Committee in 1986. Now serving as Minority Counsel for the Subcommittee, Maness is deeply involved in economic issues presented by deregulation of the railroads, as well as in improving the safety of the nation's roads.

Maness negotiated the final version of the "Commercial Motor Vehicle Safety Act of 1986" with the House staff. The purpose of the bill is to make U.S. highways safer by setting new safety standards for truck and bus drivers. Commercial drivers must now meet stringent alcohol safety standards that are similar to those established for airline and railroad crews. In addition, commercial drivers may hold only one driver's license and must earn it by passing a driver's test in a bus or a truck—not an automobile, as was previously possible.

Maness was also involved with the "Surface Freight Forwarded Deregulation Act," which improved freight forwarders' ability to compete with other shipping middlemen. He negotiated with the House on the final version and drafted floor statements explaining the legislation.

Personal: born 3/15/56 in Greensboro, North Carolina. B.A. Univ. of North Carolina at Chapel Hill, 1978 (Phi Beta Kappa). J.D. Yale Law School, 1981. 1981-1982, Judicial Clerk, the Hon. Patrick E. Higginbotham, U.S. Court of Appeals for the Fifth Circuit & U.S. District Court, No. District of Texas. 1982-1986, attorney, U.S. Department of Justice, Antitrust Division, Transportation, Energy, & Agriculture Section. 1984-1985, Special Assistant U.S. Attorney for the District of Columbia. 1986-present, Subcommittee on Surface Transportation, Committee on Commerce, Science and Transportation. Published article on state antitrust enforcement in Antitrust Bulletin, *1982.*

In addition to his involvement with the Surface Transportation Subcommittee, Maness also handles Consumer Subcommittee transportation issues. He is responsible for new car safety and fuel concerns as well as anything involving the National Highway Traffic Safety Administration.

As part of efforts to improve consumer safety, Maness is working on legislation that would lead to greater side impact protection for automobiles. The legislation would also extend passenger car safety standards to vans and pick-up trucks. He is working on legislation to encourage the use of methanol and ethanol to fuel cars and a measure to further improve commercial vehicle safety.

After working all week on transportation issues, Maness takes to the road on weekends—on his bicycle. He confesses that he has a "fanatic" interest in college basketball.

David N. Meeker
General Counsel/Legislative
  Assistant
Senator Robert W. Kasten, Jr. (R-
  WI)
110 Hart Senate Office Bldg.
225-5323

Personal: born 3/10/49 in Ann Arbor, Michigan. A.B. Dartmouth Coll., 1971. J.D. Case Western Univ., 1974. 1974-1982, Assistant General Counsel, Hobart Corporation, Troy OH. 1982-1985, owner and President, Gloucester Yachts, Inc., Gloucester, VA. 1985-present, owner and President, Zanoni Corporation, Gloucester, VA. 1987-present, General Counsel/Legislative Assistant, Sen. Robert W. Kasten, Jr.

Expertise: Product liability, business & transportation, related commerce issues

David Meeker's background in the private sector, which included corporate law and owning and operating two companies, spurred his interest in public policy. And with a particular interest in the product liability question, he was a welcome addition to Sen. Bob Kasten's staff.

Today, there is concern the tort liability situation may threaten the quality of health care, the efficiency of manufacturers fearful of lawsuits and the ability of local governments to find insurance for their most important services. In response to this dilemma, Meeker and his boss (who has supported tort reform for a half-dozen years) are intensely involved in finding ways to address this important problem.

Meeker maintains that there has been an explosion in the number of manufacturers and other businesses held liable for unfounded reasons. Add to this, he says, that judges are making decisions about these cases—decisions usually reserved for state legislatures—and Meeker finds the problem is in desperate need of federal legislation. Meeker suggests that there must be a uniformity on the federal level that would establish a more equitable, effective process. Kasten and his aide will undoubtedly continue to play an active role in this area.

Because Kasten is the ranking Republican on the Surface Transportation Subcommittee and a member of the Subcommittee on Aviation, Meeker is closely monitoring various aviation and rail issues. In that regard, he finds especially challenging the need to balance fiscal prudence with air safety and infrastructure improvements. Additionally, Meeker continues to monitor the impact deregulation has had on various transportation modes.

In the area of small business, Meeker notes the successes of minority-owned businesses and the resultant job generation. But while he believes the government must continue to be responsive to small business, he also stresses the importance of "graduation" from the 8 (A) set-aside program.

An avid outdoorsman who enjoys water and land sports, Meeker also continues to study issues involving business and industry, including legislation concerning parental leave, minimum wage and mandated health benefits. While Meeker sees some merit in the congressional attention to these issues, he also stresses the concomitant cost considerations and the fact that legislation should not be intrusive on business.

W. Allen Moore
Senior Advisor to the Minority
554 Dirksen Senate Office Bldg.
224-1251

Expertise: Commerce, finance

When elected in 1976, Senator John Danforth (R-MO) spread the word he was looking for a legislative director with Washington experience. Danforth met and liked W. Allen Moore who was then working in the Ford White House. He consequently hired Moore, and they began their Senate careers together on Danforth's first day in office. In his new position, Moore found himself drawn to the Finance Committee, working on issues such as tax, trade, Social Security, and health.

In 1982, Moore was involved in Danforth's reelection campaign, working on a part-time, voluntary basis as an issues adviser and researcher on the opponent. He has informally acted as an adviser on several other political campaigns. Moore says he is more interested in public policy than in partisan politics, but well understands the two are woven tightly together.

As Senator Danforth moved up the senatorial ladder and became Chairman of the Committee on Commerce, Science and Transportation, Moore found himself also moving up to become Chief of Staff of the committee. His new position required two tasks: handling the legislation that Danforth had little time to spend on and working on those issues that were of particular interest to the Senator. In addition, Moore had the responsibility of tending to the needs of the other Republican committee members.

Personal: born 1/25/45, in Glendale, California. B.A. Pomona Coll., 1966. M.B.A. Stanford Univ. Graduate School of Business, 1971. 1967-1969 Peace Corps volunteer, Bolivia. 1971-1973, Program Analyst, Office of the Secretary, Dept. of Health, Education, and Welfare, Washington, D.C. 1973-1975, Vice President and General Manager, Seneca Corp., Washington, D.C. 1975-1977, Associate Director for Policy and Planning, White House Domestic Council. 1977-1985, Director of Legislation, Sen. John Danforth (R-MO). 1985-1986, Chief of Staff; 1987-1988, Minority Chief of Staff; 1988-present, Senior Advisor to the Minority, Senate Committee on Commerce, Science and Transportation. Publications: "It's More Than Merit Pay," Washington Post op-ed page, July 9, 1983. Member, Board of Directors, International Rescue Committee, N.Y. (since 1980).

In 1986, Moore, who is thought to be one of the most effective legislative strategists in the Senate, was particularly pleased with the passage of a truck driver licensing bill that was included in the Omnibus Drug Enforcement Bill. The legislation will eventually create national standards for issuing licenses to truck drivers. Moore imaginatively thought to link this truck driver licensing issue to the drug bill, reasoning that drug abuse can be a problem in the trucking industry. The law is now being implemented by the states. In 1987, Senator Danforth and Moore found an "aviation consumer" bill to be a good legislative vehicle on which to attach a bill that would provide for random drug testing of public transportation operators.

Moore takes pride in several other measures enacted during his tenure as Chief of Staff: tougher drunk driving laws, the sale of Conrail, the transfer of National and Dulles Airports to local control, a new system of fees for FCC services, risk-retention (self-insurance) amendments, the reauthorization of NASA in the aftermath of the Challenger accident, and budget cuts for many programs under the committee's jurisdiction.

Moore is an avid sports participant when time allows. He and his family were featured on Japanese television last year in a program contrasting a typical American father with a typical Japanese father.

Linda Joan Morgan
General Counsel
254 Russell Senate Office Bldg.
224-0411

Personal: born 5/19/52, in Chester County, Pennsylvania. A.B. Vassar Coll., 1973. J.D. Georgetown Univ. Law Center, 1976. 1976-1978, associate, Welch & Morgan law firm, Washington, D.C. 1978-1986, Staff Counsel, Senate Committee on Commerce, Science and Transportation. 1987-present, General Counsel, Senate Committee on Commerce, Science and Transportation.

Expertise: Commerce, surface transportation

Linda J. Morgan submitted her resume to former Senator Howard Cannon (D-NV) in 1978 when she decided to move from a private law firm to Capitol Hill. Given her background in legal regulatory matters, he offered her a job working on surface transportation issues within the Committee on Commerce, Science, and Transportation, of which he was then the chairman.

While serving as staff counsel on the Subcommittee on Surface Transportation, Morgan was the a key staffer on rail and motor carrier issues. She saw the evolution of legislation from the very birth of an idea to its enactment into law. In particular, in her first years on the Committee, she was involved in the development of major rail regulatory reform legislation, enacted into law as the Staggers Rail Act of 1980. She was also a key staffer in successful efforts to retain funding for Amtrak.

When Cannon was not reelected in 1982, Senator Ernest F. Hollings (D-SC) became the Ranking Democrat on the Commerce Committee. Hollings retained Morgan on his committee staff for the rail and motor carrier issues.

During this period, she was Hollings's key staffer on legislation providing for the sale of Conrail. Because Hollings took a lead on this issue, and because of controversy surrounding the issue, this legislative effort was one of Morgan's most challenging. Development of the legislative proposal spanned some three years from the earliest studies to ultimate enactment of sale legislation in 1986. In that time, Morgan spent two weeks on the Senate floor dealing with many procedural debates and amendments before the bill was finally passed by the Senate.

In 1987, the Democrats having regained control of the Senate, Morgan was promoted to General Counsel for the committee. Her responsibilities were expanded from following the legislative activity in surface transportation to handling all issues over which the commerce committee has jurisdiction. These include aviation, consumer issues, communications, science, space, oceans and trade.

Morgan says her daily schedule involves directing and giving advice on policy and procedural matters and responding to legislative problems that require immediate attention. She spends much time in consultation with other staff on the Committee and with Staff Director Ralph Everett coordinates committee activities in accordance with Hollings' agenda and the interest of the other members of the Committee. In this regard, she directs the scheduling of committee hearings and executive sessions and reviews the materials distributed in connection with those activities. She directs committee legislation through the process, including working with other committees and the House in conference committees and advising on parliamentary procedure, Senate rules and Committee rules. In a 1987 *National Journal* profile, Morgan was characterized as "a nut-and-bolts legislative person who knows members well and has a good grasp of the programs under Commerce's jurisdiction".

Morgan spends her free time with her husband, Michael Karam and her three year-old daughter. She runs daily and plays squash and tennis frequently. She also devotes time to her alma mater and the Senate Employee Child Care Center, in which her daughter is enrolled.

Roy Meeks Neel
Administrative Assistant
Senator Albert Gore, Jr. (D-TN)
393 Russell Senate Office Bldg.
224-4944

Expertise: Communications

In 1977, Roy Neel came to Washington to serve on the staff of a fellow Vietnam War journalist, the newly elected Congressman Albert Gore, Jr. (D-TN). During the first few years, Neel held the position of Special Projects Director. His major undertaking was an unprecedented series of Tennessee statewide workshops on problem issues. Gore called them "day-of-information" programs. Some of the problem areas covered were the federal grants process, education, health care, small business problems, energy conservation, solar energy, and alcohol fuels. The programs were successful in large part because of Neel's communications expertise.

With seven years communication experience, Neel probably has been as involved in satellite television legislation as any other congressional staffer. He was a key staff participant on the 1984 bill that legalized the use of private satellite dishes in the home. Neel is also at the forefront of the staff level on the bill that moves one step further to provide programming availability for satellite dish owners. As Senator Gore's Legislative Director, Neel worked primarily on communications, transportation and energy.

Neel became Gore's Administrative Assistant in June, 1987. He heads a staff of about 50 in the Washington and Tennessee offices.

Personal: born 11/16/45, in Athens, Tennessee B.A. Vanderbilt Univ., 1972. M.P.A. Harvard, 1983. 1965-1966, newspaper sports reporter, Nashville Banner. 1966-1970, U.S. Navy journalist. 1971-1972, newspaper reporter, Nashville Banner. 1972-1974, Assistant to the Mayor of Nashville. 1975-1976, Acting Director of the Tennessee Committee on Humanities. 1974-1977, owner, management consulting firm. 1977-1985, Special Projects Director; Chief Legislative Assistant, Representative Albert Gore. 1985-1987, Legislative Director, Senator Albert Gore. 1987-present, Administrative Assistant, Senator Albert Gore. Publications: Dynamite, 1975, college basketball. Coping with the Environment, editor. "National League of Cities," article on Urban Management.

About the same time Neel accepted his new administrative duties, he also became a significant contributing member to Gore's presidential campaign. He works 40 to 50 hours a week in Gore's office and 30 hours a week on the campaign. Neel is a senior advisor to the campaign with no official title. Yet, he is involved in the campaign working on debate preparation and issues development. Neel believes that the debates are extremely significant factors in this presidential race. His firsthand experience includes traveling with Gore to the debates, briefing the Senator and managing the debate research process. Neel also travels on his own, making speeches on the Senator's behalf. He speaks to rallies of supporters, giving campaign updates and explaining the Senator's stance on issues.

Keeping his sense of perspective, Neel's personal time is saved for his three boys, ages 2,4 and 7.

J. Michael Nussman
Senior Professional Staff Member
National Ocean Policy Study
425 Hart Senate Office Bldg.
224-4912

Expertise: Marine biology/ecology

Personal: born 4/15/54 in Salisbury, North Carolina. B.S. North Carolina State Univ., 1976. M.S. Univ. of South Carolina, 1978. M.B.A. Univ. of South Carolina, 1982. 1982-1983, staff member, South Carolina House of Representatives. 1983-1985, SOuth Carolina Sea Grant Consortium. 1985-1987, staff member; 1987-present, senior professional staff member, National Ocean Policy Study (NOPS).

Since the dissolving of the Ocean and Atmosphere Subcommittee, the National Ocean Policy Study (NOPS) has functioned more as a subcommittee than simply a study group. Mike Nussman and his staff exercise oversight on all ocean-related issues, including coastal zone management, fisheries, marine mammals, ocean energy, mineral resources, ocean pollution, and marine science. In addition, NOPS exercises jurisdiction over legislation relating to weather and atmospheric activities. The principal federal agencies within the purview of the study are the National Oceanic and Atmospheric Administration (NOAA) and the U.S. Coast Guard.In 1987, NOPS saw Senate passage of the Driftnet Impact Monitoring, Assessment and Control Act of 1987, the Plastic Pollution Research and Control Act of 1987, the Sea Grant Reauthorization bill, and the Commercial Fishing Industry Vessel Anti-Reflagging Act of 1987. Nussman's goal since he assumed the study's directorship has been to increase the amount of legislation emanating from NOPS and to track related legislation more aggressively. He says, "I think it's vital, in this time of tight budgets, that we, the federal government, get the most out of every dollar we spend. That means that Congress must constantly be assessing its priorities to ensure that our federal dollars are being spent in the areas of greatest need." To that end, the study is currently reviewing legislation that would increase fishing safety as well as implementing legislation for the South Pacific Tuna Treaty.

Nussman expects the study to be a busy in the immediate future as legislation comes before them to reauthorize the Marine Mammal Protection Act, NOAA's marine sanctuaries program, and the National Aquaculture Act. Additionally, he expects the study to review carefully fishery management and enforcement in the Bering Sea since recent evidence points out that there may be substantial illegal fishing occurring in this region.

The study's agenda for 1988 includes continued oversight on global climate changes. In 1987, the Commerce Committee held hearings, through NOPS and the Science, Technology, and Space Subcommittee, to evaluate priorities for global climate change research. Additional hearings are expected this year.

Nussman describes himself as "your normal hard-working Hill staffer." He enjoys most kinds of outdoor activity, such as camping and hiking on both the East and West Coasts. Not surprisingly, he says, "fishing is the hobby I love most. Before I came to Capitol Hill, I spent quite a it of time outside either canoeing some of our local rivers or fishing offshore. However, in recent years, my time spent outdoors has been confined to sitting in traffic either going to or coming from work."

Steven O. Palmer
Senior Professional Staff Member,
Aviation
428 Hart Senate Office Bldg.
224-9350

Personal: born 2/1/56 in Bowdle, South Dakota. B.A. Kalamazoo Coll. , 1978. M.A. Lyndon B. Johnson School of Public Affairs, Univ. of Texas, 1980. 1980-82, Presidential Management Intern, DOT. 1982-83, Transportation Budget Analyst, Senate Committee on the Budget. 1983-present, Senior Aviation Staff Member, Senate Committee on Commerce, Science and Transportation.

Expertise: Aviation

"Amazingly enough, I am doing what I set out to do. When I came to Washington, the administrators of the Presidential Management Intern program required us to map out 5-, 10- and 20-year plans. My five-year plan is to do exactly what I'm doing right now."

What Palmer is "doing right now" includes staffing and holding hearings, primarily on the Airport and Airway Safety and Capacity Expansion Act. He helped draft the Senate version of that bill and its attendant reports, statements and questions. His primary concern is airline safety, and he was a major participant in drafting consumer-oriented Air Passenger Protection Act, as well as drug-testing legislation for surface transport personnel.

Palmer volunteered in 1984 for the Hollings and Mondale presidential campaigns and has served as precinct captain for his Arlington, VA, district. He still actively campaigns for local candidates. Palmer says colleagues chastise him for not having any hobbies, but he pleads, "I spend so much time here that I have little left to do anything else."

While a student at the University of Texas, Palmer wrote several published papers, including "Railroad Revenue Adequacy: The Movement of Captive Western Coal." This paper won the Transportation Research Forum national award and was presented before its annual conference in 1980.

Palmer sees his role as a committee staff member very clearly: "I don't want to see my face on the front of the Federal Page of the *Washington Post* or my name in the *Washingtonian*. Our job is to work for politicians who want the front page, want the limelight. I consider my job as a staff person to do whatever I can for my boss."

Peter B. Perkins, Jr.
Professional Staff Member
Subcommittee on Science,
  Technology & Space
554 Dirksen Senate Office Bldg.
224-8172

Expertise: Aeronautics and space policy

When Pete Perkins joined the Senate commerce committee's Subcommittee on Science, Technology & Space in 1983 he brought with him a strong business and political background. Perkins puts both of these skills to the test in managing the Committee's annual authorization bills for NASA and the National Oceanic and Atmospheric Administration (NOAA) Satellite and Atmosphere Programs.

The authorization bills require a sensitive balancing act, Perkins explains. With the NASA authorization, he helps balance funding for programs, including the shuttle and the space station, with appropriations for space science research and development. Similarly, with the NOAA authorization, Perkins works to strike a balance between a variety of interests such as the weather service, atmospheric research, satellite observation programs and air quality research.

Although the authorization bills consume much of his time, Perkins also works with the Department of Transportation on issues such as private use of government launch pads. In addition, he keeps in regular contact with NASA, the Office of Management and Budget, the Defense Department and the White House Office of Science and Technology Policy.

In his spare time he enjoys music, reading and sports.

Personal: born 11/26/51 in Jackson, Mississippi. B.B.A. Univ. of Mississippi, 1973. M.B.A. in business, economics and public policy, George Washington Univ., 1984. 1974-75, staff accountant, Ernst & Whinney. 1980-1982, researcher, National Republican Senatorial Committee. 1983-present, Professional Staff Member, Subcommittee on Science, Technology & Space, Committee on Commerce, Science, and Transportation.

Kevin V. Schieffer
Administrative Assistant & Chief of
 Staff
Senator Larry Pressler (R-SD)
411 Russell Senate Office Bldg.
224-5842

*Personal: born 2/26/58 in Yankton,
South Dakota. B.A. Univ. of South
Dakota, 1982. J.D. Georgetown
Univ.Law Center, 1987. 1981,
Securities Examiner, South Dakota
Department of Commerce, Securities
Division. 1982, investigator, District of
Columbia Public Defender's Service.
1982-1985, Legislative Assistant;
1985-1986, Chief Legislative Counsel;
1987-present, Administrative Assistant
& Chief of Staff, Senator Larry Pressler
(R-SD).*

Expertise: Commerce, agriculture, foreign relations

When Kevin Schieffer became Administrative Assistant and Chief
of Staff to Senator Larry Pressler (R-SD), he found himself plucked
from the familiar commerce issues he had been covering for five
years. Today, when most staffers his age work exclusively on
specific areas of legislation, Schieffer juggles his time between the
demands of running a Senate staff of thirty-one and working on
every aspect of the Senator's legislative agenda—the latter
remaining his major interest.

The primary thrust of Schieffer's responsibilities when he first
joined Senator Pressler's staff was to deal with commerce
legislation and to serve as liaison with the Commerce, Science
and Transportation Committee, including space development,
defense issues, and transportation. During that time, he
developed a particular interest in product liability legislation, and
has worked on tort reform efforts during the past three years. He
has co-authored a University of Denver law review article with
Senator Pressler, entitled "Joint and Several Liability: A Case for
Reform," detailing key aspects of their reform efforts (February,
1988).

In his role as Pressler's Chief of Staff, Schieffer has been paying
close attention to state issues as well the more familiar national
concerns. He has been active in fighting airline, bus, and railroad
deregulation in South Dakota. Describing the state as
"devastated" by transportation deregulation, he advocates
alternatives such as shortline railroads and is pushing for
extension of the Essential Air Service program, which provides air
service in four South Dakota cities.

Hill observers note Schieffer has a "very strong, close relationship
with the Senator; not only does he work for the Senator, but he is
also a friend and a confidante." Those who have found
themselves on the opposite side of issues from Schieffer say he
has worked hard to rise above partisan interests and to find
equitable resolutions while remaining a fierce defender of his
boss's interests.

Schieffer is also responsible for dealing with foreign relations,
agriculture, and public works issues.

In his spare time, Schieffer makes use of his pilot's license, which
he has had since 1978, to fly the deregulated skies.

Robert V. Seltzer
Legislative Director
Senator Brock Adams (D-WA)
513 Hart Senate Office Bldg.
224-2621

Personal: born 3/7/45 in Newark, N.J. B.A. Marietta Coll., 1966. M.S. Illinois State Univ., 1967. Ph.D. Wayne State Univ., 1965. 1968-1978, Professor, Univ. of Detroit. 1978, Campaign Manager, Sen. Carl Levin (D-MI). 1978-1982, Administrative Assistant, Sen. Carl Levin. 1983-1986, Political Consultant, J. Buckley & Associates, Washington, D.C. 1987 to present, Legislative Director, Senator Brock Adams (D-WA).

Expertise: Defense, War Powers Act

Bob Seltzer has been concerned about arms control "ever since I first realized the world would blow up if we didn't do something about it," he says.

As Legislative Director for Sen. Brock Adams, a member of the Committee on Foreign Relations, Seltzer handles defense issues and develops legislative strategies.

Seltzer actually began his political career through coincidence. He was a professor and debate coach at the University of Detroit, when he helped then-City Council member Carl Levin with a course Levin was teaching at the University. Levin asked him to work on his Senate campaign and, when he won, he persuaded Seltzer to move to Washington in 1972 as his Administrative Assistant.

This year, Seltzer's defense and strategic responsibilities are centering around the Intermediate Nuclear Forces treaty, which must be approved by the Senate Foreign Relations Committee.

Seltzer also handles nuclear waste issues for Sen. Adams. In 1987, he worked on an amendment establishing a special commission to recommend a scientifically-based procedure for selecting a site for the disposal of high-level nuclear waste. While that amendment was not adopted, Seltzer anticipates continuing efforts to fight changes in the 1982 Nuclear Waste Policy Act.

Seltzer's defense philosophy rests solidly on pragmatic grounds. "The Soviets are not nice people; you shouldn't trust them, he says. "But we have to live with them. We have to work out a way of operating that will allow us to work with each other and not blow each other up."

He is also a fierce proponent of shifting appropriations from nuclear to conventional forces, arguing the present emphasis on nuclear weapons "is a prescription for disaster."

Immersed in his work, Seltzer says he has no time for outside interests other than his wife and two children. "I'm just trying to stay sane," he says.

David C. St. John
Special Assistant to
Chief Counsel
254 Russell Senate Office Bldg.
224-0411

*Personal: born 2/12/58 in Orange, NJ.
B.S. Syracuse Univ., 1980. 1980-1983,
News Reporter/Editor KMOX/CBS
Radio, St. Louis, MO. 1983 to present,
Special Assistant to Chief Counsel,
Senate Committee on Commerce,
Science, and Transportation.*

Expertise: Tourism

David St.John was an award-winning reporter and editor with a deep interest in politics when he met Sen. Ernest Hollings (D-SC) in 1983. The Senator hired him, and St. John began to turn his interest into action.

As Special Assistant to the Chief Counsel of the Committee on Commerce, Science and Transportation, St. John performs a wide variety of duties, including writing and editing speeches, articles, floor statements and press releases for Chairman Hollings and other Democratic senators on the committee. St. John considers himself a "jack of all trades," and enjoys shifting his energies from project to project. His experience as a reporter enables him to focus on a single issue with great intensity and move quickly to a new subject. He finds himself frequently called upon to "translate" the legal language generated by the Committee for his former colleagues in the media.

In the area of tourism, St. John wrote the authorization for the U.S. Travel and Tourism Administration. Although he considers himself always "on call" and finds it difficult to sustain outside interests, St. John is active in Democratic politics and has worked part-time drafting major policy speeches for U.S. Rep. Richard Gephardt (D-MO) prior to and during his candidacy for the 1988 Democratic Presidential nomination. He also worked as a volunteer coordinator and advance staffer for the Hollings for President campaign in 1984. As a volunteer with Democrats for the 80s, St. John was the author of the law enforcement chapter for the *1986 Democratic Fact Book* and is currently working on a writing project for the Democratic Congressional Campaign Committee.

While at KMOX/CBS Radio in St. Louis, St. John won the coveted George Foster Peabody Award for a series of documentaries on dioxin contamination at Times Beach, Missouri. Despite his talents and achievements as a reporter, St. John describes himself as "communications-oriented" and sees his work with the Committee as a way of "directing the public stance" with an opportunity to "cover more bases" than he could as a reporter.

Sally Susman
Professional Staff Member
428 Senate Hart Office Bldg.
224-9325

Personal: born 11/24/61 in St. Louis, Missouri. B.A. Connecticut Coll., 1984. 1984-86, Legislative Aide/Staff Economist, Senator Thomas Eagleton (D-MO). 1986, Fundraiser/Coordinator, Harriett Woods Senate Campaign, Missouri and Washington. 1987 to present, Professional Staff Member, Committee on Commerce.

Expertise: Foreign commerce

Describing herself as an economist, Sally Susman does not consider her work to be "political" rather, her primary focus is on fulfilling a congressional need for more and better information on the activities of foreign investors in the U.S. To that end, she spends much of the day working with numbers and analyzing data, cooperating with the Department of Commerce in an effort to determine both the extent of foreign investment in the U.S. and methodologies to determine its impact.

Susman is far from espousing a "Stay Out" policy. "Our whole orientation is toward exporting more and building a more competitive America. Yet if we didn't have the foreign investment, on which our economy is so critically dependent now, what would we do?"

Susman's colleagues and industry representatives find this objective, non-partisan approach makes working with her an exercise in "finding consensus" instead of fighting a political battle. With her experience in economics and trade, Susman is adept at figuring out how each provision of a bill fits into a larger picture. "She has a very good overview of trade," says one lobbyist and "does her homework on the issues."

Recently Susman has spent considerable time on several proposed compromises concerning foreign investment. She worked to include a section in the 1987 Trade Bill requiring foreign investors to register their investments in the U.S. She also is looking into ways of monitoring such investments.

Susman's other areas of responsibility include textiles and apparel issues, foreign commerce, and tourism. She works with the Department of Commerce on special programs to encourage small- and medium-size businesses to export overseas.

In addition to her work, there are two major components to Susman's life. She plays tennis "every free moment I get," and she is active in "Emily's List," an organization that helps raise funds for women political candidates.

Commerce, Science and Transportation

John Timmons
Legislative Counsel
Senator John McCain (R-AZ)
SR-111 Russell Senate Office Bldg.
224-2235

Personal: born 2/5/55 in Ann Arbor, Michigan. B.A. Elbion Coll., 1977. J.D. Washington and Lee Univ., 1981. 1981, Staff Assistant Congressman Mike Oxley (R-OH). 1982, Legislative Assistant, Congressman Bob McEwen (R-OH). 1983, Legislative Assistant, Congresswoman Marge Roukema (R-NJ). 1983-1986, Legislative Director, Congressman John McCain (R-AZ). 1987, Volunteer, Bob Dole for President. 1987 to present, Legislative Counsel, Senator John McCain (R-AZ).

Expertise: Energy, communications

In 1981, Sen. John McCain of Arizona was looking for an energy and resources specialist. At the same time, John Timmons was looking for a position with a member of Congress from a Western state so that he could concentrate on the public lands. The two were introduced by a political consultant and have enjoyed a beneficial relationship for the five years. Timmons is now the second in tenure on McCain's Washington staff.

Timmons's expertise includes public lands, communications, energy and resources, foreign affairs, and aviation. At age thirty-three, he is a seasoned Capitol Hill veteran. Since McCain was elected Senator in 1986 to replace retiring Senator Barry Goldwater, Timmons has felt his ability to get things done increase.

In 1984, Timmons was involved in formulating and passing the bilingual education compromise. He was also largely responsible for Congressman McCain's strong statement on the House floor which called for the withdrawal of the "peacekeeping" Marines in Lebanon.

Recently, Timmons has worked with McCain (a member of the Senate Committees on Armed Services; and Commerce, Science, and Technology) on The National Parks Oversight Act of 1987. This bill sets up a scheme for the regulation of air traffic around national parks. One section in particular, deals with the safety and environmental concerns of the Grand Canyon. Timmons helped get the legislation passed and is now writing the regulations.

The Commerce Committee on which McCain sits, is considering a "Wilderness Bill." The disposition of Federal public lands in Arizona could stand as a model for other states. One of Timmons's goals is to help settle the issue of the disposition of Federal Lands, because it is important to all Arizonans.

Timmons believes that communications is on the "cutting edge" of changes in our society and hopes to be more involved with that issue. He is also very involved with aviation and has helped promote McCain's position supporting airline deregulation and improving the air travel industry.

Because of his work on public lands issues, Timmons takes a strong interest in rafting and whitewater canoeing. He has rafted in Colorado with McCain, whom is both friend and boss. Timmons is also a Civil War buff.

Patrick H. Windham
Professional Staff Member
Subcommittee on Science,
  Technology, and Space
427 Hart Senate Office Bldg.
224-936

*Personal: born 3/8/51 in San
Francisco, CA. A.B. Stanford Univ.,
1973. Master's in Public Policy, Univ.
of California, Berkeley, 1975. Doctoral
Work, Department of Political Science,
U. Cal. Berkeley, 1975-present. 1976-
1978, Congressional Fellow, Senate
Committee on Commerce, Science,
and Transportation. 1982-1984,
Legislative Assistant, Sen. Ernest
Hollings (D-SC). 1984-present,
Professional Staff Member, Senate
Committee on Commerce, Science,
and Transportation, Subcommittee on
Science, Technology, and Space.*

Expertise: General science and technology policy

Patrick Windham, professional staffer for Sen. Fritz Hollings for almost 12 years, believes his job on the Subcommittee on Science, Technology and Space is to help insure that the United States has "the best and the latest" technology.

His years on the Senate Commerce Committee for Hollings have exposed him to a broad range of issues, and he considers "general science and technology policy" to be his expertise. His subcommittee on science, technology and space has the authorizing responsibility for many different federal agencies," Windham handles all the legislative work load for them.

These include parts of the Commerce Department, the National Science Foundation, the White House Office of Science and Technology, and the Earthquake Hazard Reduction Programs under the jurisdiction of the Federal Emergency Management Agency (FEMA).

Windham notes that he is responsible for overseeing technology policy and industrial competitiveness, making sure that the science and technology arms of the Federal Government help U.S. industries remain competitive by supplying them with up-to-the-minute technology.

Patrick Windham was involved in the passage of the Federal Technology Transfer Act of 1986, legislation that allows federal laboratories to enter into cooperative research agreements with U.S. industries and states. He was also active in the implementation of the Japanese Technology Act of 1986, which strengthened the Commerce Department's capabilities to acquire and selectively translate Japanese technological reports.

This past year, Windham worked overtime on the Technology Competitiveness Act of 1987, enacted to upgrade efforts by the National Bureau of Standards to assist U.S. companies in technological competitiveness. He stresses this approach is not "Japanese-style," but it instead takes the U.S. expertise and technology and makes it more widely and voluntarily available.

Windham believes more can be done to help U.S. businesses. Continuing efforts must be made to maintain America's technological lead, a major priority of his chairman, Sen. Hollings.

In his "other life," Windham confesses he is a political scientist. His academic studies keep him very busy, including his yet-to-be-finished doctoral dissertation.

SENATE
COMMITTEE ON ENERGY AND NATURAL RESOURCES

Patricia J. Beneke
Senior Counsel
362 Dirksen Senate Office Bldg.
224-2383

Expertise: Minerals, mining, oil & gas

Patty Beneke's interest in public policy led her from rural Iowa to the U.S. Capitol, via Harvard Law and several years of legal practice.

Beneke knew she was interested in the Congress from her work on several of now-Senator Tom Harkin's campaigns, when he was a congressman from western Iowa. After winning a number of academic awards as an undergraduate at Iowa State University, she went east to Harvard Law School. Beneke held several internships in legal services while in law school.

After graduation, she joined the Office of the General Counsel at USDA, where she was involved in litigation, administrative proceedings, and legislative drafting relating to domestic farm programs. In 1981, Beneke moved to the Land and Natural Resources Division of the U.S. Department of Justice, where she represented federal agencies in litigation relating to environmental and public lands issues. In 1983, she became a litigation associate in the Washington office of the law firm of McDermott, Will & Emery. There her practice included general corporate, environmental and administrative litigation and client counseling.

Since joining the Senate Energy and Natural Resources Committee, Beneke's responsibilities have included oversight and legislative activities relative to federal mineral leasing, national mining and minerals policy, coal production and distribution, oil and gas production and distribution, surface mining, royalty management, and minerals exploitation, development and production from public lands.

Personal: born 7/20/55 in Ames, Iowa. B.A. Iowa State Univ., 1976 (with Distinction, Phi Beta Kappa). J.D. Harvard Univ., 1979. 1979-1980, attorney, Office of the General Counsel, Dept. of Agriculture. 1981-1983, trial attorney, Land and Natural Resources Division, Dept. of Justice. 1983-1985, associate, McDermott, Will & Emery. 1985-1986, Minority Counsel; 1987-present, Senior Counsel, Senate Committee on Energy and Natural Resources.

Beneke is widely respected for her substantive knowledge. Lobbyists and her colleagues note that she has become adept at the politics of the legislative process and is considered a proven asset to committee chairman and would-be Majority Leader, Bennett Johnston (D-LA).

Beneke is a member of the Arlington (Virginia) Symphony where she plays oboe and English horn.

Scott Cameron
Legislative Assistant
Sen. Chic Hecht (R-NV)
302 Hart Senate Office Bldg.
224-6244

Expertise: Nuclear energy, public lands and western water rights.

Ten years ago Scott Cameron thought he would be working today as an assistant regional director for the Fish and Wildlife Service somewhere in the Pacific Northwest. Instead he finds himself on the Hill handling the energy, environmental and public lands issues for Senator Chic Hecht (R-NV).

In the 99th Congress, Cameron worked hard on the Great Basin National Park Act of 1986—legislation that created a new national park in Nevada. While most bills never see the light of day, five months and six days after initial introduction, S.2506 became public law (PL99-565, S.Rept. 99-458); a rare example of the legislative process moving on the fast track.

If he could have any legislation succeed in the current 100th Congress, Cameron identified the Nuclear Waste Reprocessing Study Act of 1987 (S.1211) as his first choice. This bill would place a two-year moratorium on the high level nuclear waste disposal program in the United States pending completion of an analysis of the economics of reprocessing spent fuel rather than having it go directly to deep geological disposal.

A second favorite on Cameron's "wish-list" is the Nevada-Florida Land Exchange Authorization Act of 1987 (S.854). This bill would give the federal government private land in Florida, eventually becoming a part of the national wildlife refuge system. In exchange, a depressed area in Nevada would receive public land for economic development purposes.

Personal: born 3/17/55 in New York, New York. B.S. Dartmouth Coll., 1977. M.B.A., Cornell Univ., 1979. 1979-85, Dept. of Interior, Fish and Wildlife Service. 1985-present, Legislative Assistant, Sen. Chic Hecht (R-NV).

Energy and Natural Resources

William B. Conway, Jr.
Senior Counsel
Subcommittee on Water and Power
306 Dirksen Senate Office Bldg.
224-4971

Personal: born 6/5/57 in Providence, Rhode Island. A.B. Dartmouth Coll., 1979. J.D. Louisiana State Univ., 1982. 1982-1985, Associate with Van Ness Feldman, Sutcliffe & Curtis, Washington, D.C. 1985-1987, Minority Counsel, Senate Committee on Energy and Natural Resources. 1987 to present, Senior Counsel, Subcommittee on Water and Power, Committee on Energy and Natural Resources.

Expertise: Electric utility industry regulatory issues

Bill Conway has always been interested in public policy and in private law practice he specialized in energy regulatory issues. It was natural for him to seek a position with the Committee on Energy and Natural Resources, especially considering his Louisiana upbringing and his college internship with the chairman of the committee, Senator Bennett Johnson (D-LA). Conway describes his move to the committee in 1985 as a "perfect fit."

One of Conway's first projects was hydroelectric relicensing legislation, and he has dealt with other water-related matters including reauthorization of the Small Reclamations Projects Act and the Coordinated Operation Agreement for the Central Valley Project.

Recently his attention has been focused on uranium fuel cycle issues. The Subcommittee has reported a three-part bill (S.1846) whose first and third titles were drafted in significant part by Conway. The bill would: reorganize DOE's uranium enrichment enterprise as a government corporation, provide cost-sharing for cleanup of active uranium mill tailings sites and provide support for the domestic uranium mining industry. In addition to writing sections of the bill, Conway played an advisory role, negotiating with the staffs of Committee members and keeping the principals informed on issues and developments.

Although he concentrated on natural gas regulation in private practice, Conway has had the opportunity to develop an expertise in electricity issues in the Senate, and he has a special interest in market competition within the electric utility industry. Conway plans to continue in government service for the near future and is interested in the opportunities a Democratic administration might provide.

Growing up in New Orleans, Conway attended Dartmouth where he majored in English and creative writing, a pursuit which still interests him. The most time-consuming of his college activities were the hours he put in as oarsman on Dartmouth's crew. While in law school he wrote a casenote for the Louisiana Law Review, "Moral Damages for Breach of Contract: The Effect of an Obligor's Bad Faith."

Ben Cooper
Senior Professional Staff Member
312 Hart Senate Office Bldg.
224-5360

Expertise: Nuclear energy, research and development

It's been 15 years since Ben Cooper first came to the Hill as a Science Fellow for the American Physical Society. He joined the Senate Committee on Interior a year later in 1974 and was there when it was reorganized into the Committee on Energy and Natural Resources in 1976.

Cooper is most strongly identified with nuclear power issues but has also worked on legislation dealing with fossil energy supply and energy conservation. Although he is assigned to the full committee, Cooper has focused his efforts in recent years on subcommittee issues dealing with research and development.

During his decade and a half of service to Congress, the bills Cooper is most proud of are the Department of Energy Organization Act in the 95th Congress (S.826 sponsored by Ribicoff which became PL 95-91. See S.Rept. 95-164, H.Rept. 95-539 and Conference S.Rept. 95-367), the Nuclear Waste Policy Act of 1982 (See H.R. 3809 sponsored by Udall —PL 97-425) and the Nuclear Waste Policy Act Amendments of 1987. Cooper strongly believes the country should fulfill its responsibility to solving the problem of storing high level nuclear waste.

Cooper considers the legislative process "a pretty good system" for refining views and information on controversial issues as well as educating Members of Congress who may lack a background in high technology.

Cooper believes, "Lobbyists can be a great source of information, if they are functioning properly. They can help you cut to the core, tell you what the real issue is."

Personal: born 4/12/41 in Schenectady, New York. B.S., Swarthmore Coll., 1963. Ph.D. Univ. of Virginia, 1968. 1967-1973, Assistant Professor of Physics, Iowa State Univ. 1973-1974, Congressional Science Fellow, American Physical Society. 1974-1976, (former) Senate Committee on Interior. 1976-present, Senate Committee on Energy and Natural Resources.

James T. Fleming
Administrative Assistant
Senator Wendell H. Ford (D-KY)
173A Russell Senate Office Bldg.
224-4343

Expertise: Energy, natural resources, research and development

When weary of the egos on the Hill, one can look to James Fleming for relief, providing one can get past an initial gruffness that screens out unwanted visitors. But once this defense has been breached, an easy, Kentucky-home manner takes over—giving an accurate impression of this confidant of Wendell Ford since the Senator was Governor of Kentucky. Fleming and Ford have a solid working relationship that can go on automatic pilot because of similar perspectives and years of shared experience.

In Kentucky, Fleming ran the state Legislative Research Service and designed the streamlining of a state senate committee system that had grown cumbersome. Assisting Gov. Ford, he turned his attention to state agencies, reducing the number of departments and duplicative services. This experience has helped him develop an approach to the national capital as if it were a big county seat.

Most casework is efficiently handled by the office. Fleming is amused by other administrative assistants who become scattered by their compulsion to be in on every aspect of a senator's business. He puts in long hours, but they are focused on his main legislative concern, the Energy and Natural Resources Research and Development Subcommittee that Ford chairs. Fleming bemoans the lack of a long-term national energy policy and the mixed signals industries such as solar technology receive from government. He believes "the streets of hell are paved with Harvard MBA graduates pushing for the near-term bottom line." In his view, the United States and developing countries are the only nations with such short-term horizons, and one result will be another energy crisis, during which there will be a rapid return of synthetic fuels. Kentucky coal is central to any energy plan Fleming might advocate.

Personal: born 7/07/21 in Ludlow, Kentucky. A.B. Centre Coll., 1943. M.A. Univ. of Kentucky, 1948. Johns Hopkins Univ., 1948-49. Enlisted as midshipman, U.S. Navy in 1943; released as LT in 1946. 1963-72, KY Legislative Research Director. 1972-74, Special Assistant to Governor of Kentucky. 1975 to present, Administrative Assistant to Sen. Wendell H. Ford.

Although Fleming sees much of the acid rain controversy as generated by environmentalists who espouse an anti-industrial policy for America, he works for greater efficiency in burning coal. Along with clean coal technology, Fleming is interested in promoting fuel cell improvement and conservation. He sees potential in superconductors but doesn't see where the proposed billions of appropriation dollars will come from. He is wary of government involvement that would concentrate superconductor development for Defense Department purposes while competing nations work on commercial uses that might put the United States at an economic disadvantage.

Mitchell Foushee
Legislative Assistant
Sen. Jeff Bingaman (D-NM)
501 Hart Senate Office Bldg.
224-5521

Expertise: Energy, economic development

Mitch Foushee represents Sen. Jeff Bingaman on the Energy and Natural Resources Committee, on congressional task forces and caucuses, and with organizations such as the South/West Energy Council. He advises Bingaman in the areas of environment, agriculture, international trade, economic development, labor, transportation and small business. Foushee developed his relationship with Bingaman when he served as his campaign coordinator during the primary and general election campaigns in 1982. He supervised a volunteer staff, drafted speeches and managed the Senate transition office.

Past legislative issues Foushee has given personal attention to revolve around public lands and natural resources, and that focus will be maintained. He will also have increasing involvement with endangered species, the global climate, and the Alaska Natural Wildlife Refuge. Various labor and agricultural issues are also on his plate.

Foushee is well equipped to assist political efforts in New Mexico. He had studied the Spanish language at the Foreign Service Institute and in Cuernavaca, Mexico. Foushee has also served as executive director of the New Mexico Minority Business Opportunity Committee.

A grass-roots understanding of New Mexico comes easily for Foushee, who was a VISTA volunteer providing management and technical assistance to small businesses throughout the state. During this period, 1976-1977, he also wrote a course on entrepreneurship for the state university system. In 1977, Foushee served as chairman of the VISTA Forum that represented volunteers in the region at the national level. At the ultimate grass-roots level, Foushee doubled as Cubmaster for Pack 84 in Albuquerque. He maintains an interest in volunteerism, tutoring junior high students in mathematics and English through the Higher Achievement Program in Washington, D.C.

Foushee beefed up his grasp of government regulation while working as a senior analyst and as a project manager for the U.S. Regulatory Council from 1979-81. There he helped write *Regulatory Highlights*, which reviewed regulatory reform programs. Also, he managed the research activities of a contractor who wrote a series for regulators on the use of market-oriented alternatives to improve effectiveness of regulation.

In 1984, Foushee took some time off to work as political consultant to the ill-fated Norman D'Amours for U.S. Senate campaign in New Hampshire.

Personal: born 8/14/54 in Pine Bluff, N.C. B.A. Business Administration, Univ. of North Carolina, 1976. M.A., Public Administration, Univ. of New Mexico, 1978. 1976, Small Business Institute, Univ. of N.C. 1976-1977, VISTA volunteer; 1977-1978, Chairman, VISTA Forum, Region 6. 1977-1978, Executive Director, New Mexico Minority Business Opportunity Committee. 1978-1980, Presidential Management Intern. 1979-1980, Senior analyst and project manager, U.S. Regulatory Council. 1982-1983, Campaign Coordinator, Bingaman for U.S. Senate. 1983 to present, Legislative Assistant, Sen. Jeff Bingaman (D-NM).

D. Michael Harvey
Chief Counsel
364 Dirksen Senate Office Bldg.
224-4971

Expertise: Energy law and natural resource management

Growing up in remote upstate New York where some areas did not have electric power, Mike Harvey learned not to take electricity for granted. He has since become a leading expert on energy, Federal lands, and natural resource policy and management. He has worked closely with Chairman Bennett Johnston (D-LA) for fifteen years.

Harvey views the loss of balance in energy policy as the government's greatest mistake of the last seven years. He predicts that cutting research and development of alternative technologies such as solar, geothermal, conservation and synfuels will prove painful, and budget constraints now will make it difficult to regain lost ground. "Free-market reliance has meant relying on the Middle East," where producers have great latitude in manipulating prices. The major task is now finding less expensive ways to diversify energy policy and take a long- term perspective.

Other agenda items that Harvey foresees include arrival at a national consensus on nuclear power and waste disposal; the effects of a free trade agreement with Canada on imports of hydroelectric power, gas, and uranium; reassessing nuclear production facilities (which could be affected by arms control); the promotion of methanol alcohol as a gasoline substitute through mileage credits for car manufacturers; international energy-sharing agreements; the Persian Gulf dependence issue; and oil exploration in the Alaskan Arctic Wilderness.

Personal: born 10/1/34 in Winnipeg, Manitoba. B.A. Univ. of Rochester. J.D. Georgetown Univ. 1955-1960, Eastman Kodak Company. 1960-1973, Bureau of Land Management, Dept. of Interior (1969-1973, Chief of Division of Legislation and Regulatory Management). 1977-1981, Chief Counsel; 1981-1987, Minority Chief Counsel and Staff Director; 1987-present, Chief Counsel, Senate Committee on Energy and Natural Resources. Former Chairman of Fairfax County (VA) Park Authority. Recipient of Secretary of Interior's Meritorious Service Award. Congressional Advisor to U.S. delegation to Third United Nations Conference on the Law of the Sea. Secretary of the American Bar Association's Section on Natural Resources Law and Chairman of Section's Government Policy Liaison Committee.

Harvey predicts that oil will remain the major energy factor for the next twenty years, with natural gas free to find whatever role economics dictate. He does not see super-conductor technology as providing major changes for ten or possibly fifteen years. Programs that are costly or reduce revenues are today in deep trouble. Accordingly, he is pessimistic about the proposed "supercollider". He also believes concerns over the "Greenhouse Effect" will play a much greater role in energy policy formulation.

The Energy and Natural Resources Committee may be among the least partisan on the Hill, with votes more often determined by geographic and constituent industry alliances than by party doctrine. The Democratic margin consists of one vote instead of the usual two and a strict "party" vote is unheard of.

Harvey has played a staff role in the enactment of the Natural Gas Policy Act, the Federal Land Policy and Management Act, the National Forest Management Act, the Surface Mining Act, and the Alaskan Lands Act. However, he is equally proud of his local volunteer role in acquiring 10,000 acres of parkland for Fairfax County, Virginia, doubling its present park system.

Tucker Hill
Legislative Assistant
Senator John Melcher (D-MT)
730 Hart Senate Office Bldg.
224-2733

Expertise: Energy

Last fall when Senator John Melcher (D-MT) called Tucker Hill to offer him a job, Hill accepted, uprooting his family and leaving a comfortable job in Montana to work in Washington, D.C. Hill, who had worked as a state lobbyist in the petroleum and wood products industries, was an attractive candidate to serve as Melcher's chief staffer on the Senate Energy and Natural Resources Committee. As Melcher's assistant, Hill briefs the Senator on Committee business, tracks key issues and considers what input the office will have on legislative efforts. Hill also plays a "coordinating role" between the Senator and the Subcommittee he chairs, the Energy Subcommittee on Mineral Resources Development and Production.

Involved in state government since 1974, Hill also brings that expertise to his role in the Senate. As an Intergovernmental Advisor for Montana in the mid-1970s, Hill advised local governments throughout the state. In that role he co-authored a series of publications on "Small Town Renaissance."

In his previous position as the Executive Director of the Montana Wood Products Association, Hill "ran the association." Wood Products, Montana's second largest industry after agriculture, employs nearly 12,000 people. His chief accomplishment at the Wood Products Association was designing a Workers Compensation Reform Bill, getting industry and labor to support it, and seeing to its enactment in early 1987.

Personal: born 4/5/43 in Richmond, California. B.A. San Francisco State Coll., 1970. 1970-1972, Special Features Editor, The Marin Scope. 1974-1980, Intergovernmental and Energy Advisor, State of Montana, Office of the Governor . 1981-1983, Landman, Hill-Freeman Company. 1983-1985, Director, Project 85, Project 85 Executive Board. 1985-1987, Executive Director, Montana Wood Products Association. 1987-present, Legislative Assistant, Sen. John Melcher.

In his short tenure as a Legislative Assistant, Hill has been involved in Oil and Gas Leasing Reform legislation introduced by Senator Melcher in 1987. He has also worked on amendments to the Geothermal Act, involving efforts to protect Yellowstone National Park, and Gas Royalty issues. Currently, Hill is working on staff drafts for oil shale legislation and negotiating Montana Wilderness legislation. Hill is quick to point out that Montana, Idaho, and Nevada are the only three states that have not yet been the subjects of a federal wilderness bill. According to Hill, one of the most important issues for the Committee, and for the United States, in 1988 is whether to permit drilling for oil on the arctic coastal plain.

Although his two leading issues are oil and gas and wilderness protection, Hill covers a broad range of areas for Senator Melcher. He also has worked on environmental issues, including the Clean Water Act, as well as Interior Department issues, including grazing on public lands, and protection for threatened and endangered animals. Hill has also covered dam construction and safety and forest services. As a Democrat, Hill nonetheless believes vigorously in a bipartisan approach to problem solving.

Energy and Natural Resources

Lynn Ellen Munroe
Legislative Director
Senator Malcolm Wallop (R-WY)
237 Russell Senate Office Bldg.
224-6441

Personal: born 6/15/54 in Ft. Leonard Wood, Missouri. M.S. Boston University, 1978. B.A. Mary Washington Coll. with Final Honors, 1976. University of Vienna, Vienna, Austria, Certificate of Employee Newspaper, Potomac Electric Power Company (PEPCO). 1979-80, Editor, Information Publications, PEPCO. 1980, Speech/Financial Writer, PEPCO. 1981-86, Speechwriter/ Legislative Assistant; 1986-present, Legislative Director, Senator Malcom Wallop.

Expertise: Legislative oversight

When the Potomac Electric Power Company (PEPCO) hired Lynn as a staff writer, she viewed her job as taking complex issues and concepts, such as rate structures, fuel charges and other technical subject matter and making each understandable for the average reader. Now, as supervisor and coordinator of Senator Malcolm Wallop's legislative initiatives, including work of eight legislative staff assistants, Lynn is still simplifying the complicated—not for PEPCO but for the benefit of the half-million residents of the State of Wyoming.

A former speechwriter for PEPCO as well as for Wallop, Lynn has grown accustomed to researching and writing in diverse areas of interest, be it taxes, defense, agriculture or issues affecting the electric utility industry.

While she once worked with PEPCO's senior financial executives in selecting topics, writing articles and implementing review schedules for quarterly reports to the company's shareholders, she now assists Wyoming's senior senator in establishing issue areas, drafting legislative language and writing Senate floor statements. She is specifically responsible for handling legislation in the Energy and Natural Resources Committee, of which Wallop is a member.

With seven years of Capitol Hill experience under her belt, Munroe has worked on issues that cover the political spectrum. From advancing ideas for Wyoming public broadcasting to rewriting federal oil and gas leasing laws, she has had a hand in helping the State of Wyoming and assisting with "people problems."

The expertise that Munroe carried with her from a power company to a Senate office translates into another kind of energy even when she's away from the Hill, from her routine aerobic work-out to treks to Wyoming to learn about new coal production technologies.

Daryl Hays Owen
Staff Director
364 Dirksen Senate Office Bldg.
224-7561

Expertise: Energy and natural resources

Beginning with his first job as a summer intern for Senator Bennett Johnston (D-LA), Daryl Owen has moved steadily up the ladder of responsibility. Now, as Staff Director for the Senate Energy and Natural Resources Committee, he oversees all legislative and procedural activities of the Committee, handles intergovernmental relations between the Committee and executive agencies and departments, and supervises the Committee's internal affairs—what Owen calls, "the whole shop." Owen has held this position since the opening of the 100th Congress, when the Democrats regained control of the Senate and Johnston was named Committee Chairman.

Owen went to work permanently for Johnston after graduating from law school. At first he was Legislative Assistant in charge of all matters before the Energy Committee. Later, as Johnston's Administrative Assistant, he was also the Senator's Chief of Staff.

Owen does not feel that he should be personally identified with any particular piece of legislation. Rather, he sees the legislative process as an endeavor involving many individuals of whom he is one of many contributors. Bills on which he has worked include the Natural Gas Deregulation Act, the Price-Anderson Act and legislation involving a dispute between the state of Louisiana and the Federal Government over revenues from the outer continental shelf. Most recently he was involved in the passage of amendments to the Nuclear Waste Policy Act.

Personal: born 9/9/56 in Shreveport, Louisiana. B.A. Louisiana State Univ., 1978. J.D. Louisiana State Univ. Law School, 1981. 1981-1984, Legislative Assistant; 1984-1986, Administrative Assistant, Sen. J. Bennett Johnston (D-LA). 1987-present, Staff Director, Senate Committee on Energy and Natural Resources.

As an undergraduate at LSU Owen majored in history and was president of his fraternity, Sigma Alpha Epsilon. In law school he was a member of the LSU law review which published his article, "Waste Not Want Not: The Role of the State in Nuclear Waste Storage."

Owen's only foray into political campaigning was on behalf of his father who was elected to Louisiana's Public Service Commission in 1984. When Representative Buddy Roemer (D-LA) was elected governor in 1987, Owen was mentioned by the media as a possible candidate for Roemer's north Louisiana (Shreveport) congressional seat.

Eugene Peters
Legislative Assistant
Senator Bill Bradley (D-N.J.)
731 Hart Senate Office Bldg.
224-3224

Expertise: Energy, environment

"For the most part, I'm involved in 'meat and potato' issues, instead of Sen. Bradley's big issues which are taxes and trade," says Eugene Peters, one of four legislative assistants to Sen. Bill Bradley (D-NJ). In general, while most of Bradley's legislative staff concentrates on taxes and trade, Peters handles many of the remaining issues, including those involving Bradley's Energy Committee assignment, agriculture and environmental issues.

While his primary area of expertise is energy, Peters's work for the New Jersey Senator literally spans the North American continent. Peters has been the leading Senate staffer on legislation that would allow states to regulate and claim title to historic shipwrecks within U.S. waters. In addition, Peters envisions the creation of aquatic parks for the use of sport divers. The shipwreck issue has been controversial in Gulf Coast states, especially Florida.

At the other end of North America, Peters expects to be heavily involved this year with Bradley's bill to add millions of acres to the Arctic National Wildlife Refuge area in northern Alaska. This issue is highly debated because the land in question, adjacent to the Prudhoe Bay oil fields, is thought to hold major oil reserves.

Personal: born 5/21/55 in Bethesda, Maryland. B.A. Princeton Univ., 1976. M.S., engineering, Stanford Univ., 1977. M.P.P., public policy, Harvard Univ., 1981. 1982-1983, Staff Assistant, Energy and Environment Policy Center, Washington, DC. 1983-1985, Manager of Economic Analysis, U.S. Synfuels Corp, Washington, D.C. 1985-present, Legislative Assistant, Senator Bill Bradley.

In between Florida and Alaska, Peters has been very active in Bradley's efforts to return 1.3 million acres of federal lands in South Dakota's Black Hills to the Sioux tribe. The Sioux have pressed for return of the land in federal court under an 1877 treaty. Bradley's bill as drafted would exempt Mount Rushmore and maintain existing military uses of the land. Bradley's interest in the issue stems from his sports career, when he gave basketball clinics for youth on the poverty-stricken Sioux reservation.

Peters has also worked to oppose major water projects in the western states and to reduce price supports for domestic sugar producers, a major issue in Hawaii, Texas and Louisiana. Back home in New Jersey, Peters led Bradley's effort to repeal imposition of an admission fee at the Statue of Liberty and worked to preserve one million acres of New Jersey pinelands.

"We are players in a world market," he says. As an example, he cites the sugar price support issue. "The low cost sugar producers are mostly third world countries which have large debts to major U.S. banks," he says. "Their economies are dependent on access to U.S. markets." Thus, shutting out third world sugar producers is bad for the stability of the U.S. banking system and bad for the U.S. economy, Peters maintains.

Outside the office, Peters is an avid sailor. If not for the demands of home and office, he would have tried out for the 1988 U.S. Olympic sailing team in the Star class, one of seven Olympic sailing categories. Peters is also the proud father of an infant son.

Mark Walker
Legislative Assistant
Senator Mark Hatfield (R-Oregon)
711 Hart Senate Office Bldg.
224-3753

Expertise: Energy and natural resources

Before Mark Walker completed his Master of Management degree, he never thought of working in politics. He had earned his Master's degree in music history. He studied for the management degree because he wanted to expand his career opportunities.

Indeed, his first major position was as an auditor. In 1982, Walker moved to New York City and worked as an auditor for the Marriott Corporation. While later attending college for his M.M. at Williamette University back in Oregon, he worked for the the the Oregon Judicial Department (1984-1985). None of this work was for any political office.

As it turns out, Williamette University is Senator Mark Hatfield's alma mater. The Senator called the Dean of Williamette's Graduate School about an opening in his office. After several ensuing discussions, Mark Walker was hired as a Legislative Assistant, to focus on budget and tax issues. Later, Walker moved into his present position as Legislative Assistant for energy and natural resources, where he has been ever since.

Personal: born 1956 in Roseburg, Oregon. B.A. Linfield Coll., McMinville, Oregon, 1978. M.A., Music History, Univ. of Oregon, I982. M.M. (Master of Management) Williamette Univ., 1985.

In the 99th Congress, Walker was involved in the Columbia River Gorge National Scenic Area Act, which was signed into law in November of 1986. In 1987, he worked largely on nuclear waste legislation. This year, he is working on the Omnibus Wild and Scenic River Act for the State of Oregon. Walker predicts this will be the largest single Omnibus Wild and Scenic Rivers bill since the Wild and Scenic Rivers Act was passed by Congress in 1968. He is also involved in work on timber and public lands, as well as nuclear energy and, in line with his educational background, the arts.

He plays the piano, after giving up music as a career. He likes recreational distance running and bicycling.

Marshall E. (Mark) Whitenton
Legislative Assistant
Senator Don Nickles(R-OK)
713 Senate Hart Office Bldg.
224-5754

Expertise: Oil, gas and other energy resources

When Sen.Don Nickles (R-OK) was searching for an energy policy analyst in late 1986, he turned to Mark Whitenton, an attorney who had been an aide to the House Energy and Commerce Committee and as a lobbyist for a major oil company. Respected by colleagues both on and off the Hill for his knowledge of oil and gas issues, Whitenton has found his new relationship with Nickles to his liking. The conservative Nickles has used a seat on the Senate Energy and Natural Resources Committee to advance his philosophy of free-market allocation. That suits Whitenton just fine. Together, the two are trying to scrap the remaining vestiges of the Carter Administration's energy regulations, including the Windfall Profits Tax and the Natural Gas Policy Act.

Whitenton spent seventeen months in Carter's Department of Energy drafting orders under DOE's crude oil price and allocation regulations. He recalls, "I saw firsthand how the regs were being developed and I didn't like it. I thought it was bad energy policy." Whitenton left DOE for the Republican side of the House Energy and Commerce Committee, where he found Members more sympathetic to his views on such issues as crude oil deregulation, emergency allocation plans, the Strategic Petroleum Reserve and various energy conservation bills.

Like many other energy analysts, Whitenton is concerned the U.S. is once again importing too much oil from OPEC and may face another energy crisis in the 1990s. With the domestic oil industry in a slump, the country may again become vulnerable to OPEC price-fixing. However, he notes with relief that many of the initiatives developed by the Carter Administration to control the supply and distribution of oil and gasoline have been abandoned or repealed during the Reagan Administration. "The Carter legacy taught us what we shouldn't do during a crisis," he observes. "In part, the policy itself created long gas lines by interfering with supply and demand." Whitenton and Nickles advocate free market pricing among competing fuels and decreasing the many regulatory and tax disincentives to producing domestic oil and gas. They also favor opening the Arctic National Wildlife Refuge in Alaska to drilling, a move Whitenton says would have the effect of spurring domestic oil production and reducing imports.

Personal: born I0/25/47 in Pasadena, CA. A.B. Princeton, 1969. J.D. Georgetown Law Center, 1975. 1969-1972, Intelligence Officer, U.S. Army. 1975-1979, Legislative Assistant, U.S. Delegate A.B. Won Pat. 1977-1978, Staff Attorney, Office of Hearings and Appeals, Department of Energy. 1979-1981, Associate Minority Counsel, House Committee on Energy and Commerce. 1981-1985, Associate Director, Federal Government Affairs, Standard OIL Company of Ohio. 1986, Energy and Environmental Analyst, Strategic Research Section, National Republican Congressional Committee. 1986, Legislative Assistant, Sen.James Broyhill. 1986 to present, Legislative Assistant for Energy & Environment, Sen. Don Nickles.

SENATE
COMMITTEE ON ENVIRONMENT AND
PUBLIC WORKS

Dan Berkovitz
Assistant Counsel
458 Dirksen Senate Office Bldg.
224-4039

*Personal: born 7/28/56 in Los
Angeles, CA. A.B. Princeton Univ.
(physics) 1978, cum laude. J.D.
Hastings Coll.of Law, Univ.of
California, S.F., 1982. 1982-1985,
Attorney, Office of General Counsel to
the Nuclear Regulatory Commission.
1985 to present, Assistant Counsel,
Senate Committee on Environment
and Public Works. Publications:
"California's Nuclear Power
Regulations: Federal Preemption?" Vol
9, Hastings Constitutional Law
Quarterly, 1982; "Waste Wars: Did
Congress 'Nuke' State Sovereignty in
the Low-Level Radioactive Waste
Policy Amendments Act of 1985?", Vol
11, Harvard Environmental Law
Review, 1987.*

Expertise: Nuclear regulation, nuclear waste disposal, federal-state regulations.

Dan Berkovitz, an expert in nuclear regulation and nuclear waste disposal, also is deeply involved in federal-state relations regarding nuclear waste and nuclear power issues. His "Waste Wars: Did Congress 'Nuke' State Sovereignty in the Low-Level Radioactive Waste Policy Amendments Act of 1985?" asks whether Congress can make states legally liable for finding disposal sites for low-level nuclear wastes. His other published article examines federal preemption of nuclear power regulations in California.

Berkovitz believes the toughest tasks ahead in his field are ensuring the safe operation of nuclear power plants; and finding and operating permanent repositories for high-level nuclear waste. Though the Federal Government set up a searching program in the Nuclear Waste Policy Act of 1982, there are still enormous technical and political hurdles to be overcome. How to deposit high-level nuclear wastes which no state wants is one of the grueling issues with which Berkovitz contends.

Berkovitz was closely involved with the implementation of the Nuclear Waste Policy Act of 1982, which led to the search in Nevada, Texas and Washington for potential repository sites. He also has been involved with the Low-level Radioactive Waste Policy Amendments Acts of 1985 which established a process for developing new regional disposal sites for low-level radioactive waste. Currently he is identified with the reauthorization of the Price-Anderson Act, which deals with liability issues pertinent to nuclear accidents.

Berkovitz cites as his special interests running on the Mall, and tennis. He is also a die-hard Cubs fan.

Ronald Cooper
Professional Staff member
458 Dirksen Senate Office Bldg.
224-5031

Personal: born 5/2/48 in Doylestown, PA. B.A. Ursinus Coll., 1970. M.L.A. Univ. of Massachusetts, 1974. 1975-77, Senior Planner, Adirondack Park Agency. 1977-78, Planner, City of Bozeman, MT. 1978-82, Director, Flathead River Basin Environmental Impact Study. 1982-86, Senior Legislative Assistant to Sen. Baucus (D-MT) for Subcommittee on Hazardous Waste and Toxic Substances. 1987 to present, Professional Staff Member, Committee on Environment and Public Works.

Expertise: Hazardous waste and toxic substances

Impressed by work Ron Cooper had been doing in Montana, Sen. Baucus (D-MT), Chairman of the Hazardous Wastes and Toxic Substances Subcommittee, asked him to serve as his Senior Legislative Assistant. As Director of the Flathead River Basin Environmental Study, Cooper had been instrumental in slowing the progress of a coal mine to be located nearby Glacier National Park. His determination to preserve the purity of the Flathead River Basin, the largest natural lake west of the Mississippi, prepared him for his work on the Safe Drinking Water Act, reauthorized by Congress one and a half years ago, requiring standards for 83 contaminants.

"We need to get energy conservation back into our way of thinking . . . and reduce energy consumption by 50 percent," Cooper says with conviction. He is one of the key staffers dealing with the so-called "greenhouse effect." Cooper believes the toughest difficulties ahead are to achieve recognition of the problem and build international cooperation in developing solutions.

Cooper is identified with legislation to protect stratispheric ozone on an international scale. Cooper says the U.S. releases one-third of the chlorofluorocarbons that are destroying the ozone layer, but if the U.S. were unilaterally to cease consumption of CFCs, the world might falsely consider the problem solved. Cooper finds technological alternatives less complex than "re-education". There are other ways to make refrigerators, such as using ammonia, he notes, but industry is slow to move toward these options. Cooper's background, an unusual mixture of economics, science and landscape architecture, equips him for the conflict between economic interests and the preservation and cultivation of natural resources.

Cooper misses the skiing and mountain climbing in Montana. He is a natural yet low-keyed advocate for his Senator's state, as well as for his Subcommittee's agenda.

Katherine Y. Cudlipp
Chief Minority Counsel
410 Dirksen Senate Office Bldg.
224-8832

Expertise: Environmental and public works legislation

Katherine Cudlipp landed her first job on Capitol Hill in 1971 after knocking on doors for five months. Returning to Washington for "a change" after a few years in St. Louis, Cudlipp had no particular plan to work on the Hill. But she thought this was a natural place to look for work, and after making "the rounds" secured a job as a research assistant with the then-Public Works Committee.

Cudlipp thrived in the Hill environment. She also got strong direction in her legislative capacity. Sen. John Sherman Cooper of Kentucky, the ranking Republican on the Committee at the time, told his staff that they had to answer three questions about any solution proposed to an issue on which they were working. The first was, "Is it right?"; the second was, "Is it good for the country?"; and the third was, "Is it good for Kentucky?"

Aside from a two-year stint at the National Commission on Air Quality, Cudlipp has been a professional staffer ever since. A self-described "highway specialist" at first, Cudlipp moved on to the Clean Air Act and the Resource Conservation and Recovery Act (RCRA) in 1976, becoming especially conversant with the former. Today, as Chief Minority Counsel, Cudlipp has oversight responsibility for policy issues and programs as diverse as the Clean Water Act, Superfund, the Resource Conservation and Recovery Act (RCRA), and federal Highway legislation.

Personal: born 6/26/43 in Richmond, Virginia. B.A. Randolph-Macon Woman's Coll., 1964 (Phi Beta Kappa). Fulbright Scholar, Sydney, Australia, 1965. J.D. George Washington Univ. Law Center, 1976. 1966-1968, Staff Associate, Applied Mathematics, Chesapeake and Potomac Telephone Company. 1968-1971, Associate Director of Admissions, Webster College, St. Louis, MO. 1971-1976, Professional Staff; 1976-1979, Associate Counsel, Senate Committee on Public Works. 1979-1981, General Counsel, National Commission on Air Quality. 1981-1987, Chief Counsel; 1987-present, Minority Chief Counsel, Senate Environment and Public Works Committee.

Historically, the Environment & Public Works Committee has been a bipartisan committee. Rather than an "I win-you lose situation", the approach has traditionally been a "win-win situation" where everyone comes away from the process with something to his or her benefit. The Committee also values the acquired expertise of its professional staff; staff with less than four or five years on the Committee are the exception rather than the rule.

Cudlipp, who admittedly prefers "analysis, negotiating and compromising" to "fighting", enjoys the Committee's bipartisan approach, particularly the process of forging legislation that is both sound and satisfying to a variety of political and substantive interests.

A resident of Northwest Washington, Cudlipp is an avid cyclist. Typically she travels the six miles between her home and office on one of two bicycles. On weekends and vacations she sometimes ventures even farther afield. Although she denies being a competitive cyclist, Cudlipp says she has done more than 5,000 miles of cycling in two years including a spin through the Canadian Rockies.

Robert P. Davison
Professional Staff Member
408 Hart Senate Office Bldg.
224-6691

Expertise: Fisheries, wildlife, wetlands

Robert Davison has worked on both sides of the legislative process. He has been an advocate for a public interest group, lobbying for environmental protection, and now he is a congressional staffer, assimilating a variety of viewpoints.

In fact, as a professional staff member of the Senate Environment and Public Works Committee, he now staffs some of the same issues on which he previously lobbied as a representative of the National Wildlife Federation.

In the early 1980s, working at the Federation gave Davison the freedom to focus on a relatively narrow agenda, specializing in particular wildlife interests—endangered species and wetlands. On the difference in being on the inside of the process, he notes "it's more difficult trying to reconcile different elements. And you have more of a sense of trying to get legislation passed to improve the situation, even if it's not as much as you would have liked."

Davison's committee work involves oversight of existing laws, including Section 404 of the Clean Water Act, which covers the management of wetlands areas, and the Endangered Species Act. One of his principal legislative involvements since joining the subcommittee staff in 1985 was the passage of the Emergency Wetlands Resources Act, to increase wetlands acquisition.

Personal: born 7/26/48 in Hackensack, New Jersey. B.A. Penn State Univ., 1970. M.S. Univ. of New Hampshire, 1975. Ph.D. Utah State Univ., 1980. 1980-81, assistant professor, Dept. of Fisheries and Wildlife Sciences, South Dakota State Univ. 1981-85, legislative representative, National Wildlife Federation. 1985-present, professional staff member, Senate Environment and Public Works Committee

Recently, Davison helped draft amendments to the Endangered Species Act, which would hasten recovery of endangered and threatened species.

Upcoming activities include management of the Arctic National Wildlife Refuge, amendments to the Fish and Wildlife Conservation Act of 1980 (the "nongame" act, covering songbirds and urban wildlife), and reauthorization of the Atlantic Striped Bass Conservation Act.

After completing his PhD thesis on the management of the coyote populations in northern Utah and southern Idaho, Davison spent one year as an assistant professor in the Department of Fisheries and Wildlife Sciences at South Dakota State University.

He offers a wildlife professional's perspective when he comments that public attention to wildlife programs has declined as concern for environmental hazards to human health has risen.

For Davison, the outdoors is more than the subject of his work. He is a licensed pilot and is active in outdoor sports, including backpacking, canoeing and bicycling.

C. Ann Garrabrant
Professional Staff Member
458 Dirksen Senate Office Bldg.
224-6176

Personal: born in Washington, D.C.
B.A. Notre Dame Coll. of Maryland,
1959-1963. 1963-1965, Editorial
Correspondent, National Geographic
Society. 1965-present, various
positions on the Senate Environment
and Public Works Committee.

Expertise: Civil works program, U.S. Army Corps of Engineers

Ann Garrabrant has spent virtually all of her professional life with the Senate Environment and Public Works Committee, rising from receptionist to professional staff member. In the course of her tenure, she has worked on the full range of issues by the Committee. Her particular expertise and area of oversight is the civil works program of the U.S. Army Corps of Engineers.

Garrabrant started work at the Environment and Public Works Committee as a receptionist, and then rose to the position of secretary. In 1971, Garrabrant became a staff research assistant for the committee, specializing in air pollution legislation.

When Garrabrant attained her current position of professional staff member in 1974, her primary area of focus for the next five years was the Army Corps of Engineers. From 1979 to 1980 her work was concentrated on the Clean Water Act, and from 1980 to 1984 on the Economic Development Administration (EDA).

Garrabrant is now responsible for overseeing the work of the Committee in five major areas: the civil works program of the Army Corps of Engineers, EDA, the Tennessee Valley Authority (TVA), the Appalachian Regional Commission (ARC), and the Federal Emergency Management Agency (FEMA). The work that appeals most to her, and on which she is a leading authority, is the oversight of the Corps of Engineers civil works program. She enjoys working with the "very professional" staff of the Corps, and sometimes travels across the country to Corps' project sites.

Of the multitude of projects she has worked on, Garrabrant cites as a major recent committee accomplishment the passing in 1986 of the Water Resources Development Act, mandating increased non-Federal participation in the cost of constructing navigation, flood control, hydropower and recreation projects. This was the first major piece of legislation in this field in sixteen years. Next year a major focus of committee work will be the technical directions for this Act in the Water Resources Authorization Bill.

Although legislative activity regarding the ARC and EDA in recent years has been rather limited, Garrabrant foresees oversight hearings by the Committee in 1988. There will also be Senate action on the Disaster Relief Reform Bill, an administrative reform of the program administered by FEMA.

Garrabrant is a member of the Maryland Historical Society and Maryland Genealogical Society. She is writing three chapters of the official history of the Senate Environment and Public Works Committee that will be published next year.

Curtis A. Moore
Minority Counsel
410 Dirksen Senate Office Bldg.
224-5761

Expertise: Air pollution and toxic chemicals

Several years ago, as a staffer on the Senate Committee on Environment and Public Works, Curtis Moore found himself involved with Superfund legislation. Those same efforts prompted one chemical industry journal to criticize Moore personally, but one of his colleagues notes that Moore's strongest suit has always been his unwavering dedication to environmental protection. And while this may cause resentment throughout the chemical industry, Moore's commitment still comes highly respected by his Capitol Hill peers.

Moore makes no bones about the fact that he is dissatisfied with the safety performance of the chemical industry. As he says, there is a human toll associated with environmental matters in that about 50,0000 American males over age 40 die each year as a result of lead poisoning. Additionally, Americans per capita drop some 20,0000 pounds of chemicals—mostly, carbon dioxide— into the air each year.

While Moore embraces the concept of retaining an environmental status quo, these disturbing facts make for an unnatural environment.

Moore came to the Committee on Environment and Public Works for two reasons. The first is his unmistakable commitment to the political issues affecting the environment—a commitment that pervades both his background and conversation. Secondly, he felt comfortable with the widely-held notion that the Committee was perhaps the least partisan in the Senate. While Moore laments that this non-partisan spirit seems to be waning, he still insists that it is still issue-oriented and perhaps as non-political as congressional committees come.

Personal: born 6/15/43 in Augusta, Georgia. B.A. Univ. of North Carolina, 1966. J.D. Georgetown Univ., 1973. 1966-1970, U.S. Marine Corps. 1963-1964, reporter, Raleigh News and Observer. 1965, reporter, Associated Press. 1974, coordinator for Region X, VISTA, ACTION. 1974-1976, private attorney, Bainbridge Island, WA. 1970-1973 and 1976-1978, Legislative Director, Rep. and then Sen. William V. Roth, Jr. (R-DE). 1978-present, various positions and currently minority counsel, Senate Committee on Environment and Public Works.

Chief among Moore's duties as Republican counsel are the areas of air pollution and toxic chemicals. In terms of air pollution, Moore has directed considerable attention to the acid rain issues, global climate change and the ozone depletion. His greatest legislative concern is the annual clean air authorization; a bill with which he is altogether familiar. In the area of toxic chemicals, Moore's primary focus is the EPA's Superfund program, whose performance Moore does not rate highly.

National Journal once noted that Moore has been ranking Republican Robert T. Stafford's (R-VT) "Superfund and acid rain specialist [and] has been highly visible because of his aggressive pro-environmental stand."

Jeff Peterson
Professional Staff Member
408 Hart Senate Office Bldg.
224-7069

Personal: born 3/23/54 in Lexington, Massachusetts. B.A. Bowdoin Coll., 1976. M.A. in Public Affairs, Univ. of Washington, 1981. 1976-79, Regional Planning Commission, Bath, Maine. 1979-84, Environmental Protection Specialist, U.S. Environmental Protection Agency. 1985-1986, assignment from EPA to the Staff of Senator George Mitchell (D-ME). 1987 to present, Professional Staff Member, Senate Environment and Public Works Committee.

Expertise: Clean Water Act, ground water protection, marine and coastal protection

Although the Senate Environment and Public Works Committee has primary congressional responsibility for the EPA, the Committee has surprisingly few Agency veterans on its staff. So when the Committee needed new staff members at the beginning of the 100th Congress, EPA insiders were high on the list.

Jeff Peterson not only had the needed experience at EPA, but had a good working knowledge of Congress as well. And in the short time that he has served on the Committee staff, he has distinguished himself as one of the Hill's experts on Clean Water legislation.

With over ten years of professional experience with environmental issues, Peterson is no stranger to the problems he confronts in his position with the committee.

In 1985, Peterson began an assignment from EPA to the staff of Senator George Mitchell (D-ME), who was, at that time, the ranking minority member of the subcommittee with jurisdiction over Clean Water legislation. Peterson served as Mitchell's top aide on this issue, and, when the Clean Water Reauthorization came to the Senate floor, with Mitchell as Democratic floor manager, Peterson was an active participant.

This experience not only gave Peterson a comprehensive knowledge of that particular piece of legislation, but proved to be a valuable lesson in the politics of the Senate. In January, 1987, he left the agency and joined the Committee as a professional staff member.

Although Peterson's responsibilities are at the full committee level, he continues his association with Mitchell. His areas of expertise coincide with the jurisdiction of the Subcommittee on Environmental Protection which the Senator chairs.

As a result of his considerable experience with Clean Water legislation, Peterson's work for the Committee is primarily focused on this issue. However, he is also interested in, and involved with other Committee projects dealing with ground water protection, marine and coastal protection, radon and indoor air quality.

Colleagues note Peterson's attention to detail, understanding of the fine points of legislation, and his experience with the Environmental Protection Agency, have made him an important new addition to the Committee.

Peter D. Prowitt
Staff Director
458 Dirksen Senate Office Bldg.
224-6176

Expertise: Administration

As the energetic and enthusiastic Staff Director of the Senate Environment and Public Works Committee, Peter Prowitt oversees the work of a collegial committee where bipartisanship is the rule and the Chairman and subcommittee chairmen have active agendas. Prowitt is the Committee's manager, drawing on his background in politics and business.

Prowitt's M.B.A. Case Study in 1981 studied the entry into the U.S. food market of the Vie de France Company, which specialized in wholesale French bread, and croissants, and restaurant management. Prowitt saw the company as a success story in management and controlled growth. His two years in business following graduate school as a pharmaceutical marketing representative for Eli Lilly & Co. were satisfying, but his political interests ultimately prevailed.

Prowitt served as staff assistant to then Representative Max Baucus (D-MT) for two years and worked on his successful 1978 Senate campaign. He later rejoined Baucus's staff as a legislative assistant. Specializing in economic development, he soon became the Senator's administrative assistant.

When the Democrats regained control of the Senate in 1986, Prowitt became Staff Director of the Senate Environment and Public Works Committee chaired by Senator Quentin N. Burdick, (D-ND). As a result he said he shifted his energies from A.A., where his focus was "an inch deep and a mile wide," to a narrower area, "at least two inches deep and a quarter mile wide."

Prowitt got off to a fast start when he helped marshal the votes for passing both the Clean Water Act and the Highway Bill, overriding presidential vetoes. He said these were "enormously satisfying and challenging efforts, which took the legislative process about as far as it can go."

Prowitt said the committee is looking forward to another active year, including floor consideration of amendments to the Clean Air Act, reauthorization of the Resource Conservation and Recovery Act (RCRA), and continuing oversight of the Environmental Protection Agency (EPA) Superfund program for cleanup of toxic waste sites. In addition, the committee and its subcommittee are expected to report legislation dealing with the nation's failing infrastructure, and will examine indoor air pollution, ozone depletion, groundwater policy, biotechnology and other environmental and public works initiatives.

When he has time, he enjoys sports and reading history.

Personal: born 8/4/55. B.A., Zoology, DePauw Univ., 1977. American Univ., Aix-en-Provence, France 1975. M.B.A. Univ. of Virginia, 1981, (Dean's award for S.B.S. excellence, Phi Kappa Psi). 1977-1979, staff assistant, Rep. Max Baucus (D-Mont.). 1981-1983, marketing representative, Eli Lilly & Co., Chicago. 1983-1986, legislative assistant, administrative assistant-Sen. Max Baucus. 1986-present, staff director, Committee on Environment and Public Works.

Mark Reiter
Professional Staff Member
415 Hart Senate Office Bldg.
224-6191

*Personal: born 10/29/45 in Bronx,
New York. B.S., Temple Univ., 1967.
1973-1974, Staff Member, Office of
Rep. Bella Abzug. 1974-1976, Staff
Assistant, The National Commission
on Water Quality. 1977-1987, The
Office of Water and the Congressional
Liaison Office of the U.S.
Environmental Protection Agency.
1987-present, Professional Staff
Member, Senate Environment and
Public Works Committee.*

Expertise: Superfund and environmental oversight

When the Senate changed hands in 1987, the new Democratic leadership of the Environment and Public Works Committee decided to create a new legislative subcommittee for the Environmental Protection Agency's massive "Superfund" program. Oversight of all Environmental Protection activities was included as a major responsibility of this new subcommittee. Hence, there was a need for staff members who were seasoned EPA veterans and familiar with the inner workings of Congress. Mark Reiter was a perfect fit for the job.

Reiter had fifteen years of experience on environmental issues, working as a Hill staffer for Rep. Bella Abzug (D-NY) and as a long-time EPA "insider." He combined the experience and expertise the Committee needed to fill the staff opening created by its newest sub-panel.

Although Reiter works at the full committee level—an important distinction on Environment and Public Works—his responsibilities coincide with the jurisdiction of the Superfund Subcommittee. Consequently, Reiter is closely associated with the subcommittee's chairman, Senator Frank Lautenberg (D-NJ), and his staff.

Reiter notes that Environment and Public Works is one of the least partisan committees in the Senate–a place where issues usually take precedence over partisan politics in determining the agenda. Reiter is thus able to work closely and amicably with members of both parties—a fact facilitated by his good humor and receptive disposition.

Reiter has specialized on Superfund, but he also provides the committee with the benefit of his nine years of EPA experience in the Congressional oversight of environmental concerns.

Reiter has been conspicuously involved with the Clean Water Bill, which he followed as an EPA staffer during its 1977 and 1981 reforms. The 1987 amendments to the law greeted him again in his new job on the Committee. His colleagues consider him to be one of the most well-informed Hill staffers on clean water issues.

Like many Committee insiders, Reiter is especially concerned with international environmental issues, such as stratospheric ozone depletion, global warming and international transportation and disposition of hazardous substances. Because some of these issues are partly under the jurisdiction of the Superfund and Environmental Oversight Subcommittee, and because the Subcommittee also oversees the activities of EPA's office of International Activities, they are within Reiter's professional service. But he notes that Congress's approach to these problems remains *ad hoc*, and hopes that its response can be broadened and more effectively institutionalized.

Reiter's colleagues note that his combination of substantive expertise on the issues and his procedural insight into the workings of the EPA, made him a welcome addition to the Committee staff.

Reiter will participate in the drafting of the Superfund and Environmental Oversight Subcommittee's report on Superfund implementation. The report will be based upon the Subcommittee's extensive 1987 oversight of the Superfund program. It is expected to be a baseline from which the Subcommittee will continue to oversee Superfund. He is also expected to participate in the Committee's effort to reauthorize the Resource Conservation and Recovery Act (RCAA), during the second session of the 100th Congress.

Steven J. Shimberg
Minority Counsel
508 Hart Senate Office Bldg.
224-I063

Personal: born 3/11/53 in New York, New York. B.A. State Univ. of New York at Buffalo, 1975 (magna cum laude). J.D. Duke Univ. School of Law, 1978. 1978-1981, trial attorney, Wildlife Section, Land and Natural Resources Division, U.S. Department of Justice. 1983-1987, Director and Chief Counsel, Subcommittee on Environmental Pollution, Senate Environment and Public Works Committee. January I987-present, Minority Counsel, Senate Environment and Public Works Committee.

Expertise: Hazardous waste and major committee legislation

Steven Shimberg first came to the Senate Committee on Environment and Public Works as a specialist on wildlife issues under the "wing" of Senator John Chafee (R-RI). Now, seven years later, Shimberg is still closely associated with Chafee but has advanced to the position of Minority Counsel and has distinguished himself as one of the Hill's foremost authorities on hazardous waste.

Colleagues consistently remark on Shimberg's depth of knowledge on environmental issues. They point out this knowledge is matched by a personal commitment to the environment.

In Committee circles, Shimberg's name is often associated with RCRA, the Resource Conservation and Recovery Act, and his hand can be conspicuously seen in the 1984 rewrite of this law. It is in the general area of hazardous waste management that he has made a name for himself.

But Shimberg has increasingly come to believe, along with several other staff members, that getting our own environmental house in order may not be enough—the most important environmental problems today, according to Shimberg, are not domestic but global in nature.

Thus the Committee's Minority Counsel has broadened his legislative focus and his professional expertise to include issues such as stratospheric ozone depletion, the greenhouse effect and global climate change, and tropical deforestation.

In pursuit of this interest, Shimberg has acted as both advisor and delegate to international environmental negotiating conferences in Geneva, Vienna, Montreal, and elsewhere. Here at home, he provides the Members of the Committee with the benefit of this knowledge and experience.

Shimberg describes his job as primarily one of issue-oriented problem-solving. This description is in keeping with his reputation, widely held by both the Members and the staff of the Environment and Public Works Committee, as pragmatic and nonpartisan.

As Shimberg notes, on this Committee alliances are traditionally made along issue-lines rather than party-lines. Thus Shimberg, officially a minority staff official, constantly works closely with both majority and minority Members.

This approach to the work of the Committee reflects Shimberg's firm belief that, as he quotes his long-time boss, Sen. Chafee, "environmentalism is not a partisan issue."

Timothy E. Smith
Chief Counsel
Sen. John B. Breaux (D-LA)
516 Hart Senate Office Bldg.
224-4623

Expertise: Nuclear power, hazardous waste, energy

As an associate attorney with a downtown law firm, Tim Smith had the opportunity to work with the Congress on law-of-the-sea negotiations and issues affecting the Outer Continental Shelf (OCS). The expertise he developed in those areas brought him highly recommended to then-Congressman John Breaux. And upon his election to the Senate in 1986, Sen. Breaux retained Smith and made him his Chief Counsel.

Nuclear power, hazardous waste, and energy issues fall under Smith's bailiwick. Yet his involvement with legislation does not end there; he is also involved with tax matters, various maritime issues, and the product liability question. His familiarity with the legislative process generally also means he is frequently called on regarding other matters.

As Chief Counsel to Sen. Breaux, Smith is currently involved in assisting his boss with legislation designed to reorganize the Nuclear Regulatory Commission. Currently, the NRC is an independent agency with five commissioners. Sen. Breaux and Sen. Alan Simpson (R-WY), the other Senate author, would like to facilitate a restructuring of NRC so that it has one administrator in the executive branch. Breaux, with Smith's staff assistance, held six oversight hearings on this issue last year and found that there is sometimes a lack of accountability as a result of the NRC's having five agency heads. Smith believes such a system fortifies the perception that the NRC maintains too close a relationship with nuclear regulated industries.

Personal: born 11/11/52 in Port Chester, New York. B.A. (cum laude), Florida State University, 1973. J.D., Washington College of Law, American University, 1979, 1979-81, Associate, David P. Stang, Attorneys at Law, Washington, D.C. 1981-1986, Counsel, Subcommittee on Fisheries and Wildlife Conservation and the Environment, House Committee on Merchant Marine and Fisheries. 1987-present, Chief Counsel, Sen. John B. Breaux (D-LA).

Another nuclear issue Smith is involved with concerns the reauthorization of the Price-Anderson Act. Specifically, Smith and his boss see the need to expand indemnity coverage for both nuclear power plants and contractors who work for the Defense and Energy Departments. Smith's knowledge of hazardous waste issues was an asset in the 1984 reauthorization of the Resources Conservation Recovery Act. A primary goal of that measure was to reauthorize the regulatory regime that provides guidelines and a "cradle-to-grave" tracking program of hazardous waste.

Also active in the area of the budget, Smith played a major role in the 1985 Congressional Budget Reconciliation Act (COBRA). Of special interest to Breaux was a provision requiring the division of federal revenues from lands adjacent to coastal state seaward boundaries, including those in Louisiana. Under this provision, the federal government and various coastal states divided the revenues, of which Louisiana received some $700 million.

SENATE
COMMITTEE ON FINANCE

Richard Belas
Chief Counsel to Republican
    Leader
S-235 Capitol Bldg.
224-4638

Personal: born 4/2/48 in New Britain, Connecticut. A.B. Trinity Coll., 1970. J.D. Univ. of Virginia 1973, member, Law Review editorial board. LL.M. (Taxation) New York Univ. 1977. 1973-1974, associate, Shea and Gould. 1974-1976, associate, Day, Berry and Howard. 1977-1980, assistant tax counsel, Connecticut General Life Insurance Co. 1980, Minority Tax Counsel; 1981-1982, Tax Counsel;1983-1985, Deputy Chief Counsel, Senate Committee on Finance. 1985-1986, Counsel; 1986, Chief Counsel, Senate Majority (Republican) Leader. 1987-present, Chief Counsel, Senate Minority (Republican) Leader.

Expertise: Tax policy

Much of Senator Bob Dole's reputation as a legislative craftsman is perhaps the result of his work on the tax bills of the last seven years. Throughout that time, Richard Belas has been at his side. As Senator Dole's chief counsel on the minority leadership staff, Belas continues to devote much of his professional time to tax policy.

Belas negotiated many of the details of the 1981 tax cut and 1982 tax increase on Senator Dole's behalf. Although he closely monitored the debate over the 1986 tax package, he was not one of the staffers involved in drafting it.

"The drafting itself was done by [then-Finance Committee Chairman] Sen. Packwood and his staff," Belas said. "I was involved in helping Senator Dole formulate strategy to be sure that the bill would pass. My key role was to act as Senator Dole's representative at meetings," Belas said.

Belas shares Dole's view that having low tax rates and letting economic efficiency guide decisions is the most effective tax policy. Belas believes the system will remain basically intact at least for the next few years.

"The thrust of tax reform will be retained for several years. There won't be a need for a tax rate increase. You must assume a broad based tax system for some time. That doesn't mean you won't fine-tune things. If you sift through most of the comments on tax reform there are not many complaints on policy. Most complaints center on the effective dates of the changes," Belas says.

Although he does not think taxes will be significantly increased to reduce the federal budget deficit, Belas believes the Congress should take action to reduce the deficit. He dismisses as "foolish" the suggestion of some supply-siders that no action should be taken on the deficit, as the economy will "grow" out of it.

"People concentrate on the negative side of reducing the deficit—the belt tightening. They don't focus on why you do it. You do it so the government has the flexibility to do what it wants—such as helping the poor and improving the environment," he said. "It is the ultimate in 'feel good' attitudes to assume you will grow out of the deficit."

Belas, who describes himself as a "typical conservative Republican" on economic policy, cut his political teeth at a time when holding such views was not popular. He rang doorbells and licked envelopes during Barry Goldwater's 1964 presidential campaign while Goldwater was losing Belas' home state of Connecticut by a margin of greater than 2 to 1. However, Belas was not politically active as an adult and had no ties to Dole before joining the Finance Committee staff in 1980.

"I heard from a friend that Senator Dole was looking for someone to do tax work. I sent a resume and shortly thereafter Senator Dole interviewed and hired me," Belas recalls.

During Dole's four years as chairman of the Finance Committee, he served first as tax counsel and then as deputy chief counsel for the full committee. He was especially active in the 1981 tax cut bill, the Economic Recovery and Tax Act, and the 1982 tax reform bill, the Tax Equity and Fiscal Responsibility Act. A Democratic staff colleague calls Belas a "savvy political and technical operative who knows the tax code well and represents the interests of his boss."

Joshua B. Bolten
Minority International Trade
   Counsel
203 Hart Senate Office Bldg.
202/224-5315

*Personal: born 8/16/54 in Washington,
D.C. A.B. Woodrow Wilson School of
Public and International Affairs,
Princeton Univ., 1976 (cum laude. J.D.
Stanford Univ., 1980 (note editor of the
Stanford Law Review). 1980-1981,
law clerk to the Honorable Thelton
Henderson, U.S. District Court, San
Francisco, CA. 1981-1984, attorney-
adviser, Office of the Legal Adviser,
U.S. Department of State. 1984-1985,
attorney, O'Melveny and Myers,
Washington, DC.1985-1987, majority
international trade counsel, Senate
Finance Committee. 1987-present,
minority international trade counsel,
Senate Finance Committee.*

Expertise: International trade law, public international law

Since graduating from Stanford Law, Joshua Bolten has had a varied career in the public and private sectors. He has worked in all branches of the Federal government, and also put in a stint at private practice for a Washington, DC law firm, specializing in international trade.

Bolten's talents and interest in international trade policy and law led him to staff positions in the Senate. He has served as Republican International Trade Counsel for the Senate Finance Committee, first as the majority counsel, and then, as the minority counsel. He feels that his position with the Committee affords him the unique opportunity to help Senators advance the cause of an open and successful world trading system.

Bolten identifies closely with the views of his boss, Senator Bob Packwood, who opposes changes in the international trade laws that would increase the likelihood of barriers to free trade of imports.

Most of his time has been spent lately on the Omnibus Trade Bill before the Senate Finance Committee. He also expects to spend considerable time this year on legislation implementing the U.S.-Canada Free Trade Agreement. He is one of the main Republican trade staffers managing this bill.

Before joining the Senate Finance Committee, Bolten worked as an attorney for the US Department of State. There, he provided legal counsel primarily to the Bureau of Inter-American Affairs; he also served as Executive Assistant to the Director of the Kissinger Commission on Central America.

Bolten is a squash enthusiast and a competitive player. Also, he enjoys listening to playing music and once played guitar in a rock 'n' roll band

Mike Chakarun
Legislative Assistant
Senator Malcolm Wallop (R-WY)
234 Russell Senate Office Bldg.
224-6441

Expertise: Taxation, individual and corporate

Chakarun's area of responsibility is the Finance Committee and the subcommittees that Sen. Wallop (R-WY) is assigned to, which include Energy and Agricultural Taxation (Wallop is ranking Republican), International Trade; and Taxation and Debt Management.

Coming to work for Wallop after the Tax Reform Act of 1986 was passed means Chakarun was not involved in that lengthy and tense process. He is responsible, however, for explaining Tax Reform to constituents and industry alike now that the act is phasing into full force. And as technical corrections begin to be considered, Chakarun will be responsible for those as well—something that is bound to be of great importance to Wallop since the Senator was one of a handful who voted against final passage. Wallop was also a conferee on Tax Reform.

In the 100th Congress, Chakarun has been active in seeking the repeal of the Wind Fall Profits Tax that with the current oil slump has not generated a dime of revenue while at the same time forcing the oil industry to spend almost $100 million to comply with federal tax regulations, and costing the IRS some $14 million to administer. One other piece of legislation that is of high priority to Chakarun is the 86I R&D allocation which he would like to see resolved.

Personal: born 11/7/54 in California. B.S. Northern Arizona Univ., 1976. 1977, CPA, Idaho. 1976-1977, Accountant, Price Waterhouse, Alberta, Canada. 1977-1979, Touche Ross, Boise, Idaho. 1979-1982, Chandler Corporation. 1983-1985, AFT Express. M.B.A. Boise State Univ. 1986. 1987 to present, Legislative Assistant, Senator Malcolm Wallop (R-WY).

John O. Colvin
Chief Minority Counsel
203 Hart Senate Office Bldg.
224-5315

Personal: born 11/17/46 in Canton, Ohio. A.B. Univ. of Missouri, 1968. J.D. Georgetown Univ. Law Center, 1971. LL.B. Georgetown Univ. Law Center, 1978. 1971-1975, Counsel, Office of the Chief Counsel, U.S. Coast Guard. 1975-81, Tax Counsel, and 1982-84, Legislative Director, Sen. Bob Packwood. 1985-1987, Chief Counsel, Senate Finance Committee. 1987 to present, Chief Minority Counsel, Senate Finance Committee. Adjunct Professor of Law, Georgetown Univ. Chairman, Tax Legislation Committee, Taxation Section, Federal Bar Association.

Expertise: Tax legislation and tax reform

John Colvin works on Capitol Hill "not to be someone important, but to see important things happen." And "important things" for Colvin are taxes. After twelve years on the Hill, Colvin is a veteran of every major tax bill of the last decade. In 1987, *Roll Call* listed Colvin as one of the twenty-five most influential Hill staffers. When someone on the Hill has a question about tax policy, they call John Colvin, known for his non-partisan approach and vast knowledge on the subject.

In 1969, when future Senator John Danforth was Attorney General in the Missouri State Legislature, Colvin worked under future Senator Kit Bond, then Assistant Attorney General for the state. Colvin was involved in the consumer protection division supervised by Bond. When Kit Bond ran for State Auditor in 1970, Colvin transferred for a semester to St. Louis University Law School and worked on Bond's campaign.

Most recently, Colvin has worked on the passage of the Superfund Acts of 1985 and 1986 and the reconciliation bills of 1985-1987.

Of all the bills Colvin has worked on, the one he is most associated with is the Tax Reform Act of 1986. Colvin, as Chief Counsel of the Senate Finance Committee, played a key role in the drafting and tailoring of the bill. Colvin coordinated the efforts of eight tax attorneys in developing the materials for hearings and drafting the legislation itself. The major thrust of this legislation, as Colvin puts it, was simply "to lower rates."

He found the lengthy negotiations between the two chairmen of the House Ways and Means Committee (Rep. Dan Rostenkowski) and the Senate Finance Committee (Sen. Packwood) the most dynamic and fascinating moment in the enactment process. Colvin and Packwood communicate closely and easily. "I've worked with John for over a dozen years," Packwood said. "The depth of his understanding of tax law has made him invaluable."

Colvin finds time to lecture on the subtleties of tax law to Georgetown law students and to write for the *Journal of Taxation*. In 1981 and 1983, he was the editor of *Writing Tax Law—Tax Legislative Procedures*.

On his few free weekends, Colvin stays at home with his family in Arlington. Activities on his wish list include enjoying blue grass music and canoeing.

Alexandra Deane
Tax Counsel/Legislative Assistant
Senator Tom Daschle (D-SD)
317 Hart Senate Office Bldg,.
224-2321

Expertise: Tax, budget, banking

After winning a hotly contested election in 1986 for the Senate seat of incumbent Sen. Jim Abdnor, South Dakota's Tom Daschle gained a seat on the prestigious Finance Committee. Expressing an interest in the whole range of policy issues which fall within the panel's jurisdiction, Daschle made Finance Committee issues a high priority in assembling his legislative staff. Daschle's choice for his Finance Committee tax counsel was Alexandra Deane, an energetic attorney who says she reflects her senator's interest in contributing to the debate on national tax policy and in building a solid legislative record in the Finance Committee.

Deane, a Hill newcomer when she joined Daschle's staff in March of 1987, has developed a veteran's appreciation for the nuances of life within the Senate Finance Committee, including the importance of interpersonal relationships and the limitations inherent in representing the interests of a freshman senator in committee. "It is important to understand the institutional history and personal dynamics of the committee, and I try to advance my boss's agenda within that framework."

Personal: B.B.A. Coll. of William and Mary, 1980. J.D. Univ. of Virginia Law School, 1983. 1983-1987, attorney, Piper and Marbury law firm. 1987-present, Legislative Assistant, Sen. Tom Daschle (D-SD)

Deane shares Daschle's studied approach to choosing policy initiatives. As a junior member of the Finance Committee representing a rural state, Daschle places considerable emphasis on his staff's ability to assist him in ensuring that rural concerns are considered in the debate on tax legislation, and to ensure that his constituents are provided with timely responses to their inquiries about specific tax provisions. Alex Deane accepts this mandate with enthusiasm.

Undaunted by constituent demands or the eye-crossing complexity of tax legislation, Deane welcomes the opportunity to take on new issues. Whether drafting legislation to alleviate the burden on farmers from diesel excise tax collection procedures or briefing Daschle on the myriad of issues contained in the budget reconciliation bill, Deane clearly relishes the challenge of analyzing tax problems from both a theoretical and a pragmatic perspective.

In addition to her Finance Committee responsibilities, Deane handles Judiciary and Banking Committee issues for Daschle.

Gina Despres
Legislative Assistant/Counsel
Senator Bill Bradley (D-NJ)
731 Hart Senate Office Bldg.
224-3224

Personal: born 9/28/41 Sydney, New South Wales. B.A Univ. of Sydney, with honors, 1964. Graduate Student, Univ. of California, Berkeley, Oriental Languages, 1970. J.D. Univ. of California, Los Angeles, 1974. Member of Law Review. 1974-1976, associate, Irell & Manella. 1976-1977, associate, Caplin & Drysdale. 1977-1978, attorney/advisor, Office of Gen. Counsel. 1978-1979, director of international & security policy, acting director, finance & tax, Department of Energy. 1979-present, legislative assistant, Sen. Bill Bradley (D-NJ). Author various papers, Electric Power Institute Conference, 1979. "The Geopolitics of Oil," a staff report of Senate Committee on Energy and Natural Resources, 1980. Admitted California Bar, 1975; D.C. Bar, 1976.

Expertise: Tax issues and international affairs

Bill Bradley (D-NJ) has accomplished an often unattainable goal: he has made a celebrity-conscious town forget his previous fame as a professional athlete. By carefully selecting, and then mastering a few complicated issues, the New Jersey Democrat has placed himself at the front ranks of politicians with a national presence.

When insiders talk about Bradley, they inevitably stress taxes and tax reform—the specialty of Gina Despres, an attorney with vast experience in areas related to the tax policies of the United States.

In a self-effacing way, Gina Despres quietly points out Bradley's "collegial" staff, with each legislative assistant being given latitude in his/her area of expertise, augmented she says by the seasoned and "exceptionally talented fellows" who are attracted to the Bradley staff.

Her seniority and her position as the only lawyer on the Bradley staff give her a legislative mandate broader than many veteran staff members on the Hill. She is responsible for overall issues relating to foreign policy, the role of state and defense, as well as judicial matters, including the confirmation of federal judges.

Gina Despres spends 85 percent of her time working with Bradley on tax issues, and her work frequently has been cited by major tax journals.

As a former expert in international security policy issues, Despres has authored studies on such topics as "The Geopolitics of Oil (a staff report of the Senate Committee on Energy and Natural Resources, 1980)." A former student of Oriental languages and literature, and a National Defense and Foreign Language Fellow, she is in an ideal position to advise Bradley on a wide range of issues.

Her international experience will come in handy as she works on United States relations with Japan and the Soviet Union, and international economic issues.

Joseph H. Gale
Legislative Counsel
Senator Daniel P. Moynihan (D-NY)
464 Russell Senate Office Bldg.
224-4451

Expertise: Tax, banking, securities

Joe Gale was interviewed for the tax counsel position with Senate Finance Committee member Daniel P. Moynihan (D-NY) on the same day in November 1984 that the Treasury Department issued its "Treasury I" proposal for tax reform. The Treasury proposal, signaling major tax legislation in the upcoming 99th Congress, proved prophetic. Gale got the job and spent the next two years engrossed in the most significant re-write of the federal tax code in decades.

Gale's academic and professional careers have been marked by rapid success. Shortly after graduating from Princeton in 1976, he returned to his native Virginia to work for one year under Andrew P. Miller, Attorney General of Virginia and Democratic candidate for Governor in 1977. In 1980, he received his J.D. from the University of Virginia School of Law, where he was appointed a Dillard Fellow in 1979. He worked from 1980 to 1982 as an attorney with the New York law firm, Dewey, Ballantine, Bushby, Palmer, and Wood. From 1983 to 1984, he was an associate at the Washington firm of Dickstein, Shapiro and Morin.

Gale received high marks for his work on the historic Tax Reform Act of 1986, as an effective advocate for Moynihan's legislative concerns. As principal tax adviser to Moynihan, a member of the "core group" of Senate Finance Committee members who developed the Senate version of tax reform, Gale participated in key negotiations on the bill. He also worked on the tax provisions in recent budget reconciliation legislation, including the Budget Reconciliation Act of 1987, as well as banking legislation.

Despite his achievements, Joe Gale remains quite modest. Engaging and affable, his relaxed demeanor belies the time demands and pressures of his post.

Personal: born 8/26/53 in Smithfield, Virginia. A.B. Princeton Univ., 1976. 1976-1977, scheduler for Andrew P. Miller, Attorney General of Virginia and Democratic candidate for Governor of Virginia. J.D. Univ.of Virginia School of Law, 1980 (appointed a Dillard Fellow, Univ. of Virginia School of Law, 1979-1980). Graduate level work at Georgetown Law School master's degree program in tax law. 1980-1982, attorney, Dewey, Ballantine, Bushby, Palmer and Wood, New York City. 1983-1984, attorney, Dickstein, Shapiro and Morin, Washington, D.C. 1985-present, Legislative Counsel, Senator Daniel P. Moynihan (D-NY). Publications: "Passive Loss Limitation Rules", Federal Bar Association Taxation Section Report, Winter 1987.

James Gould
Chief Tax Counsel
205 Dirksen Senate Office Bldg.
224-4515

Expertise: Tax law

For the past nine years, Jim Gould has been intimately involved in each major change in the federal tax code. As a tax court clerk, law firm associate, and legislative counsel, Gould has built his career around tax policy. In early April Chairman Bentsen named him heir apparent to current staff director Bill Wilkinson

Gould's interest in tax law began with his first job after law school as a clerk with the United States Tax Court. He took this expert knowledge to two Washington law firms before moving on to the government.

Gould's career on Capitol Hill has been brief, which makes the powerful position he now holds especially impressive. He came to the Senate as counsel to Senator Lloyd Bentsen of Texas. When Bentsen assumed the chairmanship of the Senate Finance Committee in early 1987, Jim Gould became the committee's chief tax counsel.

During his time with Senator Bentsen, Gould has been involved in several major overhauls of the tax system. In 1984, he was a part of a House/Senate tax bill conference, and he helped write the Tax Reform Act of 1986.

Gould has also helped craft the tax portions of other bills. One Senate colleague says "he basically wrote the Superfund bill" (which cleans up toxic waste dumps). He also influenced both the highway and the catastrophic health bills of 1987.

Recently, Gould helped draft the revenue provisions of the 1987 Omnibus Budget Reconciliation Act. His knowledge of the tax code can be seen in any tax-related bill which passes through the Finance Committee.

Gould has gained a great deal of respect from his colleagues during his brief tenure on the hill. "He's a proficient, knowledgeable tax expert," and "has good political sense," says experts who have worked with Gould.

Gould is praised for his sense of humor and informal style. His relationship with Senator Bentsen has made him "learn to talk Texan." He plays tennis in his spare time.

Personal: B.A. Washington & Lee University, 1975. J.D. Harvard Law School, 1979. Clerk, United States Tax Court, 1979-1981; Lee, Toomey and Kent, 1981-1982; Lane and Edson, 1983. 1984-1986, Counsel to Senator Lloyd Bentsen (D-TX). 1987-present, Chief Tax Counsel, Senate Finance Committee.

Barbara J. Groves
Tax Counsel
205 Dirksen Senate Office Bldg.
224-4515

Expertise: Tax law

Under the leadership of Louisiana Sen. Russell B. Long (D-LA), the Senate Finance Committee held firm to an "old style" staff structure during the congressional reform period of the 1970's. This tradition is maintained today by current Chairman Sen. Lloyd Bentsen (D-TX), the Finance Committee employs no subcommittee staff members; all committee staffers answer directly to the chairman.

Beginning in her native West Virginia, Barbara Groves, built an impressive academic record during the late 1970's. She was number one in her class at New York Univ., where she earned an LL.M. to accompany her earlier J.D. Her tax experience began when she clerked for the U.S. Tax Court from 1980-1982. She took this experience to the Washington, D.C., office of the Atlanta law firm of Sutherland, Asbill, and Brennan.

In 1984, she joined the Finance Committee staff, first as tax counsel for the minority and then the majority, as the Democrats won control after the 1986 election. Groves is involved in virtually every tax matter which comes before the committee.

The most significant pieces of legislation in which Groves has been involved are the tax bills of 1984 and 1986. She staffed the 1984 tax bill conference, and she helped draft the 1986 Tax Reform Act. Groves also contributed to the Superfund, Highway and Catastrophic Health bills.

Personal: B.A. West Virginia Univ., 1975. J.D. West Virginia Univ., 1978. LL.M. New York Univ., 1980. 1980-1982, clerk, U.S. Tax Court. 1982-1984, Sutherland, Asbill, and Brennan. 1984-1986, Minority Tax Counsel; 1987-present, Tax Counsel, Committee on Finance.

The tax bills were marked by the bi-partisan consensus often found among the Senators on the Finance Committee. Groves earns high praise from both Republican and Democratic staffers as "even handed and fair".

Groves most recent work has been on the revenue provisions of the Omnibus Budget Reconciliation Act of 1987, trying to implement the "budget summit" agreement, in which Bentsen was a major player.

The remaining months of the 100th Congress should provide interesting challenges for Groves. Bentsen is committed to a narrow technical revisions bill that corrects problems left over from the 1986 Tax Reform Act. Crafting the chairman's desired bi-partisan consensus on that sort of bill will occupy most of her time.

"She is solid, a good communicator," according to a legislative assistant to a Republican committee member. "Groves is the consummate staffer," says another.

Gregory F. Jenner
Tax Counsel
Minority Staff
205 Dirksen Senate Office Bldg.
224-5315

Expertise: Real Estate, interest and passive losses; estate, gift and generation skipping taxes; depreciation and capital cost recovery

Jenner's concentration on tax-related issues in private law practice in the early 1980's helped prepare him for serving on the staff of the Senate Finance Committee. Little did he know then he would participate in the greatest overhaul of the U.S. Tax Code in fifty years.

As one of the staff players on the Tax Reform Act of 1986, Jenner was chiefly responsible for those provisions affecting real estate, interest and passive losses. Jenner directly participated in drafting two important reforms made by the Act: the new passive loss rules, which eliminate most tax sheltering, and the new alternative minimum tax, which ensures that profitable corporations and wealthy individuals pay their fair share of taxes. Then Senate Finance Committee Chairman Packwood complimented Jenner's "experience and tenacious commitment to the task at hand" in contributing to the successful inclusion of those reforms in the Act.

Jenner remarked that the 1986 Tax Reform Act was a great start down the road to a fairer and more neutral tax code. However, he noted more could be done in the way of eliminating loopholes (i.e. preferences and deductions) which would help to further broaden the base.

Personal: born 8/8/53 in Portland, Oregon. B.S. Portland State Univ., 1975, with high honors. J.D. New York Univ. School of Law, 1979, cum laude; law review note and comment editor. 1979-1983, attorney, Stoel, Rives, Boley, Fraser & Wyse, Portland, OR. 1983-1985, attorney, Weiss, DesCamp & Botteri, Portland, OR. 1985-present, Tax Counsel, Senate Finance Committee. Other experiences: Articles editor, The Tax Lawyer, American Bar Association (ABA) Section on Taxation; Member, Real Property Tax Problems Committee, ABA Section on Taxation; Member, Income Taxation Of Estates and Trusts Committee, ABA Section on Real Property.

In addition, Jenner has worked on the Technical Corrections legislation to the 1986 Tax Reform Act; the Budget Reconciliation Acts of 1985, 1986, and 1987; and the Omnibus Trade Act of 1986.

When not pouring over the tax code, Jenner likes to spend his off time outdoors and also enjoys sports, including golf, softball, racquetball, and volleyball.

Tracy Kaye
Legislative Assistant
Senator John C. Danforth (R-MO)
497 Russell Senate Office Bldg.
224-6154

Expertise: Tax

In mid-1987, Senator John C. Danforth (R-MO), needed a technical expert on taxes to help him negotiate year-end tax and budget legislation. As the fourth ranking Republican on the Finance Committee, Senator Danforth has been a conferee on every major tax bill since 1979. Tracy A. Kaye, a six-year tax veteran at Arthur Young and Company came well recommended for the key staff position.

At Arthur Young & Company, Kaye evolved from a senior tax assistant responsible for coordinating and researching tax services to a tax manager in charge of monitoring tax legislation and providing technical support to Arthur Young offices. After following the Tax Reform Act of 1986 through the Ways and Means, Finance and Conference Committees, Kaye became interested in the legislative process. She decided to move from the private to the public sector in order to participate in the legislative process.

Today, Tracy Kaye is a vital participant in the policy making process as Senator Danforth's legislative assistant on tax and budget issues. In the 100th Congress, Kaye will assist the Senator in tackling the obstacles of budget reconciliation and the technical corrections tax package to follow up the 1986 Tax Reform Act. Although a newcomer to the Hill, the Chicago native has had little difficulty adapting to her new environment. She negotiates legislation in a professional manner: "She's honest, hardworking, and extremely straight forward with staff members and lobbyists" explains one of her colleagues.

After a demanding day on tax legislation, she attends night law school at Georgetown University. She manages to juggle her job and her law education "by having a very, very supportive husband and boss."

Personal: Born 5/28/59 in New Orleans, Louisiana. B.S. Univ. of Illinois, 1981. M.A. Depaul Univ., 1984. 1981-84, Senior Tax Staff, Arthur Young & Co. Chicago. 1984-85, Tax Manager, Arthur Young & Co., Boston. 1985-1987, Tax Manager, Washington National Tax Group, Arthur Young & Co. Washington, D.C. 1987-present, Tax and Budget Legislative Assistant, Senator John C. Danforth.

David Krawitz
Executive Assistant and Legislative
  Director
Senator Donald Riegle, Jr. (D-MI)
105 Dirksen Senate Office Bldg.
224-4822

Personal: born 7/4/51 in Ocean Side, New York. B.A. Univ. of California, Santa Cruz, honors, 1973. M.A. McGill Univ., Montreal Quebec, Political Science (theory), 1979. Ph.D. in progress, McGill Univ., Political Science. 1979-1982, Legislative Aide, Subcommittee on Child and Human Development, Sen. Alan Cranston (D-CA). 1982-1984, Professional Staff Member, Committee on Labor and Human Resources, Sen. Donald Riegle, Jr. 1984-1986, Professional Staff Member, Committee on the Budget for Sen. Riegle. 1986, Senior Legislative Assistant, Sen. Riegle, Committee on Finance. 1987-present, Executive Assistant and Legislative Director, Sen. Riegle.

Expertise: Health, social service, children, budget & finance

Having developed his political point of view growing up in California in the sixties, David Krawitz studied politics at the Univ. of California at Santa Cruz.

With his coursework completed and a dissertation his only obstacle to a professorship, David planned a visit of one to two years in D.C., to "look at politics firsthand". What was intended as an experience to enhance his dissertation, has turned instead into an impressive career on the Hill.

A Democrat, Krawitz successfully sought his first position with Senator Alan Cranston (D-CA), where he was a legislative aide on Cranston's Child and Human Development Subcommittee. Three years later, Krawitz moved to the staff of the Subcommittee on Alcoholism and Drug Abuse, where he began working for his present boss, Senator Don Riegle (D-MI).

On the Senate Labor Committee, Krawitz worked on health and other social service issues. After two years, he moved to the Budget Committee for Senator Riegle, where his responsibilities included analyzing, monitoring and formulating budget policy and procedure. In 1986, he became Riegle's senior legislative assistant.

In this role, Krawitz was the staff representative for the Committee on Finance, and was responsible for programs such as health care, Social Security, children's issues, welfare and public finance. In addition, he handled all issues relating to the Federal Tax Code. After one year he was promoted to his current position as Executive Assistant and Legislative Director. As Executive Assistant, Krawitz is the key staff liaison for the Senator's constituents, and is involved in such activities as policy, political analysis and special projects. As Legislative Director, he monitors and coordinates all legislative affairs and supervises the activities of the legislative assistants.

Krawitz considers the Latch Key Children Program, enacted in 1984, and the Riegle-Danforth Amendment to the Trade Bill, adopted in 1987, two of the most important issues with which he has been involved. He has also continuously pursued health care for the uninsured, as well as legislation to provide vocational rehabilitation benefits for Social Security Disability beneficiaries.

Krawitz believes he will someday return to the academic field, and to the teaching he so enjoyed while a Ph.D. candidate at McGill Univ. in Montreal. He is currently serving a three-year elected term as President of the Board of Trustees of Group Health Association (GHA). With a membership of 140,000, GHA is the largest health maintenance organization in the District.

Jeff Lang
Chief International Trade Counsel
205 Dirksen Senate Office Building
224-4515

Expertise: Trade

When Senator Lloyd Bentsen of Texas took a trip to the Orient in January of 1988, he took only two people with him—his wife and Jeff Lang. The trip illustrates two of Lang's most distinguishing characteristics; he is very close to Senator Bentsen, and he is an expert in the field of international trade.

Lang's interest in trade began when he studied international law at the Hague Academy in 1967. He decided to postpone a legal practice after graduating from law school, however, and he served in the U.S. Army. Upon completion of his service, he worked in the field of international law for a Washington, D.C. law firm and the International Trade Commission.

Lang came to Capitol Hill in 1979 as an aide to Senator Russell Long of Louisiana, assigned to the Finance Committee, more specifically the Subcommittee on International Trade. As a minority committee staffer, Lang worked with the Republican leadership on several trade bills and trade agreement ratification.

When Senator Long retired from the Senate in 1986, Jeff Lang found himself in a new position. Incoming Finance Committee Chairman Bentsen recognized Lang's broad experience in the trade area and gave him the title of Chief International Trade Counsel.

Personal: Born 6/23/42 in Washington, D.C. A.B. Bowdoin Coll., 1964. LL.B. Univ. of Virginia Law School, 1967. Certificate, Academy of International law, 1967. 1st Lt., U.S. Army, 1968; released as Capt., 1970, 1970-75, Associate, Bridgeman & Pyeatt. 1975-77, attorney, and 1975-79, Deputy General Counsel, International Trade Commission. 1979-1986, Professional Staff Member; 1987-present, Chief International Trade Counsel, Senate Finance Committee.

Lang's foremost task in his current position has been the passage of H.R. 3, the mammoth Omnibus Trade Bill. In committee, on the floor, and in conference, Lang has helped Senator Bentsen win broad bipartisan support for the bill. "Lang's perseverance made the trade bill," one Senate colleague said, "He has a great ability to get people to agree."

Lang has been involved in other trade issues, such as the "pasta wars" import dispute and the New York/Canada timber trade pact. Most recently, he had an impact on the new customs authorization provisions.

1988 should be a busy year for Lang. The completion of the Omnibus Trade Bill is his first priority. The recent trade agreement between the United States and Canada will be thoroughly examined, as will the possibility of the North American Trade Accord advocated by President Reagan.

Lang's tenure on the hill has earned him the high regard of his colleagues. "I would describe him as scholarly," says one Legislative Assistant, "he's the guru on trade." Another Finance Committee staffer says "he has a great ability to listen and sift through ideas—and he usually has great ideas."

Finance

Michael Mabile
Trade Counsel
205 Dirksen Senate Office Bldg.
224-4515

Expertise: Trade and international economic policy

Michael Mabile handles trade issues strictly for Finance Chairman Sen. Lloyd Bentsen (D-TX). Bentsen's chairmanship makes him one of the national players on the issue of reducing the massive foreign trade deficit and improving the ability of U.S. producers to compete in world markets.

Mabile has worked closely with Bentsen to advance a more moderate position than the protectionism advocated by many Members. Bentsen seems to feel the U.S. has been taken advantage of by its foreign competitors and supports some measures to remedy the unfair trade practices of other countries.

The omnibus trade legislation in which Mabile has been immersed addresses unfair trading practices, increased congressional authority in trade matters, and additional help for businesses and workers hurt by foreign competition.

Passage of the trade bill, H.R. 3, was Mabile's top concern in 1988. Conferees on the 1,179-page bill haggled over unfair trade practices and relief for import-damaged domestic industries provisions. Mabile's efforts on the bill have been limited to the strictly trade-related parts of the bill.

Personal: Assistant general counsel for litigation, International Trade Commission. 1986-present, trade counsel, Senate Finance Committee

Bentsen, as well as other oil industry supporters, inserted in H.R. 3 the repeal of the windfall profits tax. The chairman argued that the repeal would help boost domestic oil production and thus reduce the need for imported oil. Bentsen claimed the tax was unfair and discouraged exploration and production. Mabile worked to assure this provision survived the conference. The House bill did not include the repeal of the windfall profits tax.

Mabile also worked closely with Bentsen in objecting to the Administration's negotiations with Canada on the free trade pact. Bentsen felt that the Administration had not consulted fully with Congress during the drafting of the agreement and sought to assure that it did not happen in any future trade accords.

Relatively new to the Hill, Mabile has been thrown into the fray, becoming a senior trade advisor to the chairman in an area of paramount importance.

Edmund J. Mihalski
Minority Staff Director
203 Hart Senate Office Bldg.
224-5315

Expertise: Health matters including Medicare/Medicaid, social security, pensions and catastrophic health care

Mihalski is one of the most trusted advisors of Sen. Bob Packwood (R-OR), former chairman and now the ranking Republican on the Finance Committee. Mihalski was part of the staff that allowed Packwood to make history in 1986 by proposing and helping to enact the most thorough overhaul of the tax code in 45 years.

Mihalski was one of a small group of staff close to Packwood who helped put together the radically different 1986 tax package. The proposal lowered rates drastically with a top individual tax rate of 27%. The plan stunned Washington by ignoring interest groups and pleasing politicians who were clearly unable to respond to parochial pressures.

Mihalski served as Packwood's expert on all health matters that came before the Finance Committee. He was instrumental in developing the historic legislation that instituted the Perspective Payment System (PPS) that drastically altered the Medicare reimbursement system for hospitals. The PPS was passed as a provision in the Social Security Amendments of 1983. Designed to curb soaring Medicare costs, the law set in motion a three-year transition from a cost-based reimbursement system to the PPS. At the heart of the new system were flat fees for inpatient treatment of particular illnesses or conditions, from broken bones to brain tumors. Fees varied according to the complexity and length of treatment involved for specific categories of cases, known as diagnostic related groups (DRGs).

Personal: born 7/3/41 in Minersville, Pennsylvania. B.A. in accounting Univ. of Washington, 1967. M.B.A. Univ. of Arkansas, 1974. 1967-1973, first lieutenant to captain, U.S. Air Force. 1974-1982, senior evaluator, General Accounting Office. 1982-1987, minority deputy chief of staff, Senate Finance Committee. 1988 minority staff director, Senate Finance Committee.

In 1986, Mihalski helped Chairman Packwood with a controversial provision in the fiscal year 1986 reconciliation bill which gave a preference to the hospitals in his home state Oregon. .

In early 1988 Mihalski was promoted from deputy to minority staff director when Mary McAullife resigned that position. Mihalski is considered personable by his colleagues and has a reputation for being meticulous in his work. His training as a CPA was a good background for his present position as head of the minority staff of the Finance Committee.

Finance

Lindy L. Paull
Minority Deputy Chief Counsel
203 Hart Senate Office Bldg.
224-5315

Expertise: Corporate tax, tax accounting, and minimum tax

As a tax lawyer and certified public accountant, Lindy Paull is well-qualified to serve on the Senate Finance Committee. Joining the Committee in 1986, Paull arrived just in time for the Tax Reform Act of 1986.

As one of the staffers working on the tax bill, Paull played an important role in two important reforms made by the act: the new massive loss rules' which eliminates most tax sheltering; and the new alternative minimum tax. Upon final passage of the bill, then Committee Chairman, Senator Bob Packwood (D-OR), praised Paull for her "dedication and professionalism," both of which were tested during that time.

Paull believes the underlying structure of tax reform should not be changed dramatically for several years to come. Like others, she thinks more can be done to reform the federal code by broadening the tax base and closing more loopholes.

When not analyzing and writing new tax law, Paull spends a fair amount of her off-time on photography. She is most interested in taking pictures of politicians, her first one being none other than Senator Packwood.

Personal: born 11/22/48 in Miami, Florida. B.A. Univ. of Florida, 1969. Univ. of Florida Coll. of Law, 1979. LL.M. Univ. of Florida Coll. of Law, 1980. 1974-1977, Senior Tax Specialist, Laventhol & Horwath, CPAs, Coral Gables, Florida. 1979-1980, Legal Writing and Tax Research Instructor, Univ. of Florida Coll. of Law. 1980-1982, Attorney-Advisor to Judge Herbert L. Chabot, United States Tax Court. 1982-1986, Tax Associate, Sutherland, Asbill & Brennan, Washington, D.C. 1986-1988, Minority Deputy Chief Counsel, Senate Finance Committee.

Karen Borlaug Phillips
Chief Economist for the Republican
  Staff
203 Hart Senate Office Bldg.
224-5315

*Personal: born 10/1/56, in Long
Beach, California. B.S./B.A. Univ. of
North Dakota, 1977 (summa cum
laude, Phi Beta Kappa). Graduate
training in economics, George
Washington Univ. 1977-1978, research
assistant, Department of
Transportation. 1978-1982, economist,
DOT. 1982-1985, professional staff
member, Senate Committee on
Commerce, Science, and
Transportation. 1985-1987, tax
economist, U.S. Senate Committee on
Finance. 1987-Present, Minority Chief
Economist, Senate Committee on
Finance. Publications: "Research,
Politics, and the Dynamics of Policy
Development: A Case Study of Motor
Carrier Regulatory Reform", Policy
Sciences. Dec. 1984; A Study of
Trucking Service in Six Small
Communities, Nov., 1979, U.S. DOT.*

Expertise: Economic regulation, transportation, tax code

Karen Phillips, the Minority Chief Economist on the Senate
Finance Committee, works primarily with Senator Bob Packwood
(R-OR), with whom she also worked on the Commerce Committee.
During her work on the Tax Reform Act, she appreciated his
"inquisitive nature and ability to bring out the creativity and talent
of his staff".

During the Tax Reform Act of 1986, she was responsible primarily
for the transition rules for the legislation.

Phillips acknowledges that anything coming out of the political
process is an imperfect compromise, but considers the final tax
bill a tremendous improvement over the existing code. She is
pleased by how tightly legislators kept a lid on "the ardent desires
of members to insure that constituent interests have been taken
care of." Phillips does worry that the reactive nature of politics
threatens the lag time required to properly assess the bill's effects
and hopes that short-term changes are limited to technical
corrections.

Transportation is Phillip's first love, and she contributed to the
Surface Freight Forwarder Deregulation Act of 1986, the
Hazardous Materials Transportation Act Amendments of 1984, the
Motor Carrier Safety Act of 1984, the Motor Vehicle Safety and
Cost Savings Authorization Act of 1982, and the Intercity Bus
Regulatory Reform Act of 1982. She was instrumental in DOT
studies that provided deregulation framework for the trucking and
intercity bus industries. Although Phillips endorses government
oversight in many areas, as well as activism in social programs,
she considers transportation a case study of government
regulation running amok. Phillips is currently working on
international trade legislation (H.R.3), particularly with respect to
the economic implications of various trade policies.

 Phillips feels a public duty to be accessible and to look at all
points of view. She is pleased with non-partisan atmosphere of the
Finance Committee and is comfortable with Republican policy
positions.

When unwinding, she enjoys squash and tennis with her
economist husband.

Finance

Alexander Polinsky
Legislative Assistant
Senator David Durenberger (R-MN)
154 Russell Senate Office Bldg.
224-3244

Personal: born 6/6/45 in New York, New York. B.A. New York Univ., with honors in government, 1967. J.D. New York Univ. Law School, 1970. 1972-1976, U.S. Department of Justice, Anti-Trust Division. 1976-1977, Billig Sher & Jones, P.C. 1977-1984, Prentice-Hall Publications. 1984-1985, Tax Analysts. 1985-Present, legislative assistant, Sen. David Durenberger (R-MN).
Publications: Guide to FTC Franchise Disclosure Rules, Prentice-Hall, 1980. S Corporations, Tax Choices for Business Planning, Prentice-Hall, 1983.

Expertise: Tax and international trade

When, in 1985, members of the Senate Finance Committee expected tax and international trade reform to dominate its agenda, they sought qualified personnel to assist them. Alexander Polinsky, who chose to develop an expertise in tax and trade issues instead of pursuing a career racing Formula I cars, was chosen by Sen. Dave Durenberger (R-MN) for the job. Drawing on experience and scholarship, Polinsky has helped develop several major pieces of legislation.

A New York City native, Polinsky earned a B.A. with Honors in Government at New York University in 1967. He attended NYU Law School and graduated in 1970. From 1972 to 1976, he worked for the Anti-Trust Division of the U.S. Justice Department. He practiced regulatory law at Billig Sher & Jones, P.C. in 1977. He worked for Prentice-Hall Publications from 1977 to 1984, during which time he wrote two books, and demonstrated his acumen in trade and tax issues. He was Editor of *Tax Notes* from 1984 to 1985.

As an aide to Sen. Durenberger, Polinsky was involved in the Tax Reform Act of 1986. Under the previous tax laws, capital-intensive industries paid less taxes than retail industries. Thus, some companies were rewarded and others penalized for the way in which they legitimately made money. With Polinsky's input, this imbalanced was redressed by Durenberger and others in the 1986 law, which he says is "designed to level the playing field of competition by levelling tax rates and removing tax loopholes."

Polinsky conceived and drafted parts of the Superconductivity Competition Act of 1987 that aims to coordinate government and private sector technological research and development of high temperature superconductors. He also worked hard on his boss's behalf to expunge protectionist measures from the pending Omnibus Trade Bill.

Although he has worked seven days a week, for months in a row, Polinsky's regimen is not unusual for a Capitol Hill staffer. He recalls the time that he arrived at his office in the Russell Senate Building at 3:45 a.m.—only to meet an exhausted colleague who was just leaving the building after burning the midnight oil. Despite his punishing schedule, Polinsky derives great satisfaction from the knowledge that he is furthering the public good.

Polinsky is an excellent photographer who enjoys skiing.

Julie Rabinowitz
Tax Counsel
Senator William Roth (R-DE)
104 Hart Senate Office Bldg.
224-2441

*Personal: born 7/19/57 in Des Moines,
Iowa. B.A. Univ. of Iowa, 1979. J.D.
Univ. of Iowa, 1983. 1983-1984,
attorney, Internal Revenue Service.
1985-1986, Tax Counsel, Sen. Charles
Grassley (R-IA). 1987-present, Tax
Counsel, Sen. William Roth.*

Expertise: Tax

Although still a college undergraduate when Senator Bill Roth (R-DE) co-authored his well known tax reduction plan, Julie Rabinowitz would have made few, if any, changes.

These days, Senator Roth is less visible than in 1978 when he and Rep. Jack Kemp (R-NY) first proposed to cut taxes by 30 percent over three years. The Kemp-Roth plan, which was the basis for the tax cut Congress passed in 1981, was described by some as "voodoo economics" and a "riverboat" gamble. The 1981 tax bill, however, has now largely been overshadowed by last year's tax reform legislation that Senator Roth finds troubling.

Therefore, he will be relying even more on Rabinowitz to help him implement some modifications in the tax code. She agrees that last year's legislation is severely flawed. "The 1986 tax reform bill taxed savings and investment. It failed to bring about real simplicity," she says. "The U.S. needs to have more consumption-based taxes. The tax reform bill did not do enough in this, and other areas."

Rabinowitz joined Roth's staff in January after a two-year stint as tax counsel to Sen. Charles Grassley (R-IA). She first came to Washington after law school to practice tax law with the Internal Revenue Service. She had no plans to become a legislative lawyer until she was approached by Senator Grassley, whom she had met while serving briefly as an intern in his office. Although Rabinowitz said she has never been a Democrat, she had not been politically active for any candidate or cause.

Rabinowitz also feels strongly that the tax system should tax economic income, not redistribute wealth. While not a proponent of the tax bill passed in 1986, she thinks Congress should move cautiously before making changes.

"It was fraudulent to sell the bill as fair and simple. While individual rates may have been lowered, the loss of certain tax preferences won't create more savings or disposable income."

However, she and Senator Roth are prepared to wait and see what effect the bill has before proposing substantive changes. One idea in which the Senator has a strong and longstanding interest is a consumption tax. However, Rabinowitz thinks it would be too risky to change the system so soon after the latest package takes effect—even to consider a modified consumption based tax. "You shouldn't tinker with the system on an annual basis," she says.

Reba Raffaelli
Legislative Counsel/Legislative
  Assistant
Senator John Heinz (R-PA)
277 Russell Senate Office Bldg.
224-6324

Expertise: Tax

After earning a law degree, a masters degree in tax law and practicing tax litigation for the Department of Justice, Raffaelli was well qualified to become tax counsel to a U.S. Senator and become a major staff player on the Finance Committee.

For six months, Raffaelli and her brother, John D., served on the Finance Committee together, probably the only bipartisan brother-sister team serving in the Senate or House. Raffaelli learned a great deal from her brother who was a legislative assistant to Senator Lloyd Bentsen (D-TX). "To be an effective staff member you have to have an effective Senator, and vice versa," said Raffaelli. Especially in the area of tax, Raffaelli appears to have discovered the winning formula: First, argue the policy; then you argue the politics of what you are doing; and if all else fails, round-up the votes." She adds that a staff member must also learn to form coalitions within the committee in order to obtain support through the legislative process. But most importantly, the staffer must know his or her "bottom line" compromise position. Raffaelli does not consider her work on the Finance Committee to be defined in terms of Republicans vs. Democrats. "You must be willing to compromise or nothing would get done," said Raffaelli.

She says the 1986 bill was so complex much of this year will be spent determining where we made mistakes and what can be fixed. Raffaelli should know, she was deeply involved in the 1986 bill.

Capital formation, depreciation and minimum tax structure have a great impact on Pennsylvania industries, and Raffaelli has taken a staff leadership role on behalf of Heinz on these issues during the tax reform debates.

She will continue to work on the technical corrections and the extension of the Targeted Jobs Tax Credit and other provisions which expire this year.

By her experience and expertise, it is easy to understand why she was profiled in *Cosmopolitan*, 1984, as a woman of power in government.

Personal: born 10/23/48 in Texarkana, Arkansas. B.S. Univ. of Texas, 1970. J.D. Univ. of Arkansas, 1979 (member, law review editorial board). LL.M. (Tax) New York Univ., 1980. 1980-1983, practiced tax litigation, Department of Justice. 1983-present, Legislative Counsel/Legislative Assistant, Senator John Heinz (R-PA).

Andrew Samet
Legislative Counsel
Senator Daniel Moynihan (D-NY)
464 Russell Senate Office Bldg.
224-4451

Expertise: International trade, U.S.-Canadian economic relations, budget and fiscal policy, transportation

As Legislative Counsel to the erudite senior senator from New York, Andrew Samet helps Moynihan, a member of the Senate Finance Committee, keep abreast of the details of international trade and budget issues. Samet is recognized as an authority on U.S.-Canadian trade.

Samet's experience as a Washington lawyer specializing in international trade issues served as a natural stepping-stone to his current position in 1987. He had had some previous Hill experience as a professional staff member for the Senate Appropriations Committee.

Samet plunged into action on some major trade legislation upon joining Moynihan's staff, including the Omnibus Trade Bill, the Textile Bill, and the historic U.S.-Canada free trade agreement. Work remains to be completed on these bills in this congressional session. This year Samet will also be focussing on the work of the National Economic Commission established by the Budget Reconciliation Act of 1987, a 12-member panel of prominent public and private sector leaders, including Senator Moynihan. The Commission's mandate is to examine U.S. fiscal problems and measures for increasing capital formation and to produce a major report with recommendations by March, 1989. The Commission's effort could be a catalyst for economic initiatives by a new administration, and might have an impact similar to that of the influential commission that proposed the recent reforms that were implemented in the Social Security System.

One of Moynihan's pet projects, in which Samet is involved, is the enlisting of federal support for a magnetic levitation transportation system, using vehicles with superconducting magnets to achieve speeds up to 300 miles per hour.

Personal: born 6/29/57. B.A. Yale Univ., 1978. M.A. Carleton Univ., Ottawa, Canada, 1981. Georgetown Univ. Law School, 1983. 1978-1979, Professional staff member, Senate Appropriations Committee. 1984, Foreign Investment Review Law in Canada Chapter: "U.S. Response to Canadian Economic Nationalism. 1985, Politics of Canada's Economic Relationship with the U.S. Chapter: "U.S. Response to Canadian Initiatives for Sectoral Trade Liberalization." 1983-1987, international trade lawyer, Mudge, Rose, Guthrie, Alexander & Ferdon, Washington, D.C. 1987-present, Legislative Counsel, Sen. Daniel Moynihan (D-NY)

Operating prototypes for "maglev" technology exist in Germany and Japan, and Moynihan envisions an applicable system in the Northeast corridor and nation wide. Samet's work plate is so full that it leaves him little time for outside activities, although he does enjoy playing hockey. He respects his boss as a thinker and an innovator, and feels that his job has "turned out to be everything I had expected."

Susan C. Schwab
Legislative Director
Senator Jack Danforth (R-MO)
497 Russell Senate Office Bldg.
224-6154

Personal: born 3/23/55 in Washington, D.C. B.A. Williams Coll., 1976 (cum laude). M.A. in Applied Economics, Stanford Univ., 1977. 1977-1979, International Trade Economist, Office of the President's Special Representative for Trade Negotiations (now U.S.T.R.). 1980-1981, Trade Policy Officer, U.S. Embassy in Tokyo. 1981-1986, Legislative Assistant (Economic Policy and International Trade); 1986 to present, Legislative Director, Senator John C. Danforth. Publications: "The Last U.S. Trade Bill?"; The International Economy Magazine; October/November, 1987. "Policies, Economics and U.S. Trade Policy" Stanford Journal of International Law, Stanford University; June, 1987. "Japan and the U.S. Congress: Problems and Prospects": Journal of International Affairs Columbia Univ.; Summer 1983 & 1985.

Expertise: International trade, international economic policy, U.S.-Japan relations

Reducing the trade deficit which reached an approximate $171 billion in 1987, is a goal Congress will once again attempt to achieve this year. Susan Schwab and other trade and economic policy staff experts will play a role in this process as well. In fact, Schwab is regarded by many as the most influential legislative aide on the Hill on trade issues.

As Senator John Danforth's Legislative Director, Schwab is responsible for overseeing the Senator's legislative priorities, specifically in matters relating to economic policy and international trade. Since Danforth sits on two powerful committees, Commerce, Science and Transportation and the Senate Finance Committee—which has jurisdiction over international trade—Schwab has many opportunities to pursue various trade-related agendas.

Schwab describes herself as a "free-trade pragmatist" and believes the U.S. can have an activist trade policy that isn't a protectionist policy. Recently, Schwab worked on the pending omnibus trade bill which includes a Senate provision (Super 301) based on an idea Senator Danforth and Schwab developed last year. This proposal would require the President to file trade complaints against countries that "maintain a consistent pattern of import barriers." A recent *Washington Post* profile of Schwab is headlined "Enforcer Behind the Trade Bill, Economist Schwab wants the U.S. to Get Tough and Get Reciprocity" (7/24/87). In the article, Sen. Danforth credits Schwab with developing the Super 301 Amendment. This amendment, an alternative to the House Gephardt Amendment, would give the President more discretion in determining whether to retaliate. Danforth was also quoted saying, "I did not want to go the route of protectionism, but I didn't want our trade policy to be passive. Sue has envisioned how this works out and how it is put into practice. She has an incredible foresight and ability to look into the future of a bill and see what's going to happen to it."

Some of Schwab's other initiatives are found in the Trade and Tariff Act of 1984 (P.L. 98-573), the Trade Enhancement Act of 1985 and legislation involving reciprocity, telecommunications and related issues.

Although Schwab calls Washington, D.C. home, she's lived a great deal of her life abroad. On her off-time she enjoys the theater, opera and the symphony. She's also working towards her Ph.D. in Public Administration and International Business.

Jeffery S. Trinca
Legislative Aide
Senator David Pryor (D-AR)
264 Russell Senate Office Bldg.
224-2353

Personal: born 12/8/60 in Klamath Falls, Oregon. Attended Univ. of Santa Clara., Univ. of California, Davis, 1983. International Christian Univ., Japan, 1982. J.D. George Washington Univ. Law School, 1986. 1984-1986, law firm of Nossaman Gunther Knox & Elliott. 1986-present, legislative assistant, Senator David H. Pryor (D-AR).

Expertise: Tax and related issues

Growing up in a small town in northern California, Senator David Pryor's principal legislative assistant on tax matters, Jeff Trinca, feels he understands the needs of small businessmen and "just folks" in Arkansas—core constituents of the popular and populist Pryor.

Trinca particularly enjoys working in the tax area. Since tax issues "deal across the board" with every aspect of life from charities and low-income housing to the largest corporate boardrooms Trinca knows his position gives him an insight into "what's happening" in American life.

Pryor, author of the Taxpayer's Bill of Rights, chairs the Finance Subcommittee on Pension Retirement and Oversight of the Internal Revenue, which oversaw revision of the controversial I.R.S. forms. Trinca was part of the staff team that orchestrated the congressional hearing on the issue.

Toward the end of his second year in law school, Trinca worked in the Washington office of the California-based law firm of Nossaman Gunther, Knox & Elliott. One of the senior partners of the firm was former Connecticut Congressman Bob Giaimo, noted for his legislative expertise in budgetary and fiscal matters.

Strongly influenced by Giaimo, Trinca was taken under the wing of another former Hill staffer, John Riordan from the Ways and Means Committee. Riordan frequently asked Trinca to monitor legislation, attend hearings and become familiar with the nuances of the legislative process.

During this time, Trinca continued his interest in business and tax-related areas. He came to realize early that "specialties were the name of the game." Under Riordan's tutelage, he concentrated on all angles of insurance law and pension matters while becoming more active in the firm's tax activities.

Immediately involved with the tax battle, Trinca, according to several Washington insiders, was able to effectively build coalitions in areas relating to Pryor's interest. In short, he was doing from the "inside" what he had been witnessing from the "outside."

Trinca will continue to work on the issues closest to Pryor's heart: tax and pension issues relating to Small Business issues, as well as I.R.S. oversight.

In his spare time, Trinca, whose interests range from karate to collecting first editions after "digging through dusty book shops" is also a student of Japanese history. His wife, Ann, is a tax lobbyist and attorney with the U.S. Chamber of Commerce.

Marina Weiss
Chief Health Analyst
205 Dirksen Senate Office Bldg.
224-4515

Expertise: Medicare, Medicaid, welfare reform, catastrophic health c

Widely respected throughout the health care community, Weiss works closely with Sen. Bentsen, chairman of the Committee on Finance, on all health-related issues. Her work often extends beyond legislation by offering solutions to funding problems of health care providers while at the same time drawing a difficult compromise by not unfairly burdening the beneficiaries. She assisted Bentsen in developing legislative solutions that are equitable for all providers under the complicated perspective payment system (PPS) that allows for the reimbursement of hospitals.

Weiss assisted in drafting the controversial prescription drug amendment to the Medicare Catastrophic Act of 1987, which would provide elderly and disabled Medicare beneficiaries with 80% of outpatient drug costs in excess of $600 a year. Benefits would be phased in between 1990 and 1993. The legislation authorizes the biggest expansion of Medicare since the program was enacted in 1965. Weiss has been credited with developing the financing mechanism that was the cornerstone of the expanded coverage.

Weiss worked furiously on the 1987 reconciliation package to help achieve the savings required by the November 1987 deficit-reduction summit. The committee had to cut another $500 million from the $80 billion per year Medicare and Medicaid programs. Bentsen and Weiss helped to assure that despite all the cuts, Medicaid coverage would be extended to young children and low-income pregnant women. A delicate compromise was reached with the Office of Management and Budget (OMB) to allow the add-on to survive.

Weiss has also worked with Sen. Daniel Patrick Moynihan's staff on his welfare reform proposal. The bill seeks to change the thrust of welfare from a benefit program to one that moves recipients into private sector jobs.

Insiders on the committee note that Bentsen has discouraged Weiss from accepting offers from state government to head up state human resources departments, affirming the value the chairman places on her counsel.

Personal: born 1945. 1981-1986, legislative assistant, Sen. Lloyd Bentsen (D-TX). 1987-present, chief health analyst, Senate Finance Committee.

William J. Wilkins
Staff Director and Chief Counsel
205 Dirksen Senate Office Bldg.
224-4515

Personal: born 10/04/52 in Greensboro, North Carolina. B.A. Yale Coll., 1974 (summa cum laude). J.D. Harvard Law School, 1977 (cum laude). 1977-1981, King and Spaulding, Atlanta. 1981-1985, Minority Tax Counsel; 1985-1987, Minority Chief Counsel: 1987-present, Staff Director and Chief Counsel, Senate Finance Committee.

Expertise: Tax

During the 99th Congress, under Senator Bob Packwood's chairmanship, the Finance Committee concentrated almost entirely on passage of the sweeping Tax Reform Act of 1986. In the 100th Congress, under Senator Lloyd Bentsen's chairmanship, the agenda shifted to trade.

One of Bentsen's first steps as chairman was to appoint as his top aide Bill Wilkins, whom the *Legal Times* called "one of the most highly regarded staffers on the Hill." Wilkins had five years professional experience as tax counsel and most recently as Minority Chief Counsel to the Committee under then ranking Democrat Sen. Russell Long (D-LA).

Although seasoned by Capitol Hill standards, the North Carolina native is a youthful 35 years old. Because of his senior position, his expertise and his widely acknowledged competence, lobbyists and staff often assume he is years older. His thinning hairline may also explain the confusion.

In 1981, on a tip from a friend in Washington, Wilkins learned about a rare opening on the tax staff of the Finance Committee. Applying for the position, he and Senator Long found the fit a good one. Wilkins clearly impressed Long and Senators on both sides of the aisle, as well as his peers, with his solid tax acumen and his ability to translate the esoteric into laymen's terms. As one of his Senate staff tax colleagues noted "He knows the code cold."

Fellow staffers and lobbyists state that Wilkins is a "straight shooter" and widely respected. Although it may be possible to label Wilkins as a moderate or progressive Democrat, he be can be called neither politically motivated nor partisan in the workings of the Committee, which has a tradition of bipartisanship.

In fact, during consideration of the 1986 tax reform legislation, while working for the Democrats, Wilkins was called on routinely by both sides for his knowledge and to help draft legislative language in such key areas as tax shelters. His style in addressing tax law is direct, and he is said to have no fondness for using the tax code "to play games" or to obscure the purpose of transition rules.

Bill Wilkins has recently given notice he will be leaving this year.

SENATE
COMMITTEE ON FOREIGN RELATIONS

George W. Ashworth
Professional Staff Member
521 Hart Senate Office Bldg.
224-9033

Expertise: Arms control, national security

George Ashworth has been involved with arms issues for more than twenty years. These two decades have afforded him first hand experience, ranging from a foreign correspondent assignment to a presidential appointment. At *The Christian Science Monitor*, Ashworth covered the Pentagon and national security issues. He also served a tour as Saigon Bureau Chief in 1969. In his five years with the newspaper, Ashworth wrote more than 1000 major articles. As counselor to the U.S. Arms Control and Disarmament Agency, he served as chairman of the Agency's external research council, which was responsible for development and control of a $3.8 million research program. In 1980, Ashworth was appointed Assistant Director of the U.S. Arms Control and Disarmament Agency. His responsibilities included supervising a forty person staff dealing with arms transfer, world military spending, and arms control impact issues. Ashworth received a Superior Honor Award for his excellent performance at A.C.D.A.

Personal: born 3/28/38 in Washington, D.C. B.A. Washington and Lee Univ., 1960. 1961-1963, Artillery Lieutenant, U.S. Army. 1967-1972, Staff Correspondent, Christian Science Monitor. 1972-1979, Professional Staff Member, Committee on Foreign Relations and Arms Control Subcommittee. 1979-1980, Counselor, U.S. Arms Control and Disarmament Agency. 1980-1981, Assistant Director of U.S. Arms Control and Disarmament Agency. 1981 to present, Professional Staff Member, Senate Committee on Foreign Relations. 1985 to present, Advisor, Senate Arms Control Observer Group.

Under Sen. Claiborne Pell (D-RI), Ashworth works on a variety of topics, including military assistance and arms sales. He frequently travels abroad on oversight missions. Following a recent trip to the Middle East, he co-authored a report entitled *War in The Persian Gulf: The U.S. Takes Sides*, criticizing the Reagan administration's policy in the Gulf region. His specialty remains arms control. He takes pride in his current work on the INF treaty, Defense and Space Talks and chemical weapons. Previously, he staffed the SALT I hearings and debates, as well as hearings in 1977 and 1987 on the Threshold Test Ban Treaty of 1974 and the Peaceful Nuclear Explosion Treaty of 1976.

Almost fifty years old, Ashworth claims most people his age are too concerned with job security to work in a place with a high turnover, like the Congress. A former artillery officer, Ashworth disdains the bureaucratic pace of an executive branch agency.

Thomas E. Boney, Jr.
Minority Deputy Staff Director
452 Dirksen Senate Office Bldg.
224-3941

Expertise: Child nutrition, foodstamps

After interning with Sen. Jesse Helms's office during the summer preceding his senior year of college, Thomas Boney knew he was bound for Washington after graduation. What he did not realize, though, was that the nation's capital would consume the next eleven years of his life.

Boney arrived in Washington in 1976 and embraced the conservative cause. Working as a legislative correspondent for Helms solidified his political orientation and paved the way for his future career on Capitol Hill. But he did not begin mastering his specialty until he landed a position as a legislative assistant to then Rep. Eldon Rudd (R-AZ), for whom he handled economic, tax and foreign policy issues.

As a Professional Staff Member of the Senate Committee on Agriculture, Nutrition and Forestry, Boney's duties included oversight of the food-stamp and child nutrition programs as well as the overall budget of the Department of Agriculture. By the time he became Deputy Chief of Staff, Boney was an expert on legislative procedure, negotiation and the complex mechanism of the Committee's operations.

Boney worked hard on behalf of President Reagan's budget cuts in 1981, especially on the issue of striking workers' eligibility for food stamps. Although he is pleased that a bill denying such eligibility passed, he thinks that deeper cuts must still be pursued and that verification of beneficiaries should be tightened to avoid fraud and abuse.

Personal: born 7/12/54 in North Carolina. B.A. in Journalism, Univ. of North Carolina, Chapel Hill, 1976. 1976-1979, legislative correspondent, Sen. Jesse Helms (R-NC). 1979-1981, Legislative Assistant, Rep. Eldon Rudd (R-AZ). 1981-1986, Professional Staff Member, Senate Committee on Agriculture, Nutrition and Forestry. 1987 to present, Minority Deputy Staff Director, Senate Committee on Foreign Relations.

Boney traces his affinity for Reagan's policies back to 1976, when he worked part time for the Reagan campaign. He was so impressed by Ronald Reagan's ideas that, although he comes from a traditionally Democratic family, he shifted his allegiance to the Republican Party, and now feels "personally hurt" when the President deviates from his conservative course.

Boney is a newcomer to the Committee on Foreign Relations. But his interest in Foreign Relations took him abroad even before he came to the Committee in early 1987. In 1988, he was selected as a delegate from the Southeast on a study-tour to Japan sponsored by the American Council of Young Political Leaders. He has also traveled to Finland and the U.S.S.R. Boney is an active member and deacon at the Fourth Presbyterian Church in Bethesda, Maryland and likes gardening and swimming.

Geryld B. Christianson
Staff Director
439 Dirksen Senate Office Bldg.
224-4651

Personal: born 12/31/34 in Boyd, Minnesota. B.A. Univ. of Minnesota, 1957. Johns Hopkins School of Advanced International Studies (Atlantic Affairs Studies), 1967-1968. 1958-1975, Foreign Service Officer, Dept. of State (postings in Australia, Venezuela, Canada, The Hague and served from 1973-75 as Chief, Arms Control and Strategic Affairs Bureau of European Affairs). 1975-1981, foreign policy aide, Senator Claiborne Pell (D-RI). 1981-1987, Minority Staff Director; 1987 to present, Staff Director, Senate Foreign Relations Committee.

Expertise: Arms control, NATO, and Latin America

Like Foreign Relations Committee Chairman Senator Claiborne Pell (D-RI), Geryld Christianson served in the U.S. Foreign Service. Christianson is keenly interested in legislation affecting the State Department and is an expert on NATO and arms control issues in Europe. As Staff Director for the Foreign Relations Committee, however, he is often busy planning the Committee's activities and handling administrative matters. Remarking on the change in agenda which he has witnessed since the switch to a Democrat-controlled Senate, Christianson says: "It has been dramatic. There's a much greater willingness to face Central American issues, and the Committee was able to propose a prohibition against reflagging in the Persian Gulf" (commercial tankers and other vessels under the U.S. flag.)

Christianson, who earned his undergraduate degree in international relations, says he was always interested in working on Capitol Hill, and recalls he was offered a position on Pell's staff at a time when he and his family were tired of fifteen years of itinerant life with the State Department. In 1975, he was preparing for an exposure to the Hill when he briefly attended an IPSA fellowship program for mid-career Foreign Service officers at Johns Hopkins University. The program would have involved four months of working in the Senate and House in a particular field of concentration. However, Christianson was offered a permanent position by Senator Pell and resigned from the Foreign Service shortly after the orientation portion of the IPSA program began. Christianson learned Pell was looking for a Foreign Service Officer to work for him on a long-term basis just after being accepted by the IPSA program.

After becoming Foreign Policy Aide to Pell, Christianson worked on the Foreign Service Act of 1980, helped draft legislation affecting the foreign aid program and has been deeply involved in work on the Nuclear Threshold Test Ban Treaty and the INF Treaty.

In 1987, Christianson coordinated efforts to compensate for cuts in the State Department Authorization Bill and the Foreign Assistance Authorization bill forced by the federal budget crisis. In 1986 and 1987, he traveled to Vienna, Geneva, London and Brussels for conferences and arms control delegation meetings. In November, 1987 he accompanied Sens. Pell and Pressler on their trip to Nicaragua, Costa Rica and Belize. Christianson speaks fluent Spanish and was a Latin American specialist for the State Department. He also speaks French and Dutch. In Asia and Pacific affairs Christianson's work has focused on support for democracy and an end to martial law in Taiwan, a cause which has been of particular concern to Pell.

Robin Cleveland
Legislative Assistant
Sen. Mitch McConnell (R-KY)
l20 Russell Senate Office Bldg.
224-5095

Expertise: Middle East, Africa and Asia, intelligence

When Sen. Mitch McConnell (R-KY) moved to the Foreign Relations Committee in January, 1987 after serving on the Intelligence Committee for his first two years in office, he needed a new senior legislative aide to staff the committee. Robin Cleveland, who had worked for McConnell on the Intelligence Committee, was a logical choice.

Cleveland's foreign affairs background started with Asian studies, which she gained in school and by travelling in the region as the child of a foreign service officer. While on the Intelligence Committee, she acquired expertise on African and Middle Eastern affairs. As a Legislative Assistant for McConnell, a first-term senator, she handles the full range of foreign policy and defense issues.

Cleveland was the key staffer for McConnell's work with the Anti-Apartheid Act of 1986. In addition, she is known for her involvement with the legislative language on the Iran-Iraq war which was included in the 1987 Foreign Aid bill.

Cleveland estimates she spends half her time preparing the Senator for hearings and legislation, and the rest of her day talking to Administration agencies and constituents. Recent projects have included work on the INF hearings, the Persian Gulf conflict, and the Turkish-Greek situation. She also helped McConnell prepare for hearings on the creation of a new War Powers Subcommittee.

Personal: born 6/22/55 in Furstenfeldburck, Germany, . B.A. Wesleyan Univ., 1977, cum laude. 1977-1978, legal assistant on energy and antitrust issues, Spiegel & McDiarmid law firm, Washington, D.C. 1978-1980, Assistant to Press Secretary, Senate Intelligence Committee. 1980-1984, Professional Staff Member, Senate Intelligence Committee. 1984-1987, Sen. McConnell's committee designee and Middle Eastern and African affairs specialist for all committee members, Senate Intelligence Committee. 1987 to present, Legislative Assistant for Foreign Policy & Defense, Sen. Mitch McConnell.

Gerald E. Connolly
Majority Professional Staff Member
423 Dirksen Senate Office Bldg.
224-4651

Expertise: Middle East, international development aid

Gerald Connolly's writings range from articles on *The New York Times* op-ed page to reports for the Senate Foreign Relations Committee. Although the topics he covers are as diverse as the publications themselves, Connolly generally focuses his interests on U.S. global political and economic involvement.

Before coming to the Senate Foreign Relations Committee, Connolly published mostly on refugee and hunger issues. Currently, as a professional staff member, he is entrusted by the Committee to undertake political study-tours around the world and to produce reports on U.S. policies. A recent report he co-authored, entitled *War in The Persian Gulf: The U.S. Takes Sides*, criticizes the Reagan Administration for involving itself in the Persian Gulf independently. Connolly sees the move as a "hastily made decision, motivated by the Iran-Contra scheme," and one that will eventually bring the U.S. dangerously close to war with Iran. Instead, he believes the United States should back a U.N. joint effort in the volatile region. Connolly's previous literary contributions to the Senate Foreign Relations Committee include reports on the Israeli economy, on Central America and on South Africa.

Personal: born 3/30/50. B.A. in Literature, Maryknoll Coll., Glen Ellyn, IL, 1971. M.A. in public administration with concentration in international relations and U.S. foreign policy, JFK School of Government, Harvard Univ., 1979. 1971-1972, development associate of international non-profit agency. 1972-1974, associate executive director of the American Freedom from Hunger Foundation. 1975-1978, executive director, U.S. Committee for Refugees. 1979 to present, Professional Staff Member, Committee on Foreign Relations.

Connolly's "mission" on Capitol Hill is to give decisionmakers a deeper understanding of the non-European world. He believes a U.S.-Soviet clash in Europe is unlikely and that superpower emphasis should be diverted from Europe to other regions of the world, such as the Middle East, with its intractable problems and opportunities for diplomatic initiatives by both sides.

Connolly has become an expert on foreign assistance programs, winning high marks for his role in last year's committee markup of the foreign aid bill. But under Sen. Claiborne Pell (D-RI), Connolly handles a wide range of issues, including the U.N. and narcotics. He likes to see himself as a conciliator in bipartisan meetings, using diplomatic tactics to resolve issues.

Outside work, Connolly gets involved in community activities. He is active in Virginia politics, advising the state's Attorney General on youth and drugs, working with the Fairfax County Democratic Committee and on Fairfax transportation and land use. In 1984, he was elected a Virginia delegate to the Democratic National Convention. He is also a Civil War buff.

Peter W. Galbraith
Professional Staff Member
443 Dirksen Senate Office Bldg.
224-7523

Expertise: South Asia, Persian Gulf, North Africa

When his colleagues talk about Peter Galbraith, the adjective "principled" keeps cropping up. Galbraith's nine years of experience on the staff of the Senate Foreign Relations Committee have allowed him to develop, as one Hill staffer put it, "a tenacity of principle and a genuine substantive expertise".

Galbraith is the Committee's chief advisor on South Asia, the Persian Gulf, and North African affairs and is responsible for staff work on the annual Foreign Relations Authorization bill and for oversight of the State Department and the United States Information Agency (USIA).

Galbraith has worked diligently on legislation linking U.S. aid to Pakistan both to progress in human rights and to a Pakistani commitment not to produce the highly enriched uranium used in nuclear weapons.

Galbraith is particularly proud of the key role he played in 1984 in the release from prison of Benazir Bhutto, daughter of former President Zulfikar Ali Bhutto, and a friend of Galbraith from college.

Galbraith has helped senators battle efforts to politicize the USIA. Over the last seven years, Galbraith has been deeply involved in Congressional oversight of USIA policy. He has worked to maintain the non-partisan nature of the Fulbright exchange program. These efforts to preserve the integrity of the agency have led to a doubling of funding for the Fulbright program.

Personal: born 12/31/50 in Boston, Massachusetts. A.B. Harvard Coll., 1973, magna cum laude. M.A. Oxford Univ., 1975. 1972 and 1976, delegate, Democratic National Conventions. 1975-1978, assistant professor of economics and international relations, Windham Coll., Putney, VT. Faculty, School for International Training, Brattleboro, VT. 1976, Vermont co-chairman, Morris Udall's presidential campaign. 1977-1979, chairman, Vermont State Democratic Committee. 1979 to present, Professional Staff Member, Senate Foreign Relations Committee. Publications: War in the Persian Gulf, (1987). United States Security Interests in South Asia, (1984). United States-Indian Relations, (1982). Cambodian Relief, (1980).

Galbraith recently traveled to Iraq to gather information on Iraqi vulnerability in the Iran-Iraq war. He made stops in Basra and Baghdad and was one of the very few people to visit the closed-off area of Kurdistan. The resulting report on the Persian Gulf stresses the precariousness of the current Iraqi military position and the disastrous consequences of an Iranian victory.

Galbraith describes himself as a Democrat with moderate to liberal views on most matters. He says of the Hill: "I think people should come into the public sector to serve this country and to have a role in and shaping the important decisions of the day." Galbraith adds, "working on the Hill is essentially anonymous and if you don't like not getting credit for your work, you shouldn't be working here."

He has traveled all over the globe and spent time living in India where his father was posted as U.S. Ambassador. But Galbraith calls Vermont home. He hopes one day to return there to teach and, perhaps, run for elective office.

Foreign Relations

Frances M. Goodwin
Legislative Assistant
Sen. Nancy Kassebaum (R-KS)
302 Russell Senate Office Bldg.
224-4774

Expertise: United Nations, Department of State authorization

As a result of the Nixon administration taking office, Frances Goodwin's husband, who had been appointed by then-United States Attorney General Robert F. Kennedy, was replaced in his position in Kansas. And while Guy Goodwin secured a position with the Department of Justice in Washington , Frances Goodwin subsequently launched what would be a successful Capitol Hill career.

After four years of learning the congressional process in the House, Goodwin was offered a position with her home-state senator, Nancy Kassebaum (R-KS). And in early 1987, upon her promotion as Sen. Kassebaum's legislative assistant, Goodwin began her work in the area of State Department authorization.

One of the things Goodwin finds most challenging is balancing fiscal considerations with the plethora of worthy programs contained in the yearly State Department authorization bill. Currently, that bill provides funding for some 46 different agencies, including the World Health Organization, NATO, the Organization of American States and the United Nations. Because these agencies must compete for increasingly limited funds, prioritizing within the various accounts is difficult.

Personal: born 11/13/28 in Wichita, Kansas. B.A. Oberlin Coll., 1950. M.A. Univ. of Kansas, 1952. 1960-1967, English instructor, Wichita State Univ. 1975-1979, Legislative Correspondent, Rep. Helen Meyner (D-NJ). 1979-1986, Legislative Correspondent; and 1987-present, Legislative Assistant, Sen. Nancy Kassebaum (R-KS).

As a result of Sen. Kassebaum's active involvement in the United Nations, Goodwin has developed an expertise in the area of U.N. funding.

For several years, the United Nations has been criticized for little accountability. Against this background, Kassebaum introduced an amendment in 1985 to the State Department bill calling for an annual five percentage point reduction in U.S. contributions to the U.N. budget until the U.N. adopted weighted voting in budgetary matters.

Goodwin believes this measure, now widely known as the Kassebaum Amendment, has forced the U.N. to move forward on budgetary reforms. And because of Kassebaum's continued interest in this matter, Goodwin continually monitors this important issue.

Bradley Gordon
Legislative Assistant
Senator Rudy Boschwitz (R-MN)
506 Hart Senate Office Bldg.
224-5641

Personal: born 5/22/49 in Burlington, Vermont. B.A. in politics, Brandeis Univ., 1971. M.A. Univ. of Vermont, 1974. National Defense Foreign Language Fellow in Arabic, Columbia Univ., New York, N.Y., 1975. Certificate, Middle East Institute, Columbia Univ., 1976. Ph.D. (a.b.d.) in comparative politics, Columbia Univ., 1979. 1975, Research Assistant, Bureau of Applied Research, Columbia Univ. 1975-1976, Research Assistant, Middle East Institute, Columbia Univ. 1979-1985, CIA Analyst, Office of Near Eastern/ South Asian Analysis. Spring-Summer, 1983, special assignment: Minority Staff Representative, Europe and Middle East Subcommittee, House Committee on Foreign Affairs. 1985-1987, Professional Staff Member, Senate Committee on Foreign Relations. 1987-present, Legislative Assistant for Foreign Affairs, Defense and Intelligence to Senator Rudy Boschwitz (R-MN).

Expertise: Foreign affairs, defense, intelligence

After six years with the CIA, Bradley Gordon moved to Capitol Hill. His motivation for the career change, according to Gordon, was to "get into policy making and out of simply doing analysis." His first experience on the Hill was in 1983, when Rep. Larry Winn (R-KS), then the ranking Republican on the House Europe and Middle East Subcommittee, recruited him to fill a temporary vacancy as Minority Staff Representative. At the time, Gordon was one of two principal political analysts for the CIA on Iran, and Winn needed someone with expertise in Middle Eastern affairs.

Gordon's extensive background in Middle Eastern affairs served him well. His primary responsibilities at the CIA included assessing the internal political stability and foreign policies of the countries he watched, analyzing terrorism and subversion, and writing interagency intelligence papers and National Intelligence Estimates. The regional issues Gordon covered consisted of the politics of oil, Islamic fundamentalism, the Arab-Israeli conflict and Soviet capabilities in the Middle East.

Gordon frequently briefed senior government officials, other members of the intelligence community and foreign officials on these issues.

During his special assignment with the House of Representatives, Gordon was Winn's principal advisor on the Middle East and Europe. He worked on issues involving East-West trade, economic and political relations with NATO, Central American and Middle Eastern conflicts and nuclear arms negotiations.

Gordon's responsibilities also included writing memos about American foreign policy, tracking legislation before the Subcommittee, and drafting questions for hearings.

Gordon returned to the CIA for two years before taking a position with the Senate Foreign Relations Committee. As a Professional Staff Member, Gordon was responsible for issues involving the Near East and South Asia. In 1985, he helped draft major foreign assistance legislation authorizing $6.7 billion in aid to that region.

Gordon also served as the Committee's liaison with Administration officials and the diplomatic corps on Near East and South Asian issues. In this role, he worked on arms sales authorizations as well as formulating resolutions of disapproval for potential arms sales to certain countries.

When the Republicans lost control of the Senate in 1986, Senator Jesse Helms ousted Lugar from the position he would have assumed—ranking minority member of the Committee. Helms brought his own staff to the Committee, which resulted in Gordon's transfer to Boschwitz's personal staff in February, 1987.

In 1987, Gordon served as chief advisor to Boschwitz on the INF Treaty, Central American issues and the Persian Gulf crisis.

As Boschwitz's constituent contact for foreign relations and defense issues, Gordon has assisted Minnesota companies in their efforts to promote sales abroad. He was involved, for example, in helping a Minnesota computer firm, the Cray Company, sell its supercomputers to India through an agreement with the U.S. government in 1987.

Gordon has also traveled to the Middle East on fact-finding missions and with the Senator. On these trips, Gordon has met with heads of state, defense ministers and foreign ministers of Middle Eastern countries. He is fluent in Hebrew, Arabic and French.

Mary Catherine (Kay) King
Legislative Assistant
Senator Joseph Biden (D-DE)
489 Russell Senate Office Bldg.
224-5042

Expertise: U.S.-European relations, NATO, U.S.-Soviet relations

Studying at the London School of Economics during her junior year in college made a lasting impact on Kay King's career path. King developed there an understanding and appreciation for the European perspective on world affairs. This experience later resulted in a career focused on European-American relations and the NATO alliance.

Prior to her position as Senator Joseph Biden's (D-DE.) Legislative Assistant, King was an Associate Director of the European-American Project at the Council on Foreign Relations. As Associate Director, King undertook research for and did extensive editing on a series of books, each one focusing on a different aspect of the European-American relationship. These included *The Conventional Defense of Europe, Nuclear Weapons in Europe* and *Central America as a European-American Issue*.

In June, 1987, Biden hired King as a Legislative Assistant and in November, she was promoted to his Chief Foreign Policy Legislative Assistant. During her short tenure in the Senate, King has worked on many high-profile issues, including contra aid, U.S. policy in South Africa, the War Powers Resolution and the INF treaty.

Personal: born 2/22/54 in Rye, N.Y. A.B. Vassar Coll., 1976. M.I.A. Columbia Univ. 1979. 1980-1981, Staff Assistant, Council on Foreign Relations. 1981-1982, editorial assistant ,Foreign Affairs Magazine. 1983, analyst, Congressional Research Service, Foreign Affairs and National Defense Division. 1983-1987, associate director, European American Project, Council on Foreign Relations. 1987 to present, Legislative Assistant, Senator Joseph R. Biden, Jr.

As Biden's Foreign Policy LA, King briefs the Senator on all foreign policy issues before the Senate Foreign Relations Committee. She prepares Biden's testimony and opening statements for Committee hearings, drafts questions for witnesses who appear before the Committee and writes memoranda explaining the issues. Currently, King is spending most of her time on the INF treaty hearings. She assists in researching and briefing Biden on a broad range of arms control issues relating to the Treaty. King is also working on the upcoming Committee review of the War Powers Resolution.

In 1987, King worked on the State Department Authorization Bill, which came out of the Foreign Relations Committee. She was responsible for working with other Committee staff to incorporate various provisions in the Bill.

As Biden's foreign policy advisor, King also has contact with the Senator's constituents. She travels to Delaware to meet with both public and private groups to discuss foreign policy concerns.

King wanted to work for Biden because she respects "his intelligence, knowledge of foreign policy issues and strong set of values."

In her free time, King enjoys ballet which she studied for seven years. King also confesses to being a football fan, especially a fan of the New York Jets.

Barbara Mills Larkin
Legislative Assistant/Counsel
Senator Terry Sanford (D-NC)
716 Hart Senate Office Bldg.
224-3154

Personal: born 7/26/51 in Dubuque, Iowa. B.A. Clarke Coll. (magna cum laude), 1973. J.D. Univ.of Iowa , 1977. 1973, Legislative Aide, Iowa State Senate. 1974, Coordinator, Blouin for Congress Committee. 1974-1976, Legislative Assistant, Rep. Michael T. Blouin, (D-IA). 1977-1978 Staff Attorney, North Carolina Department of Insurance. 1978-1983, associate, Sanford, Adams McCullough & Beard law firm. 1983-1986, partner, Sanford, Adams, McCullough & Beard. 1986-present, Legislative Assistant/Counsel to Sen. Terry Sanford (D-NC). Admitted to Iowa, North Carolina and the District of Columbia Bars; U.S. Tax Court; Federal District Courts in North Carolina; and Fourth Circuit Court of Appeals.

Expertise: Foreign relations

Barbara Larkin has only held her current position with Sen. Terry Sanford (D-NC) for a little more than a year, but this is not her first tour of duty on Capitol Hill. Always fascinated by politics and active in campaigns throughout high school and college, she was 23 years old and had just finished her first year of law school when she came to Washington as a legislative assistant to Rep. Michael Blouin (D-IA) in 1974.

After two years with Blouin, she finished law school and joined the Raleigh, NC, firm of Sanford, Adams, McCullough and Beard, where current Sen. Terry Sanford was the senior partner. Specializing in tax, business, securities fraud, litigation and lobbying, Larkin became a partner in 1983.

As a "big fan" of Walter Mondale, she became involved in his 1984 campaign for President. After participating in Sanford's 1986 Senate campaign, she was invited to return to Washington as his legislative assistant/counsel.

Larkin's first task was organizing a swearing-in party for 2000 guests from North Carolina on the Senate steps. Compared with that, organizing Sanford's work with the Foreign Relations Committee seems easy.

In Central America, to which she has made several trips, she sees the problems as economic and social, not necessarily military.

The Soviet Union is another area of Larkin's interest. Some of her earliest political memories were of Khruschev's infamous U.N. shoe-banging episode, his visit to an Iowa farm, and the Cuban missile crisis. She recently participated in a seminar sponsored by the American Council of Young Political Leaders which took her to Moscow, Kiev, and rest of the Ukraine. As one of 14 Americans, she discussed arms control, human rights and bilateral issues with Soviet scholars. During the past year she has also visited South Korea and the People's Republic of China. Larkin's own understanding of the Persian Gulf has convinced her that the U.S. should maintain a presence there, but that the President should invoke the War Powers Act and consult with Congress as to what form that presence should take. At the present time, she is busy with the INF treaty hearings in the Foreign Relations Committee.

Growing up in Iowa, the daughter of a Catholic Republican physician, Larkin remembers the Kennedy-Nixon and Johnson-Goldwater campaigns. These events helped catalyze a dedicated Democrat.

Larkin worked her way through college teaching tennis and still plays whenever possible.

Alan Miles MacDougall
Legislative Assistant
Senator Frank Murkowski (R-AK)
709 Hart Senate Office Bldg.
224-3378

Personal: born 1943 in Winchester, Massachusetts. B.A. Tufts Univ., 1965. M.A. Graduate School of Public Affairs, State Univ. of New York, Albany, 1967. 1967-1969, Military Intelligence Corps, U.S. Army. 1969, Graduate of U.S. Army Command and General Staff Coll. 1968-1974, Intelligence Officer, Office of the Special Advisor to the Commander in Chief, U.S. Forces, Korea. 1974-1977, Researcher, Combined Arms Combat Developments Activity; Instructor (Soviet and Korean Studies), U.S. Army Command and General Staff Coll., Ft. Leavenworth, KS. 1977-1984, Senior Intelligence Officer, Korea/Japan Branch, Directorate for Research, Defense Intelligence Agency. 1984-1987, Chief, Asia Pacific Branch, Directorate for Research, Defense Intelligence Agency. 1987, American Political Science Association Congressional Fellow. 1987-present, Legislative Assistant, Sen. Frank Murkowski.(R-AK).

Expertise: Foreign Affairs, Asia and Pacific

In light of developments in the Philippines and Korea, Sen. Frank Murkowski, the ranking minority member of the Senate Foreign Relations Committee's East Asia and Pacific Subcommittee, has made considerable use of Alan MacDougall's expertise in Asian-Pacific affairs since choosing him for his staff in October 1987. As a career defense intelligence officer, MacDougall lived in Korea and consequently employs a first hand knowledge of both the culture and the language.

MacDougall is probably one of the Senate's most knowledgeable staffers on the Philippines and Korea. He does not, however, limit himself to these areas but handles the whole range of foreign policy issues for Murkowski. He enjoys working on a relatively small Senate staff, where he can have more contact with Alaska constituents and more impact generally. MacDougall spends much of his time preparing the Senator for committee hearings, while also finding time to respond to constituents on foreign affairs matters.

MacDougall comes to foreign affairs with a practical, analytical background which serves him well in assisting Murkowski, a former banker. MacDougall strongly believes that it is important for the average citizen to understand foreign policy because it directly affects American domestic policy.

As a Congressional Fellow working as a legislative assistant, he brings a unique perspective to his job. Already familiar with the substance of foreign policy, he is enjoying his role as a "visiting student" from the executive branch, observing the Senate's operating procedures.

Outside his professional interests, MacDougall and his wife are active in Scottish-American folk activities. He also enjoys swimming, needlepoint, and traveling.

Richard McCall
Legislative Assistant
Senator John Kerry (D-MA)
358 Russell Senate Office Bldg.
224-2742

Expertise: Foreign Affairs, Central America and foreign economic aid

Having been in Washington since 1971, Dick McCall is a veteran of Capitol Hill. Two of his most formative career experiences were working for former Sen. Gale McGee (D-WY) and Hubert Humphrey (D-MN), from whom he learned both the political process and the substance of foreign policy. In particular, he calls Humphrey the "father of foreign aid."

Today as an aide to Sen. Kerry (D-MA), McCall handles all foreign policy issues with the exception of arms control. His areas of specialty include Africa, the United Nations, Central America, foreign aid and economic development, and East Asia.

Hill observers may recognize McCall's name from his work on the 1985 Senate resolution linking American aid to the Philippines to domestic reforms there. McCall is also noted for his contributions to the Panama Canal treaties, the Arms Export Control Act of 1975, and the SALT I treaty.

McCall believes that foreign affairs have grown more complicated over the years. In the early 1970s, he found much of his time as a staffer was devoted to the Vietnam War and the War Powers debate, but now he must advise Kerry on problems in areas of the world as diverse as the Philippines, Korea, Africa, China, Central America, the Persian Gulf, and the Middle East.

One of the most frustrating aspects of working on the Hill to McCall is the tug-of-war between the executive and legislative branches and between the two political parties. As he sees it, the end result of this bickering is a distorted view of foreign policy that often focuses more on short-term remedies than on long-term commitments to serious change. On the flip-side, he notes that U.S. foreign policies are never "set in cement".

McCall enjoys working for Kerry because of the Senator's abiding interest in international affairs. He appreciates the active interest Kerry's Massachusetts constituents take in foreign policy. He also appreciated Kerry permitting him to devote time to a comprehensive study of aid to Central America organized by Sen. Terry Sanford (D-NC) and Duke Univ.'s Center for International Development. The report is due to be issued this spring.

McCall travels a fair amount for his job, but he also makes time to be home to coach his sons' basketball team.

Personal: born 1942 in Detroit, Michigan. B.A. Hastings Coll., Hastings, NE, l964. Graduate work at Univ.of Nebraska, l964-l967. l968-l97l, reporter for United Press International for Wyoming. 1971-1978, staff assistant, Senators Gale McGee (D-WY) and Hubert Humphrey (D-MN). 1978-1980, deputy staff director, Senate Foreign Relations Committee. 1980-1981, assistant secretary of international organization affairs, Department of State. 1981-1985, Deputy Staff Director, Senate Democratic Policy Committee. 1985 to present, Legislative Assistant, Foreign Affairs, Sen. John Kerry (D-MA).

Douglas L. Miller
Legislative Director
Senator Larry Pressler (R-SD)
411 Russell Senate Office Bldg.

Expertise: Foreign relations, defense

The twenty-eight year relationship between Douglas Miller and Sen. Larry Pressler (R-SD) might be called "academic", beginning with their undergrad days together at the Univ. of South Dakota. In addition to his role as legislative director, Miller also advises Pressler in his activities on the Senate Foreign Relations Committee and on national defense.

South Dakota's farm economy has shaped Miller's pragmatic views, especially on international trade policy. He understands that his state's agricultural surplus depends on easy access to foreign markets and a non-protectionist trade policy by U.S. leaders. Retaliation is therefore only a last resort, when trade barriers are insurmountable and fair play simply does not work.

On defense matters, Miller displays his long-held beliefs in a credible U.S. military deterrent. He shares the concerns of conservatives over verification of U.S. arms control treaties, and believes that a reduction in nuclear arms requires a strengthening of America's conventional forces with U.S. allies sharing more of the burden than they do. He admits he is encouraged yet advises a "wait and see" attitude toward Soviet *glasnost* or openness policies. Miller believes the Strategic Defense Initiative has been oversold, but with Soviet testing of anti-missile defenses, the U.S. is obligated to follow suit.

Personal: born 6/26/42 in Bell, California. A.B. Univ. of South Dakota, 1964. M.A. Univ. of Hawaii, 1966. Ph.D., Univ.of Colorado, 1976. 1968-1970, Teaching Associate, Univ. of Colorado. 1966-1968, Assistant Professor, 1970-1979, Professor of Political Science, Northern State Coll. 1974-1979, Chairman, Dept. of Social Science, Northern State Coll. 1980-present, Legislative Director, Sen. Larry Pressler.

Among Miller's major legislative efforts for Pressler in 1980 was helping organize the Senate opposition to the Carter Administration's grain embargo against the Soviet Union in response to the Soviet invasion of Afghanistan. He feels American agriculture was devastated by this ill-advised policy, and that it has taken years to return to where the U.S. was in 1978-1979. He also played a staff role in Pressler-sponsored foreign assistance legislation to prohibit U.S. contributions to the United Nations being used by such nations and organizations as Iran, Cuba Libya and the PLO, which support terrorism.

For diversion from Capitol Hill, Doug Miller entertains himself by reading financial publications, books on world history, numerology, astrology and occasionally fiction. He remains firmly unpersuaded that running is a healthy activity. He credits Laura Ingalls Wilder's (a fellow South Dakotan) pioneer fiction with his lifetime work ethic and basic values. His South Dakota high school not only included a graduating class of seven, but an unforgettable English teacher who spurred him to recite Shakespeare as he plied milk from his family cows.

Mary Ann Richardson
Legislative Assistant
Senator Brock Adams (D-WA)
513 Hart Senate Office Bldg.
224-2621

Personal: born 11/27/52 in Erie,
Pennsylvania. B.S. Gannon Univ.,
1974. M.A. candidate George
Washington Univ., 1974-1976. 1973-
1976, Staff of Rep. Joseph Vigoritto
(D-PA). 1976-1986, Staff, House
Banking Committee's Subcommittee
on International Development,
Institutions and Finance; and
Legislative Assistant to Representative
Stan Lundine (D-NY). 1986 to present,
Legislative Assistant to Senator Brock
Adams (D-WA).

Expertise: Trade, economics and foreign policy

A self-taught expert on international and domestic trade, exchange rates and economic policy, Mary Ann Richardson says her experience working for Sen. Brock Adams (D-WA) has taught her to connect foreign relations with economics and trade issues. "The U.S. today is playing in a different arena with newly industrializing countries and other industrialized trading partners developing extensive links and interdependencies," she says.

Richardson's career on the Hill has been atypical. She worked on the House side for thirteen years and then moved to the Senate. "The rules are completely different, and I think it is an advantage to have been exposed to both sides from inside and out," she says.

Richardson was involved in her first campaign in the fourth grade. When she was eighteen years old she became the youngest Democratic committee woman in Pennsylvania. Throughout her college years she was active in local politics. Ultimately, however, she chose the legislative arena as her area of concentration.

She was Senior Contributing Editor of The National-House Democratic Caucus's Trade Task Force report entitled "Competing for the Future: A Democratic Strategy for Trade" (1984). The task force report was an important forerunner to the Omnibus Trade Bill. It included strategies for addressing the trade deficit, exchange rate imbalances, industrial competitiveness, export promotion, fair international trade and labor. In the Senate, Richardson subsequently worked on three successful amendments to the Omnibus Trade Bill: an amendment relating to a countervailing duties statute which would prevent action against an international consortium (in a case involving Boeing and Airbus Industrie); an amendment providing for a study of U.S.-China trade relations and anti-dumping laws; and an amendment designed to encourage bank-affiliated export trading companies.

Richardson has worked on a number of trade-related legislative issues, from the textile bill to sanctions on semiconductors. She describes Sen. Adams as a "free trader" but notes he will support sanctions such as those against Japanese semiconductor manufacturers when a clear violation of a bilateral agreement is involved. "He has problems with the Gephardt Amendment and legislation such as the textile bill which block free trade or artificially close borders," she says.

Assisting the Senator on the Foreign Relations Committee, Richardson has worked on issues such as the need to apply the War Powers Act in the Persian Gulf, the Arms Control Threshold Test Ban Treaty and the reinterpretation of the ABM treaty and the INF treaty.

John B. Ritch III
Deputy Staff Director
439 Dirksen Senate Office Bldg.
224-3953

Expertise: Arms control, NATO, European Affairs & international economics

When former Sen. William J. Fulbright (D-AR) hired John Ritch to work for the Senate Foreign Relations Committee fifteen years ago, he brought aboard a unique individual. He is also thought to be the only U.S. government official to have infiltrated Soviet-occupied Afghanistan in 1984.

During his first two years on the Committee staff, Ritch was one of two staffers responsible for all work on foreign aid. From 1974-1978, he was in charge of all staff work dealing with oversight of the State Department and USIA. His next nine years were spent as a top aide on NATO, European, and Soviet affairs.

As the deputy staff director, Ritch is responsible for overseeing and coordinating all of the Committee staff's activities, in addition to being directly involved with all of its hearings. He also writes speeches for Chairman Claiborne Pell(D-RI) and Sen. Biden, leading Democrats on the Committee. Ritch feels that two of his most important assets to the Committee are his broad foreign affairs experience and his institutional continuity. Ritch has been with the Foreign Relations Committee longer than any current Senator except Pell.

Personal: born 3/13/43, Oakland, CA. B.S. U.S. Military Academy, 1965. (Eastern Collegiate Athletic Association "Outstanding Scholar-Athlete", 1965; Academic All-American, basketball; Rhodes Scholarship.) M.A. in Philosophy, Politics, and Economics, Oxford University, 1968. U.S. Airborne (parachute) school, 1968. U.S. Army Infantry company commander, Korean DMZ, 1969-1970. Special assistant, office of the U.S. Army Chief of Staff, 1970-1972. Consultant to the Environmental Protection Agency, 1972. Senior staffer on Senate Foreign Relations Committee, 1972-1987. Deputy staff director, Senate Foreign Relations committee, January 1987-present.

Ritch has authored two foreign affairs articles for *The Atlantic*. Ritch is presumably the only Capitol Hill staffer to have attended West Point, received an award for excellence in real estate development from the American Institute of Architects (AIA) and written numerous published reports for the committee. Two of his best-known reports are "SALT and the NATO Allies" (1979) and "Hidden War: The Struggle for Afghanistan" (1984). Ritch is also a member of the International Institute for Strategic Studies and the Council on Foreign Relations.

Recently, Ritch was involved with the Committee's hearings on reinterpretation of the ABM treaty and the INF treaty signed by Reagan and Gorbachev in December. In January, he accompanied Sen. Joseph Biden (D-DE) to meetings with several European heads of state to discuss their views on the INF treaty. Early 1988 was devoted to ratification hearings.

Despite his hectic schedule, Ritch still finds time for an interesting hobby–he is an avid collector of art deco and art nouveau and his home was recently featured in a national fine arts magazine.

Andrew K. Semmel
Legislative Assistant
Senator Richard Lugar (R-IN)
306 Hart Senate Office Bldg.
224-4814

*Personal: born in Palmerton,
Pennsylvania. B.A. Moravian Coll.,
Bethlehem, PA. M.A. Ohio Univ.,
Athens, Ohio. Ph.D. Univ. of Michigan,
Ann Arbor. 1971-1977, assistant
professor of political science, Univ. of
Cincinnati. 1977-1981, associate
professor of political science, Univ. of
Cincinnati. 1979-1981, faculty fellow
under Intergovernmental Personnel
Act (IPA) at International Security
Affairs/Dept. of Defense (DOD). 1981-
1984, foreign affairs specialist,
programs division, plans directorate at
Defense Security Assistance Agency
(DSAA)/DOD. 1984-1985, chief,
analysis division, plans directorate,
DSAA/DOD. 1985-1987, Professional
Staff Member, Senate Committee on
Foreign Relations. March, 1987 to
present, Legislative Assistant for
foreign policy, Sen. Richard G. Lugar.*

Expertise: Foreign affairs and national security issues

Unlike many legislative staffers who get their jobs on the Hill
through political savvy and key contacts, Andrew Semmel was
approached for a job because of his expertise in foreign policy
analysis and national security affairs. He earned a Ph.D. in foreign
policy and international relations from the University of Michigan
and went on to teach at the University of Cincinnati, where he
became a tenured associate professor.

In September, 1979, he took a leave of absence under an IPA
fellowship to become a Policy Analyst for the International Security
Affairs Bureau at the Department of Defense. In 1981, he was
hired full-time by DOD's Defense Security Assistance Agency
as a foreign affairs specialist and then as chief of the
analysis division.

After three and a half years at DOD, where he specialized in
security assistance programs, budgeting, defense analysis and
arms sales, Semmel was offered a professional staff position on
the Senate Foreign Relations Committee. He coordinated and
drafted arms sales legislation, involving the Middle East (i.e., sales
to Saudi Arabia and Jordan). He also drafted the amendment that
allowed the Special Defense Acquisition Fund to continue.

When he went to work for Sen. Lugar in March, 1987, Semmel's
role and influence changed dramatically. Moving from the staff of a
key committee to serve as assistant to the second-ranking
Republican on the committee would usually mean reduced
influence. But the peculiar circumstances in which Sen. Jesse
Helms (R-NC) and Lugar vied for the ranking Republican position
on the committee put Semmel in a key position to deal with other
committee members.

As Lugar's staff representative for foreign relations, Semmel
advises on issues before the Committee or the full Senate
concerning foreign policy, defense, State Department and related
agencies, and international trade. In 1987, he worked hard to
amend the 1988 Foreign Aid Authorization bill which he says
"threatened to emasculate the State Department." Semmel
played a key role in drafting a Comprehensive Recovery Act for
the Philippines.

An accomplished political scientist, he has published more than
twenty journal articles, book chapters, monographs, and reviews.
He gives lectures, briefings and other presentations to DOD,
academic, industry and other groups and maintains contact with
the academic community.

Frank A. Sieverts
Press Spokesman
446 Dirksen Senate Office Bldg.
224-5224

Expertise: Press relations, refugees

If experience and expertise count for anything, Frank Sieverts is ideally suited for his position as Press Spokesman for the Senate Committee on Foreign Relations. Indeed, he brings to the committee a 24-year career in the State Department, as well as early experience as an overseas news correspondent. During his quarter-century involvement in foreign relations, Sieverts's major work has been the pursuit of negotiations concerning refugees as well as POWs and MIAs in Southeast Asia. As special assistant to Ambassador Averell Harriman, he handled the POW issue at the Paris Peace Talks and in Southeast Asia. Due partly to his efforts, several Americans were released with Sieverts accompanying them back to a waiting America. He was in Hanoi for the release of American POWs in 1973 and represented the United States in further meetings with the Vietnamese officials on this issue. Sieverts played a similar key role in U.S. and international programs to aid Indochinese refugees, an interest he maintains in his current work on the Foreign Relations Committee. As press spokesman Sieverts is responsible for the supervision of media activities and acts as the primary press contact for the committee. As a result of his foreign policy background, Sieverts is involved with various policy initiatives that are addressed by the committee. He expects that Senate ratification of the INF Treaty will be the committee's's greatest focus this year.

Personal: Born 6/19/33 in Frankfurt, Germany. B.A., Swarthmore Coll., 1955. M. Phil., Balliol and Nuffield Coll., Oxford Univ., England, Rhodes Scholar, 1958. 1959-1960, London and Washington Correspondent, Time. 1960, Staff Assistant, John F. Kennedy Presidential Campaign. 1962-1964, Special Assistant for Public Affairs; 1965, Staff Director, Senior Interdept. Group; 1965-1980, Liaison to American and International Red Cross; 1965-1975, Special Assistant for POW/MIA in Southeast Asia; 1975-1978, Deputy Assistant Secretary for POW/MIA; 1978-1979, Deputy Asst. Secretary for Human Rights and Refugee Affairs; 1980-1981, U.S. Mission, Geneva, Switzerland; 1982-1986, Special Asst. for Public Affairs, Bureau of Refugee Programs; 1985-1986, Staff Director, Indochinese Refugee Panel, Dept. of State. 1986-present, Press Spokesman, Senate Committee on Foreign Relations.

Paul Noble Stockton
Legislative Assistant
Senator Daniel Patrick Moynihan
  (D-NY)
464 Russell Senate Office Bldg.
224-4451

*Personal: born 8/10/54 in Los
Angeles, California. B.A. Dartmouth
Coll., 1976 (summa cum laude). 1976-
1978, 1980, Delex Systems, Inc.,
Arlington, VA, military strategy
consultant. 1981-1982, Harvard
University, Teaching Fellow in modern
political philosophy and international
relations. 1982-1983, International
Institute for Strategic Studies, London
research associate on US-USSR
strategic stability, NATO, and military
activities in space. 1986, Ph.D. in
Government, Harvard University,
dissertation on U.S. development of
strategic weapons. 1986-present,
Legislative Assistant to Senator Daniel
Moynihan (D-NY).*

Expertise: Foreign policy, national security, intelligence, arms control

In a move to which few other congressional staffers can lay claim, Paul Stockton came straight to Capitol Hill after receiving his Ph.D. in Government from Harvard in 1986.

While he is a specialist on military strategic issues, Stockton manages a variety of duties as Moynihan's top foreign policy aide. He writes Moynihan's foreign policy speeches, drafts and promotes legislation, handles press requests, oversees junior staffers, and helps prepare the Senator for committee hearings.

As a consultant to the Pentagon, Stockton had experience analyzing complex naval and air defense systems and their political uses. In addition, he has written a number of articles and studies on strategic concepts that have appeared in respected publications. As a student and teacher at Dartmouth and Harvard, Stockton received numerous prestigious awards.

In addition to his academic background on arms control and other international security issues, Stockton is very familiar with United Nations issues and aid to Ireland, two important concerns for Senator Moynihan. Stockton was a driving force for Moynihan behind a recent State Department authorization bill that prevents the denial of a visa to an immigrant on the basis of ideology. He has also spent a good deal of time lobbying for international labor organization convention treaties up for Senate ratification. Some people on Capitol Hill are also familiar with Stockton's work on a successful joint congressional resolution that countered a UN resolution declaring Zionism a form of racism.

Stockton enjoys working for Moynihan, a man he greatly respects and often praises. He is comfortable with Moynihan's politics and at ease working for another former Harvard professor.

Stockton's main complaint is the cumbersome nature of the Senate's operating system. But he enjoys the new challenges posed by working on the Hill, one of which is finding the time for his hobby, playing the cello. And he can still wax philosophical about his demanding job. It is, he says, "not a job to have twice, but to dream about having once."

Gerald Felix Warburg II
Legislative Assistant
Senator Alan Cranston (D-CA)
112 Hart Senate Office Bldg.
224-3553

Expertise: Foreign policy, defense and international trade

Gerry Warburg describes himself as an "intelligence operative" for Senator Alan Cranston (D-CA), the number two man in the Democratic leadership, member of the Senate Foreign Relations Committee and Chairman of the Subcommittee on East Asian and Pacific Affairs. "I mean intelligence operative in the sense of vote counting, analyzing the issues, assessing our strength and scouting the opposition. I always watch for areas of compromise," qualified Warburg, who adds that he spends a lot of time on the Senate floor keeping abreast of the views of opponents.

As Senator Cranston's right hand in researching and implementing foreign policy, defense and trade legislation, Warburg in 1987 worked on legislation ranging from the Intermediate Range Nuclear Forces (INF) treaty to trade issues affecting Silicon Valley to the formulation of a 'Marshall Plan' for the Philippines. Warburg's job is particularly stimulating because of Cranston's active involvement in foreign affairs. Cranston has taken the lead and has often been controversial in his policy stance on issues such as Contra aid, arms to Saudi Arabia and the sale of nuclear technology to China.

Warburg is half political operative, half fervent intellectual. His background in Soviet studies, arms control and U.S.-China relations and his experience as an advisor to the U.S. Nuclear Regulatory Commission on nuclear export licensing issues qualify him to deal with the minutia of arms control and to coordinate public outreach programs on nuclear power issues.

Personal: born 7/31/54 in San Francisco, California. B.A. Hampshire Coll., 1975. M.A. Stanford Univ., 1979. 1975, Legislative Intern to Sen. John Tunney (D-CA). 1975-1976, research assistant to syndicated columnist Tom Braden. 1976-1978, Legislative Assistant, Rep. Jonathan Bingham (D-NY). 1978-1979, consultant to U.S. Nuclear Regulatory Commission in the Office of Commissioner Peter Bradford. 1982, 1978, visiting lecturer in foreign policy, nuclear power, and legislative affairs. 1979-present, Legislative Assistant, Sen. Alan Cranston (D-CA).

Warburg's legislative career began in 1976 as Legislative Assistant to Rep. Jonathan Bingham (D-NY). He was the lead House staffer for the opposition to the Nuclear Siting and Licensing Act (1978), the Nuclear Fuel Assurance Act (1977) and the Price-Anderson Act Renewal (1976). He drafted the 1976 Bingham Amendment abolishing the Joint Committee on Atomic Energy. Reforming congressional policymaking on nuclear power issues is of special interest to Warburg, who was the principal drafter of the House-passed version of the Nuclear Nonproliferation Act of 1978, while detailed to the House Foreign Affairs Committee.

As Legislative Assistant to Cranston, Warburg played a lead staff role in a number of major congressional proceedings, including drafting and advancing such legislation as Cranston's resolution of disapproval for the U.S.-Japan Nuclear Cooperation Agreement (1987); Panama sanctions measure (1987); Democracy in South Korea resolution (1987); Anti-Apartheid Act (1984-1986); Saudi arms resolution of disapproval (1985-1986); resolution of approval for U.S.-P.R.C. Nuclear Cooperation Agreement (1985); Philippine aid legislation (1984-1986); Arms Export Control Act Amendments

(1985); Jordan arms resolution of disapproval (1984-1985); "Contra" aid resolution of disapproval (1984-1987); Export Administration Act Amendments (1984); CTB/SDI/SALT compliance/nuclear freeze legislation (1981-1987); El Salvador Human Rights Certification Act (1982); Senate investigations of nuclear proliferation in Iraq, Libya and Pakistan (1980-1987); and SALT II Treaty ratification (1979).

Warburg is the only staffer for Cranston's leadership Arms Control Study Group, which will play a central role in the INF ratification fight. Warburg has accompanied Cranston on delegations throughout Europe, East Asia and Central America. Warburg also often travels west with Senator Cranston and works on political campaigning and issues affecting his native California.

SENATE
COMMITTEE ON GOVERNMENTAL AFFAIRS

Richard E. Ashooh
Professional Staff Member
Subcommittee on Federal
  Spending, Budget and
  Accounting
448 Hart Senate Office Bldg.
224-8779

Expertise: Federal spending, federal employment

As Senator Rudman's personal staff member to the Subcommittee on Federal Spending, Budget and Accounting, Ashooh's responsibilities include government oversight, federal spending, and federal employment.

Since he came to the Committee in April, 1987, he has been especially active in oversight legislation before the Senate Governmental Affairs Committee. He considers himself a fiscal conservative, and has paid special attention to the issues of congressional and Federal pay raises.

Raised in a New Hampshire family with long traditions of Washington government service, Ashooh began his career during college, as a staffer for Senator Gordon Humphrey. Upon graduation with a degree in political science and communications, he started work as a caseworker in the New Hampshire office of Senator Warren Rudman. He simultaneously worked on Senator Rudman's campaign.

Until he moved to Washington in 1987, Ashooh coached at the Amoskeag Rowing Club in Manchester, NH. Since his arrival in Washington, he has studied karate at the Jhoon Rhee Institute.

Personal: Born 6/2/64 in Manchester, New Hampshire. B.A. Univ. of New Hampshire, 1986. 1985, staff, Sen.Gordon Humphrey (R-NH). 1986, caseworker, Senator Warren Rudman (R-NH). 1987, Professional Staff Member, Senate Governmental Affairs Committee.

Jo Anne B. Barnhart
Minority Staff Director
346 Dirksen Senate Office Bldg.
224-2627

Expertise: Government financial management, welfare reform

When Senator William V. Roth, Jr. (R-DE) named Barnhart majority staff director of the Senate Governmental Affairs Committee, she was one of only two women serving as staff director of a major Senate committee.

She brought with her an established reputation as a major player in the Reagan Administration's welfare reforms. She has worked to improve the professional expertise, financial accountability and workability of welfare services since the early 1970's when she was a founder and vice president of the Title VII Nutrition Project Directors Association.

During her tenure at Family Assistance at HHS, the AFDC program went from no states with work programs for welfare recipients to 38 states with work programs. As Associate Commissioner, she administered a staff of 750 for the largest cash assistance program in the country with a budget of $16 billion.

Since joining the Committee, she oversees a staff of eleven, coordinating with minority staff directors of five subcommittees. Barnhart's future concern will include a renewed interest in welfare and work programs, and improving the management of government. She believes strongly that her experience in the Executive Branch has provided an important perspective in working on both.

In 1976, she was in charge of literature distribution for Senator Roth's campaign. A past vice president of the Republican Women on Capitol Hill, she enjoys needlework, refinishing furniture, and gardening.

Barnhart says she's been "lucky to get involved in public service where my jobs meshed with my personal convictions."

Personal: born 8/26/50 in Memphis, Tennessee. B.A. Univ. of Delaware, 1974. 1970, advertising associate. 1973, legislative liaison for Mental Health Association of Delaware. 1975 Director of the SERVE nutrition program (Title II-C). 1977, legislative assistant to Senator William Roth, Jr. (R-DE) on health and welfare issues. 1981, Deputy Associate Commissioner for Family Assistance, HHS. 1986, consultant to White House Office of Policy Development for President's Welfare Reform Study. 1986, Majority Staff Director, Senate Committee on Governmental Affairs. 1987-present, Minority Staff Director, Senate Committee on Governmental Affairs.

Jeffrey Gilbert Berman
Counsel
340 Dirksen Senate Office Bldg
224-4751

Personal: born 5/29/57 in New York, New York. B.A. Brown Univ., 1979, magna cum laude. J.D. Harvard Law School, 1982. 1982-1984, associate, Reed, Smith, Shaw and McClay. 1984-1986, associate, Shaw, Pittman, Potts and Trowbridge. 1986, deputy campaign manager, John Glenn presidential committee. 1987 to present, Counsel, Senate Committee on Governmental Affairs. Publications: "Public Opinion and Our China Policy," Asian Affairs, Co-author, Jan/Feb, 1978.

Expertise: Nominations, rules of procedure, hearing agendas

Jeff Berman's quiet, almost shy demeanor belies his distinguished resume and his responsibilities at the Governmental Affairs Committee. Not readily forthcoming with information about himself, Berman has the political and legal experience of someone years older. A long-standing and very good relationship with Chairman John Glenn (D-OH) furthers his important role as Counsel to the Governmental Affairs Committee.

Berman's main duties include nominations which come before the Committee, rules of procedure and establishing the agenda for hearings.

He has overseen the investigation of those nominated for the positions of Director and Deputy Director of the Office of Management and Budget, the Postal Service Board of Governors, the Postal Rate Commission, the Federal Labor Relations Authority, and the Office of Government Ethics, among others. Following the completion of a nominee's investigation, Berman recommends to the Chairman whether or not the nominee should be confirmed.

Berman pays particular attention to how well the nominee meets the particular qualifications of the job. Nominees for the National Archivist, for instance, have to meet "very strict professional credentials." For the Office of Government Ethics, on the other hand, one looks more for candidates with "judgement and independence."

Berman wrote the panel's "Bible" — the Rules of Procedure for the Committee. His responsibilities include briefing the Committee chairman about all hearings, and making sure they run smoothly.

He is involved with some of the most complicated subjects under the jurisdiction of any committee—ethics legislation. Thoroughness and attention to detail are two Berman characteristics he relies upon every time he works on executive branch ethics laws. In 1987, he handled the Independent Counsel Reauthorization Act when it came before the Governmental Affairs Committee.

Those who work with Berman recognize his ability. Steve Ryan, also a Counsel to the Committee, says Berman "knows his craft, he's very thorough, and he is very competent." On a committee that cannot function unless the majority and minority work together, "Jeff works well with the minority."

Harry G. Broadman
Chief Economist
340 Dirksen Senate Office Bldg.
224-4751

Expertise: Economic analysis

Among the handful of economists on Capitol Hill who possess Ph.D.s is Harry Broadman. Under the chairmanship of Sen. John Glenn (D-OH), the Senate Committee on Governmental Affairs has experienced a number of important changes. One such change included adding two full-time economists.

One of Broadman's responsibilities is to assist the committee in defining its jurisdictional purview in terms of the role of government in economic matters. Such a definition, believes Broadman, will allow the committee to have a greater impact on national and international economic policy issues.

Recently Broadman has been involved in the House-Senate conference on the omnibus trade bill. He is also involved with Senate consideration of the recent U.S.-Canada Free Trade Agreement.

Regulatory policy is another area of concern to Broadman. The committee is evaluating the effectiveness of deregulation in a number of industries, from aviation to energy and utilities. Appraising new methods of achieving regulatory reform, such as "regulatory negotiation" is also on the committee's agenda.

Personal: born 12/23/54 in New York, New York. A.B. Brown Univ., Phi Beta Kappa, magna cum laude, 1977. A.M. Univ. of Michigan, 1978. Ph.D. Univ of Michigan, 1981. 1976, economist, U.S. Energy Research and Development Administration. 1979, economist, The Rand Corporation. 1980-1981, research fellow, Brookings Institution. 1984-1985, faculty member, Johns Hopkins Univ. 1981-1987, assistant director and fellow, Resources for the Future, Washington, D.C. 1985-1987, faculty member, Harvard Univ. 1987-present, chief economist, Senate Committee on Governmental Affairs

Broadman sees as a challenge the conflict between the need for new national technology investment initiatives in the face of fiscal constraints. Broadman will continue to devote considerable time to evaluation and analysis of the ways in which the government can best foster private sector investment in long term, high-risk technology development and application.

Broadman has also focused on assessing U.S. energy policy. Of particular importance in this area is determining the value of alternative energy sources, such as methanol, and appraising federal policy in enhancing U.S. energy security vis-a-vis the nation's dependence on imported oil.

Brian Andrew Dettelbach
Assistant Counsel
340 Dirksen Senate Office Bldg.
224-4751

Personal: born 9/11/56 in Detroit, Michigan. B.S. in Foreign Service, Georgetown Univ., 1978 (cum laude). J.D. George Mason Univ. School of Law, 1986. 1976-1979, Research Assistant, Sen. John Glenn (D-OH). 1980-1986, Professional Staff Member, Senate Subcommittee on Energy, Nuclear Proliferation, and Government Processes. 1987-present, Assistant Counsel, Senate Committee on Governmental Affairs.

Expertise: Energy, environment, federal management & nominations

Brian Dettelbach's career has been in an ascending orbit around Senator John Glenn (D-OH) since 1976, when he worked his way through undergraduate Foreign Service studies as Glenn's research assistant in international affairs.

Trained as a historian, Dettelbach is sometimes frustrated that results on the Hill aren't always readily apparent. Though many of the legal issues he deals with as Assistant Counsel are procedural, he does get involved in strategy and appreciates that much is accomplished informally, particularly if a good foundation has already been laid with other staffers.

Dettelbach has been involved in a growing examination of the storage of hazardous materials at government defense facilities, and in uncovering related threats to the health and safety of workers as well as nearby residents. This is an unfolding issue of increasing importance across the country.

In addition to the issue of handling and storage of radioactive materials at military bases, he will probably maintain some involvement in his previous areas, particularly utilities and high-tech industries affecting energy. Also, Dettelbach has recently assumed the responsibilities for handling all nominations referred to the Committee and looks forward to helping ensure that nominees for these public positions of trust are of high caliber.

Glenn has given the Committee a great deal of attention and Dettelbach expects the trend of increasing activism to continue into the future, reflecting the Senator's passions for non-proliferation, national security, health and safety, support for science and technology, economic competitiveness, and energy and environment considerations.

Paul Drayton, Jr.
Staff Counsel
346 Dirksen Senate Office Bldg
224-2627

Personal: born 10/10/59 in Philadelphia, Pennsylvania. B.A. Univ. of Delaware, 1981 (Pi Sigma Alpha Political Science Honor Society, Martin L. King Academic Excellence Award). J.D. Villanova Univ. School of Law, 1986. 1986-1987, Assistant District Attorney, Philadelphia District Attorney's Office. 1987-present, Counsel to Senate Committee on Governmental Affairs. Member of Pennsylvania Bar Association.

Expertise: Defense procurement and governmental management

In 1987, Paul Drayton moved from serving as an assistant district attorney in Philadelphia to the post of Counsel to the Governmental Affairs Committee, specializing in defense procurement and government management.

In May, 1987 he was working as an assistant district attorney in Philadelphia. In April, he was named Counsel to the Governmental Affairs Committee, specializing in defense procurement and government management.

Drayton has impressed colleagues and superiors with his abilities to quickly adapt to the complex world of defense procurement.

Steve Ryan, counsel to committee chairman John Glenn (D-OH), commends how Drayton was able to make the transition from Philadelphia to Washington. "He does a very good job on the committee and works well with the majority staff."

But Drayton soon found that a big difference between prosecuting and legislating is feedback. In the district attorney's office Drayton saw progress every day on the various cases he worked on. Not so on Capitol Hill where, "somewhere down the line, your work might result in a hearing or investigation."

Although he lacked previous experience in defense matters, Drayton's prosecutorial background has equipped him with something just as good: persistence in getting answers to tough questions.

That persistence has more than paid off for him in increased insights into the defense procurement issues facing Congress, and in his ability to deal effectively with key Pentagon players.

Drayton has spent his first year on Capitol Hill looking into the Aquila, the Army's remotely piloted vehicle. Critics contend that construction of the weapon has exceeded its budget, and that it does not work as advertised. In 1988 the committee is expected to examine alternatives to the Aquila.

Drayton has the same concern about the Aquila as he does with any other new weapons system: "We have to make sure they work before they go into full-scale production and we wind up spending millions—or billions—of dollars on them."

Linda J. Gustitus
Staff Director and Chief Counsel
Subcommittee on Oversight of
   Government Management
442 Hart Senate Office Bldg.
224-3682

*Personal: born 12/29/47 in Rockford,
Illinois. B.A. Oberlin Coll.,1969. J.D.
Wayne State Univ., 1975. 1975-1976,
attorney, Illinois Fair Employment
Practices Agency. 1976-1977, Cook
County State's Attorney's Office,
investigating narcotics corruption.
1977-1979, trial attorney, Civil Fraud
Division, Department of Justice. 1979-
1980, Legislative Assistant, Sen. Carl
Levin (D-MI). 1979 to present,
Democratic Staff Director, Oversight of
Government Management
Subcommittee, Committee on
Governmental Affairs.*

Expertise: Governmental affairs

442 Hart is practically the only office on Capitol Hill without chairs or reading material for visitors. This is a Subcommittee full of "very busy people," its Staff Director, Linda Gustitus, explains. She says of the Subcommittee's Chairman, "Senator Levin loves oversight."

Gustitus cites the Wedtech scandal to explain the Subcommittee's mandate: a program to open opportunity to the poorest in the South Bronx and to provide defense work was allegedly sold out by a few. Levin serves both on the Small Business and Armed Services Committees which share concern about the Wedtech abuses. Gustitus noted Wedtech's actions directly harmed Levin's state, Michigan, and appeared to violate the 8(a) minority set-aside program in the area of defense procurement.

A second example of the Subcommittee's action reveals the degree of its assertiveness. When the Finance Committee postponed investigating abuses of the Social Security disability program, this Subcommittee went into action. Moving quickly to adjust to the new terrain of the Social Security Administration and the Office of Management and Budget, Gustitus worked to "catch the agency at its own game." The investigation lasted from late 1981 to 1984.

Other major investigations have included a revision of the ethics legislation on Defense subcontracting kickbacks (Nov. 1985-Oct. 1986), and probes of illegal and unethical collection methods in the Internal Revenue Service in 1980.

Levin's Subcommittee also has jurisdiction over the independent counsel legislation. Efforts to strengthen the law proved necessary in the aftermath of challenges by the Attorney General, and later lawsuits by Oliver North and Michael Deaver. Gustitus emphasizes the constitutional challenge must be resolved in court, but she is hopeful her work on the law, which passed in August, 1987 will pay off.

Gustitus believes the regulator nowadays must protect the efficiency of government, because courts and the public tend to react to 'bureaucracy' by submerging well-meaning career officials in regulation. Remedial action often seems inefficient and long in coming, but to Gustitus, much of the oversight responsibilities of the Hill do not receive the detailed, patient attention they require. In her experience, political appointees have greater incentives to act unethically, and fewer bonds to the programs they are mandated to lead, than the civil servants under them.

As a working mother on Capitol Hill, Gustitus is the co-founder of the Senate Employee Child Care Center, and was its first President from 1983 to 1985.

Anthony A. R. Harkins
Legislative Aide
Senator Jeff Bingaman (D-NM)
502 Hart Senate Office Bldg.
224-5521

Personal: born 2/8/64, in Bandung, Indonesia. B.S.(cum laude), at Williams Coll. Study in Paris, 1985. 1986-present, Legislative Aide, Sen. Jeff Bingaman.

Expertise: Governmental affairs, banking, communications, tax, finance, federal employees

As a young staffer on the rise, Tony Harkins handles a wide range of issues, from finance and banking through governmental affairs.

As assistant to Senator Jeff Bingaman in the area of Governmental Affairs and Finance, Harkins has handled the issues of debt and trade, stressing the importance of the U.S. role in encouraging stimulation of the world economy. Harkins also feels strongly about the U.S. role in maintaining an open economic system, in which developing and developed nations progress side by side.

Assisting on budget issues, Harkins has helped Senator Bingaman in his efforts to toe a strong line on the federal deficit. In these capacities, he has also supported Bingaman's efforts to reduce the explosive growth of both campaign spending and the inordinate influence of PACs on the political process. Bingaman has backed the Senatorial Election Campaign Act and other legislation to curtail significantly the amounts spent on congressional campaigns and to disallow destructive financing processes such as "bundling" of funds.

Senator Bingaman has also urged strong efforts to reduce the trade deficit and the foreign-financed national debt. Harkins points out that New Mexico, with its great economic potential can play a leadership role in this effort.

On the revenue side and overlapping into the area of Governmental Affairs Committee, Harkins is involved in the issue of Internal Revenue Service abuses of taxpayer rights. He emphasizes that bureaucratic abuse of the legally defenseless is a great concern and makes tax collection more difficult as well.

Harkins has also worked on legislation to deal with the "Census undercount" issue.

Robert F. Harris
Staff Director
Subcommittee on Federal
  Spending, Budget, and
  Accounting
326 Dirksen Senate Office Bldg
224-9000

Expertise: Governmental affairs, social policy, civil rights, Florida

Making sure the Executive Branch continues to be accountable to the Legislative Branch is a difficult chore made easier by people like Bob Harris.

Harris directs the Committee's investigations into procurement, contracting and grants. Its tough assignment requires that skills of an investigative reporter and the determination of a concerned and persistent neighborhood activist. Harris is both, which makes his job easier—and also makes him a key senior adviser to Committee Chairman Lawton Chiles (D-FL).

Harris participated in the 1975 review of military meat standards and the 1977 investigation of the General Services Administration. He also held a crucial position in the probes of the Small Business Administration's Section 8a minority set-asides program, which generated many spin-off investigations, including a feature story on CBS's *60 Minutes*.

Harris is a man who does not hesitate to get involved. Beyond his duties as Staff Director, he is a staff assistant to Sen. Chiles on a number of issues, including civil rights. His previous work as a teacher and grass-roots community service organizer has propelled him into housing, education, labor, and other social policy issues.

During his free time, Harris likes to play tennis and run.

Personal: born 5/15/41 in Knights, Florida. B.S. Florida A&M Univ., 1964. M.S. Univ. of South Florida, 1972. Who's Who is American Colleges and Universities, 1963. 1964-1967, 193rd Infantry Brigade, U.S. Army. 1965, World's best 200-meter dash. 1967-1973, teacher and coach, Polk County Schools. 1969, co-founder, N.W. Lakeland Community Service Center. 1971, Lakeland Zoning Board; Wrote weekly column for The Ledger Newspaper, Lakeland, FL. 1972,78,84, supported Lawton Chiles for Senate. 1973, Professional Staff Member, Governmental Affairs Committee. 1979 to present, Staff Director, Subcommittee on Federal Spending, Budget and Accounting, Committee on Governmental Affairs. 1980, President, Black Senate Legislative Caucus.

W. Stephen Hart
Professional Staff Member
176 Russell Senate Office Bldg.
224-5344

Personal: born 1/17/55 in Washington, D.C. B.S., Arizona State Univ., 1977. M.A., Ball State Univ., 1981. 1977-1980, news anchor/reporter, WTSN (Dover, New Hampshire) and WCSM (Celina, OH). 1981, freelance journalist, Gannett, UPI and Muncie Star. 1982, campaign press secretary, Kerry for Congress. 1983-1986, Legislative Assistant, Senator George J. Mitchell (D-ME). 1987-present, Professional Staff Member, Senate Committee on Governmental Affairs.

Expertise: Veterans affairs, judicial compensation (COLAs), non-nuclear energy issues, natural resources, government affairs

While stringing for UPI, Hart was offered a legislative staff position by Sen. George J. Mitchell (D-ME). Today he is a staffer for the Senate Committee on Governmental Affairs. Hart feels his writing skills have facilitated the transition from journalist to congressional aide.

As the only Senator with assignments on both the Committee on Governmental Affairs and the Committee on Veterans' Affairs, Mitchell has been active in legislation to elevate the Veterans Administration to cabinet-level status. While the VA would undergo no structural change under this bill, the Senator and his aide see special significance in such legislation.

Beyond giving the VA greater access to the President and top White House officials, Hart points to the symbolic significance such a measure would grant to America's veterans. The change would also give a greater voice to veterans on issues ranging from budgetary concerns to medical care to insurance coverage.

Rural health care is another area with which Hart is involved. While the VA is the largest health care system in the free world with 172 medical centers and some 200 outpatient clinics, Mitchell is concerned that most of the facilities do not reach into rural America. In fact, Maine, which is predominantly a rural state, has only one VA hospital. Hart is hopeful that health care will eventually be improved and extended to rural areas.

With Hart's assistance, Mitchell is working with the Defense Department to develop a mutual arrangement whereby the VA could utilize various military installations in some non-urban areas. Additionally, they are looking at the feasibility of a pilot project that would provide some mode of transportation to veterans who are removed from the VA's urban locations. In the area of natural resources, Hart has been assisting Mitchell with his initiative involving the preservation of America's lighthouses. Last year, Congress established the Bicentennial Lighthouse Fund with the aim of distributing $1 million throughout the National Parks Service for preservation and construction renovations of lighthouses currently listed on the National Register of Historic Buildings.

In his time away from Congress, Hart enjoys running, watching college basketball and learning sign language. His wife, Beth Marchak, is the Editor of the "Federal Report" section of *The Washington Times*.

Jeffrey D. Landry
Minority Staff Director and Counsel
Subcommittee on Federal Services
601 Hart Senate Office Bldg.
224-4551

Personal: born 9/26/52 in Spokane, Washington. B.A. Univ. of Utah, 1974. J.D. Univ. of Puget Sound, 1983. 1975-1976, construction foreman, Alaska. 1976-1977, marine carpenter. 1977-1980, lobbyist, Alaska State Legislature. 1983-1985, Assistant Counsel, Subcommittee on Civil Service. 1986, Counsel, Subcommittee on Civil Service. 1987-present, Minority Staff Director and Counsel, Subcommittee on Federal Services.

Expertise: Federal personnel benefits, Alaska state government

In 1983, Jeff Landry was hired as Assistant Counsel to the Civil Service Subcommittee. At that time, he was responsible for drafting compensation legislation, including amendments to the federal health program. He also assisted in designing a new federal pension system for the federal civilian workforce. The pension bill amended title 5 of the U.S. code and established a new retirement and disability plan for Federal employees, Postal Service employees and Members of Congress. This pension system, the Federal Employee Retirement System (FERS), is probably "the single most significant legislation that this subcommittee has worked on," Landry says. Passed in June 1986, the retirement system affects all federal employees hired after 1983.

For the last five years, Landry has worked for Sen. Ted Stevens (R-Alaska). In 1987, he was promoted to Minority Staff Director of the Federal Services Subcommittee, which falls under the Committee on Governmental Affairs and is responsible for the Civil Service, the Post Office, the General Services Administration, and the Census Bureau. Last year, he worked on several pieces of legislation relating to health and life insurance payee issues.

Landry has held a variety of interesting jobs. He has restored traditional sailboats, driven a truck on the Trans-Alaska Oil Pipeline, worked on a dairy farm in Wisconsin, worked as a commercial fisherman in Alaska and finally, lobbied on Capitol Hill. As a lobbyist, he gained experience in drafting legislation and testified on a broad range of medical issues. This experience gives him special insight into legislative issues.

Landry and his wife Janet have been married for seven years. They are quite active skiers, enjoying both telemark and downhill skiing. Landry enjoys spending time outdoors, and doesn't find life in the city very appealing. His lifestyle in rural Maryland reflects his desire for a simple life. Every morning, he leaves his 200-year old cabin in Maryland, and rides his bicycle to a Metro stop where he catches a subway train to the Capitol. "Every morning I embark upon a 200-year time travel," Landry says. He finds life in the cabin the closest thing to living in Alaska, the place he'd like to move back to someday.

Lorraine Pratte Lewis
Counsel
340 Dirksen Senate Office Bldg.
224-4751

Expertise: Nominations, lobbying registration, ethics

For Lorraine Lewis, her motivation in undertaking the rigors of an exceedingly competitive law school was the possibility of later achieving a challenging career in the federal government. She has not been disappointed. Lewis' concern for individual rights directed the emphasis of her activities and studies at Harvard. She was first a staff member and later the articles editor for *The Harvard Civil Rights-Civil Liberties Law Review*.

After graduation, Lewis secured a position as Field Attorney with the National Labor Relations Board. This position, while it allowed her to gain litigation experience, also gave her practical knowledge of various labor issues. That experience eventually brought her highly recommended to the Washington, D.C. law firm of Feder and Edes, where she sharpened her expertise in labor and employee benefits matters.

Like many Capitol Hill staffers, Lewis began her congressional career as a volunteer research assistant. She then secured a spot on the Senate Committee on Governmental Affairs as an Assistant Counsel in 1986. She has since been promoted to Counsel. As Assistant Counsel to the committee, Lewis assisted Sen. Glenn for nearly a year in achieving passage of the Inspector General Act Amendments of 1988. She is also involved in reviewing the Federal Advisory Committee Act, which is the law governing various presidential commissions and other federal advisory committees.

Personal: born 2/25/56 in Springfield, Massachusetts. B.A. Yale Univ., (magna cum laude), 1978. J.D. Harvard Univ., 1981. 1982-1984, Field Attorney, National Labor Relations Board, Chicago, IL. 1984-1985, Associate, Feder & Edes, Washington, D.C. 1986, volunteer attorney, Washington Lawyers' Committee for Civil Rights Under Law, Washington, D.C. 1986, Research Assistant, Sen. John Glenn. 1987, Assistant Counsel; 1987 to present, Counsel, Senate Committee on Governmental Affairs.

Aside from playing a role in organizing committee hearings and the drafting of committee reports, Lewis assists in monitoring all of the nominations the committee receives. Nominations include D.C. Court of Appeals personnel, Superior Court judges, the Board of Governors to the U.S. Postal Service, and the OPM and OMB directors. While many may think such nominations are routine, just the opposite is true. Lewis works with her colleagues on the majority and minority staffs in reviewing scores of documents as well as the background, character and qualifications of a particular nominee. Lewis also acts as the liaison to Sen. Levin's Subcommittee on Oversight of Government Management. Of particular interest to the Subcommittee is the effectiveness of the ten-year old Ethics in Government Act.

Paul Light
Special Consultant on Public
   Management
340 Dirksen Senate Office Bldg.
224-4751

*Personal: born 12/7/52 in Sioux Falls,
South Dakota. B.A. Macalester Coll.,
summa cum laude, 1975. M.A. Univ.
of Michigan, Political Science, 1976.
Ph. D., Univ. of Michigan, Political
Science. Schattschneider Award for
Outstanding Dissertation in American
Politics, 1980. 1980-1983, assistant
professor of government, Univ. of
Virginia. 1983, 1984, 1986, 1988,
visiting associate professor of political
science, George Washington Univ.
1982-1983, congressional fellow, Rep.
Barber B. Conable, Jr. (R-NY) and
John Glenn Presidential Campaign.
1983-1984, guest scholar, The
Brookings Institution. 1984-1987,
director of studies, National Academy
of Public Administration. 1987-
present, special consultant on public
management, Senate Governmental
Affairs Committee.*

Expertise: Executive organizations and management

After participating in the American Political Science Association Fellowship program, Paul Light realized that studying and teaching political science were not enough. Instead, this motivated and energetic young professor found himself increasingly drawn into the public policy process, and eventually returned to work on Capitol Hill.

As a congressional fellow, Light worked on both legislation and political campaigns, spending time in the office of Representative Barber Conable (R-NY) and on Senator John Glenn's (D-OH) presidential campaign. While continuing to teach and research various facets of domestic politics and policy-making, Light was named Director of Studies at the National Academy of Public Administration. There he researched the presidential appointments process, regulatory review at the Office of Management and Budget, and Congressional oversight, and was responsible for program direction, proposal development, fundraising and publications.

Light says his position on the Senate Governmental Affairs Committee is a "natural fit," considering his background and interests. As Special Consultant on Public Management, he is involved in many of the same areas he previously researched including Department reorganization, OMB management, presidential appointments process, and some budget process issues. Light has worked to establish a cabinet-level department for veterans, and also has been involved with the Presidential Transition Effectiveness Bill and a comprehensive review of regulatory reform.

When one looks back on Paul Light's record in the field of academia, it seems perhaps a bit puzzling as to why he left such a promising and successful career. His list of publications is impressive, including *Artful Work: The Politics of Social Security Reform; Vice Presidential Power: Advice and Influence in the White House; The President's Agenda: Domestic Policy Choice from Kennedy to Carter*, as well as numerous research articles and chapters in various books. Additionally, he recently edited *The Baby Boomers: A Political and Social Reappraisal*. However, Light had a strong desire to more directly "influence outcomes"—a desire that he wasn't satisfying as a scholar.

Although Light hasn't escaped the long hours of many key staffers on the Hill, he does find time to play basketball with friends.

Andrew McElwaine

Minority Staff Director
Subcommittee on Government
  Efficiency, Federalism and the
  District of Columbia
613 Hart Senate Office Bldg.
224-4508

Personal: born 11/9/60 in New York, New York. B.A. Duke Univ., 1982. 1982-1983, Intern, Rep. Charles Wilson (D-TX). 1983-1984, Research Assistant, DOE contractor. 1984, Staff Assistant, Rep. Toby Roth (R-WI). 1985-1986, Legislative Assistant to Sen. John Heinz (R-PA). 1986-present, Minority Staff Director, Subcommittee on Government Efficiency, Federalism and the District of Columbia; Staff Director, Senate Republican Task Force on Education and Job Training; Minority Staff Member, Senate Coal Caucus.

Expertise: Budget, education, training policy

McElwaine focused on two issues last year: the budget summit, and education and job training. Two questions—what is enough deficit reduction and what is good policy—were foremost in his mind as he arranged hearings, drafted bills and advised Sen. Heinz on the status of legislation. "I have to know that bill line-item by line-item."

In his role with the Task Force on Education and Job Training, McElwaine writes reports on program successes and failures and works to form partnerships between the private sector and non-profit organizations to secure employment for those who have been through federal re-training programs. Accomplishing this goal is a personal concern for him. "Western Pennsylvania (the site of Heinz's old Congressional district before he was elected to the Senate) never really came out of the early 80s recession," he says. "Economic development and retraining and re-employment are critical issues. Since day one with Sen. Heinz, I've worked with the workers directly and their umbrella groups in the western end of the state to try and develop policies which will get them off unemployment."

McElwaine also works on behalf of veterans' groups, and won an award from American Ex-Prisoners of War for his efforts to pass a bill to improve their benefits. "It's very hard to say no, and it's hard for the senator to say no to people who were incarcerated by our enemies when they are not getting adequate health care," he says.

An American history buff and an active member of several historic preservation groups, McElwaine enjoys living in what he calls "the core of American history." He also serves as a precinct captain for his district in Arlington, Va. "I'm one of the only Republicans in a very Democratic precinct, so I have my hands full," he says wryly.

McElwaine says he always thought he would end up working on the Hill and shows great enthusiasm for his job. Sen. Heinz has been "a phenomenal boss." McElwaine considers himself very lucky to have landed where he has while he is still "not particularly old," and in spite of not yet having finished his "darned" Master's degree in American Political History.

Jane Jeter McFarland
Professional Staff Member
340 Dirksen Senate Office Bldg.
202-224-4751

Expertise: Budget, health care, employee benefits

Filling 27 notebooks while assisting Sen. Robert Byrd (D-WV) during the emotional debate over the Panama Canal treaties in 1978, marked Jane McFarland's initiation into the sometimes laborious world of congressional politics.

These days, much of her attention is directed to budget issues and the Gramm-Rudman-Hollings process, which she fears may preclude any examination of budget priorities and become merely a numbers game.

McFarland also is examining the concept of pay equity in the federal government, which was first advanced by Sen. Daniel Evans (R-WA). The General Accounting Office has conducted a study that indicates some disparity exists based on gender. McFarland notes that "it's never popular to raise wages," and adds that the whole matter is being watched to see if any precedents are set.

McFarland is particularly proud of her work on a bill to provide aid to the homeless, which passed Congress and was signed into law last year. She also was instrumental in achieving a compromise in 1987 that prevented large-scale cuts in benefits for postal workers. And she deals with other federal employee issues such as health care reform, the Catastrophic Health Care Bill and rising health insurance premiums.

Personal: born 1/1/55 in Rutherfordton, North Carolina. WC Honors and WC scholarship, Wellesley College, 1973-1975. B.A., Economics, Univ. of North Carolina at Chapel Hill, 1977. 1979-1983, professional staff member, Senate Democratic Policy Committee. 1983-1986, professional staff member, Senate Special Committee on Aging. 1987-present, professional Staff member, Committee on Governmental Affairs.

McFarland has spent time on a bill to revise the Hatch Act, which limits the political activities by federal workers. McFarland says the bill contains adequate sanctions to prevent federal workers from being coerced into political activity and notes that currently "a federal worker risks trouble by appearing in a family photo with a spouse who is running for office."

McFarland, 33, came to the Hill as a staffer on the Senate Democratic Policy Committee, where she worked as a speechwriter and as a liaison to interest groups, the executive branch and the House Democratic Leadership. At the committee, McFarland helped develop Democratic policy initiatives on social security, Medicare and other welfare programs, as well as women's issues and the Equal Rights Amendment.

Away from the office, McFarland likes gardening and perfecting her southern "health food" recipes that usually start with a pound of bacon.

Michael C. Mitchell
Deputy Minority Staff Director
346 Dirksen Senate Office Bldg.
224-2627

Expertise: International trade, intergovernmental relations

When Mike Mitchell was appointed Deputy Minority Staff Director of the Senate Committee on Governmental Affairs, he assumed an interesting new set of responsibilities.

Keeping on top of policy issues while tackling the added management responsibilities might appear complicated, but Mitchell says he enjoys the opportunity to manage the minority staff of the Committee in cooperation with the Staff Director. He admits that time management and balancing his diverse duties can be challenging, but says that making those management decisions is one of his favorite parts of the new jobs which he began in November, 1987.

Mitchell is a strong believer in quality writing skills and says effective writing is an invaluable tool for communication on the Hill. "It's time-consuming, but I think everyone benefits from the effort."

He takes his management duties seriously and says his most important responsibilities are making certain Senator William Roth (R-DE), the Committee's Banking Republican Member, has timely, accurate information, keeping up with the legislative agenda; and helping to determine staff responsibilities.

Personal: born: 6/13/51 in Iowa City, Iowa. B.A. Trinity Coll., Hartford, CT., 1973. M.P.A. American Univ., 1977. 1977-1981, Federal Relations Associate for the U.S. Advisory Commission on Intergovernmental Relations. 1981-1985, Professional Staff Member on the Senate Committee on Governmental Affairs. 1985-1986, Director of Government Services for the Public Affairs Council. 1986-1987, Professional Staff Member, Senate Committee on Governmental Affairs, 1987-present, Deputy Minority Staff Director, Senate Committee on Governmental Affairs.

In his only pre-Hill job after graduate school, Mitchell worked for the U.S. Advisory Commission on Intergovernmental Relations. On the Commission staff, he focused on encouraging implementation of the Commission's federal-level recommendations. In this effort he "did a good deal of writing and staff contact work on the Hill and in the agencies." The experience helped him gain expertise that has served him well since he joined the Senate Committee on Governmental Affairs.

As the Republican minority's principal player dealing with trade matters before the Committee, he is currently involved with the omnibus trade legislation. The Governmental Affairs Committee has jurisdiction over procurement and agency organizational matters in the bill.

When it comes to life outside the office, his wife and two children are the focus of Mitchell's attention. He enjoys cross-country skiing and competitive sports, including racquetball and squash.

John J. Parisi
346 Dirksen Senate Office Bldg.
224-2627

Personal: born 4/11/49 in Kalamazoo, Michigan. B.A. Kalamazoo Coll., 1971. J.D. Wayne State Univ., 1986. 1969, intern for Sen. Jacob Javits (R-NY). 1971-1973, teacher of American government. 1976-1977, attorney in private law practice. 1977-1979, Legislative Assistant for Rep. Garry Brown (R-MI). 1979-1981, Legislative Director for Rep. Thomas N. Kindness (R-OH). 1981-1987, Minority Counsel to the Subcommittee on Government Information, Justice, and Agriculture, House Committee on Government Operations. 1987-present, Minority Counsel to the Senate Committee on Governmental Affairs.

Expertise: Government information/records and administrative law

Following his family's long involvement in politics, John Parisi worked on a congressional campaign while in high school, handing out materials for his hometown candidate, Garry Brown.

While in college he served on the Hill as an intern for Senator Jacob Javits (R-NY). His professional life then took a detour away from the Hill that lasted nearly eight years. During that time, he taught American government in a public high school, earned his law degree, and practiced law before seeking a position on the Hill. A position in Congressman Garry Brown's office opened up, and he was appointed a legislative assistant.

In that and subsequent positions, Parisi has developed expertise in government information and records laws, such as the Freedom of Information Act and the Federal, and Presidential, Records Acts; in administrative law; and, in governmental accountability laws such as the Inspector General Act.

During his ten years on the Hill, his work has included the National Archives independence bill and the CIA Information Act in the 98th Congress and the Presidential Libraries Act and the Freedom of Information Act Amendments in the 99th.

In his current position as Minority Counsel to the Senate Governmental Affairs Committee, he considers his most important duties to be covering his subject areas of responsibility for Senator William Roth (R-DE), the Ranking Republican Member of the Committee, and working cooperatively with his colleagues, sharing his experience with them.

In time away from the office, Parisi likes to read about European (especially German) history and current affairs. His wife shares his interest in history and they enjoy travel to places of historic significance. A former percussionist, he regularly attends National Symphony Orchestra concerts. He is also an avid Detroit Tigers baseball fan.

Parisi has become wary of losing perspective through total immersion in the Congress. To help stave off myopia, he reads his hometown newspaper and has been very active in improving contacts with West German political leaders. To maintain a good historical perspective in one's work on the Hill, he recommends the book, *Thinking in Time: The Uses of History in Decision-Making*, by Ernest May and Richard Neustadt.

Stephen M. Ryan
Counsel
340 Dirksen Senate Office Bldg.
224-4751

Expertise: Oversight and investigation

"Essentially, I see the taxpayer as my client, and my job is to see that tax dollars are spent appropriately. That is what the goal of   congressional oversight is to me."

Responsible for oversight and investigation, in addition to providing legal advice, Ryan's portfolio is eliminating fraud, waste and abuse from agencies the committee monitors. These agencies include OPM, GSA, GAO and OMB. Investigations of telecommunication procurements, the adequacy of NCR investigations, and the inventory loss of weapons are examples of the committee's oversight activities of the past year. In his first year on the job, Ryan drafted bills to allow the GAO to audit the CIA, to extend the coverage of the Inspector General Act, and to create safety oversight of DOE's nuclear weapons complex.

Ryan is also concerned with Department of Defense logistics, particularly procurement issues. "The projects that are the most interesting to me are in the area of government management where there are many billions of dollars at stake which do not receive front line attention. When we buy a weapons system, there's a great deal of attention as to whether we're going to buy thirty helicopters. There is significantly less attention paid to how much we will spend on spare parts, maintenance and operations."

Personal: born 4/19/55 in New York City. B.S., Cornell University, 1977. J.D., Notre Dame, 1980. 1979-81, Clerk to U.S. District Judge Robert A. Grant. 1981-1984, Associate, law firm of Howrey & Simon. 1984-86, Deputy Counsel, The President's Commission on Organized Crime. 1986-87, Assistant U.S. Attorney, District of Columbia. 1987-present, Counsel, Senate Committee on Government Affairs.

Working on the hill was a goal for Ryan, but he wanted to come on board to work for a committee chairman. His work on John Glenn's Presidential campaign provided his link, and he joined the staff as counsel in 1987. As a trial lawyer in the Criminal Division of the U.S. Attorney's office, and as Deputy Counsel for the President's Committee on Organized Crime, Ryan gained considerable experience in criminal investigation and prosecution. "It was a wonderful opportunity to jail or obtain the cooperation of figures in the Mafia and Chinese organized crime. It was an interesting and colorful experience and I'm proud of those achievements."

"I really enjoy being a government lawyer. I enjoy seeing my client as the United States. It's very enjoyable to wake up in the morning when you're a federal prosecutor and say, 'Ladies and Gentlemen of the jury, I represent the United States of America'."

Ryan is an avid waterfowler on the Eastern Shore and collects antiquarian books, mostly in the area of American history and politics. He marks 1987 as a momentus year professionally and personally—his favorite activity is watching his newborn baby grow. Ryan teaches at Cornell's School of Labor Relations each semester and is active with his church and the ABA.

Randy J. Rydell

Professional Staff Member
340 Dirksen Senate Office Bldg.
224-4751

Personal: born 9/29/52 in Missoula, Montana. Univ. of Virginia, B.A. (with high distinction), 1973 (Phi Beta Kappa). London School of Economics and Political Science, England, 1973-74, M.Sc. Princeton Univ., 1975-79, M.A. 1977 and PhD., 1979. Princeton Univ., lecturer, 1977-79. 1980-86, Lawrence Livermore National Laboratory, Political Analyst. 1987-present, Professional Staff Member, Senate Committee on Governmental Affairs.

Expertise: Nuclear non-proliferation

Randy Rydell's "business" on the Governmental Affairs Committee is nuclear non-proliferation. The reason Dr. Rydell devotes his full attention to this issue requires an understanding of the committee's priorities in terms of its Chairman John Glenn (D-OH), who has focused intensively on the spread of nuclear weaponry since coming to the Senate in 1974. Given Glenn's continuing emphasis on the issue, it is natural, according to Rydell, that nuclear non-proliferation would become a top priority issue with this committee. When Glenn became Chairman after the Democrats regained control of the Senate in 1986, his staff director, Leonard Weiss, abolished a subcommittee and placed nuclear matters under the full committee. To meet the resulting need for experienced staff, Glenn hired Rydell, an expert on nuclear non-proliferation at Livermore National Lab.

Referring to the never-ending bureaucratic policies among many other agencies of government that have some piece of the nuclear non-proliferation issue, Rydell calls it a "sea of enormous icebergs banging against each other," to say nothing of "difficulties between the Executive and Legislative branches."

Paul Leventhal, a Hill veteran who now heads the non-profit, independent Nuclear Control Institute, says Rydell is "highly expert in this field," particularly with regard to the "safeguards and technology" issues. Citing his experience with the Livermore National Laboratory, where Rydell served as a political analyst for six years, Leventhal agrees with Rydell that the Committee can play a "major role" on such matters as the U.S.-Japan Nuclear Agreement and other non-proliferation areas, even when it must share jurisdiction with the Senate Foreign Relations Committee and balance conflicting opinions and political objections from the Administration.

Rydell says the concern is addressing nuclear non-proliferation as a key national security issue, one that, at times, requires hard choices involving "big political and economic stakes". Glenn feels that countries that violate international nuclear export laws—like Pakistan—should not be rewarded with massive aid programs, unless that aid is tied to significant nuclear restraints.

Rydell knows firsthand that cynicism in this area is rampant. More and more nations are trying to inch their way into nuclear "clubs." Numerous public interest groups promote solutions. The central issue from a U.S. standpoint, Rydell feels, is "how to bring the issue home to Peoria" before some major international disaster puts the issue on everyone's front burner.

Rydell relaxes by coin collecting and playing the trumpet with musical groups.

Leonard Weiss
Staff Director
340 Dirksen Senate Office Bldg.
224-4751

Expertise: Science and technology policy; Nuclear non-proliferation

In 1975, Leonard Weiss was a full professor at the University of Maryland with a sabbatical coming up. His long interest in public policy led him to apply for an IECE Congressional Fellowship. He was awarded the Fellowship (one of two given nationally that year in 1975) and applied for the position in the office of Senator John Glenn (D-OH). "I liked Senator Glenn right away. He was a freshman senator, and needed work done on energy, science and technology, arms control and nuclear policy."

Weiss returned to the University of Maryland after his fellowship was over but shortly afterward, when Senator Glenn asked him to come back, Weiss agreed. Once again on leave, Weiss became staff director of the Subcommittee on Energy, Nuclear Proliferation and Federal Services. There he was the chief staff architect of the Nuclear Non-Proliferation Act. At the end of this second sabbatical, Weiss decided he was "hooked" and resigned his post at the University. (One of his proudest moments was the White House signing ceremony for the Act in 1978.)

Personal: born 3/14/34 in New York City. BEE City Coll. of New York, 1956. MSEE Columbia Univ., 1959. Ph.D. Johns Hopkins Univ., 1962. 1962-76, consultant to industry and government, tenured and visiting academic appointments to universities including Brown University, University of Maryland, University of California at Berkeley and UCLA. 1976, Institute for Electrical and Electronic Engineers, Congressional Fellow. 1977-81, Staff Director of the Senate Subcommittee on Energy, Nuclear Proliferation and Federal Services. 1981-87, Minority Staff Director of the former. 1987-present, Staff Director, Senate Committee on Governmental Affairs.

Weiss describes his current job as staff director of the Senate Committee on Governmental Affairs as "stimulating and exciting"—we set a very ambitious agenda." In the past year, the Committee held 84 days of hearings, reported 13 bills (4 of which were enacted into law, and 5 others were passed by the Senate). One of the Senate-passed measures creates five new inspectors general at OPM, FEMA, NRC, IRS and Treasury. Another bill the committee spent much time on last year would enhance health, safety, and environmental protection at DOE nuclear facilities. The Committee has been investigating procurement practices of GSA and DOD and is also involved in the legislation to create a cabinet-level department of Veterans Affairs. The committee will also devote time in the coming months to studying intergovernmental relationships on health issues such as AIDS, alcoholism, and nutrition. With a change in administrations ahead, the Committee has drafted legislation that will streamline the presidential transition procedure. Much Committee time is also spent overseeing nominations for numerous agencies of government.

Weiss enjoys reading, music, theater and travel and tries to keep up with new scientific developments. He now serves on the IEEE Board which selects Congressional Fellows. He is the recipient of numerous awards for his scholarly writing and has lectured at Japanese, Polish and Western European universities. Weiss was a Sloan Fellow.

SENATE
COMMITTEE ON THE JUDICIARY

Edward H. Baxter
Chief Counsel and Staff Director
Subcommittee on Patents,
   Copyrights, and Trademarks
327 Hart Senate Office Bldg.
224-8178

Expertise: Antitrust and copyright law, drugs, crime

A well-worn Washington career path has been to gain Hill experience and then move to a trade association. Ed Baxter altered that pattern by first being a government affairs director for an association, then bringing his energy and skills to the Senate Judiciary Committee's Subcommittee on the Constitution.

After six years in that position, Baxter became chief counsel and staff director for Sen. Dennis DeConcini's (D-AZ) Subcommittee on Patents, Copyrights, and Trademarks.

Baxter advised the senator on the Kennedy, Rehnquist, Scalia and Bork hearings and virtually all other federal judicial nominations before the committee. As chief counsel to DeConcini, Baxter is responsible for drafting statements, newspaper opinion pieces, and preparing questions for the senator.

Baxter played a role in the reform of the U.S. criminal code, as it was modified by 1984's Comprehensive Crime Control Act. Additionally, the subcommittee has focused attention on the RICO statute, particularly in light of allegations some businesses were abusing that statute.

This year the subcommittee is conducting hearings on the International Copyright treaty under the auspices of the Berne Convention. Baxter believes the sentiment is beginning to mount that America's intellectual property rights would be better served by becoming a participant country. The subcommittee is reviewing the full implications of these changes in copyright law under the Berne Convention.

Personal: born 11/19/48 in Savannah, Georgia. B.B.A. Univ. of Georgia, 1871. J.D. Univ. Of Georgia, 1974. 1974-1977, staff attorney, U.S. Department of the Interior. 1977-1981, Director of Government Affairs, American Physical Therapy Association. 1981-1987, Minority Counsel, Subcommittee on the Constitution; 1987-present, Chief Counsel and Staff Director, Subcommittee on Patents, Copyrights, and Trademarks, Senate Judiciary Committee.

As a moderate Democrat on the committee, DeConcini often finds himself a pivotal vote. This situation allows him to create workable solutions to sometimes contentious policy issues. Baxter is the staffer who helps find this center ground. Last year, for example, Baxter assisted his boss in reaching a consensus on the Resale Price Maintenance bill. That legislation clarified the evidentiary standards and plaintiff responsibilities in resale price maintenance anti-trust suits. Sens. DeConcini and Grassley, Baxter points out, found a middle-of-the-road approach that eventually won approval.

With contentious issues ranging from immigration to copyright, a pivotal player like DeConcini, as well as his staff, will likely remain at the center of the action in the Senate Judiciary Committee.

Eddie Correia
Chief Counsel and Staff Director
Subcommittee on Antitrust,
  Monopolies and Business Rights
308 Hart Senate Office Bldg.
224-5701

Expertise: Consumer and antitrust legislation

When Eddie Correia went to work for FTC Commissioner Mike Pertschuk just after the Reagan Administration came to power, he knew what to expect. The commissioner had opted to stay on even though the change in administration meant that he could no longer be chairman. Pertschuk wanted to continue as the voice of the consumer in an otherwise pro-business atmosphere. Correia, as Pertschuk's adviser, was able to work effectively within the constraints of this minority role. When Correia moved to the Judiciary staff in 1984, he was still in the minority. Finally, when the Democrats gained control of the Senate, Correia got his chance to work for the side in power.

The years of being in the minority have helped Correia be effective in his new majority role. He is known for taking practical approaches to legislation that will get the support of a broad coalition. Some examples are the fight against the Bork nomination to the Supreme Court, legislation to ban plastic guns, and to strengthen the antitrust laws.

Upcoming issues include the Thurmond-Metzenbaum lobby bill to broaden restrictions on the "revolving door". The bill would increase restrictions on lobbying for foreign governments and on lobbying of departments in which a lobbyist was previously employed. Correia will also be working on amendments to RICO (Racketeer-Influenced and Corrupt Organizations Act) to decrease its misuse in commercial disputes. The amendments would restrict the availability of treble damages in business litigation, but would retain provisions protecting consumers.

Whatever the issues before him, Eddie Correia will certainly approach them with the pragmatism and commitment to protecting the consumer that have made him effective in both minority and majority roles.

Personal: born 7/8/48 in Chickasha, Oklahoma. B.A. Univ. of Oklahoma, 1969. Univ. of Durham, England, 1969-1970. M.P.P. Harvard Univ., 1972. J.D. Univ. of Oklahoma Law School, 1976. 1976-1978, Staff Attorney, Federal Trade Commission, Cleveland regional office. 1978-1980, Assistant Director, F.T.C., Dallas regional office. 1981-1984, senior attorney and advisor to commissioner, F.T.C. 1984-1986, Minority Chief Counsel, Subcommittee on Courts and Administrative Practice, Senate Judiciary Committee. 1987 to present, Chief Counsel and Staff Director, Subcommittee on Antitrust, Monopolies and Business Rights, Judiciary Committee.

Richard W. Day
Minority Chief Counsel and Staff
    Director
Subcommittee on Immigration and
    Refugee Affairs
807 Hart Senate Office Bldg.
224-6098

*Personal: born November 24, 1935,
Rockwood, Pennsylvania. B.A. Univ.
of Maine, 1958. J.D. Univ. of Wyoming,
1965 (board of editors of Wyoming
Law Journal, Lambda Chi Alpha).
Admitted to the Wyoming Bar, 1965.
1958-1962, high school English
teacher. 1965-1967, attorney,
Standard Oil Co. of Calif. 1967-1981,
attorney in private practice, Cody, WY.
1981-1987, Chief Counsel and Staff
Director, Subcommittee on
Immigration and Refugee Policy. 1987-
present, Minority Chief Counsel,
Subcommittee on Immigration and
Refugee Affairs, Senate Committee on
the Judiciary.*

Expertise: Immigration

Shortly after Alan Simpson (R-WY) was elected to the Senate in
1978, he began urging his old friend, Dick Day, to join him in
Washington. Day finally agreed after Simpson convinced him that
loyalty and general abilities were more important for Senate staff
than a knowledge of politics or immigration policy. Senator
Simpson wanted someone he could trust dealing with an issue
Simpson says provokes a reaction of "equal parts emotion,
racism, guilt and fear". Now, with many years on the Hill and the
passage of the Simpson-Mazzoli Immigration Bill behind him, Dick
Day has both the full confidence of Senator Simpson and a
detailed understanding of immigration and refugee issues.

Day is now working on a second major immigration bill to change
the way legal immigrants are selected for entrance into the United
States. Currently, most legal immigrants come through family
connections in the United States. The proposed bill would allow
immigrants with needed skills to enter the United States even if
they have no family here.

Day has become well-respected outside the Senate for his work on
immigration asylum and refugee issues. He has represented the
United States at numerous international conferences, and has
visited refugee camps in Europe, Central America and Asia. Being
an expert in a highly specialized field is quite a contrast from his
general law practice in Cody, Wyoming.

Day's influence on the Judiciary Committee comes from the depth
of his knowledge of issues and the fact that Simpson relies on
him. The Senator frequently calls on Day to assist him with
delicate issues such as the Bork confirmation hearings. If Senator
Simpson becomes Republican leader one day, it is a safe bet Dick
Day will be at his side.

Samuel J. Gerdano
Minority Chief Counsel/Staff
   Director
Subcommittee on Courts and
   Administrative Practice
325 Hart Senate Office Bldg.
224-6736

*Personal: born 12/11/54 in Herkimer,
New York. B.A. Syracuse Univ., 1977
(cum laude). J.D. Syracuse Univ.
College of Law, 1983 (cum laude).
1983-1985, Assistant Chief Counsel
for Advocacy, U.S. Small Business
Administration. 1985-1987, Counsel,
and 1987-present, Minority Chief
Counsel and Staff Director, Senate
Judiciary Subcommittee on Courts
and Administrative Practice.*

Expertise: Administrative law, judicial nominations

Sam Gerdano spent a summer as a law clerk in Washington, D.C.
in 1981 and caught a severe case of "Potomac Fever". A New
York native, he found his way back in 1983 as a regulatory and
legislative counsel at the Small Business Administration; and, in
1985, he landed a position with the Senate Judiciary
Administrative Practice and Procedure Subcommittee, which
became the Subcommittee on Courts and Administrative Practice
in 1987. Moving up quickly, Gerdano was appointed Minority Chief
Counsel and Staff Director of the Courts in October, 1987.

Gerdano's policy areas have included the Administrative
Procedure Act, regulatory reform, legislative veto, tort claims,
product liability and agricultural bankruptcy. He was a principal
staff author of the reauthorization of the Equal Access to Justice
Act and the Family Farmer Reorganization Act. Enacted in 1986,
this amendment was the first U.S. Bankruptcy Code provision to
apply specifically to farmers in over 50 years.

Gerdano plays a unique role because he is the chief Judiciary
Committee advisor for one of the three non-lawyers on the
Committee—Senator Charles Grassley (R-IA), a farmer by
profession.

All Judiciary Committee staffers, including Gerdano, were totally
immersed in the work on the Supreme Court nomination of Judges
Robert Bork and Anthony Kennedy. Gerdano, who "read
everything Judge Bork has ever written", described the
confirmation hearings as an intensive "CLE (Continuing Legal
Education) course in constitutional law." As advisor to Senator
Grassley, one of the most forceful advocates for Judge Bork's
confirmation and the traditional Senate nomination process,
Gerdano felt frustrated by what he called the political campaign to
derail the nomination of "one of the most qualified (persons) ever
nominated to the Court."

In his leisure time, Gerdano is a self-described "fanatic" supporter
of Syracuse University's football and basketball teams. He has
been known to travel "great distances at great expense and with
great difficulty" to root for his alma mater.

Mark Gitenstein
Chief Counsel
224 Dirksen Senate Office Bldg.
224-5225

Expertise: General judicial issues

In a city where most lawyers take their government experience to the more lucrative private sector after a few years, Mark Gitenstein is an exception. Having spent almost his entire career with the Senate Judiciary Committee, he has developed considerable expertise in virtually every issue before the Committee.

Gitenstein's Capitol Hill career began on the Subcommittee on Constitutional Rights, and he has remained personally involved in every constitutional issue facing the full committee. He was Chairman Joseph R. Biden's (D-DE) chief advisor through the confirmation hearings on Judge Robert H. Bork, including the selection of witnesses and the development of strategy.

Gitenstein's first significant role as a staff member came during his tenure as counsel to the Senate Select Committee on Intelligence. During those years, he was part of the "Church Committee's" investigation of the domestic intelligence gathering abuses of the CIA, FBI, and Defense Intelligence Agency. More specifically, Gitenstein investigated the destruction of FBI Director J. Edgar Hoover's papers after his death. He drew on this experience while drafting the 1982 "graymail" bill, which codified procedures that would allow for limited disclosure of classified information in criminal prosecutions while protecting national security secrets.

Personal: born 3/7/46 in Montgomery, AL. A.B. Duke Univ. 1968. J.D. Georgetown Univ. 1972. 1970-72, Staff, American Bar Assoc.'s Committee on Crime Prevention. 1972-75, Counsel, Subcommittee on Constitutional Rights, Senate Committee on Judiciary. 1975-76, 1976-78, Counsel, Senate Select Committee on Intelligence. 1976, grant recipient, American Civil Liberties Foundation. 1978-1980, Chief Counsel, Subcommittee on Criminal Justice; 1981-86, Minority Chief Counsel; 1987-present, Chief Counsel, Senate Committee on Judiciary.

Gitenstein's first managerial assignment came in 1978, when he became Chief Counsel fo the Subcommittee on Criminal Justice. This post gave him the criminal law background which he utilized in the development of Biden's 1984 Comprehensive Crime Control Act. This major bill, written largely by Gitenstein, represented the most expensive revision of federal criminal law in the past century, including the exactment of sentencing guidelines, bail reform, asset seizure, limitations on the insanity defense, and major revisions to the federal organized crime and drug trafficking statutes.

As Chief Counsel for the full Judiciary Committee, Gitenstein made an immediate impact by reorganizing the subcommittee structure. Several new subcommittees were formed, and an "ad hoc" task force on judicial nominations was created under his direction.

Gitenstein was a close advisor to Biden during his aborted presidential campaign. On a personal level, Gitenstein is hailed by his colleagues for his thoughtfulness and intelligence. As one Senate staffer put it, "he is not only the type to be concerned whether the summer interns need emergency lodging, but he is also brilliant."

Diana Huffman
Staff Director
224 Dirksen Senate Office Bldg.
224-5225

Personal: born 6/27/49 in Louisville,
Kentucky. B.A. Northwestern Univ.,
1971. M.S. in Journalism Columbia
Univ., 1972. J.D. Georgetown Univ.
Law School, 1976. 1974-1976, news
editor, Montgomery Sentinel. 1976-
1978, counsel, Subcommittee on
Administrative Practices, Senate
Judiciary Committee. 1977, admitted
to the District of Columbia Bar. 1978-
1980, reporter, Legal Times. 1980-
1983, editor, Legal Times. 1983-1987,
managing editor, National Journal.
1987-present, Staff Director, Senate
Judiciary Committee.

Expertise: General judicial issues

It doesn't take long to find out who is in charge at the Senate Judiciary Committee. Diana Huffman personally supervises all of the committee's day-to-day business. From judicial nomination hearings to personnel, Huffman's involvement is extensive.

Her background is marked by substantial experience in both law and journalism. With degrees from Columbia School of Journalism and Georgetown Law School, Huffman has blended the two fields. She has edited two national publications and served as counsel to a Senate subcommittee, bringing together two very different perspectives to her current position. Huffman was brought on board in early 1987 to oversee Sen. Joseph R. Biden's (D-DE) transition from ranking minority member to chairman of the Judiciary Committee. Her work included the reorganization of the subcommittees, the creation of an ad hoc judicial nominations task force, and the hiring of many new professional staff members. She is now responsible for administration of the Committee.

Huffman's involvement in issue work on the Committee has been more broad than deep. She is responsible for coordinating the work of the various subcommittees and supervising the work of ten majority chief counsels. She helps determine the legislative and executive agenda of the committee, and is involved in any policy decision by the chairman.

The one area where she has had a more specific impact is judicial nominations. She staffed the Bork and Kennedy nomination hearings, and handles the committee hearings of all nominees for lower federal court judgeships.

Huffman's press credentials have taken her into the realm of media relations for the committee. She has, on occasion, been a spokesperson for the committee and for Sen. Biden. She is also involved in media planning and strategy. Although she has been with the committee for a relatively short while, Huffman has become a trusted advisor to Biden. She has implemented many of his reform proposals in the committee structure, and she is responsible for prioritizing his chairmanship agenda.

Staffers connected with the Judiciary Committee call Huffman "demanding, but fair. She expects a lot from all of us, but I think it makes us a productive unit," says one committee counsel.

Karen Kremer
Chief Counsel/Staff Director
Subcommittee on Courts and
   Administrative Practice
223 Hart Senate Office Building
224-4022

Karen Kremer began her career on the Hill in 1983 as a counsel for Sen. Howell Heflin (D-AL) on the Subcommittee on Courts and Administrative Practice. In 1986, Kremer became the minority chief counsel for the subcommittee. Since then, Kremer has been the chief counsel and staff director for the subcommittee.

The subcommittee on Courts and Administrative Practice has jurisdiction over legislation concerning bankruptcy, court reform, matters effecting judges, bankruptcy judges and magistrates, private relief legislation, and administrative law issues such as regulatory reform, legislative veto and an independent core of administrative law judges.

Although Kremer is primarily responsible for the issues involving the Subcommittee on Courts and Administrative Practice, she also advises Sen. Howell Heflin, the chairman of the subcommittee, on all issues within the jurisdiction of the Judiciary Committee. The jurisdiction of the committee is broad and includes such diverse issues as anti-trust, and intellectual property reform.

Personal: born 6/22/57 in Birmingham, Alabama. B.A. in Political Science Univ. of Alabama, 1979, summa cum laude. J.D. Univ. of Alabama School of Law, 1983. Member of Alabama Law Review. 1983-present, Subcommittee on Courts and Administrative Practice.

Deborah Leavy
Chief Counsel and Staff Director
Subcommittee on the Constitution
524 Dirksen Senate Office Bldg.
224-5573

Personal: born 3/5/51 in New York, New York. B.A. State Univ. of New York, College at Old Westbury, 1972. J.D. Yale Law School, 1981. 1972-1975, free-lance writer and editor. 1975-1978, director, Capital Punishment Project, American Civil Liberties Union, New York. 1981-1983, associate, Hogan and Hartson, Washington, D.C. 1983-1987, counsel, House Judiciary Subcommittee on Courts, Civil Liberties and the Administration of Justice. 1987-present, chief counsel and staff director, Senate Committee on the Judiciary, Subcommittee on the Constitution.

Expertise: Constitutional law, civil liberties, civil rights enforcement, copyright

"I want to work on issues that are important to me; I really care which side wins," says Deborah Leavy. Her current position fits that bill. As chief counsel and staff director of the Senate Judiciary Subcommittee on the Constitution, Leavy holds a job where she can make a difference in the areas that matter most to her—civil liberties issues. Leavy counts herself lucky to have assumed her subcommittee duties in February, 1987, the beginning of the Constitution's 200th Anniversary.

Leavy's vocational interest in civil liberties was first sparked by a free-lance article she wrote in the early 1970's for *Ms* magazine about the only woman on death row in the U.S. Ultimately, her journalism background and devotion to civil liberties issues landed her the job with fellow journalist Sen. Paul Simon (D-IL), chairman of the Constitution Subcommittee.

Leavy came to the Senate via the House, where she worked for four years as counsel to a House Judiciary subcommittee under chairman Robert Kastenmeier (D-WI). There, Leavy developed expertise in copyright and civil liberties issues, working closely on video and audio home taping legislation and on the 1986 Electronic Communications Privacy Act, which revamped the twenty-year-old Wiretap Act to provide privacy protection to communications transmitted through new forms of technology.

Once in the Senate, Leavy was able to play a role in the Judiciary Committee's hearings on the nomination of Robert Bork for a seat on the Supreme Court—"the most fascinating discussions of constitutional law I've been involved with since law school," she says.

In addition to her "prep" work for the Bork and other confirmation hearings, Leavy monitors civil rights enforcement. She worked extensively on amendments to the Fair Housing Act to provide more vigorous enforcement of fair-housing laws. She has also worked on Sen. Simon's "hate crimes" bill and on the telephone monitoring bill that would require an audible tone on monitored calls. She has worked extensively on proposals for a balanced budget amendment and for campaign finance reform as well.

Leavy is a committed civil libertarian who enjoys working for Sen. Simon because "he cares about what I care about." She summed up her approach to the issues before the committee: "I believe strongly in what I do and Senator Simon believes you should stand up for what you believe in. Yet the legislative process is one of compromise and consensus, so I try to be true to both those sets of values."

Leavy enjoys cooking, biking, and birdwatching in her spare time.

Judiciary

Steven J. Metalitz
Chief Nominations Counsel
224 Dirksen Senate Office Bldg.
224-8191

Expertise: Judicial nominations

In his free time, Steven Metalitz enjoys being behind the controls at a Washington-based radio station as a jazz disc jockey. During the day, however, he is behind the controls on federal judicial nominations as he serves as the Chief Nominations Counsel to the Committee on the Judiciary.

Metalitz estimates he spends 90 percent of his time helping the Senate fulfill its "advice and consent" constitutional role on federal judicial nominations. "We do the investigation into all the judicial nominations, and I direct a staff of three, which includes an attorney, an investigator, and a clerk," said Metalitz.

Describing the process by which he and his staff determine the fitness and qualifications of those selected to serve on the federal judiciary, Metalitz said, "We review the FBI reports, the Judiciary Committee questionnaire (which Metalitz helped revise), Nexis and Lexis searches, as well as matters brought to our attention by private groups and people."

Personal: born 2/4/51 in Washington, D.C. B.A. Univ. of Chicago, 1972. J.D. Georgetown Univ., 1977. 1977-1982, associate, Epstein, McClain and Derfner, Charleston, S.C. 1982-1983, Counsel, Committee on Judiciary, Subcommittee on Criminal Law. 1985-1987, Legislative Director, Sen. Charles Mathias, Jr. (R-MD). 1983-1987, Staff Director, Committee on the Judiciary, Subcommittee on Patents, Copyrights and Trademarks. 1985-1987, Chief Counsel, Committee on the Judiciary, Subcommittee on Patents, Copyrights and Trademarks. 1987-present, Chief Nominations Counsel, Committee on the Judiciary.

Metalitz, who is working for one of the most liberal Senators, Patrick Leahy (D-VT), formerly spent several years working for a liberal Republican, former Maryland Senator Charles "Mac" Mathias, Jr. Metalitz notes, "The issue of judicial nominations, which I was also involved with when I worked with Senator Mathias, while a major issue, is bipartisan for the most part. While I have a particular responsibility to the Senators on the Judicial Nominations Task Force, an informal group led by Senator Leahy, I also work for the Senator who is chairing a particular nomination hearing as well as for the Judiciary Committee chairman" (Joseph Biden, Jr. (D-DE)).

Besides his work on the Judicial Nominations Task Force, Metalitz does some intellectual property and copyright work for Senator Leahy, most importantly on the Berne Convention for the Protection of Literary and Artistic Work. The intellectual property and copyright work is familiar terrain to Metalitz. Prior to his current assignment, he served as Chief Counsel and Staff Director to the Subcommittee on Patents, Copyrights and Trademarks for Chairman Mathias. Metalitz had served as that panel's staff director from 1983-1987.

Metalitz lives in Takoma Park, Maryland, with his wife and two children. For the past five years, he has enjoyed being a disc jockey for a jazz program on WDCU radio.

Carolyn Osolinik
Chief Counsel
Subcommittee on Immigration and
  Refugee Affairs
518 Dirksen Senate Office Bldg.
224-7878

Personal: born 5/18/52 in Brooklyn, New York. B.S. Lindenwood Coll., 1974. J.D. George Washington Univ. Law Center, 1977. 1977-1979, attorney, Solicitor's Office, Dept. of the Interior. 1979-1981, trial attorney, Dept. of Justice, Land and Natural Resources Division. 1981, staff, Sen. Edward Kennedy (D-MA). 1982, Chief Minority Counsel; 1987-present, Chief Counsel, Subcommittee on Immigration and Refugee Affairs.

Expertise: Environment, civil (women's) rights, crime

Despite her title, Osolinik handles absolutely no immigration or refugee affairs. Osolinik, who left her Carter administration job when Reagan was elected, is chief counsel of the Immigration and Refugee Affairs Subcommittee because she works for Senator Edward Kennedy (D-MA), who chairs that subcommittee. Actually she is Kennedy's point person on the Judiciary Committee, with oversight on all the full committee issues—including the confirmation of Supreme Court nominees.

Osolinik believes that the advice and consent role of the Senate is constitutionally equal to that of the President who nominates federal judges. She helped spearhead Kennedy's outspoken opposition to the elevation of Justice Rehnquist to Chief Justice, a battle she considers the philosophical forerunner to the successful defeat of Robert Bork.

Osolinik was instrumental in hammering out the Omnibus Crime Control Act, participating in a negotiating team comprising aides of two liberal and two conservative senators as they crafted a compromise bill to reform the criminal code. She insists it is "important to work together [with the opposition] to narrow differences" and "cooperate to the extent possible in order to focus on the main issues and clear away any tangential issues."

Osolinik has been especially active in helping draft the Civil Rights Restoration Act aimed at overturning the Supreme Court's 1984 decision in the *Grove City* case. She defines "civil rights" in the broadest sense, to mean all individual rights, thus encompassing women's struggle for equality.

A hard worker who recalls all-night sessions while eight months pregnant, Osolinik spends what little free time she has with her husband and one son and relaxes by gardening at her Alexandria home.

Randall R. Rader
Minority Chief Counsel and Staff
  Director
Subcommittee on Patents,
  Copyrights and Trademarks
229 Hart Senate Office Bldg
224-7703

Expertise: Constitutional, intellectual property

In 1981 while playing basketball, Randy Rader heard about an opening on the Senate Judiciary staff from a long-time friend who was administrative assistant to Sen. Orrin Hatch.

Rader accepted the position of Chief Counsel and Staff Director of the Constitution Subcommittee and has since played a major role in the consideration of every proposed constitutional amendment that has come before the committee.

In addition to working on balanced budget and school prayer issues, Rader directed the Committee's work—from drafting to enactment—on the Bicentennial of the Constitution Act, the Trademark Protection Act and the Trademark Clarification Act. He was also instrumental in the adoption of the Missing Children Act; the insanity defense, sentencing and other criminal reforms; collective bargaining; bankruptcy amendments; the Comprehensive Crime Control Act, and the reorganization of the Civil Rights Commission.

Rader served on Sen. Hatch's staff when the Republicans controlled the Senate, and helped direct Senate confirmation proceedings for dozens of federal judges and executive branch officials. These included Chief Justice Rehnquist, Justice Scalia, Circuit Judges Kozinski, Manion, Anderson, Buckley, Noonan, and numerous District Court appointees.

Personal: born 4/21/49 in Hastings, Nebraska. B.A. Brigham Young Univ., 1974, magna cum laude. J.D. George Washington Univ. Law Center, 1978, with honors. 1975-1978, Legislative Assistant, Rep. Virginia Smith (R-NE). 1978-1981, Legislative Director, Rep. Philip Crane (R-IL). 1981-1985, Chief Counsel and Staff Director, Senate Subcommittee on the Constitution. 1987 to present, Minority Chief Counsel and Staff Director, Senate Subcommittee on Patents, Copyrights and Trademarks, Committee on the Judiciary.

When the Democrats regained control of the Senate in 1986, Rader led the minority staff. In 1987, he advised Hatch and other Republican senators during the Judiciary Committee hearings on the nomination of Judge Robert Bork.

Since January, 1987, Rader has served as Minority Chief Counsel and Staff Director of the Subcommittee on Patents, Copyrights and Trademarks. He also has a hand in all of the committee's legal work.

A prolific writer, and author of numerous articles on judicial issues, Rader edited a book with Patrick McGuigan *Criminal Justice Reform* on which he delivered a number of public speeches.

He is recognized by lobbyists and senators on both sides of the aisle for his excellent negotiating skills and knowledge of Senate procedure. As one Judiciary Committee staffer says, "Rader's institutional knowledge is of great value. No one else on the staff knows as much about how the Committee works. He is very successful 'working the system'."

Rader enjoys tennis and basketball. But his real passion is English literature, particularly Shakespeare and Dickens. He reads a book a week and hopes one day to teach college English.

Jeffrey D. Robinson
Minority Chief Counsel and Staff
  Director
Subcommittee on the Constitution
224-6791

*Personal: born 10/13/58 in El Paso,
Texas. B.A. Lafayette Coll. J.D. Yale
Law School, 1983. 1983-1986,
associate, Wilmer, Cutler and
Pickering, Washington, D.C. 1986-
1987, Counsel, Senate Committee on
the Judiciary. 1987-present, Minority
Chief Counsel and Staff Director,
Senate Committee on the Judiciary,
Subcommittee on the Constitution*

Expertise: Constitutional law

One of the most influential Senators to consider the nomination of Judge Robert Bork to the Supreme Court was Senator Arlen Specter (R-PA). Ultimately, Specter was the only Judiciary Committee Republican to vote against Bork. Advising Specter during the grueling confirmation fight was Jeffrey D. Robinson.

As Minority Chief Counsel and Staff Director of the Subcommittee on the Constitution, Robinson's role during the Bork hearings was to collect information on the nominee and prepare memoranda detailing the Judge's position on such issues as whether the equal protection clause of the 14th Amendment is applicable to categories other than race, and the limits of the "clear and present danger" test of political speech under the 1st Amendment.

Robinson notes "Working with Senator Specter, you feel like you can make a difference and that you can see the effect of your work. The Bork hearings were a good forum for Senator Specter to display his considerable abilities." According to Senate insiders, the hearings provided an excellent opportunity for Robinson to demonstrate his considerable abilities and reaffirm his reputation as a "professional with good judgment."

Robinson also works on such other Judiciary Committee matters as antitrust legislation, retail price maintenance and criminal law issues (specifically, the Sentencing Commission). In 1987, he was involved in developing the Fair Housing Act. This legislation, co-sponsored by Specter, adds a new protected class to the 1968 act and strengthens the existing fair housing enforcement mechanisms.

Robinson came to the Judiciary Committee as a counsel to Committee Chairman Joseph R. Biden (D-DE). He was able to make the transition from Democrat Biden to Republican Specter without difficulty, noting the philosophical difference between the two legislators was "not that great." Robinson came to Capitol Hill in 1986 after three years of practicing law with the Washington, D.C. law firm of Wilmer, Cutler and Pickering. While at the firm, Robinson was involved in litigation with an emphasis on federal securities, RICO, government contract litigation and pro bono death penalty litigation. Most of Robinson's time away from the Senate is spent with his wife, Donna, and their two children.

Robert J. (Duke) Short
Minority Staff Director & Minority
  Chief Investigator
148 Dirksen Senate Office Bldg.
224-8248

Expertise: Judicial nominations

The first thing you notice when walking into Duke Short's office is the collection of hats prominently displayed along one wall. These hats are the first clue to the many roles Short has filled in his fourteen years with the Senate Judiciary Committee. From investigating terrorist activity to the varied special projects he has undertaken for Ranking Minority Member Strom Thurmond, Duke Short has a wide-ranging portfolio.

The most prominent of Short's responsibilities is that of investigating judicial nominees to the federal bench. By his own estimate, he has been involved in the confirmation process of over three-quarters of the federal judiciary including four Justices of the Supreme Court. He begins with a background check, reviewing the FBI files and IRS records of each nominee. He also "puts the hearing together" for the minority.

Short stresses fairness in the confirmation process, something he feels is a direct result of Thurmond's integrity. "We try to be fair. Senator Thurmond wants it that way and he has instilled that in me." Short has also learned to compromise and work with the majority committee staff. "The Democrats set the agenda now, so it is absolutely necessary to work with them to accomplish anything," he says with the resigned conviction of one who has worked for both majority and minority chairmen.

Personal: born 3/31/34 in Moultrie, Georgia. B.S. North Georgia Coll., 1956. Doctor of Chiropractic Medicine, Palmer Coll. of Chiropractic Medicine, 1965. 1956-1957, Industrial Engineer. 1957-1961, U.S.Army, 82nd Airborne. 1961-1962, and 1965-1972, Special Agent, Intelligence Div., Dept. of the Treasury. 1974-1976, Senior Investigator, Senate Subcommittee on Internal Security. 1976-present, Minority (1981-1987, Majority) Staff Director and Chief Investigator, Senate Judiciary Committee.

One thing on which Short will not compromise is his relationship with Thurmond. He is extremely loyal and flatly declares "he's the boss." The Senator has trusted Short with numerous special assignments over the years, including a role in both the investigations of the Atlanta child murders; and of Billy Carter's lobbying, the Robert Vesco investigation and the President's Commission of Organized Crime.

Short wants to be called "Duke" by his friends, and he has amassed a number of them during his long tenure on Capitol Hill. *The New York Times* quoted a Judiciary Committee member as saying "Duke Short is the institutional knowledge of this committee."

Originally from Georgia, Short calls D.C. home. In his spare time he enjoys boating and riflery.

George C. Smith
Minority Chief Counsel
Subcommittee on Technology and
    the Law
162 Dirksen Senate Office Bldg.
224-8254

Personal: born 2/24/45 in Wilmington, Delaware. U.S. Marine Corps, 1964-1968. B.A. Penn State Univ., 1970 (magna cum laude). J.D. Duke Univ. Law School, 1974. 1974-1983, Rogers & Wells, Washington, D.C. 1983-1984, private law practice. 1984-1987, Director of Litigation, Washington Legal Foundation, Washington, D.C., 1987-present, Minority Chief Counsel, Senate Judiciary Technology and Law Subcommittee.

Expertise: Technology, judicial nominations, civil rights legislation

When Senator Gordon Humphrey (R-NH) was elected to his second term and named to the Judiciary Committee, he needed a counsel. George Smith was a good choice because he had already had experience with several major issues, was a member of President Reagan's Transition Team in 1980-1981 and was then directing media, government and congressional relations for the conservative Washington Legal Foundation.

A soft-spoken but intense individual, Smith is Humphrey's chief advisor on judicial nominations. He has long been a student of the judicial nomination process, writing chapters for *The Judges War* on the topics of judicial qualifications and adjudication as policy-making during the Carter presidency. The book was published by the Free Congress Foundation. This experience enabled him to step in as Humphrey's right-hand during the committee's consideration of the Supreme Court nomination of Judge Robert Bork in 1987.

Humphrey also depends on Smith for his expertise on fair housing, antitrust and civil rights (especially the *Grove City* issue). In his previous legal practice, Smith had front-line experience in successful defense of EEO class actions against a major Fortune 500 corporation, and he has extensive familiarity and experience with the "comparable worth" doctrine.

Humphrey is especially interested in computer information security issues. It is expected that Smith will assist the Senator in playing a role on this issue when it is before the Judiciary Committee.

Those who know George Smith well say that his special value to Humphrey stems from the discipline he acquired when he was in the Marine Corps. He is known for his concentration and his ability to focus single-mindedly on an objective until he successfully resolves a problem.

Smith's versatility is exhibited by his extensive experience as an expert TV and radio commentator on controversial legal policy issues. He has appeared on CBS Morning News, ABC's "Nightline", NBC's "1986", MacNeill-Lehrer News Hour, CNN's "Crossfire", C-Span's "America and the Courts" and PBS's "Devil's Advocate."

Smith is competent in Japanese. He also enjoys running, tennis, swimming, weightlifting and plotting ways to attend athletic events at his alma mater, Pennsylvania State University.

Peter F. Smith
Press Secretary
240 Dirksen Senate Office Bldg.
224-5225

Personal: born 8/14/40 in New Canaan, Connecticut. B.S. Northwestern Univ., 1962. 1967-70, Graduate Instructor, Univ. of Iowa. 1970-1971, Reporter,The Telegraph Herald, Dubuque, Iowa. 1971-1972, Press Secretary, Sen. Richard Clark. 1979-1980, Press Secretary, Sen. John C. Culver. 1981-1986, Press Secretary, Sen. Joseph R. Biden Jr. 1987 to present, Press Secretary, Senate Judiciary Committee.

Expertise: Media relations

There is an unwritten maxim on Capitol Hill that former reporters make excellent press secretaries. Peter Smith's Washington experience validates that point.

As a reporter for Iowa's *Cedar Rapids Gazette*, Smith covered all city government functions. This served as a springboard to a career in Washington when Smith was recommended to Senator Dick Clark (D-IA) for the position of press secretary.

After his tenure with Senator Clark, Smith held senior positions with two other Senators, John Culver and one-time presidential hopeful Joe Biden. When the Democrats regained control of the Senate early last year, Senator Biden became chairman of the Judiciary Committee and Smith became the Committee's press secretary.

Smith acts as the chief spokesman for the chairman and primary press contact for the fourteen-member Committee. He also plans and supervises all aspects of the Committee's press operation, which includes press relations, technical arrangements for coverage of major hearings and coordination of press and legislative strategies. He is also the senior advisor to the chairman on all public relations matters.

Whether the issue is fair housing, a court nomination, or racketeering legislation, Smith is in constant communication with the Washington press corps. He estimates that he speaks to between twenty and thirty reporters per day.

Smith's philosophy about what makes a good congressional press secretary is simple: establish and maintain your credibility.

Jerry M. Tinker
Staff Director
Subcommittee on Immigration &
  Refugee Affairs
522 Dirksen Senate Office Bldg.
244-7877

Personal: born 8/29/39 in Fallbrook, California. B.A. Univ. of Redlands, 1961. Maxwell Fellowship Program in India, Syracuse Univ., 1962-1963. M.A. American Univ., 1965. Candidate for Ph.D., The American Univ., 1966. 1966-1967, Research Associate, Human Sciences Research, Inc. 1968-1969, Doctoral research in India. 1969, International Peace Research Institute, Oslo, Norway. 1970-1981, Counsel; 1981-1987, Minority Counsel; 1987-present, Staff Director, Senate Judiciary Subcommittee on Refugees (reorganized in 1979 and renamed Subcommittee on Immigration & Refugee Affairs).

Expertise: Immigration, humanitarian foreign policy issues

Since 1970, Jerry Tinker has been as involved as one staffer possibly could be in helping Senators move toward the adoption of landmark legislation in the areas of international humanitarian assistance and immigration reform.

Tinker joined the Senate Judiciary Subcommittee on Refugees, Chaired by Sen. Kennedy, that year as a foreign policy expert specializing in refugee problems in Indochina. Tinker has been a part of Kennedy's legislative team ever since. Their association over the past two decades has not been confined to the halls of Congress. Tinker has accompanied Kennedy on numerous overseas factfinding missions to regions in crisis including Bangladesh, Southeast Asia and Africa. In 1984, for example, Tinker observed a somber Christmas in famine-ravaged Ethiopia with Kennedy and his children.

In 1977, Tinker was asked by Kennedy to take on additional legislative responsibilities for immigration issues, an area of intense involvement for Kennedy from the outset of his Senate career. Two years later, as Chairman of the full Judiciary Committee, Kennedy, combined the two separate subcommittees dealing with immigration and refugees issues into a special unit of the committee.

As Tinker recalls past legislative skirmishes, one of his most enduring memories is working alongside Kennedy and the late Hubert Humphrey in 1974 to bolster support for the historic Kennedy-Pearson amendment. Albeit a symbolic victory, it was the first time the Senate had voted as a body to cut military aid to South Vietnam. The amendment was carried by one vote.

Far from symbolic were Tinker's efforts in connection with the enactment of the Refugee Act of 1980. The first major refugee reform in over a decade, this bill replaced the previous ad hoc approach with systematic admissions procedures and sustained refugee assistance programs. Kennedy and Tinker worked tirelessly with Strom Thurmond and his staff to garner widespread Senate support of the bill. Highly unusual for any foreign assistance measure, the bill passed the Senate unanimously.

Tinker also assisted Kennedy with the creation by statute in 1979 of the bipartisan Select Commission on Immigration and Refugee Policy, comprised of Members of Congress, Cabinet officers and presidential appointees. The Commission's work spanned two full years and laid the groundwork for the future overhaul of U.S. immigration policy. Another unforeseen, yet significant, result of these two years was the opportunity for Commission member Senator Alan Simpson (R-WY), who would eventually become the

Immigration Subcommittee Chairman when Republicans took control of the Senate in 1981, to gain an intensive, in-depth working knowledge of the complexities of immigration reform.

It was during Simpson's tenure as chairman that the far-reaching Immigration Reform and Control of Act of 1986, better known as the Simpson-Rodino-Mazzoli Bill, was enacted in the fall of that year. The legislation granted the opportunity for legal status to many illegal aliens, and included sanctions on employers who hired undocumented workers. Although Simpson was the bill's chief architect, Kennedy's imprint, according to Tinker, was most firmly affixed in the legislation's generous and flexible amnesty provisions and in "setting the tone" for the bill's anti-discrimination measures. Ultimately, however, those measures were not as extensive as Kennedy had hoped and, in protest, he voted against final passage.

Now that the Democrats once again hold the Subcommittee's reins, Tinker, as Staff Director, continues to work closely with Simpson and his staff on the other side of the immigration coin, changes in legal immigration law, as well as in monitoring the implementation of Simpson-Rodino-Mazzoli.

Tinker is typically generous in crediting Kennedy's ability to work effectively, over long periods of time, with his colleagues at varying planes of the political spectrum in striking necessary legislative compromises. Tinker as well enjoys the wide respect of his Senate and House counterparts, who praise his grasp of the issues and prowess at negotiating common ground.

If Tinker is battle-weary after 17 years on the frontlines, it doesn't show. According to one Senate staffer, Tinker is the "conscience of compassionate immigration reform."

Terry L. Wooten
Minority Chief Counsel
145 Dirksen Senate Office Bldg.
224-6693

Personal: born 1/20/54,in Louisville, Kentucky. B.A. Univ. of South Carolina, 1976, (magna cum laude). J.D. Univ. of South Carolina, 1980. 1976-1977, law clerk, Lexington, SC. 1978-1979, law clerk, Columbia, SC. 1979-1980, Chief Advocate, Student Government of University of South Carolina, Columbia, SC. 1980-1982, partner, Mann and Wooten, Columbia, SC. 1982-1986, Assistant Solicitor, Fifth Judicial Circuit, Columbia, SC. 1986-1987, Counsel to Senate Judiciary Committee. 1987, Legislative Director, Sen. Strom Thurmond (R-SC). 1987-present, Minority Chief Counsel, Senate Committee on Judiciary.

Expertise: Criminal law

Having been in Washington for only two years, Terry Wooten has risen to the position of Minority Chief Counsel for the Senate Judiciary Committee.

His relative newness to political life has not been a disadvantage. Wooten brings a strong background in criminal law to the Committee. His trial experience as an assistant prosecutor in his native South Carolina and extensive background in criminal litigation have given Wooten a practical view of the legislative process. He has tapped this experience in his work on the sweeping drug and gun bills passed in 1986.

He is also practical in realizing the role of the minority committee staff. Referring to the Democratic majority, Wooten admits, "They control the agenda. Some degree of compromise is necessary to get things done." The bipartisan support received by both the drug and gun bills is evidence of Wooten's contention.

Wooten is not new to Ranking Republican Senator Strom Thurmond (R-SC). Wooten served as Legislative Director to Thurmond for part of 1987, and is now the Senator's top aide for judicial issues.

Priorities for the remainder of the 100th Congress, according to Wooten, will include continuing to adjust to Democratic control of the Judiciary Committee, and the proposed limits on ex-government officials' lobbying activities.

This Washington newcomer has found much to like in this city. "It's interesting here—things change very fast—especially the dynamics of the political process."

SENATE
COMMITTEE ON LABOR AND HUMAN RESOURCES

William A. Blakey
Chief Counsel
Subcommittee on Employment and
  Productivity
644 Dirksen Senate Office Bldg
224-5575

*Personal: born 9/1/43 in Louisville,
Kentucky. B.A. Knoxville Coll., 1965.
J.D. Howard Univ., 1968. 1965-1968,
Sen. Daniel B. Brewster (D-MD). 1968-
1969, HUD. 1969-1970, the National
Urban Coalition. 1970-1971, the
TransCentury Corp. 1971-1972, A.L.
Nellum and Assc. 1972-1976, U.S.
Commission for Civil Rights. 1976-
1977, Kentucky Commission on
Human Rights. 1977-1980, assistant
secretary of legislation on education;
1980-1981, deputy assistant secretary
for legislation on human services,
HHS. 1981-1985, Counsel and Staff
Director, Subcommittee on
Postsecondary Education. 1985-1987,
Legislative Assistant, Sen. Paul Simon
(D-IL).*

Expertise: Education, minority issues

William Blakey—"Buddy" to his friends and colleagues—has
focused his career on education and minority issues for more than
twenty years. Those years have been filled with service in the
private sector, Executive agencies and on the Hill for the
advancement of civil rights for minorities, women, and the elderly.

He has authored articles on affirmative action and discrimination,
racism and sexism in American society, school desegregation,
minority access to higher education and the historically black
colleges and universities. He has taught as a visiting professor at
Illinois State University, Eastern Illinois University, and the
University of Rhode Island.

Blakey's outstanding credentials include a long list of awards:
Outstanding Alumnus, Knoxville Coll., 1980; The United Negro
College Fund Award for Honor in 1983 for his work on the
Challenge Grant Act Amendments of 1983; The Black College Act
Award for his work on the Black College and University Act. He is
listed in *Who's Who in Black America (1975-78, 1979-80).*

Blakey is a personable man who sports a bow tie like his boss,
Sen. Paul Simon (D-IL). He has worked for Simon since 1981,
when Simon served in the House. As Senior Legislative Assistant
and, later, as Minority Counsel for the Subcommittee on
Employment and Productivity, Blakey says he "has worked on
most domestic issues, specifically those with education, health
employment, civil rights, and minority interests.

As Chief Counsel to the Subcommittee, Blakey is responsible for
analyzing education and employment and job training programs
supervised by the Labor Committee. Last year, he organized
hearings on and helped draft the Economic Dislocation and
Worker Adjustment Assistant Act (S.538), a provision of the 1987
Trade Bill (H.R.3) that expands services to workers who, for
example, have lost their jobs due to plant closings.

He also worked on Simon's Guaranteed Jobs Opportunity Act
(S.777), one of the central components of the Senator's
presidential campaign platform. Modelled on Roosevelt's Work
Projects Administration, the bill provides for 32-hour-a-week jobs
on public works projects for people unemployed for five weeks or
more.

Blakey admits that underneath the credentials and the dedicated
public service, he is just "a frustrated disc jockey." He spends his
few free hours making cassette tapes—medleys of jazz, R&B and
pop tunes—for his friends and parties. "It's the only time I get to
sit for long periods of time," he says.

Amanda Broun
Chief Education Counsel
615 Hart Senate Office Bldg.
224-5501

Expertise: Elementary and secondary education

In her two years on Capitol Hill, Amanda Broun has been involved in several initiatives affecting America's education system.

One of Broun's first challenges was assisting in the crafting of the omnibus education reauthorization bill. One area she focused on in particular was the reauthorization of the bilingual education program. That provision provided states with bilingual education funding and required evaluation of the universe of students it serves.

Additionally, Broun helped draft the Star Schools proposal which authorizes grants to telecommunications networks. These grants assist in bringing courses to those in rural areas who do not have access to math, science or foreign language instruction.

For the committee's chairman, Sen. Edward M. Kennedy (D-MA), Broun drafted legislation involving early childhood education. Entitled "Smart Start," this legislation provides full work day and full calendar-year development services to four-year-old children. By advancing this kind of developmentally appropriate education program, Broun is confident this measure will build on the positive results of other early childhood programs. Additionally, Broun believes this bill would effectively address day care needs for parents with children of pre-school age.

Personal: born 3/15/58 in London, England. B.A. Barnard Coll, Columbia Univ., 1979, cum laude. J.D. New York Univ., School of Law, 1982. 1982-1983, staff attorney, New York Board of Education. 1983-1986, legislative counsel, New York City Office of Management and Budget. 1986-present, chief education counsel, Senate Committee on Labor and Human Resources

In general, Broun feels that children, especially disadvantaged children, at the pre-school level benefit greatly from early childhood educational programs, and that funds ought to be made available to augment current education and child care programs. Such a system, says Broun, could help remove the enormous barrier to parents wishing to work. In that context, Broun believes it is senseless to commence early education initiatives which do not also address day care needs.

Another area that Broun will continue to monitor is the Literacy Corps Program, which is contained in this year's omnibus trade bill. That initiative would make available $20 million to colleges whose students spend time in the community tutoring others. Broun's involvement in education issues also extends to the Subcommittee on Education, Arts, and Humanities, chaired by Sen. Claiborne Pell (D-RI), which reports most of the committee's education legislation.

James Brudney
Chief Counsel
Subcommittee on Labor
608 Hart Senate Office Bldg
224-5546

Personal: born 7/6/50 in New York, New York. B.A. Amherst Coll., 1971, Phi Beta Kappa, summa cum laude. M.A. Oxford Univ., "First Class" Degree, 1973. J.D. Yale Law School, 1979. editor, Yale Law Journal. 1979-1980, law clerk, Honorable Gerhard A. Gesell, U.S. District Court, Washington, D.C. 1980-198l, law clerk, Justice Harry A. Blackmun, U.S. Supreme Court. 1981-1985, associate, Bredhoff & Kaiser, Washington, D.C. 1985-1986, Minority Counsel, Senate Subcommittee on Labor. 1987-present, Chief Counsel, Senate Subcommittee on Labor. Publications: "Agency Shop in the Public Sector: Recent Developments in the Law," VIII Collective Bargaining Quarterly No. 1 May 1985. "The Cost of Growing Old: Business Necessity and the Age Discrimination in Employment Act," 88 Yale Law Journal, 565 (l979).

Expertise: Labor relations

James Brudney's initiation to working in the Senate in 1985 was the successful negotiation of a compromise amendment that preserved the protections of the Fair Labor Standards Act for public employees, while protecting state and local governments from undue fiscal constraints.

Brudney was also involved in the consideration and passage of the Age Discrimination in Employment Amendments of 1986, which abolished mandatory retirement in all occupations, with temporary exemptions for police, firefighters and tenured faculty in higher education. He also played an important staff role in the Economic Dislocation and Worker Adjustment Assistance Act, which requires employers of more than 100 employees to give sixty days' notice of shutdowns and long-term layoffs, and provides increased federal funds for readjustment and retraining of dislocated workers.

Brudney's colleagues note his acuity in drafting legislation that satisfies the conflicting interests of disparate factions. A good example in the Senate this year is the High Risk Occupational Disease Notification and Prevention Bill, for which Brudney has organized a range of endorsements including the AMA, labor representatives, and numerous members of the business community. The bill establishes a low-cost mechanism for identifying, notifying and monitoring employees whose health is at risk from exposure to hazardous substances in their work place.

Chief Counsel on the Committee for Labor and Human Resources, Tom Rollins, speaks for many who have worked with Brudney: "I think of him as the country's gift to government." Brudney is married and has two children. His hobby is spending time with them.

Christopher Button
Professional Staff Member/
  Legislative Assistant
Subcommittee on the Handicapped
625 Hart Senate Office Building
224-1285

Personal: born 12/4/48 in Bethesda, Maryland. B.S. Florida State Univ., 1970. M. Ed., Special Education, Univ. of Missouri, 1972. Currently Doctoral Candidate, Special Education Policy Specialist Program, Univ. of Maryland. 1972-76, Master Teacher, Mid-Missouri Mental Health Center, Colombia, MO. 1976, Intern, Bureau of Education for the Handicapped, Dept. of Health, Education and Welfare. 1977-79, Assistant Specialist-Special Education Due Process and Contract Services, Fairfax County, VA, Public Schools. 1980-84, Consultant, National Assoc. of State Directors of Special Education. 1980-84, Faculty Research Assistant/Instructor, Univ. of Maryland. 1984. Fellow, National Council on the Handicapped. 1985-present, Professional Staff Member, Subcommittee on the Handicapped, Senate Committee on Labor and Human Resources.

Expertise: Disability issues, including special education, and developmental disabilities

"It is hard to measure all the benefits of federal programs for people with disabilities," says Christopher Button. "How do you place a value on such things as personal dignity, or the ability to be an active member of your community?" These are some of the reasons why Button feels strongly about her responsibilities as a professional staff member of the Subcommittee on the Handicapped. Considered a leading expert in the Senate on special education, Button has been involved with programs for the disabled ever since junior high school, when she worked with disabled children as a volunteer. Her interest in the field also stems from a close childhood friendship with a disabled youngster. And as part of an internship program during her undergraduate years, Button spent a semester living in an institution for the mentally retarded, an experience which was critical in shaping her views on the importance of integration, rather than segregation, of people with disabilities.

In her three years with the Subcommittee, Button has been a strong advocate for initiatives which "move the system forward." She was a lead player last session in legislation which created a new state grant program for supported employment—a program which will enable many people with severe disabilities to become competitively employed. She is also very enthusiastic about changes in the recently reauthorized Developmental Disabilities' Program which acknowledge the ability of people with disabilities to make decisions for themselves.

A major legislative initiative on which Button is working is the "Home and Community Quality Services Act" introduced by Sens. Chafee and Weicker. This bill would mandate states to develop a wide range of community-based services, funded through the Medicaid system, which is currently institutionally biased. It would also freeze Medicaid funding for services for people with disabilities in large institutional settings. The bill is important because "it would make it possible for many people with disabilities to become more independent, productive members of society", says Button.

Outside the office, Button's time is consumed with raising a four-year old child and completing her doctoral degree. Her hobbies are photography and playing the piano. Her doctoral dissertation deals with integration of handicapped children into the least restrictive environment as guaranteed under the Education for all Handicapped Children Act.

David Evans
Staff Director
Subcommittee on Education, Arts
&the Humanities
648 Dirksen Senate Office Bldg.
224-7666

Expertise: Education

David Evans has been with the Subcommittee on Education, Arts and the Humanities for years, serving first as a Professional Staff Member and then as Minority Staff Director. In this capacity, Evans works with Claiborne Pell of Rhode Island. His primary issues include higher education, student financial aid, and elementary, secondary, and vocational education.

Evans's list of legislative credits include: The Education for Economic Security Act (accepted by the House without amendment); the emergency math and science legislation of 1984, which provided immediate assistance to update, train and retrain teachers in math and science; and The Carl Perkins Vocational Education Act of 1984, which re-targeted vocational education funds serving the disadvantaged, the handicapped and adults who need training or retraining. Evans was instrumental in writing and helping to enact the Higher Education Act of 1986, which directed $10 billion to extend all student aid programs for five years, and was the lead staff person for the Robert T. Stafford Elementary and Secondary Education Act, which provided $7.5 billion for an omnibus re-authorization of the elementary secondary and Adult Education programs.

Evans's duties include developing and analyzing legislation; planning and staffing hearings; serving as a primary source of information and direction to the Senate staff on issues related to federal education policy; and dealing with national education associations. He is responsible for oversight of federal education laws and the operation of the U.S. Department of Education.

Personal: born 12/9/41 in Holdrege, Nebraska. B.A. Grinnell Coll., Grinnell, Iowa, 1964. M.A. The Eagleton Institute of Politics, Rutgers–The State University, New Brunswick, New Jersey, 1966. 1965-1966, Fellowship from the National Center of Education in Politics, N.Y. 1966-1967, Penn. State Univ. 1969-1972, Administrative Assistant, Governor of Rhode Island. Consultant for business and political services, Westerly, Rhode Island. 1979-present, Professional Staff Member, Minority Staff Director, Staff Director, Subcommittee on Education, Arts and the Humanities, Senate Committee on Labor and Human Resources. Delegate to the 1968 and 1972 Democratic conventions; worked in the presidential campaigns of Eugene McCarthy, George McGovern, Morris Udall.

Evans has spent almost his entire career in public service. He grew up in a Midwest prairie state in a family whose roots are in public service. "My father was the administrator of a mental institution. There is no question that growing up in that kind of arena tended to give me an awareness and sensitivity to the disadvantaged. Since being Minority Staff Director, I feel my strength has been to pull diverse interests together to produce legislation in a spirit of consensus."

According to his colleagues, David is considered very experienced, substantively knowledgeable, politically savvy...and a gentleman.

When Evans is not actively participating in government, he spends time at the beach in Rhode Island. Evans is an avid animal lover.

Michael A. Francis
Legislative Aide
Senator Robert T. Stafford (R-VT)
l33 Hart Senate Office Bldg.
224-5141

*Personal: born 6/9/43 in Rutland, VT.
B.A. American Univ., Washington,
D.C., 1970. 1967-1969, U.S. Army.
1969, Campaign Organizer, Sen.
Winston Prouty. 1970-1971, Research
Assistant, Sen. Winston Prouty. 1971
to present, Legislative Aide, Sen.
Robert Stafford.*

"Access is the key. I don't have to write a memo to communicate with the Senator, I just walk through the door," says Michael Francis, Legislative Aide to Sen. Robert Stafford, (R-VT), with a crisp New England accent. In contrast to most Senate offices representing larger states, Stafford's legislative staff numbers only two and Francis could not be more pleased, "It really cuts out the bureaucracy."

Francis, a Vermont native, is a Capitol Hill veteran having served for Senator Winston Prouty (R-VT) and then for Senator Robert Stafford (R-VT) following Prouty's death in 1971. Francis is proud of his long tenure, "I don't view this job as a stepping stone. I see it as an opportunity for public service." Because of the small size of the staff, Francis handles a wide variety of issues ranging from taxes, trade, housing and labor, to welfare, environment and energy. Thus, Francis is more of a generalist than most staffers on the Hill.

This last year, Francis was involved with Stafford's successful efforts to reauthorize the block grant program for energy assistance for low income persons. In 1988, he expects to be involved with legislation to require worker notification of exposure to toxic chemicals.

Francis has played a part in several major legislative accomplishments over the years, and cites three in particular. First of these is the passage of the Education Act for All Handicapped Children Act of 1976, especially the provisions which gave due process rights to children who appeal denial of educational opportunity. Second on the list is the Vocational Rehabilitation Act of 1972, which extended civil rights protections to disabled persons. The third cited is the set aside of 40,000 additional acres of wilderness lands for the enjoyment of future generations in the Green Mountain National Forest in Vermont.

In general, Francis is not pleased with the changes in the Senate over the last l7 years. "Today, the issues are more polarized. A lot of new politicians are extremely oriented toward the media and have no experience with the legislative process. These people are more ideological and find it harder to compromise and get things done."

Francis is also a coach for his daughter's soccer team and his son's basketball team. Stafford has announced his retirement. However, Francis intends to remain in Washington.

F. Edwin "Win" Froelich, M.D.
Physician Advisor for Minority
835 Hart Senate Office Bldg.
224-2094

*Personal: born 8/3/57, in West
Germany. B.S. Univ. of Oklahoma,
1979. M.D. Vanderbilt Univ., 1983.
Family medicine resident, Univ. of
Oklahoma, 1983-84. J.D. Georgetown
Univ. (Expected 5/88). 1980-84,
computer programmer for Vanderbilt
Univ., the Univ. of Alabama, the Univ.
of Oklahoma and the Pensacola, FL,
education program. 1984-present,
emergency room physician, Farmville,
VA., and Lawton, OK. 1985-87,
Professional Staff Member/Physician
Advisor, Senate Committee on Labor
and Human Resources. 1987-present,
Physician Advisor for Minority, Senate
Committee on Labor and Human
Resources.*

Expertise: Health

Win Froelich's qualifications as a physician were probably
paramount when Sen. Orrin Hatch (R-Utah) first hired him in 1985
to join the staff of the Senate Labor and Human Resources
Committee. But it probably didn't hurt that Froelich also is a
lawyer, a computer programmer, a sailor, a car builder and racer, a
scuba diver and a skier. If Hatch was looking for a man of action,
he found one who, at the time, was only 28 years old.

Froelich is today one of two physicians on the committee's
minority staff. His legislative areas include acquired immune
deficiency syndrome (AIDS), tobacco, occupational diseases and
the Public Health Service. He also monitors the National Institutes
of Health, the Centers for Disease Control and the Health
Resources Administration.

Froelich takes his cue from the Utah senator whose approach, he
says, is promoting public information. In working on the
Smokeless Tobacco Act and, in particular, on provisions to ban
tobacco advertising, Froelich believes the top priority is to
recognize the public's right to make an informed decision. Even
though he favors restrictions on smoking in airplanes, Froelich
says he has an "interesting relationship" with the Tobacco
Institute, the tobacco industry lobby. He recognizes the Institute as
an important source of information to mix with other perspectives
and viewpoints that are necessary to the legislative process.

This broad approach to the process shows in his work on bills
introduced by Senator Hatch's political adversaries, including Sen.
Edward Kennedy (D-MA) and Sen. Howard Metzenbaum (D-OH),
both of whom are members of the Committee. Rather than try to
block Metzenbaum's Occupational Health Bill, which contained
many provisions unacceptable to Hatch, Froelich worked with
Metzenbaum's staff to modify those provisions and widen support
for a more acceptable bill.

Froelich is particularly proud of his work on AIDS. He advised
Hatch to encourage the creation of the President's Commission on
AIDS. He says that this and other efforts by Hatch to confront the
AIDS crisis, have resulted in Hatch being one of the few Members
of Congress who have received praise from the diverse interests
involved in the crisis.

In what might be considered by outsiders as an unusual move by
a conservative staffer, Froelich says he helped "rewrite Kennedy's
AIDS bill in order to secure bipartisan support."

Froelich's skills are admired by many of those with whom he
deals, even if they are on opposite poles on an issue. One industry
representative who agrees with Froelich that they are
"adversaries," said "I'm happy that Win was brought to the Hill.

He is neither an academician nor a politician, but he's a bit of both. He's a professional, sophisticated, able young guy. Sure, we've taken off the gloves, but Win's been reasonable when others were not."

On Labor and Human Resources, Froelich works with a broad range of health related issues including AIDS, tobacco, organ transplantation, health manpower, health care financing and oversight of federal health agencies. Among the bills in which Froelich has been active were the Smokeless Tobacco Act of 1986, which required warning labels on and banned television advertising of smokeless tobacco products, and the Drug Export Control Act.

While his position with the Committee is rooted in his medical and legal background, Froelich is also a dedicated conservative follower of his boss, Sen. Hatch. "As a staff member, my job is to advance Sen. Hatch." Froelich is also a life member of the Republican National Committee.

Yet, Froelich recognizes that bipartisan cooperation is necessary for the legislative output of the Committee. "We have a tradition of cooperation here. Very little legislation is ultimately enacted without the support of both Sen. Hatch and Sen. Kennedy."

Despite his political and legal credentials, Froelich is, first and foremost, a doctor. Among the academic degrees that decorate his office, Froelich prominently displays a picture drawn by a young patient whom he had treated. "I keep it there to remind me who we are working for. Ultimately, care for the patient is what it's all about."

Froelich's major outside interest is aviation. At the age of nineteen, he earned a commercial pilots license. Froelich is also an avid skier.

Lois Lee Fu
Staff Director
Subcommittee on Aging
404 Hart Senate Office Bldg.
224-3239

Personal: born 3/23/53 in Detroit, Michigan. B.A. Univ. of Michigan, 1974. M.P.P. Institute of Public Policy Studies, Univ. of Michigan, 1976. 1976-1979, graduate student, George Washington Univ. 1976-1977, Research Analyst, U.S. Department of Labor. 1977-1978, Labor Economist, Ketron, Inc. 1978-1979, Research Analyst, National Commission on Employment and Unemployment Statistics. 1979-1980, Research Associate, National Academy of Sciences. 1980-1985, Labor Economist, Dept. of Labor. 1983-1984, American Political Science Association Congressional Fellow, Office of Sen. John Glenn (D-OH). 1984-1987, Financial Planning Officer and Acting Director of Policy Development and Planning, American Red Cross National Headquarters. 1987-present, Staff Director, Subcommittee on Aging.

Expertise: Aging, employment and training

The distinction between the Special Committee on Aging and the Subcommittee on Aging may not be obvious at first glance. Both focus on the concerns of older Americans. The Special Committee is more visible as it strives to draw attention to those concerns in hearings and reports. But only the Subcommittee has jurisdiction over legislation affecting the elderly. And Lois Fu is responsible for the Subcommittee.

Fu came to the Committee in January, 1987 with a distinguished background in labor issues, and she was assigned to the Subcommittee on Aging. Although she had not worked specifically on seniors' issues, she learned quickly, relying on the management expertise she had developed during her years at the American Red Cross. While with the Red Cross, Fu designed and implemented a new budget system for the National Headquarters. The success of the system enabled Fu to lead a strategic plan for the organization as a whole, redirecting its focus away from many disparate services and back to its primary, traditional role as an emergency relief group.

Last year, the Subcommittee devoted most of its energies to reauthorizing the Older Americans Act of 1965 (S.887), which passed the Senate by a vote of 98-0. The bill provides funds for state and regional networks that coordinate and deliver social services to senior citizens. These services include programs such as "Meals on Wheels," which brings food to home-bound seniors, as well as transportation services and senior centers.

The philosophy behind this hallmark legislation may change by the time it comes up for reauthorization in four years. Some legislators would like to see a "means test" included in the bill, to render wealthier seniors ineligible to receive some of the services it provides. Others do not want the central tenet of the legislation—"eligibility for all seniors"—to be tampered with. Fu has been responsible for reviewing this proposal and others that would target programs for minorities and indigent seniors.

The Subcommittee changed the reauthorization period of the Act from every three to every four years, giving itself time to work on other legislation. One bill that may fall into its jurisdiction this year is the Domestic Volunteer Services Act. Three of the four programs in that bill involve the elderly.

Like the chairman of the Subcommittee, Sen. Spark Matsunaga D-HI), Fu prefers to be a quiet leader on aging issues. Staff members with whom she has worked on these issues describe her as extremely competent, professional in her work and easy to get along with.

Robert M. Guttman
Minority Counsel
Subcommittee on Labor
428 Dirksen Senate Office Bldg.
224-6306

*Personal: Born 8/9/28 in Munich,
Germany. U.S. citizen by
naturalization, 1952. A.B. Harvard
Coll., summa cum laude, Phi Beta
Kappa, 1952. Littauer Graduate
School of Public Administration, 1952-
1954. Sheldon Traveling Fellow,
Harvard University, London School of
Economics, 1954-1955. LL.B. George
Washington Univ., 1961. 1956-1970,
various administrative and legal
positions, Dept. of Labor, ending as
Associate Solicitor for Legislation and
Legal Counsel. 1970-1981, Specialist,
Social Legislation, CRS. 1981-1984,
Counsel, Subcommittee on
Employment and Productivity, Senate
Committee on Labor and Human
Resources. 1984-1985, Staff Director,
Temporary Select Committee to Study
the Senate Committee System. 1985-
1986, Chief Counsel, Sen. Dan
Quayle. 1987-present, Minority
Counsel, Labor Subcommittee, Senate*

Expertise: Labor and employment

1981 was a critical year for the nation's job training programs. The Comprehensive Employment and Training Act (CETA) of 1973 was about to expire, and President Reagan's Labor Department was anxious to eliminate federal job training programs altogether. Sen. Dan Quayle (R-IN), the chairman of the Senate Subcommittee on Employment and Productivity, needed to draft a compromise bill that would satisfy both the new Administration and the liberal members of the Senate Labor Committee, led by Sen. Kennedy.

Quayle sought out Robert Guttman to serve as counsel to the subcommittee.

Guttman, a labor and employment specialist with the Congressional Research Service at the Library of Congress for over a decade, had grown dissatisfied with the Service's shift in emphasis away from providing legislative assistance to the congressional committees towards more academic concerns. Anxious to continue his work with the Senate and House Labor Committees and sensing the challenge of creating a responsible and effective successor to CETA, Guttman joined the Subcommittee staff in 1981. Two years later, the new job Training Partnership Act was voted into law. The new Act sought to discontinue CETA's emphasis on providing employment for disadvantaged individuals at the government's expense while still providing the job training which Guttman and other experts on employment consider important.

Although Guttman is a specialist on labor and employment, he has also worked on other legislation. In 1984, Quayle was appointed chairman of the Temporary Select Committee to Study the Senate Committee System, and Guttman signed on as Staff Director. The Committee issued several proposals for improving the efficiency of the Senate, including revising committee assignment limitations, moving to a two-year budget cycle, restricting non-germane amendments and revising the cloture rule. Although the committee's report was unanimous, no substantial changes came out of the proposals. Guttman, however, is hopeful some of the committee's recommendations may yet be adopted.

Guttman also assisted Quayle in one of the Senator's other areas of interest, the procurement procedures of the Defense Department. An unqualified supporter of a strong defense, Guttman believes that the Defense Department must be efficient as well as effective.

Yet Guttman's primary interests have always remained labor and employment. Highest among Guttman's concerns while evaluating labor legislation is the impact that such legislation will have on the level of employment. While he agrees that proposals such as an

Labor and Human Resources Committee. Recent publications: "Job Training Partnership Act: New help for the unemployed," Monthly Labor Review, *March, 1983, "The Role of Data in the Formulation of Manpower Policy,"* Proceedings of Joint Canadian American Conference on Manpower Policy, *1976.*

increase in the minimum wage and mandated health benefits have appeal on an individual basis, he maintains that the cumulative effect of such policies will be a decrease in employment.

Guttman says that "an unemployed person will not really care that the job he used to have pays better." Guttman is also concerned with maintaining the integrity of the employer/employee bargaining process. "If the government mandates certain benefits or restrictions in favor of the employee, it becomes impossible to realize an agreement which is fair to the employer, he says. As examples of such legislation, Guttman cites the proposed ban on "double-breasting" by construction companies, the proposed requirements for advance notice of plant closings, and the proposed mandated health benefits and parental leave.

Guttman considers his highest immediate priority the revamping of the rules which regulate private pension funds. He acknowledges that the current Pension Benefit Guarantee Corporation is inadequately funded, and he is fearful that funds will not be available to cover the increasing number of pension funds which are not able to pay the benefits they have promised.

Guttman holds the distinction of having held three different citizenships in his lifetime: German, British and American. During his two years with the British Army, Guttman administered a program offering delinquent youths the option of serving in the Army instead of being sent to reform school.

Terry W. Hartle
Chief Advisor for Education
615 Senate Hart Office Bldg.
224-5501

Personal: born 8/4/51 in Bay Village, Ohio. B.S. Hiram Coll., 1973. M.S. Maxwell School, Syracuse Univ., 1974. Ph.D. George Washington Univ., 1982. 1975-1984, Educational Testing Service. 1984-1987, American Enterprise Institute for Public Policy Research. 1987-present, Chief Advisor on Education, Senate Committee on Labor and Human Resources.

Expertise: Elementary, secondary and higher education

Terry Hartle joined the Senate Committee on Labor and Human Resources with his views on educational policies well known. He is a prolific writer, having written chapters in six books and written or contributed to over 70 monographs and articles. He co-authored the book *Excellence in Education: The States Take Charge* which was selected as one of the ten best books of 1986 by the *American School Board Journal*. Hartle has written broadly on educational finance, governance and quality issues facing federal and state governments

Hartle came to the Senate Committee on Labor and Human Resources from the American Enterprise Institute where he was Resident Fellow and Director of Social Policy Studies. His research at AEI focused on policy-oriented studies of educational and human capital development. Prior to AEI, he worked at the Educational Testing Service for ten years as a research scientist studying education finance, governance and quality. He was also a Washington liaison for ETS, and worked in government relations with Congress, the executive branch and special interests groups.

Hartle has been a consultant to many public and private organizations. He has taught in the School of Government and Business Administration at George Washington University.

Since joining the Committee in April, 1986, he has helped write the Higher Education Technical Amendments of 1987, the education components of the Trade Bill and the Robert T. Stafford Elementary and Secondary Education Improvement Act. Among the parts of the Elementary and Secondary Education Improvement Act he worked on were the expansion of the National Assessment of Educational Programs (NAEP) and the creation of the Fund for the Improvement and Reform of Schools and Teaching (FIRST). If passed, this would provide grants to schools to develop locally oriented curricula. In addition he wrote the Comprehensive Child Development Center Act, which is an amendment to legislation on the Head Start Program. This act would provide early childhood education funding for severely disadvantaged children.

Charlotte Anne Hayes
Legislative Assistant
Senator Barbara A. Mikulski (D-
   MD.)
320 Hart Senate Office Bldg.
224-4654

*Personal: born 7/1/53 in Springfield,
MA. 1973-1974, International Law,
Univ. of Geneva, Switzerland; B.A.
Wellesley College, 1975; J.D., New
York Univ., 1978. 1985-1986, Partner
and Associate Attorney, Hart, Carroll,
Chavers, Washington, D.C. 1982-
1985, Associate Attorney, Ballard,
Spahr, Andrews and Ingersoll,
Washington, D.C. 1980-1982, Office of
Assistant General Counsel for
International Law, U.S. Department of
Transportation. 1978-1980, Associate
Attorney, Arnold and Porter,
Washington, D.C.*

Expertise: Municipal finance and international law

An expert in municipal finance, Charlotte Hayes was involved in a private law practice, but politics and national policy were her real interests. In 1986, she left her position with a D.C. law firm and volunteered part-time for Barbara Mikulski's Senate campaign. She then joined Mikulski's staff as a Legislative Assistant and has no regrets about the choice. Her job now is "incredibly consuming." she says, and "it's much more interesting than working in a law firm."

Hayes staffs the Senate Labor and Human Resources Committee for Mikulski. She has become closely linked with many education issues before the committee. Recently, Hayes assisted Mikulski in putting together the Robert T. Stafford Elementary and Secondary Education Improvement Act. Primarily, she focused on the reauthorization of programs that are important to Maryland citizens. For example, Chapter I of the Act continued federal aid to programs for the educationally and economically disadvantaged. The availability of impact aid, "magnet school" aid and the Women's Educational Equity Act were other key elements in this package. Hayes feels this legislation epitomizes good government—it is a cost-effective program that serves a genuine need.

Hayes sees education as one of the basic, looming issues for the next decade, especially as it relates to the readiness of the nation's workforce. "Many young people are inadequately trained, lacking both technical and basic skills," she says. Efforts will have to be made to match worker skills with the needs of employers, as socio-technological changes are making present skills obsolete, Hayes says.

Hayes is also responsible for monitoring banking, tax, housing, securities, welfare reform, homelessness and budget legislation.

Hayes is a big Baltimore booster, having moved there four years ago.

Kevin S. McGuiness
Minority Staff Director
835 Hart Senate Office Bldg.
224-6770

Expertise: Labor

Following an academic career which included teaching renaissance history in Florence, Italy, Kevin McGuiness settled in with his family's Washington law firm. Specializing in the area of labor law, McGuiness was eventually recruited by the United States Senate and Utah's junior senator, Orrin Hatch.

Then-Chairman of the Senate Committee on Labor and Human Resources, Hatch needed a staffer to assist him with proposed Reagan Administration legislation, particularly the Equal Employment Opportunity Act. While McGuiness joined the staff as labor counsel, he has risen through the ranks to become the committee's minority staff director. As a result, he currently coordinates all committee issues for the senator.

While labor counsel, McGuiness played a key role in a number of legislative accomplishments, including labor services legislation, anti-racketeering laws, the home health care provisions of the Older Americans Act, and legislation involving age discrimination in employment.

As a majority staffer, McGuiness was also responsible for organizing a hearing on Teamsters President Jackie Presser, as well as hearings that eventually led to corruption convictions against the local Operating Engineers Union in Lake Charles, Louisiana.

McGuiness has been active in minimum wage legislation, mandated health care and other proposals that, if passed, McGuiness felt would have had an adverse effect on the Gramm-Rudman deficit reduction bill. In general, McGuiness feels that the federal government cannot craft one labor benefit package that meets every need. Such remedies are best left to negotiations between employees and their employers.

The remainder of the 100th Congress promises to hold a number of important and controversial issues for Hatch and his aide. One bill that McGuiness will continue to be involved in concerns amending the 1935 National Labor Relations Act to bar double breasting in construction firms. McGuiness will also extend his involvement to polygraph testing legislation. Finally, continued focus will be on the Grove City bill, which passed the Senate last year and which Hatch opposes. It is obvious McGuiness takes considerable pride in the staff Hatch has assembled. Whether the issue is job training or health care matters, McGuiness is confident of the expertise of his colleagues. As he says, "They make life easier for me as staff director, and their abilities permit me to concentrate on my chief area, labor law."

Personal: born 4/I/52 in Oakland, California. B.A. Univ. of California, Irvine, 1974. J.D. George Washington Univ., 1980. 1976-1982, labor law specialist, McGuiness & Williams, Washington, DC. 1982-1987, labor counsel, Sen. Orrin Hatch (R-UT). 1987-present, Minority Staff Director, Senate Committee on Labor and Human Resources.

Terry L. Muilenburg
Minority Staff Director
Subcommittee on the Handicapped
625 Hart Senate Office Bldg.
224-1285

Expertise: Handicapped

In the tight fiscal climate of the eighties, few advocates of social programs can claim to have defended their programs successfully against cuts, much less won increases for some and established new ones. But Terry Muilenburg is proud to have played a mostly successful part in legislative battles for programs on behalf of the disabled.

Known for her political acumen, Muilenburg, like many Hill staffers, moved up through the ranks to her current position as Minority Staff Director for the Subcommittee on the Handicapped.

It has not been uncommon for Muilenburg to cross swords with conservatives as she has worked to preserve family planning programs or on behalf of the proposed Civil Rights Restoration Act. This Act would reverse the controversial 1984 Supreme Court Grove City decision by denying federal funds to institutions that discriminate in any of their programs on the basis of race or sex.

Personal: born 9/13/56 in Washington, D.C. B.A. Univ. of Virginia, 1978. 1978-1979, bilingual secretary, International Monetary Fund. 1979-1981, executive secretary to the Director, National Commission on Air Quality. 1981-1984, Staff Assistant and 1984-1986, Professional Staff Member, Subcommittee on Labor, HHS and Education, Senate Committee on Appropriations. 1986, Legislative Aide, Sen. Lowell Weicker (R-CT). 1986-87, Majority Staff Director, Subcommittee on the Handicapped, Senate Committee on Labor and Human Resources. 1987-present, Minority Staff Director, Subcommittee on the Handicapped, Senate Committee on Labor and Human Resources.

The bulk of Muilenburg's work, however, is devoted to advocacy of programs for the disabled, especially oversight of state programs. In addition to winning re-authorization of several existing programs in 1986, the subcommittee spearheaded the drive for three new programs for the handicapped, creating a new state grant program for supportive employment services for the disabled, winning a federal grant for handicapped infants, and mandating states to develop protection and advocacy programs on behalf of mentally ill persons who have been victims of abuse in state institutions.

Muilenburg is especially proud of the last program, which resulted from a nine-month investigation into conditions in state institutions for the mentally ill by Weicker's staff in 1985. In the course of the investigation, Muilenburg and four other staffers visited institutions in 31 states and uncovered many cases of abuse and neglect. The investigation culminated with three days of hearings and considerable publicity, including lead stories on all three networks on the day of the hearing.

In 1988, Muilenburg expects to be involved in two major legislative efforts. First, Weicker plans to introduce a comprehensive "Americans with Disabilities Act" which would outlaw all forms of discrimination against the handicapped. In addition, the Subcommittee will be reauthorizing Weicker's protection and advocacy program for the mentally ill. Also, the Subcommittee will be closely monitoring Finance Committee action on a "Home and Community Quality Services Act," which would provide funds for community-based care as an alternative to institutionalization for the mentally handicapped. "We do not want to see dumping, as has happened with the mentally ill," says Muilenburg.

David H. Nexon
Senior Health Policy Advisor
527 Hart Senate Office Bldg.
224-7675

Personal: born 4/10/45 in Chicago, IL. B.A. Harvard Coll., 1966. M.A. Univ. of Chicago, 1970. Ph.D. Univ. of Chicago, 1974. 1964, Johnson presidential campaign. 1966-67, Management Intern, Office of Economic Opportunity. 1967-68, Spec. Asst. to Manpower Dir., Mayor's Comm. on Human Resources, Pittsburgh, PA. 1971-73, asst. professor, Claremont Coll., Claremont, CA. 1974-75, Charles Taft Post-Doctoral Fellow, Lecturer, Univ. of Cincinnati. 1975-77, Program Mgr., Russell Sage Foundation, New York, NY. 1977-83, Senior Budget Examiner, HCFA Health Branch, OMB. 1983-86, Senior Minority Health Policy Counsel; 1987-present, Senior Health Policy Advisor, Senate Committee on Labor and Human Resources.

Expertise: Health

After twenty-five years in the Senate and countless initiatives in the realm of domestic and foreign policy, the one legislative area with which Sen. Edward Kennedy is most often and readily identified is health care. As Kennedy's senior health advisor and Staff Director for the Health Office of the Senate Labor and Human Resources Committee, David Nexon has been a driving force in shaping the Committee's health policy agenda.

Prior to working for the Committee, Nexon, a former political science professor whose credentials seem endless, served as David Stockman's chief analyst for health care financing at the White house Office of Management and Budget.

In 1983 Nexon joined the Committee as the minority staff health advisor. When Democrats regained control of the Senate in 1987, Kennedy assumed the chairmanship of the Labor and Human Resources Committee and asked Nexon to take on the added duties of Health Staff Director. As such, Nexon oversees virtually every health issue considered by the Committee, including catastrophic health insurance, organ donation, AIDS, home health care, long-term care, Medicare, Medicaid, HMO's and others. In addition to his broad oversight responsibilities, Nexon is a virtuoso in grasping the complexities of health care financing, budgeting techniques and insurance coverage.

During a time of budget cuts and Administration opposition, Nexon has been instrumental in launching a wide range of health related bills, such as the Kennedy-Gephardt Solvency Act of 1984, the Comprehensive Mental Health Service Plan Act of 1986, and the Stewart B. McKinney Emergency Homeless Assistance Act of 1987.

The second session of the 100th Congress will again find Nexon placing special emphasis on increasing citizenry access to adequate health care. More specifically, in an effort to provide basic health protection to millions of uninsured, full-time workers and their families, Kennedy has introduced the Minimum Essential Health Care Act that will mandate employers to offer employees minimal health insurance coverage.

According to one Senate colleague, "Senator Kennedy's leadership in the area of health care is in no small way a positive reflection on David Nexon's knowledge, commitment and staff work. His political coalition on the minimum health benefits proposal is a work of art."

Nexon has been a prolific author and reviewer: "Asymmetry in the Political System: Occasional Activists in the Republican and Democratic Parties, 1956-1964," *American Political Science Review*, September, 1971; "Elections, Parties and Representation," in Louis Maisel and Joseph Cooper, eds, *The Impact of the Electoral Process*, Sage Productions, 1977; "Methodological Issues in the Study of Realignment," in Richard J. Trilling, ed, *Realignment: Electoral and Policy Components*, 1979; "The Politics of Congressional Health Policy in the Second Half of the 1980's," *Medical Care Review*. Book reviewer, *American Political Science Review, American Journal of Political Science*; article referee, *American Political Science Review, American Journal of Political Science, Urban Analysis.*

Nexon is married with one child. Reading is his hobby.

Ellin J. Nolan
Minority Staff Director
Subcommittee on Education, Arts
and Humanities
727 Hart Senate Office Bldg.
224-2962

Expertise: Education

Ellin Nolan's two special concerns throughout her years on Capitol Hill have been funding of special education programs and funding of aid to lower-income students for higher education.

Having financed part of her own education through government loans, Nolan appreciates the need for financial assistance toward higher education. She believes the freedom of all students to choose their institution of higher learning without regard for its cost lies near the heart of the American educational system. In addition, Nolan believes the Pell grant program should receive greater funding so that lower-income students may be relieved of a level of indebtedness which becomes impossible to repay.

Nolan's second area of concern is special education. She has extensive professional and academic experience in special education, and considers it her highest priority. An important legislative activity has been working to resist Administration attempts to convert all special education programs to block grant programs. In that effort, opponents on the Hill have had reasonable success. While the Chapter II programs have been converted to block grants, Chapter I, which contains the programs for educating handicapped children, has remained intact. Nolan admits the block grant funding of Chapter II has met with some initial approval from individual communities because of the flexibility such funding allows, but she believes that future efforts to increase funding of block grants will cause considerable frustration.

Personal: born 1/14/47 in Bryn Mawr, Pennsylvania. B.S. Univ. of Michigan, 1969. M.S. George Washington Univ., 1973. Post-masters work at George Washington Univ. 1970-71, special education, Centreville, VA. 1971-73, teacher, Takoma Park, MD. 1973-1976, Learning Disabilities Teacher, Essex Town, VT. 1976-1982, Curriculum Coordinator and teacher, Essex Town, VT, Supervisory School District. 1978-1979, Instructor, Trinity College, Burlington, VT. 1982-1984, Legislative Assistant, Sen. Robert T. Stafford (R-VT). 1984-1987, Professional Staff Member, Subcommittee on Education, Arts and Humanities. 1987-present, Minority Staff Director, Subcommittee on Education, Arts and Humanities, Committee on Labor and Human Resources.

An experienced public speaker who often represents Sen. Stafford, Nolan is more interested in the fine points of policy and legislation than in politics. While she has served in one elected position, as School Commissioner in Burlington, VT, she does not anticipate ever holding an elected position except at the local level.

Nolan's most important future priority is to find increased funding for special education programs. An increase in the number of high-risk students entering U.S. school systems, coupled with the nation's increasing expectations and acceptance of physically challenged individuals has, according to Nolan, created educational expenses which local school systems will be unable to bear. Nolan feels the federal government must help bear responsibility for the education of these children. "Public education of special need children should begin at birth," says Nolan. With today's technology we can really help children from a very early age—and early education is also cost-effective."

Marsha E. Renwanz
Staff Director
Subcommittee on Children, Family,
    Drugs and Alcoholism
639 Hart Senate Office Bldg.
224-5630

*Personal: born 10/3/51 in
Summerville, New Jersey. B.A.
Douglass Coll., 1973. M.A. Danforth
Fellow, Anthropology, Stanford Univ.,
1974. Ph.D., Danforth Fellow,
Anthropology, Stanford Univ., 1981.
1981-1982, American Political Science
Association Congressional Fellow for
Rep. Ed Markey and Sen. Chris Dodd.
1983-1987, Minority Staff Director,
Subcommittee on Family and Human
Services. 1983-1987, Founding Staff
Director of Senate Children's Caucus.
1987 to present, Staff Director,
Subcommittee on Children, Family,
Drugs and Alcoholism, Committee on
Labor and Human Resources.*

Expertise: Child care, child abuse, parental leave

North Sea oil development in the 1970's spawned a sizeable economic boom in the Shetland Islands off the coast of Scotland. When Marsha Renwanz went to the Shetland Islands to study the repercussions on the small island communities, she was impressed by the child care facilities and parental leave provisions to deal with the flood of young working mothers. Renwanz decided if she wanted to see such child care programs instituted in the United States, she had to "go where policy was made." Within two years, she was Minority Staff Director for Sen. Chris Dodd's (D-CT) Labor Subcommittee on Children, Family, Drugs and Alcoholism.

The Senate Children's Caucus, a bipartisan committee of 34 Senators established in 1983 and co-chaired by Senators Dodd and Specter, was Renwanz' brain child. In her four years as staff director Renwanz organized fourteen hearings on children's issues, from the first congressional hearing on "latchkey children" (children who lack adult supervision, particularly after school, because one or both parents are working) to hearings on childhood poverty and child sexual victimization. During those years, she worked on a number of bills affecting child care. They include the Child Abuse Prevention Federal Challenge Grant Act of 1984, the Drug and Alcohol Abuse Prevention and Treatment Model Projects for High Risk Youth Act of 1986, the Child Development Associate Scholarship Assistance Act of 1985 and the Child Survival Fund Act of 1984.

Over the past year, Renwanz focused her attention on organizing hearings for the Parental and Temporary Medical Leave Act of 1987 (S.249), sponsored by Sen. Dodd, chairman of the Subcommittee. This bill represents a widely perceived need for a directive for employers to establish parental leave, unpaid but with job guaranteed on the parent's return, during the birth, adoption or serious illness of a child. Renwanz also drafted and oversaw the enactment of the Child Abuse Prevention and Treatment Act Reauthorization of 1987," (S. 1663). Renwanz has also organized hearings on a wide range of additional issues affecting children, from child care to children who suffer from alcohol or drug abuse.

She has done research in Mexico and Puerto Rico on women in prison, produced a film in 1970 on prostitutes in New York City called "Pro Girl," and worked in a girl's reformatory school. In November of 1987, she received the National Council of Jewish Women Congressional Staff Award for her dedication to children and family issues.

Thomas M. Rollins
Staff Director and Chief Counsel
428 Dirksen Senate Office Bldg.
224-5465

Personal: born 11/7/55, Panama Canal Zone. B.A. Georgetown Univ. (cum laude) 1978. J.D. Harvard Law School (magna cum laude) 1982. Editor, Harvard Law Review. 1978-1979, Research Assistant, Senate Committee on the Judiciary . 1978-1979, Reporter for New Times and Politics Today magazines. 1982-1983, law clerk to Judge James L. Oakes U.S. Court of Appeals for the Second Circuit. 1983-1985, attorney, Susman, Godfrey & McGowen, Houston, TX. 1983-present, Staff Director and Chief Counsel, Senate Committee on Labor and Human Resources.

Expertise: Health, education, labor, human relations

When Senator Ted Kennedy wants to brainstorm, he calls on Tom Rollins. And although Rollins administered the passage of nineteen bills in the 1987 calendar year, he prefers not to discuss his responsibilities.

Under his jurisdiction are all of the human resources issues under labor, health, and education including terms and conditions of employment such as wages, benefits, safety, health and pensions; all educational spending, teacher retraining and grants; most federal medical programs; public health service; legislation for the homeless; federal non-military research, and federal low-income assistance programs.

Rollins is known among his colleagues for his astounding energy, intellectual capacity and occasionally brusque personality. The nature of the Labor and Human Resources committee requires him to be expert in an incredibly diverse number of subjects.

Rollins cites his main frustration as the tyranny of small decisions that prevent the passing of important legislation. He also says, "I try to remember that most of the members have far more experience than I do. I constantly remind myself that I was only seven years old the day Kennedy was sworn in."

Rollins probably should be classified as a sensitive humanitarian: "When I go into battle for an important human rights issues, I know I'm on the side of the angels."

Calling himself a "gifted stereo player," Rollins' hobbies are also weight lifting, music and dancing.

Robert Silverstein
Staff Director
Subcommittee on the Handicapped
113 Hart Senate Office Bldg.
224-6265

Personal: born 2/19/49 in New York, NY. B.S. Wharton School of Finance and Commerce, Univ. of Pennsylvania, 1971,(cum laude). J.D. Georgetown Univ. Law Center, 1974. 1974-1975, Staff Attorney, Office of the Solicitor, Dept. of Labor. 1975-1978, Director, Legal Standards Project, Lawyers Committee for Civil Rights Under Law. 1978, Attorney-Advisor, Office for Civil Rights, Department of Health, Education, and Welfare. 1979-1985, Long and Silverstein. 1985-1987, Counsel to the House Subcommittee on Select Education, Committee on Education and Labor. 1987-present, Staff Director, Subcommittee on the Handicapped, Committee on Labor and Human Resources.

Expertise: Education and civil rights legislation

Those who are involved with education of the handicapped in public schools–whether a handicapped student, parent of a handicapped student, or teacher of the handicapped–have many reasons to appreciate the work of Bobby Silverstein and the Subcommittee on the Handicapped. Silverstein's best known contributions to this field include drafting reauthorizing legislation used in the House and Senate Title I of the Elementary and Secondary Education Act; the Education of the Handicapped Amendments of 1986 creating new programs for the services of handicapped infants and toddlers, and the equally important report on this bill. Silverstein's method of comprehensive research into the bills he drafts reflects his effort to write bills that meet the needs of people with handicaps to the fullest possible extent.

As an attorney for various civil rights and public interest groups, he developed an expertise in policy law and in preventing violations in statutory law. His clients included groups such as parents of handicapped children and school districts. By the time Tom Harkin (D-IA) asked Silverstein to be Staff Director of the Subcommittee on the Handicapped, Silverstein had established a substantial reputation in the field.

Silverstein is regarded by his colleagues as a top draftsman of conceptual legislation. His colleagues repeatedly stress he is a thorough and skilled legal technician who enjoys their complete confidence and respect. Silverstein values the views of the consumer, the parent, and the advocate in helping shape the philosophy and content of the bills he drafts.

The latest interests of the Subcommittee on the Handicapped are technology issues and long-term care issues. Technology issues cover devices able to improve the quality of a handicapped person's life. Silverstein is also interested in expanding anti-discrimination legislation protecting the rights of persons with physical or mental disabilities.

Silverstein is an avid tennis player who competes in local inter-club tournaments around Washington.

Nancy E. Taylor
Minority Health Policy Director
835 Hart Senate Office Bldg.
224-3191

Expertise: Health policy

A lifelong Utah resident who studied political science as an undergraduate, Nancy Taylor was teaching in Utah when Sen. Orrin Hatch became chairman of the Senate Committee on Labor and Human Resources in 1981. Anxious to contribute to the many changes being realized in Washington at the beginning of the 1980s, Taylor moved to Washington to join the Committee staff.

Taylor works primarily on health and human resources issues which fall under the jurisdictions of the Labor and Human Resources Committee and the Finance Committee. Among her areas of responsibility are health care financing issues, such as catastrophic health care, home health care, capital costs health planning, alcohol and drug abuse and mental health issues.

The first legislation Taylor tackled upon arriving in Washington was the Budget Reconciliation Act of 1981. This Act had become part of President Reagan's attempt to shift control of federal programs to the state level. The most important feature of this shift was the conversion of categorical programs into block grants, which allow the states greater administrative control.

Personal: born 4/6/56 in Salt Lake City, Utah. B.S. Univ. of Utah, 1979. Expects to receive a J.D. from the Columbus School of Law at Catholic Univ.of America in June, 1988. 1981-87, Professional Staff Member, Committee on Labor and Human Resources. 1987-present, Minority Health Policy Director, Committee on Labor and Human Resources.

Taylor worked to help advance these block grant programs in the health area. The efforts were considerably successful, as 19 existing categorical programs were converted into four block grants.

Taylor also contributed to the Child Abuse Act of 1984. This legislation sought to ensure appropriate medical care for severely handicapped infants, and includes provisions to clarify the "Baby Doe" controversy, which arose when a Bloomington, IL, infant with Down's syndrome and an incomplete esophagus was allowed to die. Hatch sponsored a compromise amendment ensuring handicapped babies adequate medical care but also recognizing limits to the extent to which doctors must go in order to save a baby that is certain to die in spite of their efforts.

In addition, Taylor worked with other staff on the Omnibus Health Act of 1986, which successfully combined nine previous bills which had failed to muster enough support on their own. The first of these was a bill designed to increase the supply of vaccines and to provide "no-fault" compensation to the parents of children who suffer ill effects as a result of vaccines. Hatch believes the prohibition of such exports presents disadvantage to smaller, more experimental drug firms. Originally introduced in 1984, Hatch's bill passed only when it became part of the Omnibus Health Bill.

Sarah von der Lippe
Legislative Assistant
527 Hart Senate Office Bldg.
224-6710

Expertise: Poverty and low income issues

When Sarah von der Lippe received a letter from the Senate labor committee asking her to come for an interview, she searched for several days before she could find a manual typewriter to write her acceptance letter. She was in Dakar, Senegal, at the time, living with an African family and doing research for a study on rural energy on a five-month grant from Stanford University. Eventually she found a typewriter at the AID office and was soon on a plane to Washington, D.C.

The first bill she worked on, the Jobs for Employable Dependent Individuals Act, or JEDI, (S.514), passed the Senate by a vote of 99-0. The legislation provides financial incentives to job training agencies which secure permanent jobs for hard-to-place individuals, including the homeless.

She was also involved in the enactment of the Stewart B. McKinney Homeless Assistance Act (S.809), comprehensive legislation providing funds for services and job training for the homeless. It was introduced the same week that JEDI passed, a week that von der Lippe recalls as hectic and exciting.

Personal: born 3/20/63 in New York, New York. B.A. Stanford Univ., 1985 . 1984-1985, Student Director, Stanford Volunteer Network; Conference Director, "You Can Make a Difference: a Conference on Hunger", Stanford Univ. 1984-1986, Consultant and Staff Member, Stanford Public Service Center. 1985, recipient of J.E. Wallace Sterling Award for outstanding volunteer service. 1986-present, Legislative Assistant, Committee on Labor and Human Resources.

She also worked on the Comprehensive Child Care Development Centers Act (S.1542), which provides continuous care for underprivileged children, beginning with prenatal care for mothers. "This bill was a joy to work on . . . If we can make an early investment in the lives of our children, we can break the cycle of poverty," she says. She helped draft Senate Resolution 303, which sets aside a day to inform and educate citizens on the problems of poverty in America.

The problems of poverty have concerned von der Lippe since she was an undergraduate at Stanford, where she organized a major conference on domestic and international poverty with experts from the private and public sectors. "This nation is too wealthy to have 32 million poor people," she maintains.

She relishes the opportunity of working for Sen. Edward Kennedy (D-MA), chairman of the Labor Committee, whom she has admired for many years for his efforts on behalf of the underprivileged. "He is one of the best in the business because he presents the injustice of poverty to the American people and demands that we respond," she says.

Although she loves the pace and challenge of life on the Hill, von der Lippe finds Washington too far from the ocean. An avid sailor in college, she has had little opportunity to pursue her sport since she came to Capitol Hill.

SENATE
COMMITTEE ON RULES AND ADMINISTRATION

William B. Canfield III
Republican Counsel
479 Senate Russell Office Bldg.
224-8923

Personal: born 5/22/46 in Detroit, Michigan. B.A. Denison Univ., 1968, Dean's List. J.D. Detroit Coll. of Law, 1973. 1968-1970, U.S. Army. U.S. Army Commendation Medal, Bronze Star medal nominee, and Republic of Vietnam Civic Action Honor Medal. 1973-1975, trust officer, Detroit Bank and Trust Company. 1975-1976, Subcommittee Counsel, Committee on House Administration. 1976-1978, Counsel to the Librarian, Library of Congress, 1978-1987, Senior Staff Counsel, Select Committee on Ethics. 1987 to present, Republican Chief Counsel, Committee on Rules and Administration.

Expertise: Federal election law

In January, 1987, Bill Canfield began his work as the Republican Chief Counsel at the Senate Rules Committee. In the short time since then, he has performed the unique task of helping educate the Senate on the cost—both economic and political of S. 2, the campaign finance reform bill. His success can be measured by the four Democratic revisions of the bill and a successful Republican filibuster that has stalled Senate floor action. Canfield attributes his success on this "apple pie and motherhood" issue to "showing how the law of unintended consequences would come into play" if the proposal were ever adopted by Congress. In addition, Canfield has drafted two alternative federal campaign finance law proposals, S.1326 and S.1672 (100th Congress).

Canfield not only enjoys working on these types of election law issues, but he is also a recognized expert in this area. During his years at the Senate Select Committee on Ethics, Canfield's work ran the gamut of the Committee's broad jurisdictional mandate. He is recognized for helping formulate the theory behind the Code of Conduct as found in the Standing Rules of the Senate.

To take full advantage of Canfield's expertise in this area, Senator Ted Stevens has assigned Canfield additional responsibilities relating to Stevens's work on the Senate Committee on Governmental Affairs.

Canfield's efforts in this area have included working on the Oversight and Investigations Subcommittee's hearings on the Wedtech scandal, writing amendments to the Bill to reauthorize the independent counsel statute, and reviewing the role of presidential transition committees.

According to Bonnie Parker, Deputy Director of the Senate Select Committee on Ethics, Canfield, who worked under an equal number of Democratic and Republican chairmen at the Select Committee, proved himself to be a "balanced, bipartisan player." She says he still gets calls at Rules about ethics questions."

Canfield's Senate colleagues joke that he has been on every page of The *Washington Post* except the front page and the obituary. Canfield collects rare Civil War books and has restored a 1954 MGTF Roadster. In addition, Canfield says he was the winner, in 1972, of a transcontinental automobile race ("The Cannonball Baker Sea-to-Shining-Sea Memorial Trophy Dash") which was the subject of three motion pictures, two of which starred Burt Reynolds.

William McWhorter Cochrane
Senior Adviser
305 Russell Senate Office Bldg.
224-0275

Personal: born 3/16/17 in Newton, North Carolina. A.B. Univ. of North Carolina, 1939; LL.B./J.D. Univ. of North Carolina Law School, 1941. LL.M. Yale Univ. Law School, 1951. 1941-1967, U.S. Naval Reserve; released as Lt. in 1945 after service as deck officer of minesweeper; 1942-1945, active duty; 1945-1954, asst. director, and from 1952, administrative director, associate research professor of public law and government, managing editor, Popular Government, Inst. of Government, Univ. of North Carolina. 1954-1958, Executive Secretary and Legislative Counsel, Sen. W. Kerr Scott (D-NC). 1958-1972, Administrative Assistant, Sen. B. Everett Jordan (D-NC). 1972-1980, Staff Director; 1981-1986, Minority (Democratic) Staff Director; 1987-present, Senior Adviser, Senate Committee on Rules and Administration.

Expertise: Administration of committees and offices

Cochrane came to the Senate as counsel to Senator Kerr Scott in 1954. While he never intended to stay on the Hill, Cochrane has become a familiar face in the sea of changing faces.

After his three and one-third years of service to Senator Scott, he went on to serve as Administrative Assistant to Senator Jordan for nearly 15 years. This led to his position on the Rules Committee. In his work with the committee, Cochrane has briefed almost every Senator on the Hill today, including former college roommate Senator Terry Sanford (D-NC).

Although the administration of the Rules Committee is Cochrane's area of "expertise" (a term he refuses to use), colleagues say he is best known for his know-how and ability to get the job done. A 1987 edition of *Roll Call* listed the key staffers in the Senate by 3 symbols–a light bulb for know-how, a key for access and a muscle for the obvious. Cochrane had both a light bulb and a key next to his name.

Cochrane is known especially for his contributions to the 1974 Budget Control and Impoundment Act, the creation of the Office of Technology Assessment and the Federal Election Commission. As staff director, he also oversaw the Rules Committee hearings of Gerald Ford and Nelson Rockefeller when the 25th Amendment was put to the test for the first time.

One is struck by his friendly and unassuming manner which greets veteran Senators and Hill newcomers alike in an office that seems to be bursting from everything that Cochrane has forced it to accommodate. The office is filled with reports and steeped in history. There are photos of him walking soon-to-be Presidents to their inauguration. Cochrane has been involved in putting together every inauguration since Lyndon Johnson. He is also active in staff work for the Joint Committee on the Library, which has guided the expansive growth of the Library of Congress into the world's largest library.

What has kept Bill Cochrane in the Senate for more than 33 years? (Longer than any senator except John Stennis.) His respect for the institution. He believes if you are lucky enough to get to know the members of the House and Senate as individuals, you'll find that they're "pretty special people."

James O. King
Majority Staff Director
305 Senate Russell Office Bldg.
224-6352

Expertise: Administrative

Jim King has worked for five Kentucky governors and several educational institutions—most particularly The University of Kentucky—overseeing policies, management, and personnel.

While a relative newcomer to the Senate Rules Committee, areas he has handled during his first ten months include telephone systems, computers, and policies affecting the Architect of the Capitol—one of the Hill's more politicized positions.

In 1988, King will play a key role in a review of the Senate rules and procedures.

Although the Rules Committee has the meticulous job of approving every voucher in the Senate, King says the Committee's biggest problem is a Senate-wide one—maintaining systems to improve the operational efficiency of the Senate. He feels since the overwhelming number of issues that come before Rules are nonpartisan, the Committee is less partisan than most. Furthermore, King notes that Senators Ford and Stevens, and their staffs, work particularly well together. Republicans agree that King's background is not in Congress but management and he brings a wealth of experience to the job. His management style is revealed as he explains that the professional staff of the Rules Committee need the freedom to accomplish their work in their individual areas of expertise.

Feeling most at home in Kentucky and in Kentucky politics, Jim King commutes to Lexington on weekends.

Personal: born 12/11/30 in Covington County, Alabama. 1951-1955, U.S. Air Force. B.S. Univ.of Alabama, 1957. M.A. Univ. of Alabama 1959. 1959-1974, various positions in Kentucky state government. 1974, Secretary of the Cabinet, Gov. Wendell Ford. 1975, Executive Director Office of Management Policy Analysis, Univ. of KY. 1975-1980, Administrative Assistant, Sen. Wendell Ford. 1981-1982, Secretary of Cabinet, Gov. John Y. Brown. 1982, Administrative Assistant to the President, Univ. of KY. 1982-1983, Secretary of Cabinet, Mayor Harvey Sloane. 1983-1986, V.P. for Admin., Univ. of KY. 1987-present, Majority Staff Director, Committee on Rules and Administration.

Charles S. Konigsberg
Minority Deputy Counsel
481 Senate Russell Bldg.
224-8923

Expertise: Budget process, Senate procedure

When Chuck Konigsberg, as an undergraduate at Kenyon College, met Wyoming Congressman Dick Cheney, he had no idea it would mark the beginning of his congressional career. After serving as a student guide for Cheney when the congressman participated in a conference on the Gambier, Ohio, campus, Konigsberg was offered an internship in Cheney's Washington office.

One internship led to another, fostering an interest in the budget process and resulting in an article on amending the 1974 budget act in Notre Dame's Journal of Legislation. That, in turn, led to a job on the Senate Budget Committee staff, where he spent three years reviewing legislation to ensure that it conformed to requirements under the Budget Act and the new Gramm-Rudman-Hollings deficit reduction act.

But like many on the Hill, Konigsberg found himself a casualty of the change in the Senate majority after the 1986 elections. With the Democrats back in control, his position on the Budget Committee was eliminated. He soon landed a job, though, with Alaska Senator Ted Stevens, who holds the ranking minority slot on the Rules and Administration Committee.

Personal: Born 7/18/58 in Cleveland, Ohio. A.B. Kenyon Coll., 1980 (Alpha Lambda Omega, Phi Beta Kappa, John Chestnut Memorial Prize). J.D. Case Western Reserve Univ. 1983 (executive editor, Law Review). 1983-87, staff attorney, Senate Committee on the Budget. 1983-1986, staff attorney, Senate Committee on the Budget. 1987-present, Minority Deputy Counsel, Senate Committee on Rules and Administration. Admitted to Ohio State Bar, 1983; DC Bar, 1984. Author: "Amending Section 2 of Voting Rights Act of 1965," Case Western Law Review; "Amending the Congressional Budget Act of 1974," Notre Dame Journal of Legislation, Winter 1984.

"I learned a lot during during my three years at the Budget Committee, but I enjoy the diversity I now have with Senator Stevens. It has worked out really well."

His primary responsibility is assisting Stevens on the Rules Committee, although he has also helped the Senator with his Governmental Affairs Committee responsibilities as a conferee on the omnibus trade bill and the Budget Reconciliation Bill. Right now, Konigsberg is in the middle of a comprehensive review of the Senate rules and committee system, with the goal of improving the chamber's efficiency and addressing frustrations that came out of last year's budget process.

Although the meeting with Cheney proved to be the impetus for Konigsberg's congressional career, public policy has always been a part of his life. His father spent many years in public serving as mayor of a town in the Cleveland suburbs.

Konigsberg enjoys spending his free time working with the Jewish community in Washington, and he recently led a group on a tour of Israel.

Wayne A. Schley
Republican Staff Director
479 Senate Russell Office Bldg.
224-8923

*Personal: born in Hamilton, Montana.
A.A. Shasta Coll. B.S. Sacramento
State Univ.,1963. Attended Univ. of
Alaska-Fairbanks. M.S. Public
Relations, American Univ., 1975.
Harvard Univ. Program for Senior
Managers in Government, 1982. 1968-
1970, High School Administrator.
1971-1977, Legislative Assistant to
Sen. Ted Stevens(R-AK). 1977-1980,
Minority Staff Dir., Subcommittee on
Civil Service, Post Office, and General
Services. 1987-present, Republican
Staff Director, Committee on Rules
and Administration.*

Expertise: Postal Service, federal personnel

A self-described "workaholic," Wayne Schley lives only four blocks from the office. As Republican Staff Director on the Senate Rules Committee, Schley continues to work on the many issues he has dealt with during his ten-year tenure with Senator Ted Stevens.

Schley is a recognized expert on Postal Service legislation and as such he was a leading candidate for appointment to the Postal Rate Commission in 1981.

Schley notes that, while many offices give postal issues to a new staffer, his ten-years' experience in this area create opportunities an inexperienced staffer would not seize. He was a major player in the passage of the Mail Consumer Fraud legislation, as well as various postal appropriations bills. In addition, Schley represents Senator Stevens at many postal and federal employee union meetings across the country. In addition, he has worked on Presidential Inaugural and Swearing-In ceremonies, co-chaired the 1973 Presidential Inaugural Ball-Natural History Museum Site, and is a member of the Congressional Intern Advisory Board.

At the Rules Committee, Schley views his position as nonpartisan and his role as providing and enhancing Senate service. As Republican Staff Director, he works on issues affecting Senate business and administration, the Library of Congress, the Government Printing Office, and the Smithsonian Institution.

One Senate colleague notes that Schley is "a low-key guy" who is extremely accessible: "he's the kind of guy that I can barge into his office, interrupt him, and always get responsive, constructive help." Furthermore, while at the Rules Committee, Schley has been a "good and persistent ally" against "a lot of inertia."

Schley is a "history buff" who travels around the Washington area visiting historical sites.

Gerald W. Siegel
Chief Counsel
305 Senate Russell Office Bldg.
224-0279

Personal: born 9/21/17 in Waterloo, Iowa. A.B. State Univ. of Iowa, 1941. LL.B. Yale Law School, 1947. 1942-1946, U.S. Army Air Force. 1947-1953, Attorney and Executive Assistant to the Chairman, U.S. Securities and Exchange Commission. 1953-1958, Chief Counsel, U.S. Senate Democratic Policy Committee. 1958-1961, Lecturer and Member of Faculty, Harvard Business School. 1961-1975, Vice President and Counsel, The Washington Post. 1975-1978, Counsel, Clifford, Warnke, Glass, McIlwain and Finney. 1979, Chief Staff Counsel, U.S. Court of Appeals for the D.C. Circuit. 1979-present, Chief Counsel, Committee on Rules and Administration.

Expertise: Rulemaking, budgetary procedure

Gerry Siegel is a man rich with memories of a productive career in government service and still going strong as Chief Counsel of the Senate Rules Committee.

In his current position, one of Siegel's primary areas of focus has been his work on a two-year budget process for Senator Wendell Ford (D-KY). These efforts have yet to bear fruit.

Siegel describes the bulk of his work as "undramatic," yet often it is the minutiae that keeps the Senate operating. On the Rules Committee, Siegel is responsible for rule-making, regulations, allowances and other administrative activities of the Committee, and all legislative matters except federal election law.

Some issues at the Rules Committee, according to Siegel, can be difficult to handle since he must balance the demands of individual Senators and their staffs.

As Counsel to the Democratic Policy Committee from 1953 to 1958, Siegel worked closely with then-Senate Majority leader Lyndon B. Johnson. According to Siegel, LBJ's jurisdiction in those days was "Chairman of Everything," which thrust Siegel into the forefront of some of LBJ's successes including two landmark Civil Rights Acts in 1957 and 1960, the Small Business Investment Company Act, the first public television law, and space legislation in 1958.

When asked about the politics of policymaking, Siegel is quick to say he prefers his legislative work—or in his words, he prefers to "stick to my knitting." Indeed, he says that LBJ always described his aptitude for politics as a man who "couldn't run for dogcatcher in Blanco County, Texas."

In his free time from the Rules Committee, Siegel enjoys theater, bridge, and tennis.

SENATE
COMMITTEE ON SMALL BUSINESS

John W. Ball III
Staff Director and Chief Counsel
428A Russell Senate Office Bldg.
224-8497

Personal: born 6/30/55 in Batesville, Arkansas. B.A. (Honors) Hendrix College, 1977. J.D. (Honors) University of Arkansas, Fayetteville, 1980. 1980-82, Law Clerk, The Hon. William R. Overton, U.S. District Judge (d). 1982-83, Law Clerk, The Hon. Richard S. Arnold, U.S. Circuit Judge for the Eighth Circuit, Little Rock, Ark. 1983-84, Legislative Assistant, Senator Dale Bumpers, U.S. Senate. 1985-86, Minority Staff Director and Chief Counsel, U.S. Senate Small Business Committee. 1986 to present, Staff Director and Chief Counsel, Senate Small Business Committee.

Expertise: Issues related to small business, appropriations, the judiciary.

As the top staffer on the Senate Small Business Committee, John Ball is the Hill expert on small business programs or any issue that affects the U.S. small business community.

Beginning with the Reagan Administration's proposal to abolish the Small Business Administration (SBA), Ball has been in the thick of discussions on small business issues since 1985. As Minority Staff Director and Chief Counsel before the Democrats won control of the Senate in 1987, he was involved in the drafting and negotiation of S. 408 (P.L. 99-272), the SBA authorization bill, and worked to ensure the interests of small business are represented in the 1986 tax reform bill.

When Senator Dale Bumpers (D-AR) took over as chairman in 1987, Ball became Staff Director and Chief Counsel for the full committee and began to examine several areas, including the cost and availability of health benefits for small business, and the impact of government-mandated benefits legislation. He also drafted the small business title to the 1987 trade bill, designed to increase participation of small business in international trade, and was responsible for two small business finance bills which have passed the Senate, H.R. 2166 and S. 437. Ball has been the principal staff member overseeing the committee's investigation of the Wedtech scandal, and supervised drafting of S. 1993, a major bill to reform and restructure SBA's Sec. 8(a) minority contract assistance program. In addition, he continues to pursue the chairman's agenda for the Second Session of the 100th Congress, including S. 1929, a bill establishing the Corporation for Small Business Investment (COSBI), as well as reauthorization of SBA programs.

Ball has served as a resource person for the Small Business Council of the Democratic National Committee and freely advised a number of 1986 Senate campaigns on small business issues.

One of the more important influences on Ball was the late U.S. District Judge William R. Overton, who died in 1987 at the age of 47. "The Judge probably shaped or encouraged my professional outlook more than anyone else", says Ball. Ball clerked for Overton during the time the judge presided over the controversial "creation-science" case, McLean v. Arkansas Board of Education, (1982), which became the focus of international attention. The Court held the Arkansas statute mandating the teaching of creation science unconstitutional following a celebrated eight-day trial in 1981.

Patricia B. Barker
Counsel
428A Russell Senate Office Bldg.
224-8495

Expertise: Banking, insurance, securities

Coming to Washington from Little Rock, Arkansas, considered to be a leading investment center, Patty Barker felt at home on the Small Business Committee covering banking, insurance and securities issues.

Judiciary issues also are among Barker's responsibilities, including school prayer legislation, bankruptcy, and antitrust issues. She also has worked on campaign finance reform legislation, such as the Senatorial Election Campaign Act of 1987.

Primarily, Barker has focused her efforts on banking and insurance issues. In the 99th Congress, she helped to attract support for the Financial Institution Integrity Act of 1985, S. 736, introduced by Senator Bumpers to close the so-called "nonbank bank loophole" in the Bank Holding Company Act which allows financial institutions to get around certain banking regulations. A more extensive nonbank bank loophole closing provision was later included in the Competitive Equality Banking Act of 1987.

More recently, Barker has focused on the liability insurance crisis, a problem the 1986 White House Small Business Conference listed as the biggest barrier facing small businesses. Barker has been Bumpers's chief aide on the issue for the last two years, and plans to work with the Committee members on possible insurance reform proposals.

Personal: born 12/7/57 in Little Rock, Arkansas. B.A. Southwestern at Memphis (Rhodes), 1980. J.D. Univ. of Arkansas, 1985. 1980-1982, Legislative Research Specialist, Arkansas Legislative Council. 1985-present, Counsel, Senate Committee on Small Business.

One of Barker's main goals on the Small Business Committee is to encourage banks to increase lending to small businesses through the use of the various small business lending and investment programs made available at the Small Business Administration (SBA). "Small business provides 80 percent of the new jobs in the country," Barker says, "It would be an even bigger boom to the economy if more banks would use SBA programs and make available the capital needed by new and growing small businesses."

Softball is a tradition on the Hill and Barker does her part as one of the top players on the Bumpers softball team, where she has earned the team's "Most Valuable Player" award. Otherwise, if she isn't playing tennis she can be found on a golf course or riding her bike around her Capitol Hill neighborhood.

Ray C. Culver III
Chief Counsel on Agriculture
428 Russell Senate Office Bldg.
224-3188

Personal: born 9/29/56 in Greenville, Mississippi. B.A. Louisiana State Univ. 1978. J.D. Univ. of Arkansas Law, 1981. LL.M., Univ. of Arkansas Law, 1982. 1980-1981, Public Defenders Office, Fourth Judicial Circuit. 1981-present, Contributing Writer, Agricultural Law Update. *1982-87, Legislative Assistant, Sen. Dale Bumpers (D-AR). 1987-present, Agriculture Counsel, Senate Committee on Small Business.*

Expertise: Agriculture, agri-business

Agriculture is to the state of Arkansas what oil is to Texas or fishing to Maine. And so it was, when Arkansas Senator, Dale Bumpers (D-AR), became chairman of a committee that plays an important role in overseeing small farmers, he naturally turned to the same person he had relied on for five years on his personal staff, Ray "Chuck" Culver.

With a degree from the only agricultural law program in the country, and part of a family rooted in an agricultural past, Culver has become an agriculture legislative and legal expert on the Hill, today serving as Chief Agriculture Counsel for the Small Business Committee and its Subcommittee on Rural Economy and Family Farming.

While a personal staffer representing the leading producing state in rice and poultry, Culver was in the thick of the battle on several fronts. He was on the floor during the famous Pryor-Bumpers "rice recipe" filibuster, which ended successfully after the two Senators read rice recipes until rice farmers were protected in the 1984 "mini-farm" bill.

In the 98th Congress, Culver helped draft the "Huxtable" bill, which waived the Flood Control Act of 1928 law exempting the Corps of Engineers from damage done to local communities by Corps' projects. The bill forced the Corps to compensate persons and businesses in eastern Arkansas which suffer damage due to Corps' activities. Culver's legislative director says the bill's passage was "nothing short of a miracle."

On the Small Business Committee, Culver has concentrated on the problems of agribusiness. More specifically, he is focusing on how small agribusinesses, e.g., fertilizer and tractor dealerships, are affected by the farm crisis, and by government programs which pay farmers not to plant crops—thus reducing demand for fertilizer and all the other goods and services which make up the rural economy.

A fan of the Arkansas Razorbacks and the Louisiana State Tigers, Culver spends the "off-season" carefully assembling and painting additions to his elaborate set of miniature Napoleonic War soldiers. He also entertains a passion for Cajun cooking—a hobby that requires knowing a lot of rice recipes.

A proud Democrat who says "if it has a 'D' in it I'm for it," he yearns for a return to the day when the government's agriculture policy was almost exclusively conducted by the "farm bloc," a small group of farm-state senators with a lot of clout. "I'm concerned that the government has allowed about every group to dictate the direction of farm policy but the farmer," says Culver.

Robert J. Dotchin
Minority Staff Director
622 Senate Hart Office Bldg.
224-8494

Personal: born 12/13/49 in Manchester, Connecticut. B.A. Univ. of Connecticut, 1971. Graduate studies, Univ. of Connecticut, 1972. 1972-74, Legislative Aide, Sen. Lowell P. Weicker, Jr. (R-CT) 1974-77, Legislative Director, Sen. Lowell P. Weicker, Jr. 1977-80, Minority Staff Director, Senate Small Business Committee. 1986 to present, Minority Staff Director, Small Business Committee.

Expertise: All issues related to small business

Beginning as Minority Staff Director in 1977, Bob Dotchin has made a name for himself in his work on small business concerns—as he begins his second decade on the Small Business Committee staff.

Over the past ten years, which included six years as Majority Staff Director under then-Chairman Senator Lowell Weicker, Jr. (R-CT), Dotchin has played a significant role on scores of small business initiatives—relating to tax, government procurement, finance, and international trade—during a period in the nation some have called the "decade of the entrepreneur."

Since 1981, among other legislative accomplishments, Dotchin was among the key players directly responsible for elevating the status of the Small Business Committee from a "select" to a "standing" committee with legislative authority. Dotchin has been instrumental in the fight to preserve the Small Business Administration (SBA), scheduled for elimination in President Reagan's Fiscal Year 1986 and 1987 budgets. Other legislative accomplishments include working on the enactment of the Small Business Innovation Research Act; the SBA Secondary Market Improvement Act; the White House Conference on Small Business Authorization Act; the Small Business and Federal Procurement Competition Enhancement Act; and certain key provisions in the Economic Recovery Tax Act of 1981, including a more graduated corporate tax rate. He also helped establish the first advisory council for a Senate Committee, consisting of twenty-five small business owners from around the country.

In his free time, Dotchin is a golf enthusiast. His favorite getaways include Hilton Head and Cape Hatteras.

Nancy H. Kelley
Professional Staff Member
428A Russell Senate Office Bldg.
224-2809

Personal: born 1/15/40 in Sheffield, Alabama. B.A. Univ. of North Alabama, 1964. M.A. Univ. of North Alabama, 1974. 1961-64, reporter, Birmingham News. 1964-1966, English Teacher, Coffee High School, Florence, Alabama. 1974-1977, Small Business Proprietor, Fabric Shop. 1979-1982, Staff Member, Tennessee Valley Authority (TVA). 1982-1986, Legislative Staffer, Sen. Dale Bumpers (D-AR). 1987-present, Professional Staff Member, Senate Small Business Committee.

Expertise: Small business, labor, FDA

When Senator Dale Bumpers became chairman of the Small Business Committee and was looking for new committee staff, he found a logical choice in a familiar face. As a member of Bumpers's staff for four years, Kelley had dealt with Food and Drug Administration (FDA) regulations and labor affairs, and continues to supervise those issues from the small business perspective as a professional staffer.

Not long after Bumpers became chairman, Kelley began to make her mark on the Committee—which she sees as the ombudsman for small manufacturers responsible for many of the medical products on the shelves of the nation's drugstores. S. 1808, a bill she champions, is cosponsored by such political opposites as Senators Kennedy and Hatch, and would prevent harmless devices, such as RGP contact lenses, from undergoing the same lengthy and costly process for approval as more risky products. As a result of this bill, such products would be more readily available to the consumer at cheaper prices, and small manufacturers would not be bankrupted by high legal costs and unwarranted bureaucratic delays.

In the field of labor, Kelley heads up the Committee's critical examination of S. 79, the High Risk Occupational Disease bill. "The goal of this bill is laudable, but it could open a 'can of worms' . . . there must be a better way."

An amateur archeologist, she follows a passion first begun as a child when she discovered scores of ancient Indian artifacts near her home on the Tennessee River, an area now well-known for being rich in paleolithic gems. When vacationing, if she isn't participating in a large archaeological dig, she might be found fly fishing in a backwoods stream somewhere.

A self-described "yellow-dog" Democrat who made her first political speech at the age of 12 for her father, a probate judge, Kelley feels right at home in politics, and isn't shy about speaking up for small business. "My goal everyday is to make the playing field level for the small businessman—to give him a chance against the big guys who operate in a world weighted in their favor," she says. And she should know. She is also one of the few Senate staffers who has actually owned a small business.

Charles E. Ludlam
Chief Tax Counsel
428A Russell Senate Office Bldg.
224-3095

Expertise: Tax, trade, economic and regulatory issues

During the tax reform hearings, while the nation's leading corporations were fighting it out in "Gucci Gulch"—the hallway outside the committee rooms where scores of lobbyists were crowded—the small business person and Sen. Dale Bumpers were being represented by Chuck Ludlam.

With 11 years on Capitol Hill behind him, beginning as an intern in 1965, combined with experience in the White House, service overseas and private law practice, Ludlam is a veteran staffer in the Senate who brings with him a broader perspective.

As a lawyer at the Federal Trade Commission (FTC), Ludlam was the trial counsel for two major deceptive advertising adjudications and won three awards for his performance. He went on to serve as a manager for the Hart-Scott-Rodino Antitrust Improvement and Ethics in Government Acts, and authored the first law on organizational conflict of interest in federal procurement. He was also the principal legal advisor to the Carter White House for the Administration's regulatory reform initiatives. While working on the Joint Economic Committee, he authored the "natural resource subsidy" provision of the 1984 House trade remedies legislation.

Personal: born 1/1/45 in Sewickley, Pennsylvania. B.A. Stanford Univ., 1967. J.D. Univ. of Michigan, 1972. 1968-1970, Peace Corps Volunteer, Nepal. 1972-1975, trial attorney, Federal Trade Commission, Bureau of Consumer Protection. 1975-1979, Counsel, Subcommittees on Administrative Practice and Separation of Powers, Senate Judiciary Committee. 1979-1981, Legal Counsel, White House Domestic Policy Staff. 1981-1982, attorney, Musick, Peeler and Garrett. 1982-1985, Assistant to the Chairman, Joint Economic Committee. 1985-present, Chief Tax Counsel, Senate Small Business Committee.

Since coming to the Small Business Committee, Ludlam has worked on tax reform and trade, and drafted the "Agenda for Competitiveness", introduced by Committee Chairman Bumpers. The agenda includes three separate bills: one regarding state and local competitiveness initiatives, S.930; one regarding capital formation for start-up small businesses and enterprises, S.931, and the last regarding cash profit sharing incentives, S. 932.

He sees all three bills as steps toward innovative alternatives for a national industrial policy: "To restore American competitiveness, we need to create active participation between government, business, labor and the non-profit sector."

Ludlam takes his hours off the Hill seriously. An experienced white water enthusiast, he is well known for organizing rafting trips for staffers.

Ludlam is a veteran in a field where many of his colleagues have left for comfortable positions in the private sector. He remains because, "the issues are important and complicated—and because one person can make a difference."

William B. Montalto
Procurement Policy Counsel
428A Russell Senate Office Bldg.
224-8490

Expertise: Government contract law

One of the most cherished commodities on the Hill is the technical expert, and Bill Montalto fits the bill in one of the most arcane subject areas—government contracting.

As a respected government contracts attorney with extensive policy experience, Montalto was recruited onto the Senate Governmental Affairs Committee staff in 1981 to assist with the Senate consideration of the comprehensive *Proposal for a Uniform Federal Procurement System*. Before joining the Senate staff, Montalto served with the American Bar Association's project that drafted the *Model Procurement Code for State and Local Governments*, a legislative proposal for revamping public purchasing by state and local governments, a set of *Recommended Regulations* to implement the model statute; a *Model Procurement Ordinance*; and a condensed version of the Code for smaller units of local government. Prior to that, Montalto was on active duty with the United States Army Reserve, with his last assignment being at HQ, US Army Materiel Command. Since leaving active service, he has continued his Reserve military service, most recently as a Mobilization Planning Officer at AMC Headquarters.

Personal: born 12/21/44 in Jamaica, New York. B.A. New York Univ., 1967. M.A. New York Univ., 1973. J.D. Washington Coll. of Law, American Univ., 1976. 1967-present, U.S. Army Reserve, Major, Vietnam Veteran, Bronze Star. 1975-1981, American Bar Association, Model Procurement Code for State and Local Governments Project, Assistant Project Director and Project Director. 1981, ABA, Director of Government Grants. 1981-1983, Procurement Policy Counsel, Senate Governmental Affairs Committee. 1983-present, Procurement Policy Counsel, Small Business Committee.

During his six years as a Senate staffer, Montalto has been deeply involved in most of the major legislation relating to fundamental changes in the federal procurement system. He was a principal staff participant in the drafting of the "Competition in Contracting Act of 1984" (P.L. 98-369), the "Defense Procurement Reform Act of 1984," Title XII of the FY 85 DoD Authorization Act (P.L. 98-525), and the "Small Business and Federal Procurement Competition Enhancement Act of 1984" (P.L. 98-577). He was also deeply involved in the 1983 reauthorization of the Office of Federal Procurement Policy (P.L. 98-191) and the passage of the "Prompt Payment Act of 1982" (P.L. 97-177)

"Despite the fact that Federal procurement expenditures represent one-fifth of the Federal budget, $197 billion in FY 87, the topic of federal procurement is not one that naturally stirs the passion or even the interest of Senators. The key to being effective is to be able to present understandable and compelling analyses of the problems and solutions, avoiding incomprehensible procurement jargon, and then to very carefully fashion workable legislative solutions, recognizing existing operational realities of the system. The greatest challenge came during the height of media attention to procurement problems at the Defense Department. With public and Member demands for immediate and sweeping solutions at their strongest, I am particularly satisfied with the effective and responsible legislative responses finally enacted."

"The challenges continue as the Committee on Small Business seeks to make the federal procurement market a more accessible market, a more user friendly market, for the small firm which wishes to participate as a federal contractor or a subcontractor. And they hope to participate despite the reality that the system remains inherently complex, prone to paperwork, and too often fraught with dangers of financial ruin, if one fails to recognize the differences from the commercial marketplace. But my satisfaction is knowing that many small firms consistently do well, and that they comprise the foundation of the nation's industrial and technological bases on which the Defense Department and the civilian agencies are dependent."

Montalto also has a substantial expertise in federal grant law, having co-authored several law review articles on legal remedies of grantees and procurement under federal grants. He served as Associate Editor of *Federal Grant Law* (ABA, 1982).

Montalto is active in a number of professional associations and activities. He is active in the American Bar Association, particularly its Section of Public Contract Law, and the D.C. Bar Association. A ten-year member of the National Contract Management Association, he serves on its National Board of Advisors. He also serves on the Advisory Board for American University's Procurement Management Program in the College of Business Administration, and as a faculty member for George Washington University's procurement courses for Government and Industry, a continuing education program sponsored by the School of Government and Business Administration. Montalto is also a Charter Life Member of the National Assistance Management Association, the professional association of grants managers, where he served three terms on the Board of Directors and two terms as national secretary.

A long-time boatman, Montalto tries to catch as many hours as possible aboard *Take Two*, which is docked at the Gangplank Marina on the Washington Channel. He is also a member of the Army-Navy Club of Washington.

SENATE
COMMITTEE ON VETERANS' AFFAIRS

Anthony J. Principi
Republican Chief Counsel/Staff
   Director
202 Hart Senate Office Bldg.
224-2074

*Personal: born 4/16/44 in New York,
NY. B.S. U.S. Naval Academy, 1967.
J.D. Seton Hall Univ., 1975. 1967-69,
Engineering Office, USS Joseph P.
Kennedy. 1969-70, Unit Commander,
River Patrol Force, Tra Cu, Vietnam.
1970-72, Staff Officer, Navy Education
and training Center, Newport, RI.
1975-79, various assignments with the
Judge Advocate General's Corps. incl.
Chief Defense Atty, San Diego, CA.
1979-80, Legislative Counsel, Dept. of
the Navy, Washington, D.C. 1980-83,
Counsel, Senate Committee on Armed
Services. 1983-84, Assoc. Dep. Adm.
for Congressional and Public Affairs,
Veterans' Administration. 1984-
present, Republican Chief Counsel/
Staff Director, Senate Committee on
Veterans' Affairs. Chairman,
Legislative Subc., General Practice
Section, American Bar Assoc. Bronze
Star with Combat "V". Vietnamese
Cross of Gallantry. Navy
Commendation with Combat "V".
Navy Combat Action Medal.*

Expertise: Veterans' issues

Sen. Alan Simpson (R-WY) found a seasoned veteran for chief
counsel and staff director of the Veterans' Affairs Committee when
he asked Principi to come to the Hill in 1984. At that time, Principi
was Associate Deputy Administrator for Congressional and Public
Affairs, as well as White House liaison, at the Veterans
Administration. A graduate of the Naval Academy, a decorated
Vietnam veteran and a former counsel to then-Armed Service
Committee Chairman John Tower (R-TX), Principi's credentials
were impeccable and his understanding of veterans' and military
affairs formidable. He not only knew the "ins and outs" of
Congress, but he was eager to return to Capitol Hill.

Principi accepted the job and began working on major legislation
to provide temporary disability payments for veterans suffering
form several diseases linked to the herbicide Agent Orange. The
effects of Agent Orange had been debated for years and were also
the subject of litigation. Under Principi's leadership, the
Committee moved forward with a bill, which was enacted into law
in late 1984.

Since then, Principi has had to deal with other issues just as
contentious, such as how to meet the growing needs of older
veterans in an era of fiscal austerity; how to better assure quality
health care at the VA's 172 hospitals and 226 out-patient clinics;
and how to reduce defaults and foreclosures in the VA's home loan
program. Through it all, he has remained open-minded and,
according to colleagues, on good terms with veterans' groups that
lobby the Committee.

Principi has also devoted a great deal of his attention to a proposal
to elevate the VA to cabinet-level status. In Principi's view, it is an
idea whose time has come. "The VA is the largest independent
federal agency, with a workforce of nearly 250,000. It administers
the world's largest health care delivery system as well as
education (GI bill) and housing (VA loans) programs that have a
tremendous impact on the economy," says Principi. "Contrary to
what the critics say, making the VA a cabinet-level department
would give us greater policy coordination and help us do more
with less," he says.

Although he was hired by Simpson, Principi now works for
Chairman Frank Murkowski (R-AK). Their relationship, Principi
says, has "grown tremendously. We spend a lot of time together
discussing defense-related issues."

Principi considers San Diego, his home and he plans to one day
return there to practice law and perhaps get involved in politics.
But for now, he says, "I feel very fortunate to be involved in
making public policy that affects a great many Americans."

Edward P. Scott
General Counsel
414 Russell Senate Office Bldg.
224-9126

Personal: born 12/17/37 in Somers Point, New Jersey. B.A. Rutgers Univ. 1959. J.D. Univ. of Pennsylvania, 1963. 1963 -1967, Staff Judge-Advocate, U.S. Air Force. 1967, Associate, Arnold and Porter, Washington, DC. 1968-1973, Peace Corps staff, Director of the Peace Corps program in Korea. 1973-1977, staff attorney, Mental Health Law Project and Director, Mental Health Legislative Guide Project. 1977-1981, General Counsel, Senate Veterans' Affairs Committee. 1981-87, Minority Counsel, Senate Veterans' Affairs Committee. 1987 to present, General Counsel, Senate Veterans' Affairs Committee.

Expertise: Veterans Administration, veterans' programs

Appointed to the Senate Veterans' Affairs Committee in 1977 by Sen. Alan Cranston (D-CA), Scott considers his role as General Counsel to be that of a team player, supportive of the Committee staff's joint efforts.

Scott is involved in virtually all committee work ranging from legislation to oversight to budget matters. He has seen the transition from majority to minority and back to majority status. His experience over the past ten years has solidified his conviction that the Veterans Affairs Committee is not as divided along partisan lines as other committees.

Among his and the committee's achievements, Scott counts the creation of the Vets Center Program for veteran readjustment in 1979; restructuring of the Veterans Administration vocational training rehabilitation project for service-disabled veterans in 1980; and the ongoing reform movement in the V.A.'s home loan program, under way now for three years.

Scott joined the staff in 1977 for two reasons: first, for the opportunity to work for Cranston, and second because of his personal belief in the importance of "the way our society fulfills its obligations to veterans," he says. By and large, in Scott's view, the U.S. has a good record in taking care of former men and women in uniform.

Scott believes the political power of veterans will grow if the Veterans' Administration is elevated to cabinet level department status. The agency, he says, will have more direct access to the White House than it has had historically, which should help ensure the agency participates directly in final decisions affecting its programs and budget.

In his spare time, Scott enjoys road running and bird watching and is a volunteer to the Achilles Track Club, a road running club for disabled persons.

Jonathan R. Steinberg
Chief Counsel and Staff Director
414 Russell Senate Office Bldg.
224-9126

Expertise: Human services

Serving under Sen. Alan Cranston, (D-CA), chairman of the Senate Veterans' Affairs Committee and a leading advocate of human resources issues, Jonathan Steinberg has had a hand in some of the most important human services legislation that has gone through the Senate since 1969.

Among Steinberg's achievements are legislation which has reformed various aspects of disability compensation and pension benefits for veterans and survivors, extended and expanded the GI Bill, made major changes in veterans' housing and health care law, and set up the special veterans center program for counselling Vietnam-era veterans. Steinberg heads up a staff charged with oversight of the $28 billion annual Veterans' Administration budget. Since 1977 he has been responsible in the Senate for twenty different veterans' bills enacted into public law.

Steinberg serves as a chief adviser to Cranston, not only on veterans' and human resource issues generally but on budgetary matters, especially as they affect human resources services under recent Gramm-Rudman belt-tightening. Steinberg is also a chief adviser to Cranston on some foreign policy and security matters, especially the Peace Corps.

Steinberg oversees all activities of the committee staff and is responsible for contact with other committees and the press.

Personal: born 1/3/39 in Philadelphia, Pennsylvania. B.A. Cornell Univ., 1960. L.L.B., Univ.of Pennsylvania Law School, 1963, cum laude. 1963-1964, Law Clerk, U.S. Circuit Judge Warren E. Burger. 1964-1968, Attorney Advisor, Office of the General Counsel, Peace Corps. 1968-1969, Deputy General Counsel, Peace Corps. 1969-1971, Counsel, Subcommittee on Veterans' Affairs. 1971-1973, Counsel, Subcommittee on Railroad Retirement; Committee on Labor and Public Welfare. 1971-1977, Counsel, Special Subcommittee on Human Resources, Committee on Labor and Public Welfare. 1977-1981, Chief Counsel, Committee on Veterans' Affairs. 1981-1987, Minority Chief Counsel, Committee on Veterans' Affairs . 1987-present, Chief Counsel and Staff Director, Committee on Veterans' Affairs.

SENATE
SELECT AND SPECIAL COMMITTEES

Alan Parker
Staff Director
Select Committee on Indian Affairs
838 Hart Senate Office Bldg.
202-224-2251

*Personal: born 8/8/42 in Fort Yates,
N.D. B.A. St. Thomas Seminary, 1964.
J.D. Univ. of California at Los Angeles,
1972. 1965-68, U.S. Army Signal
Corps. 1972-74, associate attorney,
Solicitor's office, Department of the
Interior. 1974-77, associate director,
American Indian Lawyer Training
Program. 1975-76, publisher,
University of New Mexico Law School
research projects, American Indian
Policy Review Committee. 1977-79,
Chief Counsel, Senate Select
Committee on Indian Affairs. 1979-83,
private law practice. 1983-86,
president, American Indian National
Bank. 1986-present, Staff Director,
Select Committee on Indian Affairs.*

Expertise: Indian affairs, law

Growing up on a reservation in North Dakota, Alan Parker learned
from firsthand experience about the problems that Indians face.
He is now in a key position to help people solve them.

Parker, staff director for the Senate Select Committee on Indian
Affairs, is a member of the Sioux tribe. The 45-year-old Parker
says his father instilled in him at an early age a sense of obligation
to help his people.

After college and decorated Army service in Vietnam, Parker, at
his wife's urging, chose to attend law school. At UCLA, he read
cases that heightened his interest in Indian issues and problems
and decided to channel that concern into a career that includes
Congressional staffer, publisher of material for a task
force on Indian affairs and the presidency of the American Indian
National Bank.

After working as an associate attorney in the Interior Department,
Parker served as chief counsel to the committee (which was then
a subcommittee rather than a select committee) from 1977-78.
Last year, almost a decade later, he returned as staff director. Sen.
Daniel Inouye of Hawaii is now the chairman, and the committee's
legislative agenda has almost doubled.

Parker says his chief role is to identify ways in which the federal
government can assist in the economic development of Indian
reservations and to initiate proposals that can, with the help of
experts in tribal business and finance, facilitate economic
independence for Indians.

"The Select Committee is simply another bureaucracy if it can't
help tribes to create a visible and ongoing economic base," he
says. "It should be involved in the entire spectrum of services
required to fulfill the government's responsibility to the Indian
peoples."

Parker has been working on the formation of an American Indian
Development Financial Institution, which he envisions as a World
Bank for Indians, helping them develop their resources. Parker
says he chose the World Bank as a model because he thinks it
has learned which policies are the most effective.

Parker is also working to create public awareness of problems that
Indians face. The committee produces a newsletter that offers
basic descriptions of legislation to tribes and the general public, as
well as videotapes of the committee's hearings, some of which
have been aired on public television.

The committee also has proposed a national Indian museum as a
part of the Smithsonian Institute in Washington. Parker says that

the museum would include representations from all tribes and provide recognition of Indian art, history and culture.

Indians must be able to continue in distinct tribal societies as a means to retain their identity, says Parker, who adds that a museum would add to that recognition.

The committee has no subcommittees but recently established the Special Committee on Investigations, formed after reports in the media charging that more than $5 billion owed to various tribes for mineral rights has never been paid. Parker says the Special Committee will examine that and other areas.

Parker served in the Army's Signal Corps during the Vietnam War and was awarded the Bronze Star and the Good Conduct Medal with oak leaf cluster. He and his wife, Sharon, live in Washington with their two children.

Patricia Zell
Chief Counsel
Select Committee on Indian Affairs
838 Hart Senate Office Bldg.
224-225

*Personal: born 3/1/46 in Jacksonville,
North Carolina. B.A. Washington Univ.,
1969. J.D., Georgetown Univ., 1981.
1969-1975, Director, Psychological
Information Center, American
Psychological Association. 1975-
1978, American Indian Policy Review
Committee. 1978, Research Assistant;
1981-1982, Staff Attorney; and 1982-
present, Chief Counsel, Select
Committee of Indian Affairs.*

Expertise: Indian affairs

Patricia Zell believes she has found the perfect job. She has effectively combined a former career in psychology with a law degree to become Chief Counsel to the Select Committee on Indian Affairs.

Zell approaches her responsibilities on the Committee in a very personal sense, since her grandparents were members of the Navajo tribe. As she says:, "I'm very fortunate to be working in an area that assists those people who need it so badly; people long neglected and overlooked."

Several areas of which Zell is interested include health care, education, housing and natural resources. And while she believe some improvements have been made in this area, she still points to the fact that Native Americans are still ranked lowest by very socio-economic indicator. For instance, the unemployment rate among Native Americans is approximately 75 percent and they claim the highest mortality rate.

In response to these problems, Zell has been instrumental in a five-year effort to re-enact the Indian Health Care Improvement Act. While this bill failed passage in the waning days of the 99th Congress, Zell believes this measure to be the Committee's highest priority.

Zell has also focused her attention on several pieces of legislation involving water rights. One bill, the Pyramid Lake Water Settlement bill, addresses water rights between California and Nevada. Another, the San Luis Rey Water bill, would settle claims of five mission states.

Zell sees two overriding concerns in all of the Select Committee's activities, the first being to insure that the U.S. honors the treaties entered into with Native Americans. She views these contracts as a matter of fundamental trust between the government and Native Americans.

The other concern involves the establishment of independent determination among native Americans. Zell believes that for too long the problems of these people have been resolved by Washington without prior consultation.

Even away from Committee, Zell is active in Indian affairs by being editor of the *Indian Law Reporter*. In every sense, Patricia Zell is carrying out the tradition of her Navajo grandfather by improving the quality of life of all native Americans.

G. Lawrence Atkins
Minority Staff Director
Special Committee on Aging
628 Hart Senate Office Bldg.
224-1467

Personal: born 4/20/48 in Cooperstown, New York. A.B. (magna cum laude), Kenyon Coll., 1969. M.A. Univ. of Kentucky, 1971. M.S. Univ. of Louisville, 1975. Ph.D. Brandeis Univ., 1985. 1969-1973, Teacher. 1973-1974, Phoenix Associates. 1975-1979, Human Services Coordination Alliance, Louisville. 1981-1985, professional staff member; 1985-1987, Deputy Staff Director; 1987 to present, Minority Staff Director, Senate Special Committee on Aging. Publications: "Spend it or Save it? Pension Lump-Sum Distributions and Tax Reform" (Employee Benefit Research Institute, 1986). "The Economic Status of the Oldest Old", Milbank Memorial Fund Quarterly, Health and Society, Vol. 63, No. 2, 1985. "Closing Back Doors out of Social Security", in Y.P. Chen and G. Rohrlich (eds.), Checks and Balances in Social Security. (New York: University Press of America, 1986).

Expertise: Social security, pensions, employee benefits

Before coming to Capitol Hill, Larry Atkins spent ten years in Kentucky working to improve the delivery of social services to low-income people. Using the same thoughtfully conceived, practical approaches to problem-solving in his career with the Senate Special Committee on Aging, Atkins has been instrumental in helping shape reforms in the Social Security and private pension systems.

Recruited from Brandeis University's well-regarded Social Welfare Policy Program in 1981, Atkins was "baptized by fire" into his work with the Aging Committee on May 12, 1981, his second day on the job. That day, President Reagan set off a furor in Congress and everywhere else by calling for cuts in the Social Security program, proposing early retirement penalties and decreases in disability benefits.

Atkins quickly became a key player in the Social Security debate, devoting his next two years to this issue exclusively. His work began with the Social Security Amendments of 1981. Then, serving as technical advisor to Sen. John Heinz (R-PA) in his work with the President's National Commission on Social Security Reform, Atkins helped formulate the recommendations that eventually became the Social Security Amendments of 1983. This legislation is best known as the financing vehicle credited with rescuing the Social Security system from potential insolvency. Not surprisingly, a committee colleague calls Atkins "one of the Senate's retirement security experts".

Atkins also staffs Heinz on pension and employee benefits issues in the Finance Committee. Using the unusual approach of meeting early and often with business groups, Atkins helped Heinz craft the Retirement Income Policy Act of 1985. The bill's provisions became the basis for the elaborate pension law changes contained in the 1986 Tax Reform Act. These changes broadened the pension system's coverage by addressing the problems of the low- and middle-income workers who change jobs frequently. Atkins also has worked extensively on steel industry pension funding legislation, looking for creative ways to shore up underfunded plans.

Since being promoted to minority staff director in August, 1987, Atkins has turned more of his attention to health issues as such long-term health care, physician reimbursement, health insurance coverage, and retiree health benefits.

Atkins moors what "you might call a sailboat" in Cape Cod and charters boats for closer-to-home trips on the Chesapeake.

Lloyd Duxbury
Professional Staff Member
Special Committee on Aging
G-41 Dirksen Senate Office Bldg.
224-5364

*Personal: born 2/1/22 in Caledonia,
Minnesota. B.A. Harvard Univ., 1947.
J.D. Harvard Univ. Law School, 1949.
1943-1946, U.S. Army. 1949-1969,
private law practice, Caledonia, MN.
1951-1970, member, Minnesota
House of Representatives; 1959-1962,
minority leader; 1963-1969, speaker of
the house. 1969-1981, vice president,
Burlington Northern, Inc. 1982-1986,
president, Railroad Retirement
Association. 1987-present,
professional staff member, Senate
Special Committee on Aging*

Expertise: Pensions and retirement benefits

Duxbury joined the staff of the Senate Special Committee on
Aging in mid-1987 after a period of retirement from
Burlington Northern, Inc., a natural resource and transportation
conglomerate, that he represented in Washington for twelve years.
He had also worked five years with a nonprofit association of
railroad retirees, for which he presented testimony and statements
to the Senate and House committees on railroad retirement and
social security issues.

Duxbury's committee staff involvement has included the Employee
Retirement Income Security Act and Pension Benefit Guarantee
Corporation, the Medicare Catastrophic Illness legislation,
employee and retiree health insurance benefits, Social Security
earnings limitations, taxation of Social Security benefits, the age
Discrimination in Employment Act and the enforcement thereof by
the equal Employment Opportunity Commission, and the Railroad
Retirement System.

Duxbury feels that many older Americans share his desire to
continue working not only beyond the "early retirement" age, but
also beyond the "normal retirement" age of 65. He believes that
governments and private employment policies should encourage
continued employment of those older Americans who want to work
and are physically and mentally capable of doing so, no matter
what their age.

Max I. Richtman
Staff Director
Special Committee on Aging
G41 Dirksen Senate Office Bldg.
224-5364

Personal: born 1/1/47 in Muhldorf, West Germany. B.A. Harvard, 1969. J.D. Georegetown Law School, 1973. 1973-1975, Legislative Assistant, Rep. Sydney Yates (D-IL). 1975-1977, Staff Assistant for American Indian Policy Review Commission chaired by Jim Abourezk. 1977-1979, Counsel, Senate Select Committee on Indian Affairs. 1979-1981, Staff Director, Senate Select Committee on Indian Affairs. 1981-1986, Minority Staff Director, Senate Select Committee on Indian Affairs. 1987-present, Staff Director, Senate Special Committee on Aging.

Expertise: Medicare, Social Security, disability, income security

In 1987, when Senator John Melcher (D-MT) moved from the Select Committee on Indian Affairs to the Senate Special Committee on Aging, Max Richtman went with him once again as Melcher's Staff Director.

A fourteen-year veteran of Capitol Hill, most of Richtman's past expertise has been in Indian affairs. He was at that time identified with reform in federal and Indian oil and gas royalty collections and Indian healthcare legislation.

Richtman brings to his new position a thorough knowledge of the process. Currently, he is most closely identified with catastrophic healthcare legislation and has developed an expertise in Medicare, Social Security, disability and income security.

For the future, Richtman believes his toughest tasks will be working on bringing healthcare costs under control and providing safeguards for long-term healthcare (including home care and nursing homes, neither of which was included in last year's catastrophic healthcare legislation).

Colleagues praise Richtman's approach to committee work. Says one,"I have not known anyone who has been more conscientious in looking out for his Senator, nor have I known anyone who has been more diligent and fair in working with other staff members to get the Senate's business done."

Richtman was born in Muhldorf, West Germany, and is a naturalized citizen of the U.S. In 1951, when he was four, he found himself a displaced person, immigrated by means of Jewish agencies and deposited in Omaha, Nebraska. His father survived a Nazi concentration camp. Certainly the injustices and trials of these early experiences give him a special sensitivity to questions of social justice.

Cycling is a favorite endeavour about which Max is serious to the tune of 50 miles a day on weekends and 25 miles a day during the week.

SENATE
OTHER KEY STAFF

Max McCallie Barber
Superintendent
Senate Radio and Television
  Gallery
S-325 Capitol Bldg.
224-6421

Personal: born 5/27/26 in
Chatanooga, Tennessee. B.S. in
Agriculture, Univ. of Maryland, 1952.
1944-46, U.S. Navy. l953-55,
Bacteriologist, Alexandria Dairy. 1955-
72, Third Assistant Superintendent,
House Radio and Television Gallery.
1972-present, Superintendent, Senate
Radio and Television Gallery.

Expertise: Press

1988 marks Max Barber's 33rd year working on Capitol Hill for the Radio and Television Correspondents' Galleries. The House and Senate Galleries were established in 1939, when Fulton Lewis, Jr., a radio reporter, was denied membership in the Press Galleries. Lewis convinced congressmen that radio reporters, as well as print reporters, needed an organization on the Hill to service its members. Initially, the legislation creating such an organization covered only radio reporters. After World War II, it was expanded to include television broadcast correspondents as well.

The House and Senate Radio and Television Galleries are governed by an Executive Committee of Radio and Television Correspondents, consisting of seven reporter/members for each Gallery.

In 1955, Barber was hired as the Third Superintendent to the House Gallery and tracked legislation, kept a running account of House floor proceedings and explained parliamentary procedures to correspondent/members. He also made arrangements for Gallery members to attend committee hearings and special events.

Barber moved to the Senate Gallery in 1972 when he was hired as Superintendent. According to Barber, his responsibilities as Senate Gallery Superintendent include tracking legislation for its reporter/members, providing information about Senate activities, managing space for correspondents'reporting and overseeing special projects.

The Gallery "has to change all the time to adapt to new technology," according to Barber. He is currently completing a fiber optic project, which involves running cable from the Capitol to the Senate office buildings. Barber notes that this newly developed fiber optic communications system will be ready this year According to Barber, the new system will transmit Senate news events to member/correspondents downtown, enabling them to report on Senate conferences and interviews.

In 1987, the Gallery moved into a larger space, necessitated by its rapid growth in membership. Accredited members jumped from 750 in 1979 to 2500 in 1988, Barber said. He attributes this growth to satellites, noting that members represent networks throughout the U.S. and many foreign countries. Of its 2500 members, 250 are foreign broadcasters. The Gallery space includes two television work-stations, three radio work-stations and numerous typewriters. Because the work-stations have special lights, Barber said, members can bring their own equipment and broadcast directly from the Gallery. The national networks have their own booths.

Barber's responsibilities also include accrediting reporters for the president's inauguration every four years. Every radio or television correspondent who wants to cover the inaugural has to apply through the Gallery, Barber said. He is responsible for setting up their work space and building a platform and seats. According to Barber, this process becomes his "top priority" for six weeks before each inauguration. In 1984, 1500 reporters were accredited through the Gallery; however, he expects more next time because the inaugural will not involve an incumbent president.

It is clear that Barber loves his work—judging by the length of time he has served as Superintendent and his enthusiasm for the job. When asked what has kept him there, Barber replied, "It's been fascinating."

Christina Bolton
Administrative Assistant/Legislative
  Director
Rep. Robert Dole (D-KS)
141 Hart Senate Office Bldg.
224-6521

*Personal: born 7/15/49 in Pittsfield,
Massachusetts. B.A. Smith Coll.,
1971, Deans List. J.D. Georgetown
Law Center, 1987 with specialty in
trade. 1972-1974, executive assistant,
chairman of the Department of
Romance Languages, Yale Univ. 1974-
1976, deputy national press secretary,
Lloyd Bentsen for president. 1976-
1979, director of Office of Continuing
Medical Education, Georgetown Univ.
Medical Center; concurrently, director
of news bureau. 1979-1984, legislative
assistant; 1984-1987, legislative
director; 1988, administrative
assistant/legislative director, Sen.
Robert Dole (D-KS).*

Expertise: Nutrition and education issues

Eight years ago, when Christina Bolton arrived on Capitol Hill, Robert Dole's office was the first to follow through on her resume. Since then, she has served as Dole's legislative assistant; then as his legislative director, and currently in her expanded title of administrative assistant/legislative director. She supervises five offices (four in Kansas) and 35 employees with a budget of over one million dollars. Working for Dole presents its own unique challenges and Bolton gets involved in just about every kind of legislation and administrative issue. She is considered to be a leading expert on food stamps and child nutrition programs and her special contributions relate to the Food Stamp Act Amendments of 1981 and 1982 during the budget reconciliation process.

Naturally, Bolton would like to see Bob Dole elected president, because "he is the strongest leader I know." Ultimately a realist, she's not dreaming ahead to the White House—that's a long way down the road, if at all. Currently, her ability to switch gears and set new priorities on a daily basis serves her well in an unpredictable office environment. Her greatest personal aspiration is to be able to live a well-balanced life ("maybe I'll have to leave Washington for that.")

Bolton has done volunteer work for Sen. Dole's presidential campaign. Previous political campaign involvements have been the task force on Reagan's education proposals and Lloyd Bentsen's short-lived presidential campaign in 1975.

On a more personal level, Bolton is happiest when she has a camera in her hands—her favorite subjects being landscapes, children, and political events. Although not particularly athletic, she does ski and enjoy biking and hiking.

Eugene Callahan
Administrative Assistant
Senator Alan J. Dixon (D-IL)
331 Senate Hart Office Bldg.
224-2854

*Personal: born 11/5/33 in Milford,
Illinois. B.A. Illinois Coll., 1955. 1953-
1955, staff, Jacksonville (IL) Journal
Courier, 1953-1955, staff, Jacksonville
Radio WLDS. 1957-1967, Illinois State
Register. 1965-67 downstate Illinois
stringer, New York Times and Time
Magazine. 1968-1969, assistant press
secretary to Illinois Governor Samuel
Shapiro. 1969-1972, administrative
assistant and press secretary to
Illinois Lt. Gov. Paul Simon. 1973-
1977, administrative assistant to
Illinois State Treasurer Alan J. Dixon.
1977-1980, Assistant Secretary of
State to Illinois Secretary of State Alan
J. Dixon, 1980-present, Administrative
Assistant, Sen. Alan J. Dixon.*

Expertise: Illinois politics

Anyone wanting to learn about the State of Illinois would be well advised to talk to Gene Callahan. As a man who has visited all of Illinois's 102 counties at least twice and been involved in every statewide campaign since 1958, he has the reputation of being an "expert on Illinois."

Bred, born and raised on Illinois's Democratic politics, Callahan has served both of the state's current Democratic senators. He is highly regarded by them and his colleagues on the Hill as an astute political operative whose contributions have been of great assistance to the Congressional delegation from Illinois.

His current boss, Senator Alan J. Dixon, with whom Callahan has been associated for more than 15 years, says of him, "Gene is the most remarkable guy I've ever known. He could be making three times his government salary if he wanted to go into consulting. But he is totally dedicated to working for Illinois. We're lucky to have him."

"There's nobody better," adds former boss, and Illinois junior Senator Paul Simon who still values Callahan's advice.

Callahan's career involvement with Illinois politics goes back to 1958 as a reporter covering statewide campaigns. In 1960, he covered the Kennedy-Nixon contest in Illinois as he did the Johnson-Goldwater campaign in 1964. In 1969, he began working with Lt. Governor Paul Simon as press secretary and administrative assistant and continued to assist him in his unsuccessful bid for the governorship in 1972. Callahan joined Alan Dixon in 1973 when Dixon was State Treasurer; then later served as Assistant Secretary of State when Dixon was Secretary of State.

An open and friendly man, with a passion for all sports, Callahan manages a staff of 53 among five offices in Illinois and Washington with a remarkably low turnover rate. This may be due in part to Callahan's style which puts a lot of stock in team work. A sign in his office says, "There is no letter *I* in the word team."

Robert A. Chlopak
Executive Director
Democratic Senatorial Campaign
  Committee
430 S. Capitol Street
224-2447

Expertise: Democratic politics

The Democratic Senatorial Campaign Committee (known as the "DSCC") is the official arm of the Democratic Party dedicated to electing Democrats to the United States Senate. As Executive Director, Bob Chlopak works closely with the chairman, Sen. John Kerry (D-MA), and the other senators serving on the committee.

During 1988 Chlopak and his staff are involved in assisting Democratic candidates in all 33 of the states with Senate elections this year. The DSCC provides Senate incumbents and challengers with financial, technical and strategic resources. Reflecting the rejuvenation Senate Democrats have enjoyed beginning with the 1986 election, the DSCC under Chlopak has boosted fundraising forty percent above where it was at this juncture in the last election cycle two years ago.

Prior to becoming Executive Director of the DSCC, Chlopak was the Deputy Director of its House counterpart, the Democratic Congressional Campaign Committee, chaired at that time by Rep. Tony Coehlo (D-CA), now the House Majority Whip.

Prior to his work for the campaign committees, Chlopak was in the private sector. He headed the Coalition Against Double Taxation, the lobbying group credited with successfully leading the opposition to eliminating the federal deduction for state and local taxes during the debate over the 1986 Tax Reform Act.

Chlopak is also well known in Washington environmental circles. For four years he worked with Friends of the Earth where he initiated and administered its political action committee and eventually became Director of the entire organization.

Chlopak is a graduate of George Washington University.

Jann L. Olsten
Executive Director
National Republican Senatorial
  Committee
347-0202

Expertise: International trade, campaign finance law

Olsten thought he had put a career in politics behind him when he left Washington in 1982 to return to Minneapolis to practice law and raise his three children. He had managed fellow Minnesotan Rudy Boschwitz's Republican campaign for the Senate in 1978 and then stayed on as his chief of staff, helping the freshman senator set up an office and launch a career in national politics. Olsten returned to Minneapolis after three-and-a-half years as Boschwitz's top man and a short stint in the Commerce Department.

Four years later, Boschwitz was elected Chairman of the National Republican Senatorial Committee, and asked Olsten if he would oversee the Committee's operations.

"At first I thought it was a crazy idea," Olsten says of the offer. "I had always said I wouldn't come back to Washington until our children were raised. But I thought being the executive director was one of the best jobs in Washington. It's an excellent and unusual opportunity to have an impact on your times. Your efforts are very focused, and your results are measurable. I saw it as a unique way of merging my interests in business, politics and policy."

Personal: born 5/11/48 in Minneapolis, Minnesota. B.A. Gustavus Adolphus Coll., 1970. J.D. William Mitchell Coll. of Law, 1974 (cum laude). 1975-1978, attorney, Stacker & Ravich, Minneapolis, MN. 1977-1978, Legal Counsel to People for Boschwitz Campaign. 1978, Boschwitz Campaign Manager. 1978-1982, Administrative Assistant, Senator Rudy Boschwitz (R-MN). 1982, Special Assistant, International Trade Administration. 1983-1985, partner, Stacker & Ravich. 1984, Chairman, Reelection Campaign for Senator Rudy Boschwitz. 1985, partner, Robins, Zelle, Larson & Kaplan, Washington, D.C. 1986-present, Executive Director, National Republican Senatorial Committee. Member, U.S. Senate Small Business Advisory Committee, Minnesota District Export Council, Governor's International Trade Advisory Board.

Olsten accepted the two-year appointment, and the challenge of guiding the Committee's efforts through the 1988 election cycle. The Committee is the Republican Party's fundraising and recruiting arm for senatorial races. According to Olsten, the Committee hopes to raise up to $70 million for GOP candidates by election time, and has the ambitious goal of putting the Republicans back in control of the Senate.

"Rudy and I took over at a difficult time," Olsten says of the 1988 election. "The Committee had raised record dollars in 1986 but suffered severe losses. The GOP was no longer in the majority and we knew our resources weren't going to be as much this next go around. That made it that much more important for us to take a good hard look at the Committee's activities."

One of the changes Olsten has made is to decentralize the Committee's involvement in campaigns. "We felt it was important to place added emphasis on the individual campaigns," he says, "and we are trying to give them the independence they need." Olsten also claims that one can no longer assume that the Democrats will retain their majority hold on the Senate. "There is already a lot of uncertainty about 1988 because of the presidential election," he explains, "and so if we can move enough races into the questionable category—mix things up a bit—we have a change of regaining the majority."

After the 1988 election, Olsten will return to his law practice—this time in Washington, to co-manage his firm's D.C. office.

Robert Ernest Petersen, Jr.
Superintendent, Senate Press
  Gallery
S-316 Capitol Bldg.
224-0241

*Personal: born 10/20/44 in Richland,
Washington. B.A. Virginia Polytechnic
Institute, 1968. 1969-1971, U.S. Army;
Army Commendation Medal, Good
Conduct Medal and Meritorious
Service Medal. 1971-1973, Office
Manager, Architect of the Capitol Field
Office, (now called Construction
Management Division). 1973-1974,
Secretary, Senate Press Gallery. 1974-
1981, Fourth Assistant
Superintendent, Senate Press Gallery.
1981, Third Assistant Superintendent,
Senate Press Gallery. 1981-1983,
Second Assistant Superintendent,
Senate Press Gallery. 1983-Present,
Superintendent, Senate Press Gallery.*

Expertise: Washington press corps, accreditation

During Robert Petersen's fifteen years in the Senate Press
Gallery, he has held five of its six staff positions. In 1973, Petersen
was hired as the Gallery's secretary (now called Fifth Assistant
Superintendent). Petersen moved up the ranks to assume the
Superintendent's job in May, 1983.

The Senate Press Gallery was established through an act of
Congress in 1879 to regulate press coverage of that body. A
Standing Committee of Correspondents, consisting of five
members of the Gallery, administers the Gallery. The five Standing
Committee Correspondents are elected by all Gallery reporter/
members for staggered two-year terms. Admission to the Gallery
is limited to bona fide newspaper reporters who must apply
through the Standing Committee. Applications are subject to
review and approval by the Senate Committee on Rules and
Administration.

The Standing Committee, rather than the Senate, is responsible
for hiring and firing the six Gallery superintendents, who service
the reporter/members. This process ensures that the jobs remain
professional and not political.

The Gallery currently serves 2200 reporter/members. The staff is
responsible for tracking Senate activities and providing
information to members for their reporting. It also provides work
space and equipment for members to perform their jobs efficiently.

Petersen got his first job with the Gallery because he could type
75 words a minute. As secretary, he did the office typing and other
administrative tasks. When he was promoted to Fourth Assistant,
Petersen attended committee hearings and kept logs of Senate
chamber activities for Gallery members. Tracking Senate bills and
hearings and recording information is essential for reporter/
members who are unable to attend these events in person,
according to Petersen.

The superintendents rotate which hearings they attend so that
each staff person "knows a little about everything going on in the
Senate," Petersen said. This is important because the Gallery
staff must respond to reporters' questions about provisions in bills
and their status, and all other Senate activities.

The Gallery stays open whenever the Senate is in session,
although official hours are 9:00 to 6:30. The job is "public
information, public affairs and public relations," Petersen said. He
estimates the office gets 300 to 400 telephone calls each day.

Petersen's top priority in 1988 will be to accredit all print reporters
who attend the national election campaigns. The Gallery must
certify that the reporter represents a legitimate organization before

it issues accreditation. According to Petersen, the Gallery has been doing this longer than any other agency in D.C.—since 1904 for the Democratic Party and since 1908 for the Republican Party.

Servicing the national election campaigns also involves assigning all workspace and seats for reporters attending the conventions. This year, 4500 will attend. Petersen's responsibilities also include coordinating phones and housing for the reporters and meeting with architects who will design the press stands. Petersen has already traveled to Atlanta and New Orleans to work on these objectives and he is planning future trips. Although the Senate Press Gallery staff does not receive additional pay for this work, it began working on the accreditation process for the 1988 election in 1985.

Petersen is currently involved in a project to upgrade existing space in the Senate Press Gallery. They will be getting new furnishings for the first time in twenty-two years. All of the Gallery's budget requests must first be approved by the Sergeant at Arms, who submits them to the Rules Committee. After the Rules Committee approves a request, it then goes to the Senate Appropriations Committee for final approval.

Another project Petersen is working on involves installing a mainframe computer for the Gallery's internal use. He plans to develop a program on this computer for the political conventions. Petersen envisions the Gallery's members will have access to the computer through a modem which will provide them with information about upcoming press conferences, committee lists, roll call votes and legislative summaries. According to Petersen, reporter/members will use a codeword to access this program. He hopes to implement the system shortly after the national conventions.

C. Abbott (Abby) Saffold
Secretary for the Majority
S-309, Capitol Bldg.
224-3735

Personal: born 11/22/44 in Baltimore, Maryland. B.A. Bates College, 1966. 1966-1967, school teacher, Washington D.C. 1967-1969, Post Office and Civil Service caseworker/ legislative correspondent, Rep. William Scott (R-VA). 1969-1970, part-time employee, Rep. Lloyd Meeds (D-WA) 1970-1972, Legislative Secretary to Sen. Gaylord Nelson (D-WI). 1972-1979, Chief Clerk of Judiciary Subcommittee on Constitutional Amendments, and Legislative Assistant and Designee on Appropriations Committee for Sen. Birch Bayh (D-IN). 1979-87, manager of floor staff, Democratic Policy Committee, Sen. Robert Byrd (D-WV). 1987 to present, Secretary for the Majority.

Expertise: Legislative strategy

Abby Saffold, Secretary for the Majority, is the first woman of either political party to hold this position. It is a job for which she is well-qualified.

Saffold describes herself as a legislative strategist who "looks after the interests of Democrats." However, she understands in order for the legislative process to work she must pay attention to the wants, needs, and demands of Members on both sides of the aisle. "Every Senator gets here as a result of ability," she states. "My function is to help the Senators do the very best they can in a system that is sometimes frustrating and very often unbelievably time consuming."

Saffold is a resource on the Senate floor. She manages the executive calendar and advises Senators on many aspects of legislative strategy. "My expertise is having a feel for the business of the Senate. I have to know all the options a Senator faces when introducing or debating a particular piece of legislation. I have to know how long it will be before a measure is considered as well as have a good feel for how long the debate will last."

Saffold got to this position by rising through the legislative ranks in the 1970's, a period when women were just beginning to gain access to policy positions. Saffold is understandably proud of this and of the many other women on Capitol Hill who have done the same.

David Pratt, Saffold's predecessor in the office, describes her as a master of Senate procedures. "Abby is extremely skilled in running the cloakroom. She is a veteran of the Senate and knows many of its Members. She is the person who makes sure the political signals from the Majority Leader, the Minority Leader and the Members all get translated clearly."

Pratt recalls an incident from the 98th Congress which illustrates Saffold's role in the Senate. Majority leader Baker was on the Senate floor leading the debate while Saffold was in the rear working out the legislative timetable with Baker's staff. At one point Baker could proceed no further until Saffold finished her negotiations. Baker said for the record, "We're just here waiting for Abby."

Although her job demands a great deal of time, Saffold does try to keep up with her reading, gardening, knitting and bird-watching on Virginia's Chincoteague Island.

John Robert Vastine, Jr.
Staff Director
Republican Conference
405 Hart Senate Office Bldg.
224-2764

*Personal: born 11/12/37 in Danville,
Pennsylvania. B.A. Haverford Coll.,
1959. M.A. School of Advanced
International Studies, Johns Hopkins
Univ., 1959. Fellow, Inst. of Politics,
John F. Kennedy School of
Government, Harvard Univ., 1977.
1965-1968, Economic Assistant, Rep.
Thomas B. Curtis. 1968-1969,
lobbyist, Emergency Committee for
American Trade. 1969-1971,
Washington Representative, CPC
International, Inc. 1971-1975, Minority
Staff Director, Senate Committee on
Governmental Affairs. 1975-1977,
Deputy Assistant Secretary for
International Trade and Raw Materials,
Treasury Department. 1977-1982,
consultant, Washington Pacific Group
and president, Alliance for American
Innovation. 1981, Deputy Leader for
Reagan Transition Team at Treasury
Department. 1982-1984, Legislative
Director, Sen. John Chafee (R-RI).
1985-present, Staff Director, Senate*

Expertise: Foreign trade policy, congressional budget process, media relations, satellite communications

Scholar, policy analyst, lobbyist, campaigner, administrator, politician and PR consultant, Vastine is not an average Hill staffer.

Vastine's first stint on the Hill was as an economic analyst for Representative Thomas B. Curtis, specializing in foreign trade policy. A free-trader, Vastine broadened the scope of his interests in economics and the budget process while working for Senators Percy and Chafee. As the minority staff director for the Senate Government Affairs Committee, he played a key role in helping Senator Percy draft the Budget Reform and Impoundment Act of 1974, which was Congress's first comprehensive attempt to manage the federal budget. Vastine asserts, "While this budget tool has needed a little tinkering over the years, the budget system and process are essentially sound. Any failure lies with Congress for not having the will to reduce spending."

An expert on international trade and the Congress, Vastine has published several works on these subjects and is regularly asked to share his views. In 1977, he received a fellowship from the Institute of Politics, John F. Kennedy School of Government, Harvard University where he organized a seminar entitled "The Standoff Between the World's Rich and Poor." While it is at times an unpopular position, he is firm in his view that a market-based economic policy is the best solution to the economic problems of Third World countries. In 1985 The U.S. Information Agency awarded Vastine a grant to tour Southeast Asia and lecture on U.S. foreign trade policy and the Congress, where his talks on looming protectionism and barriers to free trade were well received.

Vastine also held a number of key posts in the Nixon administration. As a Deputy Assistant Secretary at the Treasury Department, he was responsible for foreign trade and commodity policy and ran the then East-West Foreign Trade Board. Combatting international commodity agreements (or, what he terms "price fixing arrangements") was a priority agenda item. He also served as a deputy leader for the Reagan transition team at Treasury in late 1980 and early 1981.

For a time, Vastine left the government and worked as a lobbyist and consultant. He helped form the Emergency Committee for American Trade with A. K. Watson and David Rockefeller to lobby against protectionist measures. He also worked with small high-tech companies in California to advance their interests. It was during this time that Vastine volunteered to work for the Reagan-Bush Campaign. An experienced hand at political campaigns, he worked for Representative Curtis' unsuccessful bid for the Senate and Senator Percy's successful one.

Republican Conference. Publications: "The Kennedy Round and the Future of American Trade," co-author, 1972; "U.S. International Commodity Policy", Georgetown Univ. Journal of Law and Policy in International Business, *1977.*

Vastine has served as a volunteer for a number of organizations. He was appointed to the California Economic Development Council by then-Governor Jerry Brown. He served as a trustee of the World Affairs Council of Northern California and as a director of the California Council for International Trade.

Vastine's current job is director of the Senate Republican Conference. Senator Chafee gave him the task of organizing a comprehensive communications service for Republican Senators. Vastine put together an organization, including radio and television broadcasting, satellite communications and graphics and print services, that has few rivals in Washington. During last December's Reagan-Gorbachev summit, the Conference organized over sixty live interviews between Senators in its D.C. studio and their home TV and radio stations.

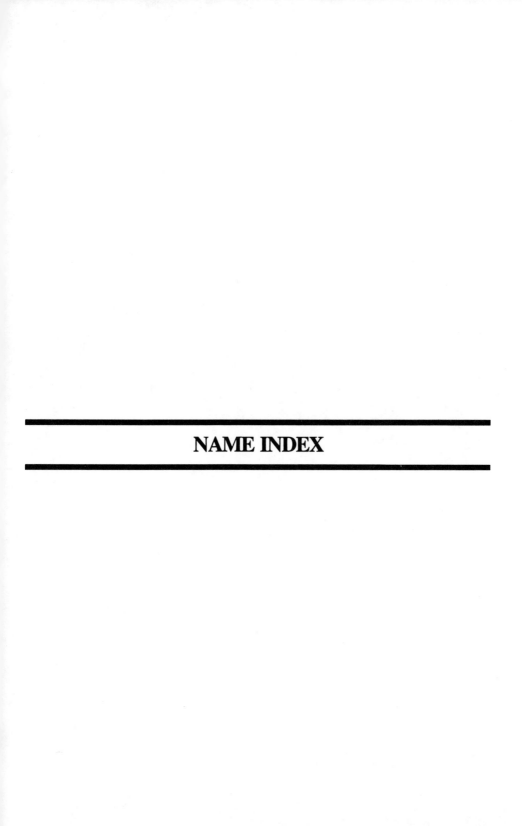

NAME INDEX

NAME INDEX

SUBJECT INDEX

This index cross-references many of the major issue areas and subjects presently before the Congress by the committees with paramount authorizing jurisdiction. Some issue areas will have fragmented jurisdiction, meaning other committees could have ancillary jurisdiction.

Note the House and Senate Committees on Appropriations have a significant impact on many of these issue areas, as policy determinations are made in the appropriations process. The Budget Committees also have an impact on many of these issues through their annual budget resolutions. Additionally, oversight jurisdiction for many of these issues is found in the House Government Operations, Senate Governmental Affairs, and select and special committees.

— A —

— B —

— C —

— D —

— E —

— F —

— G —

— H —

— I —

— O —

— P —

— S —

— V —

— W —

— Y —

APPENDIX

RESEARCHERS & WRITERS

Jeri Hessman Allen
Dan Amon
Sarah Anderson
Diane Ballard
Joseph Barry
Brett Bates
Stephen Beachy
Charles Blackburn
Gary Bland
Page Blankingship
Christine Brim
Donna Brodsky
Janet Bruce
Janis Budge
Leanne Buttrick
Stan Cannon
Lisa Carr
Alan Carter
Larry Cerignano
Chino Chapa
Laura Chapin
Becky Christenson
William Claire
Torie Clark
Ed Clement
Jeanne Clendenin
Michael Codel
Roz Coleman
Jamie Cook
Mitchell Cooper
Dale Curtis
Gloria Danziger
Joan Davis
Charles Dervarics
John Dougherty
Linda Dougherty
Barbara Drake
Peter Duveen
Debbie Evans
John Falardeau
John Fedewa
Lee Feldstein
Joe Feuer
Janice Fischer
Kelly Fitzgerald
Barbara Fox
Stephen Garber
Jane Garner
Pamela Gault
Susannah Gaylord
Martha Glenn
Mark Goldstone
Rob Goodling
Stuart Goodman

Andrew Gordon
Bezalel Gordon
Jeffrey Gordon
Peter Gordon
Ethel Hammer
Margaret Harned
Maureen Hart
Diane Hatcher
Doug Hatcher
Douglas Hattaway
Tim Heaphy
Fred Helm
Leigh Hennessey
Andrea Herman
James Hickey
Susannah Hill
Scott Hughes
Timothy Hugo
Julia Jackson
Kathleen James
Thomas James
Paul Jentel
Skip Kaltenheuser
Frank Kane
Elizabeth Klumpp
Jane Kubeja
Kate Kulesher
Miles Lackey
Pam LaLonde
Anita Lawson
Susan Lehman
Melinda Lloyd
Peter Loach
Steve Long
Tracey Longo
Joanne Lukens
Elizabeth Maier
Claude Marx
Rosina Mason
Stacy Mason
Elizabeth Massie
Margie McAllister
Patrick McCaffrey
Mary Lou McCormick
Colin McGinnis
Karen McIntosh
Andy Mcleod
Pam McQuay
Scott Miller
Anita Mintz
Dan Moll
Christine Moore
Jay Morris
Katherine Noble

Kalika Novoa
Nancy O'Brien
Sean O'Brien
Nina Ostrovitz
Susie Paige
Howard Park
Richard Parker
Heather Perram
Peggy Peterson
Jeanne Pettenati
Jim Pinkleman
Abigail Porter
Sarah Potts
Denise Roach
Thomas Robinson
Helen Rojas
Nancy Ross
Adam Sachs
Lorna Schmidt
Gill Schor
Edward Segal
Mark Sharpe
Daniel Sheehan
Kathe Simpson
Tony Sims
Tracy Sinnott
Zophia Smardz
Brendon Smith
Kevin Andrew Smith
Dan Soso
LeAnne Steincipher
Judith Sullivan
Joseph Tarver
Ruth Thaler
Dave Thibault
Merrell Tuck
Teresa Tucker
Patrick Turner
Monique Van Landingham
Trina Vargo
Harrison Wadsworth
Dan Walt
Elizabeth Waters
Mary Webber
Reede Webster
Tina Westby
Lisa Western
Justin Whittington
Kevin Winston
Jean Wright
Tracey Wright
Ted Zeggers

For additional copies of The Almanac of the Unelected fill out this page and send to :

The Almanac of the Unelected
P.O. Box 3785
Washington, D.C.   20007

Personal, in-depth profiles: What you need to know about 600 key Congressional staffers.

[] Yes, please send me ___ copies of The Almanac of the Unelected at $250.00 per copy (D.C. residents add 6% sales tax.)   Add $2.50 shipping fee

[] Check enclosed

[] Bill me upon delivery

Signature:_____

For additional copies of The Almanac of the Unelected fill out this page and send to :

The Almanac of the Unelected
P.O. Box 3785
Washington, D.C.   20007

Personal, in-depth profiles: What you need to know about 600 key Congressional staffers.

[] Yes, please send me ___ copies of The Almanac of the Unelected at $250.00 per copy (D.C. residents add 6% sales tax.)   Add $2.50 shipping fee

[] Check enclosed

[] Bill me upon delivery

Signature:_____

For additional copies of The Almanac of the Unelected fill out this page and send to :

The Almanac of the Unelected
P.O. Box 3785
Washington, D.C.   20007

Personal, in-depth profiles: What you need to know about 600 key Congressional staffers.

[] Yes, please send me ___ copies of The Almanac of the Unelected at $250.00 per copy (D.C. residents add 6% sales tax.)   Add $2.50 shipping fee

[] Check enclosed

[] Bill me upon delivery

Signature:_____

───

For additional copies of The Almanac of the Unelected fill out this page and send to :

The Almanac of the Unelected
P.O. Box 3785
Washington, D.C.   20007

Personal, in-depth profiles: What you need to know about 600 key Congressional staffers.

[] Yes, please send me ___ copies of The Almanac of the Unelected at $250.00 per copy (D.C. residents add 6% sales tax.)   Add $2.50 shipping fee

[] Check enclosed

[] Bill me upon delivery

Signature:_____

For additional copies of The Almanac of the Unelected fill out this page and send to :

        The Almanac of the Unelected
        P.O. Box 3785
        Washington, D.C. 20007

Personal, in-depth profiles: What you need to know about 600 key Congressional staffers.

[] Yes, please send me ___ copies of The Almanac of the Unelected at $250.00 per copy (D.C. residents add 6% sales tax.) Add $2.50 shipping fee

[] Check enclosed

[] Bill me upon delivery

Signature:_____

==

For additional copies of The Almanac of the Unelected fill out this page and send to :

        The Almanac of the Unelected
        P.O. Box 3785
        Washington, D.C. 20007

Personal, in-depth profiles: What you need to know about 600 key Congressional staffers.

[] Yes, please send me ___ copies of The Almanac of the Unelected at $250.00 per copy (D.C. residents add 6% sales tax.) Add $2.50 shipping fee

[] Check enclosed

[] Bill me upon delivery

Signature:_____